Common Law and Civil Law Today

Convergence and Divergence

Editor

Marko Novakovic

Institute of International Politics and Economics, Serbia

Series in Law

VERNON PRESS

Copyright © 2019 Vernon Press, an imprint of Vernon Art and Science Inc, on behalf of the authors.

All rights reserved. No part of this publication may be reproduced, stored in a retrieval system, or transmitted in any form or by any means, electronic, mechanical, photocopying, recording, or otherwise, without the prior permission of Vernon Art and Science Inc.

www.vernonpress.com

In the Americas:
Vernon Press
1000 N West Street,
Suite 1200, Wilmington,
Delaware 19801
United States

In the rest of the world:
Vernon Press
C/Sancti Espiritu 17,
Malaga, 29006
Spain

Series in Law

Library of Congress Control Number: 2019934592

ISBN: 978-1-62273-507-5

Product and company names mentioned in this work are the trademarks of their respective owners. While every care has been taken in preparing this work, neither the authors nor Vernon Art and Science Inc. may be held responsible for any loss or damage caused or alleged to be caused directly or indirectly by the information contained in it.

Every effort has been made to trace all copyright holders, but if any have been inadvertently overlooked the publisher will be pleased to include any necessary credits in any subsequent reprint or edition.

Cover design by Vernon Press

Painting by Jelena Novakovic http://www.jelenanovakovic.com/

Editor: Dr Marko Novakovic LL.M.

Editorial Board:
1. Prof. David Law, Sir Y.K. Pao Chair in Public Law, The University of Hong Kong Charles Nagel Chair of Constitutional Law and Political Science, Washington University in St. Louis, USA
2. Prof. Gianluigi Cecchini, University of Trieste
3. Prof. Ezzio Benedetti, University of Trieste
4. Prof. Bojan Milisavljević, Faculty of Law, University of Belgrade
5. Prof. Vladimir Čolović, Director of the Institute of Comparative Law, Belgrade
6. Prof. Vasilka Sancin, Faculty of Law, University of Ljubljana
7. Prof Pawel Kowalski, SWPS University of Social Sciences and Humanities
8. Prof. Senad Ganić, State University of Novi Pazar
9. Prof. Emir Ćorović, State University of Novi Pazar
10. Dr. Kwanele Pakati, South African Human Rights Commission

To my wife Jelena.

I will never be able to thank you enough for the time, love and attention you devoted to our family and especially that you accepted, without ever mentioning it, neglecting your amazing artistic career so that I could pursue my professional dreams.

Table of Contents

Introduction		xi
Part 1 **International and European Law**		xiii
Chapter 1	**International Law as a Wedge between Legal Systems** Paul B. Stephan	1
Chapter 2	**Internal Law and International Law: From Common Law To Civil Law** Augusto Sinagra Anna Lucia Valvo	17
Chapter 3	**Territorial Knowledge, Sociality and the Convergence of International and Constitutional Law** William E Conklin	27
Chapter 4	**Convergence and Divergence in Statutory Interpretation** Jeffrey A. Pojanowski	55
Chapter 5	**Common Law Constitutionalism and Popular Sovereignty: A Matter of Public Trust** Anne Richardson Oakes	69
Chapter 6	**Legal Globalization through the Constructivist and Poststructuralist Lenses** Luka Martin Tomažič	93

Chapter 7	**With or Without You. Thoughts on Brexit and European Private Law**	105
	Cristina Poncibò	
Chapter 8	**Are European Security Policies Learning some Lessons from the United States on Migration and Human Rights?**	137
	Paolo Bargiacchi	

Part 2
The Role of the Judicial Bodies — 163

Chapter 9	**A few thoughts on various legal traditions, forms of civilization and the ICJ**	165
	Marko Novaković	
Chapter 10	**Anglophone and Civilian Legal Cultures: Global Governance by Corporation and State**	173
	Joseph P Garske	
Chapter 11	**Case-Law Relevance in the European Union Law: The Triumph of reason over Precedent**	197
	Letizia Seminara	
Chapter 12	**The General Principle of 'Abuse of Rights': Its Roots in Domestic Law and Impact on Investment Arbitration**	221
	Philipp Janig	
Chapter 13	**The Court of Justice of the European Union and the European Court of Human Rights Procedures: On the Quest for a more Coherent Approach in Human Rights Protection**	247
	Vesna Ćorić	
Chapter 14	**The ECHR's Influence on Convergence between Common Law and Civil Law Systems**	263
	Brice Dickson	

Part 3
National implications 287

Chapter 15 **Common Law and Civil Law Approaches to Excessive Group Crimes** 289
Marjolein Cupido

Chapter 16 **The Concept of Fault in the Regulation of International Responsibility – Reception or Rejection of Domestic Law Analogy** 317
Anna Czaplińska

Chapter 17 **A Mixture of Civil and Common Legal Systems? An Example of Trend of Taiwan's Legal Development on Information Technology** 351
Chun Hung Lin

Chapter 18 **Conceptions of Contract in German and English Law and their Legal Traditions** 363
Marin Keršić

Chapter 19 **Institutional Transplants in Serbia – the Stories of Success and Failure** 381
Ana Knežević Bojović

Chapter 20 **Supreme Audit Institutions of the Republic of Serbia and the United Kingdom – Comparative Legal Analysis** 413
Jelena Kostić

Chapter 21 **Influence of the Eurasian Integration Process on the Legal System of the Russian Federation** 437
Dmitriy V. Galushko

Chapter 22 **Convergence and Divergence of International Law in Slovak Judicial System** 465
Lucia Mokrá

Index 487

Introduction

Coming from the continental law system, I was always fascinated with that "other" legal tradition, founded on different pillars and with a somewhat different path to the fairness, justice and order. Elements such as precedents, different - adversarial approach, and other main features were notions that I was familiar with from my bachelor studies. However, it is very hard to present all finesses of the interaction and intersections of two legal systems to the scholar, let alone to the student. Several approaches were on my mind in addressing this subject in this collection. However, I rejected immediately classical approach: Listing first the common law articles, then civil law (or vice-versa) articles, followed by "meeting point" articles. Moreover, I did not want to have a structure where this common law/civil law dichotomy is in the focus *prima facie*. I feel that having different subject from different areas of law in the focus would is the more viable option. Uncovering common law-civil law relation within the frame of different, more concrete issues is the best way to demonstrate its layers and profoundness. And that is the point – although we can scatch some main situations of the common law-civil law elements and their encounters, every case in the vast area of law is case for itself, and it should be observed just like that.

The aim of this collection is to present to the reader every article as a separate legal situation and later to allow the (careful) reader to grasp the "common law and the civil law" picture by putting together dots from each article. Alternatively, I am sure that every article is interesting enough *per se*.

Part 1
International and European Law

Chapter 1

International Law as a Wedge between Legal Systems

Paul B. Stephan[1]

Abstract

The newly emerging field of comparative international law identifies areas of systematic divergence in the determination, interpretation, and application of international law among national legal systems. This field can inform the question of whether international law might serve to mediate between the common law and the civil law. In the abstract, international law, or more precisely international institutions that interpret and apply international law, might bridge divergences between common-law and civil-law legal structure by uncovering general principles that embrace both systems. In practice, international institutions may widen rather than bridge these gaps. The judges who serve on international courts, for example, typically lack a thorough grounding in both legal systems. They thus are vulnerable to confusing the familiar with the universal. Specialists in international law and international human rights may fail to distinguish neutral, fundamental principles particular to one system from pretexts designed the undermine respect for international obligations. The resulting judgment may confound and irritate officials in the legal system concern, undermining respect for international law heightening tensions between domestic legal systems. We can see this dynamic at work in two cases involving criminal justice in the United States and the United Kingdom. With respect to the United States, the International Court of

---

[1] John C. Jeffries, Jr., Distinguished Professor of Law and John V. Ray Research Professor, University of Virginia. This paper has benefited from comments received at the Conference on the Common Law and the Civil Law Today – Convergence and Divergence, masterfully organized by Dr. Marko Novaković. I am grateful to the participants, and bear sole responsibility for errors, misjudgments, and other blunders.

Justice determined that the United States had violated its obligation to ensure that arrested aliens are informed of their right to contact a consulate to obtain assistance in the criminal proceeding and, because of these violations, had to provide a new hearing for each affected person to determine whether the violation affected the outcome of the proceeding. The United States conceded the treaty violation but maintained that the persons concerned had waived their claim under the generally applicable rules of U.S. criminal procedure. The International Court of Justice failed to understand how a lawyer's failure to make a timely claim could bind a criminal defendant. With respect to the United Kingdom, legislation reformed the rules for introducing hearsay evidence in criminal trials. The British courts applied strict procedural safeguards before allowing a jury to hear such evidence but did not require a separate determination at the 18 end of submission of all evidence to determine if the submission was justified. The Strasbourg Court has ruled that an end-of-trial determination is necessary, overlooking the difficulty of undoing the submission of evidence to a jury, a procedure unique to common-law criminal trials. In both cases, the failure of mostly civilian judges to understand how common law criminal proceedings work may have led to interpretations of international law that the subject states found both incomprehensible and unacceptable.

The big question that this volume addresses is whether international law can bridge gaps between the world's principal legal systems. There are many pathways that such bridging might take, and others explore them in this book. What I want to do is discuss the ways that international law might serve as an obstacle to convergence between the common law and civil law.

This essay draws on a larger scholarly enterprise in which I have played a part, namely the exploration of the concept of comparative international law.[2] International law aspires to universality and uniformity. It applies independently of municipal (domestic) law. Yet in practice states and regions have distinct, and sometimes radically different, approaches to both the process of making international law and the products of that

---

[2] Anthea Roberts, Paul B. Stephan, Pierre-Hugues Verdier and Emilia Versteeg, eds. *Comparative International Law*, (Oxford: Oxford University Press 2017); Symposium. 2015. "Exploring Comparative International Law." *Am. J. Int'l L.* 109, No. 3, 467-550. For a related work by a collaborator, see Anthea Roberts,. *Is International Law International?* (Oxford:Oxford University Press 2017)

process. Claims about what international law requires and how one can tell vary a lot, depending on who makes the claim.

Many forces contribute to this variation in international law. One is the background norms and predispositions that particular legal systems create and reinforce. The people who produce international law come out of these systems and carry these traits. Because to some extent background assumption about what law is and does are taken for granted and thus unconscious, these actors produce international law that confirms and extends their local understandings of how law works.

This paper first will outline the general features of comparative international law. It then will discuss the particular features of the international human rights system that can exacerbate the gaps between common-law and civilian jurists. It demonstrates how these features play out through an example, an important human rights dispute that implicates the differences between the common law and civil law. It concludes by showing how these differences bring about discord and block international cooperation to the detriment of the international law project.

1. Comparative International Law

The root of the problem is that international law depends on international lawyers. These people are necessarily products of a specific legal culture. They begin their education and training in particular national institutions, no matter how soon and how deeply they throw themselves into the field of international law. Moreover, most of them function in particular national institutions as either formal or informal advisers to national governments. Almost all international law involves nation states, either as participants in transactions with other states or as subjects of international law charged with certain duties regarding persons, legal and natural. States use international lawyers both to understand their rights and obligations but, perhaps even more importantly, to shape international law to their liking.

The national dimension of international law becomes even starker when one looks at courts as producers of international law. Most judges in domestic courts lack much training or background in international law. A national supreme court might have one or two members who have some professional investment in international law, but few if any have a substantial number of such specialists. The persons who serve on international tribunals tend to have a specific international legal focus, corresponding to the nature of the tribunal involved. Human rights courts in particular tend to fill up with persons with a substantial interest in human rights law, but not taxation, commercial transactions, or even criminal adjudication.

Moreover, international law lacks a canon, and perhaps even a rule of recognition. One can take the discipline seriously and still admit that a lot of room exists for contentious claims about what counts as international law and what constitutes its hierarchy as well as the existence and content of particular rules or obligations.[3] This flexibility makes it easier to mold claims about international law to reflect the interests of particular states.

I do not mean to make the simplistic observation that individual states will tailor their versions of international law to meet their needs – that should be obvious and not especially interesting – but rather that where a state sits in the complex web of international relations strongly influences its account of international law. A hegemon, for example, makes very different assertions about international law than does a subordinated state.[4] During the period of bipolar superpower competition, the United States and Europe, on the one hand, and the Soviet Union and the People's Republic of China, on the other hand, constructed very different versions of international law, including divergent accounts of state sovereignty, *jus cogens*, treaty interpretation, customary international law, the definition of aggression, and other fundamental matters.[5] In the contemporary world, these patterns of difference endure.

2. Comparative International Human Rights

The centrifugal forces pulling on international law take on added force in the field of international human rights. To begin with, a large number of people – perhaps a majority of those on this planet – live in regimes that believe that sovereign equality and noninterference in domestic affairs are the core values of international law, indeed enjoying the status of *jus*

---

[3] I explore these issues at greater length in Paul B. Stephan. 2018. "Overlapping Sovereignty and Laws' Domains." *Pepperdine L. Rev.* 45, No. 2 (forthcoming).

[4] Paul B. Stephan.. "Symmetry and Selectivity: What Happens in International Law When the World Changes." *Chi. J. Int'l L.* 10, No. 1 (2009): 91-123.

[5] Paul B. Stephan. "The Impact of the Cold War on Soviet and US Law: Reconsidering the Legacy." In *The Legal Dimension in Cold War Interactions: Some Notes from the Field*, edited by Tatiana Borisova and William B. Simons, (Leiden, Martinus Nijhoff Publishers. 2012), 141-58.

cogens.[6] For these regimes, human rights obligations exist, but enforcement by any means other than an express treaty commitment, such as that found in the European Convention on Human Rights, is problematic if not illegal.

This existential issue aside, international human rights interact with municipal law in a manner that is unusual, if not unique, within public international law. Almost all human rights issues involve domestic officials, who either do something bad or fail to prevent something bad from happening. Assessment of these officials necessarily requires a sense of what normal official conduct looks like so that one can detect a deviation. Not all injuries inflicted on people by the state implicate human rights law. For example, the conduct of a criminal proceeding that results in conviction and punishment harms the convict – that, after all, is its purpose – but this harm stems from a human rights violation only if the proceeding departed from some standard. What this standard is, however, can be embedded in unconscious assumptions about the right way to do things, assumptions that may vary among the lawyers who make up the international legal system. Moreover, in many instances international human rights involve not simply the prescription of primary rules, but also of obligations to redress. Access to justice, for example, is one of the entitlements protected by this body of law, but determining what counts as sufficient access necessary requires an assessment of municipal law.

Complicating this picture is the role of courts and tribunals in defining and enforcing international human rights. To a greater extent than in other areas of international law, judges are the stewards of this corpus. Their limitations as products of national legal systems become even more salient. In the international tribunals that enforce human rights, there exists yet another layer of limitations. Almost without exceptions, the persons who serve on these bodies are specialists in either human rights or international law, but not in the body of municipal law that a claim may implicate.

A common failing of both domestic and international judges is the absence of experience or training in comparative law, and especially in comparative procedural law. More often than not, these judges have experience with international or regional institutions and have worked for many years in the field of human rights. What they mostly lack is

---

[6] Declaration of the Russian Federation and the People's Republic of China on the Promotion of International Law, Jun. 23, 2016, points 2, 4, 6, 8, available at http://www.mid.ru/en/foreign_policy/position_word_order//asset_publisher/6S4RuXfeYlKr/content/id/2331698.

experience with other legal systems generally, as distinguished from their human rights practice. On matters of both substance and procedure, they typically lack a basic sense of normal variation in the way legal systems dispose of specific matters.

Procedure is especially salient, because legal actors tend to take these ways of doing things for granted. Although common lawyers and civilians might profess loyalty to shared values such as fairness and expediency, they do not commonly explore how particular procedural rules fit within an entire system. They especially lack much insight into the interlocking features of rules and practices in other regimes. As a result, they may fail to understand how a particular approach, not used in their own system, may advance the values that they see as undergirding all processes.

Jurists within public international law have explored, and largely bemoaned, the phenomenon of fragmentation, namely the development of different cultures, norms and methodologies in different parts of the discipline.[7] Human rights specialists, including especially judges on international tribunals, belong to a distinct subculture. Part of what distinguishes these actors from other international lawyers is focus and values, but different expertise, and necessarily gaps in expertise, also plays a role. And when these specialists fall back on often unstated assumptions about what it is to "think like a lawyer," the gap between civil law and the common law often manifests itself.

These differences would not present a problem if they were transparent, theorized, and incorporated into the analysis underlying the legal task at hand. But the pretension of international law to universality and uniformity leads to suppression of these steps, if actors consider them at all. What we instead tend to see is confusion and recrimination based on misunderstandings. Such misunderstandings in turn can lead to charges of incompetence and even bad faith, as actors will fail to get at the root of their mutual incomprehension. Such irruptions can in turn provoke systemic challenges to the value and integrity of international legal regime, human rights in particular.

3. An Example

Specific examples can bring into focus these general observations. I discuss here an episode where an international tribunal looked at municipal

---

[7] Paul B. Stephan. "Comparative International Law, Foreign Relations Law and Fragmentation: Can the Center Hold?" *Comparative International Law*, note 2 (2017).

criminal justices processes and found them wanting.[8] The municipal law reflected the habits and assumptions of the common law system, and civilian-majority tribunal found a violation of international human rights law. The episode can be understood as an instance of mutual miscomprehension that complicates the divide between the common law and civil law as well as undermining the international law project.

For twenty years, individuals protected by the Vienna Convention on Consular Relations have sought redress in U.S. courts for violations of their right of access to consular assistance after arrest. Article 36(1)(b) of the Vienna Convention obligates a state party to inform "without delay" a person arrested for a crime of the state's obligation to inform the relevant consular official of the arrest. Consular assistance is thought necessary to enable a person, perhaps a stranger to the municipal legal system, to navigate the challenges poses by a detention connected to a criminal investigation or prosecution. Most law enforcement in the United States occurs at the State or local level, and the police officers and local magistrates who administer arrest and detention did not always carry out their duty to inform a detained person of his right to consular access.

Litigation in U.S. courts and the International Court of Justice (ICJ) focused mostly on cases where a person who had not received notice of the right to consular assistance later was sentenced to capital punishment for the crime committed. Although the international obligation did not turn on the outcome of the proceedings, claimants sensibly argued that the severity of the punishment made the issue of the legality of the process that led to conviction more salient. Consular assistance, they maintained, would have provided persons charged with crimes another layer of advice, including identification of experienced counsel, that might have helped these persons to avoid the death penalty.

Three states brought cases to the ICJ claiming that U.S. practice violated the Vienna Convention to the detriment of their nationals. In the first proceeding, the Court did not address the merits because the United States executed the person in question, in spite of provisional measures provided by the Court to bar carrying out the sentence.[9] In the second

---

[8] My discussion here tracks my earlier treatment of the case. Paul B. Stephan. "The Political Economy of Judicial Production of International Law." *The Political Economy of International Law: A European Perspective*, edited by Alberta Fabbricotti, (Cheltenham, Edgar Elgar, 2016), 219-20.

[9] Case Concerning the Vienna Convention on Consular Relations (Paraguay v. U.S.). 1998., *I.C.J. Rep.* 426.

case, the Court retained jurisdiction after the execution of the persons in question and determined that the United States had not complied with its obligations under the Convention.[10] In the third case, the Court mandated that the United States not execute any person until a new judicial proceeding had determined whether that person had suffered a material detriment from the absence of notification of the right to consular access.[11]

One of the arguments made by the United States in defense of its conduct was that in all of the cases at issue, counsel for the accused had failed to raise in a timely fashion the issue of the Convention violation. The procedural law applicable to the trials imposed deadlines after which claims of the sort that the Vienna Convention issue implicated – a question not directly implicating the accused's guilt or innocence – were deemed waived. In most, if not all cases, counsel for the accused had not brought up the Vienna Convention until after direct appeals of the conviction had been exhausted.[12] The ICJ's respond to this argument was brief to the point of terseness: Because the right to learn of consular access belonged to the detained person, decisions after the fact made by that person's lawyer could have no bearing on questions of the right's violation:

> [T]he procedural default rule prevented [U.S. courts] from attaching any legal significance to the fact, inter alia, that the violation of the rights set forth in Article 36, paragraph 1, prevented Germany, in a timely fashion, from retaining private counsel for them and otherwise assisting in their defence as provided for by the Convention.[13]

The effect of this part of the ruling was to give the victim of a treaty violation a nonwaivable right of access to a judicial determination as to whether the violation affected the outcome of the trial, even if as a matter of municipal law the victim had surrendered that right.

---

[10] LaGrand Case (Germany v. U.S.). 2001. *I.C.J. Rep.* 466.

[11] Case Concerning Avena and Other Mexican Nationals (Mexico v. U.S.). 2004. *I.C.J. Rep.* 12.

[12] U.S. law almost uniquely has a system of post-conviction judicial review of criminal sentences that applies once all direct appeals have been exhausted. This review, colloquially known as *habeas corpus*, is a matter of right but limited as to the kinds of claims that can be raised. If most if not all of the cases addressed by the ICJ, the municipal legal issue was the scope of *habeas* review.

[13] LaGrand Case ¶ 91. The Court repeated the point, quoting LaGrand, in Avena ¶ 112.

U.S. courts, in contrast, insisted that the power of a criminal accused's lawyer to make binding decisions about the assertion of claims, including choices that had the consequence of waiving a claim was a fundamental aspect of U.S. criminal procedure. The Supreme Court of the United States observed that insistence of a timely assertion of a claim was one of the "established principles of domestic law."[14] It found it inconceivable that a right based on a treaty would enjoy greater protection in the U.S. legal system than do individual rights based on the Constitution.

What fundamentally divided the ICJ from the Supreme Court were assumptions about the power of the accused's lawyer. For the ICJ, once a person had suffered from a violation of a right provided by international law, only that person could decide how to seek redress. A convicted person presumably could decide not to seek relief due to a belief that the argument had no merit. But because the notice right was personal to the accused, the ICJ appeared to conclude that the accused's lawyer lacked the power to forfeit the right, even if a clear procedural rule of the local forum otherwise were to require that outcome.

The Supreme Court, by contrast, could not understand how an accused's lawyer could not have the power to bind his or her client. U.S. law imposes a constitutional standard of competency on the representatives of criminal accuseds, which means that incompetent blunders will entitle the client to additional proceedings, and perhaps a new trial. But the system takes for granted that a competent lawyer may choose not to pursue particular avenues in defending a case and that the lawyer's choices bind the client. This is particularly true of rules about the timing of claims. If a competent lawyer had all the information needed to assert a claim during the course of a trial and had no good reason for not raising that claim before the case went to a jury, the system regards it as intolerable not to close the matter out. Were the rule otherwise, the lawyer could present a case to a jury while retaining viable claims in reserve, knowing that a favorable verdict would bind the government but that an

---

[14] Sanchez-Llamas v. Oregon. 2006. 548 *U.S.* 331, 360. Two years later the Court stated that "a contrary conclusion would be extraordinary, given that basic rights guaranteed by our own Constitution do not have the effect of displacing state procedural rules." Meddelín v. Texas. 2008. 552 *U.S.* 491, 523. The Court ruled in multiple cases that U.S. law did not provide for judicial enforcement of orders or judgments of the ICJ, thus obligating courts to defer to Congress in determining how to bring the United States into compliance with the ICJ's mandate. Breard v. Greene. 1998. 523 *U.S.* 371, 375); Meddelín, *supra*; Meddelín v. Texas. 2008. 554 *U.S.* 759; Garcia v. Texas. 2011. 564 *U.S.* 940.

unfavorable outcome could be reversed by a belated presentation of the reserved claim.

These different assumptions about the lawyer's role rest on fundamental differences between the common law and the civil law. At least as members of the system conceive of their roles, a judge in a civil law proceeding maintains greater control and more closely supervises the actions of the other participants, including the advocates of the parties. Advocates may propose things, but across a wide range of issues the judge controls the course of the proceedings. The judge in particular is supposed to intervene in the interests of justice, asking questions and making arguments that the advocates may not have raised. The difference may be one of degree, and realization of these conceptions in actual practice may be uneven. But the lawyers in the system, judges perhaps most of all, believe these things to be true, and indeed take them for granted.

The common law system, by contrast, gives greater responsibility to the advocate and expects the judge to defer more to the choices of a competent counsel. Absent concerns about competence or on matters of fundamental fairness, a common-law judge will not call for evidence and arguments on issues that the accused's lawyer has not chosen to raise. Lawyers have greater discretion to act or not without having to account to the judge.

Two distinct features of the common law system reinforce this tendency – plea bargaining and jury trials. Plea bargains maximize the discretion of the lawyer and limit the role of the judge, who supervises but generally does not undo or redo these deals. A jury trial, where the jury carries out a distinct role and functions in the judge's absence, makes irreversible acquittals a possibility. This possibility in turn increases the need for forfeiture rules that prevent unnecessary multiple trials. Together these features inculcate in the participants a culture of greater lawyer autonomy and reduced judicial intervention in the criminal trial.

These observations are, of course, only generalizations about the culture of the two systems. The common law has known active, even domineering trial judges, and particular civil law proceedings may give advocates greater room to play than the cultural account might indicate. It remains the case that these features are accurate depictions of different mindsets, that these mindsets are shared by most actors in the system, and that they support assumptions about the proper way of doing things that generally are taken for granted rather than critically examined.

What results are significantly different appraisals of a conventional procedural rule. A civilian judge will assume that the judge, as representative of the state, ultimately has the responsibility to ensure that a criminal proceeding has addressed critical issues, including (where relevant) access to consular assistance. It should not be left to the advocate to draw the court's attention to this problem, because the judge has ultimate responsibility for ensuring the realization of justice. In the common law, by contrast, the powerful lawyer, who may bypass a trial altogether by inducing the client to plead guilty, or instead insist on a jury trial that may turn on factors not formally recognized by the law ("jury nullification"), must have room to make critical decisions and to bind the client to them.

The point is not, I hasten to add, that one approach is superior to the other. Incomprehension entails mutual responsibility. Perhaps the judges on the ICJ, only one of whom would have had any familiarity with the characteristics of the U.S. criminal justice system (and he was not a specialist in the field), should have tried harder to understand the work that procedural default rules do in a common law system and not jump to the conclusion that they had no bearing on the protection of a right. Perhaps the U.S. judges should have considered whether the issue of consular assistance should be left up to the accused's lawyer, or instead if the trial judge should be compelled to play a more proactive role with respect to the issue. For my purposes, it suffices to note that neither of these expectations might be realistic. Rather, the structure of this aspect of international law opens the path to conflict, and the divergence of the two legal systems then fuels the conflict.

This analysis does not address a different point, namely whether the United States had an obligation to comply with the judgment of the ICJ whether or not that judgment was persuasively reasoned. A growing phenomenon in the contemporary world is the refusal of municipal courts to require their governments to comply with the judgments of international tribunals, no matter how clear the conventional obligation to submit. The United Kingdom has paid judgments for compensation ordered by the European Court of Human Rights (Strasbourg Court) but has refused to amend its laws in instances where its courts believed that the Strasbourg Court had misunderstood the European Convention on Human Rights.[15] Italy's Constitutional Court has invalidated legislation meant to bring the country into compliance with an order of the ICJ because, it believed, the legislation infringed constitutional guarantees

---

[15] Moohan v Lord Advocate. 2014. *U.K.S.C.* 67; Regina v Horncastle. 2009. *U.K.S.C.* 14.

regarding access to justice.[16] Most recently, the Constitutional Court of the Russian Federation barred payment of a judgment of the Strasbourg Court that, in the view of the Russian court, violated Russia's constitutional order.[17]

These instances suggest a disturbing pattern of states invoking municipal law to bar compliance with the demands of international courts to which these states had agreed to submit their disputes. Perhaps the actions of the United States made it easier for other countries to go down the same road. What these cases do not do, however, is sort out in a way the distinguishes civil-law states from common-law ones. The United States and the United Kingdom exemplify the common law system. Italy and the Russian Federation are both civilian jurisdictions that have made constitutional commitments to hierarchical supremacy of international law. These acts of resistance indicate that, if there is a pattern of erosion of international norms, it reflects not the differences between civil and common law systems so much as a general disenchantment with international legal institutions.[18]

4. Revisiting the Wedge

That misconceptions based on the common-law/civil-law divide might lead to a dispute over the content of a particular international legal obligation need not concern us much. Disagreements over the interpretation and application of international law happen all the time

---

[16] Italian Constitutional Court, Judgment No. 238 of October 22, 2014. Unofficial English translation by Alessio Gracis, available at http://italyspractice.info/judgment-238-2014.

[17] Resolution No. 1-P of the Constitutional Court of the Russian Federation of January 19, 2017, http://www.ksrf.ru/en/Decision/Judgments/Documents/2017_January_19_1-P.pdf (official English translation).

[18] Pushing back slightly against the statement in the text, one can observe that the two common-law jurisdictions identified problems that the legislature remained free to fix. The U.S. Congress may create the hearing right that the ICJ demanded, and the British Parliament might amend the law to allow felons to vote (pace Moohan) and to make it easier to exclude hearsay testimony (pace Horncastle). The Italian and Russian decisions, by contrast, created barriers to compliance with an international tribunal's order that only a constitutional amendment might eliminate. It is not clear to me, however, however this difference relates to the civil-law/common-law divide.

and help to keep the field dynamic and relevant. But some disputes matter more than others and can endanger the system.

The controversy between the ICJ and the United States over the Vienna Convention illustrates the kind of dispute that can have collateral harmful effects. First, although international law embraces the principle of sovereign equality, clearly some states matter more than others. When a large and powerful state, something close to a hegemon, that also has played a major role in shaping the current international legal regime rejects the demands of the preeminent judicial body attached to the United Nations, others take note. When the background to the dispute involves a practice that important communities, the European in particular, regard as barbaric – here capital punishment – the dispute takes on even greater salience.

As noted above, the specific grounds for U.S. refusal to comply with the ICJ judgment was a matter of municipal public law that had nothing to do with the civil-law/common-law law divide. In the view of the Supreme Court of the United States, creation of the mechanism that the ICJ required – a judicial hearing on the question of whether a violation of the Vienna Convention notice right had an impact on the subsequent criminal proceeding – required a legislative act, and could not be adopted by either an order of the President or by judicial fiat. The Court conceded that legislative inaction would leave the United States in default on its clear international obligation, but placed separation-of-powers principles above the imperative of honoring the mandate of international law.

The problem with separation-of-powers arguments is that they lack clear resonance with other states. Although most modern states embrace some version of the principle, variation in practice is profound and sometimes subtle. Distinguishing, for example, between truly independent judiciaries that enforce separation of powers and those that endorse whatever the transient local power wishes can be challenging. As a result, much of the relevant audience will discount such justifications for noncompliance with international law, no matter how persuasive the arguments might seem to internal audiences.

To repeat, this is not a problem of the civil-law/common-law divide. Issues of public law do not fit so nicely into categories of legal systems. But the issue of enforcement never arises if key decisionmakers avoid a confrontation over the interpretation of the obligation.

Here the ICJ-US controversy has important lessons to teach us. First, a failure to take account of the differences in domestic legal systems, especially as to procedural rules, can more easily produce an escalation of resistance. Second, this resistance can affect not just the parties, but the entire international legal regime. Third, applications and rejections of international law require thick justification to convey the sense that actors take the issues seriously, whatever they choose to do. A failure to grapple with differences in procedural aspects along the civil-law/criminal-law divide results in thin justification and a loss of legitimacy. Fourth, and conversely, attention to these differences in the course of justification can produce collateral benefits for the international legal regime.

On the first point, one can tie the economical, to put it gently, manner in which the ICJ dealt with the issue of procedural default to the rather indignant reaction of the Supreme Court. If the ICJ's approach seemed inexplicable to the U.S. court, at least some of the responsibility lies with the ICJ's failure to provide an explanation. That apparent indifference to what the U.S. audience saw as a fundamental point may have contributed to the Supreme Court's later unwillingness to find space within the U.S. separation-of-powers system for the ICJ's mandate.

Second, it may be impossible to assess conclusively the impact of the U.S. defiance of the ICJ, but assigning it some responsibility for the later trend of resistance to international tribunals seems plausible. Without unpacking the gist of the U.S. position or demonstrating causal links, one still can note the recent willingness of constitutional courts in various states to interpose fundamental municipal law between a state and its international legal obligations. Law-based international cooperation is a fragile enterprise, and defiance by a powerful actor can inspire others to ask, "Why not me?" Once a U.S. court invoked its domestic constitutional order as a basis for its failure to bring the United States into compliance, other jurisdictions might have embraced the broader point of municipal law not as a means of allocating authority to bring about compliance, but as an absolute barrier to compliance.

Third, the burden to give plausible accounts of rulings that grapple with the interpretation and application of international law seems greatest when high profile issues involving high profile actors are in play. We may have gotten past the point where the absence of direct resources to enforce international law by itself confirms the claim that there is no international law. But the effectiveness of international law as a genuine social force still depends on persuasion. International law must convince relevant actors before its demands have any traction. Thinly argued rulings, and in particular rulings that do not attempt to encompass the divide between the civil law and common law, fail at the fundamental mission of engaging those whose cooperation is needed.

Fourth, a failure to provide a thick justification that accounts for differences in legal systems represents a missed opportunity. The structural differences between the common law and the civil law are not going away. Their influence on international law will be enduring. Those engaged in the international law enterprise must confront this problem and seek to overcome it. Serious reasoning about the implications of different features of the legal process for the formulation of international legal norms is essential. Where it is absent, all the negative effects discussed here can occur. Conversely, serious reasoning can inspire further serious work, changing the norms for justification and argument within the field.

To conclude, the divide between the civil law and the common law has the capacity to make mischief in the formulation and application of international law. Rather than bridging gaps between the two systems of municipal law, international law might make matters worse. But what follows is not despair, but rather a mandate to work harder. Those of us laboring in the fields of international and comparative law must do more to explore how our disciplines overlap, interact, and to depend on each other. Not to do this would shortchange not only ourselves but the greater social projects that we hope to launch and nourish.

Bibliography

Breard v. Greene. 1998. 523 *U.S.* 371, 375); Meddelín, *supra*; Meddelín v. Texas. 2008. 554 *U.S.* 759; Garcia v. Texas. 2011. 564 *U.S.* 940.

Case Concerning Avena and Other Mexican Nationals (Mexico v. U.S.). 2004. *I.C.J. Rep.* 12.

Case Concerning the Vienna Convention on Consular Relations (Paraguay v. U.S.). 1998., *I.C.J. Rep.* 426.

Declaration of the Russian Federation and the People's Republic of China on the Promotion of International Law, Jun. 23, 2016, points 2, 4, 6, 8, available at http://www.mid.ru/en/foreign_policy/position_word_order//asset_publisher/6S4RuXfeYlKr/content/id/2331698.

Italian Constitutional Court, Judgment No. 238 of October 22, 2014. Unofficial English translation by Alessio Gracis, available at http://italyspractice.info/judgment-238-2014.

LaGrand Case (Germany v. U.S.). 2001. *I.C.J. Rep.* 466.

LaGrand Case ¶ 91. The Court repeated the point, quoting LaGrand, in Avena ¶ 112.

Meddelín v. Texas. 2008. 552 *U.S.* 491, 523.

Moohan v Lord Advocate. 2014. *U.K.S.C.* 67; Regina v Horncastle. 2009. *U.K.S.C.* 14.

Resolution No. 1-P of the Constitutional Court of the Russian Federation of January 19, 2017, http://www.ksrf.ru/en/Decision/Judgments/Documents/2017_January_19_1-P.pdf (official English translation).

Roberts, Anthea, Paul B. Stephan, Pierre-Hugues Verdier and Emilia Versteeg, eds. *Comparative International Law*.Oxford, Oxford University Press, 2017.

Roberts, Anthea. *Is International Law International?*.Oxford:Oxford University Press, 2017.

Sanchez-Llamas v. Oregon. 2006. 548 *U.S.* 331, 360.

Stephan, Paul B. "Comparative International Law, Foreign Relations Law and Fragmentation: Can the Center Hold?"*Comparative International Law*, note 2.2017.

Stephan, Paul B. "Overlapping Sovereignty and Laws' Domains."*Pepperdine L. Rev.* 45, No. 2.2018.(forthcoming).

Stephan, Paul B. "The Impact of the Cold War on Soviet and US Law: Reconsidering the Legacy." In *The Legal Dimension in Cold War Interactions: Some Notes from the Field*, edited by Tatiana Borisova and William B. Simons, 41-58. Leiden: Martinus Nijhoff Publishers. 2012,

Stephan, Paul B. "The Political Economy of Judicial Production of International Law." *The Political Economy of International Law: A European Perspective*, edited by Alberta Fabbricotti, 219-20. Cheltenham:Edgar Elgar, 2016.

Stephan, Paul B."Symmetry and Selectivity: What Happens in International Law When the World Changes." *Chi. J. Int'l L.* 10, No. 1 (2009): 91-123.

Symposium. 2015. "Exploring Comparative International Law." *Am. J. Int'l L.* 109, No. 3, 467-550.

Chapter 2

Internal Law and International Law: From Common Law To Civil Law

Augusto Sinagra[1]
Anna Lucia Valvo[2]

Abstract

The paper examines the process of progressive adaptation of national legal systems to the "civil law" legal system. Such a process is confirmed by the steady and more and more widespread process of drafting legal instruments for legislative purposes at an international level in order to "unify" private law of the national legal systems. In that regard it is to be highlighted the activity conducted for many years by the International Institute for the Unification of Private Law. The same phenomenon is happening within international public law through its progressive and steady "codification" by way of multilateral international treaties. The process of progressive harmonization and unification of national legal systems implies a basic choice for "civil law" instead of "common law" whose raison d'etre and purpose is to guarantee a higher legal certainty in the interindividual legal relationships either of private or of public persons. The "codification" of private international law has the purpose of harmonizing national legal systems of States so as to facilitate legal relationships and international "circulation" of national legal acts. Yet, the "codification" of international public law raises some doubts because the attempt to create "positive law" or to "crystallize" legal relationships between States at international level is not convincing as a matter of law and fact. In fact, inter-State legal relationships are highly variable due to the ever-changing underlying political and economic grounds. As regards means, forms and timings the

---

[1] Full Professor of European Union Law at the University "La Sapienza" of Rome.
[2] Full Professor of European Union Law at the University of Central Sicily "Kore" of Enna.

way international public law adapts to such grounds and related changes is very different from the way States' legal systems adapt to new requests coming from national societies. The paper also examines the role played by case-law in the relationships between "civil law" legal systems and "common law" legal systems.

1

Despite its multiple implications, the topic concerning possible convergences and divergences between common law and civil law in this particular historical and political moment of international cooperation, also from the legal point of view, cannot be separated from considering the deep relations existing between those two big and historic legal systems. This consideration not only applies to single national legal orders but also to the international legal one, that should be the normative expression of the States' International Community, and that should address the regulation of its relations.

This paper aims to highlight the process of "civilization" or "continentalization" of the common law system. This system should be understood as a legal system that regulates the relations existing between the States in the framework of a general International Community, both at the level of national legal orders and at the international legal one.

In terms of "competition", the "civil" or "continental" law system seems to prevail over the "common" law system.

2

At this point in our analysis, a retrospective consideration on the origins of the common law system may be useful. This legal model characterized the Roman legal order in its different political and institutional "moments" and historical developments: the Monarchy, the Republic, the Empire and all those *interim* "moments" of autocratic or dictatorial management of political power. Considering the latter, the most proper term to use should be "consular" management of power, in its different declination of single consul or triumvirate.

In order to highlight a similar, even if brief, political and juridical experience it will be useful to recall the 1920 Italian Regency of Fiume Charter[3] (the Constitution of the Autonomous Regency of Fiume – nor

---

[3] Augusto Sinagra, Lo Statuto della Reggenza italiana del Carnaro: tra storia, diritto internazionale e diritto costituzionale,(Milano:Giuffrè editore, 2009)

Republic neither Reign – characterized in its essence by a desired provisional nature, as the word *regency clearly indicates*, as the final goal of this political experience was the union of Fiume and its province to the Reign of Italy). This constitutional charter foresaw that the representative popular assembly could have given mandate to a *Commander* to temporarily take the powers of the *regency* in case of emergency, as it happened in the ancient Roman political system, in which the Senate was called to take such a decision even if there were no constitutional provisions regulating this situation.

Originally, the Roman Senate did not have a specific and primal legislative normative function. It had, on the other hand, a primal decision-making and political guidance functions for the general issues and the power to nominate, both in time of peace and war, the figure of the Consul, tasked with resolving the issues defined by the Senate, foreseeing also the use of the military force if needed.

As is well known, a "legislative" function did not exist at that time with the current meaning we give to this process. The "normative" function was absolved by the *Praetor* adopting for the resolution of each concrete case the most relevant legal discipline needed. According to the general unwritten principles that characterized the legal and political order in the Roman system,[4] the *Praetor* absolved this function. He was appointed to apply the most suitable legal regime for the resolution of each specific case.

In this way, the jurisprudential development of the law evolved in a manner which was indisputably connected to the *precedent* approach. This justified the *edictum tralatricium* of the ancient Roman *praetor*.

The current common law system originates from that historical, political and legal context. It is not an autonomous and original characteristic of the Anglo-Saxons or similar legal systems, but it is the resumption of the original Roman legal order. All these systems are born from the same socio-political characteristics of those communities, although they were primitive societies and their political institutions were not developed.

At a certain historical moment, the Roman common law system bent towards the formal "positivization" of law, namely its evolution towards what we nowadays call the civil law system. This evolution process was constant in its historical development that origins from the Roman laws:

---

[4] Vicenzo Arangio Ruiz, Istituzioni di diritto romano, (Napoli Casa Editrice Dott. Eugenio Jovene, 1984)

since *lex Julia*, *lex Claudia*, *Lex Cilicia*, *lex Gaja*, ecc. to the constitutionalization and formalization of the Justinian age. This slow but constant evolution continued with the establishment of the "*communal charters*", and with the claim of autonomy and formalization for States' legal orders and it culminated with the great Napoleonic codifications.

The common law systems survived in those countries, namely the Anglo-Saxons countries, which had not experienced these fundamental processes of political transformation and political restructuring of the State.

In brief, the ancient Roman common law system moved to Great Britain where it survived.

3

It is, however, indisputable that this transformation process of the common law's legal systems in civil law's legal orders is still evolving.[5]

While examining this process, it has to be pointed out that an ongoing and a wider process of elaboration of the legal texts, which have the legislative goals of ruling the relations between individuals and those between individuals and the public authority, is the evidence of the progressive adaptation of the common law legal orders to the civil law one. These legal texts are elaborated in response to the interstate legal cooperation efforts aimed to unify and harmonize the private law that differs from State to State.

In this context, the work of the *International Institute for the Unification of Private Law* is fundamental.

Likewise, it has to be recalled the codification of the private law and the civil procedural law done by the *Hague Conferences on Private International Law*.

In the general context of the globalization and its implications, International Organisations like the European Union take the lead of the ongoing codification process of the private and – in some cases – the public law. The International Organisations are requested to "legislate" on issues traditionally falling within the competences of the national legal order of the States: from contracts to transport obligations, from

---

[5] Giuseppe Morbidelli, Lucio Pegoraro, Angelo Rinella and Mauro Volpi, *Diritto pubblico comparato*, (Torino:Quinta Edizione, 2016)

parentage to succession, from trade to financial relations, from research to education, etc.

It is worth thinking about the legislation of the trade relations between States introduced by the World Trade Organisation Treaty.[6] In this case, relevant aspects of the public law are involved in the process of codification of the law at a supranational level. The process gets involved also those State legal orders – like Great Britain's one – that are traditionally common law systems.

Some important Conventions confirm the evolution of the legal orders towards the civil law system. For example, international multilateral treaties set up a different process of constitutionalization of the international law and a different internationalization of the constitutional systems of the States – tackling the wider issue of the limits and content of the state sovereignty and the relations between citizens and foreigners with the public authorities of the State.

The international multilateral treaties created jurisdictional bodies to protect their own provisions. A few examples: the Convention for the Protection of Human Rights and Fundamental Freedoms signed in Rome on 4 November 1950; and the American Convention on Human Rights, also known as the Pact of San José, signed on 22 November 1969.

4

On the one hand, the needs and the purpose of the process aimed at fostering the unity of the subject and more certainty of the inter-individual legal relations – between public and private individuals – are clear. On the other hand, the "codification" of the international public law[7] raises concerns because of the improbability of the proactivity of the "positivization" or the "freezing" of the legal relations among the States due to the changing political and economic demands of the relations themselves. The nature of the international public law made necessary its adaptation to those demands. Concerning the means, forms and timings that characterize the adaptation of international public law to such

---

[6] Antonio Parenti, *Il WTO*,(Bologna:Il Mulino, 2011)

[7] The codification of the international private law does not raise any doubt because it is contextual to the harmonisation process of each national legal order aiming to facilitate the inter-individual relations and the "circulation" of the States' national legal acts.

demands and related changes is very different from the way States' legal systems adapt to new requests coming from national societies.

An *ad hoc* United Nations Commission leads the codification work of the international public law. The Commission has undoubtedly an important role in the codification process that aims to define a more legal certainty of the States' legal relations in the frame of their international relations.

Since it will be pointless listing all the relevant codifications treaties made by the Commission, we need only to recall, among the many, the Vienna Convention on Diplomatic and Consular relations, the Vienna Convention on the Law of Treaties, the Draft Articles on the Responsibility of States for Internationally Wrongful Acts, and the conventions on jurisdiction.

It cannot be denied that this work of codification has gone beyond the limit of the "positivization", namely the codification in a written and definite form of the customary law or the general principles of the international legal order. Apart from excusable errors in the codification that strayed from the original meaning of the customary law, the point is that "new" norms were introduced in the international multilateral acts. These norms have exclusively a covenantal nature because these written rules do not find any evidence in the pre-existing and effective norms of international customary law.

In addition, apart from the systematic and logical *blackout* of codifying the Law of Treaties with an international treaty that a successive bilateral agreement can modify, the idea of codifying the general principles of the international legal order concerning the order itself seems to raise some doubts. As an example, the codification of the general principle *pacta sunt servanda* or other general principles concerning the structure of the International Community[8] is a risky operation, also considering a very general perspective that discusses the very essence of the codification work that distorts the essence itself of a "codification".[9] The process cannot be entrusted to the members, albeit authoritative, of the International Law Commission or to the participants to an international intergovernmental conference that gathers a large majority of the States. They cannot be entrusted with the task and the function of interpreting

---

[8] As few examples of these general principles: the State sovereignty, the horizontal structure of the International Community, the territorial integrity, the political independence, the autonomy in the political economy decisions, etc.

[9] Rolando Quadri, *Diritto internazionale pubblico,*(Napoli: Libri Liguori 1989), 134

the international legal collective conscience that is characterized by its ability to suddenly *express* itself as a new and different general principle of the international legal order. Thereby the general principles set themselves apart from the customary laws because the former do not need the requirement of *diuturnitas* from which infers the necessity of a legal regulation, namely the *opinio juris*.

5

It is well known that the general international law norms – both customary laws and general principles – are not the product of an institutionalized process of normative production, as it happens in the domestic legal order of the States by the Parliaments that detain the legislative power. The general principles[10] arise suddenly from the international legal collective conscience of the International Community. Instead, the interaction of the *diuturnitas*, namely the general practice of the States, and the *opinio juris sive necessitates*,[11] namely the belief that an action was carried out as a legal obligation, creates customary laws.[12]

The conclusion is that the *rate* or adaptability of the overall general international law's norms to the changing social and political needs and perceptions of the International Community of the States is fundamentally instantaneous for the general principles and it is rapid for the customary laws.[13]

In addition, it is useful to remind that this codification exercise may produce the involuntary effect of freezing the norms, in contrast with the changing needs and perceptions of the reference society.

However, this disconnection between the will and the perceptions of the society and the failure to immediately adaptation of its legal order is *institutionalized* in those national legal orders where the amendment of the laws requires waiting for the decisions of the Parliaments.

---

[10] Augusto Sinagra, "I principi generali di diritto nelle concezioni socialiste del diritto internazionale", *Comunicazioni e studi.*, (1978): 417-468; Augusto Sinagra and Paolo Bargiacchi, *Lezioni di diritto internazionale pubblico*, (Milano:Giuffrè editore, 2016): 179.; Umberto Leanza and Ida Caracciolo, *Il diritto internazionale: diritto per gli Stati e diritto per gli individui*, (Torino:G.Giappichelli Editore, 2012),139.

[11] Mario Giuliano, *La Comunità internazionale e il diritto*, (Padova: CEDAM, 1950), 161 and 223.

[12] Quadri, *Diritto internazionale public*, 129.

[13] Tito Ballarino, *Diritto internazionale pubblico*, (Padova: CEDAM, 2014), 39.

Not always, the "positivization" of the general international law produce acceptable effects in terms of relations between legal order and *social* will. Nevertheless, we highlight that the legal certainty rate is higher in the international relations States' systems that are the product of the codification exercise.

In particular, the general principles cannot be objects of codification not only for the aforementioned reasons but also for the baseless and implicit claim of identifying the representatives of the States during the international conferences with the international legal collective conscience of the International Community.

With regard to the international public law[14] that is made whether by the international institutionalized jurisprudence or by the non-institutionalised jurisprudence,[15] the common law systems strive for the civil law system when the codification attempts are experienced, as it happens for the international private law.

6

The overall issue, so far examined in its legal aspects, raises serious doubts also in its political and economic implications existing in the framework of interstate relations, namely between so-called 'strong' and 'weak' States.

These doubts derive from the fact that the States try to impose on the political level, and then on the written law level, normative choices in the frame of the international public law. The States want to use those norms in a specious way or to use them speciously in order to grant legitimacy to some actions that otherwise would be wrongful. As an example, we recall the undue interference in the internal affairs of States – in contrast with the general principle of the domestic jurisdiction – that can escalate into the military intervention aimed at damaging the territorial integrity, the political independence or the legitimate exercise of the political economy instruments.

In this framework, the specious use of the alleged defense of the individuals' and fundamental rights, namely the political and civil rights, becomes dramatic when Western ideas, models, and norms are exclusively

---

[14] The international public law can be understood as a typical expression of the common law system.

[15] We refer to the Hague International Court of Justice for the institutionalised jurisprudence; instead, we refer to the *ad hoc* Arbitral Tribunals called upon to decide the international disputes for the non-institutionalised jurisprudence.

applied.[16] The same we can state for the claim for a change of the structure of the International Community that look at the State as an autonomous political organization of the society in the frame of a definite and limited territory in which the State exercises legitimately its sovereign powers.

Regarding the last example taken from the empirical observation, there was any codification of the principle of the structure. However, the claim consists of replacing the essence and will of the legal collective conscience of the States concerning the way of being of the States themselves with a political *option* in need of legal legitimacy.

Nowadays, the claim - clearly aimed to legitimate any wrongful act against a State including the armed aggression – rejects the traditional constitutive elements of the State: government, people and territory. It denies the possibility for a community to organize itself politically and to express a sovereign, legitimate and exclusive capacity to rule over a limited territory.

The territory – where the government power is exercised exclusively – is not considered a proper *constitutive* element of the State, but it is a *necessary* element that defines the spatial limits of the different legislative spheres of the States.[17] Given that, those who support the changing of the general principle that identifies the State as subject to international law pretend to apply the democratic conditionality for the aforementioned identification.

Referring at the "democratic" internal political asset of the State (as a condition, as said, confirming its international legal subjectivity) is not only contradicting the completely different and still valid general principle of self-determination of people entangled in international law also related to the choice they made of their internal political organization, but it has not any defined content or logical justification if we consider in addition that we cannot identify a unique *model* of democracy, or, better to say, it does not exist only the liberal representative democracy, but it exists also participatory democracy as well as corporative democracy, or other models and forms of democratic organization of the State.

---

[16] Anna Lucia Valvo, "Diritti e libertà fondamentali e sospensione degli Stati membri dell'Unione europea", *Rivista della Cooperazione Giuridica Internazionale* (2003): 21.

[17] The juridical function of the border is the physical identification of the space beyond which the State cannot claim any sovereignty, sovereignty that for its nature tries to affirm beyond any spatial limit.

It is easy to see that this claim hides the unbearable chance to interfere, also with violent means, in the internal affairs of a State. The democratic conditionality as a requirement for the international legal subjectivity, not only contradicts the general principle of the right of people to self-determination, concerning in particular the right to choose its political organization, but also does not have a clear content or meaning because it does not exist a unique *model* of democracy.[18] In addition, according to Eduardo Cimbali, the issue of the "democratization" of the internal politics of a State, the issue of the democratic nature of a State, or in general the *struggle against the tyranny* belong to each people. These issues cannot justify in any way the interference of third States in the name of the defense of the civil and political rights of the Liberal State,[19] according to the Western models.

Bibliography

Ballarino, Tito.*Diritto internazionale pubblico*.Padova:CEDAM, 2014.

Cimbali, Eduardo.*Lo Stato secondo il diritto internazionale universale*.Milano: Kessinger Legacy reprints,1891.

Giuliano, Mario,.*La Comunità internazionale e il diritto*.Padova:CEDAM, 1950.

Moribelli, Giuseppe, Lucio Pegoraro, Angelo Rinella and Mauro Volpi.*Diritto pubblico comparator*.Napoli: Quinta Edizione, 2016.

Parenti, Antonio.*Il WTO*.Il Mulino, 2011.

Quadri, Rolando.*Diritto internazionale pubblico*.Napoli: Libri Liguori, 1989.

Ruiz, Vicenzo Arangio.*Istituzioni di diritto romano*.Napoli:Casa Editrice Dott. Eugenio Jovene, 1984.

Sinagra, Augusto and Paolo Bargiacchi.*Lezioni di diritto internazionale pubblico*.Milano: Giuffrè editore, 2016. Leanza, Umberto and Ida Caracciolo.*Il diritto internazionale: diritto per gli Stati e diritto per gli individui*.Torino: G.Giappichelli Editore, 2012.

Sinagra, Augusto."I principi generali di diritto nelle concezioni socialiste del diritto internazionale", *Comunicazioni e studi.*, (1978): 417-468

Sinagra, Augusto.*Lo Statuto della Reggenza italiana del Carnaro: tra storia, diritto internazionale e diritto costituzionale*.Milano:Giuffrè editore, 2009.

Valvo, Anna Lucia, "Diritti e libertà fondamentali e sospensione degli Stati membri dell'Unione europea", *Rivista della Cooperazione Giuridica Internazionale* (2003): 21.

---

[18] There are different model of democracy: the liberal representative democracy, the participative democracy, the corporative democracy, etc.

[19] Eduardo Cimbali, *Lo Stato secondo il diritto internazionale universale*, (Milano: Kessinger Legacy reprints ,1891)

Chapter 3

Territorial Knowledge, Sociality and the Convergence of International and Constitutional Law

William E Conklin[1]

Abstract

The issue of the possible convergence of international law and domestic constitutional law in a common law state raises the issue of the obligatory character of a law, whether international or domestic. I shall retrieve the traditional approach, of recent years, to such an issue. I shall argue that this approach is misdirected. Instead, I shall retrieve a missing element of the obligatory character of something to be a law. This missing element, I shall argue, is critical for an understanding as to whether there is a possibility for the convergence of international legal norms and domestic constitutional laws in common law states. The clue to the traditional approach to the binding character of a law has rested in the justification of any possible legal unit with reference to intellectually transcendent concepts. A rule, right, principle, doctrine, policy or other intelligible standards, for example, are concepts. Such concepts are the objects of reflection, deliberation and a decision. A legacy has characterized such consciously represented concepts as 'written law'. In the context of the possible convergence of international and domestic constitutional law, the reflection, deliberation, and decisionism about what is binding have taken for granted that the convergence involves intellectually transcendent concepts over the acts and concepts of domestic constitutional regimes. When a general concept has been the object of express or implied consent of a state, a unit of international or constitutional law has been framed in the form of such a

---

[1] William E Conklin, Professor at the Faculty of Law, University of Windsor, Canada, Royal Society of Canada member.

concept. Social events have been represented as falling inside the territorial-like boundary of the conceptual unit. If a social event falls outside the territorial-like boundary of the concept of an international or national tribunal, then the possible convergence between public international law and domestic constitutional law dissipates. The acts of intellectualization in 'written law', I argue, conceal something which is very important. I shall argue that the missing feature of a binding law has concerned 'sociality'. Sociality, I shall argue, justifies the obligatory character of both international and domestic legal orders of common law jurisdictions. Drawing from the notion of 'sociality' in early modern (eg Grotius, Pufendorf, Hegel) and Roman (eg Cicero and Seneca the Younger) juristic writings, I shall also retrieve how sociality has figured in recent judgments of international and domestic tribunals concerning stateless peoples (Conklin 2014, 2015) and peremptory norms (Conklin 2012). The issue of the nature of legal obligation, I argue, must be addressed before one can consider whether an intellectually transcendent concept is obligatory for the one system of law (the international) and not for the other (the domestic). The problem is that if one understands convergence with reference to intellectually transcendent concepts, some concepts will abstract from context-specific phenomena of sociality, select other social phenomena, ignore other social phenomena and forget still other social phenomena as elements of a legal order. What jurists take as 'written law', as a consequence, risks lacking the sociality needed for a law to be binding. In the brief time available, I shall elaborate on the conditions for the existence of sociality and, therefore, for the possibility of convergence of public international law and domestic constitutional law. Without a focus upon sociality, the risk is that the absence of sociality leaves an alleged legal order non-existent.

A pivotal issue confronting international law and constitutional law doctrines concerns whether the doctrines are converging into each other. This issue has been plagued by a paradox. On the one hand, the sovereign state, its institutions, and its officials have been said to possess legal obligations to the international community only if the state expressly or impliedly consents to such obligations. Such obligations have been said to transcend and to trump the content of domestic laws as well as the actions of officials. Universal human rights and international criminal law have been said to possess a peremptory character of international law. On the other hand, the international legal doctrines have manifested a special reserved space to the sovereign state's law-making, adjudication and law enforcement. Such a reserved space has privileged the institutional and doctrinal sources of domestic constitutional law. The legislature and the courts have been said to be such institutional sources. The precedents of higher domestic courts have been said to bind lower court decisions. Such institutional and doctrinal sources have presumed the sovereign state as the ultimate or final author referent of the justification of legal rules and other intelligible standards. How is it possible for the state to be considered sovereign and yet to be obligated to a community that is said to transcend the sovereign state and its officials? Hans Kelsen framed this issue in the context of a paradox: "[t]he sovereign seems to be incompatible with being subject to a normative order."[2] HLA Hart described the paradox in this way:

> One of the persistent sources of perplexity about the obligatory character of international law has been the difficulty felt in accepting or explaining the fact that a state which is sovereign, may also be 'bound' by or have an obligation under international law.[3]

The paradox has raised the deeper issue, however. 'How can domestic constitutional law be congruent in content with public international law if the sovereign state is the ultimate referent of justification of domestic and international laws?'

In order to address such an issue, a distinction needs to be made. Lawyers and judges are usually preoccupied with the identity of a law. That is, is a law a rule? Or is it a principle, a policy, doctrine or custom? The identity of such a law, however, differs from the question, 'why is an identifiable law binding upon its inhabitants?' The usual response since the emergence of constitutionalism after the French and American Revolutions has been that the binding character of a law rests with the 'written Constitution'. But what renders authority to the framers or the ratifiers of such a text? Why are the identifiable customs of a traditional or nomadic community historically prior to the basic text not binding upon the framers or the ratifiers of the text?

I wish to suggest that the binding character of an identifiable law has presupposed two different approaches. The first approach has assumed that 'the Law' is a territorial space and that familiar doctrines of constitutional law presume a territorial-like space in legal consciousness. This sense of legal knowledge as territorial and territorial-like has been seriously problematic for the possibility of the congruence of constitutional and international law. The second response to the issue of the binding character of an identifiable law has rested upon the

---

[2] Hans Kelsen, "Sovereignty and International Law" in *Georgetown LJ* 48 (1960) 627-40.

presupposition that sociality binds inhabitants into a legal bond.[4] By sociality, I mean the social relationships of natural persons and their groups. The territorial space and the state's claim to constitutional authority over an individual where one finds oneself is a mere coincidence, as Grotius once wrote. Sociality is analytically independent of the territoriality and territorial-like legal knowledge. I shall address the territorial sense of legal obligation in Section 1. Section 2 will identify a series of obstacles to congruence in such a territorial sense of the binding character of a law. Section 3 will turn to an alternative grounding of a binding law: namely, sociality. I shall conclude that only the second sense of a legal bond – that is, the social relationships of individuals inter-se – raises the possibility that constitutional and international laws are congruent.

1. Territorial Knowledge

Now, international and constitutional legal analysis has presupposed that the legally binding character of a law is conditioned by a territorial sense of legal space. I wish to outline two such senses of legal space. The one concerns physical territory. The other relates to a territorial-like space in the doctrines, rules, principles and other intellectual standards of international and constitutional law. These standards constitute a legal consciousness.

a) The Identity of an Internationally Recognized Legal Person in Territorial Space

Returning to the paradox of sovereignty mentioned a moment ago, a sovereign state represents a territorial sense of space. As an example of how important territorial space has been to jurists, the Arbitrator Huber in *Palmas* (1928) stated in an oft-cited opinion that "territorial sovereignty is, in general, a situation recognized and delimited in *space* ... ."[5] A state's legal claim of absolute title to a territorial space, Huber wrote, hinges upon the extent to which a state controls the "space",[6] "*places*" or a "*given*

---

[3] HLA Hart, *Concept of Law* 3rd ed *(*Oxford: Clarendon Press, 2013 [1961]), 220.

[4] See the argument generally and the documentation in William E Conklin, *Statelessness: the Enigma of the International Community* with a Foreword by William Twining and Preface by William Conklin (Oxford: Hart, 2015 [2014]), 190-301.

[5] *Island of Palmas Case (Netherlands v United States)* 2 RIAA 829, 838-39; (1928) 4 ILR 3.

[6] *Ibid*, 839.

zone".[7] Such a space represents the "point of departure in settling most questions that concern international relations... ."[8] A few years later, Article 1 of the *Montevideo Convention on the Rights and Duties of States (1936)* listed four requisites for the recognition of a state as a legal person in the international community: a permanent population, a defined territory, a government and the capacity to enter foreign relations with other states. Each of the four elements of a state expressly or implicitly focused upon territoriality as an element of statehood. Only the control and claim to own a territorial space possessed the capacity of the space's representative government to enter into foreign relations. The United Nations now recognizes 220-odd such autonomous territorial spaces on the globe. The presumed territorial space itself, as the condition of the international community, has become increasingly difficult to question the more often it has been cited as a presumption in international law.[9]

This territorial sense of legal space has been presupposed in critically important doctrines about the binding character of international law. So, for example, the territoriality of the legal person (that is, the state) of the international community can be ceded, conquered or occupied. The form of a state's acquisition of territory impacts upon how a lawyer, judge or other official understands why a law is binding. From the international doctrinal delineation of the globe into territorial spaces, each space has become an intrinsically valued entity, an end-in-itself. As Zygmunt Bauman writes, the globe is "fully and exhaustively divided into national domains . . . [with] no space left for internationalism."[10] Borders separate the territorial spaces (and therefore the universal claims about law). Legal knowledge has become a territorial knowledge.

---

[7] *Ibid*, 848.

[8] *Ibid* 839.

[9] Even Kant makes this point. See Immanuel Kant, *Metaphysical Elements of Justice*, trans with Intro and Notes, John Ladd. 2nd ed. (Indianapolis: Hackett, 1999 [1797]), 123-25, lines 318-320; *Metaphysics of Morals*, trans by Mary Gregor (Cambridge, Cambridge University Press, 1996), 95. See Fitzpatrick, "'Gods Would be Needed . . .": American Empire and the Rule of (International) Law' in *Law as Resistance Modernism, Imperialism, Legalism* (Burlington Va: Ashgate, 2008), 167-204; 'What are the Gods to us Now? Secular Theology and the Modernity of Law' in *Law as Resistance* 293-322, at 293, 299, 305, 315.

[10] Zygmunt Bauman, *Modernity and the Holocaust*, Cambridge: Cambridge University, 1989) 53 as quoted in Fitzpatrick, "Latin Roots: Imperialism and the Making of Modern Law" in *Law as Resistance ibid* 275-291, at 289.

b) The Identity of Discrete Laws as Territorial-like Spaces

Now, territorial knowledge has conditioned the binding character of a law in a second way. This has concerned how various international doctrines have been constructed as if the boundary of the doctrine protected a territorial-like space. This space is not physical in that it cannot be seen or heard. Rather, this sense of space has manifested a territorial-like character. I say 'territorial-like' because the sense of physical territorial space has been transcribed into the language of legal consciousness.

i) The Reserved Domain as Territorial-like Space

In the late 18th century, Emir de Vattel introduced a term for the territorial space associated with the binding character of law. He coined the phrase, the *domaine réservé* of the international community.[11] By this, the international community reserved legal spaces where the representative states of each space could enact legislation, adjudicate disputes and administer the laws. Each state was thereby free to make laws and to render decisions without interference by an external constraint. Indeed, Vattel connected such a freedom to the state's very claim to own the territorial space under its control.[12] The international community has never deferred all law-making to the reserved domain. But some crucial elements of law-making and governmental decisions have been protected from external interference by virtue of their being located inside the reserved domain. Examples are a Declaration of war, an emergency Declaration, the determination as to one's alleged allegiance to the state, the conferral, expulsion or withdrawal of nationality and the like. The reserved domain has functioned as a residuary of law-making in the international community.

What is important to appreciate is that the doctrine of the reserved domain is juridically constructed. The Permanent Court of the League affirmed this juridical construction as central to the very possibility of international law in the *Austro-German Customs Union Case* (1931).[13] The association of international law with a residual territorial-like space for

---

[11] Emer de Vattel, *The Law of Nations*, ed. with Intro. Béla Kapossy and Richard Whitmore (Indianapolis: Liberty Fund, 2008 [1797]); also in full trans. G Fenwick (New York, Klaus Reprint, 1916; 1797 [2008]), Bk I, ss 77-81.

[12] *Ibid.* Bk 2, c 7, para 82. See also paras. 81, 86 and 88. Note Vattel's description of internal jurisdiction as territorial knowledge, paras. 79–97.

[13] *Austro-German Customs Union Case* (advisory opinion), PCIJ Ser A/B, No 41 (1931), p 36, at 57-58; also reported in 6 ILR 26.

law-making and law-enforcement has continued into recent judicial decisions.[14] In this regard, the reserved domain of the international community is often cited as if it were a legal fact and therefore juridically uncontrollable. As an example, jurists have continually quoted one famous *dictum* – that is the Permanent Court's *Lotus* judgment – as if a 'given' in international law:

> International law governs relations between independent States. The rules of law binding upon States therefore emanate from their own free will as expressed in conventions or by usages generally accepted as expressing principles of law and established in order to regulate the relations between these co-existing independent communities with a view to the achievement of common aims. Restrictions upon the independence of States cannot therefore be presumed.[15]

International law governs relations between independent States. The rules of law binding upon States therefore emanate from their own free will as expressed in conventions or by usages generally accepted as expressing principles of law and established in order to regulate the relations between these co-existing independent communities with a view to the achievement of common aims. Restrictions upon the independence of States cannot therefore be presumed.[16]

But despite its oft-repeated quotation in Memorials and judgments of international tribunals, the *dicta* may no longer be sustained as a

---

[14] *Taiem v Minister for Immigration & Multicultural Affairs* [2001] FCA 611, para 17 (Federal Court of Australia). One can also read the conflict between Israel and the Palestinian Authority, as interpreted by the International Court in the *Wall* judgment (2004), in terms of the claims of each entity to space or what the Court called a "territorial sphere". *Legal Consequences of the Construction of the Wall in the occupied Palestinian Territory* I.C.J. Rep. (2004), 135. See also 'Summary Legal Position of the Palestine Liberation Organization', App ll, as discussed in *Wall* ibid, 181 para 115; *Beit Sourik Village Council v Government of Israel*, HCJ 2056/04, Israel; See, eg, *Bankovic and others v Belgium and others*, Applic'n 52207/99 [2001] ECHR 390, Grand Chamber, Epn Ct Human Rts, 12 December 2001, para 59, 6671, 78, 80; *Issa and others v Turkey*, Application no 31821/96, [2004] ECHR 629, (2005) 41 EHRR 27, 17 BHRC 473, Epn Ct Human Rts, 16 November 2004; *R (Al-skeini) v Secretary of State for Defence* [2005] EWCA 1609, Capp, Epn Ct, para124192, 196, 205-06.

[15] *The SS 'Lotus'*, (1927) PCIJ, Ser. A, No. 10, p. 1

[16] *The SS 'Lotus'*, (1927) PCIJ, Ser. A, No. 10, p. 1

presumption according to James Crawford.[17] If it is no longer sustainable, then why is it that such a presumption has been considered binding in the first place?

My response to that question is that jurists have taken for granted that the globe could be divided into bounded territorial spaces and territorial-like spaces reserved for law-making, adjudication and law-enforcement. The intellectual production of the reserved domain has even been considered essential for the very idea of a state as a territorial entity.[18] But how can there be a congruence of such a transcendent legal duty and the same duty in both international and constitutional doctrinal law if binding laws in legal knowledge are assumed to possess a territorial-like character? Let us turn to the basic texts of the League of Nations and the United Nations for evidentiary support of the presupposed territorial-like character of binding laws.

ii) Territorial-like Space in the League's Covenant

Article 3 of the *Covenant* held out that the globe was divided into territorial spaces, each equal before the international law. Each state, as a territorial-like space, was protected from external intervention (Art 8). Some social matters, for example, were considered "solely" within internal jurisdiction of a state. The state's conferral, withdrawal or withholding of nationality, for example, was held to be one such matter. A Declaration of war was another. So too arguably were internal state practices such as torture and genocide. The League's Council could not even address such "sole" matters [Art 15(8)].[19] Such a residuary of the international law was justified by the Rapporteur in the *Aaland Islands Report* (1921) as necessary for the "order and stability" of the international community.[20]

---

[17] James Crawford, Chance, Order, Change: The Course in International Law: General Course on public International Law (HAGUE Academy of International Law AIL-Pocker 2014), para 95-98.

[18] The point has recently been affirmed by the Inter-American Court of Human Rights. Proposed Amendments to the Naturalization Provisions of Constitution of Costa Rica (advisory opinion), OC-4/84, Inter-Am Ct HR, Ser A, No 4, Decision of 19 January 1984; (1984) 5 HRLJ 161; 79 ILR 28.

[19] League of Nations Covenant, *Treaty of Versailles*, Pt 1, Art 1-26, in force 10 January 1920; BFPS (British Foreign Service Cases) 112: B, 316, 28 June 1919. The Council, however, could refer the dispute to the Assembly.

[20] League of Nations, "The Aaland Islands Question: Report Submitted to the Council of the League of Nations by the Commission of Rapporteurs", Document of Council B.7.21/68/106 (Geneva: 16 April 1921), LNOJ Spec Supp No 3 (1921), 22-23.

The Permanent Court explained two years later in *Tunis and Morocco* (1923) that without Article 15(8) of the *Covenant*, noted above, the content of the state's reserved domain would open to scrutiny from sources external to the domain.[21] In addition, even harm during armed conflict was understood as harm to the reserved domain of the other state in military conflict.[22] Further, aside from such "sole" matters lying in the international community's reserved domain, "advanced nations" were said to possess a "tutelage" over colonies and mandated territories. A colony or mandated territory lacked a reserved domain because it was not yet considered a self-creative and self-determinative author of a territorial space on the globe [Art 22(1)].[23]

iii) Territorial-like Space in the UN Charter

Let us turn to the UN *Charter* as a further example of how a territorial-like residuary was assumed to be the core of the International law. Article 2(7) of the *Charter* states that "[n]othing contained in the present Charter shall authorize the United Nations to intervene in matters which are *essentially within* the internal jurisdiction of any State ... ."[24] This essential element of the reserved domain is described by the *Charter* as "inherent", "inviolable", and "fundamental". Notwithstanding a "faith in fundamental human rights, in the dignity and worth of the human person, in the equal rights of men and women", the *Charter* defers to the jurisdiction of a state as the sole legal person in the international community [Art 18(1) and 27(1)]. But jurisdiction is a territorial-like space within which an official or institution is free to enact, adjudicate or enforce laws. By Article 2(1), each state is considered equal with the next. The international community is constituted from "the principle of equal rights and self-determination" (Art 55). Further, although each legal person (that is, each state) has the right of "*self*-government". Some territorial spaces may not necessarily be

---

[21] *Tunis and Morocco Nationality Decrees*, PCIJ (Ser B), No 4 (1923), p 7, at 24; (1922-25) 1 *Advisory Opinions* 1-32. Also reported in 2 ILR 349.

[22] Pursuant to Article 11(1) of the League's *Covenant*, "[a]ny war or threat of war, whether immediately affecting any of the members of the League or not, is hereby declared a matter of concern to the whole League." Although not considered a grave harm to another state, mass de-naturalization, if accompanied with expulsion, arguably caused harm to "the whole League"'.

[23] *Official Journal, League of Nations*, (23 April 1923) 604. See also D P O'Connell, "Nationality in 'C' Class Mandates" (1954) 31 *Brit Ybk Int'l L* 458.

[24] *UN Charter*, TS No 993, 59 Stat. 1031, 3 Bevans 1153, Signed 26 June 1945. Entered into Force: 24 October 1945. Emphasis added.

"*self*-governing" (Art 73). When one state militarily interferes in the reserved domain of another state, harm is caused to the reserved domain of the latter state. Accordingly, the state possesses "the inherent right of individual or collective self-defence". "Peace and security" are challenged when the reserved domain of a state is the object of external interference (Chap Vll). "Universal peace" involves the relations between the territorial-like reserved space of each legal person. A "people" is not a legal entity unless recognized as a state with a defined territorial border. Once that moment of recognition arises, the "people" can defend itself as a state. Until that moment, the members of "the people" are considered stateless unless their members possess the nationality of some state claiming radical title to a territorial space.

Now, one might respond to my above argument that a territorial-like space is reserved for state action by claiming that various human rights treaties 'protect' universal human rights. One might also claim that international and regional human rights tribunals have recognized peremptory norms which render domestic laws and actions void. A close reading of such treaties leaves one with the conclusion that a territorial-like space is reserved for the state to act freely of other state members and of the international organizations as a whole.[25] At best, the peremptory norms have been considered customary norms. Being customary norms, though, they may dissipate through time.[26] They may also be consciously modified by express or implied state action. How can norms be peremptory, then, if they are variable through the action of the governmental structures of territorial spaces?[27] And how can such a variability hold out peremptory norms as transcendent *vis-a-vis* domestic laws if once again, the international community is an aggregate of the wills of states?

c) Constitutional Doctrines as Territorial-like Spaces

So, territorial space and territorial-like spaces characterized the international legal community. Constitutional common law doctrines are also steeped in a presupposed sense of a territorial-like bounded space. Let us identify a series of constitutional doctrines manifesting the territorial-like spaces in legal consciousness.

---

[25] See in particular, Conklin, *Statelessness supra* note 3, 138-51.

[26] See Conklin, *Statelessness supra* note 3, 162-76.

[27] Conklin, 'The Peremptory Norms of the International Community' in *European J Int'l L* 23 (2012): 837-61.

i) Radical Title to the State's Control of Land

To begin with, the state has been said to actually possess title to all land which the state claims as its own. The claim to title, initially elaborated in *Campbell v. Hall* (1774), authorized a state to appropriate all *terra nullius* ("the land of no-one").[28] The vacancy, being an intellectual construct, has had the effect of excluding inhabitants whose social origins lacked the character of a state.[29] As Huber stated in his *Palmas* Arbitration judgment, international law functions as "the guardian" of the title to a state's property.[30] But title is a concept, not an observed possession of land. In this vein, Kant insightfully described the ownership of property as an "intellectual possession."[31] Once a state claims title to land, rightful exclusive and absolute possession are presumed to follow. The text of the American Constitution adds legitimacy to such a doctrine by providing that representatives of the territorial-like space could enact "all needful rules and regulations respecting the territory" (Art. 4, §3, cl. 2).

ii) The Pyramidal Governmental and Doctrinal Structures

There is another example of the association of a constitutional structure with a territorial-like space in legal culture. Here, a constitutional structure is assumed to be represented by a pyramidal institutional bureaucracy and a pyramidal hierarchical structure of constitutional doctrines. Again, this structure and hierarchy of doctrines is a construct of legal consciousness. Individuals situated in a community lacking such a structure are excluded from legal recognition as legal persons. This has particularly been the case for Nomadic peoples. Lacking a fixed situs on land and lacking a centralized, pyramidal institutional structure, Nomadic peoples have been excluded from legal recognition since Roman times.[32] Conversely, some

---

[28] *Campbell v. Hall* (1774) 1 Cowp. 204, 98 E.R. 1045.

[29] See the documentation in Conklin, "The Exclusionary Character of the Early Modern International Community" in *Nordic J Int'l L* 81 (2012) 133-173; "The Myth of Primordialism in Cicero's Theory of *Jus Gentium*" in the *Leiden Journal of International Law* (2010): 479-506. See also the important American judgements of *Johnson and Graham's Lease v M'Intosh* (1823), 8 Wheaton 543, at 588; 21 US 240 at pp. 590-91. See also Marshall's judgments in *Worcester v State of Georgia* (1832), 6 Peters 515, 31 US 530; *Cherokee Nation v United States*, US Sup Ct, (1831) 30 US 1.

[30] *Island of Palmas Case (Netherlands v. United States)*, (1928) 2 RIAA 829, 839; 4 ILR 3.

[31] Kant, *Justice supra* note 8, line 254.

[32] This is documented in Conklin, "Early Modern International Community" *supra* note 27; "Cicero's Theory of *Jus Gentium*" *supra* note 27.

communities have been characterized as 'nomadic' and therefore subject to the legal 'reality' of state ownership even though they were agrarian and therefore settled on a territory. Such is exemplified by Chief Justice Marshall's erroneous claim in his *Worcester* (1832) that all "natives" in North America were nomadic – that is, as he put it, they were "roaming" and "wandering" over the territories.[33] And yet, the very traditional community at issue in the case before him belied such a categorization of the "natives" in that they lived in an agricultural culture rather than being nomadic.[34] Absent a familiar intellectual characterization, common law courts have been quick to represent their legal interest as *inchoate* – that is, as "lacking a legal category" or lacking a "complete category". At best, any Indigenous or Nomadic group lacking the pyramidal representative structure has been said to constitutionally possess a *usufructuary* right to property.[35] By this, the inhabitant can use the land but not own it, sell it, or exchange it for some other object. Such an inhabitant must first obtain the consent of the Monarch or President or other Head of the governmental structure of the territorial space before the indigenous or nomadic inhabitant can "sell" it.

iii) Membership in the Territorial-like Spaces

To take a further example of the territorial-like space reserved by the international community, some inhabitants of the globe even lack a usufructuary right due to the territorial-like space of the concept of radical title of the state, itself a territorial space. Of course, such inhabitants of the globe are *de jure, de facto* and effectively stateless in the international community.[36] The dominant international and constitutional discourses have protected the state's freedom inside its bounded territorial space to exclude human beings from entering its territory, to expel others, to withdraw membership (nationality) from others, and to allow still others to inhabit the state's territory on certain conditions. Without a nationality and, with it, the freedom to inhabit a state's territory without conditions, stateless persons have found themselves subject to prolonged detention,

---

[33] *Worcester v Georgia*, (1832) 31 US 530, 6 Peters 515.

[34] Barker, "For whom sovereignty matters", *Sovereignty Matters* ed. Joanne Barker (Lincoln & London: University of Nebraska Press, 2005), 1-32, 12.

[35] *Guerin v The Queen* [1984] 2 SCR 335 at 403; 13 DLR (4th) 321 as discussed in *Delgamuukw v British Columbia*, [1997] 3 SCR 1010, paras. 131- 132.

[36] For the statistics and various forms of such stateless persons, see Conklin, *Statelessness supra* note 3, 7-10, 96-135.

forced displacement, expulsion to the place of birth and *refoulement*. Despite this frame of reference being manifested in many contemporary states including the United States, a competing structure of language is also apparent, a language, that is, that has been grounded in sociality. I shall address the latter in a moment.

iv) Federalism as the Division of Two Territorial Spaces

One prominent doctrine in contemporary constitutional discourses has been federalism. But this doctrine too has presupposed that constitutional law is a matter of territorial-like spaces in legal consciousness. Both Provinces and a Central governmental structure exist on the same territorial space. And yet, each possesses an autonomous territorial-like space in legal consciousness. Within the boundary of the latter territorial-like space, the institutions of the Province or of the Central Government are free to enact, adjudicate and enforce its laws. An interference of the one from the other governmental structure opens the door to an unconstitutional act.

v) Rights and other Territorial-like Constitutional Spaces

Aside from *terra* nullius, radical title, *usufructuary* interests, statelessness, constitutional rights and federalism, other constitutional doctrines manifest a territorial-like character in legal consciousness. Indeed, common concepts in constitutional law also presuppose a bounded territorial-like space. Such concepts, for example, are the concepts of property, title, a right, the state, the state's sovereignty, jurisdiction, a legal person, the independence of the courts, the separation of powers, and freedom. So, for example, a court is said to possess jurisdiction or territorial-like space to adjudicate over certain subject-matters and not others. Similarly, a right is bounded around a territorial-like space within which the natural person is free to think, express, assemble and act. It is just that the space exists in legal consciousness, not in the physical world of nature.

2. The Congruence Issue

Now, as a consequence of territorial knowledge, the international community is condensed into an aggregate of the wills of reserved autonomous spaces. The binding character of domestic laws of each state has presupposed rights, duties, jurisdiction and other concepts as if they bounded territorial-like spaces in the legal mind. If international and constitutional laws are congruent, then there must be some other sense of law than that of territorial knowledge. As long as there are boundaries to such a freedom of state laws and action, there will be effective, *de jure* and diplomatically stateless inhabitants on the globe. They will inhabit non-spaces. That is, they will live outside the boundary of legal consciousness. At best, once we assume that legal reality is synonymous with the constructed territorial-like space, we can only imagine the identity of human beings experienced outside the boundary and then only, because of the contingently and analytically prior belief in law as territorial-like space. Such an imagined exteriority to the boundary of territorial knowledge posits the outside and the outsiders as if one is perceiving and observing the outsider as legal fact. The identity of the outsiders will have to be imagined. Despite this imagined world in which outsiders live, they are subject to our passports, border control cards, work visas, and other documentary *indicia* signifying whether they may enter into or return to the territorial space of state-owner of the territory. The state's claim to be free inside the international community and with that freedom, the governmental structure of its territorial space may construct a wall between its territory and that of other territorial units in the aggregated international community.[37]

As long as jurists presume that the Law as a whole or a discrete law manifests a territorial or a territorial-like character, such a legal space cannot explain nor justify the possibility of congruence of international and constitutional laws. The possibility of congruence begs that the jurist examine something that is contingently and analytically prior to the presumption of reserved territorial and territorial-like spaces of an international community.

There is an ironic twist to the universality claimed for human rights and peremptory norms. Neither an international legal order nor a constitutional legal order can possess universal norms as long as each norm is deemed 'existent' inside the bounded territorial and territorial-like spaces. The claim of the universality of human rights is even more ironic in that the products of intellectual construction – the state, rights, federalism and the like – are considered "legal facts". Justice Read, dissenting in the leading International Court precedent, *Nottebohm* (1955), for example, described the territorial space of the state in just such a manner: "municipal laws are merely facts which express the will and constitute the activities of States and ... the court does not interpret the

---

[37] For photos and explanation of this 'freedom', see Wendy Brown, *Walled States, Waning Sovereignty* (New York: Zone Books, 2010).

national law as such".[38] Guggenheim, again in *Nottebohm*, insisted that domestic law must be regarded *as a fact*.[39] One not infrequently finds Anglo-American jurists of Conceptual Jurisprudence describing such spaces as "legal facts" – that is, as just 'given's in legal analysis.[40]

Pushing this point further, jurists may well agree that a certain principle, such as say, human dignity, is shared in both international and constitutional legal orders. Such a possibility has traditionally been said to characterize a peremptory norm. But any such principle is an *a priori* concept (that is, a concept that is prior to experience). Since it is an *a priori* or pure concept in acts of justification, it must lack any contingent or social-cultural content. But any concept itself manifests a bounded territorial-like space in one's legal consciousness.

The problem of congruence so far is that a concept – territorial-like space – is presupposed to represent legal reality and therefore to being prior to any context-specific social relationships.[41] And so, legal reality – better known by lawyers, judges, law students, law professors and law deans as 'legal practice' – has been said to involve the application of a rule (that is, a concept) to any particular context-specific experienced event. Thus, we end up erroneously intellectualizing *about* the boundary of the multiplicity of territorial-like spaces as if the spaces are synonymous with the experiential world. This experiential world is what Cicero, Grotius, Pufendorf, Hegel and many other jurists have considered as "sociality".[42]

---

[38] *Nottebohm (Liechtenstein v Guatemala)* (second phase) (1955) ICJ Rep 4, p 36 (also reported in (1955) 22 ILR 349). Available at: www.refworld.org/docid/3ae6b7248.html

[39] *Nottebohm* (1955) ICJ Rep 4, at 23; (1955) 22 ILR 349, para 2. aff'g *Brazilian Loans Case*, Perm't Crt Int'l Justice, Ser A 20/21, 124.

[40] See eg, Joseph Raz, *Between Authority and Interpretation* (Oxford: Oxford University press,2009) 344-447; Neil MacCormick, *Institutions of Law: an Essay in Legal Theory* (Oxford: Oxford University press, 2007)11-142-43, 289-93, 304.

[41] See Bernard Waldenfels, *Order in the Twilight*, trans. DJ Parent (Athens Ohio: Ohio University Press, 1996), 64.

[42] See eg Conklin, 'Peremptory Norms" *supra* note 25; *Hegel's Laws: the Legitimacy of a Modern Legal Order* (Stanford: Stanford University Press, 2008); 'Lon Fuller's Phenomenology of Language' in *International J for Semiotics of Law* 19 (2006): 93-125; 'A Phenomenological Theory of the Human Rights of the Alien' in *Ethical Perspectives* 13 (2006): 245-301; *The Phenomenology of Modern Legal Discourse* (Aldershot UK/ Brookfield, USA/ Singapore/ Sydney, Australia: Dartmouth, 1998).

I am not suggesting that there is an alternative sense of a legal bond in some idealizing world 'out there', independent of the 'is' of the residuary of international law. To any response that I am describing as an idealized world, I say that I am describing an 'is' world concealed inside the idealization and reification of reality as territorial knowledge. The conclusion is warranted that we lawyers will never know whether there is a congruence between international and domestic constitutional law as long as we take legal reality as a territorial-like space that encloses social life. Indeed, the assumed analytic displacement of sociality by territorial-like legal space has reinforced a self-referential character to international and domestic constitutional law. Why are the legal structures of an international and constitutional community self-referential? Because a boundary has been accepted as the key to the delimitation of legal analysis. Such a boundary is neither legal nor illegal, neither inside law (the reserved domain) nor outside it (as extra-legal or non-legal). What counts as a law can only refer to other norms, rules, principles and other intelligible standards *inside* the space's boundary. Since territorial-like space has been presupposed as the form of law in general and of discrete laws in particular, what we have taken as law cannot be anything other than internal to the boundary. The boundary encircles an institutional structure as if the structure were a fortress or castle that excludes other fortresses from interfering into the territorial-like space of the first fortress.

My point is that if a law is identified in or as if a territorial-like space, such a law ultimately depends upon the experiential sociability for its obligatory character. Such a sociality is buried inside the territorial-like spaces in legal consciousness. Again, a space cannot exist, we have been led to believe, unless the space has a boundary. With such a boundary, there has to be an inside and an outside. The law – whether international or domestic constitutional – takes for granted that there remains an outside as well as an inside, a "pre-legality" as well as a "legality", a "sociality" as well as a "law", an extra-law as well as a law. But in each rhetorical division, there is a presumption that one knows what is excluded from the law. One cannot differentiate or exclude sociality from territorial knowledge without such a presumed knowledge. Without a knowledge of the sociality, that is, there just cannot be an international or constitutional legal community. Once the jurist interrogates how territorial and territorial-like space has been constructed as the dominant historical *a priori* of international law and its presumed framework of domestic constitutionalism, the jurist is driven to understand the very legal culture which has fomented such a historical *a priori*.

3. Sociality

The pivotal problem with the possibility of the congruence of the International and Constitutional legal orders is that the boundary of a territorial or territorial-like space ends the need to justify any legislative, judicial or executive action. The boundary forecloses further legal issues. Such a boundary sets the condition for the identity of laws in a way which excludes as well as includes. Without a focus upon sociality concealed in the territorial-like spaces reserved for states by the international community, the risk is that the absence of sociality leaves the international or constitutional legal order lacking binding laws.

a) The Contemporary Deference to Sociality in International Law

What I wish to do now is to retrieve how courts have focussed upon an experiential knowledge as an alternative to the territorial legal knowledge. In the early 19th century, the English judicial decisions were faced with two legal traditions concerning the nature of the binding character of a law. The one path, outlined in Section 1, took for granted that a binding law was situated inside a territorial space represented by a state. The other path focussed upon the place of social relationships as determinative of the binding character of a law.[43] Such a sociality is pre-intellectual. It is unstated and unwritten. It draws from the pre-intellectual memories and expectations which natural persons experience and have experienced with others. Intermediate constitutional and international doctrines flowed from such a presupposed sense of the Law and of laws as grounded in sociality. Sociality has continued into the judgments of the International Court, regional human rights tribunals and domestic constitutional judgments.[44] If one turns to higher court judgments in Asia, South America, and Africa, however, one finds many examples of a preoccupation with the social basis of the bond of natural persons.[45] I now aim to flesh out the binding sense of law as grounded in sociality. I do so because it opens up the possibility of congruence of international and constitutional law.

---

[43] For documentation, see Conklin, *Statelessness supra* note 3, 179-80, 198-99; "Peremptory Norms" *supra* note 25.

[44] For documentation see *Ibid* 186-96, 199-219, 220-301.

[45] For examples, see my *Statelessness supra* note 3, 199-301.

i) Nottebohm

The International Court's Majority judgments in *Nottebohm* opinion (1955) manifest the importance of sociality as the basis of a binding law.[46] Here, the binding character of a law was buried in the notion of a legal bond. The Majority expressed that "*a legal bond having as its basis a social fact ...*".[47] Such a bond, the Majority continued, "constitutes *a translation into juridical terms* of the individual's connection which has made him its national." What constitutes the nature of such a "translation"? The Majority's response to such a question concerns "*a social fact of attachment, a genuine connection of existence, interests and sentiments, together with the existence of reciprocal rights and duties. ...*" of a natural person *vis-à-vis* other natural persons (not with the state). The *Nottebohm* Court went further: social relationships (family, religious, linguistic, educational, professional, labor and other groups) were said to be "translated" into the legal conception of nationality. Further, in addition to habitual residence, the Court was obligated to examine one's family ties, participation in public life, attachment to one's children, and the state's own recognition of a natural person as possessing legal status, legal rights and legal duties. Such factors, ironically, constituted what the Court described as the "establishment of *a new bond of allegiance*".[48] I say 'ironic' because the "new" legal bond radically differs from any sense of allegiance as that term has been used to describe the nature of the territorial-like space reserved for states. The "new" form of a legal bond exists independent of such a space although the space is dependent upon the "new" bond as a condition precedent for the existence of binding international and constitutional laws.

Nottebohm does not stand alone in this regard. International and regional human rights tribunals and refugee tribunals have continued this focus upon sociality as the basis of the binding character of a domestic law.[49] As the ILC suggests, nationality is no longer "conferred" onto an individual. Instead, nationality is an "attribute" of an individual's social life. Such social relations impact the role of the judiciary. A law effectively exists by virtue of experiences with others. At one point, the ILC described effective nationality as a "personal" "emotional attachment to a particular

---

[46] *Nottebohm* (1955) ICJ Rep 4, at 23.

[47] *Nottebohm* (1955) ICJ Rep 4, at 23. Emphasis added.

[48] *Nottebohm* (1955) ICJ Rep 4, at 24; (1955) 22 ILR 349, at p. 361).

[49] Conklin, *Statelessness supra* note 3,199-219.

country".⁵⁰ On another occasion, Crawford states in one ILC proceeding that the relation of a natural person to a territory constitutes "a *social reality* in the link between people and territory".⁵¹ The ILC has added further factors manifesting the sociality of the individual claimant to constitutional or international law protection: the individual's place of residence, the unity of a family, military obligations, and the entitlement to pensions.⁵² The ILC has explained that a "personal" "attachment" and "genuine link" of an individual with others involves an individual's "emotional attachment to a particular country".⁵³ Such a complex of social factors embodied Nottebohm's own life-world, not the judiciary's. The ILC *Draft Articles on Diplomatic Protection* has added a further series of *indicia* of a social bond:

> [t]he authorities indicate that such factors include habitual residence, the amount of time spent in each country of nationality, date of naturalization (i.e. the length of the period spent as a national of the protecting State before the claim arose); place, curricula and language of education; employment and financial interests; place of family life; family ties in each country; participation in social and public life; use of language; taxation, bank account, social security insurance; visits to the other State of nationality; possession and use of passport of the other State; and military service.⁵⁴

Again, effective nationality concerns "[the] *social reality* in the link between people and territory."⁵⁵

Contrary to the traditional readings of the works of Grotius, Hobbes, Locke, Kant, and Hegel, the legal bond is not between a natural person and the state as early modern jurists have assumed about the emergence

---

⁵⁰ ILC, Report, 'Summary Records of the Meetings of 47th Session: State Succession and its Impact on the Nationality of Natural and Legal Persons', UN Doc A/CN.4/SER.A/1995, *ILC Yearbook 1995*, vol I, p. 37, para 186.

⁵¹ Crawford, in *ILC Yearbook* 1997, vol. 2 (1), 52. Also see Mikulka, Third Report on nationality in relation to the succession of States, UN Doc A/CN.4/480 & Corr.1 and Add.1 & Corr.1-2, 12, para 9. Emphasis added.

⁵² ILC, *Yrbk Int'l L Comm'n* 1997, v 2 (Pt 1), Art 5, Comm 4.

⁵³ ILC, Report 47th Session above n 48, para 186, p. 37.

⁵⁴ ILC, "Draft Articles on Diplomatic Protection, with Commentaries", UN Doc A/61/10, reprinted in *ILC Yearbook 2006*, vol 2 (2), Art 8, Comm 5.

⁵⁵ Crawford *supra* note 15. Emphasis added.

of the sovereign state.⁵⁶ The legal bond, again, rests in the social relationships inter-se. It just happens that this rather than that state claims to own the territorial space where one's social relationships were experienced. Sociality impacts the sorts of evidence that domestic and international tribunals have admitted into the record. Such evidence has included personal and collective memories, statistical evidence, the social biography of a complainant, the context-experiences of group members, and individual and group expectations.

In effect, before one can ever entertain a sense of international or constitutional law as a territorial-like space, such a sense of law is conditioned by one's social relationships. Such a sociality experientially and analytically also precedes any legal category. Put differently, the legal bond *post facto* translates into "reciprocal rights and duties" experienced as social relations with others.⁵⁷ One's social relationships embody (that is, give body to) one's legal identity as well as the very nature of a binding law. The place of one's social experiences is not some territorial space. One experiences a place (as opposed to a space) through one's social relations with others.⁵⁸

b) The Constitutional Deference to the Cultural Features of Sociality

i) The Constitutional Protection of a Culture Independent of Territorial Knowledge

I wish to highlight to areas of Canadian constitutionalism where sociality has played a critical role. Against the background of the Supreme Court's recognition that unwritten laws are binding because of their role independent of state sovereignty or a text,⁵⁹ two contexts have especially highlighted the Court's recognition of sociality.

---

[56] See Conklin, *Statelessness supra* note 3, 179-80, 198-99; Conklin, *Hegel's Laws supra* note 40, 51-56, 162-87; *The Invisible Origins of Legal Positivism: a re-reading of a tradition* (Dordrecht: Kluwer, 2001) 95-98; "Early Modern International Community" *supra* note 27; "Cicero's Theory" *supra* note 27.

[57] *Nottebohm* (1955) ICJ Rep 4, at 23; (1955) 22 ILR 349, at p. 360-61).

[58] The difference between territorial space and a place is examined in Edward S. Casey, *Getting Back into a Place* (Bloomington: Indiana U. Press, 2009 [1993]); M. Merleau-Ponty, *Phenomenology of Perception*, trans. C Smith (London, Routledge & Kegan Paul, 1962).

[59] *Secession Reference*, [1998] 2 SCR 217, paras. 49-54, 70-80.

The one context emerged in the 1950s when the Supreme Court, through the judgments of Justices Rand and Abbott, highlighted how sociality explains why the freedoms of expression and assembly are binding upon state officials. Justice Rand explained in one judgment (*Saumur*) that the freedoms of speech, religion and the inviolability of the person are justified by virtue of their being "the necessary attributes and modes of self-expression of human beings and the primary conditions of their community life within a legal order."[60] In another judgment (*Switzman*), Rand explained that without sociality (what Rand described as "social life"), one could not possess a binding legal order.[61] The Court continued that "the primary condition of social life, thought and communication by language" was "little less vital to man's mind and spirit than breathing is to his physical existence." My point is that one cannot understand the thrust of human rights judgments in Canadian constitutional law without appreciating how sociality trumps territorial knowledge. Such a displacement of territorial knowledge, confirmed in recent Canadian judgments,[62] raises the possibility of a congruence between international and constitutional law.

This takes me to a second general area of constitutional discourse where the Canadian Supreme Court has highlighted the importance of sociality independent of the territoriality of the state as the basis of constitutional obligation. This has concerned the Court's preoccupation with the sociality of Nomadic and Indigenous inhabitants independent of any territorial knowledge associated with the state. Here, as the Court has put it, independent of the possession or use of territory claimed by the state, state officials have a constitutional obligation to "protect" an Indigenous or Nomadic group even if that group has not provided evidence of "their connection with the piece of land on which the activity was taking place was of a central significance to their distinctive culture."[63] The traditional, contemporary *indicia* of territorial possession by an individual or a group – the construction of buildings or the enclosure of fields – matters little in

---

[60] *Saumur v City of Quebec*, [1953] 2 SCR 2999, [1953] 4 DLR 641.

[61] *Switzman v Elbling*, [1957] SCR 285, 7 DLR (2d) 337.

[62] See eg *R v Hape*, [2007] 2 SCR 292, 2007 SCC 26, at para. 34-39, 53-56. Available at: https://scc-csc.lexum.com/scc-csc/scc-csc/en/item/2364/index.do. *Ezokola v. Canada (Citizenship and Immigration)* (SCC 2013), para 42-49, 51. Available at: https://scc-csc.lexum.com/scc-csc/scc-csc/en/item/13184/index.do

[63] *R v Adams*, [1996] 3 SCR 101, para 26; *R v van der Peet*, [1996] 2 SCR 507, 74, cited approvingly in *Adams*, [1996] 3 SCR 101, para 29.

comparison with the social relationships drawn from "hunting, fishing or otherwise".[64] The latter forms of livelihood have been highlighted due to their critical role in the social relationships of Indigenous inhabitants.

More generally, "a sensitive and generous approach to the evidence" is required in assessing the context-specific sociality of a particular Nomadic or Indigenous group.[65] The key requisite to establish such sociality is the signification of "a certain practice or event" in "their world and value system".[66] This requires the study of "the traditional way of life", including "the group's size, manner of life, material resources, and technological abilities, and the character of the lands claimed" and "the manner in which the society used the land *to live*, namely to establish villages, to work, to get to work, to hunt, to travel to hunting grounds, to fish, to get to fishing pools, to conduct religious rites, etc."[67] Added to such evidence is the need to study "the means of survival, their socialization methods, their legal systems, and, potentially, their trading habits".[68] Justice L'Heureux-Dubé, dissenting in one judgment, has clarified this principle by emphasizing that the social context-specific culture must be understood "through the eyes of aboriginal people, not through those of the non-native majority or the distorting lens of existing regulations."[69] Most importantly, what one means by "culture" is "inherently cultural".[70] Several South American human rights judgments have followed up with the recognition that sociality is not important in its relation to the survival of a group but in "their worldview, of their religiousness, and consequently, of their cultural identity".[71] Sociality has also played a role in other jurisdictions.[72]

---

[64] *R v Marshall; R v Bernard*, Sup Ct Ca [2005] 2 SCR 220, para 56, 66; *Adams*, [1996] 3 SCR 101, paras. 26-30; *Delgamuukw* [1997] 3 SCR 1010, per Lamer, para 39; *Peet*, [1996] 2 SCR 507, para 74.

[65] *Bernard*, [2005] 2 SCR 220, para. 68.

[66] *Bernard*, [2005] 2 SCR 220, para. 68-69; *Guerin v The Queen* [1984] 2 SCR 335; 13 DLR (4th) 321, para 388.

[67] *Delgamuukw* [1997] 3 SCR 1010, para. 149 as quoted approvingly in *Bernard*, [2005] 2 SCR 220, para 49, emphasis in original. See also para. 193 in *Bernard*.

[68] *R v Sappier; R v Gray* [2006] 2 SCR 686, para 45.

[69] *Peet*, [1996] 2 SCR 507, para 162.

[70] *Sappier* [2006] 2 SCR 686, per Bastarche para 44.

[71] *Rameshbhai Dabhai Naika v States of Gujarat and others*, (Civil), Civil App 654 (2012), Sup Ct India; *Xákmok Kásek Indigenous Community v Paraguay*, Ser C no 214, 24 August 2010, Inter-Am Ct H Rts; *Saramaka People v Suriname*, IACHR, Ser C, no

4. Conclusion

The congruence of international law and constitutional law does not rest with the sources of law traditionally accepted by common law lawyers and judges. Nor does the express or implied consent of a state set the stage for a response to the congruence of international and constitutional laws. Nor, for that matter, does a congruence rest in the rational justification of any institutional sources in the territorial-like spaces reserved for the state by identifiable international laws. Nor is congruence between the two areas of law congruent with a presupposed sense of law as territorial knowledge. Nor is congruence possible if one focuses upon basic texts such as treaties, statutes, and precedents. Nor is congruence possible as the product of rational deduction from prior rationally justified principles. The congruence is not possible as a consequence of comparing the content of constitutional and international laws.

If congruence is possible as I have argued, it rests upon the shared reciprocal social relations heretofore excluded from 'law' as extra-legal to the boundary of territorial knowledge. Without a sociality amongst natural persons, an identifiable international legal norm or other intelligible standard would not exist as legally binding. Nor would a domestic constitutional concept exist as legally binding. To be sure, there might well be groups of people governed by rulers. There might be a political system, a state of exception, or a moral system. But there would not be a legal order. If congruence is possible, this possibility rests in the shared pre-analytic expectations and memories so conducive to the sociality of natural persons. The factors making for sociality in the International Court's *Nottebohm* raise the possibility of convergence of public international law and domestic constitutional law. Recent developments in Canadian constitutional law reinforce the importance and practicality of sociality and therefore of the possibility of the congruence of

---

172, 28 November 2007; *Sawhoyamaxa Indigenous Community v Paraguay*, 29 March 2006, para 118, Inter-Amer. Ct Hum Rts; *Indigenous Community Yakye Axa v Paraguay*, Merits, Reparations and Costs, para. 135; Inter-Amer Ct HR Series C No 125, 17 June 2005, Inter-Amer Ct HR; *A v Agawa*, Ont CA, 1988, 53 DLR (4th) 101, 215-216: *Olga Tellis v Bombay Municipal Corporation*, India Sup Ct, AIR 1986 SC 18, Sup Ct India.

[72] See eg *Jalang ak Paran & Kampong anak Amih v Govt of state of Sarawak & Borneo and Pulp and Paper sdn, bhd*, CA Malaysia, Civil no Q-01-133-06, p 419; *Mabo v Queensland (No 2)*, (1992) 175 CLR 1, 3 June 1992, H Ct Austl per Brennan para 41; *Members of the Yorta Aboriginal Community v Victoria* (2002) 214 CLR 422, H Ct Austl; *The Wik Peoples v Queensland*, H Ct Australia, (1996) 141 ALR 129, H Ct Austl.; *Milirrpum v Nabalso Pty Ltd* High Ct Australia, (1971) 17 FLR 141, H Ct Austl.

International and Constitutional Law. The jury is out. If sociality is the crux of the binding character of a law, much depends upon the duty of jurists to address sociality as raising the importance of sociality in the possibility of the congruence of constitutional and international law.

Bibliography

A Phenomenological Theory of the Human Rights of the Alien' in *Ethical Perspectives* 13 (2006)

Austro-German Customs Union Case (advisory opinion), PCIJ Ser A/B, No 41 (1931)

Banković and others v Belgium and others, Applic'n 52207/99 [2001] ECHR 890, Grand Chamber, Epn Ct Human Rts, 12 December 2001,

Barker, Joanne. "For whom sovereignty matters", *Sovereignty Matters* ed. Joanne Barker (Lincoln & London: University of Nebraska Press, 2005)

Bauman, Zygmunt. *Modernity and the Holocaust*, Cambridge: Cambridge University, 1989) in Fitzpatrick, "Latin Roots: Imperialism and the Making of Modern Law" in *Law as Resistance*

Beit Sourik Village Council v Government of Israel, HCJ 2056/04, Israel;

Brown, Wendy. *Walled States, Waning Sovereignty* (New York: Zone Books, 2010).

Campbell v. Hall (1774) 1 Cowp. 204, 98 E.R. 1045.

Cherokee Nation v United States, US Sup Ct, (1831) 30 US 1.

Conklin, William. "The Myth of Primordialism in Cicero's Theory of *Jus Gentium*" in the *Leiden Journal of International Law* (2010)

Conklin, William. 'The Peremptory Norms of the International Community' in *European J Int'l L* 23 (2012):

Conklin, William. "The Exclusionary Character of the Early Modern International Community" in *Nordic J Int'l L* 81 (2012) 133-173;

Conklin, William. *Statelessness: the Enigma of the International Community* with a Foreword by William Twining and Preface by William Conklin (Oxford: Hart, 2015 [2014]).

Crawford, in *ILC Yearbook* 1997, vol. 2 (1),

Crawford, James. *Chance, Order, Change: The Course in International Law: General Course on public International Law* (HAGUE Academy of International Law AIL-Pocker 2014).

Delgamuukw v British Columbia, [1997] 3 SCR 1010.

Casey, S. Edward. *Getting Back into a Place* (Bloomington: Indiana U. Press, 2009 [1993]);

de Vattel, Emer. *The Law of Nations*, ed. with Intro. Béla Kapossy and Richard Whitmore (Indianapolis: Liberty Fund, 2008 [1797]);

Ezokola v. Canada (Citizenship and Immigration) (SCC 2013) Available at: https://scc-csc.lexum.com/scc-csc/scc-csc/en/item/13184/index.do

Fenwick, Charles G. (New York, Klaus Reprint, 1916; 1797 [2008]), Bk I

Fitzpatrick, Peter."Gods Would be Needed . . .": American Empire and the Rule of (International) Law' in *Law as Resistance Modernism, Imperialism, Legalism* (Burlington Va: Ashgate, 2008)

Guerin v The Queen [1984] 2 SCR 335 at 403; 13 DLR (4th) 321

Hegel's Laws: the Legitimacy of a Modern Legal Order (Stanford: Stanford University Press, 2008); *International J for Semiotics of Law* 19 (2006):

HLA Hart, *Concept of Law* 3rd ed *(*Oxford: Clarendon Press, 2013 [1961]).

ILC, "Draft Articles on Diplomatic Protection, with Commentaries", UN Doc A/61/10, reprinted in *ILC Yearbook 2006*, vol 2 (2), Art 8, Comm 5.

ILC, Report 47th Session above n 48, para 186, p. 37.

ILC, Report, 'Summary Records of the Meetings of 47th Session: State Succession and its Impact on the Nationality of Natural and Legal Persons', UN Doc A/CN.4/SER.A/1995, *ILC Yearbook 1995*, vol I.

ILC, *Yrbk Int'l L Comm'n* 1997, v 2 (Pt 1), Art 5, Comm 4.

Inter-Amer Ct HR; *A v Agawa*, Ont CA, 1988, 53 DLR (4th) 101.

Inter-Amer. Ct Hum Rts; *Indigenous Community Yakye Axa v Paraguay*, Merits, Reparations and Costs, para. 135; Inter-Amer Ct HR Series C No 125, 17 June 2005,

Island of Palmas Case (Netherlands v United States) 2 RIAA 829, 838-39; (1928) 4 ILR 3.

Island of Palmas Case (Netherlands v. United States), (1928) 2 RIAA 829, 839; 4 ILR 3.

Issa and others v Turkey , Application no 31821/96, [2004] ECHR 629, (2005) 41 EHRR 27, 17 BHRC 473, Epn Ct Human Rts, 16 November 2004;

Jalang ak Paran & Kampong anak Amih v Govt of state of Sarawak & Borneo and Pulp and Paper sdn, bhd, CA Malaysia, Civil no Q-01-133-06.

Johnson and Graham's Lease v M'Intosh (1823), 8 Wheaton 543, at 588; 21 US 240

Kant, Immanuel.*Metaphysical Elements of Justice*, trans with Intro and Notes, John Ladd. 2nd ed. (Indianapolis: Hackett, 1999 [1797]).

Kelsen, Hans Kelsen."Sovereignty and International Law" in *Georgetown LJ* 48 (1960).

League of Nations Covenant, *Treaty of Versailles*, Pt 1, Art 1-26, in force 10 January 1920; BFPS (British Foreign Service Cases) 112: B, 316, 28 June 1919.

League of Nations, "The Aaland Islands Question: Report Submitted to the Council of the League of Nations by the Commission of Rapporteurs", Document of Council B.7.21/68/106 (Geneva: 16 April 1921), LNOJ Spec Supp No 3 (1921).

Legal Consequences of the Construction of the Wall in the occupied Palestinian Territory I.C.J. Rep. (2004),

Merleau-Ponty, Mauric.*Phenomenology of Perception*, trans. C Smith (London, Routledge & Kegan Paul, 1962).

Mabo v Queensland (No 2), (1992) 175 CLR 1, 3 June 1992, H Ct Austl per Brennan.

Marshall's judgments in *Worcester v State of Georgia* (1832), 6 Peters 515, 31 US 530;

Members of the Yorta Aboriginal Community v Victoria (2002) 214 CLR 422, H Ct Austl.

Metaphysics of Morals, trans by Mary Gregor (Cambridge, Cambridge University Press, 1996)

Mikulka, Third Report on nationality in relation to the succession of States, UN Doc A/CN.4/480 & Corr.1 and Add.1 & Corr.1-2, 12,

Milirrpum v Nabalso Pty Ltd High Ct Australia, (1971) 17 FLR 141, H Ct Austl.

MacCormick, Neil. *Institutions of Law: an Essay in Legal Theory* (Oxford: Oxford University Press, 2007)11-142-43.

Nottebohm (1955) ICJ Rep 4, at 23; (1955) 22 ILR 349, para 2, aff'g *Brazilian Loans Case*, Perm't Crt Int'l Justice, Ser A 20/21, 124.

Nottebohm (Liechtenstein v Guatemala) (second phase) (1955) ICJ Rep 4, p 36 (also reported in (1955) 22 ILR 349). Available at: www.refworld.org/docid/3ae6b7248.html

Official Journal, League of Nations, (23 April 1923) 604. See also D P O'Connell, "Nationality in 'C' Class Mandates" (1954) 31 *Brit Ybk Int'l L* 458.

Olga Tellis v Bombay Municipal Corporation, India Sup Ct, AIR 1986 SC 18, Sup Ct India.

Proposed Amendments to the Naturalization Provisions of Constitution of Costa Rica (advisory opinion), OC-4/84, Inter-Am Ct HR, Ser A, No 4, Decision of 19 January 1984; (1984) 5 *HRLJ* 161; 79 ILR 28.

Raz, Joseph.*Between Authority and Interpretation* (Oxford: Oxford University press,2009)

R (Al-skeini) v Secretary of State for Defence [2005] EWCA 1609, Capp, Epn Ct, para124192

R v Adams, [1996] 3 SCR 101,

R v Hape, [2007] 2 SCR 292, 2007 SCC 26., Available at: https://scc-csc.lexum.com/scc-csc/scc-csc/en/item/2364/index.do.

R v Marshall; R v Bernard, Sup Ct Ca [2005] 2 SCR 220.

R v van der Peet, [1996] 2 SCR 507, 74, cited approvingly in *Adams*, [1996] 3 SCR 101

Rameshbhai Dabhai Naika v States of Gujarat and others, (Civil), Civil App 654 (2012), Sup Ct India. *Xákmok Kásek Indigenous Community v Paraguay*, Ser C no 214, 24 August 2010, Inter-Am Ct H Rts. *Saramaka People v Suriname*, IACHR, Ser C, no 172, 28 November 2007.

Saumur v City of Quebec, [1953] 2 SCR 2999, [1953] 4 DLR 641.

Sawhoyamaxa Indigenous Community v Paraguay, 29 March 2006.

Switzman v Elbling, [1957] SCR 285, 7 DLR (2d) 337.

Taiem v Minister for Immigration & Multicultural Affairs [2001] FCA 611, para 17 (Federal Court of Australia).

The Invisible Origins of Legal Positivism: a re-reading of a tradition (Dordrecht: Kluwer, 2001)

The Phenomenology of Modern Legal Discourse (Aldershot UK/ Brookfield, USA/ Singapore/ Sydney, Australia: Dartmouth, 1998).

The SS 'Lotus', (1927) PCIJ, Ser. A, No. 10, p. 1

The Wik Peoples v Queensland, H Ct Australia, (1996) 141 ALR 129, H Ct Austl.

Tunis and Morocco Nationality Decrees, PCIJ (Ser B), No 4 (1923), p 7, at 24; (1922-25) 1 *Advisory Opinions* 1-32. Also reported in 2 ILR 349.

UN Charter, TS No 993, 59 Stat. 1031, 3 Bevans 1153, Signed 26 June 1945. Entered into Force: 24 October 1945.

Waldenfels, Bernard. *Order in the Twilight,* trans. DJ Parent (Athens Ohio: Ohio University Press, 1996).

Worcester v Georgia, (1832) 31 US 530, 6 Peters 515.

Chapter 4

Convergence and Divergence in Statutory Interpretation

Jeffrey A. Pojanowski[1]

Abstract

I will focus on statutory interpretation and the common law tradition, with a slight comparative touch, looking at modern civil law interpretation as well. My tentative thesis is that the stereotypes regarding both (in the U.S. at least) have it backward: usually the casual academic identifies the common law tradition with creative interpretation and the civil law tradition as rejecting judicial creativity. I'm inclined to think that one plausible understanding of the common law tradition requires formalism--one accepts imperfection even when reason points judges toward improving the regime (essentially, the paper of mine you read). On the other hand, the modern civil systems' embrace teleological interpretation that seeks reasoned coherence, even when that means moving beyond strict adherence to formal text. My tentative thought is that systems of interpretation mirror styles of legislation: Americans typically legislate in a common law way: lumpy, reactive, non-systematically, whereas the civilian tradition aspires to systematic, reasoned codes.

Introduction

The usual story about statutory interpretation in the Anglo-American legal world is that the common law tradition supports judicial creativity. The stereotype of civilian interpretation returns the favor, emphasizing the

---

[1] Professor of Law, Notre Dame Law School. The author is grateful for comments and questions by the participants at the conference "The Common Law and the Civil Law Today: Convergence and Divergence," graciously organized and hosted by the Southern European Center for Legal Research. He is also grateful for the editorial assistance of his student, Meredith Holland.

limited role of the judge and the supremacy of legislation over case law. These pairs of received wisdom tell plausible stories, but the whole truth is more complicated than that. Civilian scholars are well aware of the limits to the claim that judges just mechanically apply the law. Less familiar to both civilian and common law scholars is the notion that the common law tradition also has a counter-story, namely that it can support an argument in defense of formalist approaches to statutory interpretation.[2] This chapter will present that story and bring it into discussion with civilian learning on statutory interpretation.

I. Common Law Statutory Interpretation: The Standard Account

In the United States, the standard account about the relationship between statutory interpretation and the common law presents a neat dichotomy. Non-formal approaches to interpretation build upon the spirit of the common law tradition, whereas formalist approaches to interpretation are a rejection of that tradition in favor of a more civilian method. Whether such a rejection of the common law tradition is a good thing will depend on one's views on the common law or formalism more generally, but those are the choices.

Allow me to first clarify my terms. At risk of oversimplification, we can track *"formalism"* in terms of the interpreter's willingness to privilege a legal text's letter over its spirit or broader purpose.[3] When confronted with a reasonably clear rule—whether the metric is plain meaning or historical intent at a low level of generality—the formalist is more inclined to implement the rule even if it is at odds with what the interpreter thinks is the rule's animating purpose or policy. The nonformalist, by contrast, identifies the background purpose or policy as the true legal norm; when formal features of legislation conflict with its background purpose or policy, sound interpretation points toward giving force to the latter considerations over the letter.[4]

Relatedly, and even more pertinent from the perspective of common lawyers, we can also understand formalism and non-formalism in terms of

---

[2] For an extended argument along these lines, see Pojanowski, "Statutes in Common Law Courts," 1357. This chapter's discussion on the common law and statutes draws heavily on my prior work in that article.

[3] See Schauer, "Formalism," 509.

[4] Manning, "What Divides Textualists from Purposivists?," 70.

the interpreter's willingness to supplement or even *'update*" legislation.[5] Although both sides of the spirit/letter distinction just discussed presuppose a judicial norm of faithful agency, non-formalist interpretation may go further and claim that the interpreter has the power or obligation to infuse legislation with norms that go beyond the historical framers' particular intentions, purposes, or principled aims. More modestly, this might include extending a statute by analogy to cover cases not clearly contemplated by the legislation.[6] More ambitiously, it could include the power to supplement legislation with contemporary norms that the legislation's drafters never would have even considered, or would have rejected had they considered them.[7] A formalist rejects such an approach as violating separation of powers, overstepping the limits of the judicial office, and disrespecting any compromises the legislature struck when it acted.

So much for a rough distinction between formalist and non-formalist interpretation.[8] In the United States, there is a pronounced tendency for defenders of non-formal interpretation to claim the common law tradition.[9] In courts, especially state courts with common law powers, non-formalists emphasize how their authority to issue judge-made law overrides separation-of-powers concerns about supplementing, extending, or updating legislation beyond the four corners of the statute. Similarly, they claim that such powers at least allow them to regard themselves as partners in dialogue with the legislature, rather than mere agents.[10]

Scholars sound a similar tune. Professor William Eskridge pushes back against interpretive formalism in federal law by arguing that the United States Constitution's judicial power incorporates the common law powers

---

[5] See, e.g., Aleinikoff, "Updating Statutory Interpretation," 20.

[6] For arguments for such approach, see Pound, "Common Law and Legislation," 383; Traynor, "Statutes Revolving in Common-Law Orbits," 401.

[7] See, e.g, Calabresi, *A Common Law*.

[8] The distinction is far less sharp when a statute is unclear. There, both formalists and non-formalists will look to purpose and more general legal values. See Manning, "What Divides Textualists from Purposivists?," 79–85 (discussing the common ground between the two camps). It is fair to say, however, that formalists are more likely to rely on historical purpose than contemporary norms the original drafters would not have countenanced.

[9] See Pojanowski, "Statutes in Common Law Courts," 494–507.

[10] See Kaye, "State Courts," 1; Abrahamson and Hughes, "Shall We Dance?," 1045.

of English courts, which construed legislation far more liberally than modern federal textualists. Judge Guido Calabresi invokes the common law tradition to ground his theory of updating legislation. Ronald Dworkin, a common law "*romantic*"[11] and antiformalist par excellence, holds that courts should construe statutes much in the same way that they develop precedent.[12] Little surprise that Dworkin centers his theory of statutory interpretation on *Riggs v. Palmer*,[13] a New York appellate decision that rejected the plain meaning of a statute in light of countervailing, background common law principles.[14] And such non-formalists have classical common law maxims at hand, most usefully Lord Coke's articulation of the mischief rule in *Heydon's Case*.[15]

Most formalists in the United States accept this conflict between the common law and formalism, only they argue that the common law tradition should give way. Federal law formalists emphasize that federal courts are courts of limited jurisdiction and thus lack the general common law powers upon which more dynamic theories rely.[16] It is no coincidence that the late Justice Antonin Scalia entitled his formalist manifesto "*Common Law Courts in a Civil Law System.*"[17] Professor John Manning, moreover, argues that the English common law Professor Eskridge musters is inapposite to the particular features of the United States federal context.[18] State court formalists, moreover, look to non-common law federal courts for guidance on interpretive method and sometimes even rail against the common law more generally.[19]

2. Reconsidering the Standard Account

The received wisdom linking non-formalist statutory interpretation with the common law is oft-received because there is a lot of truth to it. But the

---

[11] Dyzenhaus and Taggart, "Reasoned Decisions and Legal Theory," 134.

[12] Dworkin, *Law's Empire*, 313.

[13] 22 N.E. 188 (N.Y. 1889).

[14] Dworkin, *Law's Empire*, 15-20.

[15] Heydon's Case, (1584) 76 Eng. Rep. 637 (Exch.) 638-39.

[16] See, e.g., City of Milwaukee v. Illinois, 451 U.S. 304, 312 (1981) ("Federal courts, unlike state courts, are not general common-law courts and do not possess a general power to develop and apply their own rules of decision.").

[17] Scalia, "Common-Law," 3.

[18] See Manning, "Textualism and the Equity of the Statute," 8–9.

[19] See, e.g., Young, "A Judicial Traditionalist," 302.

whole truth is more complicated. The common law tradition is a contested one, and a plausible interpretation of that tradition points toward a more humble, less heroic, and more formal approach to statutory interpretation. To understand this reinterpretation, however, we first need to grasp two related ideas: the classical common law's implicit model of law and its understanding of legal reasoning.

First, its model of law. Drawing on the work of Walter Ullmann, Jeremy Waldron has helpfully distinguished between descending and ascending models of legislation. Descending, top-down approaches understand legislation as being handed down from a sovereign legislator or group of legislators. This traces back to the Roman law notion that the prince makes the law, runs through strains of European monarchism, and emerges in the Anglo-American tradition in the theories of Hobbes, Bentham, and Austin.[20] By contrast, an ascending, bottom-up understanding of law and legislation conceives of legal norms as bubbling up from the shared norms and deliberation among a wider base of people.[21] Waldron argues, persuasively, that the English model of legislation has roots in the ascending model, starting with the requirement of monarchs consulting with the nobility before legislating.[22]

This bottom-up understanding of legislation flowing from custom and assembly informs its relationship with the common law. Though some notable classical common lawyers were hostile to legislation, a sophisticated practitioner-theorist like Matthew Hale understood legislation as a *source* of common law alongside custom and judicial decisions.[23] If legislation, like judicial decisions, both respond to and seek to instantiate shared customary norms, and if the common law as a whole is a manifestation and working out of those norms, legislation and judicial decisions are simply two manifestations of the same common law. And that is, indeed, how theorists like Hale and John Selden understood the common law: not as a rationalist working out of universal principles (or handing them down from the top), but an attempt to have the law represent the reasonable custom of the realm percolating up from below.[24]

---

[20] Waldron, *Law and Disagreement*, 40–45.

[21] Waldron, *Law and Disagreement*, 56.

[22] Waldron, *Law and Disagreement*, 56–60.

[23] See Postema, "Classical Common Law Jurisprudence (Part II)," 11.

[24] See Postema, "Classical Common Law Jurisprudence (Part I),' 172–76.

This coalesces with my second point, namely the common lawyer's method of legal reasoning. Classical common law reasoning was pragmatic, reactive, and contextual, not abstract, programmatic, and systematic. The measure of a doctrine's merits was its rough reasonableness and widespread acceptance, not its congruence with a theologian or moral philosopher's system. Thus, although common sense moral evaluation played an important role in adjudication, the common lawyer was willing to accept inelegant or imperfectly just doctrines and did not demand systemic coherence across the entirety of common law.[25]

Although this reconstruction of common law addresses judicial decisions—one of the three sources of law—we can combine it with Waldron's understanding of top-down lawmaking and offer a more general understanding of legislation within a common law system. Here, I will focus on federal law in my jurisdiction, the United States of America.

American federal legislation is, like classical common law adjudication, piecemeal, reactive to context, and (often frustratingly) unsystematic. This is, in part, a product of American legislation's bottom-up character, which focuses deliberation and forging an agreement among a cacophony of legislators, rather than what Waldron calls "*Hobbesian decisiveness.*"[26] The United States Constitution's requirement that legislation must pass both houses of Congress and receive presidential approval effectively imposes a supermajority requirement for any law to pass.[27] In the absence of shared, widespread norms, this structure forces compromise—a finding of common ground or at least acceptability—and reduces the chances of systematic, cross-cutting, and rigorously coherent legislation.[28]

Relatedly, the bottom-up legislative process rarely permits a neat transition from policy ideal to legislation outcome.[29] Like the "*disciplined,*" "*solemn*" (and perhaps obscure) practice of common law argument, where moral argument and principle take on the character of

---

[25] See Pojanowski, "Statutes in Common Law Courts," 1385–89. The cited discussion draws heavily on the work of philosopher and historian of the common law Gerald Postema.

[26] Waldron, *Law and Disagreement*, 40.

[27] See Manning, "Competing Presumptions," 2039.

[28] Pojanowski, "Statutes in Common Law Courts," 1392–95.

[29] Cf. Manning, "Absurdity Doctrine," 2451 (arguing that American legislative process does not "seamlessly translate social values (and legislative purposes) into statutory commands").

law only running through the gauntlet of the common law's *"artificial reason,"*[30] policy goals become legislative policy only after disciplining, often-obscure, and sometimes frustrating legislative procedure that forges a solution that is acceptable to a super-majority of participants. The critic may view this as an irrational way to make law—just as a scholar once commented that judicial common law is *"chaos with a full index."*[31] But the common lawyer might respond that just as the shared, artificial reason of the common law is more reliable than *"the moral vision of any individual,"*[32] the outputs of bottom-up legislation may reflect *"a practical intelligence that outstrips the intelligence"* of any sole legislator.[33]

In short, legislating in the common law tradition is a bottom-up, path-dependent, consensual, and, yes, clunky approach to developing the law. It is the polar opposite of the stereotypical Continental ideal of a comprehensive, internally coherent Code produced after years of careful study, commentary, and expert drafting. (And it is worth noting that, in this respect, the United States' federal legislation tends more toward the common law tradition than Commonwealth jurisdictions that rely more heavily on law reform commissions and expert legislative drafting offices.)

The question remains what to do with the sometimes-messy outputs of legislating in the common law tradition. As noted, those who reject interpretive formalism seek to round the sharp corners of legislation or even update legislation to meet contemporary mores claim the common law tradition. But as the previous discussion suggests, this draws on a partial or contested understanding of the tradition. What Matthew Hale said in defense of the common law against Hobbes' rationalistic critique could just have been offered by an American textualist resisting calls to smooth the rough edges of clear statutes pointing toward awkward results:

> *It is not necessary that the reasons of the institution should be evident to us. It is sufficient that they are instituted laws that give a certainty to us, and it is reasonable to observe them though the particular reason of the institution appear not.*[34]

---

[30] Postema, "Classical Common Law Jurisprudence (Part II)," 8.

[31] Holland, *Essays upon the Form of the Law*, 171.

[32] Postema, "Classical Common Law Jurisprudence (Part II)," 10.

[33] Waldron, *Law and Disagreement*, 72.

[34] Hale, "Reflections by the Lord," 504–05.

To the extent the nonformalist alternative relies on the common law giving judges power to make law, it risks trading on the top-down model of lawmaking, John Austin's model of the common law judge who legislates in the gaps as a deputy sovereign. To the extent it relies on the broad moral vision of the judge, it risks replacing the pragmatic, contextual, artificial reason of the common law with the dictates of a Dworkinian philosopher king. More importantly, in its aspiration to improve the awkward outputs of common-law-style legislation, nonformalists seek to interpose their individual reason between the artificial reason of a legislative process that favors consensual compromise over broad coherence and moral perfectionism.

Such nonformalists, therefore, draw on a contested vision of the common law, one that emphasizes reason and coherence over contingency and local consensus. And, of course, the common law tradition is broad enough that one can find expositors emphasizing both poles of this antimony. Yet this alternative take on the sympathetic relationship between interpretive formalism and the common law has a number of potential payoffs for theorists and jurists within those systems.

First, the formalist interpretation offers a story of—perhaps necessary—realignment within the common law tradition. Whereas lawyers traditionally emphasize the role the common law's artificial reason plays in adjudication, a formalist approach to statutes in common law systems indicates a migration of that peculiar form of reasoning from the courts to the legislatures. In fact, such a shift in the center of gravity may be necessary for the common law to survive as a tradition, for adjudication by generalist judges may be unable to provide sound and reliable legal guidance in response to the polycentric problems our complex world presents.[35] That said, it is also in an important sense a return to the roots of the English legal system: the rise of classical common law adjudication was preceded by statutes like the Magna Carta and the Provisions of Oxford, which both codified customary obligations between the Crown and the barony, as well as memorialized compromises between them.

Second, the common law tradition offers interpretive formalists more than they appreciate. By linking interpretive formalism to the common law tradition, American formalists no longer need to repudiate the centuries of legal heritage that preceded them. Law, by its nature, is a traditional and conservative enterprise, and any theory that requires a

---

[35] Fuller, "The Forms and Limits of Adjudication," 353; Schauer, "Do Cases Make Bad Law?," 883.

rethinking of the entire legal heritage starts off on its back foot. Furthermore, the common law tradition offers a more complete theory of interpretation. Even formalists appeal to background purpose, the broader fabric of the law, and extrastatutory values when legislation is unclear. Situating interpretation as part of common law development can explain such creativity when more formal indicia are lacking, thus offering a unified theory that embraces faithful agency and more creative, integrative approaches when necessary. Formalism does not abolish unwritten law,[36] and reintegrating this approach with the common law tradition can help explain and justify unwritten norms' persistence and limits.

Third, this reinterpretation poses challenges to nonformalist interpreters who claim the common law tradition. At the very least, they grasp onto one interpretation of a contested tradition. In doing so, they arguably embrace an anachronistic interpretation that tradition, replacing the peculiar, particular character of its "artificial reason" with the philosophical ambitions classical common lawyers rejected in adjudication. Indeed, Lord Coke claimed that "*Casuists, Schoolmen,*" and "*Moral [sic] Philosophers*" make for particularly bad common lawyers.[37] It is therefore possible that the interpretive formalists' unwillingness to correct awkward legislation out of respect for the "artificial reason" of the legislative process has as much a foot in the common law tradition as Herculean judges offering moral readings of statutes. In fact, as I will suggest in the next section, it is possible that the American nonformalist interpreters may have more in common with civilian lawyers than they expected.

3. Civil Law Comparisons

The previous section complicates the standard understanding of formalist statutory interpretation in common law systems. Contrary to the late-Justice Scalia's understanding, formal faithful agency may be quite consistent with the common law tradition, such that one need not appeal to civil law analogs to justify one's practice. More broadly, understanding the contested character of the common law tradition indicates that the two systems share a similar tension between formalist and nonformalist approaches to statutory interpretation.

---

[36] Nelson, "The Persistence of General Law," 503.

[37] See Coke, "Prohibitions del Roy," 64–65.

Just as one finds received wisdom about nonformalist statutory interpretation as part and parcel of the common law tradition, there is a standard story about formalism and the civilian tradition. Namely, the goal is to keep judges out of the business of making law or, even possibly, having to engage in interpretation at all. One thinks of the quixotic, 17,000-provision Prussian *Landrecht* of 1794, which sought to provide rules of decisions for any possible situation a judge might confront. Similarly, the fear of "*government des juges*" led to the Code Napoléon's strict separation of powers and the related aspiration to make legislation "*complete, coherent, and clear.*"[38] In line with some contemporary American formalists' aim of abolishing uncodified background law, some post-Revolutionary French legal scholars not only sought to abolish interpretation but to treat the new Code as displacing all prior civil law.[39]

But even a superficial familiarity with the civil law tradition (and my encounter is superficial indeed!) reveals another side of the story. There are scholars and jurists who are skeptical, to say the least, of the notion that civilian judges neither interpret legislation nor develop law in the gaps of codes.[40] The codes past and present contain references to interpretation according to the spirit of the statute, general principles of legal order, or principles of natural law.[41] Objective teleological interpretation, as used in German courts for example, is not radically different from nonformal interpretation in the United States.[42] Finally, one might see a parallel between the common law's ascending, bottom-up approach to legislation and the 1896 German Civil Code's historical orientation and concomitant rejection of top-down rationalism.[43] In a similar vein, one might see resemblances between the common lawyer's

---

[38] Merryman and Pérez-Perdomo, *The Civil Law Tradition*, 30.

[39] Merryman and Pérez-Perdomo, *The Civil Law Tradition*, 29–30.

[40] See, e.g., Merryman and Pérez-Perdomo, *The Civil Law Tradition*, 43; Alexy and Dreier, "Statutory Interpretation," 76.

[41] Merryman and Pérez-Perdomo, *The Civil Law Tradition*, 44–46. Remarkably, the Swiss code instructs judges to adopt the rule they would choose as a legislator in the even the usual interpretive tools run out. Ibid., 46.

[42] Alexy and Dreier, "Statutory Interpretation," 88–89. Although teleological arguments over and against the text are exceptions in Germany, see ibid., 93, such "*contra legem*" decisions are also rare in the United States, even among less formal courts.

[43] Merryman and Pérez-Perdomo, *The Civil Law Tradition*, 31–32.

devotion to artificial reason and German, lawyer-focused legal science (in contrast to, say Benthamite *and* French jurisphobia).

This tension between the formal and nonformal approaches of civil law statutory interpretation resembles the same contrast in the common law tradition. That said, one could argue that in some respects dynamic and creative interpretation is more at home with the presuppositions of the civilian system than the common law. If one accepts the (admittedly stylized) notion that civilian codes are complete and coherent, it is meaningful to say that these features permit and may even demand teleological development in new cases. Interpreters can more plausibly impute to the systematically, academically crafted code a unified, organized set of principles that they can expound when they face unprovided-for cases; the premise of completeness, furthermore, demands that interpreters engage in such development. If common-law-style legislation lacks such broad coherence and completeness, such systematic development may be less warranted.

Ronald Dworkin rejects the notion that we should view legislation as a "*checkerboard*"[44] of "*negotiated compromises that carry no more or deeper meaning than the text*"[45] and suggests we are to treat "*legislation as flowing from the community's present commitment to a background scheme of political morality.*"[46] This work of reading legislation as a unified, principled scheme might require much less strain with respect to, say, the French Civil Code than the hodgepodge products the United States Congress produces. No wonder that an American scholar who grounds his defense of nonformal interpretation in common law discovered that his French colleague saw strong resemblances between American nonformalism and civilian interpretation.[47] On the other hand, one can see how the decidedly non-rationalistic approach of the common law tradition can point toward a formalist interpretive method whose commitments to legislative supremacy are similar to the Enlightenment philosophes who feared the tyranny of judges.

---

[44] Dworkin, *Law's Empire*, 179.

[45] Dworkin, *Law's Empire*, 345–46.

[46] Dworkin, *Law's Empire*, 338.

[47] Strauss, "The Common Law and Statutes," 235–236. The French scholar explained "[T]he actual practice of civil law judging is less alien to [the American] tradition than is usually supposed, in ways that I think actually support your basic argument about the relationship between judging and statutes."

But it is also important to not oversimplify matters. Although legal philosophers like Ronald Dworkin carry an aura of civilian rationalism, many common law defenders of nonformal interpretation call for careful, incremental, and episodic interventions, much in the way the classical common law developed. Thus, nonformal interpretation in the Anglo-American world may appear more empiricist and pragmatic than some civilian legal science.[48]

Similarly, as noted above, compared to the stereotype of the formalist civilian rejecting judicial creativity and insisting the Code abolished all prior law, the common law formalist has far more comfort with a purposivist interpretation of unclear statutes and the use of background law to fill gaps and inform interpretation. By the same token, the common law formalist who dismisses Dworkin's approach as a civilian transplant must face the challenge of teleological interpretation of the German code, whose historicist character bears a family resemblance to the traditionary, customary cast of classical common law. In short, as with all systemic comparisons, subtle complexities abound.

Nevertheless, we should not be surprised to see the tension between formalism and non-formalism arising in both systems. The struggle over letter versus spirit, rule versus reason, and settlement versus justice in individual cases is one of the central problems of law.[49] Lon Fuller spoke of the ineliminable antimony between reason and fiat in case law.[50] It is fair to say that those two poles pull interpreters of statutes as well, in common law and civilian jurisdictions alike.

Bibliography

Abrahamson, Shirley S. and Robert L. Hughes. "Shall We Dance? Steps for Legislators and Judges in Statutory Interpretation." *Minnesota Law Review* 75, no. 4 (April 1991)

Aleinikoff, T. Alexander. "Updating Statutory Interpretation." *Michigan Law Review* 87, no. 1 (October 1988):

Alexander, Larry. "The Gap." *Harvard Journal of Law and Public Policy* 14, no. 3 (Summer 1991): 695–701.

---

[48] On the distinction between empiricist and rationalist thinking, and linking the former to the Anglo-American tradition of philosophy, see Hayek, "Freedom, Reason, and Tradition," 229.

[49] See, e.g., Alexander, "The Gap," 695.

[50] Fuller, "Reason and Fiat in Case Law," 376.

Alexy, Robert and Ralf Dreier. "Statutory Interpretation in the Federal Republic of Germany." In *Interpreting Statutes: A Comparative Study*, edited by Robert S. Summers and D. Neil MacCormick, 73–121. Brookfield: Dartmouth Publishing, 1991.

Calabresi, Guido. *A Common Law for the Age of Statutes*. Cambridge: Harvard University Press, 1982.

Coke, Edward. "Prohibitions del Roy." In *The Reports of Sir Edward Coke* 12, edited by George Wilson, 63–65. London: E. & R. Nutt & R. Gosling, 1727.

Dworkin, Ronald. *Law's Empire*. Cambridge: Harvard University Press, 1986.

Dyzenhaus, David and Michael Taggart. "Reasoned Decisions and Legal Theory." In *Common Law Theory*, edited by Douglas E. Edlin, 134–168. New York: Cambridge University Press, 2007.

Fuller, Lon L. "Reason and Fiat in Case Law." *Harvard Law Review* 59, no. 3 (February 1946).

Fuller, Lon L. "The Forms and Limits of Adjudication." *Harvard Law Review* 92, no. 2 (December 1978).

Hale, Matthew. "Reflections by the Lord Chief Justice Hale on Mr. Hobbes His Dialogue of the Law." In Holdsworth, William Searle, *A History of English Law* 5, 499–513. London: Methuen & Co., 1927.

Hayek, Friedrich A. "Freedom, Reason, and Tradition." *Ethics* 68, no. 4 (July 1958).

Holland, T.E. *Essays upon the Form of the Law*. London: Butterworths, 1870.

Kaye, Judith S. "State Courts at the Dawn of a New Century: Common Law Courts Reading Statutes and Constitutions." *New York University Law Review* 70, no. 1 (April 1995).

Manning, John F. "Competing Presumptions about Statutory Competence." *Fordham Law Review* 74, no. 4 (March 2006): 2009–2050.

Manning, John F. "Textualism and the Equity of the Statute." *Columbia Law Review* 101, no. 1 (January 2001).

Manning, John F. "The Absurdity Doctrine." *Harvard Law Review* 116, no. 8 (June 2003).

Manning, John F. "What Divides Textualists from Purposivists." *Columbia Law Review* 106, no. 1 (January 2006).

Merryman, John Henry and Rogelio Pérez-Perdomo. *The Civil Law Tradition*, 3rd ed. Stanford: Stanford University Press, 2006.

Nelson, Caleb. "The Persistence of General Law." *Columbia Law Review* 106, no. 3 (April 2006)

Pojanowski, Jeffrey. "Statutes in Common Law Courts." *Virginia Law Review* 101, no. 5 (September 2015)

Postema, Gerald J. "Classical Common Law Jurisprudence (Part I)." *Oxford University Commonwealth Law Journal* 2, no. 2 (Winter 2002).

Postema, Gerald J. "Classical Common Law Jurisprudence (Part II)." *Oxford University Commonwealth Law Journal* 3, no. 1 (Summer 2003).

Pound, Roscoe. "Common Law and Legislation." *Harvard Law Review* 21, no. 6 (April 1908)

Scalia, Antonin. "Common-Law Courts in a Civil-Law System: The Role of the United States Federal Courts in Interpreting the Constitution and Laws." In *A Matter of Interpretation: Federal Courts and the Law*, edited by Amy Gutmann, 3–48. Princeton: Princeton University Press, 1997.

Schauer, Frederick. "Do Cases Make Bad Law?" *University of Chicago Law Review* 73, no. 3 (Summer 2006):

Schauer, Frederick. "Formalism." *The Yale Law Journal* 97, no. 4 (March 1988):

Strauss, Peter L. "The Common Law and Statutes." *University of Colorado Law Review* 70, no. 1 (Winter 1999):

Traynor, Roger. "Statutes Revolving in Common-Law Orbits." *Catholic University Law Review* 17, no. 4 (1968):

Waldron, Jeremy. *Law and Disagreement*. New York: Oxford University Press, 1999.

Young, Robert P. Young, Jr. "A Judicial Traditionalist Confronts the Common Law." *Texas Review of Law & Politics* 8, no. 2 (Spring 2004).

Chapter 5

Common Law Constitutionalism and Popular Sovereignty: A Matter of Public Trust

Anne Richardson Oakes[1]

Abstract

Writing for the Guardian in 2012, UK Supreme Court justice Robert Carnwath commented on a "decade of progress" that followed the "unequivocal" recognition by the UNEP sponsored global judges' symposium that took place in Johannesburg in 2002 that judges have a crucial role to play in the development and enforcement of environmental law at both national and international level.[2] The "widespread acknowledgment of an international 'common law' of the environment based on principles such as sustainability, and inter-generational equity"[3] represented a major achievement. Ten years later, the presence in Rio of "more than 150 judges, prosecutors, public auditors, and enforcement agencies from some 60 countries" was testament to the efforts of "judges in courts and tribunals across the world .... to give practical effect to laws for the protection of the environment"[4] but as Lord Carnwath recognized, what is required is a system of "common laws of the environment," i.e. doctrinal mechanisms that can operate within different

---

[1] Associate Professor of American Legal Studies in Birmingham City University's School of Law

[2] Robert Carnwath, *Judges for the Environment: We Have a Crucial Role to Play*, https://www.theguardian.com/law/2012/jun/22/judges-environment-lord-carnwath-rio Friday 22 June 2012 19.28 BST.

[3] Id.

[4] Robert Carnwath, *Judges for the Environment: We Have a Crucial Role to Play*, https://www.theguardian.com/law/2012/jun/22/judges-environment-lord-carnwath-rio Friday 22 June 2012 19.28 BST.

legal frameworks albeit tailored where necessary towards specific constitutions or statutory codes.[5] This paper argues that one such mechanism with potential for repositioning environmental discourse in both common law and civil law jurisdictions is the doctrine of public trust.

The public trust doctrine, write Michael Blumm and Mary Wood, "is an ancient property law doctrine which first surfaced in Roman law in the Justinian Code, was revived in medieval England largely through the efforts of Sir Mathew Hale, and became entrenched in American law in the nineteenth century through the process of statehood."[6] Drawing on "a civic and judicial understanding that some natural resources remain so vital to public welfare and human survival that they should not fall exclusively to private property ownership and control" the doctrine of public trust has the capacity to reconceptualize the discourse of environmental protection in terms of fiduciary responsibilities and governmental obligations. Its potential to both promote public access to natural resources and justify public regulation of them for the benefit of current and future generations is currently being tested in the United States in what may prove to be groundbreaking litigation aimed at forcing the U.S. federal government to uphold its duty to protect the atmosphere.[7]

In 2015, sitting as justice of the UK Supreme Court, Lord Carnwath explored but ultimately did not pursue, the capacity of the doctrine of public trust to resolve English common law disputes concerning public rights of access to the foreshore for recreational use. This paper uses the doctrine of public trust as it is currently deployed in U.S. jurisdictions to ask the question whether the judicial resourcefulness once so characteristic of the common law can transform a transatlantic hybrid of uncertain common and civil law parentage into a transformative tool of a 'common law of the environment'.

Recent experiments with referendums in the U.K. have tempted some commentators to suggest a new constitutional dynamic in which popular sovereignty now trumps that of the sovereign parliament.[8] In *R (Miller) v*

---

[5] Robert Carnwath, Judges and the Common Laws of the Environment – At Home and Abroad, J. Envtl. L. 1(2014)

[6] The Public Trust Doctrine in Environmental and Natural Resources Law, Carolina Academic Press, pp. 1-56, 2013.

[7] Juliana v. United States, 6:15-cv-1517-TC.

[8] *See* Les Green, *Should Parliamentary Sovereignty Trump Popular Sovereignty*, SEMPER VIRIDIS (2016-11-03), https://ljmgreen.com/2016/11/03/should-parliamentary-sovereignty-trump-popular-sovereignty/

Secretary of State for Exiting the European Union,[9] the suggestion was roundly refuted by the U.K. Supreme Court, and, as the British Government recently affirmed, "the sovereignty of Parliament is a fundamental principle of the UK constitution."[10] So much, so constitutionally uncontroversial. Nevertheless, as the Government White Paper conceded, "[w]hilst Parliament has remained sovereign throughout our membership of the EU, it has not always felt like that."[11] Indeed, although for the British Prime Minister, Brexit meant Brexit, for the 52%[12] of who voted to leave the European Union, Brexit was largely about popular sovereignty conceptualised in terms of borders and "taking back control" from remote and democratically unaccountable European institutions. The *Miller* decision may indeed represent constitutional orthodoxy; in the U.K.'s nebulous constitutional arrangements, the fictional device of the "sovereign Parliament" is the way in which formal constitutionalism reconciles popular sovereignty with the traditional narrative of inherited regal authority. However, as the *Daily Mail* intuited and Professor Green explains, when formal constitutionalism threatens to turn our most senior judges into "enemies of the people," they should remind themselves that "Parliamentary sovereignty is an institutional device, helpful where it secures important values, but a hindrance when it does not."[13]

If Brexit and the referenda that preceded it[14] require a reframing of constitutional thinking, the concern for this paper is what a change of emphasis in favor of popular sovereignty might look like and, more specifically, what might or could be the normative basis for a new framework of governance and legitimate authority going forward. In this connection, we could do worse than look across the pond to the United States where an action group of activist scholar advocates is currently engaged in framing sovereignty in terms of public trust encompassing duties to preserve not just the material world but also the natural world for

---

[9] [2017] UKSC 5.

[10] Dept. for Exiting the European Union, *The United Kingdom's Exit from and New Partnership with the European Union White Paper, available at* https://www.gov.uk/government/publications/the-united-kingdoms-exit-from-and-new-partnership-with-the-european-union-white-paper.

[11] *Id.*

[12] Technically 51.89%.

[13] Green, s*upra* note 8.

[14] I include here the referendum offered to the people of Scotland to determine whether Scotland should continue to be part of the United Kingdom.

the benefit of the current generation of young people and for those generations still to come.[15] As Professor Finn has observed, "the most fundamental of fiduciary relationships in our society is that which exists between the community (the people) and the State and its agencies" but, the United States apart, this "most elementary principle" has more or less receded from the public discourse of the common law world.[16] This paper now asks, is public trusteeship a metaphor whose time has come? Or to rephrase Professor Green, can popular sovereignty now "trump" parliamentary sovereignty?

1. The Public Trust Background

The background to my thinking here is a ground-breaking climate change lawsuit currently underway in the U.S. District Court for the District of Oregon. On November 10, 2016, federal judge Ann Aiken issued an opinion and order denying the U.S. government and fossil fuel industry's motions to dismiss a claim filed by 21 youth, age 9 to 20 and from all over the United States. Filed initially against the United States, President Barack Obama, and numerous executive agencies, plaintiffs allege that despite knowledge "for more than fifty years" that the use of fossil fuels "was destabilizing the climate system in a way that would 'significantly endanger plaintiffs, with the damage persisting for millennia' ... defendants, '[b]y their exercise of sovereign authority over our country' s atmosphere and fossil fuel resources, ... permitted, encouraged, and otherwise enabled continued exploitation, production, and combustion of fossil fuels, ... deliberately allow[ing] atmospheric C02 concentrations to escalate to levels unprecedented in human history[.]'"[17] Plaintiffs argue defendants' actions violate their substantive due process rights to life, liberty, and property. Plaintiffs also allege defendants have violated plaintiffs' Fifth Amendment equal protection rights by denying them protections afforded to previous generations and by favoring short term economic interests of certain citizens. Plaintiffs further allege that defendants' acts and omissions violate the implicit right, via the Ninth Amendment, to a stable climate and an ocean and atmosphere free from dangerous levels of CO_2. Finally, and most significantly for this paper,

---

[15] Juliana v. United States, No. 6:15-cv-01517-TC (Dist. OR. 10 Nov. 2016).

[16] Paul Finn, *The Forgotten "Trust": The People and the State*, in EQUITY: ISSUES AND TRENDS, 131 (Malcolm Cope ed. 1995).

[17] Juliana v. United States, No. 6:15-cv-01517-TC, 2016 WL 183903, at 1 (Dist. OR. 10 Nov. 2016).

plaintiffs allege that defendants have violated the public trust doctrine, secured by the Ninth Amendment, by denying future generations essential natural resources.[18]

Both sets of arguments seek to break new ground; the constitutional arguments derive from the guarantees of the Fifth Amendment of the U.S. Constitution and the Ninth Amendment preservation of the unenumerated rights of the people. The assertion of a federal obligation of public trust derives from common law principles and is the most significant for this paper. All arguments will be heavily contested and the stakes are high; the relief sought includes an order compelling the defendants to prepare and implement an enforceable national remedial plan to phase out fossil fuel emissions and to draw down excess atmospheric carbon dioxide to stabilize the climate system. Plaintiffs also ask the court to retain jurisdiction "to monitor and enforce" defendants' compliance with the remedial plan. Unsurprisingly, the Trump administration in conjunction with fossil fuel companies is currently seeking a reversal of Judge Aiken's order.

Backing the litigation for the plaintiffs is Our Children's Trust, an environmental nonprofit with a mission "to protect earth's atmosphere and natural systems for present and future generations."[19] Its founder is Julia Olsen, now Executive Director and Chief Legal Counsel, who represents the Trust in the *Juliana* litigation and leads a team of lawyers committed to advocating on behalf of youth and future generations and for legally-binding, science-based climate recovery policies. Influencing their strategy and arguments is the work of University of Oregon law professor Mary Wood, and specifically her conception of what she terms atmospheric trust litigation. Atmospheric trust litigation finds its roots in the public trust doctrine, which Wood calls "the oldest doctrine of environmental law"—the idea that governments must hold certain things in trust for public use, such as rivers, seas, and the seashore. It's a concept, she claims, "as old as the Romans, but in the United States, it was used to first great effect by the Supreme Court in 1892 to declare that navigable waters and submerged lands constituted part of the public trust—the government, in other words, had to preserve them for its citizens."[20] For

---

[18] *Id.*

[19] *See* https://www.ourchildrenstrust.org/mission-statement/, last accessed 20 Apr. 2017.

[20] https://thinkprogress.org/can-this-group-of-kids-force-the-government-to-act-on-climate-change-349abc0809ab. (The case she is referring to is *Illinois Central R.R. v. Illinois*, 146 U.S. 387(1892)).

Wood and the scholar advocates of Our Children's Trust the doctrine has a much broader application with transformative potential for fighting climate change. "What [the Oregon] litigation does is it fast forwards that... principle to the modern urgency of climate crisis, ... It's a very simple extension of logic. If navigable waters were crucial to the public back then, certainly the air, atmosphere, and climate systems warrant protection as public trust systems as well."[21]

The *Juliana* case is not the first to make these claims, and as counsel for amici in a predecessor case pointed out, in the United States "[t]he terms "public trust" and "Public Trust Doctrine" carry a range of meanings."[22] In its narrowest sense, the doctrine refers to a set of principles governing the nature of state ownership and the extent of public rights of navigation, commerce, and fishing in respect of navigable waters and the submerged lands under such waters. In this sense, as the U.S. Supreme Court recently affirmed in *PPL Montana, LLC v. Montana*, the public trust is a matter of state law[23] with significant variations across the fifty states, in terms both of substance and jurisprudential underpinnings.[24] However, as the "lodestar" case of *Illinois Central Railroad Co. v. Illinois*[25] asserted and subsequent U.S. Supreme Court decisions have repeated, the doctrine finds its origins in conceptions of sovereignty that are central to U.S. constitutional arrangements.[26]

From this perspective, *Alex L.* amici argued, in its broadest sense, "the term "public trust" refers to a fundamental understanding that no legislature can legitimately abdicate its core sovereign powers.[27] The public trust argument mounted in this case represents, they suggest, a

---

[21] *Id.*

[22] Brief of Law Professors as Amici Curiae in Support of Plaintiffs-Appellants Seeking Reversal at 4, Alec L. v. McCarthy, 2013 WL 6672484 (C.A.D.C. Dec. 18 2013).

[23] 132 S.Ct. 1215

[24] *See e.g.* Thomas W. Merrill, *The Public Trust Doctrine: Some Jurisprudential Variations and Their Implications*, 38 U. HAW. L. REV. 261 (2016); Robin Kundis Craig, *A Comparative Guide to the Eastern Public Trust Doctrines: Classifications of States, Property Rights and State Summaries*, 16 Penn ST. ENVTL. L. REV. 1 (2007).

[25] 146 U.S. 387 (1892). The term is that of Professor Joseph Sax, whose seminal article effectively resurrected an all but forgotten nineteenth century case. *See* Joseph Sax, *The Public Trust Doctrine in Natural Resource Law: Effective Judicial Intervention*, 68 MICH. L. REV. 471 (1970).

[26] "uniquely implicate sovereign interests,"

[27] Brief of Law Professors, *supra* note 22, at 4.

limitation on the power delegated to legislatures by a sovereign people and a specific application to the federal government of a broader reserved powers doctrine that prevents a legislature from seeking to infringe the equal sovereignty of later legislatures, a recognized example being the rule against legislative entrenchment or the enactment of irrepealable laws.[28] Amici draw on Supreme Court dicta in *Stone v. Mississippi*[29] and Thomas Jefferson's words to James Madison[30] to derive from reserved powers analysis both an "ancient, axiomatic principle of government" and a vindication of "basic notions of generational sovereignty:" "[e]ach sitting legislature derives its legitimate authority from the particular public that elects it." [so that] [r]ecognizing the rights and powers of later legislatures secures the rights and powers of the later citizens who will elect those later legislatures.[31] Both claims depend upon assumptions of popular sovereignty to which legislatures are accountable and by whom their powers are limited via posited models of social or foundational contract. I return to this point presently.

The immediate point is that *Alec L.* amici move from these principles to extrapolate a principle of trusteeship of natural resources as an inalienable attribute of sovereignty and indeed there is Supreme Court support for this argument at state level.[32] The doctrine of state trusteeship of certain natural resources does have constitutional underpinnings that depend upon a narrative of common law descent and regal title[33] inherited by the post-revolutionary thirteen colonies and extended to the others via the so-called Equal Footing doctrine which governs their admission to the

---

[28] *Id.* at 5 -6 (citing Stone v. Mississippi, 101 U.S. 814, 817-20 (1879)) :

[29] 101 U.S. 814, 817-20 (1879) : "No legislature can bargain away the public health or the public morals.... The supervision of both these subjects of governmental power is continuing in its nature.... [T]he power of governing is a trust committed by the people to the government, no part of which can be granted away.".

[30] *Id.* (citing Jefferson to James Madison, September 6, 1789, *Papers of Thomas Jefferson*, Ed. Julian Boyd XV, 392-98 (1950) : between society and society, or generation and generation, there is ... no umpire but the law of nature, ... [and] one generation is to another as one independent nation to another"

[31] *Id.* at 6.

[32] *See* Arnold v. Mundy, 6 N.J.L. 1, 13 (1821); Illinois Central Railroad Co. v. Illinois, 146 U.S. 387 (1892); Idaho v. Coeur d'Alene Tribe of Idaho, 521 U.S. 261(1997); PPL Mont., LLC v. Montana, 565 U.S. 576,603 (2012).

[33] For a discussion of the asserted origins of the narrative see Anne Richardson Oakes, Judicial Resources and the Common Law: The Public Trust Doctrine in the Age of Trump and Brexit (forthcoming).

Union.[34] The novelty of the *Alec L.* and *Juliana* cases lies in the attempt to extend the public trust duty to the federal government. Here the twin narratives of common law descent and inherited regal authority do not work so well; the federal government is entirely the creature of the federal constitution. If the doctrine is to succeed it must be cast in broader terms, hence the attempt of current advocates to frame their claims as "inherent limits of sovereignty." Our Children's Trust scholars locate these limits by reference to a higher imperative of "nature's law," or, in the words of Mary Wood, an approach that "defines government's duty in natural resources management as obligatory and organic to governmental power [and suggests] a trust limitation as an attribute of government itself." [35]

As Professor Huffman points out, appeals to natural law, which this must be, are by no means unknown in U.S. constitutional jurisprudence but carry with them a history that has not always been positive and remains controversial.[36] Should a higher U.S. court rule favorably on these grounds, the case will indeed be the case of the century. The question for this paper, however, is whether similar arguments can satisfactorily be deployed in the UK alma mater and if not, why not. I want to suggest that trust arguments of the *Alex L.* and *Juliana* cases are frameable (albeit not necessarily successfully so) because they tap into and are engrafted upon a dynamic of limited sovereignty which derives from the post-revolutionary settlement, was intended to and did mark a break with the British model and which would in terms of conventional UK constitutional understandings be regarded as unreplicable, albeit post-Brexit, not necessarily inconceivable.

2. Sovereignty and Public Trust in U.S. and U.K. Constitutionalism

It is one of the ironies of U.S. constitutional arrangements that while the terms 'sovereign' and 'sovereignty' do not appear in the text, the power-

---

[34] *See* Kennedy, J. in *Coeur d'Alene Tribe of Idaho*, 521 U.S. at 283-84: "The Court from an early date has acknowledged that the people of each of the Thirteen Colonies at the time of independence "became themselves sovereign; and in that character hold the absolute right to all their navigable waters and the soils under them for their own common use, subject only to the rights since surrendered by the Constitution to the general government." The Equal Footing doctrine is not found expressly in the Constitution but is derived from the Admissions Clause of Art. IV § 3, Cl. 1. *See* Pollard v. Hagan, 44 U.S. 212 (1845).

[35] Mary Christina Wood, *"You Can't Negotiate with A Beetle" : Environmental Law for A New Ecological Age*, 50 NAT. RESOURCES J. 167, 203 (2010).

[36] James L. Huffman, Why Liberating the Public Trust Doctrine is Bad for the Public, 45 Envtl. L. 337, 363 (2015).

sharing dynamic that the Framers put in place has produced a fragmented model of governmental sovereignty that differs significantly from the Blackstonian model still prevailing in the British alma mater.[37] The U.S. dualist system whereby sovereignty is located with the people but is shared with the several states, each of which is to be regarded as sovereign within its borders, came out of a post-revolutionary hinterland driven by an imperative of popular sovereignty and an understanding of its relationship with government that marked a profound rejection of the colonial past. If, as Professor Amar explains, "[t]he conventional British position understood 'sovereignty' as that indivisible, final, and unlimited power that necessarily had to exist somewhere in every political society," the constitutional framers of eighteenth-century America in effect brought about a relocation of sovereignty with the concept of a sovereign people and with it an agency or trust explanation of the relationship between government and governed:[38]

> As sovereign, the People need not wield day-to-day power themselves, but could act through agents on whom they conferred limited powers. Within the sphere of these delegated powers, government agents could legitimately compel obedience in the name of their sovereign principal, but those agents lacked authority to go beyond the scope of their agency. So long as the People at all times retained the ability to revoke or modify their delegations, such agency relationships were in no sense a surrender or division of ultimate sovereignty.[39]

By analogy with the corporate charters of the colonial era whereby the British King-in-Parliament delegated limited sovereign privileges to the American colonists, so too could the people delegate to their state and federal governments authority that would be limited by the terms of the delegation, or in other words as evidenced by the terms of their foundational constitutions. True sovereignty, however, which was

---

[37] *See* 1 W. BLACKSTONE, COMMENTARIES *49: "In every government, 'there is and must be... a supreme, irresistible, absolute, uncontrolled authority, in which the *jura summi imperii*, or the rights of sovereignty reside." Since the 'sovereign and uncontrollable authority in the making, confirming, enlarging, restraining, abrogating, repealing, reviving, and expounding of laws' resided in Parliament, *id.* at *160, that body could "do everything that is not naturally impossible... [W]hat the parliament doth, no authority upon earth can undo." *Id.* at *161.

[38] Akhil Reed Amar, *Of Sovereignty and Federalism*, 96 YALE L.J. 1425, 1436 (1987).

[39] Id.

inalienable and non-delegable and included the right to alter or remove their governments, remained with the people. In this way, explains Amar, "Americans domesticated government power and decisively repudiated British notions of 'sovereign' governmental omnipotence."[40]

My point is that whatever the outcome of the *Juliana* case, an argument based on a limitation of sovereignty by reference to considerations of public trust is not totally without traction. However, for contemporary British lawyers schooled in the traditions of Dicey and Bagehot, sovereignty remains unitary, indivisible and unlimited by considerations of agency or trust. In its narrowest sense the term is nothing more than a legal doctrine about the relationship between acts of Parliament and the Courts; English courts accord the highest legal authority to that which has been enacted by the sovereign Parliament –which in this context means the Monarch acting by and with the consent of the (now democratically elected) House of Commons and the (largely appointed) House of Lords. The fact that the House of Commons is now democratically elected and the House of Lords now largely appointed (as opposed to constituted by hereditary entitlement) makes it possible to reconcile the exercise of inherited regal authority with changing ideas concerning the location of power within the polity while the resulting near fusion of the executive with the legislature, which permits the government of the day to both wield what remains of regal prerogative power and to control the legislative activity of the parliament, continues to be applauded as the British constitution's 'efficient secret.'[41] Can this the kind of constitutional background sustain a doctrine of public trust?

3. Can Public Trusteeship Transcend Political Metaphor?

"'Fiduciary political theory'" argue Professors Leib et al., "is an intellectual project that seeks to recover the fiduciary foundations of public authority. It takes seriously the idea that political office is a public trust, which must be administered with sensitivity to the implied fiduciary role officers serve" and has been a "fertile project" for theorizing the basis of

---

[40] *Id.* at 1436.

[41] *See* Walter Bagehot, The English Constitution (1st ed. 1867).

democratic relationships within the polity.[42] The project owes much to the work of Paul Finn who more than thirty years ago wrote of a common –law world "collective amnesia" concerning that "most fundamental of fiduciary relationships in our society [namely] that which exists between the community (the people) and the State and its agencies."[43] The "amnesia," he conceded, does not extend to the United States where a constitutional narrative of popular sovereignty supports both a public trust doctrine of state ownership and responsibilities in relation to submerged waters of navigable waters, and standards of trusteeship and an imposition of fiduciary obligation in relation to the conduct of public office.[44] Given a different narrative, however, the parallels are not so easy to draw. In Professor Finn's native Australia and similarly in the United Kingdom, where the legacy of Dicey continues to prevail, posited inherited fiduciary obligations of kingship are difficult to reconcile with a constitutional narrative of parliamentary sovereignty.[45]

While it is true that as Professor Finn recognizes, Australian and U.K. courts no longer subscribe to the traditional view that members of Parliament are not holders of public office subject to obligations of trust,[46]

---

[42] Ethan J. Leib, David L. Ponet & Michael Serota, *Mapping Public Fiduciary Relationships* in THE PHILOSOPHICAL FOUNDATIONS OF FIDUCIARY LAW (Andrew Gold & Paul Miller eds., Oxford University Press, 2014) available at SSRN: https://ssrn.com/abstract=2320548. See also Ethan J. Leib, David L. Ponet &Michael Serota Translating Fiduciary Principles into Public Law 126 HARV. L. REV. FORUM 91 (2013).

[43] Paul Finn, *The Forgotten "Trust": The People and the State*, in EQUITY: ISSUES AND TRENDS 131 (Malcolm Cope ed.1995).

[44] We can fit Professor Natelson's work within this tradition. His analysis of the literary and political canon with which the Founders must be presumed to have been familiar, together with the language of the state constitutions that preceded the Philadelphia Convention and of the ratifying debates that followed supports his claim that fiduciary language and principles were already found in most state constitutions and that "leading proponents of the new government repeatedly characterized officials as the people's servants, agents, guardians, or trustees." Moreover, he continues "[t]his was a subject on which there was no disagreement from the Constitution's opponents. They very often used the same kind of language, and based their own arguments on fiduciary principles as well." See Robert G. Natelson, *The Constitution and the Public Trust*, 52 BUFF. L. REV. 1077, 1083–85 (2004).

[45] *See* A.V. Dicey, The Law of the Constitution 75 (10th ed., 1960): "Parliament is [not] in any sense a 'trustee' for the electors.'

[46] *See* Finn, *supra* note 43, at 134; Law Commission, Misconduct in Public Office Issues Paper 1: The Current Law¶¶ 2.46 -2.48 (2016) available at

in both jurisdictions the language of trust, when used in respect of government and agency responsibilities, now operates by way of political metaphor only.[47] As Sir Robert Megarry explained in *Tito v Waddell (No.2)*[48] governmental obligations, such as those owed by the British Government to Ocean Islanders in respect of royalties due under mining agreements, while they may give rise to what might be termed 'trusts in a higher sense,' do not, in general, give rise to fiduciary obligations enforceable in a court of law.[49] In this context, observes Professor Finn, a "bleak question" concerning the concept of parliamentary sovereignty itself requires an answer: can the exercise of *legislative* power be subject to some restraints by reference to rights deeply rooted in our democratic system of government and common law?"[50]

Professor Finn prefaced his question with the rider "the Constitution apart."[51] The U.K. of course has no written Constitution and, the U.K. Human Rights Act notwithstanding, no entrenched rights that can withstand the clearly expressed will of the Westminster Parliament to remove them. As Lord Hoffman explained in *R. v. Secretary of State for the*

---

www.lawcom.gov.uk/app/uploads/2016/.../misconduct_in_public_office_issues-1.pdf *(citing English (Greenway)* (1992) (unreported, Central Criminal Court)), *Australian (Boston* [1923] 33 CLR 386 at 411) *and Canadian (Hurlburt* [2012] NSSC 291) *authority and the view of then British Home Secretary Jack Straw* giving evidence to the Joint Committee on Parliamentary Privilege on 20 January 1999, that "the government's thinking at that time – considering a proposal to place misconduct in public office on the statute books – was that a "there should be an offence of Misuse of Public Office which should apply to ministers, should apply to councillors, to other members of public bodies and should also apply to Members of Parliament" and "it is vitally important that the same checks on unacceptable behaviour should apply to Members of Parliament as we in Parliament impose on members of the public": *Joint Committee on Parliamentary Privilege* (30 March 1999) HC 214-I; HL Paper 43-I para 107 and 110. It has also been indicated to us by the Standards Committee of the Welsh Assembly that Assembly Members consider themselves to be public office holders. We consider that, following *Greenway*, there would seem to be no reason why the position would not also be the same for Members of the House of Lords.

[47] Paul Finn, *Public Trusts and Fiduciary Relations*, in FIDUCIARY DUTY AND THE ATMOSPHERIC TRUST, 34 (Coghill et al. eds. 2012).

[48] (1977) Ch. 106 (Megarry, J.) (discussing Kinloch v. Secretary of State for India (1882) 7 App. Cas. 619).

[49] *Id.* at 211-216.

[50] Finn, *supra* note 43, at 135(emphasis added).

[51] *Id.*

Home Department ex parte Simms, parliamentary sovereignty means that the constraints upon its exercise by Parliament are ultimately political, not legal.[52] His words have given rise to an interpretive principle of legality requiring that Parliament must "squarely confront what it is doing and accept the political cost."[53] In other words, Parliament can if it chooses enact legislation or confer delegated powers that curtail or abrogate human rights, but as an interpretive principle, its instructions cannot be "general or ambiguous." Lord Hoffman explained:

> This is because "there is too great a risk that the full implications of their unqualified meaning may have passed unnoticed in the democratic process. In the absence of express language or necessary implication to the contrary, the courts therefore presume that even the most general words were intended to be subject to the basic rights of the individual.

In this way, he claimed, "the courts of the United Kingdom, though acknowledging the sovereignty of Parliament, apply principles of constitutionality little different from those which exist in countries where the power of the legislature is expressly limited by a constitutional document."[54]

Common law constitutionalism, or the view that the U.K. Parliament does not possess absolute sovereign legislative power but should be regarded as constrained within a common law matrix of fundamental principles which sustain the operation of the rule of law owes much to the work of Trevor Allan whose attempt to reconcile political values with legal doctrine has much in common with a Dworkinian interpretivist methodology.[55] There is a distinction, he argues, between an "external" perspective which sets out to describe the constitution in a non-evaluative way and an "internal" or interpretive approach to statutes and common law which "present[s] reasons of justice or political morality for reading them in one way rather than another."[56] In this way, he suggests, "legal

---

[52] [2000] 2AC 115, 131.

[53] *Id.*

[54] *Id.*

[55] *See* T.R.S. Allan, The Sovereignty of Law: Freedom, Constitution and Common Law 340-41 (2015).

[56] *Id.* at 6.

analysis cannot be detached from ... constitutional theory,"[57] and "*legality* is always connected to *legitimacy*."[58] Like Dworkin, he is at pains to point out that the constitutional interpreter does not choose the moral theory she brings to the task but is herself fundamentally constrained by the legal and political principles that are latent within current constitutional practice.[59] The question then is, what are these principles and how are they to be found? The answer to the first lies in Professor Allan's conceptions of the "public good": "Parliament's authority is confined by the limits of our ability (in any concrete context) to interpret its enactments as contributions to the public good."[60] In this conception, he argues, it must follow that a statute is only recognizable as such if it can be read in a way that is compatible with the principle of equal citizenship.[61] The interpretive task is for the judiciary whose job it is to construct the intent of the "ideal or representative legislator" who seeks to reconcile "current policy and overarching legal principle."[62] In this way, there is no conflict between Parliamentary supremacy and the rule of law because the ideas are interdependent, and embody the twin imperatives of democracy and respect for individual dignity and autonomy.[63]

In judicial quarters, the view that there can be common law rights whose "existence would not be the consequence of the democratic political process but would be logically prior to it"[64] is associated with the judicial and extra-judicial writings of Sir John Laws[65] but reached members of the U.K. Supreme Court in *Jackson* [2006].[66] Lord Steyn stated:

---

[57] *Id.* at 22.

[58] *Id.* at 23.

[59] *Id.* at 340-46.

[60] *Id.* at 12.

[61] *Id.* at ch. 4, 33.

[62] *Id.* at 194.

[63] *Id.* at ch.5, 168.

[64] Id.

[65] R. v. Lord Chancellor ex p. Witham, [1998] QB 575, 581 (Laws, J.). See also Thoburn v. Sunderland Council [2002] EWHC 195 (Admin), [59] (Laws, L.J.): "the traditional doctrine [of Parliamentary sovereignty] has in my judgment been modified. It has been done by the common law, wholly consistently with constitutional principle." See also Sir John Laws, *Law and Democracy* [1995] PUBLIC LAW 72.

[66] Jackson v. Attorney General [2006] 1 AC 262.

the supremacy of Parliament is still the general principle of our constitution. It is a construct of the common law. The judges created this principle. If that is so, it is not unthinkable that circumstances could arise where the courts may have to qualify a principle established on a different hypothesis of constitutionalism.[67]

Lord Hope expressed the same idea:

Our [United Kingdom] constitution is dominated by the sovereignty of Parliament. But Parliamentary sovereignty is no longer, if it ever was, absolute. It is not uncontrolled in the sense referred to by Lord Birkenhead LC in *McCawley v. The King* [1920] AC 691, 720. It is no longer right to say that its freedom to legislate admits of no qualification whatever. Step by step, gradually but surely, the English principle of the absolute legislative sovereignty of Parliament which Dicey derived from Coke and Blackstone is being qualified. ... [T]he concept of a Parliament that is absolutely sovereign is not entirely in accord with the reality. ... The principle of parliamentary sovereignty which, in the absence of higher authority, has been created by the common law, is built upon the assumption that Parliament represents the people whom it exists to serve.[68]

The problem is that common law constitutionalism or legal constitutionalism as it is sometimes called, is inherently susceptible to the criticism that, because it is the tool of judges who are unelected, unaccountable and unguided by any formal expression of the values with which they are to work, it is both undemocratic and unpredictable. Moreover, as Aidan O'Neill Q.C. points out in a review of more recent U.K. Supreme Court decisions[69] a move back to "common law basics" may

---

[67] *Id.* at ¶102.

[68] *Id.* at ¶¶104, 126

[69] He cites specifically Lord Mance (joined by Lord Neuberger, Lady Hale & Lord Wilson) in *Pham v. Home Secretary* [2015] UKSC 19 [90]-[91] warning against the CJEU reaching decisions which 'overstep jurisdictional limits which member states have clearly set at the European Treaty level and which are reflected domestically in their constitutional arrangements' and affirming that 'a domestic court must ultimately decide for itself what is consistent with its own domestic constitutional arrangements, including in the case of the European Communities Act 1972 what jurisdictional limits exist under the European Treaties and on the competence conferred on European institutions including the Court of Justice', while suggesting that direct confrontation might be avoided if 'all concerned ... act with mutual

represent a "canny response... to a political climate of ever-increasing hostility toward all things European and legal, and an oft-expressed distaste by certain politicians and journalists for un(der)qualified foreign judges making judgment on British ways" [70] but it has involved resorting to a "decontextualised and ahistorical" legal archaeology whereby English common law judges mine "historic statutes and ancient charters" and produce a "mythistory"[71] with "oligarchic, phallocratic and sectarian"[72] eighteenth-century origins that still largely depends upon a constitutional canon beginning with Magna Carta and telling of milestones in a narrative of transformed regal authority.

In an extra-judicial speech to the Friends of the British Library given to mark the 800 anniversary of Magna Carta, U.K. Supreme Court justice and medieval historian Lord Sumption, commenting on its contribution to a "mythistory" of English liberties, had this to say:

> Magna Carta as we know it was reinvented in the early seventeenth century, largely by one man, the judge and politician Sir Edward Coke... Coke transformed Magna Carta from a somewhat technical catalogue of feudal regulations, into the foundation document of the English constitution, a status which it has enjoyed ever since among the large community of commentators who have never actually read it. ... [W]hen we commemorate Magna Carta, perhaps the first question that we should ask ourselves is this: do we really need the force of myth to sustain our belief in democracy? Do we need to derive our belief in democracy and the rule of law from a group of muscular conservative millionaires from the north of England, who

---

respect and with caution in areas where member states' constitutional identity is or may be engaged' all done in 'the spirit of cooperation of which both the *Bundesverfassungsgericht* and this court have previously spoken.'

[70] Aidan O'Neill, *Not Waving but Drowning?: EU Law, Common Law Fundamental Rights and the UK Supreme Court*,6 available at UKSCBlog (Monday 22 June 2015) http://ukscblog.com/not-waving-but-drowning-eu-law-common-law-fundamental-rights-and-the-uk-supreme-court/.

[71] Mythistory" is a term coined by American historian W. H. McNeill, *Mythistory, or Truth, Myth, History, and Historians* 91 AM. HISTORICAL REV. 1, 10 (1986) to describe the way in which historical 'truths' abstracted from context can acquire the status of myth if "if they fit both what a people want to hear and what a people need to know well enough to be useful."

[72] O'Neill, *supra* note 70, at 15.

thought in French, knew no Latin or English, and died more than three-quarters of a millennium ago? I rather hope not.[73]

He raises the question but does not answer. Commentators have seen in the British experience of Brexit and the US phenomenon of Donald Trump a common theme of cultural anxiety in the face of changing political values. We are operating, claims Professor Kaufman "in a new political era in which the values divide between voters – especially among whites – is the main axis of politics:

> In a period of rapid ethnic change, this cleavage separates those who prefer cultural continuity and order from novelty-seekers open to diversity. Policymakers and pundits should face this instead of imagining that old remedies – schools, hospitals, jobs – will put the populist genie back in the bottle."[74]

What we need to do now, he suggests, is to address cultural anxieties with new ways of framing our political communication.[75] My question is can common law constitutionalism help us find a new but principled basis for framing a discourse of the relationship between governments and governed, one which does not depend upon a 'mythistory' drawn from an elitist and exploitative past but speaks a language of public obligation and fiduciary responsibilities and can reflect the popular intuition that government exists to serve its people? In other words, can a discourse of public trust step up to the mark?

Evan Fox-Decent has recently claimed that common law constitutionalism "is the theory that legal principles such as fairness and equality reside within the common law, are constitutive of legality and inform (or should inform) statutory interpretation on judicial review .... [It] is usually understood as a theory about the rule of law and the role of judges as the rule of law's guardians."[76] To underpin these principles he

---

[73] Jonathan Sumption, Magna Carta Then and Now (2015) available at *https://www.supremecourt.uk/docs/speech-150309.pdf.*

[74] Eric Kaufmann, *Trump and Brexit: Why it's Again NOT the Economy,Stupid*, British Politics and Policy, http://blogs.lse.ac.uk/politicsandpolicy/trump-and-brexit-why-its-again-not-the-economy-stupid/, Nov. 9 2016.

[75] Eric Kaufmann, Presentation to APG Conference, Brexit & Trump: What's Next for the UK EU and US, U.C. Berkeley August 30 2017.

[76] Evan Fox-Decent, *Democratizing Common Law Constitutionalism*, 55 McGill L.J. 511, 513 (2010).

articulates a theory of popular sovereignty that he terms relational because it is grounded in "respect for the agency of persons subject to irresistible public power."[77] The dependency of the citizen upon government authority, he argues, gives rise to a trustee-beneficiary parallel and brings with it Kantian-based imperatives of non-instrumentalization (the idea that persons are to be treated as ends and not means) and non-domination (the idea that individuals should not be subject to arbitrary power) capable of generating determinate legal principles of fiduciary obligation in so far as decision-making affects the citizen.[78] Where duties towards specific individuals conflict with those owed elsewhere he suggests that in general terms these might include:

> a prohibition on fraud and corruption; procedural fairness; formal equality or even-handedness; solicitude in the sense of taking seriously the legitimate interests and human rights of individuals subject to public power; transparency; proportionality; reason-giving where important interests are at stake; and purposiveness in the sense.... that public powers must be used exclusively for the purposes for which they are conferred.[79]

As a normative account of legitimate authority within the modern state which reconciles an assumption of popular sovereignty with legislative constraints based upon principles of trust, this articulation does not suffer from the counter-factual difficulties associated with social contract theory. The difficulty comes with Fox-Decent's claim of normative independence from judicial review:

> By distinguishing legality from judicial review, the theory democratizes common law constitutionalism by showing that its favoured principles are not the result of judicial fiat. Rather, they are the constitutive norms of a shared legal order that all public bodies are responsible for maintaining on behalf of the people[80]

My problem with this is exactly the same as that outlined above; in the absence of a written constitution or code how are our U.K. judges to know what exactly the values of a shared legal order; a problem that, in the context of an increasingly diverse polity is only likely to intensify.

---

[77] *Id.* at 523.

[78] *Id.* at 521-22.

[79] *Id.* at 523.

4. A Public Trust Post-Brexit Settlement?

The point of this paper has been to consider what place there might be, if any, for a U.K. doctrine of public trust post-Brexit. I want to answer this question by first returning to the environmental doctrine of public trust as it is currently recognized in the United States with which I began. The work of Robin Kundis Craig and Thomas Merrill discussed earlier has been extremely helpful in uncovering the breadth and variety of U.S. state environmental public trust doctrines.[81] What is significant is that those states with the most expansive doctrines also have environmental rights and guarantees enshrined in their constitutions.[82] The same is also true of non-U.S. jurisdictions where the doctrine of environmental public trusteeship may be regarded as established. U.S. public trust advocate Michael Blumm and his co-researcher Rachael Guthrie have recently claimed that the public trust has become "internationalised"[83] and leads "a vibrant and significant life abroad."[84] They identify "ten diverse countries on four continents: India, Pakistan, the Philippines, Uganda, Kenya, Nigeria, South Africa, Brazil, Ecuador, and Canada" in which in their view "the doctrine has become equated with environmental protection."[85] However, what is clear is that, Canada apart where the environmental trust is embryonic, the doctrine in these countries is at least supported by and in many cases explicitly derives from constitutional or statutory provisions or both. In other words the doctrine of public trust works best to date when its rhetorical allure can be tied to specific guarantees set out in an entrenched constitution which the U.K. significantly does not as yet have.

---

[80] Id.

[81] See Kundis Craig; Merrill supra note 24

[82] Kundis-Craig, supra note 24, at 19-20. In addition to Hawaii – which has the most extensive constitutional guarantees, Kundis Craig identifies Alabama, Minnesota, Mississippi, South Carolina, Tennessee, Wisconsin with constitutional guarantees of access to navigational waters and Florida, Illinois, Louisiana, Pennsylvania, Virginia, Rhode Island, & Vermont with broader constitutional environmental guarantees.

[83] Michael C. Blumm & Rachael D. Guthrie, Internationalizing the Public Trust Doctrine: Natural Law and Constitutional and Statutory Approaches to Fulfilling the Saxion Vision, 45 U.C. DAVIS L. REV. 741 (2012).See also David Takacs, The Public Trust Doctrine, Environmental Human Rights, and the Future of Private Property, 16 N.Y.U. ENVTL. L.J. 711, 737 (2008).

[84] Id. at 741.

[85] Id.

My second point is one of speculation. Constitutional reforms require 'constitutional moments', moments which capture a public mood or zeitgeist, so the question arises for consideration: could Brexit represent such a moment? David Greenberg, of the Constitutional Reform Group (CRG) is not alone in suggesting that the process to date has already highlighted significant constitutional weaknesses not least of which is the relationship between the different constituent parts of the U.K.[86] CRG proposes a more direct form of federalism and a draft Act of Union which describes itself in its preamble as an opportunity to provide

> a renewed constitutional form for the peoples of England, Scotland, Wales and Northern Ireland to continue to join together to form the United Kingdom; and to affirm that the peoples of those nations and parts have chosen to continue to pool their sovereignty for specified purposes, and to provide universal citizenship with social and economic rights.[87]

As I intimated earlier, it is entirely possible that when the dust of Brexit comes to be swept away and the divisions that have ensued fall to be repaired, constitutional reform will be on the agenda and with it an opportunity for rethinking and rearticulating the basis of legitimate authority within the polity. Should that situation arise and – with all the usual caveats that accompany speculation of this kind - should the British people decide to ground their public relationships in the language of popular sovereignty capable of sustaining obligations of public trust, my third point is the cautionary one of constitutional indeterminacy and is prompted by an atmospheric trust case recently decided last year in a Pennsylvania state court.[88]

The Pennsylvania Constitution contains an Environmental Rights Amendment which provides:

> The people have a right to clean air, pure water, and to the preservation of the natural, scenic, historic and esthetic values of the environment. Pennsylvania's public natural resources are the common property of all the people, including generations yet to

---

[86] David Greenberg, We Need a New Act of Union to Meet the Challenges of Brexit, Constitution Reform Group, http://www.constitutionreformgroup.co.uk/brexit-new-act-union/ 21 April 2017.

[87] *Id.*

[88] Funk v. Wolf, 144 A.3d 228 (2016).

come. As trustee of these resources, the Commonwealth shall conserve and maintain them for the benefit of all the people.[89]

Like the *Juliana* case, *Funk v. Wolf* was brought by a group of minor Plaintiffs seeking various forms of declaratory and mandamus relief to require the Pennsylvania Public Utilities Commission (PUC) and responsible Pennsylvania executive agencies to develop and implement a comprehensive plan for the regulation of Pennsylvania's emissions of carbon dioxide and other greenhouse gases "consistent with and in furtherance of the Commonwealth's duties and obligations under Article I, Section 27" of the Pennsylvania Constitution.[90] Petitioners alleged that in light of the contribution of CO_2 and greenhouse gas emissions to global climate change, Respondents had failed to discharge their constitutional obligations to the people of Pennsylvania and had not adequately acted as trustees of the Commonwealth's public natural resources, including the atmosphere.

Dismissing the petition, Judge Cohn Jubelirer for the Court had this to say: "[j]udicial review of governmental decisions implicating the ERA 'must be realistic and not merely legalistic.'"

> While expansive in its language, the ERA was not intended to be read in absolutist terms so as to prohibit development that enhances the economic opportunities and welfare of the people currently living in Pennsylvania. [...] Instead, the ERA places policymakers in the "constant and difficult" position of "weighing conflicting environmental and social concerns" and "in arriving at a course of action that will be expedient as well as reflective of the high priority which constitutionally has been placed on the conservation of our natural, scenic, esthetic and historical resources."[91]

My point is that as Fox-Decent points out, the fiduciary conception is inherently legal in nature.[92] This means that although, as he argues, the obligation goes to the issue of authority, so that it operates to constrain the exercise of legislative power, the obligation is inherently indeterminate so that the arbiters of what those constraints might mean in any given set of

---

[89] PA. CONST. art. I, § 27.

[90] *Id.* at 233. PA. CONST. art. I, § 27.

[91] *Id.* at 234 (internal citations omitted).

[92] Evan Fox Decent, *The Fiduciary Nature of State Legal Authority*, 31 QUEEN'S L.J. 259 (2005).

circumstances are necessarily unelected (at least in the U.K.) and thereby democratically unaccountable judges. How much of an issue this is will depend on the view that one takes of the desirability or otherwise of moving further in the direction of U.S-style Platonic constitutional guardians, a path down which the United Kingdom has been notoriously reluctant to tread. The attempts in recent years to make the composition of the judiciary more representative of the community as a whole, in terms of gender and ethnicity and indeed, most recently, sexuality represent a partial response to the most obvious of these concerns, as Haydn Davies and I have commented elsewhere.[93] In this paper I simply raise the potential of sovereignty discourse for a normative reframing of relations between government and governed in a way that can take account of popular expectations or understandings concerning the formal locus of power within the British polity.

Extrapolating from a discourse of public trust which in the United States is closely tied to conceptions of popular sovereignty I have wanted to consider the extent to which a current interest in common law constitutionalism as a matrix for circumscribing the exercise of legislative power can supply the philosophical tools for theorizing an account of fiduciary obligation which can be accommodated within UK constitutional discourse. As contributors to a recent collection of essays uncontroversially point out, in twenty-first century formulations, the terms "sovereignty" and "sovereignty discourse" occupy so many different disciplinary positions that their meaning can be both unstable and contested.[94] Professor Allan's repositioning of legal authority within this discourse grounds Fox-Decent's attempt to democratize rule of law theory but translating "sovereignty's promise" into deliverable solutions for resolving specific problems of governance without thereby necessarily increasing judicial power is another matter.

Welcoming Professor Allan's "reinvigoration" of sovereignty discourse, Dr. Stuart Lakin has observed that "[t]hese are exciting times for scholars of the British constitution. What had been a rather arid, doctrinal, area of study is now rich with philosophical interest."[95] His context was not Brexit

---

[93] Anne Richardson Oakes & Haydn Davies, *Justice Must Be Seen to Be Done: A Contextual Reappraisal*, 37 ADELAIDE L. REV. 461 (2016).

[94] *See* Melea Lewis et al., *Introduction* in RE-ENVISIONING SOVEREIGNTY: THE END OF WESTPHALIA? 1 (Trudi Jacobsen et al., eds. 2008).

[95] S. Lakin, 'Review: TRS Allan's *The Sovereignty of Law* (OUP, 2013)' U.K. Const.L. Blog (4th February 2014) (available at https://ukconstitutionallaw.org/).

which he may or may not have foreseen. In a post-Brexit world, for CRG and reform-minded supporters, the task will be to translate theory into practice, and the difficulty will be as perhaps it has always been: "[t]he philosophers have only *interpreted* the world, in various ways. The point, however, is to *change* it. [96]

Bibliography

Allan, T.R.S. The Sovereignty of Law: Freedom, Constitution and Common Law (Oxford University Press, 2015).

Amar, Akhil Reed, *Of Sovereignty and Federalism*, 96 Yale L.J. 1425 (1987).

Blumm, Michael C. & Guthrie, Rachael D., *Internationalizing the Public Trust Doctrine: Natural Law and Constitutional and Statutory Approaches to Fulfilling the Saxion Vision*, 45 U.C. Davis L. Rev. 741 (2012).

Craig, Robin Kundis, *A Comparative Guide to the Eastern Public Trust Doctrines: Classifications of States, Property Rights and State Summaries*, 16 Penn St. Envtl. L. Rev. 1 (2007).

Dicey, A.V., An Introduction to the Law of the Constitution 75 (10th ed., Palgrave MacMillan, 1960).

Fox-Decent, Evan, *Democratizing Common Law Constitutionalism*, 55 McGill L.J. 511 (2010).

Fox-Decent, Evan, *The Fiduciary Nature of State Legal Authority*, 31 Queen's L.J. 259 (2005).

Finn, Paul, *The Forgotten "Trust": The People and the State*, in Equity: Issues and Trends (Cope, Malcolm ed., The Federation Press, 1995).

Finn, Paul, *Public Trusts and Fiduciary Relations*, in Fiduciary Duty and the Atmospheric Trust, 34 (Coghill, Ken, Sampford, Charles & Smith, Tim, eds., Routledge, 2012).

Green, Les, *Should Parliamentary Sovereignty Trump Popular Sovereignty*, Semper Viridis (2016-11-03), https://ljmgreen.com/2016/11/03/should-parliamentary-sovereignty-trump-popular-sovereignty/.

Greenberg, David, *We Need a New Act of Union to Meet the Challenges of Brexit*, Constitution Reform Group, http://www.constitutionreformgroup.co.uk/brexit-new-act-union/ 21 April 2017.

Huffman, James L., *Why Liberating the Public Trust Doctrine is Bad for the Public*, 45 Envtl. L. 337 (2015).

Kaufmann, Eric, *Trump and Brexit: Why It's Again NOT the Economy,Stupid*, British Politics and Policy,

---

[96] Karl Marx, Eleven Theses on Feuerbach The Eleventh Thesis is engraved in the entryway of Humboldt University on Unter den Linden in Berlin. The Eleventh Thesis is also Marx's epitaph, engraved on his tombstone in Highgate Cemetery in London,

http://blogs.lse.ac.uk/politicsandpolicy/trump-and-brexit-why-its-again-not-the-economy-stupid/, Nov. 9, 2016.

Lakin, S., *Review: TRS Allan's* The Sovereignty of Law (OUP, 2013) U.K. Const. L. Blog (4th February 2014) (available at https://ukconstitutionallaw.org/).

Laws, John, *Law and Democracy* [1995] Public Law 72.

Leib, Ethan J. Ponet, David L. & Serota, Michael, *Translating Fiduciary Principles into Public Law* 126 Harv. L. Rev. Forum 91 (2013).

Leib, Ethan J., Ponet, David L. & Serota, Michael, *Mapping Public Fiduciary Relationships* in The Philosophical Foundations of Fiduciary Law (Gold, Andrew & Miller, Paul eds., Oxford: Oxford University Press, 2014)

Lewis, Melea et al., *Introduction* in Re-envisioning Sovereignty: The End of Westphalia? (Jacobsen, Trudi, Sampford, Charles & Thakur, Ramesh, eds., London & New York: Routledge, 2008).

McNeill, W. H., *Mythistory, or Truth, Myth, History, and Historians* 91 Am. Historical Rev. 1, 10 (1986).

Merrill, Thomas W., *The Public Trust Doctrine: Some Jurisprudential Variations and Their Implications*, 38 U. Haw. L. Rev. 261 (2016);

Natelson, Robert G., *The Constitution and the Public Trust*, 52 Buff. L. Rev. 1077 (2004).

O'Neill, Aidan, *Not Waving but Drowning?: EU Law, Common Law Fundamental Rights and the UK Supreme Court*,6 available at UKSCBlog (Monday 22 June 2015) http://ukscblog.com/not-waving-but-drowning-eu-law-common-law-fundamental-rights-and-the-uk-supreme-court/.

Richardson Oakes, Anne & Davies, Haydn, *Justice Must Be Seen to Be Done: A Contextual Reappraisal*, 37 Adelaide L. Rev. 461 (2016).

Sax, Joseph, *The Public Trust Doctrine in Natural Resource Law: Effective Judicial Intervention*, 68 Mich. L. Rev. 471 (1970).

Sumption, Jonathan, *Magna Carta Then and Now* (2015) available at *https://www.supremecourt.uk/docs/speech-150309.pdf*.

Takacs, David *The Public Trust Doctrine, Environmental Human Rights, and the Future of Private Property*, 16 N.Y.U. En Envtl. L.J. 711 (2008).

Wood, Mary Christina, *"You Can't Negotiate with A Beetle": Environmental Law for A New Ecological Age*, 50 Nat. resources J. 167 (2010).

Chapter 6

Legal Globalization through the Constructivist and Poststructuralist Lenses

Luka Martin Tomažič[1]

Abstract

The process of globalization has been variously defined as a time-space compression, as a rise of supra-territorial relations or as the intensification of worldwide social relations, which link distant localities in such a way that local happenings are shaped by events occurring many miles away and vice versa. In the present paper, the author will focus on the legal aspects of globalization. He identifies legal globalization to proceed in three main forms; progressive development of international law, emergence of supranational legal norms and gradual convergence of differing types of legal systems. The author is especially interested in the explanatory possibilities that two differing but somewhat related sets of theories, namely the constructivist and poststructuralist theories, possess regarding different aspects of legal globalization. He will analyze the merit of constructivist accounts through the application of the norm life-cycle theory of Sikkink and Finnemore in the above-mentioned areas of legal globalization. Their theory, if applied to legal globalization, could potentially explain the creation of international and supranational legal norms as well as dissemination of norms in different legal systems and perhaps even the so-called legal transplants. The notion of norm tipping point could potentially be used to analyze which norms will be retained in the domestic legal systems and which are not to find widespread acceptance. Post-structuralism on the other hand probably has great explanatory potential especially in terms of convergent development of different legal systems, for

---

[1] Assistant at the School of Advanced Social Studies, Nova Goricia, Slovenia

example, the common law and continental ones. As Derrida claims, the possibilities which are not included as meaningful language is produced always mean that there is a seed of subversion in the meaning of each word. Similar can be claimed of domestic legal systems, which are always haunted by the excluded differences. Under the pressure of globalization, Derrida's theory could explain how the dominant forms of domestic legal systems are being deconstructed so that legal systems of different States gradually become more and more similar.

1. Globalization and its Legal Dimension

Globalization is the overarching trend in the social environment into which the legal systems are embedded. It is a process driven by economics, politics, and technics,[2] which has its origins in the Westphalian order[3] and has been, in terms of a general trend, broadening and deepening ever since. Especially useful in coming to grips with its historical development is the approach taken by Thomas Friedman, who separates it into three distinct eras, namely globalisations 1.0, 2.0 and 3.0, each with its own distinct characteristics.[4] Although no single agreed upon definition of the notion exists, it is clear that at the heart of it is the idea of a growing interconnectedness between different societies and between individuals around the globe.[5] It is also a multidimensional process,

---

[2] Anthony McGrew, "The Logics of Economic Globalization", in John Ravenhill, *Global Political Economy* (Oxford: Oxford University Press, 2011), 295.

[3] Immanuel Maurice Wallerstein, *"World-systems analysis: an introduction,"* (Durham: Duke University Press, 2004), 42.

[4] Thomas L. Friedman, *The World is Flat: A Brief History of the Twenty-First Century* (New York: Farrar, Straus and Giroux, 2005) and Thomas Friedman, "Globalization 3.0 Has Shrunk the World to Size Tiny", *Yale Global Online*, April 7, 2004, https://yaleglobal.yale.edu/content/globalization-30-has-shrunk-world-size-tiny.

[5] For different definitions, see: Robert Cox, "*Multilateralism and the Democratization of World Order*", paper for the International Symposium on Sources of Innovation in Multilateralism, Lausanne, May 26-28, 1994, as cited in J. A. Scholte, "The Globalization of World Politics", in J. Baylis and S. Smith (eds.), The Globalization of World Politics, An Introduction to International Relations (New York: Oxford University Press, 1999), 15; Scholte, Defining Globalisation, 1471–1502; Giddens, The Consequences of Modernity, 64; Harvey, The Condition of Postmodernity: An Enquiry into the Origins of Cultural Change, 240; David Held, Anthony McGrew, David Goldblatt & Jonathan Perraton, "Contents and Introduction" in David Held, Anthony McGrew, David Goldblatt & Jonathan Perraton (eds.), *Global Transformations: Politics, Economics and Culture* (Stanford: Stanford University Press, 1999), 2.

Legal Globalization through the Constructivist 95

encompassing aspects such as social, cultural, economic, political and also legal globalization.

The legal dimension of the process of globalization is the consequence of a broader international but also transnational discourse emerging, which enables new legal solutions to be applied and which enables national legislators to look for inspiration and for relevant legal tools even in distant corners of the globe. Legal globalization seems to proceed in three main forms, which will be addressed in turn, namely the development of public international law, the emergence of transnational legal norms and a slow, uneven, but gradual convergence of differing types of legal systems.

The crucial characteristic of the first form is that different specialized areas of international law are converging, according to Antonio Cassese, in the process of gradual interpenetration and cross-fertilization, as the international community is becoming more integrated than ever before.[6] The correlation between the growth of the body of norms of international law and the process of globalization can be asserted from the fact that as the global interconnectedness increased, so did the canon of international law. Increased intensity and extensiveness of inter-state relations namely increase the need for norms which regulate their behavior, a timeless truth nicely summarized by the Latin saying "ubi societas, ibi ius". International law can even be seen as one of the chief institutions (in terms of the English-school terminology), upon which the Westphalian and post-Westphalian international society was created.[7] Such a relatively sophisticated system of norms was not present in the international society before Westphalia - as the process of globalization advances, so the public international law develops.

State-state and emerging state-individual relationships in public international law are not the only form of legal globalization occurring, cross-border relationships between subjects acting in terms of *iure gestionis* are also on the rise. Transnational law is thus law "*that transcends or crosses borders but may not be formally enacted by states*"[8] Under the umbrella term are included such diverse legal frameworks as the ICSID system and the FIFA law. It is in our opinion difficult to argue against the

---

[6] Antonio Cassese, "International Law " (Oxford: Oxford University Press, 2001), 22- 45.

[7] Hedley Bull, "The Anarchical Society", (Basingstoke: Palgrave Macmillan, 2002).

[8] Carrie Menkel-Meadow, "Why and How to Study "Transnational" Law," UC Irvine Law Review, 1-1 (2011), 103.

increase in the number of different legal frameworks in the era of Globalization 3.0, which is evidenced by the sheer fact that such a plethora of transnational legal frameworks did not exist before the start of the contemporary period of globalization.[9]

The third dimension of legal globalization is the gradual convergence of differing types of legal systems, for example, the common law and civil law ones. Such a convergence is predicted by the globalization theory in that if the economics, politics, and technics cause a long-term increase in interconnectedness, societies which share an environment and hold increasingly similar values, would in time become more similar.[10] Since globalization is geo-spatially and temporally an uneven process, the degree of such a convergence depends very much on the trends of increasing and decreasing global interconnectedness. What can be said however is, that since the long-term trend since the formation of nation-states is one of increase in interconnectedness (as argued by Friedman),[11] a long-term convergence and an increase in legal transplants is to be expected.

2. Constructivism and Post-Structuralism

Constructivism and post-structuralism are social "science" theories, both building on the foundations of a relativist philosophy of science (but relativist to different degrees) and on an interpretivist sociology of knowledge.[12] They both see social activity as analogous to language, however, while poststructuralists view such a language as vague to the degree of the objective reality being unknowable, constructivists build on

---

[9] A nice overview of transnational law and its emergence is offered in Peer C. Zumbansen, "Transnational Law, Evolving," in Jan Smits (ed.), *Encyclopedia of Comparative Law* (Cheltenham: Edward Elgar, 2012), 899-925. Many differing opinions however still do exist, especially in the field of comparative law. It has also been argued that the whole notion of legal globalization is the consequence of the U.S. unipolarity. See for example Ugo Mattei & Laura Nader, "*Plunder: When the Rule of Law is Illegal*" (Hoboken: Wiley-Blackwell, 2008).

[10] Frank J. Lechner, "*Globalization: The Making of World Society,*" (South Gate: Wiley, 2009), xv.

[11] Thomas L. Friedman, *The World is Flat: A Brief History of the Twenty-First Century* (New York: Farrar, Straus and Giroux, 2005) and Thomas Friedman, "Globalization 3.0 Has Shrunk the World to Size Tiny", *Yale Global Online*, April 7, 2004, https://yaleglobal.yale.edu/content/globalization-30-has-shrunk-world-size-tiny.

[12] Emanuel Adler, "Seizing the middle ground: Constructivism in world politics," *European Journal of international relations*, 3 (1997), 321.

Arthur Schopenhauer's notion of "*Verstehen*" and on its ontological implications.[13] They thus claim that the social and political discourses are in the end based on an objective reality, which however is constantly a subject of interpretation, influencing reality itself. Ideas from both theories seem especially useful in the legal domain since law itself is a form of a language game. Such a game itself is, in a Gramscian fashion,[14] constituted through a political and social discourse on a macro level and on the micro level the particular political and social discourses enter through what Nikola Visković would term semantic ambiguities.[15]

At the core of constructivism is its commitment to holism. The agents are partly autonomous, in that their actions construct, reproduce and transform the social environment. Nevertheless, they seem to be produced and shaped by nurture, not nature. Especially important is the constructivist distinction between social and brute facts. While brute facts exist independently of human activity, social facts are produced through collective activities of individuals. Norms which shape human activity, are of two types, namely regulative and constitutive rules. Constitutive norms create the social space for the activities, which the regulative rules regulate. Most constructivists retain their commitment to causality and explanation, subscribing to a Popperian theory of science.[16]

Post-structuralism is generally identified in relation to its predecessor, structuralism. While the latter retains the idea of human nature as a specific object and as an explanatory principle, the former denies such a conception of the subject and entails an abandonment of the modernist principle regarding the transcendental subject. Thus most of the poststructuralist viewpoints fall beyond the modern paradigm and into postmodern sphere.[17] In language arts, such as law, poststructuralist accounts focus especially on the moment in which meaning is ascertained in the language space. The meaning itself, regarding content, is not

---

[13] Ibid 326.

[14] See Esteve Morera, "Gramsci and Democracy", *Revue canadienne de science politique*, 23-1 (1990), 28, 29.

[15] Žaklina Harašić, "Viskovićeva teorija tumačenja u pravu", *Zbornik radova Pravnog fakulteta u Splitu*, 48-1 (2011), 57-72.

[16] Largely summarized after Michael Barnett, "Social constructivism," in John Baylis, Steve Smith and Patricia Owens, *The globalization of world politics*, (Oxford: Oxford University Press, 214) 155 – 168.

[17] Glyndwr Williams, "French discourse analysis: The method of post-structuralism" (Oxford: Routledge, 1999), 63.

defined through social consensus. Poststructuralist theorists try to explain how we fill such gaps in knowledge and for what distributive price, taking into account the society and the subject of the interpreted legal norms.[18]

3. Norm Life-Cycle Theory

Sikkink's and Finnemore's constructivist "norm life-cycle theory" could be a useful explanatory tool for the analysis of which legal norms will be accepted in the international community, in the transnational legal frameworks and which norms will gain enough traction to be accepted in individual national legal systems in terms of legal transplants. While their theory is well established and well received in the academic circles in international relations, it has not found its way to mainstream legal theory. This is even more interesting, since Sikkink and Finnemore themselves have noted that:

> "...legal norms are structured and channel behaviour in ways that create precisely the types of patterns political scientists seek to explain. Understanding which norms will become law ("soft" law as well as "hard" law) and how, exactly, compliance with those laws comes about would seem, again, to be a crucial topic of inquiry that lies at the nexus of law and international relations." [19]

The concept of norm entrepreneurs is used to explain the emergence of individual norms in the international and transnational sphere. According to Sikkink and Finnemore, norm entrepreneurs are rational actors, who more or less successfully engage in strategic social construction. They try to achieve the highest utility for themselves possible, but in this way attempt to change the utility function of other players, so that they would reflect norm entrepreneurs' normative commitments.[20] They are critical for the emergence of new norms, since they are the ones that either call attention to certain issues, or even create additional issues. This occurs especially using language, interpretation, and dramatization.[21] An example is the formation of the General Agreement on Tariffs and Trade system, where groups formed around John Maynard Keynes and Harry

---

[18] Bernard E. Harcourt, "An answer to the question: "What is poststructuralism?", University of Chicago, Public Law Working Paper No. 156 (2007), 1.

[19] Martha Finnemore and Kathryn Sikkink, International norm dynamics and political change. *International Organization*, 52 (1998), 916.

[20] Ibid. 910.

[21] Ibid. 897.

Dexter White pushed for certain international legal norms to be created or to be perhaps even more exact, for new norms to be created in a certain way.[22]

After the emergence, an individual norm begins to cascade through the society of states, in a process of dynamic imitation.[23] If a sufficient quantity of relevant actors accepts an emerging legal norm or if the norms are accepted by sufficiently powerful actors, the "norm tipping point" is reached. The relative power of actors in the international system or society is also relevant. The "norm tipping point" is the moment in time, when the critical mass of state actors accepts a certain legal norm. Such a form of norm influence has been confirmed in legal research, quantitative research made by sociologists, as well as research performed by academics in the discipline of international relations.[24] The idea of norm tipping point can be a useful starting point in further quantitative research, aimed at determining which norms will gain traction and be retained either in national legal systems, in transnational legal frameworks or in general public international law, since it can serve as a basis of distinction and research into qualities of the accepted norms and the broader social and political circumstances in which certain norms are accepted by the relevant actors.

The last phase of the norm life-cycle is the internalization of norms, when norms become accepted by the majority of relevant actors and are no more subjected to intense political debate.[25] Examples of such internalized norms could be the prohibition of torture,[26] suppression and punishment of apartheid,[27] or even rules such as the FIFA legal framework rule that "the basic compulsory equipment must not have any political,

---

[22] See Robert Skidelsky, "Keynes, Globalisation and the Bretton Woods Institutions in the Light of Changing Ideas about Markets", *World Economics*, 6-1 (2005), 15 – 30.

[23] Sikkink and Finnemore, International norm dynamics and political change, 895.

[24] Ibid. See also *Cass* R. *Sunstein, "Behavioral Analysis of Law"* (Coase-Sandor Institute for Law & Economics Working Paper No. 46, *1997*); and John W. Meyer and Michael T. Hannan, "National Development and the World System: Educational, Economic and Political Change, 1950 – 1970 (Chicago: University of Chicago Press, 1979.

[25] Sikkink and Finnemore, International norm dynamics and political change, 895.

[26] Convention Against Torture and Other Cruel, Inhuman or Degrading Treatment or Punishment, 10 December 1984, United Nations, Treaty Series, 1465, 85.

[27] International Convention for the Suppression and Punishment of the Crime of Apartheid, 30 November 1973, 1015 UNTS 243.

religious or personal slogans, statements or images."[28] It is clear that the scope of the notion is far broader than merely international custom or just peremptory norms of international law.

The "new" period of globalization has brought with itself greater interconnectedness in terms of communication, transportation and planetary interdependence, which is in a way influencing the degree of normative change and causing its acceleration.[29] According to the "norm life cycle" theory in connection with the globalization studies, norms are more easily disseminated and the norm cascade and internalization processes are shortening. Sikkink and Finnemore note that in the case of women's suffrage, where the norm emergence phase lasted eighty years and the norm cascade phase lasted forty years, the time needed for normative change has more than halved in the emergence of more contemporary norms addressing violence against women.[30] If we take the broader process of globalization and the increasing interconnectedness of the world into account, this does indeed seem to make sense.

Constructivist ideas such as 'norm life cycle theory' can therefore explain the emergence of individual norms, as well as which norms will gain traction and be internalized by the relevant actors. It also hints at the possibility that the normative change is accelerating and that it is becoming easier for norm entrepreneurs to influence, either directly or indirectly, a wider array of national legal systems.

4. Deconstruction

The potential for the use of poststructuralist ideas in explaining legal globalization stems from the fact that post-structuralism as a theory is rooted in the claim of indeterminacy of meaning in language through which individuals perceive the world. Since law itself is a language game, constituted and retained through social discourse, notions like deconstruction offer explanatory possibilities. According to poststructuralists, interpretation is dependent on a web of language and meaning. Because signifiers are not isolated, but co-dependent on each other, there is not a single epistemology in which meaning of an individual word can be

---

[28] See "IFAB Laws of the Game 2017/18" – AFC" IFAB, accessed November 10, 2017, http://www.the-afc.com/uploads/afc/files/IFAB-laws-of-the-game-2017-2018.pdf.

[29] Sikkink and Finnemore, International norm dynamics and political change, 909.

[30] Ibid.

determined once and for all.[31] In simpler terms, each word and each phrase retains its socially agreed upon meaning because the subjects it addresses accept it as such, either voluntarily or due to coercion. Deconstruction is essentially the activity of uncovering alternative possibilities in order to challenge the dominant assumptions regarding meaning, or in Derrida's own words: *"problematisation of the foundation of law, morality and politics."*[32]

What is thus important in keeping the legal language games stable is the Foucaultian idea of discourse. It denotes an interaction between legal subjects, legislators and societies at large, ordering interpretations and legal solutions in a way that has political significance. Regarding the construction of legal rules or their interpretation, poststructuralists often view that both are performed through discourses of power. The dominant interpretation or solution (in terms of legislative activity) means that all alternative interpretations are marginalized. Power itself is thus all-pervasive, and there is no distinction between discourses of power and truth-seeking inquiries,[33] or in case of law, between discourses of power and interpretation or creation of legal norms.

As an individual legal system is created and maintains its stability through social interaction, *"différance"* is ever-present.[34] What this means, on the other hand, is that there is always a potential for subversion, for an alternative interpretation or an alternative legislative solution to become dominant, if there is a sufficient political force to bring it into being.

Globalization is one such force. *"The meaning changes in accordance with permanent conditions and the meaning does that by itself."*[35] As the global interconnectedness increases in terms of a "longue durée" trend, more incentives exist for dominant tendencies of individual legal systems

---

[31] Philipp W. Rosemann, "Poststructuralism," in Robert L. Fastiggi, Joseph W. Koterski, Trevor Lipscombe, Victor Salas, Brendan Sweetman (eds.), *New Catholic Encyclopedia Supplement 2013: Ethics and Philosophy, Volume 3* (Farmington Hills: Gale, 2013) 1246.

[32] Jacques Derrida, "Force of Law: The Mystical Foundation of Authority" in Cornell et al (eds.), *Deconstruction and the Possibility of Justice* (London: Routledge, 1992) 8.

[33] More on the above see Michel Foucault, "Discipline and Punishment: the birth of a prison," (London: Penguin, 1991).

[34] Jacques *Derrida, "Differance"* (1968), accessed November 9, 2017, http://projectlamar.com/media/Derrida-Differance.pdf.

[35] Ceren Yegen, Memet Abukan, "Derrida and language: Deconstruction", *International Journal of Linguistics*, 6-2, (2014), 54.

to be deconstructed according to discourse, which is pervasive in a particular society. The excluded differences, which exist between for example common law and civil law legal systems, are brought to light and the dominant modes of understanding what law is, which are maintained through social discourse and practice, become deconstructed for new modes of understanding to emerge. Such an example is the increasing calls for taking steps towards a "stare decisis" doctrine, occurring in certain individual continental legal systems by prominent individuals, educated in legal systems of the common law type.[36] This does not mean however that each such attempt will be successful; application of poststructuralist thought on the problem at hand only predicts that with the advancement of globalization, new ideas will enter the national discourses and thus increase the likelihood of a common discourse emerging over time. If this indeed does occur, deconstruction will naturally guide the legal systems towards greater uniformity.

5. Conclusion

In the face of legal globalization, constructivism and post-structuralism can indeed offer certain theoretical insights. Constructivism's insights are especially in terms of the idea of a life-cycle of norms and the possibilities for further research into norm tipping points, in order to better understand, which norms will be retained in the international and transnational legal frameworks and which legal transplants are likely to be accepted in individual national legal systems. Constructivist ideas also have normative value, since they can help "norm entrepreneurs" be more efficient in their efforts, by better understanding the strategies, which will cause a successful norm cascade and internalization by relevant actors.

Poststructuralism, on the other hand, explains the process of deconstruction, by which the globalization theory predicts, that individual national legal systems will gradually converge.

Of course, since globalization is an uneven process, such a convergence is likely to be a "long durée" one and increases and decreases of interconnectedness can be expected in short to medium- term intervals. It is, however, difficult to claim that long-term, since the 16th century, the general social trend has not been one of increasing interconnectedness.[37]

---

[36] Boštjan M. Zupančič, "Stare decisis", Pravna praksa, 7-8 (2015).

[37] Kofi Annan, speech in the United Nations Summit Meeting in September of 2000, 53rd Annual DPI/NGO Conference, "Final Report," August 28-30 New York: United Nations, 2000).

In the words of Kofi Annan: *"...arguing against globalization is like arguing against the laws of gravity."* It is no different in the legal domain.

Bibliography

Adler, Emanuel, "Seizing the middle ground: Constructivism in world politics," *European Journal of international relations*, 3 (1997), 319-363.

Annan, Kofi, speech in the United Nations Summit Meeting in September of 2000, 53rd Annual DPI/NGO Conference, "Final Report," August 28-30 New York: United Nations, 2000.

Barnett, Michael. "Social constructivism." In: *The globalization of world politics*, edited by Baylis, John, Smith, Steve and Owens, Patricia, 155 – 168. Oxford: Oxford University Press.

Bull, Hedley, *The Anarchical Society*. Basingstoke: Palgrave Macmillan, 2002.

Cassese, Antonio, *International Law*. Oxford: Oxford University Press, 2001.

Cox, Robert. "*Multilateralism and the Democratization of World Order*", paper for the International Symposium on Sources of Innovation in Multilateralism, Lausanne, May 26-28, 1994.

Derrida, Jacques. "*Differance*" (1968), accessed November 9, 2017, http://projectlamar.com/media/Derrida-Differance.pdf.

Derrida, Jacques. "Force of Law: The Mystical Foundation of Authority." In: *Deconstruction and the Possibility of Justice*, edited by Cornell et al, 3-67. London: Routledge, 1992.

Finnemore, Martha and Sikkink, Kathryn. "International norm dynamics and political change." *International Organization*, 52 (1998), 887-917.

Foucault, Michel, *Discipline and Punishment: the birth of a prison*. London: Penguin, 1991.

Friedman, Thomas L., "Globalization 3.0 Has Shrunk the World to Size Tiny," Yale Global Online, accessed April 7. 2004, https://yaleglobal.yale.edu/content/globalization-30-has-shrunk-world-size-tiny.

Friedman, Thomas L., *The World is Flat: A Brief History of the Twenty-First Century*. New York: Farrar, Straus and Giroux, 2005.

Giddens, Anthony, *The Consequences of Modernity*. Stanford, CA: Stanford University Press, 1991.

Harašić, Žaklina. "Viskovićeva teorija tumačenja u pravu", *Zbornik radova Pravnog fakulteta u Splitu*, 48-1 (2011), 57-72.

Harcourt, Bernard E. "An answer to the question: "What is poststructuralism?" University of Chicago, Public Law Working Paper No. 156 (2007).

Harvey, David, *The Condition of Postmodernity: An Enquiry into the Origins of Cultural Change*. Malden, MA: Blackwell, 1990.

Held, David, McGrew, Anthony et al. "Contents and Introduction." In: *Global Transformations: Politics, Economics and Culture*, edited by Held, David, McGrew, Anthony, Goldblatt, David & Perraton, Jonathan, 1-30. Stanford: Stanford University Press, 1999.

Lechner, Frank J. *Globalization: The Making of World Society.* South Gate: Wiley, 2009.

Mattei, Ugo & Nader, Laura. *Plunder: When the Rule of Law is Illegal.* Hoboken: Wiley-Blackwell, 2008.

McGrew, Anthony. "The Logics of Economic Globalization." In: *Global Political Economy,* edited by John Ravenhill, 255-286. Oxford: Oxford University Press, 2011.

Menkel-Meadow, Carrie, "Why and How to Study "Transnational" Law," *UC Irvine Law Review,* 1-1 (2011), 97-130.

Meyer, John W. and Hannan, Michael T., *National Development and the World System: Educational, Economic and Political Change, 1950 – 1970.* Chicago: University of Chicago Press, 1979.

Morera, Esteve. "Gramsci and Democracy", *Revue canadienne de science politique,* 23-1 (1990), 23-37.

Rosemann, Philipp W. "Poststructuralism." In: *New Catholic Encyclopedia Supplement 2013: Ethics and Philosophy, Volume 3,* edited by Fastiggi, Robert L., Koterski, Joseph W., et al. 1246. Farmington Hills: Gale, 2013.

Scholte, Jan A. "Defining Globalisation." *The world economy* 31-11 (2008), 1471–1502.

Scholte, Jan, A. "The Globalization of World Politics." In: *The Globalization of World Politics, An Introduction to International Relations,* edited by Baylis, J. and Smith, S., 13-30. New York: Oxford University Press, 1999.

Skidelsky, Robert. "Keynes, Globalisation and the Bretton Woods Institutions in the Light of Changing Ideas about Markets", *World Economics,* 6-1 (2005), 15-30.

Sunstein, Cass R. "Behavioral Analysis of Law," Coase-Sandor Institute for Law & Economics Working Paper No. 46, *1997.*

Wallerstein, Immanuel Maurice, *World-systems analysis: an introduction.* Durham: Duke University Press, 2004.

Williams, Glyndwr, *French discourse analysis: The method of post-structuralism.* Oxford: Routledge, 1999.

Yegen, Ceren & Abukan, Memet. "Derrida and language: Deconstruction," *International Journal of Linguistics,* 6-2 (2014), 48-61.

Zumbansen, Peer C., "Transnational Law, Evolving," In: *Encyclopedia of Comparative Law,* edited by Smits, Jan, 899-925. Cheltenham: Edward Elgar, 2012.

Zupančič, Boštjan M. "Stare decisis", *Pravna praksa,* 7-8 (2015), 3.

Convention Against Torture and Other Cruel, Inhuman or Degrading Treatment or Punishment, 10 December 1984, United Nations, Treaty Series, 1465, 85.

"IFAB Laws of the Game 2017/18" – AFC" IFAB, accessed November 10, 2017, http://www.the-afc.com/uploads/afc/files/IFAB-laws-of-the-game-2017-2018.pdf.

International Convention for the Suppression and Punishment of the Crime of Apartheid, 30 November 1973, 1015 UNTS 243.

Chapter 7

With or Without You. Thoughts on Brexit and European Private Law

Cristina Poncibò[1]

Abstract

In the aftermath of the Brexit, the paper first takes a critical look on the role played by European legal elites in the process of Europeanisation of private law. The paper argues that such a process has been driven without having much regard for its impact on domestic legal environments', neglecting lawyers, notaries and judges' discursive reactions in the Member States. It also briefly discusses the legacy of English Common Law. In conclusion, the paper makes a case for reorienting the study of law in the EU away from legal positivism and towards methodology, away from legal rules and towards principles and shared values, in the hope of developing a more respectful and inclusive approach to our national legal cultures and identities.

1. Europeanisation of Private Law as an Elite Process

It is a widely shared view and oft-quoted criticism that the process of European integration has been steered and driven by the initiative of elites.[2] European legal elites played a central role in designing European private law. These elites included, for example, a group of academics and

---

[1] Professor of Comparative Law, University of Turin. E-mail: cristina.poncibo@unito.it I am grateful to the participants of the international conference organised by the Southern European Center for Legal Research (SECLR), 'The Common Law and the Civil Law Today - Convergence and Divergence', Ĉanj, Montenegro, 27-29 May 2017, who provided insightful feedbacks and comments on my conference report.

[2] H. Best, G. Lengyel, and L. Verzichelli (eds) The Europe of Elites: A Study into the Europeanness of Europe's Political and Economic Elites (Oxford University Press: 2012).

international law firms, position holders in the central institutions of the European Union and in 'substitute bureaucracies' working towards EU institutions in the member states. A self-interest in European integration seems to be more evident in the European legal elites than among national lawyers, judges, notaries, whose work and attention remained mainly focused on domestic laws and deeply rooted in domestic legal cultures.

Unfortunately, dissenting voices that attempt to theorize differently and advocate another European trajectory have been largely excluded and left unheard in mainstream discussions over the past decade of scholarship and analysis.[3] As a result, mainstream EU scholarship has accepted, for quite a long time, the premise that the European Union ('EU') should be a neoliberal, state-like political system and that Europeanisation of private law was a one-way process prevailing over domestic legal traditions of the Member State.[4]

In particular, European academic elites have embarked on the study of national private laws of Europe with the aim of fostering legal harmonization. They gathered initially in research groups that were the result of the private initiative of academics, which had different working methods and tried to give substance each to their own idea of harmonization that resulted limited to legal positivism (i.e. the adoption of new regulations, directives, or more ambitiously, codification or re-codification).

The first enterprise of this kind has been the so-called 'Lando Commission', set up in 1982 under the direction of Professor Ole Lando of the University of Copenhagen to prepare a body of rules on general contract law and, partially, the general law of obligations: the Principles of European Contract Law ('PECL'). They have reached a remarkable degree of success as an authoritative reference for the development of national legal systems in Europe. In the mind of their authors, the PECL were

---

[3] H. W. Micklitz (ed) The Many Concepts of Social Justice in European Private Law (Cheltenham: Edward Elgar, 2011). U. Mattei, M. Bussani, 'In Search of the Common Core of European Private Law' (1994) 2:3 ERPL 485-486.

Recently, C. Joerges, 'Il diritto privato nella politica economica europea dopo la crisi finanziaria' (2017) 2 Politica del diritto, 197-230. L. Niglia, 'Taking Comparative Law Seriously: Europe's Private Law and the Poverty of the Orthodoxy' (2006) 54:2 The American Journal of Comparative Law, 401-427.

[4] J. Borneman and N. Fowler, 'Europeanization' (1997) 26 Annual Review of Anthropology, 487-514.

deemed to serve a variety of goals, such as being the initial basis for a European Civil Code, or a model law to be referred to by national legislators aiming to modernize their law. They could be also used as a model both for future EU legislation and for judges and arbitrators in the adjudication of legal disputes, or as the governing law which the parties may choose in private agreements, according to the applicable rules of international private law.

Later, a group of scholars established the Study Group on a European Civil Code in 1998 as the successor of the 'Lando Commission', under the leadership of Professor Christian von Bar of the University of Osnabrück. The name itself of this Group shows that its initial goal was to develop the idea expressed by the European Parliament to foster the creation of a European Civil Code. The comprehensiveness of the codification scheme led this undertaking to enlarge the scope of the research from the general law of obligations and contracts to most of private patrimonial law. Therefore, the work of the Study Group includes not only specific contracts, but also benevolent intervention in another's affairs, unjustified enrichment, tort law, and some matters relating to property law, such as transfer of movables, security rights over movables and trust. The overall aim is to elaborate a basic set of rules for Europe, composed of principles deriving from comparative research and distillation of the best rules by way of scholarly analysis. At the root of the project is the belief that European law can emerge only as Professorenrecht, a belief that the methods of the Study Group's work, aimed at developing a shared legal culture in Europe, confirm.[5]

Simultaneously to the developments in European private law scholarship, from the end of the 1980's also the European Community institutions started expressing their interest for the harmonization of private law as a means to achieve a single market among member States. Initially, at the end of the 1980s, the driving force was the European Parliament, which voted a number of resolutions (which are politically,

---

[5] Another academic group, the Académie des Privatistes Européens, has adopted the codification idea also. Since 1992, this Group is working on a Code Européen des Contrats, under the coordination of Professor Giuseppe Gandolfi of the University of Pavia. The Académie chooses the traditional concept of codification used in continental Europe, as a set of specific rules, intended to leave less scope to interpretative activity. The provision of the Code Européen des Contrats employ as a starting point the Italian Civil code, but are sometimes open to solutions coming from other civil law systems and the common law tradition. The official language of the text is peculiar: French supersede English, now working as a global language.

not legally, binding) advocating the start of a process which could lead to a codification of European private law. The Commission joined to the Parliament initiatives in a series of Communications between 2001 and 2004, and it finally decided to finance research activities for the elaboration of a Common Frame of Reference within the Sixth Framework Programme for Research and Technological Development.

Under that call, the "Joint Network on European Private Law – Network of Excellence" (CoPECL) started working in 2005. It was the widest research network ever created in Europe. This group gathered two among the most prestigious academic research groups in Europe, the Study Group on a European Civil Code and the Research Group on the Existing EC Private Law ('Acquis Group'), together with the Project Group on a Restatement of European Insurance Contract Law and some other supporting groups. The task of the network was to deliver to the EU Commission the "Common Principles of European Contract Law" (CoPECL) that would constitute a possible basis for a future Common Frame of Reference of European Union law.[6]

These Principles have been published in 2009, and their drafters called them the "academic" Draft (i.e. not final) Common Frame of Reference ('DCFR'), in order to distinguish the results from what was termed the "political" (and final) Common Frame of Reference ('CFR'). CRF is a tool – whatever its form, scope and purpose – that the EU institutions could possibly adopt in the future, because of a political decision. The DCFR is in all but name a codification like effort. Other features aside, it is sufficient to look at its scope, which is as wide as that of many national codifications, covering contractual and non-contractual obligations, specific contracts and some matters relating to property of movables.

Yet, shortly after its completion, it has become apparent that the DCFR would not constitute the last step nor the final word in the EU legal integration process. Indeed, the EU Commission made clear that after many years of elaboration and after having spent a large amount of European research funds, the political agenda changed to a much more limited scope of intervention. In April 2010 the EU Commission set up the Expert Group on a Common Frame of Reference in the area of European Contract Law which was entrusted with the task of carrying out a Feasibility Study and making further progress on the development of a

---

[6] C. von Bar and E. Clive (eds), Principles, Definitions and Model Rules of European Private Law: Draft Common Frame of Reference (Sellier 2009 and OUP 2010) vols I-VI. N Jansen and R Zimmermann, 'A European Civil Code in All but Name' [2010] CLJ 98.

possible future European contract law instrument, starting from the DCFR.[7] Although the EU institutions have not adopted this product as far as binding legislation, it remains, to date, the most notable step of the EU private law integration project driven by academic elites as noted before.[8]

This Feasibility Study was published on 3 May 2011, and from it the EU Commission made a Proposal for a Regulation on a Common European Sales Law, which was presented on 11 October 2011.[9] This proposal for an Optional Instrument contains rules applicable to cross-border transactions for the sale of goods, for the supply of digital contents and for related services, if the parties to a contract agree to do so. Clearly, it would have introduced into every Member State an optional common European law governing cross-border contracts for the sale of goods and digital content.[10]

Although the withdrawal of Common European Sale Law (CESL) in December 2014 might have suggested that there would be a period of inaction in the field of EU Consumer and Contract Law, there were soon indications that there would be a new initiative in the context of one of the EU Commissions' priority areas: the Digital Single Market.[11]

An author correctly notes that 'The CESL provides a solution to a problem that does not really exist' (p 33) and proposes the Commission consider prioritizing the modernization of the legislation on enforcement which was considered part of the review of the Regulation No. 2006/2004 on consumer protection cooperation.[12]

---

[7] Study Group on a European Civil Code/Research Group on EC Private Law (eds), Principles, Definitions and Model Rules of European Private Law, Draft Common Frame of Reference (Full Edition), Sellier, Munich, 2009.

[8] G. Dannemann and S. Vogenauer (eds), The Common European Sales Law in Context: Interactions with English and German Law (Oxford University Press 2013).

[9] Proposal for a regulation on a Common European Sales Law COM (2011) 635 final.

[10] Comments by English legal scholars were not very positive, see G McMeel, 'The Proposal for a Common European Sales Law: Next Stop a European Contract Code?' (2012) 27 BJIB&FL 3; M. Kenny, 'The 2004 Communication on European Contract Law: Those Magnificent Men in Their Unifying Machines' (2005) 30 *ELR* 724.

[11] Communication from the Commission to the European Parliament, the Council, the European Economic and Social Committee and the Committee of the Regions, A Digital Single Market Strategy for Europe, COM/2015/0192 final

[12] A. Cygan, 'Introduction: EU consumer and contract law at a crossroads?' in C. Twigg-Flesner, *Research Handbook on EU Consumer and Contract Law* (Cheltenham (UK) and Northampton (US): Edward Elgar Publishing Limited 2016) 33 and 34.

In early May 2015, the EU Commission published its Digital Single Market Strategy containing a set of proposed actions. Surprisingly, in the most recent proposals of December 2015, the EU Commission followed the approach that has failed with the Consumer Rights Directive.[13] It is not easy to foresee whether legal scholars and politicians will successfully receive such a proposal.

The European Commission's recent proposals are made in a political climate of rising nationalism. In fact, it is disintegration, not integration of law, which seems to be the dominant motive behind contemporary politics in Europe. In our view, the Commission's argument is unlikely to convince the opposition as it focuses exclusively on the internal market. The reason is that it fails to address the principal unanswered question whether Member States should remain sovereign in matters of Contract and Consumer Law as private law is a matter of national identity. For quite a long time, any criticism against full harmonization has been dismissed as the outcome of a kind of critical legal studies exercise. This was the result of 'an age of rising nationalism' and 'ignorance, myopia or fear of the foreign and the new'.[14] Indeed, within the Western part of the European continent, the liberal democratic tradition had locked nationalist ideas in the clockwork of legal constitutional constraints and moral obligations towards history: nevertheless, this was possible until liberal democracy in the EU were challenged by the stronger and more diverse migration flows of the past couple of decades. To date, identity-based antagonisms have thus become an integral element in shaping political contestation in Europe and national legal traditions are part of such identity in each member state.

According to some private law scholars, the process of 'Europeanisation' should 'finally' step away from 'the obfuscatory shadow of the Volksgeist'.[15] So if the French prefer their Civil Code to a European equivalent, they are

---

[13] Directive 2011/83/EU of the European Parliament and of the Council of 25 October 2011 on consumer rights, amending Council Directive 93/13/EEC and Directive 1999/44/EC of the European Parliament and of the Council and repealing Council Directive 85/577/EEC and Directive 97/7/EC of the European Parliament and of the Council, OJ L 304, 22 November 2011, 64–88.

[14] M. Hesselink (ed.), The Politics of a European Civil Code (The Netherlands: Kluwer Law International 2006). In particular, the contribution of D. Kennedy, *Thoughts on Coherence, Social Values, and National Tradition in Private Law* in M. Hesselink (ed.), *The Politics of a European Civil Code* (The Netherlands: Kluwer Law International 2006), 93.

[15] G. Comparato, *Nationalism and Private Law in Europe* (Oxford: Hart Publishing 2014).

defending a 'pre-modern artefact', while their reaction to a possible European civil code could be compared to the American reaction to Pearl Harbour in 1940.[16] Traditional French reluctance to European private, and common law and civil law rivalry could be seen as evidence of a 'crypto nationalistic' discourse, containing hidden Europhobic rhetoric and resting on 'sentimental and irrational argumentation'.[17] Lastly, another author was also right in arguing for a 'democratic contract law' by urging that legal experts should not exclusively create rules of Contract Law, but must be the subject of an inclusive democratic debate.[18]

Few academics have been able of recognizing the limitations that were characterizing previous analysis, by seriously challenging and reconsidering the role legal scholarship in the process of Europeanisation. In particular, two authors note that '(...) Europe is in troubled waters. What does the unfortunate state of the European Union (EU) reveal about the state of the scholarly study of the integration project?' In such a perspective, they conclude that 'legal scholarship is in short supply of normatively convincing theoretical paradigms'.[19]

In fact, it is possible to question how the political project of a European research area has really affected national legal scholarship: the point is that European integration has generated a 'club' of EU-wide academic experts, but cast aside other legal scholars to focus on domestic laws in their 'national clubs'. It would be interesting (and might produce surprising results) to research domestic authors of European literature.

Our point here is that, as an author suggests in his 'Manifesto' for the creation of a European legal area, scholars and researchers should promote the intensification of comparative legal analysis, the

---

[16] R. Micheals quoted by S. Weatherill, EU Consumer Law and Policy (Cheltenham, Northampton: Edward Elgar Publishing 2013), 211 fs.

[17] R. Sefton-green quoted by S. Weatherill, *EU Consumer Law and Policy* (Cheltenham, Northampton: Edward Elgar Publishing 2013), 211 fs.

[18] M.W. Hesselink, 'Democratic Contract Law' (2014) 11 (2) ERCL, 81-126. On the contrary, J.M. Smits, 'Democracy and (European) Private Law: A Functional Approach', (2010) 2 *European Journal of Legal Studies*, 26-40.

[19] C. Jorges, C. Kreuder-Sonnen, 'Europe and European Studies in Crisis, Inter-disciplinary and Intra-disciplinary Schisms in Legal and Political Science' (2016) Berlin Social Science Centre Discussion Paper SP IV 2016 No. 109.

The authors conclude their contribution by saying: 'We are confident that contestation and critique will generate new ideas and perspectives for a European future beyond the present emergency politics'.

Europeanization of methods and transformation of our disciplinary identities.[20] This makes a case for reorienting the study of Law in Europe away from legal positivism and towards methodology, away from legal rules and towards principles and shared values. Hoping to find a way for connecting the 'clubs' of European legal elites with 'national clubs'.

Doubtless, in both the European Union and the United States, the question of the distribution of competence between federal and state levels of government over Private Law has been (and still is) contentious. Each system has experimented (and continues to experiment) with a range of competing regulatory strategies, including harmonization ('top-down' or 'bottom-up') and hybridization. Put in a broader historical context, the trajectories of federalized private law in each system initially seem markedly different. The days of general federal common law under Swift v. Tyson are well and truly in the past for the United States, since Erie rejected general federal court competence in developing private law. By contrast, further harmonization of Contract and Consumer Law failed for the EU.

In both the EU and the US, early developments in the federalization of certain areas of private law were met by counter-movements, emphasizing the importance of balancing constitutional imperatives toward harmonization and unification with decentralizing principles. These ideas have pointed towards the need for matters of substantive Contract Law to be mainly governed by subsidiary legal orders, as part of the balance of regulatory competence in the federal system. Summed up, it seems that the potential benefits of looking again across the Atlantic, in both directions in a comparative perspective.[21]

---

[20] A. Von Bogandy, 'National legal scholarship in the European legal area – A manifesto' (2012) 10:3 *International Journal of Constitutional Law*, 614–626.

[21] T. Bourgoigne and D. Trubeck, Consumer Law, Common Markets and Federalism in Europe and the United States (New York: Walter de Gruyter and Co. 1987). D. Augenstein (ed.) 'Integration Through Law' Revisited: The Making of the European Polity (Edinburgh/Glasgow Law and Society Series, Farnham: Ashgate 2012). Recently, D. Augenstein (ed.) 'Integration Through Law' Revisited: The Making of the European Polity (Edinburgh/Glasgow Law and Society Series, Farnham: Ashgate 2012). L. Azoulai 'Integration Through Law' and Us', (2016) 14:2 International Journal of Constitutional Law, 449-463.

2. Resistance and Containment

The process of Europeanisation of private law has faced some degree of resistance and containment from domestic legal environments (judges, lawyers, and notaries) in the member states. National parliaments and national law courts have been forced to accept that law is increasingly made and developed outside their realm, in the centers of Europe in Brussels, Luxembourg, and Strasbourg, and that European law is increasingly superseding national law, even within the confines of the nation-state.

The reaction was particularly evident with respect to the Common Law before Brexit. Common lawyers have attempted to resist in the name of their legal culture and, when inevitable, they have operated a sort of 'containment' of EU Law concepts, rules, and principles.

Clearly, European legal elites have underestimated these processes, nor noted their potential risks, at least until the Brexit. Mainstream legal scholarship has focused on the design of new EU regulation and directives, has commented them, being mainly absorbed by a new legal positivism. In proceeding in this way, they seemed to neglect the lessons of Comparative Law. In particular, the legal cultures of the Member States also reflected in Civil Codes when present, have remained on the background as nice but elusive concepts. [22] They were like reeds that must bow with the European wind.

In the Oxford English Dictionary (1933) 'Common Law' is described as 'The unwritten law of England, administered by the King's courts, which purports to be derived from ancient usage, and is embodied in the older commentaries, and the reports of abridged cases'. In this sense, it is opposed, in that sense, to statute law, and as distinguished from the equity administered by the Chancery and similar courts, and from other systems such as ecclesiastical law, and admiralty law'.[23]

---

[22] J. L. Gibson, G.A. Caldeira, 'The Legal Cultures of Europe' (1996) 30:1 *Law & Society Review* 55-86.
See also, A. L. Young, 'The Constitutional Implications of Brexit' (2017) 23:4 *European Public law*, 757–786.

[23] P. Glenn, *Legal Traditions of the World* (OUP 2014), 260-1. 'The common law, though identifiable, is a weak identifier. It can float around the world, but in so doing it provides little reinforcement for national identities, and leaves much room for accommodation with other (personal) laws'.

For leading comparative lawyers Zweigert and Kötz, the factors of a shared history, common mode of thought in legal matters, similar institutions and use of legal sources, and a shared ideology serve to identify a distinct legal tradition which distinguish it from 'rival' legal families such as those based on the civil law, Islamic, Hindu or indigenous legal traditions.[24] In particular, the authors juxtapose the common law with its focus on case law and preference for experience over theory with the systematic approach of the civil law marked by a tendency to use abstract legal norms. Private law in common law systems may thus be characterized as a law of practice, not theory, with the judge playing a particularly significant role.

Commentators equally note that the part of the strength of the common law tradition rests on its hostility to 'foreign civil law', which can be traced back to the early rejection of the continental reception of Roman law in favor of a highly developed domestic system of law.

However, this straightforward common law-civil law divide has become increasingly blurred in the EU process of 'forced' converge. In 1973, the United Kingdom joined the European Union (then, the European Economic Community) and, by virtue of the European Communities Act 1972, European Union law has obtained legal effect within the national legal system.[25]

In the words of Lord Denning 'But when we come to matters with a European element, the Treaty is like an incoming tide. It flows into the estuaries and up the rivers. It cannot be held back. Parliament has decreed

---

[24] K. Zweigert, H. Kotz, *An Introduction to Comparative Law* (oxford University Press 1998).

There is a wealth of literature discussing the meaning of 'legal family' and whether it is better described as a 'legal tradition' or 'culture' or even 'mentalité' to use the phrase of Pierre Legrand (see e.g. 'European Legal Systems Are Not Converging' (1996) 45 *ICLQ* 52). This article will not explore this debate, save to recognize the limitations of taxonomy in providing a definitive determinative link between any grouping of States.

[25] Case 6/64 Costa v ENEL [1964] ECR 585, 593. See, generally, P Craig and G de Búrca, EU Law: Text, Cases and Materials (5th edn, OUP 2011) ch 9. See also art 19 TEU: 'Member States shall provide remedies sufficient to ensure effective legal protection in the fields covered by Union law.'

that the Treaty is henceforward to be part of our law. It is equal in force to any statute'.[26]

On this basis, national courts were required to apply EU law, subject to review by the CJEU itself. Provisions of EU law that are directly applicable or have a direct effect are automatically enforceable in the United Kingdom without the need for any further enactment.[27] The doctrine of indirect effect further requires that national courts should interpret existing legislation in line with EU law.[28] The leading case is Factortame, at the instance of a company of Spanish fishermen, the House of Lords restrained UK's Secretary of Transport from enforcing the terms of UK's Merchant Shipping Act, 1988, which required ships to have a majority of British owners if they were to be registered in the UK. The judgment was given solely because of the European Court of Justice's opinion that the UK Act was incompatible with European Law.[29] While such judgments considered provisions of EU law that were directly applicable to the issue involved, a parallel body of case law emerged which required English courts to interpret domestic legislation in the light of European law even when it was not directly effective to a dispute.[30]

In addition, Article 288 TFEU further provides for EU legislation to exercise the Union's competences, EU institutions may adopt regulations, directives, decisions, recommendations, and opinions. In private law, intervention has primarily been by way of directives and, noticeably, more

---

[26] The citation is from Bulmer v Bollinger, 1 [1974] Ch 401, a leading case at the time. It was about the protection of the designation "champagne" under what is of course now EU law. Judgment was delivered only 16 months after the United Kingdom acceded to what was then known as the Common Market in January 1973.

[27] Case 26/62 Van Gend en Loos v Nederlandse Administratie der Belastungen [1963] ECR 1, [1964] CMLR 105 and Case 41/74 Van Duyn v Home Office [1974] ECR 1337. See, generally, Craig and de Búrca (n 31) ch 7.

[28] Case 14/83 Von Colson v Land Nordrhein-Westfalen [1984 ECR 1891; Case C-106/89 Marleasing SA v La Comercial Internacional de Alimentacion SA [1990] ECR I-4135; Cases C-397-403/01 Pfeiffer v Deutsches Rotes Kreuz, Kreisverband Waldshut eV [2004] ECR I-8835.

[29] The Factortame litigation highlighted that the principle of effectiveness requires that it should not be practically impossible to exercise EU rights in the national law. See Case C-213/89 R v Secretary of State for Transport, ex parte Factortame Ltd [1990] ECR I-2433 (full effectiveness of EU law impaired if rule of national law prevented court from granting interim relief against the Crown). See P. Craig, 'Sovereignty of the United Kingdom Parliament after Factortame' (1991) 11 YEL 221.

[30] See Ebb Vs. EMO Air Cargo, 1995 4 ALL ER 577.

focussed on contract law than the law of tort. Thus, the European Commission's objective of boosting the internal market and removing barriers to cross-border trade has led to a number of initiatives which have as their goal economic growth by means of improvement to existing modes of contracting.

After, much has been made of the United Kingdom's insular location, its political trajectory during the past years, and not the least debates about the effects of immigration.

An English professor was writing already in 1997 that 'Now, although one of my nightmares is that our position as a common law system on the fringe of a civil law continent and our response to international developments will mean that we will only have a marginal influence and will in effect become the Louisiana or, given our relationship with the European Union, the Quebec of Europe'.[31]

Arguably, the 'leave' campaign exhibited a very limited understanding of EU Law, that the quotation before seems to confirm, and the impact of Brexit on the United Kingdom, and the vote may ultimately represent just another example of populist outrage that seems to have gripped many Western democracies.[32]

Since the UK electorate voted to leave the European Union on June 23, 2016, legal scholars and practitioners have intensely discussed the institutional and constitutional consequences of 'Brexit', especially the operation of Art. 50 of the Treaty on European Union ('TEU'), on the one hand, and the impact of the United Kingdom's impending departure on specific areas of law on the other.[33]

2.1 Human Rights Law

European law has had an impact on English Common law, notably (but not solely) in different areas of the law. Moreover, Common Law courts were required to be conversant with a large (and expanding) body of case

---

[31] J. Beatson, 'Has the Common Law a Future?' (1997) 56 *CLJ* 291, 292-5.

[32] M. Dougan, 'Editor's Introduction', in The UK after Brexit. Legal and Policy Challenges (Intersentia, 2017) 1-12.

[33] 'Brexit Means Brexit' (2016) 22:4 *European Public Law*, 589-593. In details, J. Armour, H. Eidenmüller, *Negotiating Brexit* (Baden-Baden, Nomos 2018).

law, which they must apply when relevant, and subject to the supervision of an external court: the Court of Justice of the European Union ('CJEU').[34]

From 2000, however, English private law has faced a further challenge: the enactment of the Human Rights Act 1998 (HRA). The UK, as signatory of the convention, is bound by judgments to which it is a party, but it is the enactment of the HRA, which has made a significant difference to the Common Law and raised difficult questions about the relationship between the courts, Parliament and the European Court of Human Rights ('ECtHR').

Section 3(1) provides that 'so far as it is possible to do so' the courts should interpret primary and subordinate legislation in a compliant way with the European Convention on Human Rights ('ECHR'). This gives the UK courts a 'constitutional' role in examining the Convention-compatibility of legislation. Further, section 2(1) of the Act requires the court, in determining a question, which has arisen in connection with a Convention right, to 'take into account' judgments of the ECtHR. Section 6(1) also provides that it is unlawful for a public authority to act in a non-Convention-compliant way and sections 7 and 8 provide a cause of action by which victims may seek a remedy. Individual litigants may thus bring an action against a public authority that has violated one of the Convention rights contained in Schedule 1 of the Act. In both contract and tort law, early cases suggested that these measures have brought to some changes to existing law, triggered to a large extent by the ECtHR decision in Osman v UK.[35] In this case, the Strasbourg court had been prepared to find a breach of Article 6 ECHR (right to a fair trial) where a negligence claim against the police had been struck out for reasons arising from substantive law. While the Strasbourg court subsequently accepted in Z v UK that this represented a misunderstanding of English law, the shadow of Osman remained.[36]

---

[34] C. Twigg-Flesner comments: 'Legal reasoning at the national level cannot be purely domestic in areas affected by EU measures, with national courts required to adopt an interpretation which respects the autonomous status of EU law'. C. Twigg-Flesner, *The Cambridge Companion to European Union Private Law* (CUP 2010) 6.

[35] Osman v United Kingdom [1998] EHRR 101.

[36] Z v UK [2002] 34 EHRR 3.

An author has commented that: 'Convention rights may yet turn out to be a time bomb ticking away under the law of contract and private law generally.'[37]

In contract at least, the scope of Convention rights is limited in that their primary focus is not the protection of economic rights. In contrast, the very nature of Convention rights--which protect fundamental rights to life, freedom from torture, liberty - suggests a potentially greater role in tort law. The challenge for the courts may be seen as twofold. First, public authorities may face claims under section 7 of the HRA 1998 for breach of Convention rights (with a potential remedy under section 8 in damages).

As noted, under the much-debated doctrine of 'indirect horizontal effect', the courts, as 'public authorities' under section 6(3) of the Act, arguably have an obligation, or at least should attempt, to interpret the common law in a Convention-compliant manner.[38]

Indirect horizontal effect presented English courts, therefore, with an opportunity to utilize Convention rights as a springboard for change. This would move the English common law closer to a Convention-based framework of rights. It would, however, require the English courts to utilize European Law and not Common Law in the development of domestic private law.[39]

Interestingly, the most intense attack on the influence of European jurisprudence on English institutions came, from some of the most respected judges of the country. This was particularly so in the field of human rights law. In a series of judgments, Lord Reed criticized the tendency among English lawyers to cite Strasbourg Court judgments and provisions of the ECHR when English common law principles could protect the human rights in question. Consider, for example, the

---

[37] E. McKendrick, *Contract Law* (Palgrave Macmillan 2013) 14. See also H. Collins, 'The impact of Human Rights Law on Contract Law in Europe' [2011] *EBLR* 425.

[38] A helpful summary of their differences of opinion may be found in Conister Trust Ltd v John Hardman & Co [2008] EWCA Civ 841, [2009] CCLR 4, paras 110-111 per Lawrence Collins LJ. See also H Beale (ed), Chitty on Contracts (31st edn, Sweet and Maxwell 2012) para 1-065; G McMeel, 'Contract, Restitution and the Human Rights Act 1998' [2004] LMCLQ 280; Shanshal v Al-Kishtaini [2001] EWCA Civ 264; [2001] 2 All ER (Comm) 601 (any breach of art 1 Protocol 1 justified on basis of public interest exception).

[39] See M. Hunt, 'The Horizontal Effect of the Human Rights Act' [1998] *PL* 423; G Phillipson, 'The Human Rights Act, "Horizontal Effect" and the Common Law: A Bang or a Whimper?' (1999) 62 *MLR* 824.

comments of Baroness Hale noting '[Strasbourg's] tendency is to state the principle in very broad terms, without defining precisely the circumstances in which it will apply. Such broad statements of principle are hard to interpret and even harder to apply'.[40]

2.2 Contract Law

Whilst in the field of contract law, EU law, in particular, has brought changes to matters as fundamental as implied terms of quality and remedies in consumer sales contracts and the striking out of unfair terms in standard term consumer contracts; it is noticeable that the courts have not generally chosen to apply these legal rules outside these contexts. While this article focuses on contract law and consumer law, there is no need to note that EU law has also influenced other areas of private law.[41]

From the perspective of English contract law, perhaps the directives are Directive 93/13/EEC on unfair terms in consumer contracts[42] and Directive 1999/44/EC on the sale of consumer goods and associated guarantees[43], although contract textbooks may also briefly refer to the Package Travel, Package Holidays and Package Tours Directive[44], or the Unfair Commercial Practices Directive.[45]

---

[40] Rabone v Pennine Care NHS Foundation Trust [2012] UKSC 2, [2012] 2 AC 72, paras 96-97.

[41] One example is the law of unjust enrichment where the impact of the San Giorgio principle for illegally levied taxes has long been acknowledged: see Case 199/82 Amministrazione delle Finanze dello Stato v SpA San Giorgio [1983] ECR 3595 and the key English case of Woolwich Equitable Building Society v Inland Revenue Commissioners [1993] AC 70. Also with respect to conflicts of laws and commercial law, the impact of EU law has also been particularly significant, see P Stone, *EU Private International Law* (3rd edn, Edward Elgar 2014) and L. Gullifer and S. Vogenauer (eds), *English and European Perspectives on Contract and Commercial Law* (Oxford: Hart Publishing 2014).

[42] Council Directive 93/13/EEC of 5 April 1993 OJ L 95, 21 April 1993, 29-34.

[43] Directive 1999/44/EC of the European Parliament and of the Council of 25 May 1999 OJ L 171, 7 July 1999, 12-16.

[44] Directive (EU) 2015/2302 of the European Parliament and of the Council of 25 November 2015 on package travel and linked travel arrangements, amending Regulation (EC) No 2006/2004 and Directive 2011/83/EU of the European Parliament and of the Council and repealing Council Directive 90/314/EEC.

[45] Directive 2005/29/EC of the European Parliament and of the Council of 11 May 2005 OJ L 149, 11 June 2005, 22-39. Note also Directive 2000/31/EC on electronic commerce OJ L 178, 17 July 2000, 1-16

All the said provisions, and more generally European contract and consumer law[46], have had an impact on English contract law which goes beyond the superficial and technical. For example, the 1993 Directive, transposed into English law by means of the Unfair Terms in Consumer Contracts Regulations 1994 (now 1999),[47] introduced, a 'legal irritant' in the common law, consisting in the concept of good faith to determine the enforceability of unfair terms in standard term consumer contracts.[48] Legal scholars noted the activism of the CJEU with respect to the 1993 directive.[49] Another example comes from the 1999 Consumer Sales Directive: the implementation of the directive implied to modify some statues to include a set of new consumer-friendly remedies in addition to those already existing in Common Law.[50]

Recently, the 2011 Consumer Rights Directive has, as of 13 June 2014, been implemented in Member States, replacing Directive 97/7/EC on distance contracts and Directive 85/577/EEC on off-premises contracts.[51]

---

[46] For an overview R. Schulze, F. Zoll, *European Contract Law* (Baden- Baden: Nomos 2018).

[47] SI 1994/3159 (replaced by SI 1999/2083 due to problems with transposition).

[48] H. Collins, 'Good Faith in European Contract Law' (1994), 14 OJLS 229.
Reg. 5(1) UTCC Regulations 1999 precises: 'A contractual term which has not been individually negotiated shall be regarded as unfair if, contrary to the requirement of good faith, it causes a significant imbalance in the parties' rights and obligations arising under the contract, to the detriment of the consumer.'

[49] Case C-203/99 Veedfald v Arhus Amtskommune [2001] ECR 1-3569, [2003] 1 CMLR 1217 (Product Liability Directive) and C237/02 Freiburger Kommunalbauten GmbH Baugesellschaft & Co KG v Hofstetter [2004] ECR I-3403 (Unfair Terms Directive). Micklitz and Reich note more recently a more proactive approach by the CJEU to the 1993 Directive: H-W Micklitz and N Reich, 'The Court and Sleeping Beauty: The Revival of the Unfair Contract Terms Directive' (2014) 51 CMLR 771.

[50] Sale and Supply of Goods to Consumers Regulations SI 2002/3045, amending the Sale of Goods Act 1979, the Supply of Goods and Services Act 1982, the Supply of Goods (Implied Terms) Act 1973 and the Unfair Contract Terms Act 1977.

[51] Directive 2011/83/EU of the European Parliament and of the Council of 25 October 2011 OJ L 304, 22 November 2011, 64-88. See also, Green Paper on the Review of the Consumer Acquis COM (2006) 744 final. For a taste of some of the criticism accompanying earlier versions of the Directive, C. Twigg-Flesner, 'No Sense of Purpose or Direction? The Modernisation of European Consumer Law' (2007) 3 *ERCL* 198.

The directive is far narrower, primarily covering only two of the original eight directives, a failed opportunity according to legal scholars.[52]

2.3. Tort Law

The impact of EU Law on the Common Law has been less evident with respect to tort law (and property law).[53] Core tort law principles remain primarily for the domestic courts, and only a limited number of directives have brought changes to national law. The best-known example of change by directive remains that of Council Directive 85/374/EEC, commonly known as the 'Product Liability Directive', which imposes strict liability on manufacturers for damage caused by their defective products[54]. The Product Liability Directive is a maximum harmonization directive from which no divergence is permitted, and it may be seen as symbolic in highlighting the potential impact of EU law, supplementing the classic common law authority of Donoghue v Stevenson with EU-sourced strict liability.[55]

In addition, developments in privacy law following the enactment of the HRA 1998 indicate the ability of the courts to generate new rights in the law of tort (e.g. the 'tort' of misuse of private information). Clearly, the content of the tort at issue is shaped by the rights provided for by the Convention (here Articles 8 and 10, ECHR).[56] According to English authors, additional changes to the well-established principles of domestic tort law would have required the courts to make policy choices as to the very nature of tort law rights.[57]

C. Twigg-Flesner and D. Metcalfe, 'The Proposed Consumer Rights Directive--Less Haste, More Thought?' (2009) 5 *ERCL* 368; H-W. Micklitz and N Reich, 'Crónica de una muerte anunciada: The Commission Proposal for a 'Directive on Consumer Rights" (2009) 46 *CMLR* 471.

[52] S. Weatherill, 'The Consumer Rights Directive: How and Why a Quest for "Coherence" Has (Largely) Failed' (2012) 49 *CMLR* 1279.

[53] P. Giliker, *The Europeanisation of English Tort Law* (Oxford: Hart Publishing 2014) Chapter 3.

[54] Council Directive 85/374/EEC of 25 July 1985 on the approximation of the laws, regulations and administrative provisions of the Member States concerning liability for defective products: [1985] OJ L 210, 29.

[55] Donoghue v Stevenson [1932] AC 562.

[56] McKennitt v Ash [2006] EWCA Civ 1714, [2008] QB 73, para 11.

[57] Clift v Slough BC [2010] EWCA Civ 1484, [2011] 1 WLR 1774, noted by K Hughes, 'Defamation and the Human Rights Act 1998' [2011] CLJ 296.

Further, EU Law has shown itself capable of creating new areas of tort law, such as State liability for breach of EU law (i.e. the above mentioned Francovich liability).[58]

3. Law and National Identity

European integration is commonly thought of as a political and economic project, but the making of Europe is to a considerable degree obtained through law.[59]

In sum, these processes of European legal integration involve considerable changes to the national legal systems in Europe.[60] Hence, the topic of legal integration by European legal elites and the reactions of national lawyers is central while it has received limited attention until Brexit. An English judge is not only a judge; she is also English. In fact, she was English long before she became a judge. As a result, it is only to be expected that the law she makes should be a reflection of her culture.

When studying the relationship between law and national identity, the metaphor of 'legal transplants' commonly applied by experts on comparative law to describe 'foreign' legal rules adopted by domestic law, is revealing. National legal rules are seen as a 'body of laws', as it is sometimes actually called, and legal rules and concepts stemming from a foreign legal system – a foreign body of laws – cannot easily be 'transplanted' into the national legal 'body'. The 'legal transplant' will hardly ever interact successfully with other elements in the 'legal organism'; the most likely reaction will be one of 'irritation', perhaps even rejection.[61]

'Negligence and Human Rights Law: The Case for Separate Development' (2013) 76 *MLR* 286, distinguishing between public law/human rights norms and those of private law, remarking at 302: 'the process of convergence would serve to distort the law of negligence both by undermining established principles and by introducing alien concepts'.

[58] ECJ, C-6/90 Francovich v Italian Republic [1991] ECR I-5357, [1993] 2 CMLR 66.

[59] Doubtless, the project Integration Through Law (precisely the third volume), launched over than 30 years ago, remains unrivalled in exploring the making of Consumer Law by putting together the European and the American perspectives. See before at note 20.

[60] J.A. Weiler, 'A Quiet Revolution: The European Court of Justice and its Interlocutors' (1994) 26 *Comparative Political* Studies,510–34.

[61] A. Watson, *Legal Transplants: An Approach to Comparative Law* (University of Georgia Press 1993). See also, P. Glenn, *Legal Traditions of the World* (Oxford University Press 2004).

The image of national law as a living body is no new invention – it dates back to the natural law thinking of the Enlightenment and penetrated romantic discourse in Europe of the nineteenth century. Great influence emanated from the legal thinking of the French philosopher Montesquieu who in his classic book De l'Ésprit des Lois from 1748 introduced the notion of 'the spirit of the law', i.e. the dependency of law on the physical, cultural and political factors characteristic of a country and its people. Because of this environmental dependency of law, it is in Montesquieu's opinion only in the most exceptional of cases that the laws of one country may serve those of another country.

A similar conception of the relationship between law and nation was developed by the Von Savigny who in his historical theory of law applied the idea of Volksgeist, claiming that law has been intrinsic to national identity and culture at least since the advent of the nation-state. This was in many ways a reaction to the idea of positivizing law in the form of codified and systemized law books advocated by French jurists and statesmen in the early nineteenth century. Their objective was to assemble existing legal practices, and customs and against that background devise detailed law books.[62]

Interestingly, the ideas of nineteenth-century legal philosophy have been applied by the comparative lawyer Pierre Legrand in his critique of the political and scientific endeavor to harmonize the national legal systems of Europe; see for example the following statement of the interdependency of national belonging and legal thinking in Legrand.[63]

With respect to French experience, the Civil Code aimed not only a better certainty of law and its uniform application on a national level with the objective of enhancing individuals' rights, but also to national integration and identity around a centralizing state. Consequently, the Napoleon Code of 1804 was precisely titled 'le Code civil des Français'.[64] Moreover, the debates in favor and against some form of codification generally ended out in the 20th century. Consequently, the law, culture and national identity argument lost some of its centrality and was mainly mobilized in the context of rights for national minorities and separatist

---

[62] Montesquieu, *De l'ésprit des lois* (Geneva, Barillot 1748).

[63] P. Legrand, 'European Legal Systems Are Not Converging', The International and Comparative Law Quarterly (1996) 45 52-81.

[64] M. Madsen, Mikael, 'The Clash: Legal Culture, National Identity and European Law' (2016) iCourts Working Paper Series, No. 71, 2016. Accessed 10 July 2018 at <https://ssrn.com/abstract=2798556 or http://dx.doi.org/10.2139/ssrn.2798556>

movements. Then, in the aftermath of World War II, came the question of European integration. Now on a much larger scale, the arguments already devised in the beginning of the 19th century were once again mobilized again European law, especially a European civil code, a new form of codification in conflict with national customs and culture, was sought to be slipped in through the back-door by 'Eurocrats'. The very idea of codification was even resuscitated, although attempts at compiling an actual European Civil Code so far have generally failed beyond academic discourse (see before at paragraph 1).

In light of the above, ideas about the relationship between law and national identity seem to have played a major part in the making of the modern nation states. In the nationalistic discourse of Europe in the nineteenth century the conception of national spirits of law was helpful in the construction and invention of the nation-state, just like notions of national languages, cultures, traditions, and histories).[65] Thus, it is no coincidence that at that time many European nations were equipped with constitutions, defining the fundamental principles of law and government of the nation-state. Even today, the constitution of a country is sometimes highlighted as a national symbol on par with the Crown, the currency and the flag.

Furthermore, in the consciousness of people, the laws and legal institutions of their country play a significant part in their identification with the nation. Nevertheless, the specific role that law and legal institutions play in constructing national identity is hardly explored in discourse studies with few exceptions.[66] An author notes, for example, that if the sovereignty of a national parliament is conveyed to institutions outside the national borders, this is seen as a threat to national identity. '[P]arliaments [like currencies and borders] are far more than economic and political technicalities. In the public domain they are symbols of nationhood, and for the individual they function as symbols of national identity'.[67]

In other research areas, the relationship between law and the nation-state has been on the agenda, albeit from other theoretical perspectives. Thus, as referred to earlier, two legal historians have analyzed the roles of

---

[65] S. Jacobson, 'Law and Nationalism in Nineteenth-Century Europe: The Case of Catalonia in Comparative Perspective', (2002) 20 Law and History Review, 307–47.

[66] G. Hardt-Mautner, 'How Does One Become a Good European?' The British Press and European Integration' (1995) 6 *Discourse & Society*, 177-205.

[67] G. Hardt-Mautner before at 179.

lawyers in the making of Europe's modern nation-states in the nineteenth century,[68] and a sociologist has underlined the so-called 'boomerang' effect of European human rights law on national legal systems, has scrutinized the key position of international legal elites in the shaping of the European Court of Human Rights as a kind of European Supreme Court.[69] In addition, legal professionals' special relationship with the nation-state has been analyzed in a sociological analysis of the impact that European harmonization and globalization have on the professional identity of German lawyers.[70]

In reading the above-mentioned contributions by scholars, it emerges that the discursive conventions of nineteenth-century lawyers were not only helpful in constructing the nation states. Their discourse also worked the other way around and bounced favorably back on the professional society of lawyers, who found themselves in new and stronger positions of social power. The nation states' need for constructing a unique nationality of law gave rise to the construction of a unique nationality of legal systems, thus establishing tight conceptual and social bonds between nation, nation-state, national legal institutions, and national lawyers. Thus, the explicit relationship between law and national identity on which the modern nation-states were founded, may explain the implicit and explicit nationalism.

Surely, European integration has changed that. By pooling national sovereignty, it established an alternative center of power that over the years led scholars to imagine a supranational 'community of Europeans'. But the majority of analysts now list evidence of decreasing popular support for integration and citizens' growing distance from the EU. The most common claim made on the basis of such evidence is that European citizens want less Europe. Another claim, usually in dissent, argues that European citizens simply want a different kind of Europe and more say in deciding its course. In any case, there is a strong indication that debates about integration are increasingly being taken down to the level of

---

[68] S. Jacobson, before. See also S. Harty, 'Lawyers, Codification, and the Origins of Catalan Nationalism, 1881–1901', (2002) 20 (2) *Law and History Review*, 349-84.

[69] M.R. Madsen, 'France, the UK, and the "Boomerang" of the Internationalization of Human Rights (1945–2000)', in S. Halliday and P. Schmidt (eds) *Human Rights Brought Home: Socio-Legal Perspectives on Human Rights in the National Context* (Oxford, UK: Hart 2004), 57-86.

[70] G. Shaw, 'German Lawyers and Globalization: Changing Professional Identity' (2005) 58 *German Life and Letters*, 211-25.

national politics, where they are meeting resistance to the visions of supranational political community claimed by Habermas.[71]

Exploring the process of integration in a socio-legal perspective highlights the central role of legal elites (and obviously political) in demarcating community and belonging within the context of Europeanisation. At the same time, it cannot be 'imposed' from the top: national identity needs to reflect adequately the national legal communities composed by lawyers, judges, notaries, law students who daily work with their old-fashioned Civil Codes on their hands.[72]

Indeed, Brexit campaigners have relied on greatly on the intellectual 'difference' of the Common Law from EU Law and Member States Law. [73] Interestingly, the paper notes that the most intense attack on the influence of European law and case-law on English institutions and courts came, not from Brexit campaigners but, from some of the most respected judges of the country. As noted before, this was particularly so in the field of human rights law. The ECtHR had expanded the scope of the ECHR to illegitimate children, criminal sentencing, immigration, extradition, homosexuality, abortion, prisoner's rights, assisted-suicide in a manner that is not envisaged by the express terms of the Convention, thereby imposing values that the United Kingdom never intended to bind themselves with. In a series of judgments, Lord Reed criticized the tendency among English lawyers to cite the judgments of ECtHR and

---

[71] J. Habermas, *The crisis of the European Union: A response* (Polity 2012). Of the same author, 'Democracy in Europe: Why the Development of the EU into a Transnational Democracy Is Necessary and How It Is Possible' (2015) 21 *EUR. L.J.* 546. In his recent work, Jürgen Habermas has put forth one of the most influential theories of supranational constituent power. Habermas argues that the great "innovation" of European integration is the "complementary dependence and interconnection" between the national and the supranational levels of government. Nation states survive the process of supranational integration and coexist alongside the Union their citizens have created.

[72] S. Law, S., 'From Multiple Legal Cultures to One Legal Culture? Thinking About Culture, Tradition and Identity in European Private Law Development' (2015) 31:8 *Utrecht Journal of International and European Law*, 68-89.

[73] Nigel Farage, the UKIP leader who spearheaded the 'Vote Leave' campaign on a largely anti-immigration platform, said he has a "slight preference" for Indians and Australians over other immigrants because they are more likely to "speak English, understand common law and have a connection with this country". For these fighters of British nationalism therefore, common law is as much a part of British identity as speaking English itself.

provisions of the ECHR when the human rights in question could well have been protected by reference to English common law principles. He elucidates this approach in this speech to the Inner Temple where he says, 'But there are more fundamental reasons for our courts to take our domestic law as their starting point and to check compliance with Convention rights at a later stage in the analysis. One factor is the reputation of the common law. The domestic law of the United Kingdom has protected human rights more consistently, and over a longer period of time, than any other legal system I know'.[74]

This sentiment is echoed by UK's longest-serving judge of the appeal court, Lord Justice Laws, in his Hamlyn Lecture, where he says: 'now I will move from Brussels and Luxembourg to Strasbourg. As I said at the start, the common law's catholicity is threatened not only by the perceived effects of EU law, but also those of the law of human rights. However the perceived effects of human rights law also threatens another virtue of the common law: its restraint. The charge is that the law of human rights has got too big. It has pushed the judges into the field of political decisions'.[75]

In this well-publicized speech, Lord Sumption blames the ECtHR for undermining the democratic processes in the UK. Elsewhere, he draws on his expertise as a historian to show why Britain is unsuited to be a part of any straight-jacket legal system. He says 'We are less inclined to be told what to do by outside authorities than most countries. That is because of our physical location... that we have never been invaded or had a revolution since the middle of the 17th century, and we have a system of government and a legal system that has very gradually evolved and has unique features shared by no other country ... we were the only country in Europe apart from Spain which was not overrun by the Nazis and we were

---

[74] Master Reed (The Rt Hon Lord Reed), The Common Law and the ECHR Lord Reed, Lecture, 13 November 2013 at 14. Accessed 10 July 2018
<https://www.innertemple.org.uk/education/education-resources/readers-lecture-series/previous-lecture-series-and-speakers>

[75] Lord Justice Laws, Lecture III: The Common Law and Europe, Hamlyn Lectures 2013, 27 Novembre 2013. Accessed 10 July 2018
<https://www.globalgovernancewatch.org/docLib/20140213_laws-lj-speech-hamlyn-lecture-2013.pdf>

the only one among the European countries that was among the victors at the end'.[76]

While Brexit does not mean Britain's exit from the ECHR (which is not a part of the EU treaties), the general resentment against the EU was fuelled in no small measure by the case-law of the ECtHR. Therefore, it doesn't sound unreasonable that a country with such a different legal framework from other European countries felt uncomfortable about remaining in a political union that requires uniform laws and legal administration. EU legal elites failed to understand the relationship between law and national identity until the ultimate consequence, Brexit.

4. The legacy of English Common Law

Doubtless, the Common Law of England has influenced EU Law and policies. Indeed, legal scholars have devoted scarce attention over time to this aspect, with few exceptions.[77]

One may argue that the common law tradition contributed to EU law and policies under several aspects. The pathways through which British ideas had an influence differ among sources of law – legislation, domestic judicial interpretation of EU instruments, Commissioners and Advocates General, and, maybe most subtly, the outlook of judges as reflected in judicial style.

In many areas close to business, such as financial regulation, insolvency law, and some areas of company law and antitrust, English Law has taken the lead or offered many ideas. In some fields, such as consumer protection or some areas of company law, the United Kingdom often put

---

[76] Lord Sumption gives the 27th Sultan Azlan Shah Lecture, Kuala Lumpur, The Limits of Law, 20 November 2013. Accessed 10 July 2018 <https://www.supremecourt.uk/docs/speech-131120.pdf>

[77] M. Dougan, 'Editor's Introduction', in M. Dougan, *The UK after Brexit. Legal and Policy Challenges* (Michael Dougan ed., Intersentia, 2017), 1-12.

J. Basedow, *BREXIT and business law*, China-EU Law Journal (2017) (3), 101-118P.

S. Morris, The modern transplantation of continental law in England: how English private international law embraces Europeanisation, 12:3 (2014) Journal of Private International Law, 587-607.

the brakes on the legislative harmonization train.[78] Doubtless, Common Law drafting style remains prevailing in international contract drafting.[79]

Overall, the contributions show that the influence of the Common Law legal culture on European Union policies has been considerable. The pathways through which British ideas had an influence differ among sources of law – legislation, domestic judicial interpretation of EU instruments, Commissioners and Advocates General, and, maybe most subtly, the outlook of judges as reflected in judicial style. In many areas close to business, such as financial regulation, insolvency law, and some areas of company law and antitrust, the United Kingdom has taken the lead or UK ideas have predominated over time. In some fields, such as consumer protection or some areas of company law, the United Kingdom often put the brakes on the harmonization train. While in most areas UK law's influence has increased over time, equality law provides an interesting counterpoint, as the CJEU has increasingly moved away from the UK model.

With particular reference to the 'judicial style', legal scholars note that English common law influence had a significant impact on the judicial style of the Court of Justice of the European Union and was a source of preoccupation for the Commission since the early 1960s. While the French Conseil d'Etat was initially the greatest influence on the court in Luxembourg, it began to use common law techniques such as stare decisis and careful analysis of its own precedents after the UK accession in 1973. The combination of civil and common law style still resulted in minimalist *per curiam* decisions that allowed the court to make policy while giving relatively few justifications.[80] It is also true, that at the same time, Luxembourg also affected English statutory interpretation, as UK judges became more inclined to espouse purposive over purely literal interpretation, and at times depart from relying solely on the tradition of

---

[78] On Monday, February 27, 2017, Fordham's International Law Journal and the Center on European Union Law jointly held the symposium '*EU Law with the UK – EU Law without the UK*'. The symposium organizers attempted to take a different approach, asking what sets the United Kingdom and its laws apart from other European jurisdictions, and what impact the UK's membership had on the trajectory of EU law.

[79] B. Gessel-Kalinowska Vel Kalisz, 'Mixing Legal Systems in Europe; the Role of Common Law Transplants (Polish Law Example)' (2017) 25:4 *ERPL* 789-812.

[80] F. G. Nicola, Luxembourg Judicial Style With or Without the UK, 40 Fordham Int'l L.J. 1505 (2017).

parliamentary sovereignty through the mechanism of preliminary references. Even if preliminary references are no longer possible after Brexit, the common law influence on the Luxembourg judicial style will persist whereas the UK judiciary will continue to monitor the jurisprudence of the CJEU closely.

5. Conclusions

European Union law has affected the legal systems of its members by mixing in a reciprocal way, infusing solutions or ideas from various legal jurisdictions into the EU system and then disseminating them back into the national systems via directives, regulations, and soft law-type guidelines, as well as CJEU and European Human Court of Human Rights judgments.[81] The relationship between the common law tradition, the civil law tradition, and European Union law is a circular one. Relying on the words of Lord Neuberger, it is a process of cross-fertilization based on European law as a community of legal traditions.[82] Unfortunately, Brexit seriously jeopardizes such a fruitful process.

In the aftermath of the Brexit, the paper first takes a critical look on the role played by European legal elites in the process of Europeanisation of national private laws. Elites, in particular academic elites, have driven the 'Europeanisation' without having much regard to the impact of such process on domestic 'legal environments', neglecting lawyers, notaries and judges' discursive reactions at the national level. This approach has ended in the creation of two communicating, and often conflicting, legal environments between European and domestic legal cultures and identities. Second, the paper notes the tendency of English Common Law for 'resistance' and 'containment' of European Law that has been disregarded until the Brexit.

While the goal of integration remains valid, the context, however, has dramatically changed. The difficulty is to find a way to pursue integration in a context not only in a deep and multifaceted crisis but also in an atmosphere of widespread mistrust in the positive forces of the law. We are therefore free to question the full harmonization of EU Consumer and Contract Law with respect to minimum harmonization, and the harmonization by directive in the light of the process of spontaneous

---

[81] Lord Steyn, 'The Challenge of Comparative Law' (2006) 8 EJLR 3, 4. See also TH Bingham, 'There Is a World Elsewhere': The Changing Perspectives of English law' (1992) 41 *ICLQ* 513.

[82] 'Editorial comments: EU law as a way of life' (2017) 54:2 *CMLR* 357–367.

harmonization. It may seem obvious in these times of EU crisis, but it verges on a Copernican Revolution in comparison with what has become the dominant school of thought in EU legal scholarship. A revolution in taking national legal environments and identities for serious.

Bibliography

'Editorial comments: EU law as a way of life' (2017) 54:2 *CMLR* 357–367. 20 November 2013. Accessed 10 July 2018 <https://www.supremecourt.uk/docs/speech-131120.pdf>

Basedow, Jurgen.*BREXIT and business law*, China-EU Law Journal (2017) (3), 101-118P.

Beatson, Jack."Has the Common Law a Future?"(1997) 56 *CLJ* 291, 292-5.

Best, Heinrich, G. Lengyel, and L. Verzichelli (eds) *The Europe of Elites: A Study into the Europeanness of Europe's Political and Economic Elites* (Oxford University Press: 2012).

Borneman, John and N. Fowler."Europeanization"(1997) 26 *Annual Review of Anthropology*, 487-514.

Bourgoigne, Thierry and D. Trubeck, Consumer Law, *Common Markets and Federalism in Europe and the United States* (New York: Walter de Gruyter and Co. 1987). D. Augenstein (ed.) *'Integration Through Law' Revisited: The Making of the European Polity* (Edinburgh/Glasgow Law and Society Series, Farnham: Ashgate 2012). Recently, D. Augenstein (ed.) *'Integration Through Law' Revisited: The Making of the European Polity* (Edinburgh/Glasgow Law and Society Series, Farnham: Ashgate 2012). L. Azoulai 'Integration Through Law' and Us', (2016) 14:2 *International Journal of Constitutional Law*, 449-463.

Bulmer v Bollinger, 1 [1974] Ch 401,

Case 14/83 Von Colson v Land Nordrhein-Westfalen [1984] ECR 1891; Case C-106/89 Marleasing SA v La Comercial Internacional de Alimentacion SA [1990] ECR I-4135; Cases C-397-403/01 Pfeiffer v Deutsches Rotes Kreuz, Kreisverband Waldshut eV [2004] ECR I-8835.

Case 199/82 Amministrazione delle Finanze dello Stato v SpA San Giorgio [1983] ECR 3595

Case 26/62 Van Gend en Loos v Nederlandse Administratie der Belastungen [1963] ECR 1, [1964] CMLR 105

Case 41/74 Van Duyn v Home Office [1974] ECR 1337. See, generally, Craig and de Búrca (n 31) ch 7.

Case 6/64 Costa v ENEL [1964] ECR 585, 593

Case C-203/99 Veedfald v Arhus Amtskommune [2001] ECR I-3569, [2003] 1 CMLR 1217 (Product Liability Directive)

Case C-213/89 R v Secretary of State for Transport, ex parte Factortame Ltd [1990] ECR I-2433 (full effectiveness of EU law impaired if rule of national law prevented court from granting interim relief against the Crown).

Case C237/02 Freiburger Kommunalbauten GmbH Baugesellschaft & Co KG v Hofstetter [2004] ECR I-3403 (Unfair Terms Directive).

Clift v Slough BC [2010] EWCA Civ 1484, [2011] 1 WLR 1774,

Collins, Hugh"Good Faith in European Contract Law"(1994), 14 OJLS 229.

Communication from the Commission to the European Parliament, the Council, the European Economic and Social Committee and the Committee of the Regions, A Digital Single Market Strategy for Europe, COM/2015/0192 final

Comparato, Guido.*Nationalism and Private Law in Europe* (Oxford: Hart Publishing 2014).

Conister Trust Ltd v John Hardman & Co [2008] EWCA Civ 841, [2009] CCLR 4, paras 110-111 per Lawrence Collins LJ. See also H Beale (ed), Chitty on Contracts (31st edn, Sweet and Maxwell 2012) para 1-065

Council Directive 85/374/EEC of 25 July 1985 on the approximation of the laws, regulations and administrative provisions of the Member States concerning liability for defective products: [1985] OJ L 210, 29.

Council Directive 93/13/EEC of 5 April 1993 OJ L 95, 21 April 1993, 29-34.

Craig P and G de Búrca, EU Law: Text, Cases and Materials (5th edn, OUP 2011) ch 9

Craig P."Sovereignty of the United Kingdom Parliament after Factortame"(1991) 11 *YEL* 221.

Cygan, A."Introduction: EU consumer and contract law at a crossroads?" in C. Twigg-Flesner, *Research Handbook on EU Consumer and Contract Law* (Cheltenham (UK) and Northampton (US): Edward Elgar Publishing Limited 2016) 33 and 34.

Dannemann, Gerhard and S. Vogenauer (eds), The Common European Sales Law in Context: Interactions with English and German Law (Oxford University Press 2013).

Directive (EU) 2015/2302 of the European Parliament and of the Council of 25 November 2015 on package travel and linked travel arrangements, amending Regulation (EC) No 2006/2004

Directive 1999/44/EC of the European Parliament and of the Council of 25 May 1999 OJ L 171, 7 July 1999, 12-16.

Directive 2000/31/EC on electronic commerce OJ L 178, 17 July 2000, 1-16

Directive 2005/29/EC of the European Parliament and of the Council of 11 May 2005 OJ L 149, 11 June 2005, 22-39.

Directive 2011/83/EU of the European Parliament and of the Council of 25 October 2011 on consumer rights, amending Council Directive 93/13/EEC and Directive 1999/44/EC of the European Parliament and of the Council and repealing Council Directive 85/577/EEC and Directive 97/7/EC of the European Parliament and of the Council, OJ L 304, 22 November 2011, 64–88.

Directive 2011/83/EU of the European Parliament and of the Council and repealing Council Directive 90/314/EEC.

Directive 2011/83/EU of the European Parliament and of the Council of 25 October 2011 OJ L 304, 22 November 2011, 64-88.

Donoghue v Stevenson [1932] AC 562.

Dougan, Michael, 'Editor's Introduction', in The UK after Brexit. Legal and Policy Challenges (Intersentia, 2017) 1-12. 'Brexit Means Brexit' (2016)

22:4 *European Public Law*, 589-593. In details, J. Armour, H. Eidenmüller, *Negotiating Brexit* (Baden-Baden, Nomos 2018).

Dougan, Michael.'Editor's Introduction', in M. Dougan, *The UK after Brexit. Legal and Policy Challenges* (Michael Dougan ed., Intersentia, 2017), 1-12.

Ebb Vs. EMO Air Cargo, 1995 4 ALL ER 577.

ECJ, C-6/90 Francovich v Italian Republic [1991] ECR I-5357, [1993] 2 CMLR 66.

Gessel-Kalinowska Vel Kalisz, Beata."Mixing Legal Systems in Europe; the Role of Common Law Transplants (Polish Law Example)".(2017) 25:4 *ERPL* 789-812.

Gibson, J.L. G.A. Caldeira."The Legal Cultures of Europe"(1996) 30:1 *Law & Society Review* 55-86.

Giliker P. *The Europeanisation of English Tort Law* (Oxford: Hart Publishing 2014) Chapter 3.

Glenn P. *Legal Traditions of the World* (OUP 2014), 260-1.

Green Paper on the Review of the Consumer Acquis COM (2006) 744 final.

Gullifer, Louisse and S. Vogenauer (eds), *English and European Perspectives on Contract and Commercial Law* (Oxford: Hart Publishing 2014).

Habermas, Jurgen. *The crisis of the European Union: A response* (Polity 2012). Of the same author, 'Democracy in Europe: Why the Development of the EU into a Transnational Democracy Is Necessary and How It Is Possible' (2015) 21 *EUR. L.J.* 546.

Hardt-Mautner, Gerlinde"How Does One Become a Good European?' The British Press and European Integration"(1995) 6 *Discourse & Society*, 177-205.

Harty S."Lawyers, Codification, and the Origins of Catalan Nationalism, 1881–1901", (2002) 20 (2) *Law and History Review*, 349-84.

Hesselink, W Martijn (ed.), The Politics of a European Civil Code (The Netherlands: Kluwer Law International 2006).

Hesselink, W Martijn."Democratic Contract Law" (2014) 11 (2) ERCL, 81-126. On the contrary, J.M. Smits, 'Democracy and (European) Private Law: A Functional Approach', (2010) 2 *European Journal of Legal Studies*, 26-40.

Hunt, M."The Horizontal Effect of the Human Rights Act' [1998] *PL* 423; G Phillipson, 'The Human Rights Act, "Horizontal Effect" and the Common Law: A Bang or a Whimper?' (1999) 62 *MLR* 824.

Jacobson S."Law and Nationalism in Nineteenth-Century Europe: The Case of Catalonia in Comparative Perspective".(2002) 20 Law and History Review, 307–47.

Joerges, Christian and Christian, Kreuder-Sonnen, 'Europe and European Studies in Crisis, Inter-disciplinary and Intra-disciplinary Schisms in Legal and Political Science' (2016)

Joerges, Christian."l diritto privato nella politica economica europea dopo la crisi finanziaria"(2017) 2 *Politica del diritto*, L. Niglia, Taking Comparative Law Seriously: Europe's Private Law and the Poverty of the

Orthodoxy' (2006) 54:2 The American Journal of Comparative Law, 401-427.

Law S"From Multiple Legal Cultures to One Legal Culture? Thinking About Culture, Tradition and Identity in European Private Law Development"(2015) 31:8 *Utrecht Journal of International and European Law*, 68-89.

Legrand P."European Legal Systems Are Not Converging", The International and Comparative Law Quarterly (1996) 45 52-81.

Lord Justice Laws, Lecture III: The Common Law and Europe, Hamlyn Lectures 2013, 27 Novembre 2013. Accessed 10 July 2018 <https://www.globalgovernancewatch.org/docLib/20140213_laws-lj-speech-hamlyn-lecture-2013.pdf>

Lord Steyn, 'The Challenge of Comparative Law' (2006) 8 EJLR 3, 4. See also TH Bingham, 'There Is a World Elsewhere': The Changing Perspectives of English law' (1992) 41 *ICLQ* 513.

Lord Sumption gives the 27th Sultan Azlan Shah Lecture, Kuala Lumpur, The Limits of Law,

Madsen, M Mikael, 'The Clash: Legal Culture, National Identity and European Law' (2016) iCourts Working Paper Series, No. 71, 2016. Accessed 10 July 2018 at <https://ssrn.com/abstract=2798556 or http://dx.doi.org/10.2139/ssrn.2798556>

Madsen, M.R."France, the UK, and the "Boomerang" of the Internationalization of Human Rights (1945–2000)', in S. Halliday and P. Schmidt (eds) *Human Rights Brought Home: Socio-Legal Perspectives on Human Rights in the National Context* (Oxford, UK: Hart 2004), 57-86.

Master Reed (The Rt Hon Lord Reed), The Common Law and the ECHR Lord Reed, Lecture, 13 November 2013 at 14. Accessed 10 July 2018 <https://www.innertemple.org.uk/education/education-resources/readers-lecture-series/previous-lecture-series-and-speakers>

Mattei Ugo and M. Bussani, 'In Search of the Common Core of European Private Law' (1994).

McKendrick, Ewan.*Contract Law* (Palgrave Macmillan 2013) 14. See also H. Collins, 'The impact of Human Rights Law on Contract Law in Europe' [2011] *EBLR* 425.

McKennitt v Ash [2006] EWCA Civ 1714, [2008] QB 73, para 11.

McMeel, Gerard."The Proposal for a Common European Sales Law: Next Stop a European Contract Code?"(2012) 27 BJIB&FL 3; M. Kenny, 'The 2004 Communication on European Contract Law: Those Magnificent Men in Their Unifying Machines' (2005) 30 *ELR* 724.

McMeel, Gerard."Contract, Restitution and the Human Rights Act 1998' [2004] LMCLQ 280

Micheals R. quoted by S. Weatherill, EU Consumer Law and Policy (Cheltenham, Northampton: Edward Elgar Publishing 2013), 211 fs.

Micklitz, W Hans and N Reich, 'Crónica de una muerte anunciada: The Commission Proposal for a 'Directive on Consumer Rights" (2009) 46 *CMLR* 471.

Micklitz, W Hans, and N Reich, 'The Court and Sleeping Beauty: The Revival of the Unfair Contract Terms Directive' (2014) 51 CMLR 771.

Micklitz, W Hans.(ed) The *Many Concepts of Social Justice in European Private Law* (Cheltenham: Edward Elgar, 2011).

Montesquieu, *De l'ésprit des lois* (Geneva, Barillot 1748).

Morris P Sean, The modern transplantation of continental law in England: how English private international law embraces Europeanisation, 12:3 (2014) Journal of Private International Law, 587-607.

Nicola, G Fernanda."Luxembourg Judicial Style With or Without the UK", 40 Fordham Int'l L.J. 1505 (2017).

Osman v United Kingdom [1998] EHRR 101.

Proposal for a regulation on a Common European Sales Law COM (2011) 635 final.

R. Sefton-green quoted by S. Weatherill, *EU Consumer Law and Policy* (Cheltenham, Northampton: Edward Elgar Publishing 2013), 211 fs.

Rabone v Pennine Care NHS Foundation Trust [2012] UKSC 2, [2012] 2 AC 72, paras 96-97.

Reg. 5(1) UTCC Regulations 1999

Schulze R and F. Zoll.*European Contract Law* (Baden- Baden: Nomos 2018).

Shanshal v Al-Kishtaini [2001] EWCA Civ 264[2001] 2 All ER (Comm) 601

Shaw, Gisela."German Lawyers and Globalization: Changing Professional Identity"(2005) 58 *German Life and Letters*, 211–25.

SI 1994/3159 (replaced by SI 1999/2083 due to problems with transposition).

Stone P.*EU Private International Law* (3rd edn, Edward Elgar 2014)

Study Group on a European Civil Code/Research Group on EC Private Law (eds), Principles, Definitions and Model Rules of European Private Law, Draft Common Frame of Reference (Full Edition), Sellier, Munich, 2009.

Twigg-Flesner, Christian and D. Metcalfe.'The Proposed Consumer Rights Directive--Less Haste, More Thought?' (2009) 5 *ERCL* 368;

Twigg-Flesner, Christian, 'No Sense of Purpose or Direction? The Modernisation of European Consumer Law' (2007) 3 *ERCL* 198.

Twigg-Flesner, Christian, *The Cambridge Companion to European Union Private Law* (CUP 2010) 6.

von Bar, Christian and E. Clive (eds), Principles, Definitions and Model Rules of European Private Law: Draft Common Frame of Reference (Sellier 2009 and OUP 2010) vols I-VI. N Jansen and R Zimmermann, 'A European Civil Code in All but Name' [2010] CLJ 98.

Von Bogandy, Armin."National legal scholarship in the European legal area – A manifesto"(2012) 10:3 *International Journal of Constitutional Law*, 614–626.

Watson, Alan.*Legal Transplants: An Approach to Comparative Law* (University of Georgia Press 1993). See also, P. Glenn, *Legal Traditions of the World* (Oxford University Press 2004).

Weatherill."The Consumer Rights Directive: How and Why a Quest for "Coherence" Has (Largely) Failed".(2012) 49 *CMLR* 1279.

Weiler, H.H. Joseph"A Quiet Revolution: The European Court of Justice and its Interlocutors"(1994) 26 *Comparative Political* Studies,510–34.

Woolwich Equitable Building Society v Inland Revenue Commissioners [1993] AC 70.

Young, L. Alison."The Constitutional Implications of Brexit' (2017) 23:4 European Public law, 757–786.

Z v UK [2002] 34 EHRR 3.

Zweigert, Konrad, H. Kotz.*An Introduction to Comparative Law* (Oxford University Press 1998).

Chapter 8

Are European Security Policies Learning some Lessons from the United States on Migration and Human Rights?

Paolo Bargiacchi[1]

Abstract

If we compare American and European legal systems, differences are essentially due to the different way of dealing with the culture of security and the relationship between politics and law. Today, that gap is narrowing because Europe is changing its approach to security and, in the field of migration, its political quest for more security also involves the limitation of the judicial check and a more formalistic approach to interpreting and applying the law, i.e. two legal solutions that are typical of the US approach to security. Following decades of strong and wide protection of human rights in any situation, States and the European Commission are seeking for a new and different balance between human rights and security and are ready to trade some political idealism and legal functionalism in the field of migration and human rights for more political pragmatism and legal formalism in the field of security.

1. First Major Difference between Europe and the US: the Culture of Security. Consequences in Terms of Judicial Check over the Executive Branch and Admissibility of the Balancing Test between Human Rights and State Security

If we compare American and European legal systems, there are some remarkable differences which essentially depend on the different way of dealing with two general issues: the culture of security and the

---

[1] Professor of International Law, Faculty of Economic and Legal Sciences, Kore University of Enna.

relationship between politics and law. Yet, the central thesis of the article is that such differences are slowly lessening and the gap in dealing with them is narrowing between the two sides of the Atlantic Ocean. By examining differences (paragraphs 1-2.2) and detecting new similarities (paragraphs 3-4) between European civil law systems and the US common law system in fostering and strengthening the culture of security and interpreting and applying the general relationship between politics and law, the article suggests that European security policies are learning some lessons from the American approach and that a gradual process of convergence is underway by which European civil law systems are resembling more and more the US common law system.

As regards the first major difference between these legal systems, one should underline that security is a core issue in US politics to such an extent that some related notions (imminent threat, continuing threat, etc.) are so widely interpreted that sometimes human rights are severely limited. For instance, some Guantanamo detainees "*who cannot safely be transferred to third countries in the near term [...] and who are not currently facing military commission charges*" are subject to continued indefinite detention without charge or trial because their detentions "*remains necessary to protect against a continuing significant threat to the security of the United States*".[2] Even in Europe security is a core issue but its goals are accomplished within a more comprehensive framework of values and interests in which human rights and the rule of law are equally important.

The first consequence that follows from such difference affects the scope and content of the judicial check over the Executive Branch.

Judicial deference has been (and still is) a long-established doctrine throughout the political and legal history, culture, and tradition of the United States. Above all in cases of national security, foreign affairs and immigration the judicial power yields its competence to the executive and legislative powers.

In the area of immigration deference "*is particularly powerful [...] because 'the power to expel or exclude aliens* [is] *a fundamental sovereign attribute exercised by the Government's political departments largely*

---

[2] White House, "Plan for Closing the Guantanamo Bay Detention Facility," February 2016,
https://www.defense.gov/Portals/1/Documents/pubs/GTMO_Closure_Plan_0216.pdf, 1 and 4.

immune from judicial control.' Shaughnessy v. United States ex rel. Mezei, 345 U.S. 2016, 210 (1953)".[3]

Also in the area of war-making, national security, and foreign relations "*the judiciary has an exceedingly limited role*" because courts cannot "*impermissibly draw* [...] *into the 'heart of executive and military planning and deliberation,' Lebron, 670 F.3d at 550, as the suit would require the Court to examine national security policy and the military chain of command as well as operational combat decisions regarding the designation of targets and how best to counter threats to the United States*". In one word, the Judiciary cannot hinder the ability of the Congress and the Executive "*to act decisively and without hesitation in defense of U.S. interests*".[4]

Of course, the limited judicial check does not mean that a state of war is "*a blank check for the President when it comes to the rights of the Nation's citizens*"[5] and political branches may "*switch the Constitution on or off at will and govern without legal constraints*".[6] American judges have not abdicated their constitutional functions, and Guantanamo decisions confirm it. Yet, as discussed below, the Guantanamo jurisprudence - when compared to the bicentennial interpretation by US governments and courts of the relationship between power, law, and territory - seems like a "drop" of European-style functionalism in a "sea" of American-style

---

[3] U.S. Court of Appeals, *U.S. v. Peralta-Sanchez*, 868 F.3d 852 (9th Cir. 2017).

[4] U.S. District Court for the District of Columbia, *Nasser Al-Aulaqi et al. v. Leon C. Panetta et al.*, 35 F.Supp.3d 56 (2014), 34 and 36. See also U.S. Court of Appeals, *Vance v. Rumsfeld*, 701 F.3d 193 (7th Cir. 2012) (*en banc*), 200 (Congress and the President, not judges, should make the "*essential tradeoffs*" required to manage national security) and U.S. Supreme Court, *Johnson, Secretary of Defense, et al. v. Eisentrager, alias Ehrhardt, et al.*, 339 U.S. 763 (1950), 774 ("*Executive power over enemy aliens, undelayed and unhampered by litigation, has been deemed, throughout our history, essential to wartime security*") and 789 ("*It is not the function of the Judiciary to entertain private litigation – even by a citizen – which challenges the legality, wisdom, or propriety of the Commander in Chief in sending our armed forces abroad*").

[5] U.S. Supreme Court, *Youngstown Sheet & Tube Co. v. Sawyer*, 343 U.S. 578 (1952), 587; see also *Hamdi v. Rumsfeld*, 542 U.S. 507 (2004), 536.

[6] U.S. Supreme Court, *Lakdhar Boumediene, et al. v. George W. Bush, et al.*, 553 U.S. 723 (2008), 757.

formalism.[7] In the United States, in fact, protection of human rights and judicial check over the Executive Branch are more limited than in Europe.

In Europe there is no room for judicial deference. The primacy of law and judicial interpretation over politics is absolute, and politics must defer to the considered opinion of the Judiciary, especially of the European supranational courts, i.e. the European Court of Justice (ECJ) and the European Court of Human Rights (ECtHR).

The second consequence that follows from the different culture of security concerns the admissibility of the balancing test between human rights and State security.

In the United States the balancing test is allowed to such an extent that the extrajudicial killing in a foreign country of an American citizen who is a senior operational leader of al-Qa'ida is lawful if the US Government "*has determined, after a thorough and careful review, that the individual poses an imminent threat of violent attack against the United States*". According to the Attorney General, in fact, "*based on generations-old legal principles and Supreme Court decisions handed down during World War II*" and the global war on terror, the "*US citizenship alone does not make such individuals immune from being targeted*" and the government has the right to use lethal force "*to protect the American people from the threats posed by terrorist*" when capture is not feasible.[8]

The balancing test is also applied in the expedited removal procedure, i.e. the process by which an alien can be denied entry and physically removed from the United States. In this case the balance, inter alia, is between "*the nature of the private interest at stake*" (the claim for the Fifth Amendment due process right to counsel) and "*the government's interest, including the additional financial or administrative burden*" the granting of such right would impose on the government (costs of detention,

---

[7] On the relationship between power, law, and territory, see Kal Raustiala, *Does the Constitution Follow the Flag?* (New York: Oxford University Press, 2009); Paolo Bargiacchi, *Orientamenti della dottrina statunitense di diritto internazionale* (Milano: Giuffré Editore, 2011), 262-75.

[8] U.S. Office of the Attorney General, "Letter to the Chairman of the Committee on the Judiciary of the United States Senate," May 22, 2013, https://www.justice.gov/slideshow/AG-letter-5-22-13.pdf. See U.S. Department of Justice, "White Paper. Lawfulness of a Lethal Operation Directed Against a U.S. Citizen Who Is a Senior Operational Leader of Al-Qa'ida or an Associated Force," no date, document leaked in February 2013, accessed November 19, 2017, http://msnbcmedia.msn.com/i/msnbc/sections/news/020413_DOJ_White_Paper.pdf.

government's lawyers, "*pay for the increased time the immigration officer must spend adjudicating such cases, distracting the officer from any other duties*", etc.).[9]

The *Peralta-Sanchez* ruling confirms previous case-law in holding that individuals facing expedited removal procedure under 8 U.S.C. § 1225 have no right to counsel or to a hearing before an immigration judge because they only "*have a limited interest at stake*" having not been, inter alia, present in the United States "*for some period of time longer than a few minutes or hours*". In other words, as discussed below, it is just a formalistic matter of time. In accordance with the formalism that characterizes the US legal system and its interpretation (see § 2.1), in fact, during the inspection and the expedited removal procedure aliens are treated as if they were not within the United States for the purposes of applying some constitutional rights. In fact, an arriving alien, even if has "*technically effected entry into the United States*", has a very limited interest in remaining (because he has established only a limited presence) compared to that of an alien already living in the United States and placed in a removal proceeding other than that under § 1225. The consequence is that the former, unlike the latter, has no Fifth Amendment due process right to counsel. As time does *not* go by, the scope of human rights protection severely narrows while the "*presence of lawyers will inevitably complicate*" the procedure: human rights protection cannot thwart the government in pursuing its goal to exclude quickly aliens who are inadmissible and once again human rights must yield to national security.[10]

In Europe, on the contrary, the balancing test between human rights and national security is not allowed. Even when the security risk posed by an individual is so high to threaten public order and national security, States

---

[9] U.S. Court of Appeals, *U.S. v. Peralta-Sanchez*, 868 F.3d 852 (9th Cir. 2017). Such balancing test was articulated by the U.S. Supreme Court in *Mathews v. Eldridge*, 424 U.S. 219 (1976).

[10] The Executive Order 13767 issued by President Donald Trump on January 25, 2017 further enhanced the expedited removal procedure on the grounds that border security is "*critically important*" to national security and "*aliens who illegally enter the United States without inspection or admission present a significant threat to national security and public safety*". See White House, "Executive Order 13767 of January 25, 2017, Border Security and Immigration Enforcement Improvements," *Federal Register* vol. 82, no. 18, 8793-97. See also Memorandum from John Kelly, Secretary of Homeland Security, "Implementing the President's Border Security and Immigration Enforcement Improvements Policies" (memorandum, February 20, 2017).

cannot find a balance between their security risk and the real risk that fundamental rights might be infringed in case of extradition, return or removal to another State. The absolute prohibition against torture or cruel, inhuman or degrading treatment or punishment must be respected "*even in times of emergency or war*". The ban on the balancing test articulated by European supranational courts is always upheld including when deportation orders are taken against those who play an active role in terrorist organizations and threaten national security.[11] The ban applies to everyone (including third-country nationals who illegally arrive at EU external borders or illegally enter and reside within the EU) regardless of his legal status (asylum-seeker, displaced person, migrant, suspected or sentenced person) and of the requested measure (return, removal, extradition, etc.).

To deny or grant the balancing test also affects the scope and content of procedural rights of the person concerned and powers of national and supranational courts.

In Europe supranational courts strictly enforce and widely protect procedural rights and full judicial review is in principle guaranteed pursuant to Articles 6 (right to a fair trial) and 13 (right to an effective remedy) of the European Convention on Human Rights (ECHR) and Article 47 (right to an effective remedy and to a fair trial) of the EU Charter of Fundamental Rights. In order to assess whether or not a trial or a remedy is fair, the effectiveness is the main criterion used by courts and not even the Security Council binding resolutions can displace application and enforcement of human rights. In *Al-Jedda* ruling the ECtHR held that Security Council resolutions have primacy only if they are "*in line with human rights*" and that the ECHR is not displaced.[12] In *Kadi* judgment of July 2013, the ECJ held that EU regulations did not enjoy immunity from

---

[11] ECtHR (Grand Chamber), Judgment of 15 November 1996, *Chahal v. the United Kingdom*, Application no. 22414/93; ECtHR (Grand Chamber), Judgment of 28 February 2008, *Saadi v. Italy*, Application no. 37201/06. Saadi, a Tunisian national already arrested in Italy on suspicion of involvement in international terrorism, had been sentenced to twenty years in prison for terrorist charges by a military court in Tunisia. Italy had issued a deportation order because "*the applicant had played an 'active role' in an organization responsible for providing logistical and financial support to persons belonging to fundamentalist Islamist cells in Italy and abroad* [and] *consequently, his conduct was disturbing public order and threatening national security*". The deportation order was stayed by Italian courts and by the ECtHR.

[12] ECtHR (Grand Chamber), Judgment of 7 July 2011, *Al-Jedda v. the United Kingdom*, Application no. 27021/08.

jurisdiction even if they are only designed to give effect with no latitude to one's black-listing mandated by the Security Council. The ECJ vindicated its own right to *"ensure the review, in principle the full review, of the lawfulness of all Union acts in the light of the fundamental rights"*. Notwithstanding *"overriding considerations"* concerning the security of the EU or its Member States and the conduct of their international relations, in fact, such judicial review remains *"indispensable to ensure a fair balance between the maintenance of international peace and security and the protection of the fundamental rights and freedoms of the person concerned"*.[13] In *Abu Qatada* ruling the ECtHR stayed the extradition to Jordan of a person wanted on terrorism charges due to the real risk that evidence obtained by torture might be admitted during the trial in violation of Article 6 of the ECHR. The Memorandum of Understanding between the United Kingdom and Jordan (concerning the protection of Articles 3 and 5 of the ECHR) had to be amended by also including protection of Article 6.[14]

2. Second Major Difference between Europe and the US: the Relationship between Politics and Law. Consequences in Terms of Interpretation and Application of the Legal System

2.1 The American Formalism

The second major difference relates to the relationship between politics and law, i.e. how courts and governments interpret, apply and implement the rules of the legal system and the related circumstances of fact.

In the United States the relationship is essentially imbued with formalism rather than with functionalism. In our reasoning the phrase *"US formalism"* means that legal interpretation is closer to the letter of the law (its literal interpretation) than to the spirit of the law (its teleological interpretation). Formalism often narrows human rights protection because sometimes it makes it possible to split the exercise of powers (especially abroad) by the government and the application of law. Formalism may indeed lead more easily to a strictly territorial (or intra-territorial) interpretation of the relationship between power, law, and

---

[13] ECJ (Grand Chamber), Judgment of 18 July 2013, *European Commission & Council of the EU v. Yassin Abdullah Kadi*, Joined Cases C-584/10 P, C-593/10 P and C-595-10 P, §§ 97-98 and 125.

[14] ECtHR, Judgment of 17 January 2012, *Othman (Abu Qatada) v. The United Kingdom*, Application no. 8139/09..

territory, as shown, for instance, by the Indian Tribes and the Insular Cases decided by the US Supreme Court.[15]

The general political rationale behind this kind of formalism lies in the fact that the Constitution and, more generally, the law *"follows the flag"* (i.e. the exercise of powers by the government) but at times *"doesn't quite catch up with it"*, especially in case of extraterritorial exercise of that power.[16] Based on this premise, for a long time the Judiciary interpreted *"American law instrumentally, in a manner that generally enhanced the autonomy and power of the United States government"* when acting abroad, in order to not *"overly fetter the projection of American power, and American commerce around the globe"*.[17] Since the 1940s the relationship between power and law was partially reinterpreted by the courts, the formalism, and its rigid *"hermetic territorialism"*, gave more way to the functional approach, and the Constitution was more often able to catch up with the Flag when abroad.

As anticipated, the Guantanamo jurisprudence recognized some constitutional rights of foreign prisoners by taking a functional rather than a formal approach to the legal status of the continued American presence at Guantanamo. Piercing the veil of formalism (Guantanamo is abroad) and looking functionally at reality (the US exercises *de facto* sovereignty over the area), the Supreme Court recognized the US effective control and jurisdiction rather than the Cuban formal sovereignty and granted the Constitution's extraterritorial application. In any case, as anticipated, such jurisprudence on the relationship between power, law, and territory, is just a "drop" of European-style functionalism in a "sea" in which legal

---

[15] Indian Tribes were considered as "domestic dependent nations" living in a territory with respect to which "though plainly sovereign American territory, Congress could draw intra-territorial distinctions". Indian territory was American "as far as other sovereigns were concerned" but remained foreign for the purpose of domestic law. Raustiala, Does the Constitution Follow the Flag?, 84-85. See also U.S. Supreme Court, Cherokee Nation v. Georgia, 30 U.S. 1 (1831), 16-18. In the Insular Cases, Puerto Rico and other overseas territories were not regarded as being part of the United States for the purposes of applying the Constitution but "foreign to the United States in a domestic sense" although "appurtenant and belonging to the United States". See U.S. Supreme Court, Downes v. Bidwell, 182 U.S. 244 (1901), 341-342.

[16] It was the Secretary of War Elihu Root who said in relation to the Insular Cases that "as neas as I can make out the Constitution follows the flag – but doesn't quite catch up with it". Philip C. Jessup, Elihu Root (New York: Dodd, Mead & Company, 1938), I, 348.

[17] Raustiala, Does the Constitution Follow the Flag?, 61 and 67.

formalism is still the strongest tide as demonstrated by the three examples set out below.

First example: in habeas corpus cases concerning indefinite administrative detention abroad of foreign nationals [18] the extraterritorial reach of the writ can be limited by "*practical concerns or obstacles*" that would make "*impractical or anomalous*" its issuing. The reality on the ground (i.e. the circumstances of fact surrounding the situation) is used for limiting the protection of human rights while in Europe, as discussed in § 2.2, it is interpreted instrumentally in a manner that broadens that protection. For instance, in *Eisentrager* ruling (German soldiers detained at Landsberg prison in post-war occupied Germany) the Supreme Court held that the need to "*transport the petitioners across the seas for hearing*" would have diverted the field commander efforts and attention "*from the military offensive abroad to the legal defensive at home*" and required allocation of human and economic resources: the right of habeas was denied to the prisoners for this reason too.[19] Even in *Al Maqaleh* decision (foreign nationals detained at US Military Base in Bagram, Afghanistan) the "*circumstances of fact surrounding*" the military base exerted a decisive influence in denying the habeas corpus to the prisoners: the armed conflict raging outside the walls of the base stripped away that constitutional right which had been instead granted to Guantanamo prisoners because Guantanamo does not lie in a theater of war and there is a peaceful situation. Notwithstanding all the prisoners are in the same situation (namely under the complete and unfettered control of the detaining power), those held in Bagram are beyond the reach of the Constitution because, inter alia, troops "*are actively engaged in a war with a determined enemy*".[20] The paradoxical consequence is that the scope of human rights protection depends on the formalistic assessment of factual circumstances.

Second example: in *Sale* decision the Supreme Court held that non-refoulement principle did not apply outside the national territory and

---

[18] Paolo Bargiacchi, "Power, Law and Territory: Extraterritorial Application of the United States Constitution at Landsberg Prison in Occupied Germany, at Guantanamo Bay Naval Base in Cuba and at Bagram Airfield Military Base in Afghanistan," in *International Institutions and Co-operation: Terrorism, Migrations, Asylum*, eds. Giancarlo Guarino and Ilaria D'Anna (Napoli: Satura Editrice, 2011), 495-540.

[19] U.S. Supreme Court, *Johnson, Secretary of Defense, et al. v. Eisentrager, alias Ehrhardt, et al.*, 339 U.S. 763 (1950), 778-779.

[20] U.S. Court of Appeals, *Al Maqaleh v. Hagel*, 738 F.3d 312 (D.C. Cir. 2013), 349-350.

government may return asylum-seekers provided they have not reached or crossed the national border (for instance, in case of interdiction and return of asylum vessels on the high seas). The Court upheld the formalistic, textual interpretation of the word "*return*" in Article 33(1) of 1951 Refugee Convention advanced by a Presidential Executive Order. Whilst conceding that such strictly territorial interpretation of Article 33(1) "*may even violate* [its] *spirit*", the Court however concluded that "*a treaty cannot impose uncontemplated extraterritorial obligations on those who ratify it through no more than its general humanitarian intent. Because the text of Article 33 cannot reasonably be read to say anything at all about a nation's actions toward aliens outside its own territory, it does not prohibit such actions*".[21] Once again, the Supreme Court split the exercise of power (the Flag) and the application of the law (the Constitution).

Third example: diplomatic assurances are required by the US Government before transferring foreign nationals to countries whose human rights record displays a real risk of human rights violations. The US only gets the promise from the receiving State that "*appropriate humane treatment measures*" (a lower standard than full protection of human rights) will be guaranteed but there is no substantive assessment of the real risk of human rights violations occurring after the transfer.[22] The US only relies on the formal assurance offered by the receiving State and the seeking of such formal promise is the only legal requirement to abide by the human rights obligations.

2.2 The European Functionalism

In Europe the general approach to these issues is different because European courts (especially supranational courts) assess the relationship between politics and law in functional rather than formalistic terms.

---

[21] U.S. Supreme Court, Sale v. Haitian Centers Council, Inc., 509 U.S. 155 (1993), 183. The word "return" in Article 33(1) would only be "referred to the defensive act of resistance or expulsion at the border rather than to transporting a person to a particular destination". Anthony North, "Extraterritorial Effect of Non-refoulement," accessed November 19, 2017, http://www.fedcourt.gov.au/digital-law-library/judges-speeches/justice-north/north-j-20110907.

[22] "The United States coordinated with the Government of the United Arab Emirates to ensure these transfers took place consistent with appropriate security and humane treatment measures". See U.S. Department of Defense, "Detainee Transfers Announced," Press Release No: NR-438-15, November 15, 2015, accessed November 19, 2017, http://www.defense.gov/News/News-Releases/News-Release-View/Article/628980/detainee-transfers-announced.

In our reasoning the phrase "*European functionalism*" means that legal interpretation is closer to the spirit of the law (to its teleological interpretation) than to the letter of the law (to its literal interpretation). Functionalism often extends human rights protection also because it makes it almost always possible to link the exercise of powers (especially abroad) by governments and the application of law. Functionalism may therefore lead more easily to an extraterritorial interpretation of the relationship between power, law, and territory.

Whenever European judges are called upon to protect individuals against human rights violations committed by governments, as discussed below, they always apply the "reality on the ground test" and reject literal and formal interpretations of the law. The main consequence is that functionalism almost always links the Flag and the Constitution (ECHR, EU legislation, domestic laws, etc.) and States are usually held accountable for their actions wherever in the world (at home or abroad) those actions may have been committed or their consequences felt. It is no coincidence that personal and territorial models of jurisdiction are widely interpreted and applied so that almost anyone might fall within the jurisdiction of States. For instance, the ECtHR is not far from recognizing that even the simple power to kill exercised abroad brings the victim under State jurisdiction. In *Jaloud* ruling the Court stopped just one step before reaching that conclusion and only a "drop" of American-style formalism in a "sea" of European-style functionalism pushed the Court - at least for the time being - to still "*draw a distinction between killing an individual after arresting him and simply shooting him without arresting him first, such that in the first case there is an obligation to respect the person's right to life yet in the second case there is not*".[23]

European functionalism also makes circumstances of fact surrounding human rights violations irrelevant to the courts. Human rights may be infringed by a policeman patrolling the peaceful streets of London as well as by a soldier during security operations carried out in occupied Iraq in the aftermath of the war. In the latter case it is also irrelevant whether the violation occurred within a military base under the exclusive control of a State or in the whole region for whom the State had assumed authority and responsibility for the maintenance of security.[24] Judicial assessment

---

[23] ECtHR (Grand Chamber), Judgment of 20 November 2014, *Jaloud v. The Netherlands*, Application no. 47708/08.

[24] ECtHR (Grand Chamber), Judgment of 7 July 2011, *Al-Skeini and Others v. The United Kingdom*, Application no. 55721/07.

of "*surrounding circumstances*" is therefore one of the greatest differences between American formalism and European functionalism: they weigh too much for American judges (and habeas corpus is denied to Bagram prisoners), and they weigh too little for European judges (and the result is *Al-Skeini* case-law).

As a general rule, in Europe situations concerning human rights are always assessed on a case-by-case basis and with regard to the existing reality on the ground in order to detect any possible real risk of human rights violations for individuals.

The main consequence of the judicial application of the "reality on the ground test" is that - in case of return, extradition, and removal - the test rules out any probative value to the fact that the receiving State is party to relevant international human rights treaties.[25] Given that functionalism prohibits formalistic and literal interpretations of human rights rules and concepts, the sending State must always demonstrate that the receiving State is a "*safe country*", i.e. a country where human rights are generally and consistently protected and there are no substantial grounds "*for believing that there was a real risk that the applicants would be subjected to treatment contrary to Article 3*" (Prohibition of torture, inhuman or degrading treatment or punishment) of the ECHR.[26] The safe country test

---

[25] "*the existence of domestic laws and the ratification of international treaties guaranteeing respect for fundamental rights are not in themselves sufficient to ensure adequate protection against the risk of ill-treatment where* [...] *reliable sources have reported practices resorted to or tolerated by the authorities which are manifestly contrary to the principles of ECHR*". See ECtHR (Grand Chamber), Judgment of 23 February 2012, *Hirsi Jamaa and Others v. Italy*, Application no. 27765/09, §§ 128 and 136.

[26] According to Article 38(1) of Directive 2013/32/EU of the European Parliament and of the Council of 26 June 2013 on common procedures for granting and withdrawing international protection, a State is "*safe*" when "*(a) life and liberty are not threatened on account of race, religion, nationality, membership of a particular social group or political opinion; (b) there is no risk of serious harm as defined in Directive 2011/95/EU; (c) the principle of non-refoulement in accordance with the Geneva Convention is respected; (d) the prohibition of removal, in violation of the right to freedom from torture and cruel, inhuman or degrading treatment as laid down in international law, is respected; and (e) the possibility exists to request refugee status and, if found to be a refugee, to receive protection in accordance with the Geneva Convention*".

also applies to EU Member States because there is no presumption they would respect fundamental rights only because are members of the EU.[27]

Against this background, furthermore, it is no coincidence that diplomatic assurances offered by receiving States to European sending States almost never pass the "reality on the ground test" even if a memorandum of understanding is in place between States. US-style generic and thin assurances are never allowed by European courts, and a substantial case-by-case assessment is always required: assurances may only be accepted if they are enough "*detailed*", "*reliable*" and "*specific*" and provide "*individual guarantees*" that the person, if returned, "*would be taken charge of in a manner adapted to*" his personal situation.[28]

Lastly, European functionalism recognizes the extraterritorial scope of the non-refoulement principle. In line with the UN High Commissioner for Refugees (UNHCR) advisory opinion, "*the decisive criterion*" for applying the principle is whether asylum-seekers "*come within the effective control and authority*" of the State wherever it happens including interdictions at sea.[29] Such interpretation is consistent with the overriding humanitarian object and purpose of the principle and perfectly matches the European teleological approach to human rights legal instruments.

---

[27] ECtHR (Grand Chamber), Judgment of 21 January 2011, *M.S.S. v. Belgium & Greece*, Application no. 30696/09; ECtHR, Judgment of 21 October 2014, *Sharifi and Others v. Italy & Greece*, Application no. 16643/09; ECJ, Judgment of 21 December 2011, *N.S. v. Secretary of State for the Home & M.E. and Others v. Refugee Applications Commissioner and Others*, Joined Cases C-411/10 and C-493/10.

[28] «*Swiss authorities were obliged to obtain assurances from their Italian counterparts that on their arrival in Italy the applicants would be received in facilities and in conditions adapted to the age of the children, and that the family would be kept together* [...] *Without detailed and reliable information* [...] *the Swiss authorities did not have sufficient assurances* [and in case of return] *there would accordingly be a violation of Article 3 of the Convention*". ECtHR (Grand Chamber), Judgment of 4 November 2014, *Tarakhel v. Switzerland*, Application no. 29217/12, §§ 120 and 122.

[29] UNHCR, "Advisory Opinion on the Extraterritorial Application of Non-Refoulement Obligations under the 1951 Convention relating to the Status of Refugees and its 1967 Protocol," Geneva, January 26, 2007, § 43. accessed November 19, 2017, http://www.unhcr.org/4d9486929.pdf.

3. Narrowing the Gap between Differences: An American Model for European Security Policies?

The analysis carried out so far shows, on the one hand, that the US formalism often facilitates the splitting up between the extraterritorial exercise of powers by the government and the application of law and, on the other, that the European functionalism almost always makes that power fall under the law's rule. It goes without saying that the scope and content of human rights protection as well as the overall security model vary depending on the chosen approach.

In the United States, the formalism is still the main methodology and legal ideology in assessing facts and circumstances and interpreting and applying rules and procedures of domestic and international legal systems, and there is no meaningful convergence towards the European functionalism.

In Europe, instead, perhaps a process was set in motion through which the gap between the two sides of the Atlantic Ocean is slowly narrowing with the European side coming a little bit closer to the American one in terms of management of security threats. What is probably changing in Europe is the way of dealing with those two general issues we mentioned above: the culture of security and the relationship between politics and law.

In times of growing terrorist threats and unprecedented irregular migration flows, there is an increasing securitization of European politics and legislation and some States, right or wrong, are wondering whether the highest level of human rights protection afforded by European courts in the last decades is still "sustainable" with respect to the need for defending their own security from these new threats.

The increasing securitization is also confirmed by: *a)* the amendment or suppression of some fundamental principles of European integration (EU citizens no longer undergo a minimum check when crossing an EU external border and reintroduction of border controls within Schengen is no longer a truly exceptional measure);[30] *b)* the massive-scale data

---

[30] Since April 2017 EU Member States are obliged to carry out systematic and enhanced checks against relevant databases on all persons, including EU citizens, at all external borders (air, sea and land borders), both at entry and exit. On September 2017, the European Commission also proposed to update the Schengen Borders Code to adapt the rules for the reintroduction of temporary internal border controls and better tackle new security challenges such as terrorist threats. Time limits for internal border controls will be prolonged to a maximum period of two

collection, treatment and analysis to identify previously unknown likely suspects and create general assessment criteria for criminal profiling (see, for instance, EU Directive 2016/681 on the use of passenger name record for the prevention, detection, investigation and prosecution of terrorist offenses and serious crime); *c)* the renewal and enhancement of EU return policy to make it more effective on the basis of principles (wider use of accelerated, swifter and simplified procedures, of presumptions and inadmissibility grounds, of detention, etc.) and goals (curbing abuses of asylum procedures, prevent and combat irregular migration, etc.) which are similar to those of the US's return policy;[31] *d)* the enhanced cooperation with non-EU States to prevent and manage irregular migration, including the possible establishment of processing centers funded by the EU in African countries (Libya, Chad, Niger, etc.) to identify refugees and hold and turn back migrants. The externalization or offshoring processing policy echoes the widely criticized Australian policies of regional resettlement and increases the risk of violations of international human rights law and of the EU turning a blind eye to that reality.

As anticipated, the latest European policies of securitization underpin a different way of dealing with security and with the relationship between politics and law. All of this is having far-reaching legal consequences and serious implications. In fact, the political quest for more security also involves the limitation of the judicial check and a more formalistic approach to interpreting and applying the European legal systems. In other words, it involves two legal solutions that are typical of the US approach to security issues and threats.

As regard to the limitation of the judicial check (especially of the ECtHR), for different reasons but with the same goal of better protecting their own security, States such as France, Ukraine and Turkey derogated from the obligations under the ECHR according to Article 15 (also the UK might soon derogate from these obligations). Furthermore, the ECHR system will be amended by Protocol no. 15, once in force, and an explicit reference to the principle of subsidiarity and the doctrine of the margin of appreciation will become part of the ECHR. It will be then clearer that *"the Convention*

---

years in order to respond to evolving and persistent serious threats to public policy or international security.

[31] European Commission, "EU Action Plan on return," CCM(2015) 453 final, Brussels, 9.9.2015; Id., "Communication on a more effective return policy in the European Union – A Renewed Action Plan," COM(2017) 200 final, Brussels, 2.3.2017.

system is subsidiary to the safeguarding of human rights at national level and that national authorities are in principle better placed than an international court to evaluate local needs and conditions" and apply and implement the Convention.[32] The reform will shift the present balance between national courts and ECtHR in favor of the former also because States, right or wrong, believe that the legal understanding of the ECHR as a "living instrument" has gone too far in that it expanded rights and freedoms too much beyond what the framers of the Convention had in mind in 1950.

In other words, derogations, reforms and States' attitude suggest that in times of increasing security threats the European States feel a degree of unease with the present balance of power between governments and supranational courts and are looking for a different judicial framework in which national courts might apply more often the margin of (national) appreciation than the (international) "living instrument" understanding.

As regards to a more formalistic approach to interpreting and applying rules and procedures, several policies and provisions recently proposed or adopted in the field of migration seem to distance themselves from European functionalism (and the related "reality on the ground test") and get a little bit closer to American-style formalism. After all, this shift is almost inevitable once simplification and swiftness of asylum and return procedures and cooperation with third countries become key instruments of the European migration and return policies.

On the one hand, in fact, simplification and swiftness sit uncomfortably with that thorough and careful examination of situations concerning asylum-seekers and migrants required by the "reality on the ground test" and are more easily secured by literal than teleological interpretation of the law. On the other, the enhanced partnership with African countries requires a greater reliance and respect for other nations' sovereignty, assurances and commitments.[33] Partnership inevitably allocates and distinguishes competencies, tasks, duties and responsibilities between counterparts and this may weaken the European goal to uphold and promote its own values "*in its relations with the wider world*" (Article 3(5)

---

[32] "Protocol No. 15 amending the Convention for the Protection of Human Rights and Fundamental Freedoms," CETS No. 213, Explanatory Report, § 9, http://www.echr.coe.int/Documents/Protocol_15_explanatory_report_ENG.pdf.

[33] European Commission, "Communication on establishing a new Partnership Framework with third countries under the European Agenda on Migration," COM(2016) 385 final, Strasbourg, 7.6.2016.

of the Treaty on European Union) and to "*develop a special relationship with neighboring countries [...] founded on the values of the Union*" (Article 8(1)). In fact, the more the EU relies on cooperation and assurances from third countries, the less it can command respect for absoluteness and universality of human rights standards. After all, outsourcing human rights protection inevitably lowers these standards, and it might eventually lead Europe to turn a blind eye or claim no liability for violations occurring abroad.

In other words, managing irregular migration by relying on simplified and accelerated procedures and cooperation with third countries materializes the risk of lowering human rights standard and formalism and literal interpretation and application of the law might allow Europe to shirk its responsibilities while pursuing the final goal of strengthening security.

A number of recent developments in the field of migration support these findings and submissions.

First example: in September 2015, the European Commission proposed the establishment of an EU common list of safe countries of origin which includes Turkey and Balkan countries.[34] Whilst continuing to be assessed on an individual case-by-case basis, applications for international protection lodged by nationals of safe countries would also be fast-tracked for allowing faster returns if refused. The fear is that the safe-country assumption will actually make the assessment of the application too fast and cursory and the need for faster returns will prevail over the effective protection of human rights. In this respect, it is thought-provoking the Action Plan on measures to support Italy in reducing migratory pressure presented by the European Commission on July 2017. The Commission, in fact, urges Italy to develop "*a national list of 'safe countries of origin', prioritising the inclusion of the most common countries-of-origin of migrants arriving in Italy*".[35] With this recommendation the Commission reverses the logic of the list of safe countries: third countries should be included on the list following a thorough and careful assessment of their

---

[34] European Commission, "Proposal for a Regulation of the European Parliament and of the Council establishing an EU common list of safe countries of origin for the purpose of Directive 2013/32, and amending Directive 2013/32/EU," COM(2015) 452 final, Brussels, 9.9.2015.

[35] European Commission, "Action Plan on measures to support Italy, reduce pressure along the Central Mediterranean route and increase solidarity," SEC(2017) 399, Brussels, 4.7.2017, § 2 at 4.

being "*safe*" but in this case the inclusion depends only by the fact that certain countries are the most common countries-of-origin of migrants arriving in Italy. In doing so, however, the true objective of the list becomes to reduce migratory pressure and protect European security at any cost while it should be the other way around, namely to reduce the abuses of the asylum system (clearly unfounded claims, subsequent applications, etc.) after a careful assessment of the human rights situation in foreign countries.

The case of Nigerian nationals is a telling example. In 2016 Nigeria was one of the most common countries-of-origin of migrants arriving in Italy, and the recognition rate of asylum application lodged by its nationals (more than 47,000) was so low (8% in the first three quarters) that the abuse of the asylum system is seemingly clear. At the same time, however, the International Organization for Migration "*estimates that 70% of the Nigerian women and children who arrived in Italy in 2015 and the first five months of 2016 were victims of trafficking*".[36] The difference between these two data exposes a failure in the asylum system notwithstanding Italian authorities would apply ordinary asylum procedures which require careful and thorough examination of the application. If Nigeria were included in the list of safe countries, accelerated and streamlined asylum and inadmissibility procedures would then apply, and the risk of not being able to identify a victim of trafficking would become considerably greater.

Second example: on March 2016 the EU and Turkey issued a joint statement ("*EU-Turkey Statement*") in order to have all irregular migrants crossing from Turkey into Greek islands returned to Turkey.[37] It is quite clear the formalistic approach towards interpretation and application of the Statement. The European Council and the Commission deny any binding value to the Statement because it would be a simple press communique setting only political commitments. Such interpretation of the Statement runs counter to the reality on the ground given that the content of its "*action points, thereby enumerating the commitments to which the parties have consented*", the active involvement of EU

---

[36] GRETA, "Report on Italy under Rule 7 of the Rules of Procedure for evaluating implementation of the Council of Europe Convention on Action against Trafficking on Human Beings," GRETA(2016)29, published on 30 January 2017, § 15. GRETA stands for Group of Experts on Action against Trafficking on Human Beings.

[37] "EU-Turkey Statement," 18 March 2016, Press Release 144/16, accessed November 19, 2017, http://www.consilium.europa.eu/en/press/press-releases/2016/03/18/EU-Turkey-statement/.

Institutions in its implementation and relevant international law suggest that it is an internationally binding agreement.[38] Furthermore, the ECJ dismissed an action for annulment of the Statement on the ground of its lack of jurisdiction. Whilst qualifying the Statement as a binding international "*agreement*", the ECJ held that it "*cannot be regarded as a measure adopted by the European Council*" (or by the EU) but by the EU Member States in their own capacity.[39] The thin and somewhat ambiguous distinction drawn by the ECJ between EU agreement and EU Member States agreement reveals a formalistic approach to the reality that it would have been unthinkable just a few years ago in Europe.

The formalism underpinning the Statement is also demonstrated by the generic and undetailed assurances that returns take place "*in full accordance with EU and international law*" (Turkey for its part, assures the respect of human rights once irregular migrants are returned), that "*all migrants will be protected in accordance with the relevant international standards and in respect of the principle of non-refoulement*", and that "*any application for asylum will be processed individually by the Greek authorities*". This kind of diplomatic assurances (not even binding according to EU Institutions) are much more similar to the formal ones sought by the US Government than to the substantive ones required by the ECtHR in *Tarakhel* decision. It seems equally formalistic the behavior of the Commission insofar as it laconically responds to the criticism of human rights violations[40] by confirming that returns "*are carried out strictly in accordance with the requirements of EU and international law, and in full respect of the principle of non-refoulement*" and that the situation in the Turkish centers "*complies with required standards*".[41] Political and legal ambiguities surrounding the EU-Turkey Statement raise doubts on true objectives of European States and Institutions. The

---

[38] Mauro Gatti, "The EU-Turkey Statement: A Treaty That Violates Democracy (Part 1 of 2)," published on April 18, 2016, accessed November 19, 2017, ejiltalk.org /the-eu-turkey-statement-a-treaty-that-violates-democracy-part-1-of-2/.

[39] ECJ, Order of 28 February 2017, *NF v. European Council, NG v. European Council, NM v. European Council*, Joined Cases T-192/16, T-193/16, T-257/16, par. 71-72.

[40] Council of Europe (Parliamentary Assembly), "The situation of refugees and migrants under the EU-Turkey Agreement of 18 March 2016," Report of the Committee on Migration, Refugees and Displaced Persons, Doc. 140128, April 19, 2016, §§ 3.2-3.3.

[41] European Commission, "Fifth Report on the progress made in the implementation of the EU-Turkey Statement," COM(2017) 204 final, Brussels, 2.3.2017, § 2, at 5.

Statement seems to be a political *escamotage* and a legal shortcut to institutionalizing the US-style scant diplomatic assurances, avoiding a strict application of EU and international law and achieving at any cost the goal of halting irregular migration flows.

4. Conclusion

Differences between US and European approaches to security still exist as well as between the overall legal framework and principles of common law and civil law systems. The gap is, however, narrowing insofar as Europe is increasingly adopting US-style attitudes and policies in dealing with the culture of security and the relationship between politics and law. As a result, a developing process of convergence of European civil law systems towards the US common law system is underway with regard to these particular issues.

All of this is causing a legal identity crisis given that formalism and limited judicial check are far from European legal culture and tradition. Following decades of strong and wide protection of human rights in any situation, States and the European Commission are seeking for a new and different balance between human rights and security. It is almost like States and Commission are nowadays ready to trade some political idealism and legal functionalism in the field of migration and human rights for more political pragmatism and legal formalism in the field of security. Derogations and reform of the ECHR and Schengen systems, the revised and enhanced return policy, the controversial legal nature and paternity of the EU-Turkey Statement and the increasing reliance on cooperation and assurances from third countries are emblematic clues of the European renewed approach to security. Even if Europe has substantially stayed true to a high standard of human rights protection for the time being, the quest for more security through less judicial control and more legal formalism might eventually lead to instability within the European legal cultures and systems.

Should the formalistic approach of governments clash with the functionalist approach of courts in the near future, there would be the risk that the former might not be so willing to settle the dispute with the latter. The first testing ground might be the lawfulness of enhanced cooperation with third countries in the field of migration. European Institutions and governments have been accused of complicity in abuses committed in Libya against migrants:[42] should a European supranational court uphold these charges, how would governments react? Would they respect and implement the ruling as always happened in the past or would they take a critical and challenging stance as Visegrad States did in the *affaire* of mandatory relocation of asylum seekers decided by the ECJ against their interests?[43]

It is too early to draw a conclusion, but courts and governments should agree on a new balance between security and human rights so as to avoid, on the one hand, any kind of institutional conflicts and, on the other, the risk that European governments would sooner or later start following more closely some US policies (hearsay evidence, expedited removal procedures, enhanced interrogation techniques, etc.) which, right or wrong in that legal culture, are however far away from the European one in terms of a *"decent respect to the opinions of mankind"* and to... human rights.

Bibliography

"EU-Turkey Statement," 18 March 2016, Press Release 144/16, accessed November 19, 2017, http://www.consilium.europa.eu/en/press/press-releases/2016/03/18/EU-Turkey-statement/.

"Libya's detention of migrants 'is an outrage to humanity', says UN human rights chief Zeid," November 14, 2017, http://www.un.org/apps/news/story.asp?NewsID=58084.

"Protecting Human Rights in the UK - The Conservative Proposals for Changing Britain's Human Rights Law," London, October 2014, https://www.theguardian.com/politics/interactive/2014/oct/03/conservatives-human-rights-act-full-document

"Protocol No. 15 amending the Convention for the Protection of Human Rights and Fundamental Freedoms," CETS No. 213, Explanatory Report, § 9, http://www.echr.coe.int/Documents/Protocol_15_explanatory_report_ENG.pdf.

Bargiacchi, Paolo."Power, Law and Territory: Extraterritorial Application of the United States Constitution at Landsberg Prison in Occupied Germany, at Guantanamo Bay Naval Base in Cuba and at Bagram Airfield Military Base in Afghanistan," in *International Institutions and Co-operation: Terrorism, Migrations, Asylum*, eds. Giancarlo Guarino and Ilaria D'Anna (Napoli: Satura Editrice, 2011), 495-540.

---

[42] Nikolaj Nielsen, "EU accused of complicity in Libya migrant abuse," *EU Observer*, September 7, 2017, https://euobserver.com/migration/138932.

[43] ECJ (Grand Chamber), Judgment of 6 September 2017, *Slovakia and Hungary v. Council*, Joined Cases C-643/15 and C-647/15.

Council of Europe (Parliamentary Assembly), "The situation of refugees and migrants under the EU-Turkey Agreement of 18 March 2016," Report of the Committee on Migration, Refugees and Displaced Persons, Doc. 140128, April 19, 2016, §§ 3.2-3.3.

Duffy Burnett, Christina and Burke Marshall (eds.), *Foreign in a Domestic Sense: Puerto Rico, American Expansion, and the Constitution* (Durham: Duke University Press, 2001).

ECJ (Grand Chamber), Judgment of 18 July 2013, *European Commission & Council of the EU v. Yassin Abdullah Kadi*, Joined Cases C-584/10 P, C-593/10 P and C-595-10 P, §§ 97-98 and 125.

ECJ (Grand Chamber), Judgment of 6 September 2017, *Slovakia and Hungary v. Council*, Joined Cases C-643/15 and C-647/15. The Visegrad Group is formed by Poland, Hungary, Slovakia and the Czech Republic.

ECJ, Judgment of 21 December 2011, *N.S. v. Secretary of State for the Home & M.E. and Others v. Refugee Applications Commissioner and Others*, Joined Cases C-411/10 and C-493/10.

ECJ, Order of 28 February 2017, *NF v. European Council, NG v. European Council, NM v. European Council*, Joined Cases T-192/16, T-193/16, T-257/16, par. 71-72.

ECtHR (Grand Chamber), Judgment of 15 November 1996, *Chahal v. the United Kingdom*, Application no. 22414/93

ECtHR (Grand Chamber), Judgment of 20 November 2014, *Jaloud v. The Netherlands*, Application no. 47708/08. London High Court, Judgment of 17 March 2015, *Al-Saadoon & Others v. Secretary of State for Defence* [2015] EWHC 715 (Admin), §§ 95 and 106.

ECtHR (Grand Chamber), Judgment of 21 January 2011, *M.S.S. v. Belgium & Greece*, Application no. 30696/09;

ECtHR (Grand Chamber), Judgment of 23 February 2012, *Hirsi Jamaa and Others v. Italy*, Application no. 27765/09, §§ 128 and 136.

ECtHR (Grand Chamber), Judgment of 28 February 2008, *Saadi v. Italy*, Application no. 37201/06.

ECtHR (Grand Chamber), Judgment of 4 November 2014, *Tarakhel v. Switzerland*, Application no. 29217/12, §§ 120 and 122.

ECtHR (Grand Chamber), Judgment of 7 July 2011, *Al-Jedda v. the United Kingdom*, Application no. 27021/08.

ECtHR (Grand Chamber), Judgment of 7 July 2011, *Al-Skeini and Others v. The United Kingdom*, Application no. 55721/07.

ECtHR, Judgment of 17 January 2012, *Othman (Abu Qatada) v. The United Kingdom*, Application no. 8139/09.

ECtHR, Judgment of 21 October 2014, *Sharifi and Others v. Italy & Greece*, Application no. 16643/09;

Ekins, Richard, Jonathan Morgan and Tom Tugendhat.*Clearing the Fog of Law – Saving our armed forces from defeat by judicial diktat.*(London: Policy Exchange, 2015).

European Commission, "Action Plan on measures to support Italy, reduce pressure along the Central Mediterranean route and increase solidarity," SEC(2017) 399, Brussels, 4.7.2017, § 2 at 4.

European Commission, "Communication on establishing a new Partnership Framework with third countries under the European Agenda on Migration," COM(2016) 385 final, Strasbourg, 7.6.2016.

European Commission, "EU Action Plan on return," COM(2015) 453 final, Brussels, 9.9.2015; Id., "Communication on a more effective return policy in the European Union – A Renewed Action Plan," COM(2017) 200 final, Brussels, 2.3.2017.

European Commission, "Fifth Report on the progress made in the implementation of the EU-Turkey Statement," COM(2017) 204 final, Brussels, 2.3.2017, § 2, at 5.

European Commission, "Proposal for a Regulation of the European Parliament and of the Council establishing an EU common list of safe countries of origin for the purpose of Directive 2013/32, and amending Directive 2013/32/EU," COM(2015) 452 final, Brussels, 9.9.2015.

Gatti, Mauro."The EU-Turkey Statement: A Treaty That Violates Democracy (Part 1 of 2)," published on April 18, 2016, accessed November 19, 2017, ejiltalk.org /the-eu-turkey-statement-a-treaty-that-violates-democracy-part-1-of-2/, at 3.

GRETA, "Report on Italy under Rule 7 of the Rules of Procedure for evaluating implementation of the Council of Europe Convention on Action against Trafficking on Human Beings," GRETA(2016)29, published on 30 January 2017, § 15. GRETA stands for Group of Experts on Action against Trafficking on Human Beings.

Kinsella v. Kruger, 351 U.S. 470 (1956).

Memorandum from John Kelly, Secretary of Homeland Security, "Implementing the President's Border Security and Immigration Enforcement Improvements Policies" (memorandum. February 20, 2017).

Nielsen, Nikolaj."EU accused of complicity in Libya migrant abuse," *EU Observer*, September 7, 2017, https://euobserver.com/migration/138932. As of November 19, 2017,

Nikolaj Nielsen, "EU-Turkey deal not binding, says EP legal chief," *EU Observer*, May 10, 2016, https://euobserver.com/justice/133385.

Paolo Bargiacchi, *Orientamenti della dottrina statunitense di diritto internazionale* (Milano: Giuffré Editore, 2011), 262-75.

Philip C. Jessup, *Elihu Root* (New York: Dodd, Mead & Company, 1938), I, 348.

Raustiala,Kal.*Does the Constitution Follow the Flag?* (New York: Oxford University Press, 2009)

Reid v. Covert, 354 U.S. 1 (1957)

Stephan.Paul, "International law as a wedge between the common and civil law," in *The Common Law and the Civil Law Today – Convergence and Divergence*, ed. Marko Novaković (Wilmington: Vernon Press, forthcoming).

The British Court of Appeals, Judgment of 9 April 2008, *AS & DD (Libya) v. Secretary of State for the Home Department and Liberty*, [2008] EWCA Civ. 289.

The Executive Order 13767 issued by President Donald Trump on January 25, 2017

U.S. Court of Appeals, *Al Maqaleh v. Gates*, 605 F.3d 84 (D.C. Cir. 2010), 107.

U.S. Court of Appeals, *Al Maqaleh v. Hagel*, 738 F.3d 312 (D.C. Cir. 2013), 349-350.

U.S. Court of Appeals, *U.S. v. Aluminium Co. of America*, 148 F.2d 416 (2nd Cir. 1945))

U.S. Court of Appeals, *U.S. v. Peralta-Sanchez*, 868 F.3d 852 (9th Cir. 2017).

U.S. Court of Appeals, *U.S. v. Peralta-Sanchez*, 868 F.3d 852 (9th Cir. 2017).

U.S. Department of Defense, "Detainee Transfers Announced," Press Release No: NR-438-15, November 15, 2015, accessed November 19, 2017, http://www.defense.gov/News/News-Releases/News-Release-View/Article/628980/detainee-transfers-announced.

U.S. Department of Justice, "White Paper. Lawfulness of a Lethal Operation Directed Against a U.S. Citizen Who Is a Senior Operational Leader of Al-Qa'ida or an Associated Force," no date, document leaked in February 2013, accessed November 19, 2017, http://msnbcmedia.msn.com/i/msnbc/sections/news/020413_DOJ_White_Paper.pdf.

U.S. District Court for the District of Columbia, *Nasser Al-Aulaqi et al. v. Leon C. Panetta et al.*, 35 F.Supp.3d 56 (2014), 34 and 36. See also U.S. Court of Appeals, *Vance v. Rumsfeld*, 701 F.3d 193 (7th Cir. 2012) (en banc), U.S. Supreme Court, *Johnson, Secretary of Defense, et al. v. Eisentrager, alias Ehrhardt, et al.*, 339 U.S. 763 (1950),

U.S. Office of the Attorney General, "Letter to the Chairman of the Committee on the Judiciary of the United States Senate," May 22, 2013, https://www.justice.gov/slideshow/AG-letter-5-22-13.pdf.

U.S. Supreme Court in *Mathews v. Eldridge*, 424 U.S. 219 (1976).

U.S. Supreme Court, *Cherokee Nation v. Georgia*, 30 U.S. 1 (1831), 16-18.

U.S. Supreme Court, *Downes v. Bidwell*, 182 U.S. 244 (1901), 341-342.

U.S. Supreme Court, *Johnson, Secretary of Defense, et al. v. Eisentrager, alias Ehrhardt, et al.*, 339 U.S. 763 (1950), 778-779.

U.S. Supreme Court, *Lakdhar Boumediene, et al. v. George W. Bush, et al.*, 553 U.S. 723 (2008), 757.

U.S. Supreme Court, *Sale v. Haitian Centers Council, Inc.*, 509 U.S. 155 (1993), 183. accessed November 19, 2017, http://www.fedcourt.gov.au/digital-law-library/judges-speeches/justice-north/north-j-20110907.

U.S. Supreme Court, *Youngstown Sheet & Tube Co. v. Sawyer*, 343 U.S. 578 (1952), 587; see also *Hamdi v. Rumsfeld*, 542 U.S. 507 (2004), 536.

UK Court of Appeals , Judgment of 9 September 2016, *Al-Saadoon & Others v. Secretary of State for Defence* [2016] EWCA Civ. 811, § 70.

UNHCR, "Advisory Opinion on the Extraterritorial Application of Non-Refoulement Obligations under the 1951 Convention relating to the Status of Refugees and its 1967 Protocol," Geneva, January 26, 2007, § 43, accessed November 19, 2017, http://www.unhcr.org/4d9486929.pdf.

Vagts, Detlev. "A Turnabout in Extraterritoriality," *American Journal of International Law* 76, no. 3 (July 1982): 591-94.

White House, "Executive Order 13767 of January 25, 2017, Border Security and Immigration Enforcement Improvements," *Federal Register* vol. 82, no. 18, 8793-97.

White House, "Plan for Closing the Guantanamo Bay Detention Facility," February 2016, https://www.defense.gov/Portals/1/Documents/pubs/GTMO_Closure_Plan_0216.pdf,

Part 2
The Role of the Judicial Bodies

Chapter 9

A few thoughts on various legal traditions, forms of civilization and the ICJ

Marko Novaković [1]

The ICJ is a court with a very distinctive position and is considered the most respected international court for a number of reasons. Its status is elevated at the international law stage by including its Statute in the United Nations Charter and making it one of the main UN organs. Even with this very prominent position within the UN system, the fact remains that ICJ has a dreadfully demanding task – to settle disputes between states. It is very important to understand that with every judgment, ICJ is testing the limits of the international community and adherence of the (especially the most powerful) countries to international law.[2] There is no doubt that having representatives of all major legal traditions is not only important but also necessary. Two major legal traditions – the common law and the civil law – are the most prominent ones and without any doubt the most important, but ICJ cannot hesitate to introduce a judge from any legal system that reaches a prominent position in the future – and there are some in the pool already.

1. Introduction

In retrospect, I realize that my work on this Collection of papers started many years ago at the criminal law study group at the Faculty of Law, University of Belgrade. At that time, the debate on the potential changes of

---

[1] Dr. Marko Novaković LL.M. is a Research Fellow at the Institute of International Politics and Economics, Belgrade and lecturer at Diplomatic Academy.

[2] Marko Novaković, "The Relevance Of The International Court Of Justice And International Security", Serbian Political Thought, 2/2018, Vol. 60, 2018.pp. 257-271.

the Criminal procedure code of the Republic of Serbia started and this issue was discussed as well in some extent at the above-mentioned study groups. The process of the "Americanization of the Serbian criminal procedure", as some authors put it, received more than a few critiques. My view[3] on that issue was more focused on the way those novelties are introduced and what are potential gains and possible hazards. This normative reform started me thinking and researching differences, similarities and meeting points of the two biggest and most widespread legal traditions – the common law and the civil law. It is not always possible to take some legal solutions characteristic of one legal tradition to another. This process can include a number of contraindications and many of them are result of the fact that legal traditions are more than just a sum of different norms. Simply put, some common law elements were welcome (and some were present for decades within the Serbian legal system even before 2013), and some were just inadequate or wrongly implemented. The best solution is to investigate and research every potential change on a case-by-case basis.

Unfortunately, as often happens, the whole debate on this issue was reduced to two views: those who were absolutely against introducing common law elements at all and those who blindly supported every common law feature. Siding in any kind of discussion in those absolute, general categories is rarely a good idea, especially for the researcher. It is obvious that the relationship is much more complex and with the idea to investigate these layers of complexity I started this comparative project.

I would like now to consider one interesting aspect of this discrepancy. In the international law and more specifically within the ICJ[4] we can see the dominant and effective role of the common law and the civil law legal traditions on a world stage. Apart from summing up those features I will, a bit unexpectedly considering the title of this book, refer to other legal traditions and their potential place in the ICJ bench.

2. Different legal traditions

The ICJ as the most important international court has a very demanding task to settle disputes between states. This position of the Court is *per se* very difficult, but when states' attitude towards ICJ judgments and

---

[3] Luka Breneselović, Marko, Novaković, "On General Conception of Draft Criminal Procedure Code of the Republic of Serbia", Review of criminology and criminal law, vol.48, Issue 2, pp.191-225, 2010

[4] International Court of Justice

jurisdiction in general is taken into account,[5] the task in front of the ICJ is nothing short of strenuous. This is why the bench has to be composed in such a manner, to leave no doubt in its legitimacy and representation of both "big and small" and "the east and the west".

There are two provisions of the ICJ Statute that are of crucial importance to the composition of the bench. The first rule promulgated is that "(a)t every election, the electors shall bear in mind not only that the persons to be elected should individually possess the qualifications required, but also that in the body as a whole the representation of the main forms of civilization and of the principal legal systems of the world should be assured."[6]

An additional condition regarding the Court composition can be found in article 3, where is stated that "The Court shall consist of fifteen members, no two of whom may be nationals of the same state."[7]

In analyzing these (and other relevant provisions) Shabtai Rosenne noted that it "introduces the political factor into the composition of the court"[8] or in words of Fassbender, article 9 is "rooted in power politics".[9] While nowhere mentioned in the Statute, five permanent members of the Security Council are always represented by the P5 convention. And this raises the first question – what is the nature of this informal obligation, is it helping or diminishing the request that "main forms of civilization and…principal legal systems" are represented? There is no doubt that, considering countries that are P5 members, they will have to find its place at the bench even without P5 convention, in order to maintain the provision from the article 9 of the ICJ Statute.

---

[5] Marko Novakovic, "The Relevance Of The International Court Of Justice And International Security", Serbian Political Thought, 2/2018, Vol. 60, 2018.pp. 257-271.

[6] Article 9, Statute of the International Court of Justice

[7] Article 3, Statute of the International Court of Justice

[8] Rosenne, Shabtai, *The World Court: What it is and how it Works*, Martinus NIjhoff Publishers, 2003: 44.

[9] Bardo Fassbender, "Chapter one. Organization of the Court: Article 9" in, *The statute of the International Court of Justice: A Commentary*, Ed. A. Zimmerman at al., Oxford, Oxford University Press, 2006, 316.

These two phrases were used in 1920 to solve the problem of how the principle of equality of the states could be reconciled with the wish of the "Great powers" to be always represented on the Court.[10]

Is there any use of these provisions today or was their purpose fulfilled in 1920 with the fulfillment of the wish of the "Great powers"? Can these phrases, especial the one referring to the "main forms of civilization", solve some contemporary issues? And should ICJ use it for?

Introducing the new developments through the concept of the "main forms of civilization" might be used to make the place on the bench accessible for the people representing those "civilizations forms" that emerged at the international level since 1945.

3. Other legal traditions

There is no disputing that the common law and the civil law are the two most influential and the most widespread legal traditions. Consequently, they have the most prominent place in the ICJ.

According to the adopted practice of the ICJ, Western European and Others Group has 5 seats, Africa 3 seats, Asia 3 seats, Latin American and Caribbean Regional Group 2, Eastern Europe 2. When we deduct P5[11] judges, Western Countries are left with 2 seats, as well as Asia. If we add Japan and Germany to that, we have 1 seat left for the non-P5 Western European and Others Group member and one non-P5 Asian seat.[12] This simple calculus demonstrates that almost half of the bench is coming from the countries that are known upfront and remaining 8 are divided among the rest of the World.

However, this does not mean that representation of the legal traditions other than the common law and the civil law should not be considered. The Sharia law is certainly among those that should be considered, but there is another developing tradition that has more certain future in the sense of development and potential influence. India has been developing in various aspects in the last decades, including its legal system. Some

---

[10] Bardo Fassbender, The Representation of the "Main Forms of Civilization" and of "the Principal Legal Systems of the World" in the International Court of Justice, Chapter 26 in Unité et diversité du droit international/Unity and Diversity of International Law, ed. Dennis Alland et al, Brill, 2014, 582

[11] Group of 5 countries that permanent members of the Security Council (USA, UK, France, Russia and China)

[12] Ibid.

A few thoughts on various legal traditions 169

future, Indian version of the common law – if it reaches an adequate level of specialty (for example through social justice paradigm development) might fall into category "principal legal system" and certainly it already is "the main form of civilization". Alongside its growing influence in the international arena it certainly might be next state that will continuously have a judge on the bench.

3.1 Current composition and education vs. legal system of the country of origin

Current Judges of the ICJ (at the beginning of 2019) are President Abdulqawi Ahmed Yusuf, **Somalia**, Vice-President Xue Hanqin, **China**, Judge Peter Tomka, **Slovakia**, Judge Ronny Abraham, **France**, Judge Mohamed Bennouna, **Morocco,** Judge Antônio Augusto Cançado Trindade, **Brazil**, Judge Joan E. Donoghue, **United States of America**, Judge Giorgio Gaja, **Italy**, Judge Julia Sebutinde, **Uganda**, Judge Dalveer Bhandari, **India**, Judge Patrick Lipton Robinson, **Jamaica**, Judge James Richard Crawford, **Australia**, Judge Kirill Gevorgian, **Russian Federation**, Judge Nawaf Salam, **Lebanon**, Judge Yuji Iwasawa, **Japan.**

One can easily divide judges, according to their country of origin, in common law or in civil law. However, it is hardly ever so simple. A good example of this claim is the case of President of the court, Abdulqawi Ahmed Yusuf. He comes from Somalia, a county that has influences of the Common Law system, of the (Italian) civil law, Sharia law and Somali customary law. And that is only to start with. He was educated in Florence and Graduate Institute of International Studies in Geneva. So, it is hardly a clear picture, although there is some civil law predominance. However, using and representing other traditions is an added value that must be always on the mind of the judges coming from such a diverse legal background.

Instead of conclusion – is the women's involvement in the ICJ a form of civilization?

Although the topic of this article and the book in general are legal traditions, one cannot neglect quite an unfortunate tradition of other kind that has been established over the decades within the ICJ. In the current composition of the Court, women are represented through the three judges (Xue Hanquin, Julia Sebutine and Joan E. Donaghue). The saddest thing in this calculus is the fact that having 3 out of 15 judges being a woman (20%) is by far the biggest number ever and it actually does not provide the real picture. From its foundation, ICJ allocated only 3% of its slots to the women (The percentage was calculated by dividing the total number of women judges each year by the total number of male and female judges per year).[13] The first woman became an ICJ judge in 1995, and since then there were three more – the same three women currently in the bench. This situation is justified by the fact that women make up a much smaller percentage of the available pool of candidates than men. Grossman has rightfully rebutted this argument.[14] Very similar arguments are used to answer the question why there are so few female high UN officials (not the mention the Secretary-General position).[15] There is no doubt that it is time to enable a much more important role for women in the ICJ and other international courts and tribunals – putting this issue as one of the prime goals is *condition sine qua non* of the development of the ICJ. After all, is not the emancipation of the women also a form of civilization?

Bibliography

Breneselovic, Luka, Novakovic, Marko, "On General Conception of Draft Criminal Procedure Code of the Republic of Serbia"x Review of criminology and criminal law, vol.48, Issue 2, pp.191-225, 2010

Fassbender, Bardo "Chapter one. Organization of the Court: Article 9" in, *The statute of the International Court of Justice: A Commentary*, Ed. A. Zimmerman at al., Oxford, Oxford University Press, 2006.

Fassbender, Bardo, The Representation of the "Main Forms of Civilization" and of "the Principal Legal Systems of the World" in the International Court of Justice, Chapter 26 in Unité et diversité du droit international/Unity and Diversity of International Law, ed. Dennis Alland et al, Brill, 2014.

Grossman, Nienke, Shattering the Glass Ceiling in International Adjudication (September 7, 2015). Virginia Journal of International Law Vol. 56.2 2016, Forthcoming; University of Baltimore School of Law Legal Studies Research, 23.

Mackanzie Ruth et al, *Selecting International Judges, principles, process and politics,* Oxford, Oxford University Press, 2010.

Novaković, Marko, "Some remarks regarding the procedure of the appointment of the secretary general of the United Nations.", Anali Pravnog fakulteta u Beogradu 64, 2016.

---

[13] Grossman, Nienke, "Shattering the Glass Ceiling in International Adjudication" (September 7, 2015). Virginia Journal of International Law Vol. 56.2 2016, Forthcoming; University of Baltimore School of Law Legal Studies Research, 23.

[14] Ibid.

[15] Novaković, Marko, "Some remarks regarding the procedure of the appointment of the secretary general of the United Nations", Anali Pravnog fakulteta u Beogradu 64, Belgrade 2016

Novaković, Marko, "The Relevance Of The International Court Of Justice And International Security", Serbian Political Thought, 2/2018, Vol. 60, 2018

Shabtai, Rosenne, *The World Court: What it is and how it Works,* Martinus NIjhoff Publishers, 2003.

Statute of the International Court of Justice

Chapter 10

Anglophone and Civilian Legal Cultures: Global Governance by Corporation and State

Joseph P Garske[1]

Abstract

This paper sets forth a way to understand, how technology has enabled Anglophone legality to employ both the structure of the state and the structure of the corporation in its project of globalization. The paper does so by comparing the origins, development, and fundamental differences between the two Western legal traditions, Civil and Common. It describes Civil law as a philosophical system, and Common law as a collegial system: the scholar central to the former, the judge central to the latter. This comparative approach is used to explain how the Civilian method is assimilated to the state, and how its Anglophone counterpart holds an elevated position of equal and independent judicial predominance over both state and corporation. It shows how, compared to the principled predictability of the Continental method, the pragmatic adaptability of the English method is an advantage in constructing a global regimen. This paper concludes by discussing how technical advance has made possible the two halves of a legal culture - adjudicative and educative - to produce a global Rule of Law.

1. Medieval Laws

Both the Anglophone and Civilian traditions of law were born nearly a thousand years ago, during the medieval period. They arose out of convulsive changes taking place across Latin Christendom during the

---

[1] Chairman of "The Global Conversation", Harvard (B.A.).

eleventh century. In fact, however, their origins were very different, and the two traditions remained apart, often regarding one another with hostility and derision. To a remarkable extent, their simultaneous beginnings, their parallel development into the modern age, and their very different conceptions of law, can explain their divergent roles in the project of globalization today.[2]

Historians mark the origin of Continental law with the founding of the University at Bologna, Italy in 1088. At that time, the university was a new type of institution, a place for academic study of the ancient Roman Code. Eventually, the European university would also become a location for the study of all the ancient arts and sciences, the heritage of culture and learning in the West.[3] Thus, over centuries the legal methods of Europe became assimilated to the underlying tradition of values and ideals that prevailed among the educated public, and that descended down through the population generally. The scholar of the university was the center and source of legal development.

By contrast, historians usually mark the beginning of an Anglophone legal tradition with the Norman Conquest of England in 1066. This violent episode would be the single greatest turning point in English history. Thousands, perhaps tens of thousands of innocent victims were killed, whole regions depopulated, the land distributed among the Norman invaders. From that time forward, during the next two centuries, England would be ruled mostly by absentee kings. They wielded their authority over their vassal domain, primarily through the Royal Courts of Justice, located in London.[4]

Originally, those courts were presided over by jurists trained at the University of Bologna. They, in turn, were assisted in mundane aspects of their work by a retinue of functionaries - scribes, messengers, recorders, servants - who in the practice of the time, organized themselves into guilds of trade. However, within a century after the Conquest, in dispute with King Henry II, the learned justices were expelled, and the guild

---

[2] Manlio Bellomo, *The Common Legal Past of Europe: 1000-1800* (Washington, DC: Catholic University of America Press, 1995), p. 112.

[3] Charles M. Radding, *The Origins of Medieval Jurisprudence* (Yale University Press, 1988), p. 37; Randall Lesaffer, *European Legal History* (Cambridge University Press, 2010).

[4] John Hudson, *The Formation of the English Common Law* (London: Longman, 1996), p. 18.

members were granted a monopoly on administering the courts among themselves.

The English court lawyers, like all men joined in fellowships of trade, protected their exclusive privilege through particular forms of knowledge and technique, which were held closely among themselves. There came to be universities in England, at Oxford and Cambridge, but the internal learning of the law guilds had no necessary connection with what was studied at the university, nor with the values of the public generally. The judicial doctors of Bologna were considered unwelcome competitors and their Romanist teachings anathema. From the medieval period forward, the English tradition remained irreconcilably separated from its European counterpart. The judge, as royal arbiter and oracle of law, became the center and source of all legal development.[5]

2. Legal Methods

This arrangement with the central courts in London worked well because they operated at no expense to the king. The guildsmen were self-supporting, collecting fees and gratuities they exacted from their clients. At the same time, a constant flow of bails and fines were supplied to the Royal Treasury. Originally, the main purpose of the guildsmen was to litigate matters of dispute between noble landholders. Land was important because it was the primary form of wealth and the main source of revenue for the Crown. Thus, from the beginning, the work of the guildsmen joined their knowledge of law with the power of material wealth in the work of the dispensing royal justice.[6]

There were at least three aspects of the Anglophone approach to law that separated it from its Civilian counterpart. At its inception, and continuing to its most modern form, those aspects would remain basic to its nature: First, it was a collegial method of law, anchored in the fellowship of its members and in the punitive authority wielded by its judges. Because its approach was fraternal and pragmatic, maintaining unity among its members was necessarily the overriding premise of its work. Moreover, unlike the Civil law, which came to be taught at many universities and applied in numerous languages, the cohesion of Anglophone law required that all its members speak English.

---

[5] Harry Potter, Law Liberty, and the Constitution: A brief history of Common Law (Woodbridge: Boydell Press, 2015), p. 46.

[6] F.W. Maitland, *State, Trust, and Corporation* (Cambridge University Press, 2003), p. 17.

A second important trait of the Common law was its essential purpose as a medieval fellowship of trade.[7] Unsurprisingly, in the pattern of the time, that purpose was the enrichment of its members. Every type of guild provided either a product or a service; in the case of the law guilds, they provided law court proceedings. Like other guilds, from their inception, the fraternities of law worked to ensure the perpetuation of their trade and the exclusion of unwanted competition. Also, by maintaining a stern internal discipline they were able to protect their collective sources of influence and revenue.

A third characteristic of the Common law was its independence as a fellowship, both in relations with the Church and with other councils and orders of the King and his nobles. Because Norman England was originally ruled mostly by absentee monarchs, the Royal Courts quite naturally came to function without close oversight. Even though the guildsmen imposed the law of the realm, their collective purpose was not precisely identical with the purposes of the King. Instead, they worked to profit from transacting the procedures of law. This and several other aspects of the guild fellowship--its closed assemblages, opaque knowledge, and collectively, the astonishing wealth of its membership—insured its independence.[8]

As the two rival traditions of law, Civilian and Anglophone, developed in different ways, each method had particular advantages over the other. Civil law could offer the virtue of being both understandable and predictable in matters of litigation. The work of the Civilians rested on well-understood principles of rationality and clarity, and they followed the law laid down by enacted statute. On the other hand, the Common lawyers, because of their self-directed independence, had the advantage of adaptability in any situation. Moreover, as a source of legal innovation they had an advantage as well: just as the independent scholar was the guiding hand of a developing Civil law, each independent judge shaped the advancing features of Common law. Beyond even that, the judge, unlike the scholar, had the power to enforce both his opinions and his innovations.[9]

---

[7] J. H. Baker, *An Introduction to English Legal History* (London: Butterworths, 1971), p. 23.

[8] Michael Tigar, *Law and the Rise of Capitalism* (New York: Monthly Review Press, 1977), p. 187.

[9] Arthur R. Hogue, *Origins of the Common Law* (Indianapolis: Liberty Fund: 1986), p. 200.

3. Legal Cultures

To understand the role of Anglophone and Civilian legal cultures in the project of globalization today, it is useful to return to the second phase of their parallel development, during the sixteenth and seventeenth centuries. Beginning in that period, several elements converged that would have a decisive impact on how medieval legal practices eventually took on their modern form. In many ways, those events provide an excellent way to understand the legal basis of global governance being constructed in the present day.[10]

When looking back to that period, it is important to remember that every regimen of law is comprised of two essential parts: an adjudicative aspect, and an educative aspect. In the short term, a mode of rule might impose order by sheer force, *in terrorim*. But, over time, establishing an atmosphere of stability and continuity, requires the public to understand legal authority in terms of the benefits it confers; the public must also be taught a habit of compliance. Combining the methods for bringing order to human life and shape to human thought forms the basis of a legal culture.[11]

The modern version of both Western legal regimes began almost five hundred years ago. The change occurred during an age shaped by a dramatic technological revolution taking place across all of Latin Christendom. That signal event was precipitated by three great inventions: the maritime compass, gunpowder weapons, and the printing press.[12] Each of these three innovations had a dramatic effect: The improved compass brought an increase in sea trade and enormous wealth, the new weaponry brought mass armies and catastrophic warfare, while the mechanical production of books brought a proliferation of knowledge and learning.

Moreover, the impact of the new inventions also coincided with the rise of a powerful merchant class. Suddenly medieval institutions, long established, were thrown into a protracted period of conflict and decline.[13] The formerly unified legal culture of Latin Christendom was shattered by

---

[10] Jurgen Habermas, *The Divided West* (Cambridge: Polity Press, 2008), p. 115.

[11] Habermas, *Communication and the Evolution of Society* (Boston: Beacon Press, 1976), p. 178.

[12] Thomas J. Misa, *Leonardo to the Internet: Technology and Culture* (Baltimore: Johns Hopkins University Press, 2011), p. 20.

[13] Philip S. Gorski, *The Disciplinary Revolution* (University of Chicago Press, 2003), p. 26.

internecine wars, with the Continent finally breaking up into hostile enclaves. England, geographically detached and with a tradition of centralized monarchy different from its Continental neighbors, began to grow more insular in its religious as well as its legal composition. A fundamental gulf continued to enlarge between Europe and England as emphatic as the ocean channel that separated them. In fact, the way in which the two legal methods began to further diverge at that time had a great deal to do with the new technology of print.[14]

It was not only important that books of law could now be produced in quantity and with exact uniformity. Equally important, with the innovation of moveable type, those books could be published in multiple European languages, just by changing the order of the characters. A legal treatise no longer needed to be published only in the universal language of Latin. Instead, it could be published in one of the many European vernaculars. With the new techniques, regional jurisdictions began to arise with their own books published, for example, in French, German, Italian - and English. The beginning of the breakup of Christendom into nation-states had begun.[15]

During the convulsive sixteenth and seventeenth centuries a merchant class - already highly evolved on the Continent - began to develop in England as well, and the fellowship of the Royal Courts began to litigate issues of both landed and monetary wealth. Moreover, as their legal acumen converged with the new financial interests, the jurisdiction of the guildsmen began to enlarge. Their authority eventually came to predominate in all the courts of England, including the criminal courts, the High Court of Parliament and, finally, within the Monarchy itself. Ultimately, the Common law became an integral part of the English unwritten constitution.

Out of this convulsive period there also arose new approaches to governance and new methods of legality. Some of the old forms of rule - the kingdom, parliament, court, nation, estate, and profession - would survive, but usually in an altered version. Equally important, the two Western traditions of law began to take on their modern forms. The Common lawyers continued as an independent fraternity in their guilds of trade but were now assimilated to the monarchy itself. At the same time, beginning in the seventeenth century, Civil advocates on the Continent,

---

[14] Eric Nelson, *The Hebrew Republic* (Harvard University Press, 2010), p. 23.

[15] Lesaffer, *op.cit.*, p. 307.

began to wield their authority through the structure of the newly founded nation-state. These two very different placings of the law, one distinct from, and one assimilated to the state, would have profound implications—even into the global age.[16]

4. Two Foundations

Actually, it had been Romanist scholars on the Continent who had made dramatic advances in the workings of the law, especially during the time when new forms of government and commerce were being attempted. Yet, often their novel concepts and innovations were easily adopted by the pragmatic English lawyers as well.[17] There were no better examples of this opportune borrowing than two seventeenth-century innovations, the nation-state and the corporation. Although these legal entities had been both originated by Civil law scholars, eventually, both would also become widely established within the English-speaking realm.

During the seventeenth century legal revolution taking place both in England and on the Continent, the search for new instruments of rule by law broadened. Most frequently this concerned methods for ordering relations of property and persons, both matters urgently important to those who governed. At the time, quite naturally, there was a reliance on old forms that were familiar and had, by experience, proven to be reliable. There was also a proliferation of scholarship, in an attempt to adapt two inherited legal traditions - the Roman Codes (following on the *Jus Commune*) and the Merchant Law (the *Lex Mercatoria*) - to fit the new circumstance. Out of this search were developed new techniques by which sovereign power could be exercised, controlled, delegated, and extended.[18]

At the time, in both England and on the Continent, these emergent forms of administering and enforcing were not always clearly defined. Especially, for example, the difference between what in modern times would become a state, an estate, a corporation, a commonwealth, or a company, were not precisely distinguished from one another. In fact, in different contexts, each term might have a different meaning, while, in other situations, certain of these terms could be used almost interchangeably. These confusions were

---

[16] Habermas, *Europe, the Faltering Project* (Cambridge: Polity Press, 2009), pp. 38-39.

[17] Peter Stein, *Roman Law in European History* (Cambridge University Press, 2004), p. 97.

[18] A. Clair Cutler, *Private Power and Global Authority* (Cambridge University Press, 2003), p. 108.

even more pronounced in English practice because its jurisprudence was by nature both inexplicit and opaque.

In the Anglophone realm, this lack of distinction can be seen in two well-known examples: one concerns the manner by which England was ruled from 1653 to 1659, under a form of government called The Commonwealth.[19] It was a harsh militaristic and theocratic rule, but it had many of the standard features of a modern state. It held unquestioned authority over the land and people within its borders. It had a judiciary and a parliament, a means of taxation, as well as an army to fight wars and to quell domestic rebellion.

But in an era when the term sovereignty often meant virtual ownership, the Commonwealth also had many properties typical of the modern corporation. Its circle of regents, including the Lord Protector, Oliver Cromwell, acted very much like the officers and proprietors of an enterprise for amassing property and wealth. Under The Commonwealth, tens of thousands of small freehold farmers were driven from their lands and villages - holdings that, by right of tenure, had often been in the same family for generations. Whole regions were impounded, their chapels, markets, and dwellings leveled, as the arable land was divided among members of the newly emergent ruling caste.

In the process, the mechanisms of this state structure produced the material benefits of a modern business conglomerate, and all was accomplished with scrupulous attention to the requirements of a newly propounded law. An enormous population of destitute and disenfranchised people were expelled from the countryside, reduced to abject poverty, and forced to live in the hovels and tenements of the city. Great landed estates were assembled out of what had once been many separate farmsteads. Over decades, the effects of these expulsions amounted to one of the great transfers of wealth and property in both English and Irish history.

In contrast to government under The Commonwealth, the British East India Company, founded in 1600, was expected to operate very much like a modern multi-national corporation. It was the creature of its stockholders and was intended to exploit the servile labor and seemingly inexhaustible resources of distant regions, especially India. In fact, for more than two centuries, the East India Company became the conduit by which wealth was extracted from the Indian sub-continent. What had been an empire of ancient and fabulous opulence became a war-ravaged

---

[19] Cynthia B. Herrup, *The Common Peace* (Cambridge University Press, 1989), p. 75.

territory overrun by an impoverished and subjugated population. One reason for these effects was that the East India Company also had many of the characteristics of a modern totalitarian state.[20]

It held absolute and unquestioned authority over the land and peoples of India. Under its appointed officials, it had its own law courts, its own municipal bodies, as well as offices of tax and tariff. It had a military force to resist invasion from outside and to suppress rebellion from within. One of the most astonishingly successful commercial endeavors of all time, it was said to have provided the initial capital by which the Industrial Revolution was launched in England. But it was also, until its dissolution in 1857, a remarkable example of governance wielded through a corporate entity, established for the purpose of stockholder enrichment. The experience of the East India Company would also provide lessons applicable to strategies of global governance, during the twenty-first century.[21]

5. Modern Progress

Two legally defined structures, the state and the corporation - both methods for ordering property and persons - would become central institutions in the progress of Western legal development. The Treaty of Westphalia in 1648 marked the symbolic establishment of the nation-state as the sovereign means, by which populations and territories would be governed on the Continent.[22] At the same time, legal scholars at various universities continued to develop the instrument of the corporation. As a subordinate institution intended for purposes of large-scale finance and trade, it was especially suitable for the modern enterprise, conducted on a broad territorial or maritime basis.

The importance of both legal structures was multiplied, however, by a second wave of technical advance that began early in the nineteenth century, especially innovations that had to do with traversing distance. These included the steamship, railroad, and electronic telegraph. Although the new inventions would not have profound effects equal to those of the fifteenth century, they were even more important in one other

---

[20] R.W. Kostal, *A Jurisprudence of Power* (Oxford University Press, 2005), p. 205.

[21] Philip J. Stern, *The Company-State: Corporate Foundations of The British Empire* (Oxford University Press, 2011).

[22] John Micklethwait, *The Company: A short history of a revolutionary idea*, (New York: Modern Library, 2003), p. 159.

respect: They would make it possible to extend Western methods of governing, of finance and trade, around the entire world.

Their most tangible effect was to introduce an era of imperial conquest and competition among the Western powers, an unfriendly contest that resulted in the rise of several modern empires. With the new machines it had become possible to not only conquer at a great distance but also to dominate and control. By the end of the nineteenth century, virtually every remaining unclaimed territory on every distant continent had been annexed and colonized, or at least brought to subjection. In this period of imperial aggrandizement and rivalry, Western methods would be imposed on nearly all regions of the earth. Without the new inventions of that period, such an expansion of influence could not have occurred.[23]

But the inventions had another result as well: they led to a strengthening and consolidation of the already existing nation-states. With rail and telegraph, national polities were able to connect distant cities and localities. With steam power and transportation they could promote industrial growth. With new mobility and armaments and increased military power they could defend their borders.[24] Perhaps, most of all, by these means of travel and communication, they could centralize governing authority as well. Nonetheless, as dramatic as the impact of the new inventions was, on both the empire and on the nation-state, the nineteenth century would be merely a prologue.

The twentieth century became a period of even more rapid technical development, rising to an entirely new level, introducing the automobile, airplane, telephone, and mechanized weaponry. More than that, for the nation-state, especially important were new modes of mass communication: radio and cinema. These electronic methods of broadcast and dissemination, employed in separate languages, made it possible to create a single atmosphere of awareness and understanding within each nation. To an extent never before possible, during the nineteen thirties, entire populations could be united and mobilized for purposes of production and warfare.

---

[23] Raymond Vernon, *Consequences of Multinational Enterprises* (Harvard University Press, 1972), p. 143.

[24] Misa, *op.cit.*

6. States of Crisis

During the early twentieth century, the nation-state reached the height of its development and, in its various forms, had come to include within its iterations nearly the entire habitable surface of the earth. It was precise in its dimensions, defined by recognized borders, and entitled to defend itself according to codified rules of war. It was sovereign in its domestic policies, wielding exclusive authority over its people and resources. Each state was recognized as a member of the family of nations, able to enter into relations with any one of its counterparts as an equal polity.[25]

One reason for the successful proliferation of the nation-state, as a form of governance, had been that the stage of technological advancement was well adapted to its limited territorial dimension. During the twentieth century, the state had been grounded in well-tested doctrines and practice, but it also fitted the level of technology prevailing at that time. This included not only the means of transport and trade, but also the printed book and journal in the national language, and, of new importance, radio and cinema—with their astonishing ability to shape public awareness.[26] Combined together, they were able to create a total environment of public understanding and national purpose, within a region of common language and custom.

In fact, by mid-century this ability to unify national populations for purposes of production and warfare had brought catastrophic consequences. Because of this, a new international movement would take shape, to restrain the individual state as a locus of power, and bring it under the authority of an international legal framework. Such a plan was inevitably fraught with complication and hazard, and not only because of deeply rooted animosities between states. There was also lacking an overarching authority, with the power to actually enforce programs of deliberation and cooperation in world affairs.[27]

However, even more fundamental difficulties with the mechanism of the state began to emerge in the late twentieth century, especially with the advent of television and the computer networks. It is difficult to exaggerate

---

[25] Barry Buzan, *From International to World Society* (Cambridge University Press, 2006), p. 214.

[26] Niklas Luhmann, *The Reality of the Mass Media* (Stanford University Press, 2000), p. 25.

[27] John Jackson, World Trade Organization Constitution and Jurisprudence (London: Chatham House, 1998), p. 36.

the impact of these two innovations at both the national and international level. Sound and image could be broadcast across borders and around the world, penetrating the family domicile at any location on earth. Computerized information of any quantity on any topic could be transmitted from any one location to any other location, at any time by any person. Suddenly, capital could be organized, labor assembled, and resources marshaled, without regard to distance or topography.[28]

For the state, these new developments marked a dramatic challenge not only to its functioning as a territorial authority and to its foundation of national law, but also to its self-sufficiency as a productive entity. Among the first problems to be confronted, was the effective negation of its borders, its protection against unregulated communication and trade. The former conception of the border as an absolute and defined barrier, separating not only territories but also legal jurisdictions, was becoming untenable. Overseeing the affairs of its own citizens had been rather easy, because both they and their property generally existed within the region marked by national boundaries. Matters were less simple with those entities whose primary assets and ownership lay outside territorial limits, and beyond the reach of authority.

But the impact of these technical innovations proved, once again, to be simply a prelude to what would come. The approach of the twenty-first century marked not only the advent of a new millennium but also the onset of a new age. It was termed the age of technology, of information, and of globalization. It was sometimes referred to as the postmodern age to distinguish it from the period of modernity that preceded it. In fact, because of remarkable advances in technology - and the way it was employed - many conventional forms of governance and rule were coming to be reconsidered and displaced. In particular, the nation-state seemed to be undergoing a profound decline and regression.[29]

7. The Corporation Rises

As the new millennium approached, the problems roiling the state were being more than offset by the exhilarating impact the new technologies were having on the corporation. For that legal construct, electronic transmission of sound and image, telephonic communication, information systems, and computerization were unqualified positives. An

---

[28] Thomas Piketty, Capital in the Twenty-First Century (Harvard University Press, 2017), p. 174.

[29] Vernon, *Sovereignty at Bay* (New York: Basic Books, 1971), p. 143.

explosion of networking infrastructure around the world reached into the most remote and inaccessible regions. Worldwide television broadcasting brought enormous commercial opportunity with its combination of entertainment and advertising. The new ability to travel, to transport, and to trade, to reach a world market of entire populations, opened unheard of opportunities for expansion and consolidation.[30]

These technical advances accelerated even more the expansion of decentralized multi-national corporations, strengthening their ability to manage and control. From the perspective of Anglophone governance, certain advantages of the corporation over the state were also becoming obvious. Moreover, the influence of technical applications had begun to blur the old divisions between corporation and state, public and private, economic and political. But for Anglophone legal practice, this posed no special difficulty, because, from its viewpoint, both the state and the corporation were equally subject to oversight by collegial adjudication.[31] Beyond that, for the purpose of giving force to directives of an elevated legal authority, each type of construct had advantages particular to itself.

From the nineteenth century, in the Anglophone realm, the corporation had been a highly favored means of extending legal authority. Compared to the state, it was less bound by statutory obstacles, as well as the impediment of constitutional questions and political meddling. It could be utterly pragmatic in its operations. Corporate proprietors, with their unchecked oversight, generally operated outside of view, not directly accountable to the public. Most of all, the corporate agility in adapting to change was another great key to its usefulness. For purposes of ordering human action and shaping human thought, the advantages of the corporation over the state were numerous.[32]

From this perspective, an entirely new overarching legal regime, anchored less in the state and more in the corporation, was also possible. The supra-territorial corporation was able to extend its operations without geographic limit. At the same time hundreds of territorial states covered the earth, a single modern corporation could cover the same territories - easily transcending state jurisdictions, its extensiveness unimpeded by any national border. This malleable structure was a natural vehicle for

---

[30] Geoffrey Jones, *Multinationals and Global Capitalism* (Oxford University Press, 2005).

[31] Anthony Giddens, *Modernity and Self-Identity* (Stanford University Press, 1991), p. 78.

[32] Micklethwait, *op.cit.*, p. 161.

strategies of Economic Development, Open Markets, Interdependency, and Free Trade. Viewed in a certain way, these terms were very often, in fact, merely inverted ways to explain the process of corporatizing the properties and persons of various countries and continents.[33]

8. Transcendence

But the corporation offered other advantages as well. For example, through that instrument, legal jurisdictions might reach far beyond their own national boundaries. It offered a solution for those situations, in which the authority of one state was prohibited from reaching across its national border into the territory of another state. The corporation could provide, in effect, an extraterritorial reach from one legal regime into the domestic affairs of another.[34] With the new technical abilities, the corporation could provide all the necessary provisions and resources for the feeding and clothing of populations. It might provide a military presence in the form of weapons, strategic advice, and in extreme circumstances, even mercenary soldiers.

In the past, the role of education had fallen to the state. But with the new advances, nothing could equal the various electronic media as instruments for shaping public behavior, norms, and values. The corporation was able to provide an atmosphere for understanding political and world affairs, and information the public needed to acclimate and participate in a worldwide regimen of governance. Unlike the old brick and mortar national school system, with its instilled ideology and its laborious method of rote learning, the new media could create an atmosphere of understanding that was continuous and ubiquitous in its effects and required little effort on the part of the learner.[35] Nothing could match this potential ability to instill habits of acceptance and compliance - a crucial necessity for an established Rule of Law.

From the perspective of English legality, all of these factors served to blur the artificial dichotomy of public and private, political and economic, national and international. A perhaps irresistible challenge to the existing state system of the world had arisen; the corporation was technologically based and fully compliant with requirements of the law, because it was

---

[33] Gabrielle Marceau, ed., *A History of Law and Lawyers in the GATT/WTO* (Cambridge University Press, 2018), p. 60.

[34] Jones, *op.cit.*

[35] Bill Readings, *The University in Ruins* (Harvard University Press, 1997), p. 61.

legal in its composition. In fact, in the case of Anglophone legal practice, the converging elements of technology, state, and corporation allowed a kind of reversion to its primitive, more essential form as a medieval fellowship.[36]

The Common law was based on a guild model that had long pre-existed both state and corporation and had come from a world far removed from modern times. It was formed as an organic fellowship of members, neither an abstract construction nor an articulated system. It was human in its composition, established in a bond between persons. From its collegial perspective, both political and economic institutions could be equally useful beneath the independent supremacy of its judicial hierarchy. Viewed pragmatically, the two structures might be employed to form a transcending legal culture around the globe. All that was needed to bring this enveloping tandem into being was a coercive means of enforcement.

9. The Hegemon

An undisputed Anglophone world predominance first arose during the nineteenth century of the *Pax Britannica*. No nation or group of nations could match the industrial, financial, and naval power of the British Empire. In the twentieth century, following the two great worldwide wars, the groundwork of Anglophone predominance was established once again, but on a different basis; it rested primarily on the Atlantic alliance between Britain and America.[37] In conflicts that had left much of the world in ruin, the combined strength of the English-speaking nations had only been increased. Especially, after the worldwide war of the mid-century, their industrial and military capacities had been virtually untouched, and both were operating at peak efficiency.

Traditionally, the hallmark of Anglophone influence in the affairs of the world had been the Balance of Power. This strategy was especially effective when employed against the Continental states. Europe, after all, was a collection of small and large nations divided by language, culture, and religion. Fomenting hostilities between any two of them was often rather easy. Britain normally sided with the weaker of two protagonists, keeping Europe perpetually on the brink of conflict. In the generation following the second Great War, in fact, the entire world had come to be divided into

---

[36] David Kennedy, *A World of Struggle* (Princeton University Press, 2016), p. 171.

[37] Adam Watson, *The Evolution of International Society* (New York: Routledge, 2009), p. 299.

such a balance - the Cold War, a stalemate of crisis and provocation, between the Soviet Union and the United States.[38]

During this period the Anglophone alliance, united by a common legal heritage, would continue to enlarge its already enormous corporate, media, and military influence. It combined British diplomatic sophistication going back centuries, with almost limitless natural resources, dispersed around the world. The combined financial, commercial, and industrial power, together with its far-reaching system of marketing and management, produced an irresistible force - what in the nineteen seventies was frequently condemned as Anglo-Saxon capitalism.

However, after the collapse of the Soviet Union in the last decade of the twentieth century, there existed, once again, the unusual situation of a single power predominant in world affairs. That great world power was, of course, the United States. But it seldom needed to act entirely alone. Invariably it moved in partnership with its more sophisticated British mentor. Beyond Britain, the U.S. had an inherent kinship with all the other countries and polities that shared in the Common law heritage: especially, Canada, Australia, New Zealand, as well as Singapore, Hong Kong, and Israel. Out of public view these partners asserted a broad underlying legal influence in world affairs. In the aggregate, this influence and its various permutations amounted to the skeletal basis for an alternative system of world order.[39]

The Europeans, of course, had already begun their experiment in building a union of nations within a geographic region of shared history and culture. It was being assembled, quite naturally, on the explicit principles of reason and universalism that typified its Civil law traditions. In this undertaking, the sovereign state was subsumed within the outlines of a unity, having some of the properties of a confederation. The European Union was able to assimilate elements of statehood into a larger collective because the new technical advances made this possible. The project was limited to Europe - with the inclusion of anomalous Britain - but the hope was that it might provide an example for the consolidation of other geographic and cultural regions around the world.[40]

---

[38] Quinn Slobodian, *Globalists: The end of Europe and the birth of Neoliberalism* (Harvard University Press, 2018), p.121.

[39] *Ibid.*, p. 146.

[40] Habermas, *Europe, the Faltering Project* (Cambridge: Polity Press, 2009), p. 47.

From the perspective of Anglophone legality, the European approach, as a prototype of world order, was as much problematic as it was helpful. It was, after all, premised on the state. Moreover, even though this Civilian initiative provided a wide allowance for recognizing and assimilating the many cultures and religions within a region of states, the Anglophone approach could do more. In the vacuum of power left by the collapse of the Soviet Union, the English fellowship might piece together the elements of a seamless world order, on a different basis. Their approach could be carried out in a way that would include all regions around the world in a single regimen, precisely because it was indifferent to any particular cultural, religious, or ethnic composition.[41]

To put in place such a regime, across every nation and people, the initial requirement was a worldwide mechanism of enforcement, wielding coercive power, not only over individuals and institutions but also over the various nation-states. This cumulative force could be asserted benignly, in the form of diplomatic persuasion. Toward more recalcitrant polities, the device of economic reprisal could be employed. Finally, in the most extreme cases, military force was the ultimate means of unquestioned dominance. With the new technologies of warfare, the Anglophone nations could intervene immediately, efficiently, and at any location on earth.

Yet, experience showed that for any regime, including a hegemonic power, the instrument of brute force alone, as a means of rule, was only useful in the short term. Ultimately, for purposes of governance on a global scale, a very substantial legal foundation must be combined with extensive channels of public acculturation and education. This would include ties of material interdependency, contract, treaty, judicial institutions, policing authority, universities, schools, and electronic media. In effect, a wholly functioning, immersive reality, an enveloping frame of global legal culture, that would overlay the system of ordered states. In the Anglophone approach this required one more element: a universal understanding and use of the English language.[42]

10. A Global Language

Among the unique features of the aged Common law tradition, including its collegiality, its esoteric complexity, and its oracular judiciary, one factor

---

[41] Ronald Dworkin, *Law's Empire* (Harvard University Press, 1986), p. 87.

[42] Thomas Pogge, ed., *Global Justice: Seminal Essays, Vol. 1* (St. Paul: Paragon House, 2008), p. 288.

remained constant as the single essential of its operation: all its unique attributes required that its members use the same language. The collegial nature of the English law - its bond of personal familiarity, its attachments of common experience, its loyalties, its disputatious methods of trial, and its hierarchy of judicial obeisance - could operate in no other way.[43]

Since its inception in the eleventh century, its method of legal rule relied on two modes of communication. During its earliest medieval stages, when printed documents and the ability to read were exceptional, its procedures and methods relied almost entirely on the spoken word - beginning with the oath of admission to the guild. The collegial aspect of the tradition was personal in nature, and the spoken word, person to person, face to face, among its fellows, was basic to its nature. But its internal directives were hand inscribed, *forms* and *writs,* and after the onset of printing and the wider use of printed charters and ordinances in the seventeenth century, written expressions of legal authority became more important. Also, at that time, public education in the legal culture came to be more reliant on the printed book - especially the Bible. But as a continuing judicial presence, the guild was, from its inception, anchored in the written or printed text.[44]

The Anglophone approach to global adjudication would not necessarily require establishing a fixed structure, or set of principles - and, especially, not a structure resembling some kind of world state. Instead, in the English pattern of legal rule, governance would consist of an organic panoply of authority. It might include associations, firms, partnerships, initiatives, societies, clubs, associations, and schools.[45] Rather than a clearly defined federation of states, or a clearly defined structure of political administration on the model of the European Union, it would comprise a much less explicit form of cohesiveness. The presiding edifice of legal rule would amount to personal bonds of obligation and opportunity, within a transcendent collegium of practitioners joined by a common language.

The rise of English to the status of a universal language began to occur during the first decades of radio broadcast, especially in the nineteen twenties and thirties. With the victory of the English-speaking peoples following both great wars, the advantage in commerce and

---

[43] David Crystal, *English as a Global Language* (Cambridge University Press, 2012).

[44] Walter Ong, *Orality and Literacy* (New York: Routledge, 2003).

[45] Anne-Marie Slaughter, *A New World Order* (Princeton University Press, 2004), p. 216.

communication made the English language, almost by default, the world language of both finance and trade, even encroaching on the domain of French as the language of diplomacy. But the great leap in the extent of English fluency around the world came with the onset of the technological revolution that was underway in the late twentieth century.

There was only one superpower in the world, America. Its values, appetites, and amusements were broadcast virtually everywhere. Suddenly, a rising generation was immersed in an atmosphere of transmitted sound and image, almost an alternative reality. Along with that, the availability of information by way of computer, followed by the advent of computer networks, was another great step. Because the initiative of technical transformation was so much in the hands of the English-speaking world, especially America, quite naturally, much of this electronic ephemera was broadcast, stored, and transmitted in the English language.[46]

To construct a regimen of legal rule requires that both those who rule and those who are ruled over, understand each other. To a minimal extent, that means they must speak the same language. An Anglophone regimen can only become fully manifest among practitioners who speak English fluently, and among a population that can, at least to a basic level, understand it as well. Although the initial importance of the language had been as the internal basis of a legal practice, it became equally important in the other half of the legal culture - shaping the thought and habits, the appetites and aspirations of the public. The possibility of a global Anglophone legal culture began to emerge when English had become a technologically transmitted global language, on both a professional and a public level.[47]

11. Global Governance

There are many ways to understand the project of globalization as it is being advanced to include all localities and all peoples of the world. But no way of understanding is complete without including the foundation of legality on which it is being constructed. That foundation will include the same basic elements that have been employed for nearly a thousand years: an adjudicative method that brings order to human life, coupled with an educative method that gives shape to human thought. Together, the two elements - coercive and persuasive - will form a global legal

---

[46] Crystal, *op.cit.*

[47] Luhmann, *op.cit.*

culture. Anglophone law, in its efforts to construct its own Rule of Law, approaches the project in a characteristic manner. But with advancing technical abilities, it is able to both extend its authority and shape public understanding in a new way and on a far wider scale than ever before.[48]

Historically, the English language law, both in its domestic application and while enlarging its influence throughout the realm of world affairs, has followed a consistent pattern. That pattern corresponds to three fundamental elements of its makeup. First, the approach is collegial, not structural; it is bound by pledge, and although it employs institutions, it is not, itself, institutional. Second, because its place of rank and privilege is grounded in a combination of knowledge and wealth, its outlook necessarily remains pragmatic in maintaining its basis of material strength. Finally, the English legal method is independent. That is, both the fellowship of practitioners and its hierarchy of jurists act as an elevated and detached presence. In this respect, they follow on the omnicompetent High Court of Parliament; that is, their jurisdiction is potentially without limit, and they recognize no authority superior to themselves.[49]

However, in and of itself, the Anglophone fellowship of law would not be capable of extending its rule on a global scale. To accomplish this great objective, it must rely on other subordinate and subsidiary agencies and institutions. Of primary importance among these is the fixed territorial structure of the state. Its construct is especially useful as a regulatory body and as a basis for civil order among the separate national populations. The other structure of especial importance is the corporation, with its flexible adaptability and veiled autonomy. Together, this tandem of highly developed legal constructs provides mechanisms adaptable to the many requirements of global governance.

Nonetheless, advances on a global scale would not be possible without the remarkable progress of technology. During the sixteenth century, the period of the three great inventions—gunpowder weapons, the maritime compass, and printing press—ingenious tools and devices have made possible unprecedented concentrations of power and wealth. During that early period, these concentrations were manifest in the nation-state on the Continent and Parliamentary rule in England. Later, in the nineteenth century, new innovations - including steamship, railroad, and telegraph - provided the means by which empires could be constructed and

---

[48] Habermas, *op.cit.*, 1976, p. 178.

[49] Stephen Breyer, *The Court and the World* (New York: Knopf, 2015), p. 89.

administered. Among their effects was the rise of great imperial powers, culminating, especially, in the British Empire that once included nearly a quarter of the land surface and population of the earth.[50] Most importantly, by means of these inventions, Western methods of law and government, of finance and trade, were implanted in virtually every part of the habitable world.[51]

However, the Anglophone approach to global governance during the twenty-first century will not precisely replicate the methods of the eleventh century, the sixteenth century, the nineteenth century, or even the twentieth century. This is especially true in the educative, or persuasive, aspect of its rule. The old nation-state was well adapted to the printing press, book, and journal, as a means of shaping the public mind, instilling a fixed structure of belief. But now there are much more highly evolved channels and networks for shaping human consciousness - not by instilled belief but by a continuous flow of information. The ability to construct, in effect, a virtual reality of transmitted sound and image, provides entirely new possibilities for creating an atmosphere of public acceptance and compliance. Moreover, these methods are easily adaptable to all regions and peoples of the earth.

When examining the Anglophone alliance and its globalization project, several impressive achievements become obvious. Not only does it have enormous hegemonic power to advance its method, but it also has pragmatic flexibility to establish a transcendent authority. By its collegial approach, it can adapt to changing circumstance with agility, even absorbing and employing the concepts and methods of its rival, the Civil law. In the process it need only retain two essentials: one is the cohesion of its membership, beneath the authority of its judges around the world; the other is the willing compliance of all those peoples subject to its authority.[52] With advanced technology, it is possible to marshal the many instruments of legal order, including both state and corporation, to advance this collegial purpose. By these varied means, an Anglophone legal culture can be developed, and by these means its global Rule of Law can be established.[53]

---

[50] Stern, *op.cit.*
[51] Marceau, *op.cit.*, p. 275.
[52] Slaughter, *op.cit.*, p. 261.

Bibliography

Baker, J. H. *An Introduction to English Legal History*. London: Butterworths, 1971.

Bellomo, Manlio, translated by Lydia G. Cochrane. *The Common Legal Past of Europe: 1000-1800*. Washington, DC: Catholic University of America Press, 1995.

Breyer, Stephen: *The Court and the World*. New York: Knopf, 2015.

Buzan, Barry: *From International to World Society*. Cambridge: Cambridge University Press, 2006.

Crystal, David. *English as a Global Language*. Cambridge: Cambridge University Press, 2012.

Cutler, A. Claire. *Private Power and Global Authority*. Cambridge: Cambridge University Press, 2003.

Dworkin, Ronald. *Law's Empire*. Cambridge: Harvard University Press, 1986.

Giddens, Anthony. *Modernity and Self-Identity*. Stanford: Stanford University Press, 1991.

Gorski, Philip. *The Disciplinary Revolution*. Chicago: University of Chicago, 2003.

Habermas, Jurgen. *Communication and the Evolution of Society*. Boston: Beacon Press, 1976.

----------. *The Divided West*. Cambridge: Polity Press, 2008.

----------. *Europe, the Faltering Project*. Cambridge: Polity Press, 2009.

Herrup, Cynthia B. *The Common Peace*. Cambridge: Cambridge University Press, 1989.

Hogue, Arthur. *Origins of the Common Law*. Indianapolis: Liberty Fund, 1986.

Hudson, John. *The Formation of the English Common Law*. London: Longman, 1996.

Jackson, John. *World Trade Organization Constitution and Jurisprudence*. London: Chatham House, 1998.

Jones, Geoffrey. *Multinationals and Global Capitalism*. Oxford: Oxford University Press, 2005.

Kennedy, David. *A World of Struggle*. Princeton: Princeton University Press, 2016.

Kostal, R.W. *A Jurisprudence of Power*. Oxford: Oxford University Press, 2005.

Lesaffer, Randall. *European Legal History*. Cambridge: Cambridge University Press, 2010.

Luhmann, Niklas, translated by Kathleen Cross. *The Reality of the Mass Media*. Stanford: Stanford University Press, 2000.

---

[53] Kennedy, *op.cit.*, pp. 1-20.

Maitland, F.W. *State, Trust, and Corporation*. Cambridge: Cambridge University Press, 2003.

Marceau, Gabrielle, ed. *A History of Law and Lawyers in the GATT/WTO*. Cambridge: Cambridge University Press, 2018.

Micklethwait, John. *The Company: A short history of a revolutionary idea*. New York: Modern Library, 2003.

Misa, Thomas J. *Leonardo to the Internet: Technology and Culture*. Baltimore: Johns Hopkins University Press, 2011.

Nelson, Eric. *The Hebrew Republic*. Cambridge: Harvard University Press, 2010.

Ong, Walter. *Orality and Literacy*. New York: Routledge, 2003.

Piketty, Thomas. *Capital in the Twenty-First Century*. Cambridge: Harvard University Press, 2017.

Pogge, Thomas, ed. *Global Justice: Seminal Essays, Vol. 1*. St. Paul: Paragon House, 2008.

Potter, Harry. *Law, Liberty, and the Constitution: A brief history of Common law*. Woodbridge: Boydell Press, 2015.

Radding, Charles. *The Origins of Medieval Jurisprudence*. New Haven: Yale University Press, 1988.

Readings, Bill. *The University in Ruins*. Cambridge: Harvard University Press, 1997.

Slaughter, Anne-Marie. *A New World Order*. Princeton: Princeton University Press, 2004.

Slobodian, Quinn. *Globalists: The end of Europe and the birth of Neoliberalism*. Cambridge: Harvard University Press, 2018.

Stein, Peter. *Roman Law in European History*. Cambridge: Cambridge University Press, 2004.

Stern, Philip J. *The Company-State: Corporate Foundations of the British Empire*. Oxford: Oxford University Press, 2011.

Tigar, Michael. *Law and the Rise of Capitalism*. New York: Monthly Review, 1977.

Vernon, Raymond. *Sovereignty at Bay*. New York: Basic Books, 1971.

----------. *Consequences of Multinational Enterprises*. Cambridge: Harvard University Press, 1972.

Watson, Adam. *The Evolution of International Society*. New York: Routledge, 2002.

Chapter 11

Case-Law Relevance in the European Union Law: The Triumph of reason over Precedent

Letizia Seminara[1]

Abstract

The Court of Justice of the European Union reflects the learnings of both common and civil schools of law. According to Article 19 TEU, the Court "shall ensure that in the interpretation and application of the Treaties the law is observed", but this provision does not give notice on the relevance of precedent in the decision-making process. This paper aims at studying whether case law is relevant in the European Union law, and if so, to what extent it is important in the process of constructing and supporting a judgment within the CJEU, enquiring particularly on the question whether the latter's judgments are law-making decisions. It further sustains that the Court has created, in a kind of dialectical process, a 'synthetical' system of law in which precedent is not constraining, but it is relevant for constructing and upholding a decision. The present paper will thus scrutinize this system of law in which the European judges can be guided by precedent without being compelled by it, because this is not the only pertinent criterion in the decision-making process.

When Andrea Lo Bianco first appeared to the *Beati Paoli* –the famous secret society that, in the 18th century acted "in service of justice, in defence of the weak, against any violence and against the insolence of government, lords and priests"- its members talked to him in the following terms: "If you have *reason*, if you are a poor oppressed person, if you've been offended, confide in us, may be we could be of use. What's your

---

[1] PhD, Sapienza University of Rome and University of Strasbourg

name?".[2] Although it is open to question whether the concept of justice close to the *Beati Paoli* is the ideal of justice as we perceive it today, this story tells us that justice intrinsically contains the idea of 'reason'. Justice is such because it is based on reason and not on arbitrariness. But what is the operation made by a modern judge if his decision is to be based on reason? What are therefore the number of elements which are taken into account to compose a legal reasoning in support of a judicial decision, and what is the relevance of each of the elements considered?

In modern democratized societies (based on the rule of law), the motivations grounding a judgment must follow from what the law is. The legal reasoning is therefore governed by the rule of law. The judge must discern and apply the law to the case presented to him, and the goodness of his judgment will depend on the correctness of that reasoning.

In the common law systems, the rule of law has justified the great relevance conferred to precedent.[3] In fact, the 'doctrine of precedent' is based on the principle that "decided cases which laid down a rule of law are authoritative and must be followed".[4] According to this doctrine, cases alike deserve the same treatment, regardless of any reasoning operation. It has been observed in that regard that in common law systems the court is in the positive obligation to "abide by a precedent just because of its status of precedent, without reasoning at all about the content and value of the precedent itself".[5] In those systems, the decision made would be therefore the product of an assimilation or ordering process, rather than the fruit of a reasoning process; it has to do more with tradition than with reason. Case-law systems (based on the strict respect of precedents) may be characterized, from this point of view, as somewhat opposite to reason: precedent must be followed no matter the reason is.

On the other hand, in a statutory-law system the assumption that the legislation applicable must be applied in the case presented to the judge is based on the (also, dogmatic and, somewhat, unreasonable) assumption that that statute must be applied no matter the reason is. Precedent is peremptory in the case-law systems and legislation is imperative in the

---

[2] Luigi Natoli, *I Beati Paoli* (Palermo: Flaccovio, 1972), 112 ff. Our translation. Italics added.

[3] Jeremy Waldron, "Stare Decisis and the Rule of Law: A Layered Approach", *Mich. L. Rev.* 111 (2012): 1-32.

[4] See, D. H. Laird, "The Doctrine of Stare Decisis", *Can. B. Rev.* XIII, n. 1 (1935): 2.

[5] See, Stefano Civitarese, "A European convergence towards a *stare decisis* model?", *Revista digital de Derecho Administrativo* 14 (2015): 175.

statutory-law systems, as a consequence of the rule of law. Both systems are similar on that point. It has been observed in that regard that while in case-law systems the rule enounced in a case must be applied in all alike successive cases although judges are persuaded that that rule is the fruit of an error, in statutory-law systems a judge will be bound to apply a clear and pertinent statutory provision even if he is personally convinced that it is the result of a moment of collective insanity of the parliament.[6]

The first question to approach the subject of the relevance of case-law in EU law is, therefore, a question that aims to establish what the law to be applied is. In particular, what is the law that the Court of Justice of the European Union must apply in its judicial decisions? This will give us a first clarification on the role of case law in the EU law. Another (more important) question to elucidate whether and to what point case-law is relevant in the European Union law is the manner in which the applicable law is extricated, and it is further applied in the judicial methodology of that Court. The manner in which the judge discern and 'manipulates' the law to apply it to the case at hand is decisive, as it is intimately related to the *reasoning* grounding his decision. This is a crucial question to our study because, as we will attempt to prove, the European judge is much more concerned with the reasoning grounding their decisions than with the sources of law, be this case law or statutory law. In other words, we will inquire about the reasoning methodology that grounds a decision, to identify its elements and the way they are related in this operation. Briefly, we will try to describe how legal reasons are articulated in EU law, taking always in mind that our objective is to know whether and to what point case law is relevant in this legal system.[7]

In Part I, we argue that the European Union law is a statutory-law system, that the rule of *stare decisis* has not been incorporated in that system of law as a principle ruling its legal method and that therefore precedents are not binding for the Court of Justice of the EU. However, we do not exclude the importance of case law in the European judicial

---

[6] For this latter comparison, see Carlo Augusto Cannata and Antonio Gambaro, *Lineamenti di storia della giurisprudenza europea*, 4th ed. (Torino: Giappichelli, 1989), 114-115.

[7] We limit our study to the relevance of 'horizontal' precedent, taking exclusively into consideration the respect that the Court of Justice of the European Union has itself for its previous judgments. The relevance of 'vertical' precedent (thus, both the respect for CJEU's precedents by its inferior tribunals, such as the General Court and the Civil Service Tribunal, and the respect for EU law by domestic Courts), is therefore excluded from the scope of this work.

reasoning. In fact, a certain relevance has been recognized to case law also in those systems of law, and we will show that the European judge and, especially, the General Advocates, use case law in their legal reasoning. In that regard, we reach in Part II, the commonly agreed position of scholars recognizing that case law is to a certain extent relevant in EU law. It has been sometimes maintained in that regard that the importance of case law in EU law is persuasive,[8] but we support a slightly different position, which tends to establish that case law is neither relevant as a constraining precedent nor as persuasive jurisprudence. We argue in part III that case law is relevant in EU law simply as an *element of legal reasoning*.

In fact, we are of the view that the Court of Justice of the European Union rejects the idea of applying precedent without any reasoning operation grounding its decision and with the only motivation of respect for precedent. We will attempt to show that EU law, and its European *Beati Paoli* in the Court of Justice, who are now based on the rule of law as well as on the principle of proportionality, are more concerned with 'reasons' than with 'tradition', two values that not always can be conciliated. This article aims therefore to show that this idea has lead the Judges in Luxembourg to look at case law as one (but not the only) element of the reasoning that inevitably will ground its decision, so that it is neither constraint nor persuasive, but simply an (important) part of the judicial process.

1. EU Law as Statutory Law

According to Article 19 TEU, the Court of Justice of the European Union "shall ensure that in the interpretation and application of the Treaties the law is observed". What this 'law' is in the European Union? A first important answer to the matter will depend in great measure on whether this 'law' is based –or at least predominantly based- on case law (judge-made law) or whether it is mainly the product of a legislative procedure and can be therefore characterized as statutory law.

The problem with answering this question is that, as it has been highlighted by scholars, the Treaties "do not provide any indication of the

---

[8] See the references, mainly citing Barcelò, in Urška Šadl and Ioannis Panagis, "The force of EU case law: An empirical study of precedential constraint", in *Legal Knowledge and Information Systems* 279 (2015): 71-80; Gundega Mikelsone, "The Binding Force of the Case Law of the Court of Justice of the European Union", *Jurisprudencija/Jurisprudence* 20, n. 2 (2013): 488.

sources of law which the Court of Justice should apply".[9] It is, however, a common consolidated understanding that the law that the Court must primarily apply is the European Union law, i.e. the law commonly intended as coming from the EU sources of law.[10] It seems, moreover, that this law excludes the judgments of the CJEU from the formal sources of EU law. This view was explicit in *Internationaler Hilfsfonds v. Commission*, where AG Trstenjak explained this point: "[t]he term 'law' within the meaning of that provision covers all binding written and unwritten rules of Community and Union law. These include, in addition to primary and secondary legislation, general legal principles and custom. However, the sources of Community law do not include the judgments of the Community Courts. Judgments are an expression of the interpretation which the Community Courts give to the law, but they should not be confused with the law itself".[11]

A number of reasons lead us, therefore, to affirm that the European Union law fits much more with a statutory-law system than with a case-law system. Statutory law is usually defined as the "law that is derived from statutes, as opposed to common law, constitutions, custom, etc", being a 'statute' "a written law passed by a legislative body".[12] It is

---

[9] See, Kieran Bradley, "Vertical Precedent at the Court of Justice of the European Union: When Push Comes to Shove", in *Liber Amicorum in Honour of Nial Fennelly*, ed. Kieran Bradley, Noel Travers and Anthony Whelan (Oxford: Hart Publishing, 2014), 50.

[10] For a detailed description of these sources, see Anna Lucia Valvo, *Lineamenti di diritto dell'Unione europea*, 2nd ed., (Padova: Amon, 2017), 177-212; Paolo Bargiacchi, *Diritto dell'Unione europea*, (Rome: Aracne, 2015), 225-274. For the respective literature in English, see Allan Rosas, "The European Court of Justice: Sources of Law and Methods of Interpretation", in *The WTO at ten: the contribution of the dispute settlement system*, ed. Giorgio Sacerdoti, Alan Yanovich and Jan Bohanes (Cambridge: Cambridge University Press), 482-489. Naturally, the fact that the CJEU must apply the EU law does not exclude the possibility to apply norms coming from other systems, such as international law, the general principles of law or the 'common constitutional traditions" of the Member States, as the Court did apply already, especially in the field of fundamental rights. See, for the respective CJEU's judgments and, in general, for this subject, our work, Letizia Seminara, "Tutela dei diritti fondamentali e Corte di Giustizia dell'Unione europea, con particolare riguardo alla limitazione dell'esercizio dei diritti", *Foroeuropa* 3 (2016).

[11] See, Opinion of Advocate General Trstenjak delivered on 28 March 2007, Case C-331/05 P, *Internationaler Hilfsfonds v. Commission*, par. 84.

[12] See, *Oxford Living Dictionaries*, the terms "statutory law" and "statute".

characterized by two elements. On the one hand, it is mainly composed of written law. On the other hand, it is legislatively enacted.[13]

First, EU law is mostly based on written law. Both primary law and derived law are mainly written law. Although –as in any legal system- there is a part of unwritten law, such as general principles of law, legal customs and agreements between the Member States, no one would contest that the sources of law of the European Union are mainly composed of written law.[14] Second, derived law –which constitutes a substantial part of EU law- is largely the result of a 'legislative procedure'.

Notwithstanding the failure of the Constitutional Treaty in defining certain normative acts as "European laws" and "European framework laws", which later implied that the Treaty of Lisbon opted for defining the legal acts adopted through the legislative procedure as "legislative acts",[15] it is possible to characterise these acts as "legislatively enacted". The so-called 'democratic deficit' criticism of the EU methodologies does not change the nature of these acts.[16] As E. Triggiani put it, the fact they have been called as 'legislative acts' instead of 'European laws' or 'European framework laws' was an inevitable homage to Mr de la Palisse, for not consenting 'bad thoughts' on the existence of a para-constitutional system.[17] The system stays on the side of statutory law even in the case of non-legislative acts,[18] if one considers that these acts are none the less written law and that they can be assimilated to delegated acts in one case and to administrative acts of a statutory-law system in the other (executive acts).

Furthermore, the Treaties do not refer to any value or legal status of case law in the EU law. Neither the status of case law nor that of precedent are

---

[13] See, in this regard, *Merriam-Webster Law Dictionary*, the terms "statutory law".

[14] This is in the ABC of European Union Law. See, therefore, Klaus-Dieter Borchardt, *The ABC of European Union Law* (Luxembourg: Publications Office of the European Union, 2010), 85.

[15] According to Article 289 (3) TFEU, "[l]egal acts adopted by legislative procedure shall constitute legislative acts".

[16] For a position defending the legitimacy of EU methods, see Andrew Moravcsik, "In Defence of the 'Democratic Deficit': Reassessing Legitimacy in the European Union", *JCMS* 40, n. 4 (2002): 606-624.

[17] See, Ennio Triggiani, *L'Unione europea dopo la riforma di Lisbona* (Bari: Levante Editori, 2011), 25.

[18] For the nature of these acts, see Giuseppe Tesauro, *Diritto dell'Unione europea*, 7th ed. (Padova: Cedam, 2012), 136.

addressed by the Treaties provisions.[19] Moreover, one could argue that the content of Article 19 on the exercise of the jurisdiction of the Court of Justice, that puts on its charge the function of 'interpretation' and 'application' of the Treaties, is closer to a system that relies on written law rather than case law, as the process of 'interpretation' and 'application' of the former has been traditionally related to statutory law and less to the process of creation of law by judges, which is typical of a case-law system.[20] In that regard, the function of the Court of Justice of the European Union has been characterized as an activity of 'legal interpretation' that would involve an activity of interpretation of *legal texts* supplemented by principles of law "where texts are silent".[21] And this is what a judge in a statutory-law system does. In the same sense, AG Bobek has pointed out in *Cussens and Others* that "the Court's interpretations of legal provisions 'graft themselves' onto those provisions". Particularly, he highlighted on that occasion that, "[i]n accordance with the separation or 'horizontal and vertical allocation' of powers, the Court's mission is to find the law, not to create it".[22] As J. Komárek has explained, reasoning with previous decisions in the 'classical' common law context is different from reasoning statutes or the constitution: "the latter often leaves facts behind and focuses on *interpreting legal provisions* in a fairly abstract context of

---

[19] The Declarations annexed to the Final Act of the Intergovernmental Conference which adopted the Treaty of Lisbon, contain a number of references to case law, but none of them confer to the latter an exact status within the EU law. The 17th Declaration concerning primacy is the most precise, where it recalls that "in accordance with well settled case law of the Court of Justice of the European Union, the Treaties and the law adopted by the Union on the basis of the Treaties have primacy over the law of Member States, under the conditions laid down by the said case law". Primary and secondary EU law have therefore primacy "under the conditions" laid down by case law, but this is still not enough to determine the legal status of case law in EU law.

[20] See, Fernanda G. Nicola, "National Legal Traditions at Work in the Jurisprudence of the Court of Justice of the European Union", *Am. J. Comp. L.* 64 (2017): 873: "In the civil law tradition, judges, at least at the declaratory level, are mere interpreters of a piece of legislation or codes, writing in a style that is succinct and short, but otherwise they have more discretion than their common law counterparts".

[21] This is even the point of view of an Advocate General coming from a common law system. See, Nial Fennelly, "Legal Interpretation at the European Court of Justice", *Fordham Int. Law Journal* 20, n.3 (1996): 656-679, this quotation at p. 679.

[22] See, Opinion of Advocate General Bobek delivered on 7 September 2017, Case C-251/16, *Cussens and Others*, par. 36.

the case behind".[23] Written texts and their interpretation are more relevant than precedent in European Union law, to the point that the importance of what is written is also extended to the text (instead of, or at least not only, the *ratio decidendi*) of judgments. As the above quoted Author also observes, "the text of judicial decisions matters in adjudication before European Courts".[24]

This state of affairs cannot but be confirmed by the fact that, unless for the effects among the parties, the Treaties do not confer to the judgments of the Court of Justice any other vertical or horizontal binding effect on itself, the inferior EU Courts or domestic courts. Therefore, legally speaking, judgments are in principle only binding on the parties. This is commonly accepted by scholars, who generally agree that "the principle of *res judicata* extends only to matters of fact and law actually or necessarily settled by the judicial decision in question"[25] and that the Court's judgments are only binding to the addressee.[26]

It is noteworthy that the fact that European law should be applied by domestic courts, including the interpretations given by the CJEU, is not the result of any general binding effect of its judgments nor an obligation to respect precedents, but it has to do more with the primacy of EU law. This follows from the circumstance that what is binding for domestic courts is, in fact, the application of the European Union law and not the respect of precedents in itself, in the sense that the obligation of domestic courts consist in interpreting domestic law in conformity with the European legal texts, even if, naturally, judges in the Member States may consider that the interpretation of those legal texts already given by the

---

[23] See, Jan Komárek, "Reasoning with Previous Decisions: Beyond the Doctrine of Precedent", *Am. J. Comp. L.* 61 (2013): 157. Italics added.

[24] *Ibidem*, 156.

[25] See, Koen Lenaerts, Ignace Maselis and Kathleen Gutman. Janek Tomasz Nowak (Editor), *EU Procedural Law* (Oxford: Oxford University Press, 2014), 782.

[26] See, also, similarly, Sonja Boelaert, "European Union Courts", in *The Rules, Practice, and Jurisprudence of International Courts and Tribunals*, ed. Chiara Giorgetti (Leiden: Brill, 2012), 430: "Judgments are binding to the addressee, which means that the addressee needs to take all necessary steps to comply with it". While treating the matter of the effects of a CJEU's judgment, mention is not usually made in the works of scholars of any binding effect of the *ratio decidendi* in cases other than the case at hand.

Court of Justice is authoritative.[27] But, again, this is the result of the primacy of EU law and not the consequence of an eventual constraining effect of precedents in the EU law.[28]

2. The Relevance of Precedent in EU Law

It is an agreed opinion among scholars of both schools of law (common law and civil law) that, although precedent is not a formal source of law in statutory-law systems,[29] it is still relevant in the decision-making process of its courts.[30] As scholars have underlined, no one would seriously contest today the role of case law in civil law systems.[31] It has been observed in that sense that the value of precedent is universal.[32] The role of case law in modern continental European law can be summarised, as F. Muller brightly did, in the following maxim: "the earlier decision provides me with food for thought, but it does not 'pre-decide' for me".[33]

---

[27] See, Giuseppe Tesauro, *Diritto dell'Unione europea*, 7th ed (Padova: Cedam, 2012), 183 ff., who links "strictly and necessarily" the obligation to interpret domestic law in conformity with EU law, to the primacy of the European Union law over domestic law.

[28] The reasoning methodology in case-law systems is different: the constraining element is there the *ratio decidendi* and not the conforming interpretation of legal texts.

[29] See, Stefano Civitarese, "A European convergence towards a *stare decisis* model?", *Revista digital de Derecho Administrativo* 14 (2015): 181: "The ECJ regularly refers to its 'settled' case law, but it does not treat its past rulings as formally binding". The Author refers here to T. Tridimas, "Precedent and the Court of Justice. A Jurisprudence of Doubt?", in *Philosophical Foundations of European Union Law*, ed. J. Dickinson and P. Eleftheriadis (Oxford University Press, 2012).

[30] See, Jan Komárek, "Reasoning with Previous Decisions: Beyond the Doctrine of Precedent", *Am. J. Comp. L.* 61 (2013): 167; Friedrich Muller, "Observations on the Role of Precedent in Modern Continental European Law from the Perspective of Structuring Legal Theory", *Stellenbosch L. Rev.* 11 (2000): 426-436; Elisabetta Vianello, "La relatività della regola "stare decisis" nella pratica del precedente giudiziario", *Rivista trimestrale di diritto e procedura civile* XLVI, n. 2 (1992): 644; Charles C. Soule, "Stare Decisis in Continental Europe", *Green Bag* 19 (1907): 460-431.

[31] See, Vincenzo Varano and Vittoria Barsotti, *La tradizione giuridica occidentale*, 5th ed. (Torino: Giappichelli, 2014), 187.

[32] See, Carlo Augusto Cannata and Antonio Gambaro, *Lineamenti di storia della giurisprudenza europea*, 4th ed., II (Torino: Giappichelli, 1989), 110.

[33] See, referring particularly to the continental model, Friedrich Muller, "Observations on the Role of Precedent in Modern Continental European Law from the Perspective of Structuring Legal Theory", *Stellenbosch L. Rev.* 11 (2000): 428.

Case law is, therefore, a relevant element of the legal reasoning in statutory-law systems, and it is as well in EU law. From this perspective, the attitude of the European judge is not so far from the position of a domestic judge in such a system of law. Nor it is from the position of the international judge who insists on previously settled jurisprudence and sometimes mentions judgments previously rendered.[34] The attitude of the International Court of Justice, to give an example (the approach of other international judges is similar), is in the direction of not recognizing any binding value to its own precedent, but to take it "into great consideration".[35]

The importance of case law has been in that sense relativized in EU law. In *Sürül*, AG La Pergola set aside the emergence of any rule, in the European law, which would have conferred to the *ratio decidendi* of judgments the constraining force representative of the common law system (overwritten statements, such as obiter dicta), recalling that the rule *stare decisis* "has not been incorporated in the Community judicial system". The Advocate General also underlined on that occasion that "the Court does not of course fail to ensure that its case-law displays continuity and that its judgments are logically compatible and not contradictory with each other. However, the Court is not technically bound by its earlier judgments, and may therefore –as far as the present case is concerned as well - give a different answer to a preliminary question dealt with in an earlier decision, if such a result is justified by new matters brought to its attention in the later proceedings".[36]

AG La Pergola arguments provide us with a good explanation on what exactly the relevance of case law is in EU law. Precisely, one point of this explanation let us know more about its role in the European Union law. The fact is that the Court's necessity to ensure that its judgments are "logically compatible and not contradictory one each other" reveals that it is deeply and ultimately concerned with safeguarding the correctness of its reasoning. What matters is, in the end, the rectitude of the reasoning that grounds the solution given by the Court to a certain legal problem.

---

[34] See, as regards the position of the International Court of Justice, Gilbert Guillaume, "The Use of Precedent by International Judges and Arbitrators", *Journal of International Dispute Settlement* 2, n.1, (2011): 9-10.

[35] *Ibidem*, 12.

[36] See, Opinion of Advocate General La Pergola delivered on 12 February 1998, Case C-262/96, *Sürül v. Bundesanstalt für Arbeit*, par. 36.

This 'way of deciding' (or 'legal methodology', in formal terms) is based on the principle that the most important value guiding the decision-making process of the Court is not 'tradition' but 'reason'. This concern was too clear, for instance, in *King*, where AG Tanchev was of the view that the case should not be solved by following the Court's established precedents and that it rather approach the problem to hand by considering a question. The question, as it was formulated, took naturally into account the Court's interpretation of the applicable provision, but, especially, it was put with the aim to *reason around a legal problem*, instead of automatically applying the previous interpretation given by the Court.[37]

A relative importance to case law was also conferred in *Stichting Brein* by AG Campos Sánchez-Bordona. Here, despite his statement that the "requirement of certainty in the application of the law obliges the court, if not to apply the *stare decisis* in absolute terms, then to take care to follow the decisions it has itself, after mature reflection, previously adopted in relation to a given legal problem", he made it clear that he shall adopt the propositions previously set down by the Court as the "*basis for his arguments*". Therefore, the Advocate General did not take case law as constraining in absolute terms, but as a part of a *mature reflection* that would not have been the decisive element that provided the solution to the case in his reasoning.[38] He, therefore, 'reasoned around' relevant case law.

In the end, what the Court refuses to accept is the fiction on which the common law is based, that consists in assuming that two legal cases can be truly alike. Whilst in a case-law system subsequent cases tend to be assimilated to or distinguished from previous cases, the Court is instead concerned with treating and solving each case alone, in relation to what (complexly) the European Union law is. This was the position adopted by

---

[37] See, Opinion of Advocate General Tanchev delivered on 8 June 2017, Case C-214/16, *King*. The question made by the domestic court in a preliminary ruling procedure was whether a worker like Mr King could claim that he was prevented from exercising the right to paid annual leave when he had not taken the annual leave to which he was entitled in the relevant leave year because the employer refused to pay him for any period of leave he took (par. 65). The Advocate General put the question in these terms: "All this being so, I am of the view that *the Court can put to one side its established precedents* on Member State temporal and other restrictions on the exercise of paid annual leave, and *rather approach the problem to hand by considering the following question*" (par. 75). Italics added.

[38] See, Opinion of Advocate General Campos Sánchez-Bordona delivered on 8 December 2016, Case C-527/15, *Stichting Brein*, par. 41-42.

AG Kokott in *Fresh Del Monte Produce v. Commission*, where she took the view that "since any case may have its own peculiarities, the issue of whether precedents exist in the case-law of the Court of Justice or of the General Court, the circumstances of which are identical or similar to those of the present case, likewise cannot be a determining factor".[39] Advocate General Kokott has been so clear in that regard, to the point that she stated in *Répertoire Culinaire* that "in European Union law, the Court's judgments do not constitute binding precedents. Although the Court is naturally hesitant to depart from previous judgments, it has had occasion in the past, in a number of important cases, to re-examine its earlier case-law and, if necessary, amend or clarify it".[40]

It is worth adding that the Court is not obliged to have recourse to precedent to solve a legal problem. For instance, in *Regione Autonoma della Sardegna v. Commission*, even if referring to its own case law, the General Court reach a solution to the legal problem concerned "regardless of those precedents".[41] The words used by Poiares Maduro in *Ordre des barreaux francophones and germanophone and Others*, were allusive, where he considered that "the Court *may* profitably rely on some of its own precedents", but, clearly did not refer to any duty for the Court to rely on them.[42] In a similar position, in *Van Parys* AG Tizzano considered it "advisable" to see how the Court had defined the exception in question by examining the line of case law.[43] In those cases, none of them considered it mandatory to refer to the Court's case law to solve the legal problem presented to them.

The CJEU is moreover reluctant to the inclination –emblematic in case-law systems- to assimilate (or distinguish) cases. In *Meilicke and Others* the Court, answering to the arguments of one of the parties that the German tax rules were the same as the rules in Finland, which had been already

---

[39] See, Opinion of Advocate General Kokott delivered on 11 December 2014, Joined Cases C-293/13 P and C-294/13 P, *Fresh Del Monte Produce v. Commission*, par. 80.

[40] See, Opinion of Advocate General Kokott delivered on 15 July 2010, Case C-163/09, *Répertoire Culinaire*, par. 61.

[41] See, Judgment of 20 September 2011, *Regione Autonoma della Sardegna v. Commission*, Case T-394/08, par. 214.

[42] See, Opinion of Advocate General Poiares Maduro delivered on 14 December 2006, Case C-305/05, *Ordre des barreaux francophones and germanophone and Others*, par. 2. Italics added.

[43] See, Opinion of Advocate General Tizzano delivered on 18 November 2004, Case C-377/02, *Van Parys*, par. 87.

declared incompatible with EU law in *Manninen*, refused to accept this comparison and therefore rejected the argument.[44] A similar averse attitude was evident in *European Commission v. Aer Lingus and Ryanair*, where AG Mengozzi refused to give the solution given in a number of precedents followed by the General Court, as "those precedents would appear to be of questionable relevance in the present proceedings".[45]

In this framework, precedents may be therefore a part of a complex of elements that compose a legal reasoning. It is inevitably a relevant part of the latter. Its function is to understand what the law is and how it has been applied in previous cases, but it is not the decisive element of the legal reasoning. It *interacts* with other elements of the same reasoning, and its relevance is limited to this role because the judge feels free to make a different decision if that is necessary to safeguard the righteousness of his reasoning. Therefore, precedents 'assist',[46] they can be used as 'guidance',[47] but do not constrain as AG Kokott has repeatedly made it clear. This is possible because, talking in mathematical terms, a number of 'variables' that are not taken into account to solve a problem in a case-law system, take part instead in the CJEU's reasoning. This approach was apparent, for instance, in the reasoning of AG Bot in *Essent Belgium* where he used precedent to *infer* the solution given by the Court in that precise matter, but this was only a part of a reasoning composed of more elements.[48]

---

[44] Judgment of 6 March 2007, *Meilicke and Others*, Case C-292/04. The case is reported by Jan Komárek, "Reasoning with Previous Decisions: Beyond the Doctrine of Precedent", *Am. J. Comp. L.* 61 (2013): 154-5.

[45] See, Opinion of Advocate General Mengozzi delivered on 5 July 2016, Joined Cases C-164/15 P and C-165/15 P, *European Commission v. Aer Lingus and Ryanair*, par. 79.

[46] See, for instance, the Opinion of Advocate General Campos Sánchez-Bordona delivered on 17 March 2016, Case C-207/15 P, *Nissan Jidosha v. EUIPO*, par. 46, for whom case-law precedents represent an instrument of 'assistance': "Since this is an unprecedented legal problem, it will have to be resolved — without the assistance of case-law precedents — using the traditional criteria for interpretation, including the adjustments derived from EU law".

[47] See, similarly, the Opinion of Advocate General Saugmandsgaard Øe delivered on 17 December 2015, Case C-528/14, *X*, par. 30, where he refers to precedents as 'guidance'. Previously, AG Mengozzi had referred to two judgments of the Court as "important interpretative guidance", in his Opinion delivered 31 March 2011, Case C-195/09, *Synthon*, par. 60.

[48] See, Opinion of AG Bot delivered on 14 April 2016, Case C-492/14, *Essent Belgium*, par. 71, where he uses exactly the terms "infer from those precedents".

The result is that a judgment of the Court of Justice of the European Union is not the fruit of the maxim 'decide as it has been previously decided' but 'decide consequently with reason', a situation that can be somewhat seen as a triumph of reason over precedent.

3. The Triumph of 'Reason' over 'Precedent' in EU Law: Concluding Remarks on Precedent as a Non-constraining but Relevant Element of the European Legal Reasoning

The practice of the CJEU shows that this Court is much more concerned with the necessity of 'giving reasons' to ground its judgments, rather than with 'standing by its decisions'. This can be explained by a number of reasons. First, it can be explained by the fact that the Court is interested in legitimating its decisions, and, in its logic, this could be better done through reason, as the doctrine of precedent could lead the Court to results that would be seen as contrary to justice. F. Emmert explains in that regard that the European Court "cares about its reputation, or as we say as lawyers, it cares about its legitimacy".[49] Also, the Court's interest in safeguarding the healthiness of its reasoning could be found in the considerations made by V. Perju, who recalls a duty of the CJEU to justify the exercise of its public power. The Court would be, in that operation of justification of its judicial activity, in the position of taking elements of both a 'justification model' and a 'command model'.[50]

In reality, this 'need to rationalise' which is the essence of the European judgments, seems to be motivated, of course, by the political and technical reasons mentioned above, but it is especially rooted in a (legal) cultural motivation which is strictly related to the notion of justice to which we

---

[49] This has lead this Author to relativize the importance of case law in the EU law. As he put it, "if the Court wishes to decide a case differently from a similar earlier case, it has to explain why the facts are different, why and how the law is no longer the same, why or how the times have changed, or why the earlier decision was incorrect to begin with. Unsurprisingly, therefore, the European Court makes regular and extensive references to its own earlier case law to make abundantly clear how that case law is overall consistent and coherent, and very rarely deviates from an earlier line of cases, unless the facts can clearly be distinguished or the law has changed. The question whether or not the European Court of Justice is or sees itself in a civil, statutory, or common law tradition really makes no difference at all in this respect". See, Frank Emmert, "Stare Decisis: A Universally Misunderstood Idea", *Legisprudence* 6 (2012): 226-227.

[50] See, Vlad F. Perju, "Reason and Authority in the European Court of Justice", *Virginia Journal of International Law* 49 (2009): 307-378.

referred at the beginning of this work. As we highlighted since the departure, in European legal culture the notion of justice is intimately related to reason and, therefore, the Court is attentive both to making decisions that must be the result of a rational operation and to departing from approaches that can lead to an irrational result. The Court's judicial methodology (and especially those of the Advocates General) consists in fact in the articulation of legal motivations in a coherent manner because this is the basis of the rule of law in European (continental) legal culture.[51] Relying on a precedent without 'reasoning around' other legal motivations would not only be contrary to the rule of law, but particularly contrary to that legal culture which tells us that a just solution cannot but be based on reason. The same could be said if the Court reasoned around motivations without taking account of precedents at all.

There is, therefore, an enormous difference between using case law to reason around a legal problem and using case law as a constraining factor. In this sense, the Court refuses, in fact, to "see a world dominated by precedent"[52] because this could bring it to a nonsense result which would

---

[51] For the European legal culture, see ed. Volkmar Gessner, Armin Höland and Csaba Varga, *European legal cultures* (Aldershot: Dartmouth, 1996); Martijn Willem Hesselink, *The new European legal culture* (Deventer: Kluwer, 2001); Sylvaine Poillot-Peruzzetto, "Vers une culture juridique européenne, le pont de l'Europe", in *Les échanges entre les droits, l'expérience communautaire: une lecture des phénomènes de régionalisation et de mondialisation du droit*, ed. Sophie Robin-Olivier and Daniel Fasquelle, (Bruxelles: Bruylant, 2008), 173-196; Vagn Greve, "The historical roots: European legal culture traditions", *Tidskrift utvigen av Juridiska Föreningen i Finland* 146, n. 5 (2010): 482-492; Kjell Åke Modéer, "The historical roots of European legal culture: transitions due to diversities and differences", *Tidskrift utvigen av Juridiska Föreningen i Finland* 146, n. 5 (2010): 493-500; Michael Stolleis, "The historical roots of European legal culture", *Tidskrift utvigen av Juridiska Föreningen i Finland* 146, n. 5 (2010): 501-503; Markku Kiikeri, "Legal-cultural approach to European law", in *Interdisciplinary research in jurisprudence and constitutionalism*, ed. Stephan Kirste, Anne van Aaken, Michael Anderheiden, and Pasquale Policastro (Stuttgart: Franz Steiner Verlag, 2012); António Manuel Hespanha, *La cultura giuridica europea*, trans. by Giovanni Damele (Bologna: Il Mulino, 2013); ed. Geneviève Helleringer and Kai Peter Purnhagen, *Towards a European legal culture* (München: Beck, 2014); Åse Berit Grødeland and William Watts Miller, *European legal cultures in transition* (Cambridge: Cambridge University Press, 2015).

[52] See, in this regard, the severe criticism of Steven Stark, "Why Lawyers Can't Write", *Harv. L. Rev.* 97 (1983-1984): 1391, on the lawyers' attitude of giving an excessively protagonist role to precedent: "[lawyers] see a world dominated by precedent. It is one of the law's timeless truths that everything is merely an extension or alteration

enormously weaken the strength of the European legal reasoning. The relevance of case law in EU law is therefore relativized in function of other important factors.

It has been none the less observed that, to complain of the reliance of courts on precedent "at the expense of matters of interest that should be included in the opinion is to misunderstand the function of precedent in shaping an idea" and that, therefore, "Judges do not, nor should they, write on a clean slate, even when addressing issues of first impression. The law is an organic whole, making it imperative that judges plug themselves into the broader cultural context".[53] The European judges know that. But taking law as an *organic whole* that is composed of several elements has led them to give a balanced (relative) importance to precedent.

One should also take in mind that in the conception of the European judge, the judgments of the Court of Justice are not a part of law.[54] Even when the importance of case law was recognised to the greatest extent, this has not been made in detriment of reason. *Merck v. Prime-crown* is illustrative in this sense, if we look at the arguments advanced by AG Fennelly on the importance of case law in EU law.[55] Indeed, on that occasion he took the view that "the Court should, as a matter of practice, follow its previous case-law except where there are strong *reasons* for not so doing", therefore recognising that, as many important aspects of the (at that time) Community law were not comprehensively dealt with in the Treaty, the applicable principles and rules of Community law were thus "to a large extent 'judge-made law'", and, as interpretations of Treaty provisions, were not amenable to modification or qualification through legislative means.[56] Here, even if recognizing the importance of the Court's case law to its greatest legal force, reasons prevailed over precedents.

---

of what has appeared before. Thus, in their briefs and legal opinions, lawyers constantly explain things in terms of the past; they reason that they are doing nothing and only following existing precedent".

[53] See, William Domnarski, "The Opinion as Essay, the Judge as Essayist: Some Observations on Legal Writing", *J. Legal Prof.* 10 (1985): 143. Domnarski is actually reacting to the position of Steven Stark mentioned above.

[54] See, above, our reference to the Opinion of AG Trstenjak in *Internationaler Hilfsfonds v. Commission*.

[55] The case is commented by Tamas Szabados, "Precedents in EU law - The problem of overruling", *ELTE L. J.* (2015): 128.

[56] See, Opinion of Advocate General Fennelly delivered on 6 June 1996, Joined Cases C-267-95 and C-268/95, *Merck*, par. 142. Italics added.

The case was also paradigmatic where AG Kokott suggested that the so-called 'Marks & Spencer exception' should be reviewed because that regime "proved to be impracticable" and she gave 'four reasons' that justified her assertion, before grounding its proposition by more than 'three reasons'. Particularly, she was of the advice that a review as to the appropriateness of the *Marks & Spencer* exception was "both possible and necessary".[57] More recently and, similarly, AG Bot observed in *Asklepios Kliniken Langen-Seligenstadt*, that it seemed necessary "to revisit" two precedents and further proposed the considerations on what "the Court should base its reasoning".[58]

Another strong (complementary but very significant) motivation for the CJEU to stay far from the 'cult of precedent' can be finally found in the remarks made by international judges and scholars as regards the use of precedent in the international jurisdiction. G. Guillaume has observed in this regard that constantly following precedent "also freezes the law, and prevents it from progressing according to new demands of society".[59] The European Court seems, therefore, to be aligned to this position, according to which "a balance must be found for the judge and arbitrator between the necessary certainty and the necessary evolution of the law".[60] In the end, as Guillaume states, "the cult of the precedent is thus just as dangerous as the rejection of precedent".[61]

The fact that in the European Union the integration of different legal orders is continuously *in progress* and that it keeps pursuing objectives to achieve its final purpose bolsters this position. If other EU organs are legitimately carrying forward this process, putting itself in the condition of a 'freezing actor', would not only be a counterproductive attitude of the

---

[57] See, Opinion of Advocate General Kokott delivered on 23 October 2014, Case C-172/13, *European Commission v. the United Kingdom*, par. 42 ff.

[58] See, Opinion of Advocate General Bot delivered on 19 January 2017, Joined Cases C-680/15 and C-681/15, *Asklepios Kliniken Langen-Seligenstadt*.

[59] See, Gilbert Guillaume, "The Use of Precedent by International Judges and Arbitrators", *Journal of International Dispute Settlement* 2, n.1, (2011): 6. See, similarly, with regard to the difficulties faced to revert a precedent, Ewoud Hondius, "Precedent and the Law", *Electronic Journal of Comparative Law* 11, n. 3 (2007): 15: "The changes in norms and values, in theories as to finding the law, are nowadays so rapid that case law –which often takes a long time to be submitted to a legal system's highest court– simply cannot cope with them".

[60] *Ibidem*.

[61] *Ibid.*, p. 23.

Court, but also a too vast understanding of its functions. As AG Bobek made it clear: the function of the Court is not that of creating law.[62] A too expansive role of judges, to the point of the appropriation of politics by law, has been even interpreted as a 'suicidal' attitude of the European Union.[63]

The evolving function of law was a strong point in the arguments of AG Trstenjak *Internationaler Hilfsfonds v. Commission*. On that occasion, the appellant's arguments aimed to consider it possible to infer legal consequences for the pending case from a previous judgment of the Court. The Advocate General rejected the idea that that judgment could bind the Court and she explained the motivations that had lead the EU law to take distance from the common law systems, alluding to the necessity of the European Union law to be elastic: "[t]he binding authority of precedent is not an inherent feature of the Union's judicial system. Although, in the interest of legal certainty and the uniform interpretation of Community law, the Community Courts endeavor in principle to give a coherent interpretation to the law, the general structure of both the Community legal order and the judicial system means that the Community Courts are not bound by their previous decisions. Historically, this can be explained by the fact that the Community was originally founded by States belonging to the family of continental European civil law systems, with the result that the supranational legal order thereby created has similar characteristics. Another reason is the fact that the Court of Justice was originally set up as a court of first and last instance before a further judicial body was added by the Council decision establishing a Court of First Instance. Accepting the binding authority of precedent along common law lines would have been inappropriate in so far as it would have been possible to alter judgments having the force of *res judicata* only by amending the founding treaties. Against the background of the associated constitutional obstacles in the Member States, the Court of Justice had to be put in a position to depart from its previous case-law if necessary and to steer developing Community law in a different direction".[64]

---

[62] See, his Opinion cited above in *Cussens and Others*.

[63] See the view of Agostino Carrino, *Il suicidio dell'Europa: Sovranità, Stati nazionali e 'grandi spazi'* (Modena: Mucchi Editore, 2016).

[64] See, Opinion of Advocate General Trstenjak delivered on 28 March 2007, Case C-331/05 P, *Internationaler Hilfsfonds v. Commission*, par. 84-85.

This position seems to be in the sense of the previous position expressed in *Cipolla* by AG Poiares Maduro, on the need for *adaptability* of the EU law, even if in this position he gave clearly more relevance to precedents, recognising none the less that the stability that would result from the force that the Court has given to its judgments as an instrument to secure the values of cohesion, uniformity and legal certainty inherent in any system of law, "is not and should not be an absolute value".[65] The Advocate General took in his Opinion an important position that is worth reporting: "28. [t]he Court has always shown itself to be circumspect with regard to reversing an interpretation of the law given in earlier judgments. Without determining whether those judgments constituted legal precedents the Court has always shown deference to a line of well-established case-law. The force awarded by the Court to judgments it has delivered in the past may be considered to derive from the need to secure the values of cohesion, uniformity and legal certainty inherent in any system of law. Those values are all the more important within the context of a decentralized system of applying the law such as that of the Community legal system. The acknowledgment in *CILFIT* that there is no longer an obligation to make a reference for a preliminary ruling if the question raised has already been interpreted by the Court and the option for the Court provided for in Article 104(3) of its Rules of Procedure to adopt an order if 'a question referred to the Court for a preliminary ruling is identical to a question on which [it] has already ruled' can only be understood in the light of the interpretative authority granted the Court for the future. Even though the Court is not formally bound by its own judgments, by the deference it shows them it recognizes the importance of the stability of its case-law for its interpretative authority and helps to protect uniformity, cohesion and legal certainty within the Community legal system. 29. It is true that stability is not and should not be an absolute value. The Court has also recognized the importance of adapting its case-law in order to take account of changes that have taken place in other areas of the legal system or in the social context in which the rules apply. It has also accepted that the appearance of new factors may justify adaptation or even review of its case-law. The Court has none the less agreed only cautiously to depart from its earlier judgments in as radical a way as is suggested by the Commission in the present case".

---

[65] See, Opinion of Advocate General M. Poiares Maduro delivered on 1 February 2006, Case C-94/04, *Cipolla*, par. 28-29.

Conclusion

It could be finally presumed that this relativized relevance of case law, which allows the latter to govern the European law as long as it does not impair the Court's concern for reasonability, will be corroborated with the departure of the British components of the Court of Justice. The circumstances reported by scholars on the situation that had taken place years ago with the access of the British members, leading to a shift from a Court initially modeled on the French *Conseil d'Etat* to the use of common law reasoning,[66] will probably no longer be maintained in the future. Further shift of the European judges in the sense of giving more relevance to case law is improbable because, as it has been observed, the imposition of a system of binding precedent "would be a significant departure both from the practice followed in the Member States in their own legal orders, and from international practice".[67]

Bibliography

Barcelò, in Urška Šadl and Ioannis Panagis, "The force of EU case law: An empirical study of precedential constraint", in *Legal Knowledge and Information Systems* 279 (2015).

Bargiacchi, Paolo.*Diritto dell'Unione europea*, (Rome: Aracne, 2015)

Boelaert, Sonja.European Union Courts.in *The Rules, Practice, and Jurisprudence of International Courts and Tribunals*, ed. Chiara Giorgetti (Leiden: Brill, 2012)

Borchardt, Klaus-Dieter.*The ABC of European Union Law* (Luxembourg: Publications Office of the European Union, 2010)

Bradley, Kieran.Vertical Precedent at the Court of Justice of the European Union: When Push Comes to Shove.in *Liber Amicorum in Honour of Nial Fennelly*, ed. Kieran Bradley, Noel Travers and Anthony Whelan (Oxford: Hart Publishing, 2014)

---

[66] See the situation as described in Fernanda G. Nicola, "National Legal Traditions at Work in the Jurisprudence of the Court of Justice of the European Union", *Am. J. Comp. L.* 64 (2017): 871. It is possible to find a good example depicting this situation in the position of British AG Warner, in his Opinion delivered on 20 September 1977, Case C-112/76, *Manzoni*, p. 1662 ff., where he took the view that the principle of *stare decisis* "must come into play", particularly as regards the binding character of the *ratio decidendi* of the Court's judgment, for all the domestic Courts throughout the Community.

[67] See, Kieran Bradley, "Vertical Precedent at the Court of Justice of the European Union: When Push Comes to Shove", in *Liber Amicorum in Honour of Nial Fennelly*, ed. Kieran Bradley, Noel Travers and Anthony Whelan (Oxford: Hart Publishing, 2014), 51.

Carlo Augusto Cannata and Antonio Gambaro, *Lineamenti di storia della giurisprudenza europea*, 4th ed. (Torino: Giappichelli, 1989).

Carrino, Agostino.*Il suicidio dell'Europa: Sovranità, Stati nazionali e 'grandi spazi'* (Modena: Mucchi Editore, 2016).

Civitarese, Stefano.A European convergence towards a *stare decisis* model?.*Revista digital de Derecho Administrativo* 14 (2015)

Domnarski, William.The Opinion as Essay, the Judge as Essayist: Some Observations on Legal Writing. *J. Legal Prof.* 10 (1985)

Emmert, Frank.Stare Decisis: A Universally Misunderstood Idea.*Legisprudence* 6 (2012)

Fennelly, Nial.Legal Interpretation at the European Court of Justice.*Fordham Int. Law Journal* 20, n.3 (1996): 656-679

Fernanda G. Nicola, "National Legal Traditions at Work in the Jurisprudence of the Court of Justice of the European Union", *Am. J. Comp. L.* 64 (2017)

Gessner, Volkmar, Armin Höland and Csaba Varga (eds.), *European legal cultures* (Aldershot: Dartmouth, 1996)

Greve, Vagn.The historical roots: European legal culture traditions.*Tidskrift utvigen av Juridiska Föreningen i Finland* 146, n. 5 (2010)

Grødeland, Åse Berit and William Watts Miller.*European legal cultures in transition* (Cambridge: Cambridge University Press, 2015).

Guillaume, Gilbert. The Use of Precedent by International Judges and Arbitrators.*Journal of International Dispute Settlement* 2, n.1, (2011)

Hespanha, António Manuel. *La cultura giuridica europea*, trans. by Giovanni Damele (Bologna: Il Mulino, 2013); ed. Geneviève Helleringer and Kai Peter Purnhagen, *Towards a European legal culture* (München: Beck, 2014)

Hesselink, Martijn Willem.*The new European legal culture* (Deventer: Kluwer, 2001);

Hondius, Ewoud.Precedent and the Law.*Electronic Journal of Comparative Law* 11, n. 3 (2007)

Judgment of 20 September 2011, *Regione Autonoma della Sardegna v. Commission*, Case T-394/08, par. 214.

Judgment of 6 March 2007, *Meilicke and Others*, Case C-292/04.

Kiikeri, Markku.Legal-cultural approach to European law.in *Interdisciplinary research in jurisprudence and constitutionalism*, ed. Stephan Kirste, Anne van Aaken, Michael Anderheider, and Pasquale Policastro (Stuttgart: Franz Steiner Verlag, 2012)

Komárek, Jan.Reasoning with Previous Decisions: Beyond the Doctrine of Precedent.*Am. J. Comp. L.* 61 (2013)

Laird, D. H.The Doctrine of Stare Decisis, *Can. B. Rev.* XIII, n. 1 (1935)

Lenaerts, Koen, Ignace Maselis and Kathleen Gutman. Janek Tomasz Nowak (Editor), *EU Procedural Law* (Oxford: Oxford University Press, 2014)

Mikelsone, Gundega.The Binding Force of the Case Law of the Court of Justice of the European Union. *Jurisprudencija/Jurisprudence* 20, n. 2 (2013)

Modéer, Kjell Åke.The historical roots of European legal culture: transitions due to diversities and differences. *Tidskrift utvigen av Juridiska Föreningen i Finland* 146, n. 5 (2010)

Moravcsik, Andrew.In Defence of the 'Democratic Deficit': Reassessing Legitimacy in the European Union", *JCMS* 40, n. 4 (2002).

Muller, Friedrich.Observations on the Role of Precedent in Modern Continental European Law from the Perspective of Structuring Legal Theory.*Stellenbosch L. Rev.* 11 (2000)

Natoli, Luigi.*I Beati Paoli* (Palermo: Flaccovio, 1972)

Opinion of Advocate General Bot delivered on 19 January 2017, Joined Cases C-680/15 and C-681/15, *Asklepios Kliniken Langen-Seligenstadt.*

Opinion of Advocate General Campos Sánchez-Bordona delivered on 17 March 2016, Case C-207/15 P,

Opinion of Advocate General Fennelly delivered on 6 June 1996, Joined Cases C-267-95 and C-268/95, *Merck*, par. 142.

Opinion of Advocate General Kokott delivered on 11 December 2014, Joined Cases C-293/13 P and C-294/13 P, *Fresh Del Monte Produce v. Commission*

Opinion of Advocate General Kokott delivered on 15 July 2010, Case C-163/09, *Répertoire Culinaire*,

Opinion of Advocate General Kokott delivered on 23 October 2014, Case C-172/13, *European Commission v. the United Kingdom*

Opinion of Advocate General La Pergola delivered on 12 February 1998, Case C-262/96, *Sürül v. Bundesanstalt für Arbeit*

Opinion of Advocate General M. Poiares Maduro delivered on 1 February 2006, Case C-94/04, *Cipolla*

Opinion of Advocate General Mengozzi delivered on 5 July 2016, Joined Cases C-164/15 P and C-165/15 P, *European Commission v. Aer Lingus and Ryanair*

Opinion of Advocate General Poiares Maduro delivered on 14 December 2006, Case C-305/05, *Ordre des barreaux francophones and germanophone and Others*

Opinion of Advocate General Saugmandsgaard Øe delivered on 17 December 2015, Case C-528/14, *X*

Opinion of Advocate General Tanchev delivered on 8 June 2017, Case C-214/16,

Opinion of Advocate General Tizzano delivered on 18 November 2004, Case C-377/02, *Van Parys*,

Opinion of Advocate General Trstenjak delivered on 28 March 2007, Case C-331/05 P, *Internationaler Hilfsfonds v. Commission*

Opinion of AG Bot delivered on 14 April 2016, Case C-492/14, *Essent Belgium*,

Perju, Vlad F.Reason and Authority in the European Court of Justice.*Virginia Journal of International Law* 49 (2009)

Opinion of Advocate General Bobek delivered on 7 September 2017, Case C-251/16, *Cussens and Others*, par. 36.

Poillot-Peruzzetto, Sylvaine.Vers une culture juridique européenne, le pont de l'Europe.in *Les échanges entre les droits, l'expérience communautaire: une lecture des phénomènes de régionalisation et de mondialisation du droit*, ed. Sophie Robin-Olivier and Daniel Fasquelle, (Bruxelles: Bruylant, 2008)

Rosas, Allan.The European Court of Justice: Sources of Law and Methods of Interpretation, in *The WTO at ten: the contribution of the dispute settlement system*, ed. Giorgio Sacerdoti, Alan Yanovich and Jan Bohanes (Cambridge: Cambridge University Press).

Seminara, Letizia.Tutela dei diritti fondamentali e Corte di Giustizia dell'Unione europea, con particolare riguardo alla limitazione dell'esercizio dei diritti.*Foroeuropa* 3 (2016).

Soule, Charles C.Stare Decisis in Continental Europe, *Green Bag* 19 (1907)

Stark, Steven.Why Lawyers Can't Write.*Harv. L. Rev.* 97 (1983-1984)

Stolleis, Michael.The historical roots of European legal culture.*Tidskrift utvigen av Juridiska Föreningen i Finland* 146, n. 5 (2010)

Szabados, Tamas.Precedents in EU law - The problem of overruling.*ELTE L. J.* (2015)

Tesauro, Giuseppe.*Diritto dell'Unione europea*, 7th ed. Padova: Cedam, 2012)

Tridimas,T.Precedent and the Court of Justice. A Jurisprudence of Doubt?.in *Philosophical Foundations of European Union Law*, ed. J. Dickinson and P. Eleftheriadis (Oxford University Press, 2012).

Triggiani, Ennio.*L'Unione europea dopo la riforma di Lisbona* (Bari: Levante Editori, 2011)

Valvo, Anna Lucia.*Lineamenti di diritto dell'Unione europea*, 2nd ed., (Padova: Amon, 2017).

Varano, Vincenzo and Vittoria Barsotti.*La tradizione giuridica occidentale*.5th ed. (Torino: Giappichelli, 2014)

Vianello, Elisabetta.La relatività della regola "stare decisis" nella pratica del precedente giudiziario. *Rivista trimestrale di diritto e procedura civile* XLVI, n. 2 (1992).

Waldron, Jeremy.Stare Decisis and the Rule of Law: A Layered Approach.*Mich. L. Rev.* 111 (2012)

Chapter 12

The General Principle of 'Abuse of Rights': Its Roots in Domestic Law and Impact on Investment Arbitration

Philipp Janig[1]

Abstract

Principles developed in domestic legal systems can influence general international law – namely as 'general principles of law'. By including this source of law into Article 38(3) PCIJ Statute, the drafters of the Statute allowed the possibility to take certain recourse to principles enshrined in national legal orders. While it has initially also been argued that general principles stem from natural law, today the positivistic position finds overwhelming support among scholars, calling for a comparative analysis of domestic legislation. Though the identification process of general principles is a complex task in itself, one of the general principles which has been firmly identified is the principle of 'abuse of rights'. While it clearly stems from civil law (in particular in systems influenced by the German civil code), it has also been argued that the principle is an underlying rationale reflected in various specific legal principles of the common law system. With regard to its content, the principle has been termed 'an application of [the principle of good faith] to the exercise of rights'.[2] Thus, if a right is exercised for a different end than the one intended or unduly interferes with the rights of others, the right-holder may not enjoy the privileges associated with the respective right. However, judicial engagement therewith has remained limited. Only in recent years has the

---

[1] Researcher and Lecturer, Bundeswehr University Munich. The author may be contacted via philipp.janig@unibw.de.

[2] Bin Cheng, General Principles of Law as Applied by International Courts and Tribunals (Stevens & Sons Limited 1953), 121.

principle gained renewed importance in the field of investment arbitration, where tribunals have applied the principle to address the issue of treaty shopping. This contribution will examine how the 'abuse of rights' principle functions with regard to the issue of treaty shopping and how far it has, in the process, detached from its roots in domestic law. Based on these points, it will make observations on the normative structure of general principles of law at large.

Introduction

The nature of 'general principles of law' has long been an object of scholarly debate. By including this source of law in the catalog of Article 38 PCIJ Statute (later Article 38 (1) ICJ Statute), its drafters opened the door for certain recourse to principles enshrined in national legal orders. This position, while not entirely unanimous, finds overwhelming support among today's scholars and requires a comparative analysis of domestic law. However, beyond the task of identifying the existence of general principles, questions have arisen to what extent that process may determine their content.

One principle that has attracted scholarly interest in this regard is 'abuse of rights', which is generally considered as extending the good faith principle to the exercise of rights. As a principle that was developed in civil law countries, it often is regarded as barring the exercise of rights if they are pursued solely to harm another party or for a different purpose than the one intended. Although international judicial bodies generally rarely engaged with that principle, it gained renewed importance in recent years within investment arbitration. Starting with *Phoenix Action Ltd v Czech Republic* in 2009, arbitral tribunals have resorted to 'abuse of rights' to address the issue of treaty shopping and nationality planning and, partly, decline their jurisdiction.

Starting with a brief discussion on the conceptual framework of general principles of law, this contribution will undertake a comparative analysis to examine the normative basis of 'abuse of rights'. In the second part, it will explore how investment tribunals have applied the principle to the issue of nationality planning. From these discussions, the contribution will discuss how far the principle has detached from its roots in domestic law and attempt to extrapolate observations on the normative structure of general principles of law at large.

1. 'Abuse of Rights' as a General Principle of Law: A Comparative Analysis

Overview

Apart from conventional and customary international law, the sources of international law, as enumerated in Article 38(1) ICJ Statute, include the 'general principles of law recognized by civilized nations'.[3] That phrase originally stems from the PCIJ Statute, and its exact meaning has been subject to heated debate already at the time of the provision's drafting.[4] While these debates have been partly mirrored in scholarly writing since, and never been fully resolved,[5] it appears to be general consensus within current scholarship that 'general principles of law' may arise from principles common to the domestic legal orders of states.[6] As a result, the methodology for their determination consists of two parts: As a first step, a comparative analysis of the main legal families of the world (or certain domestic orders representative of these families) is undertaken to determine whether a certain principle is common to them all. In a second step, it is examined whether the principle is transposable to international law. That is, the principle may not contradict already established rules or principles. As a result, the principles undergoes (at least) two processes of abstraction, one to account for differences between the different domestic systems and a second to account for (structural) differences between domestic law and international law. When drafting the Statute, such a source within international law appeared necessary to prevent *non liquet* situations, especially in light of the scarcity of treaties and well-established customary law in that period.[7]

---

[3] Article 38(1)(c) Statute of the International Court of Justice, 1 UNTS XVI.

[4] See Cheng, *General Principles of Law*, 6-21.

[5] Alain Pellet, "Article 38," in *The Statute of the International Court of Justice: A Commentary*, ed. Andreas Zimmermann et al. (Oxford: OUP, 2012), 832.

[6] This position has already been advocated for by Albert de Lapradelle and Lord Phillimore within the Advisory Committee of Jurists, the body tasked with drafting the PCIJ Statute, see Jan Vos, *The Function of Public International Law* (Dordrecht: Springer, 2013), 112.

[7] Alain Pellet, "Article 38," in *The Statute of the International Court of Justice: A Commentary*, ed. Andreas Zimmermann et al. (Oxford: OUP, 2012), 834; Catherine Redgwell, "General Principles of International Law," in *General Principles of Law: European and Comparative Perspective*, ed. Stefan Vogenauer and Stephen Weatherill (Oxford and Portland: Hart Publishing, 2017), 16-17 (identifying three

The following sections will focus on the principle of abuse of rights within national legal orders, including its procedural dimension.[8] As common law jurisdictions do not recognize this legal institution as such, it will be explored whether and how far other solutions have developed that might serve the same or similar functions. That is, to limit the exercise of rights in cases of intent to harm or for other reasons of social interest. This contribution understandably does not strive to undertake an exhaustive comparative analysis. Most importantly, it will limit its focus to four Western jurisdictions – Austria, Germany, France, and the United States – and thereby exemplary examine the civil law (in its Germanic and Romanistic tradition) and the common law. By doing so, the analysis might nevertheless give some guidance on pertinent similarities and difference.

Civil Law Jurisdictions

Introduction

The abuse of rights principle is clearly one of civil law heritage[9] and contained in numerous national legal systems.[10] While some Civil Codes enshrine a general pronouncement of the principle (Germany and Austria), other legislative systems only have provisions of limited application from which courts deduced a more general principle (France). Among all those jurisdictions, the specific circumstances of its application differ. For instance, in determining 'abuse' jurisdictions may employ a

---

steps, with the same content); Jaye Ellis, "General Principles and Comparative Law," *EJIL* 22, no. 4 (2011): 954-959.

[8] Arturo Ricci-Bussatti, the Italian member of the Advisory Committee of Jurists, already considered 'abuse of rights' to be one of the general principles of law, see Michael Byers, "Abuse of Rights: An Old Principle, A New Age," *McGill Law Journal* 47 (2002): 402.

[9] Byers notes that the principles appears to stem from Roman law, see Byers, "Abuse of Rights," 391-392 (fn 3).

[10] See, *e.g.*, Canada (Quebec) (Article 7 Civil Code of Quebec); Mexico (Article 1912 Mexican Civil Code); Netherlands (Article 3:13 (New) Civil Code); Philippines (Article 19-21 Civil Code); Byers, "Abuse of Rights," 392-395 (citing Austria, France, Germany, Italy, Japan, the Netherlands, Spain, Switzerland); Annekatrien Lenaerts, "The General Principle of the Prohibition of Abuse of Rights: A Critical Position on Its Role in a Codified European Contract Law," *European Review of Private Law* 18, no. 6 (2010): 1125-1126 (citing Belgium, France, Germany, Greece, Luxembourg, the Netherlands, Portugal, Spain).

subjective test (Austria) – requiring the intent to harm – or an objective test (Germany) – only examining the harmful effects of the conduct.[11]

The following section explores more deeply the commonalities and differences of the principle and its application within one jurisdiction from the Romanistic tradition (France) and two from the Germanic tradition (Germany and Austria).

France

France is considered the birthplace of the modern conception of abuse of rights, where courts developed the legal doctrine of *abus de droit* beginning from the nineteenth century.[12] One early landmark case is the *Affaire Clément Bayard* from 1915, which concerned a landowner's use of his property. He had erected a 16-meter high fence with spikes that served no purpose for his property, but was built to impede and harm balloons launching from a nearby airfield and flying over his land. The French Court of Cassation considered that to be an abuse of the right to ownership, which could give rise to damages on the basis of tortious liability under Article 1382 Civil Code.[13] While French legislation knows no provision on the abuse of rights, French courts subsequently based themselves on general tort law to develop a principle of general application. As a result, courts applied abuse of rights also to contract law, labor law or procedural law.[14] In the context of procedural law, specific provisions deal with the abusive use of legal remedies *i.a.* allowing judges to impose fines for requests that are 'abusive or dilatory'.[15] In the case of a

---

[11] See also Lenaerts, "The General Principle of the Prohibition of Abuse of Rights," 1125-1128.

[12] Michael Taggart, Private Property and Abuse of Rights in Victorian England: The Story of Edward Pickles and the Bradford Water Supply (Oxford: OUP, 2002), 145; Julio Cueto-Rua, "Abuse of Rights," Louisiana Law Review 35, no. 5 (1975): 976.

[13] Case Coquerel v Clément-Bayard, Req. 3 August 1915, D.P. 1917 I 79; S. 1920, I, 300; Julio Cueto-Rua, "Abuse of Rights," 981 (noting that this was done to extract a higher price for his property); John Prebble and Zoe M Prebble, "Comparing the General Anti-Avoidance Rule of Income Tax Law With the Civil Law Doctrine of Abuse of Law", Victoria University of Wellington Legal Research Papers No 133/2017 7, vol. 32 (2017): 158.

[14] Byers, "Abuse of Rights," 392.

[15] Hervé Ascensio, "Abuse of Process in International Investment Arbitration," Chinese Journal of International Law 13 (2014): 765; see, e.g., Arts 32(1), 550, 559, 581, 628 Code of Civil Procedure, Art 91 Code of Criminal Procedure; Art R 741-12 Code of Administrative Justice.

contractual relationship, the principle is based on the limitative function of the obligation to perform agreements in good faith under Art 1134 (3) Civil Code.

French courts consider the exercise of a right to be abusive, if it occurs with the sole intention to harm another party (subjective test; *intentional abuse*) or if it is careless and unreasonable (objective test; *social abuse*).[16] Under the objective test, the conduct of the right-holder may be compared to that of a 'reasonable man'.[17] In doing so, courts take into account elements of proportionality and the social function of a right, thus including cases of *abuse in social terms*.[18] Should a person pursue goals alien to the social objectives of a right, this may amount to an abuse of right and thus fail to enjoy legal protection.[19]

Germany

The principle of abuse of rights is enshrined in three provisions in the German Civil Code (*BGB*).[20] Underlying these provisions is the notion that the principle of good faith provides for an innate limit to the content of every subjective right (*Innentheorie*).[21] The most explicit expression of the principle is found in Section 226 German Civil Code (prohibition of chicanery; *Schikaneverbot*), according to which '[t]he exercise of a right is not permitted if its only possible purpose consists in causing damage to

---

[16] Lenaerts, "The General Principle of the Prohibition of Abuse of Rights," 1127; David Anderson, "Abuse of Rights," Judicial Review 11, no. 4 (2006): 349.

[17] Amandine Léonard, "'Abuse of Rights' in Belgian and French Patent Law: A Case Law Analysis," Journal of Intellectual Property, Information Technology and E-Commerce Law 7, no. 1 (2016): 33; Lenaerts, "The General Principle of the Prohibition of Abuse of Rights," 1126-1127; Anderson, "Abuse of Rights," 349.

[18] Léonard, "'Abuse of Rights' in Belgian and French Patent Law," 33; Prebble and Prebble, "Comparing the Anti-Avoidance Rule With Abuse of Law," 158.

[19] Léonard, "'Abuse of Rights' in Belgian and French Patent Law," 33; Prebble and Prebble, "Comparing the Anti-Avoidance Rule With Abuse of Law," 158.

[20] See Vera Bolgár, "Abuse of Rights in France, Germany, and Switzerland: A Survey of a Recent Chapter in Legal Doctrine," *Louisiana Law Review* 35, no. 5 (1975): 1023-1030.

[21] Reiner Schulze, "§ 242 Leistung nach Treu und Glauben," in *Bürgerliches Gesetzbuch*, ed. Reiner Schulze *et al.* (Baden-Baden: Nomos, 2017), MN 21; Heinz-Peter Mansel, "BGB § 242 Leistung nach Treu und Glauben," in *Kommentar zum BGB*, ed. Othmar Jauernig (München: C.H. Beck, 2015), MN 32-36.

another'.²² Due to the high evidentiary burden to show that the conduct had no other purpose than causing damage, the provision only has limited practical relevance.²³ Section 826 German Civil Code (intentional damage contrary to public policy; *sittenwidrige vorsätzliche Schädigung*) provides that '[a person who, in a manner contrary to public policy, intentionally inflicts damage on another person is liable to the other person to make compensation for the damage'.²⁴ This also prohibits the abusive exploitation of a formal legal position (*formale Rechtsstellung*) to the detriment of another person insofar that is contrary to public policy.²⁵ Similarly to the *Schikaneverbot*, this provision also has a limited practical significance.²⁶

German jurisprudences rather took recourse to Section 242 German Civil Code (performance in good faith; *Leistung nach Treu und Glauben*) to further develop the issue:

> An obligor has a duty to perform according to the requirements of good faith, taking customary practice into consideration.²⁷

The principle of good faith enshrined in the provision applies to legal relations in general, thus to the entirety of private law as well as public and procedural law.²⁸ It shall serve to prevent outcomes that are deemed unacceptable.²⁹ Whether that is the case is assessed by balancing the

---

²² See "German Civil Code: BGB," Ministry of Justice and Consumer Protection, accessed January 25, 2018, http://www.gesetze-im-internet.de/englisch_bgb/englisch_bgb.html.

²³ Helmut Grothe, "§ 226 Schikaneverbot," in *Münchener Kommentar zum BGB*, ed. Franz-Jürgen Säcker *et al.* (München: C.H. Beck, 2015), MN 1.

²⁴ "German Civil Code".

²⁵ Arndt Teichmann, "§ BGB 826 Sittenwidrige vorsätzliche Schädigung," in *Kommentar zum BGB*, ed. Othmar Jauernig (München: C.H. Beck, 2015), MN 24.

²⁶ Schulze, "§ 242 Leistung nach Treu und Glauben," MN 8.

²⁷ "German Civil Code".

²⁸ Schulze, "§ 242 Leistung nach Treu und Glauben," MN 1, 4; Mansel, "BGB § 242 Leistung nach Treu und Glauben," MN 1, 10; Claudia Schubert, "§ 242 Leistung nach Treu und Glauben," in *Münchener Kommentar zum BGB*, ed. Franz-Jürgen Säcker *et al.* (München: C.H. Beck, 2016), MN 2.

²⁹ Schulze, "§ 242 Leistung nach Treu und Glauben," MN 1.

interests of all persons involved in the specific circumstances of the case,[30] on the basis of objective criteria, *i.e.* customary practice as well as values recognized by the legal order.[31] In doing so, courts shall take into account the specific characteristics of the pertinent legal field, as well as possible public interests.[32] While no intention or fault is required, subjective elements may be also taken into account when balancing interests.[33] Contrary to Sections 226 and 826 Civil Code, which have a general scope of application, Section 242 Civil Code requires the existence of a certain legal relationship, although the bar is rather low.[34]

Despite its explicit wording, the provision not only applies to the performance of obligations, but also to the exercise of subjective rights or the utilization of any legal situation.[35] Also with regard to rights, it should prevent outcomes that are unacceptable, thus irreconcilable with considerations of fairness and law.[36] As a result, the exercise of rights (or utilization of a legal position) is impermissible if the right-holder has no interests worthy of (legal) protection or if the interests of the other party are predominantly worthy of (legal) protection.[37] The first issue entails situations in which the right-holder pursues goals that are dishonest or alien to the underlying agreement or legal order.[38] Any legal consequences

---

[30] Schulze, "§ 242 Leistung nach Treu und Glauben," MN 14; Mansel, "BGB § 242 Leistung nach Treu und Glauben," MN 1-4; Schubert, "§ 242 Leistung nach Treu und Glauben," MN 50.

[31] Mansel, "BGB § 242 Leistung nach Treu und Glauben," MN 1-4; Schubert, "§ 242 Leistung nach Treu und Glauben," MN 11.

[32] Mansel, "BGB § 242 Leistung nach Treu und Glauben," MN 10-11; Schubert, "§ 242 Leistung nach Treu und Glauben," MN 56.

[33] Schulze, "§ 242 Leistung nach Treu und Glauben," MN 14, 23; Schubert, " § 242 Leistung nach Treu und Glauben," MN 54-55.

[34] Schulze, "§ 242 Leistung nach Treu und Glauben," MN 3, 8; Mansel, "BGB § 242 Leistung nach Treu und Glauben," MN 10-11; Schubert, "§ 242 Leistung nach Treu und Glauben," MN 93-95.

[35] Schulze, "§ 242 Leistung nach Treu und Glauben," MN 21; Mansel, "BGB § 242 Leistung nach Treu und Glauben," MN 32-36; Schubert, "§ 242 Leistung nach Treu und Glauben," MN 84.

[36] Mansel, "BGB § 242 Leistung nach Treu und Glauben," MN 32-36.

[37] Schulze, "§ 242 Leistung nach Treu und Glauben," MN 22; Mansel, "BGB § 242 Leistung nach Treu und Glauben," MN 37.

[38] Mansel, "BGB § 242 Leistung nach Treu und Glauben," MN 37-43; Schulze, "§ 242 Leistung nach Treu und Glauben," MN 31.

that would lead to an unacceptable result will not arise.[39] Also, prior conduct may be relevant. Thus, if the right-holder acquired a right through conduct that is unlawful, dishonest or in breach of a contract, the exercise of this right may be impermissible.[40] Therefore, any exercise of rights that is objectively in bad faith is impermissible and unable to generate legal consequences.

Austria

The principle of abuse of rights (*Rechtsmissbrauch*) is enshrined in Section 1295 (2) Austrian Civil Code (*ABGB*), in the context of general tort law. The provisions have been closely modeled after Sections 226 and 826 German Civil Code:[41]

> Also, whoever intentionally inflicts damages in a way that contravenes good morals is liable therefore, however if that occurred in the exercise of a right, only if the exercise of the right clearly had the purpose of harming the other [party].[42]

Similarly to the German theory (*Innentheorie*), the provision is considered as an expression of an unwritten principle that good morals (*gute Sitten*) provide for a limit to the content of subjective rights in general (*Schikaneverbot*).[43] That principle applies to all fields of law, including

---

[39] Schulze, "§ 242 Leistung nach Treu und Glauben," MN 22; Holger Sutschet, "§ 242 Leistung nach Treu und Glauben," in *BeckOK BGB*, ed. Heinz Georg Bamberger *et al.* (München: C.H. Beck, 2017), MN 52.

[40] Schulze, "§ 242 Leistung nach Treu und Glauben," MN 26-27; Mansel, "BGB § 242 Leistung nach Treu und Glauben," MN 44; Sutschet, "§ 242 Leistung nach Treu und Glauben," MN 58.

[41] Friedrich Harrer and Erika M Wagner, "zu § 1295 ABGB," in *ABGB Praxiskommentar – Vol. 6*, ed. Michael Schwimann and Georg E Kodek (Wien: LexisNexis, 2016), MN 144.

[42] Section 1295 (2) Civil Code, as amended by Imperial Law Gazette No 69/1916 ('Auch wer in einer gegen die guten Sitten verstoßenden Weise absichtlich Schaden zufügt, ist dafür verantwortlich, jedoch falls dies in Ausübung eines Rechtes geschah, nur dann, wenn die Ausübung des Rechtes offenbar den Zweck hatte, den anderen zu schädigen.'; translation by the author).

[43] Alexander Wittwer, "zu § 1295 ABGB," in *ABGB Taschenkommentar*, ed. Michael Schwimann (Wien: LexisNexis, 2015), MN 54; Georg E Kodek, "§ 1295 ABGB," in *ABGB-ON*, ed. Andreas Kletečka and Martin Schauer (Wien: Manz, 2016), MN 85.

procedural law and public law.[44] The provision deals with two related but distinct issues. Its first part relates to acts offending good morals – where the conduct is neither explicitly prohibited by law nor based on a subjective right towards the other party; its second part concerns the abuse of subjective rights itself.[45] With regard to both, the person concerned must have acted with actual malice (intent to harm), whereby *dolus eventualis* suffices.[46] Conduct falling under the provision entails liability to pay damages.[47]

While courts made little general statements with regard to the first issue, scholars identified different categories of cases that are relevant. These include the abuse of a formal legal position (*formale Rechtsstellung*), the unfair discrimination of other persons, fraudulent behavior, abuse of power, or the violation of fundamental ethical principles.[48] Insofar as a person seeks to create a right through acts offending good morals, the right will generally not emerge.[49] Any procedural act (such as lawsuits or appeals) are only considered under the first issue – and not as abuse of rights proper – as they do not include the exercise of a subjective right towards another person.[50]

In the context of the second issue (abuse of rights proper), an additional criterion must be fulfilled, namely that the conduct 'clearly had the purpose of harming the other'. In earlier jurisprudence, courts required that harming the other party must have been the only purpose for the relevant. However, more recent jurisprudence has lowered the bar, finding it sufficient if unfair purposes clearly outweigh the legitimate motives to exercise a certain right (a 'flagrant imbalance').[51] Despite this more lenient stance, the intention to harm the other party taken by itself is irrelevant, as

---

[44] Kodek, "§ 1295 ABGB," MN 86; Wittwer, "zu § 1295 ABGB," MN 54.

[45] Kodek, "§ 1295 ABGB," MN 76; Rudolf Reischauer, "§ 1295 ABGB," in *ABGB – Vol. 3*, ed. Peter Rummel (Wien: Manz, 2007), MN 54.

[46] Kodek, "§ 1295 ABGB," MN 77; Wittwer, "zu § 1295 ABGB," MN 53; Harrer and Wagner, "zu § 1295 ABGB," MN 146; Reischauer, "§ 1295 ABGB," MN 58.

[47] Wittwer, "zu § 1295 ABGB," MN 54.

[48] Kodek, "§ 1295 ABGB," MN 80; Harrer and Wagner, "zu § 1295 ABGB," MN 148.

[49] Reischauer, "§ 1295 ABGB," MN 54.

[50] Reischauer, "§ 1295 ABGB," MN 54.

[51] Kodek, "§ 1295 ABGB," MN 88; Wittwer, "zu § 1295 ABGB," MN 53; Harrer and Wagner, "zu § 1295 ABGB," MN 169a.

soon as the person concerned has a justified interest to exercise his or her right.[52]

Common Law

Introduction

Generally speaking, common law knows no principle of abuse of rights. Courts have in principle been reluctant to restrict the exercise of contractual or property rights, if it falls within the objective boundaries of law, even where the underlying motive is objectionable.[53] This is exemplified by the UK House of Lords case *Mayor of Bradford v Pickles*, in which Lord Watson stipulated that '[n]o use of property which would be legal if due to a proper motive can become illegal because it is prompted by a motive which is improper or even malicious'.[54] Similarly, in *Allen v Flood* Justice Wills declared that '[a]ny right given by contract may be exercised against the giver by the person to whom it is granted, no matter how wicked, cruel or mean the motive may be which determines the enforcement of the right.'[55] With regard to abuse of process, the situation is somewhat different in English law, as judges may dismiss civil claims that are 'an abuse of the court's process or is otherwise likely to obstruct the just disposal of the proceedings'.[56]

While common law jurisdictions generally do not explicitly recognize the abuse of rights principle, commentators have argued that it nevertheless serves as an underlying rationale of specific legal principle or rules.[57] Thus, other concepts are used to find 'pragmatic solutions' that lead to similar results.[58] Hersch Lauterpacht, as an early proponent of the principle in international law, argued that the law of torts is essentially

---

[52] Harrer and Wagner, "zu § 1295 ABGB," MN 169a.

[53] Julio Cueto-Rua, "Abuse of Rights," 967.

[54] The Mayor of Bradford v Pickles [1895] AC 587, 598.

[55] Allen v Flood [1898] AC 1.

[56] Civil Procedures Rules, Rule 3.4; Ascensio, "Abuse of Process in International Investment Arbitration," 765.

[57] Anna di Robilant, "Abuse of Rights: The Continental Drug and the Common Law," Boston University School of Law Working Paper No 14-28 (20 June 2014): 12-28

[58] Lenaerts, "The General Principle of the Prohibition of Abuse of Rights," 1125.

based on a prohibition of abuse of rights.[59] More specifically, the torts of abuse of process and nuisance have been considered expressions of the principle.[60] Next to the law of torts, other scholars pointed to principles of equity,[61] or 'malice' and 'reasonableness' tests in legal subfields that serve as 'functional equivalents of abuse of rights'.[62]

However, abuse of rights might have failed to gain acceptance as a general doctrine not necessarily due to an outright rejection of the underlying notion, but rather due to structural differences between common law and civil law. As Michael Byers argued, 'abuse of rights is of limited utility in those legal systems [...] in which the rights themselves have been framed in precise or qualified terms'.[63] Thus, in civil law systems – in which rights are often defined in broad terms – there is a greater need for restricting the exercise of rights in specific cases than in common law jurisdictions, in which rights are more qualified in the first place.[64]

---

[59] Hersch Lauterpacht, The Function of Law in the International Community (Oxford: OUP, 1933, reprint 2011) 303-305.

[60] Ibid, 303-305; Byers, "Abuse of Rights," 395-397; on abuse of process see similarly Anderson, "Abuse of Rights," 350 ('extending not only to fraudulent conduct but to improper use of the court's procedures').

[61] Anderson, "Abuse of Rights," 350 ('the principles of Equity were developed largely for the specific purpose of preventing the abusive exercise of common law rights', further citing the law of defamation/contempt of court, anti-tax avoidance provisions, and fraud).

[62] See, for a historical account see Robilant, "Abuse of Rights," 12-28.

[63] Byers, "Abuse of Rights," 397; see also Cueto-Rua, "Abuse of Rights," 969-970 (citing several reasons stemming from structural differences between the legal traditions that account for the lack of acceptance of abuse of rights within common law).

[64] Byers, "Abuse of Rights," 396 (with further references); *cf.* Elspeth Reid, "The Doctrine of Abuse of Rights: Perspective from a Mixed Jurisdiction," *Electronic Journal of Comparative Law* 8, no. 3 (2004): 13 ('An overarching doctrine of abuse of rights may be required in Civil Law systems to circumscribe the exercise of rights proclaimed in generous terms. But if, as in the Common Law, rights 'contain their own qualifications' within the case-law by which they are defined, then such a doctrine is unnecessary.' [fn omitted]); see also Jukka Snell, "The Notion of and a General Test for Abuse of Rights: Some Normative Reflections," in *Prohibition of Abuse of Law: A New General Principle of EU Law?*, ed. Rita de la Feria and Stefan Vogenauer (Oxford & Portland: Hart, 2011), 220-221; Anderson, "Abuse of Rights," 350 (ascribing the lack of acknowledgment to 'the traditional reluctance of English law to think in terms of rights at all').

United States

Nuisance is a class of torts arising from the interference with the use or enjoyment of property rights, dealing with both interferences of private property (private nuisance)[65] and the rights common to the general public (public nuisance).[66] These torts may also arise where in principle lawful activities lead to the injury of another person (*e.g.* as qualified nuisance).[67] Thus, also lawful activities may lead to liability if they are considered unreasonable or unwarrantable under the circumstances.[68]

The tort of abuse of process concerns the use of procedural tools and stems from the more general principle of due process.[69] The Restatement (Second) of Torts defined it as:

> One who uses a legal process, whether criminal or civil, against another primarily to accomplish a purpose for which it is not designed is subject to liability to the other for harm caused by the abuse of process.[70]

The elements that must generally be fulfilled is the (1) wrongful and willful use of process, to (2) obtain a result that is wrongful or beyond the process's scope and that (3) results in damages.[71] Thus, the notion of abuse of rights – restricting the exercise of rights if considered not justifiable in the specific circumstances – is, at least to a limited extent, reflected in the parts of the US legal order.

---

[65] See, *e.g.*, *Dunlap v. Daigle*, 122 N.H. 295, 298 (1982).

[66] See, *e.g.*, *Robie v. Lillis*, 112 N.H. 492, 495 (1972); Bryan Garner ed., *Black's Law Dictionary* (St. Paul: Thomson Reuters, 2014) 1233-1235.

[67] Garner ed., *Black's Law Dictionary*, 1235 ('A condition that, though lawful in itself, is so negligently permitted to exist that it creates an unreasonable risk of harm and, in due course, actually results in injury to another.').

[68] See, *e.g.*, *Feeley v. Borough of Ridley Park*, 551 A.2d 373, 375 (Pa. Commw. Ct. 1988).

[69] Ascensio, "Abuse of Process in International Investment Arbitration," 765.

[70] Restatement (Second) of Torts § 682 (1977), as cited in Garner ed., *Black's Law Dictionary*, 12-13 (abuse of process).

[71] Jeffrey J Utermohle, "Look What They've Done to My Tort, Ma: The Unfortunate Demise of "Abuse of Process" in Maryland," *University of Baltimore Law Review* 32, no. 1 (2002): 8; Garner ed., *Black's Law Dictionary*, 12.

'Abuse of Rights' in General International Law

The differences between the legal families remain apparent. While the civil law jurisdictions of France, Germany, and Austria – despite their differences – have developed doctrines that apply to rights in general, comparable approaches within common law jurisdictions, such as the United States, arose only in specific, qualified sets of circumstances. The absence of a principle from a number of domestic legal orders (or a legal family) has often been considered as baring the emergence of a general principle of law.[72] Others, however, have argued that this might not necessarily be considered as a rejection of that principle if the 'circumstances justifying its application in one system are absent from the other'.[73] As already noted above, the necessity of an abuse of rights doctrine in common law countries is uncertain. Such a line of argumentation would presuppose that the nature (or design) of *rights in international* law more closely resemble *rights in civil law systems* than those in common law. While this position has some support,[74] its examination would go beyond the scope of this contribution.

Another point of contention concerns to what extent the contents of general principles of law are (or are able to be) predetermined by such a comparative analysis. International judicial bodies have not imported domestic law principles 'lock, stock and barrel',[75] but rather developed 'a body of international law the content of which has been influenced by domestic law but which is still its own creation'.[76] In part, scholars have

---

[72] Jan Willisch, *State Responsibility for Technological Damage in International Law* (Berlin: Duncker & Humblodt, 1987), 163 ('it cannot be denied that no legal principle qualifies as a general principle of law unless its underlying general concept together with its essential ingredients can be found in the different national systems of law').

[73] Cheng, *General Principles of Law*, 265-266; *cf.* Michael Akehurst, "Equity and General Principles of Law," *International and Comparative Law Quarterly* 25, no. 4 (1976): 817, fn86; *South West Africa (Ethiopia v South Africa; Liberia v South Africa)* (Second Phase; Dissenting Opinion Judge Tanaka) [1966] ICJ Rep 250, 299 ('the recognition of a principle by civilized nations [...] does not mean recognition by all civilized nations').

[74] Sara McLaughlin Mitchell and Emilia Justyna Powell, *Domestic Law Goes Global: Legal Traditions and International Courts* (Cambridge: CUP, 2011), 51-52.

[75] *International Status of South-West Africa* (Advisory Opinion; Separate Opinion Judge McNair) [1950] ICJ Rep 146, 158.

[76] James Crawford, *Brownlie's Principles of Public International Law* (Oxford: OUP, 2012) 35.

called for determining the content of general principles in greater detail through more rigorous comparative analysis, in order to enhance their 'legitimacy' and thus facilitate their application by international judicial bodies.[77] This might have considerable implications for the content of abuse of rights. Consensus among domestic legal systems might arguably be found to limit rights where the respective party *solely* exercises it to cause harm to another party. However, this is far less certain with regard to imposing limits on rights in social terms, such as reasonableness or appropriateness.

Irrespective of these issues, the principle of abuse of rights has gained recognition within international law.[78] Both scholars and international judicial bodies have generally framed abuse of rights as an expression of the principle of good faith.[79] Discussions on the content of the principle have partly mirrored domestic approaches. Thus, an abuse should occur when the exercise disproportionately favors the right-holder in light of a balance of interest[80] or when a right is exercised 'for a purpose [...] different from that for which that right was created'.[81]

---

[77] Stephan Schill, "General Principles of Law and International Investment Law," in *International Investment Law: The Sources of Rights and Obligations*, ed. Tarcisio Gazzini and Eric De Brabandere (Leiden: Martinus Nijhoff, 2012), 146.

[78] The principle also found expression in treaty law, see Art 300 UNCLOS; on its status as a general principle of EU Law see Case C-110/99 *Emsland-Stärke* [2000] ECR I-11569.

[79] See Cheng, *General Principles of Law*, 121 (abuse of rights constitutes 'an application of [the general principle of good faith] to the exercise of rights'); Ascensio, "Abuse of Process in International Investment Arbitration," 764-765; see also WTO Appellate Body – Decision WT/DS58/AB/R of 12 December 1998, *US Shrimp*, para 158.

[80] Ascensio, "Abuse of Process in International Investment Arbitration," 764-765.

[81] *Saipem S.p.A. v. The People's Republic of Bangladesh*, ICSID Case No. ARB/05/07, Award, 30 June 2009, para 160; Ascensio, "Abuse of Process in International Investment Arbitration," 764-765; see generally Cheng, *General Principles of Law*, 121-136.

2. Abuse of Rights as a Jurisdictional Objection before Investment Tribunals following Corporate Restructuring

Foreign Nationality as Prerequisite of Jurisdiction and the Practice of Nationality Planning

The jurisdiction of investor-state tribunals is based on treaties, most importantly Bilateral Investment Treaties (BITs) and, in ICSID arbitration, the ICSID Convention. Under these treaties, the possibility to take recourse to investment arbitration against a host state is only open to investors of foreign nationality. Thus, investors wishing to rely on the jurisdictional clause in a BIT (or within the investment chapter of a multilateral trade agreement), must have the nationality of the relevant state party.[82]

Similarly, Article 25 (1) ICSID Convention provides that the 'jurisdiction of the Centre shall extend to any legal dispute arising directly out of an investment, between a Contracting State [...] and a national of another Contracting State [...]'.[83] With regard to legal entities, the provision further defines a 'national of another Contracting State' as

> any juridical person which had the nationality of a Contracting State other than the State party to the dispute on the date on which the parties consented to submit such dispute to conciliation or arbitration and any juridical person which had the nationality of the Contracting State party to the dispute on that date and which, because of foreign control, the parties have agreed should be treated as a national of another Contracting State for the purposes of this Convention.[84]

Thus, while the ICSID Convention establishes foreign nationality as a basic requirement to bring investment claims, it does not provide for criteria to determine corporate nationality. Most definitions within BITs only rely on formal criteria, namely the place of incorporation or seat (*siège social*). In some case, states have narrowed these definitions through the inclusion of (additional) substantive criteria in BITs, in particular,

---

[82] Rudolf Dolzer and Christoph Schreuer, *Principles of International Investment Law* (Oxford: OUP, 2012), 252.

[83] Art 25 (1) ICSID Convention.

[84] Art 25 (2) (b) ICSID Convention.

The General Principle of 'Abuse of Rights' 237

denial-of-benefit clauses.[85] However, insofar as nationality is mainly defined by the place of incorporation,[86] it remains an issue governed by the domestic law of the home state.[87] As such, the question of nationality is one of fact, to be objectively determined before international arbitral tribunals.[88]

This framework makes it comparatively easy for corporate investors to acquire a new nationality. Thus, corporations may restructure themselves in order to achieve more favorable protection under investment treaties.[89] This practice has been characterized as 'treaty shopping', 'treaty planning', 'nationality planning', or 'corporate manoeuvering'.[90]

In *Tokios Tokelés v Ukraine*, a landmark case on nationality planning, the tribunal examined this issue.[91] Tokios Tokelés was a Lithuanian legal entity founded in 1989 and almost exclusively owned by Ukrainian nationals. In mid-2002 the claimant lodged its request for arbitration, complaining about governmental measures taken from early-2002 onwards against its Ukrainian subsidiary, which was founded in 1994.[92] While Ukraine

---

[85] By way of which only corporations with a 'substantial business activity' in a state may claim nationality of that state, *e.g.* Article 17(1) Energy Charter Treaty (adopted 17 December 1994, entered into force 16 April 1998) 2080 UNTS 95, see Dolzer and Schreuer, *Principles of International Investment Law*, 55-56.

[86] *Cf. Case Concerning the Barcelona Traction, Light and Power Company, Limited* (*Belgium v Spain*) [1970] ICJ Rep 3, at 42, para 70 [dealing with the issue of diplomatic protection]; Christoph Schreuer *et al*, *The ICSID Convention: A Commentary* (Cambridge: CUP, 2009), 281 ('ICSID tribunals have uniformly adopted the test of incorporation or seat rather than control when determining the nationality of [...] juridical persons').

[87] Dolzer and Schreuer, *Principles of International Investment Law*, 252.

[88] While domestic law might be (part of) applicable law in the merits stage, the issue of jurisdiction is in principle governed by international treaties as a distinct system. Thus the determination of jurisdiction is not subject of the law applicable to the merits, see *CMS Gas Transmission Company v. The Republic of Argentina*, ICSID Case No. ARB/01/8, Decision of the Tribunal on Objections to Jurisdiction, 17 July 2003, para 87-88; *cf* Dolzer and Schreuer, *Principles of International Investment Law*, 252.

[89] Schreuer *et al.*, *The ICSID Convention*, 292.

[90] Jorun Baumgartner, *Treaty Shopping in International Investment Law* (Oxford: OUP, 2016), 7-8.

[91] *Tokios Tokelés v. Ukraine*, ICSID Case No ARB/02/18, Decision on Jurisdiction, 29 April 2004.

[92] *Ibid*, paras 1-3.

disputed the nationality of Tokios Tokelés,[93] the tribunal found no legal reason to pierce the corporate veil. The tribunal considered it of particular relevance that the entity was not established for the purpose of gaining access to ICSID arbitration, as it was incorporated years before the BIT entered into force and the dispute arose.[94]

The basic conclusion of *Tokios Tokelés* – i.e. that nationality planning is in principle permissible – has been upheld by numerous other tribunals.[95] Nevertheless – if understood as a system for the purpose of reciprocal benefits – 'nationality planning' potentially creates a notable issue for the legitimacy of the investment framework,[96] as states might be obliged to afford protection to corporations without benefiting from any additional investment.[97] This becomes particularly pertinent where previously purely domestic disputes are 'internationalized' by corporate restructuring.

'Abuse of Rights' as Applied in Investor-State Arbitration

Within investor-state arbitration, 'abuse of rights' (or, insofar as it concerns procedural rights, 'abuse of process') has been invoked as a preliminary objection in issues such as multiple parallel arbitrations or claims brought by remote shareholders, largely to no avail.[98] However, in cases where issues of nationality planning have been examined under the heading of 'abuse of rights', arbitral tribunals partly declined their jurisdiction.[99]

---

[93] *Ibid*, paras 21-23.

[94] *Ibid*, paras 54-56.

[95] See, e.g., *CME Czech Republic B.V. v Czech Republic*, UNCITRAL Arbitration, Partial Award (13 September 2001) para 419 (in the context of parallel arbitrations of a corporate investor and its owner regarding the same dispute).

[96] *Saluka Investments B.V. v Czech Republic*, UNCITRAL, Partial Award (17 March 2006) para 240.

[97] *Cf. Tokios Tokelés v. Ukraine*, ICSID Case No ARB/02/18, Dissenting Opinion of Chairman Prosper Weil, 29 April 2004, para 30.

[98] See Ascensio, "Abuse of Process in International Investment Arbitration," 766.

[99] See Filip Černý, "Short Flight of the Phoenix: A Few Thoughts on Good Faith, the Abuse of Rights and Legality in Investment Arbitration," *Czech Yearbook of International Law* 3 (2012): 194-202.

The first case in which an arbitral tribunal dismissed an entire claim on the basis of 'abuse of rights' was *Phoenix Action Ltd v Czech Republic*.[100] The claimant, an Israeli corporation held by a Czech national, argued that its rights under the Czech-Israeli BIT were violated due to a lengthy domestic legal dispute involving two Czech companies it controlled. These two companies, however, were acquired from, and in part subsequently sold back to, other family members of the shareholder of Phoenix Action. The tribunal considered that for the determination of an 'investment' under Article 25 (1) ISCID Convention it has to take into account, as an additional requirement,[101] whether the investment was made in good faith.[102] After finding that all other criteria were fulfilled, the tribunal turned to good faith, examining several elements. In doing so, it highlighted that when acquiring the Czech companies the domestic proceedings were already ongoing (*timing of the investment*); that the claimant's initial (but subsequently abandoned) submissions would have amounted to bringing a pre-existing domestic dispute (*initial request to ICSID*); that the claimant notified the respondent of an investment dispute already two months after acquiring the Czech companies and prior to registering the change in ownership (*the timing of the claim*); that all transfers occurred between members of a single family, all of which were Czech citizens (*the substance of the transaction*); and that the claimant apparently had neither performed nor intended any economic activity (*the true nature of the operation*).[103]

Based on these considerations, the tribunal concluded that the investment was made 'for the sole purpose of bringing international litigation'.[104] As the claimant created 'a legal fiction' to gain access to ICSID arbitration, the tribunal found that to constitute an abuse of rights (a '*détournement de procédure*'). As a result, the 'initiation and pursuit of this arbitration is an abuse of the system of international ICSID investment

---

[100] *Phoenix Action Ltd v Czech Republic*, ICSID Case No ARB/06/5, Award, 15 April 2009.

[101] According to the tribunal, in addition to the investment having been made in conformity with the laws of the host state, as well as the *Salini* criteria, see *Salini Costruttori S.p.A. and Italstrade S.p.A. v. Kingdom of Morocco*, ICSID Case No. ARB/00/4, Decision on Jurisdiction, 31 July 2001, 42 ILM 609 (2003), para 52.

[102] *Phoenix v. Czech Republic*, paras 73, 113.

[103] *Ibid.*, paras 136-140.

[104] *Ibid.*, para 142.

arbitration'[105] and the tribunal therefore lacked jurisdiction *ratione materiae.*[106]

The *Phoenix* case sparked considerable debate within arbitral jurisprudence. In particular, it was criticized for determining 'good faith' as a criterion of a protected 'investment' under Art 25 ICSID Convention, thus establishing abuse of rights as an element barring jurisdiction *ratione materiae.*[107] In more recent cases, tribunals usually considered abuse of rights as an autonomous and distinct objection.[108]

As that doctrine is not enshrined in the underlying treaties or procedural rules,[109] it must 'exist independently of specific language [...] in the treaty'.[110] However, from the vantage point of arbitral jurisprudence, the specific legal basis appears somewhat unclear. By tying the issue to the determination of an 'investment', the *Phoenix* tribunal in essence interpreted and applied Art 25 ICSID Convention. Similarly to the German *Innentheorie*, however, the tribunal also held that 'every right includes an implied clause that it must not be abused'.[111] Most tribunals that have not followed the *Phoenix* approach found the doctrine (or 'theory') to be 'an expression of the more general principle of good faith'.[112] In contrast, the

---

[105] *Ibid.*, para 143-144.

[106] *Ibid.*, paras 145.

[107] *Metal-Tech Ltd. v. Republic of Uzbekistan*, ICSID Case No. ARB/10/3, Award, 4 October 2013, para 217.

[108] Ascensio, "Abuse of Process in International Investment Arbitration," 779.

[109] Ascensio, "Abuse of Process in International Investment Arbitration," 764; *cf Mobil Corporation, Venezuela Holdings, B.V., et al. v. Bolivarian Republic of Venezuela*, ICSID Case No. ARB/07/27, Decision on Jurisdiction, 10 June 2010, paras 169-175.

[110] *Gustav F W Hamester GmbH & Co KG v. Republic of Ghana*, ICSID Case No. ARB/07/24, Award, 18 June 2010.

[111] *Phoenix v. Czech Republic*, para 107.

[112] *Abaclat and Others (Case formerly known as Giovanna a Beccara and Others) v. Argentine Republic*, ICSID Case No. ARB/07/5, Decision on Jurisdiction and Admissibility, 4 August 2011, para 646; *Churchill Mining PLC and Planet Mining Pty Ltd v. Republic of Indonesia*, ICSID Case No. ARB/12/14 and 12/40, Award, 6 December 2016, para 492; similarly *Mobil Corporation, Venezuela Holdings, B.V., et al. v. Bolivarian Republic of Venezuela*, ICSID Case No. ARB/07/27, Decision on Jurisdiction, 10 June 2010, paras 169-176; *Pac Rim Cayman LLC v. Republic of El Savador*, ICSID Case No. ARB/09/12, Decision on Jurisdiction, 1 June 2012, para 2.44.

tribunal in *Saipem v Bangladesh* considered it to constitute a general principle in its own right.[113]

In determining which (procedural) right the investor might exercise abusively in this context tribunals have resorted to rather broad terms. Generally, tribunals might point to the acquisition of nationality and/or to the initiation of a claim. The *Phoenix* tribunal invoked both and held that the abuse consisted 'in the Claimant's creation of a legal fiction in order to gain access to an international arbitration procedure'[114] and thus the 'Claimant's initiation and pursuit of this arbitration is an abuse of international ICSID investment arbitration'.[115] In *Gremcitel v Peru*, the tribunal explicitly held that the 'corporate restructuring [...] constitutes an abuse of process'.[116] Other tribunals similarly pointed to an 'abuse [...] of the investment treaty system by attempting to create artificial international jurisdiction'[117] or held that '[a]n investment will not be protected if its creation itself constitutes a misuse of the system of international investment protection under the ICSID Convention'.[118]

Nevertheless, building on the *Phoenix* case, arbitral jurisprudence has developed several pertinent criteria, although rarely making general statements on an applicable standard.[119] In particular, tribunals examined the *foreseeability of the dispute* and the *motivation for restructuring* when applying the principle of abuse of rights.[120] In addition, tribunals have taken into account various other factors based on the specific circumstances of the case.

---

[113] *Saipem. v. Bangladesh*, para 145; see also the rather extensive comparative analysis in *Mobil v. Venezuela*, paras 169-175.

[114] Phoenix v. Czech Republic, para 143.

[115] Ibid, para 144.

[116] Renée Rose Levy and Gremcitel S.A. v. Republic of Peru, ICSID Case No. ARB/11/17, Award, 9 January 2015, para 182, see also ibid, para 195 ('the corporate restructurings [...] constitutes and abuse of process').

[117] Transglobal Green Energy, LLC and Transglobal Green Energy de Panama, S.A. v. The Republic of Panama, ICSID Case No. ARB/13/28, para 118.

[118] Hamester v. Ghana, para 124.

[119] See, however, *Saipem v. Bangladesh*, para 160 ('It is generally acknowledged in international law that a State exercising a right for a purpose that is different from that for which that right was created commits an abuse of rights').

[120] Jorun Baumgartner, *Treaty Shopping in International Investment Law* (Oxford: OUP, 2016), 205.

With regard to *foreseeability*, tribunals examine whether the dispute underlying a claim was foreseeable already at the time of corporate restructuring. In an attempt to clarify the standard, the tribunal in *Pac Rim v El Salvador* considered whether the investor 'can see an actual dispute or can foresee a specific future dispute as a very high probability and not merely as a possible controversy'.[121] Nevertheless, tribunals have employed different tests to determine the (temporal) existence of a 'dispute' and relied on a combination of objective and/or subjective factors to assess their foreseeability.[122]

Regarding *motivation*, tribunals will examine for which purposes corporate restructuring occurred, *i.e.* whether a new nationality was acquired in order to gain access to the system of investment arbitration.[123] With regard to the threshold, the *Phoenix* tribunal held that gaining access to investment arbitration was the 'sole purpose' for restructuring.[124] Other tribunals generally found it sufficient that it was the 'main purpose' or 'one of the principal purposes'.[125] These approaches, however, are difficult in their application as they focus on the subjective motives of the investor.[126] As a result, if a dispute is considered foreseeable, some tribunals have apparently operated with a rebuttable presumption regarding the *motivation*, thus allowing the investor to prove that other reasons were determinative for the restructuring.[127]

---

[121] *Pac Rim v. El Savador*, para 2.99; similarly, *Lao Holdings N.V. v. Lao People's Democratic Republic*, ICSID Case No. ARB(AF)/12/6, Decision on Jurisdiction, 21 February 2014, para 76 ('when things have started to deteriorate so that a dispute is highly probable')

[122] See more specifically Baumgartner, *Treaty Shopping*, 222-227; Ascensio, "Abuse of Process in International Investment Arbitration," 773-774.

[123] *Cf* already *Tokios Tokelés v. Ukraine*, para 56.

[124] *Phoenix v Czech Republic*, para 93; see also *Tokios Tokelés v. Ukraine*, para 56.

[125] *Pac Rim v. El Savador*, para 2.41-2.42; Arbitrator Stern in *Alapli Elektrik B.V. v. Republic of Turkey*, ICSID Case No. ARB/08/13, Excerpts of Award, 16 July 2012, para 393.

[126] Baumgartner, *Treaty Shopping*, 227-228; Ascensio, "Abuse of Process in International Investment Arbitration," 774.

[127] *Philip Morris Asia Limited v. The Commonwealth of Australia*, UNCITRAL, PCA Case No. 2012-12, Award on Jurisdiction and Admissibility, 17 December 2015, paras 570-584.

3. Conclusions

The application of the abuse of rights principle within jurisdictional disputes in investment law shows the continuing practical relevance of general principles of law, even in fields that are almost exclusively regulated by treaties. It further exemplifies that general principles may be suitable to grant international judicial bodies a flexible tool to address situations arguably not foreseen by states at the time of drafting treaties.

With regard to the normative foundations of the abuse of rights principle, the above discussions show that the elements employed by investment tribunals do not appear to stem directly from any elements developed in domestic law. Thus, the specific application is largely detached from its background within domestic law. Naturally, these differences should not be overstated. To a large degree, they merely reflect the international character of such a general principle of law, applied to a specific sub-field of international law. Most importantly, similar situations – *i.e.* jurisdictional disputes in which claimants only have access to a forum due to their nationality or legal form – are arguably unlikely to arise within national law. What appears of greater relevance is to what extent the general standards of determining an 'abuse' within domestic law resemble those applied by investment tribunals. As the brief comparative analysis above shows, a number of domestic systems prohibit the exercise of a right with the (sole) intention of harming the other party. Within investment law, however, investors carry out nationality planning not out of malice to harm the respondent state, but merely out of self-interest, *i.e.* to safeguard economic interests. In the cases described, most investors rather seek to secure the right to bring international investment claims with regard to disputes that tribunals considered as being domestic in nature. Thus by exercising their right to bring investment claims, these investors utilize the system of investment arbitration for a purpose it was not established, namely to adjudicate domestic disputes. On a more general level, one might argue that this affects the balance of interests underlying international investment law, *i.e.* granting special rights to a specific category of natural and legal persons (*foreign* investors) in the expectation of attracting additional investment. Whether these issues – exercising rights to pursue other goals then envisaged or disrupting the balance of interests – are considered to be 'abusive' or otherwise impermissible within all legal families appears somewhat questionable.

Another issue concerns how tribunals have dealt with the legal basis for the application of abuse of rights. At least from a dogmatic (positivist) standpoint, this appears to be particularly problematic. In a number of cases, tribunals were satisfied in basing themselves on abuse of rights as an element of the general principle of good faith. By sidestepping the question on the legal nature of abuse of rights – potentially due to its uncertain status in certain legal traditions – and invoking good faith, arbitral tribunals ascribe a content to the latter principle that they might well not be able to derive from domestic legal orders.

These considerations allow some observations on the normative structure of general principles of law at large. While it appears that general principles of law emanate from domestic law in terms of their *existence*, their specific *normative content* is generally un(der)determined by their process of formation. Although more rigorous comparative analysis may allow specifying (and thus 'legitimize') their application to a certain degree, it arguably will hardly enable scholars to draw conclusions on their normative content that go beyond general statements. In terms of normative determinability, the general principle of law might thus be compared to fundamental and human rights, which are often couched in indeterminate language and are left to be shaped through jurisprudence. This appears to be in line with the purpose general principles of law shall serve within international law, *i.e.* to award international judicial bodies some flexibility in particular situations. However, within this flexibility lies also the greatest pitfall. In particular, general principles of law award great discretionary power to international judges and arbitrators and might well be used as a tool of judicial law-making.

Bibliography

Akehurst, Michael. "Equity and General Principles of Law," *International and Comparative Law Quarterly* 25, no. 4 (1976)

Anderson, David. "Abuse of Rights," *Judicial Review* 11, no. 4 (2006): 349.

Ascensio, Hervé. "Abuse of Process in International Investment Arbitration," *Chinese Journal of International Law* 13 (2014)

Baumgartner, Jorun. *Treaty Shopping in International Investment Law* (Oxford: OUP, 2016)

Bolgár, Vera. "Abuse of Rights in France, Germany, and Switzerland: A Survey of a Recent Chapter in Legal Doctrine," *Louisiana Law Review* 35, no. 5 (1975)

Byers, Michael. "Abuse of Rights: An Old Principle, A New Age," *McGill Law Journal* 47 (2002)

Černý, Filip. "Short Flight of the Phoenix: A Few Thoughts on Good Faith, the Abuse of Rights and Legality in Investment Arbitration," *Czech Yearbook of International Law* 3 (2012)

Cheng, Bin. *General Principles of Law as Applied by International Courts and Tribunals* (Stevens & Sons Limited 1953)

Crawford, James. *Brownlie's Principles of Public International Law* (Oxford: OUP, 2012)

Cueto-Rua, Julio. "Abuse of Rights," *Louisiana Law Review* 35, no. 5 (1975)
di Robilant, Anna. "Abuse of Rights: The Continental Drug and the Common Law," Boston University School of Law Working Paper No 14-28 (20 June 2014)
Dolzer, Rudolf and Schreuer, Christoph. *Principles of International Investment Law* (Oxford: OUP, 2012)
Ellis, Jaye. "General Principles and Comparative Law," *EJIL* 22, no. 4 (2011)
Gaillard, Emmanuel. "Abuse of Process in International Arbitration," *ICSID Review* 32, no. 1 (2017)
Garner, Bryan ed. *Black's Law Dictionary* (St. Paul: Thomson Reuters, 2014)
Grothe, Helmut. "§ 226 Schikaneverbot," in *Münchener Kommentar zum BGB*, ed. Franz-Jürgen Säcker *et al.* (München: C.H. Beck, 2015)
Harrer, Friedrich and Wagner, Erika M. "zu § 1295 ABGB," in *ABGB Praxiskommentar – Vol. 6*, ed. Michael Schwimann and Georg E Kodek (Wien: LexisNexis, 2016)
Kodek, Georg E. "§ 1295 ABGB," in *ABGB-ON*, ed. Andreas Kletečka and Martin Schauer (Wien: Manz, 2016)
Lauterpacht, Hersch. *The Function of Law in the International Community* (Oxford: OUP, 1933, reprint 2011)
Lenaerts, Annekatrien. "The General Principle of the Prohibition of Abuse of Rights: A Critical Position on Its Role in a Codified European Contract Law," *European Review of Private Law* 18, no. 6 (2010)
Léonard, Amandine. "Abuse of Rights' in Belgian and French Patent Law: A Case Law Analysis," *Journal of Intellectual Property, Information Technology and E-Commerce Law* 7, no. 1 (2016)
Mansel, Heinz-Peter. "BGB § 242 Leistung nach Treu und Glauben," in *Kommentar zum BGB*, ed. Othmar Jauernig (München: C.H. Beck, 2015)
Mitchell, Sara McLaughlin and Powell, Emilia Justyna. *Domestic Law Goes Global: Legal Traditions and International Courts* (Cambridge: CUP, 2011)
Pellet, Alain. "Article 38," in *The Statute of the International Court of Justice: A Commentary*, ed. Andreas Zimmermann *et al.* (Oxford: OUP, 2012)
Prebble, John and Prebble, Zoe M. "Comparing the General Anti-Avoidance Rule of Income Tax Law With the Civil Law Doctrine of Abuse of Law", *Victoria University of Wellington Legal Research Papers No 133/20177*, vol. 32 (2017)
Redgwell, Catherine. "General Principles of International Law," in *General Principles of Law: European and Comparative Perspective*, ed. Stefan Vogenauer and Stephen Weatherill (Oxford and Portland: Hart Publishing, 2017)
Reid, Elspeth. "The Doctrine of Abuse of Rights: Perspective from a Mixed Jurisdiction," *Electronic Journal of Comparative Law* 8, no. 3 (2004)
Reischauer, Rudolf. "§ 1295 ABGB," in *ABGB – Vol. 3*, ed. Peter Rummel (Wien: Manz, 2007)
Schill, Stephan. "General Principles of Law and International Investment Law," in *International Investment Law: The Sources of Rights and

Obligations, ed. Tarcisio Gazzini and Eric De Brabandere (Leiden: Martinus Nijhoff, 2012)

Schreuer, Christoph *et al. The ICSID Convention: A Commentary* (Cambridge: CUP, 2009)

Schubert, Claudia. "§ 242 Leistung nach Treu und Glauben," in *Münchener Kommentar zum BGB*, ed. Franz-Jürgen Säcker *et al.* (München: C.H. Beck, 2016)

Schulze, Reiner. "§ 242 Leistung nach Treu und Glauben," in *Bürgerliches Gesetzbuch*, ed. Reiner Schulze *et al.* (Baden-Baden: Nomos, 2017)

Snell, Jukka. "The Notion of and a General Test for Abuse of Rights: Some Normative Reflections," in *Prohibition of Abuse of Law: A New General Principle of EU Law?*, ed. Rita de la Feria and Stefan Vogenauer (Oxford & Portland: Hart, 2011)

Sutschet, Holger. "§ 242 Leistung nach Treu und Glauben," in *BeckOK BGB*, ed. Heinz Georg Bamberger *et al.* (München: C.H. Beck, 2017)

Taggart, Michael. *Private Property and Abuse of Rights in Victorian England: The Story of Edward Pickles and the Bradford Water Supply* (Oxford: OUP, 2002)

Teichmann, Arndt. " BGB § 826 Sittenwidrige vorsätzliche Schädigung," in *Kommentar zum BGB*, ed. Othmar Jauernig (München: C.H. Beck, 2015)

Utermohle, Jeffrey J. "Look What They've Done to My Tort, Ma: The Unfortunate Demise of "Abuse of Process" in Maryland." *University of Baltimore Law Review* 32, no. 1 (2002)

Vos, Jan. *The Function of Public International Law* (Dordrecht: Springer, 2013)

Willisch Jan. *State Responsibility for Technological Damage in International Law* (Berlin: Duncker & Humblodt, 1987)

Wittwer, Alexander. "zu § 1295 ABGB," in *ABGB Taschenkommentar*, ed. Michael Schwimann (Wien: LexisNexis, 2015)

Chapter 13

The Court of Justice of the European Union and the European Court of Human Rights Procedures: On the Quest for a more Coherent Approach in Human Rights Protection

Vesna Ćorić[1]

Abstract

The objective of this paper is to analyze procedural divergences between the Court of Justice of the European Union and the European Court of Human Rights. As their inconsistent case law has already gained enough attention in the literature, the paper will primarily focus on other aspects of divergences manifested in different characteristics of available remedies. The key argument of the paper is that the procedural rules of both systems are inconsistent and need to be modified in order to contribute to the establishment of a coherent and efficient European human rights protection system, which would contain only legitimate limitations stemming from the pluralistic character of the human rights protection system and demands to provide an effective protection to individuals.

The first section addresses the stance promoted by the International Law Commission on the fragmentation of international law and aims to apply it to the European field. The second section explores the scope and nature of the doctrine of equivalent protection to determine the *specific level of procedural divergences between the two supranational courts which the European Court of Human Rights tolerates. The third section identifies the*

---

[1] Research Fellow, Institute of Comparative Law, Belgrade

procedural divergences which exist between the European Court of Human Rights and the Court of Justice of the European Union and offers concrete proposals for the improvement of the existing rules as to enable the creation of more consistent frameworks regulating procedural aspects of human rights protection before these courts. The article concludes that the efficient, coherent and transparent European human rights protection system requires not only the removal of divergences in legal procedures but also the improved level of transparency of procedural rules applied by both courts. In addition to that, in the concluding part of the paper, it is proposed to change the existing approaches of the European Court of Human Rights and that of the International Law Commission respectively as to motivate the competent bodies of the European Union to improve the set of procedural remedies which are available before the Court of Justice of the European Union.

While conducting the analysis, the author will use doctrinal methods. Primarily, the analysis will focus on the case law of two courts, relevant acts of the Council of Europe and the European Union as well as on documents of the International Law Commission. In addition, the author will rely on the available academic and expert literature in this field, which will provide additional grounds for critical assessment of procedural aspects of the operation of these courts and assist in opening up a debate for challenging the existing settings and practices.

Introduction

The Court of Justice of the European Union (CJEU) delivered its Opinion 2/13 on the Compatibility of the Draft Agreement on the Accession of the European Union to the European Convention on Human Rights with European Union law (Opinion 2/13) in December 2014. This Opinion renders the potential European Union (EU) accession to the European Convention on Human Rights (ECHR) very difficult if not impossible. This negative Opinion 2/13 is quite surprising given that the CJEU had been deeply involved in the accession negotiations. Namely, it substantially influenced the content of the prepared Draft Agreement on the Accession of the EU to the ECHR (Draft Agreement on the Accession) by means of producing a discussion document and joint communication with the President of the European Court of Human Rights (ECtHR).[2]

---

[2] Tobias Lock, "Oops! We did it again – the CJEU's Opinion on EU Accession to the ECHR", *VerfBlog*, 2014/12/18, http://verfassungsblog.de/oops-das-gutachten-des-eugh-zum-emrk-beitritt-der-eu-2/, accessed November 11, 2017.

The EU is still required by the terms of Article 6(2) of the Treaty on European Union (TEU) to accede to the ECHR, and the European Commission is exposed to a potential infringement action if it fails to do so.[3] This surely strongly motivates the EU negotiators to return to the negotiation table. There are already some official initiatives of the European Parliament to continue to work on the accession. However, its prospects at this stage are still very fragile.[4] The success of further negotiations is quite uncertain as it is hardly conceivable that states parties to the ECHR, which are not member states of the EU will accept to renegotiate the Draft Agreement on the Accession under the restrictive terms of Opinion 2/13.[5]

Both practitioners and academics who advocate in favor of accession of the EU to the ECHR claim that an accession model constitutes the optimal

---

[3] Sionaidh Douglas-Scott, "Opinion 2/13 on EU accession to the ECHR: a Christmas bombshell from the European Court of Justice", *VerfBlog*, 2014/12/24, http://verfassungsblog.de/opinion-213-eu-accession-echr-christmas-bombshell-european-court-justice-2/, accessed October 19, 2017.

[4] In its 2016 and 2017 work programmes, the Commission announced that it will continue its work on accession, taking 'full account' of the Opinion 2/13. For the European Parliament, the principal benefit of EU accession to the ECHR lies in the possibility for individual recourse against the actions of the Union, similar to that already enjoyed against member states' actions. Moreover, in the Parliament's view, accession to the ECHR will send a strong signal concerning the coherence between the EU and the Council of Europe's human rights system. On 20 April 2016, Parliament's Committee on Constitutional Affairs (AFCO) organized a hearing on "Accession to the European Convention on Human Rights (ECHR): stocktaking after the ECJ's opinion and way forward", to explore ways of relaunching the accession process. The Committee reiterated its commitment to continue work on the ECHR accession in its opinion for the Committee on Civil Liberties, Justice and Home Affairs (LIBE) on the situation of fundamental rights in the EU in 2015, of 9 November 2016, where it invites the Commission to identify the steps necessary for accession. See "Completion of the EU Accession to the ECHR", http://www.europarl.europa.eu/legislative-train/theme-area-of-justice-and-fundamental-rights/file-completion-of-eu-accession-to-the-echr, accessed October 21, 2017.

[5] See Sionaidh Douglas-Scott, (2014).

method for enhancing coherence in human right protection in Europe.[6] However, the detailed analysis of the initial Draft Agreement on the Accession, which was already determined as incompatible with EU law, demonstrates its limited capability to eliminate the divergences within the European human rights system. Moreover, the strict terms of Opinion 2/13 even additionally undermined the prospects for successful negotiations on accession aimed at creating a more coherent European system.[7]

Due to the apparent failure of the draft accession instruments, this paper is aimed to offer some other alternatives which would be beneficial for eliminating procedural divergences between the CJEU and the ECtHR. To that end, the first and second sections analyze stances on coherence which are taken by the International Law Commission (ILC) and the ECtHR respectively in order to apply them to the area of procedural inconsistencies between the CJEU and the ECtHR. In doing so, the notions of "achievable coherence" and "equivalent protection" coined by the ILC and the ECtHR respectively are to be clarified as they provide a good insight into the minimum level of coherence which is needed within the European human rights system as to be considered as coherent and effective. In other words, particular attention is paid to the identification of the maximum extent of the procedural divergences which are to be tolerated by the ILC and the ECtHR respectively. The third section identifies the procedural divergences which exist between the ECtHR and the CJEU and offers proposals for the improvement of the applicable rules. The article concludes that the efficient, coherent and transparent European human rights protection system requires not only the removal of divergences of legal procedures but also the improved level of transparency of procedural rules of both courts. In addition to that, it is suggested to modify the existing approaches of the ECtHR and the ILC respectively as to motivate the competent bodies of the EU to improve the set of procedural remedies which are available before the CJEU.

---

[6] Koen Lenaerts and Eddy de Smijter, "The Charter and the Role of the European Courts," *Maastricht Journal of European and Comparative Law* vol. 8, no. 1 (2001): 101; Dean Spielmann, "Human Rights Case Law in the Strasbourg and Luxemburg Courts: Conflicts, Inconsistencies, and Complementarities", in *The EU and Human Rights*, eds. Philip Alston, Mara R. Bustelo and James Heenan, (New York: Oxford University Press, 1999) 757-778.

[7] Vesna Ćorić, "Autonomy of the European Union Law in the Context of Signing an International Agreement Providing for Another Court", *Legal Review* no. 12, (2015): 257-272.

The offered proposals predominantly concern the improvement of procedural remedies which are available before the CJEU, while the analysis of limitations of procedural remedies which are available before the ECtHR remained out of the scope of this article. The chosen approach is based on the assumption that, at this stage of development, procedural coherence in human rights protection shall be achieved by aligning the procedural rules of the CJEU with procedural rules of the ECtHR as only the latter is particularly specialized for human rights issues. In addition, the importance of the ECtHR and its case-law for the correct application of the fundamental rights by the CJEU was enshrined in the preamble of the Charter of Fundamental Rights of the EU (Charter). Furthermore, the terms of Article 6(2) of the TEU still anticipates the accession of the EU to the ECHR implying that the ECtHR will become a superior court in relation to the CJEU when it comes to human rights issues.

1. "Achievable Coherence" in the Light of the Report of the International Law Commission

The ILC in its report pertaining to the fragmentation of international law elaborates on the phenomenon of European fragmentation, and in particular to its procedural aspect.[8] According to the ILC, the full coherence has not been achieved so far within the international legal system including European.[9] However, although the full coherence is also not, realistically speaking, achievable within the European system of human rights, each legal system has to aim to achieve the highest possible level of coherence. The notion of "achievable coherence" which is desirable within each international legal system, including the European human rights protection system, means that only those limitations to the coherence that stem from the pluralistic character of the human rights protection system are legitimate, as well as those that stem from the reasonable demands to provide the efficient protection of the individuals.[10] The achievable level of coherence does constitute a goal which should also be attained within European human rights systems

---

[8] International Law Commission, "Fragmentation of International Law: Difficulties Arising from the Diversification and Expansion of International Law", Report of the Study Group of the International Law Commission Finalized by Martti Koskenniemi, A/CN.4/L.682, 13 April 2006, paras. 15 and 140.

[9] *Ibid.*, para. 493.

[10] *Ibid.*, paras. 186, 191 and 493.

since it is graded positively as a constitutive value of the system which contributes to the predictability, legal security, and legal equality.

Taking into account that an achievable level of coherence is considered a formal and abstract virtue, the ILC in its report refers to more concrete positive effects which are attributable to coherent systems in order to explain in a more concrete manner their benefits. In that context, the ILC mentions that a lack of coherence leads to the emergence of conflicting jurisprudence, forum-shopping, conflicting rules as well as to overlapping legal regimes. All these result in the loss of legal security.[11] For all these reasons, the ILC finds that the elimination of the existing incoherence which exceeds legitimate exceptions among different systems is highly recommendable and mutually beneficial. However, it seems that the ILC in its report failed to specify more precisely the criteria which should be applied in assessing whether the level of "achievable coherence" is reached.

2. "Equivalent Protection" in the Light of the Case Law of the European Court of Human Rights

The doctrine of equivalent protection was developed through the case law of the ECtHR in the 1990s. In *M. & Co. v. Federal Republic of Germany*, the ECtHR introduced the equivalent protection doctrine for the first time. In the given case, the ECtHR found that the transfer of powers to an international organization is not incompatible with the ECHR provided that within that organization fundamental rights will receive "equivalent protection".[12] Accordingly, the European Commission of Human Rights in the given case declared the application inadmissible on the ground that the legal system of the EU (at that time Community) guaranteed the protection of fundamental rights at a level equivalent to that provided by the ECHR. However, the European Commission of Human Rights failed to specify the precise content of the "equivalent protection" test. In their subsequent cases, the European Commission of Human Rights and the ECtHR continued to use similar language.

Almost fifteen years after *M. & Co. v. Federal Republic of Germany*, the ECtHR rendered the *Bosphorus* judgment. It was a turning point in the development of the equivalent protection doctrine, as it introduced some

---

[11] *Ibid.*, paras. 9, 489, 491 and 492.

[12] European Commission of Human Rights. "M. & Co. v. Federal Republic of Germany", application no. 13258/87, decision on admissibility of 9th February 1990, p. 7.

clarifications to the scope of its application. This case still represents the most advanced attempt in shaping the doctrine of equivalent protection. The *Bosphorus* case is of key importance for analyzing procedural divergences between two supranational courts, as the ECtHR in the given ruling for the first time clarifies the procedural aspect of "equivalent protection" test along with its substantive aspect. Namely, the ECtHR applies a two-fold approach stating that the presumption of equivalent protection is founded on the following "two pillars": substantive and procedural requirements of equivalent protection.[13] In that context, the ECtHR in paragraph 155 of the *Bosphorus* judgments described these "pillars" stating that the relevant organization offers equivalent protection of human rights only if respective protection is provided as regards both the substantive guarantees offered and the mechanisms controlling their observance.

By doing so, the ECtHR shows that it is also aware of the importance of the problem of procedural divergences between two courts which has to be overcome. Most scholars argue that the substantive requirements will not give rise to problems in practice in general, as the enactment of the Charter significantly contributed to the fulfillment of the substantive requirement of equivalent protection. On the other hand, it is more likely that compliance with its procedural requirements will create more problems in practice.[14]

Contrary to the ICL, the ECtHR does not use the term "achievable coherence" but the notion of "equivalent protection". However, the ECtHR also underlines that full coherence between two European judicial systems is not realistically achievable. Instead of full coherence, the ECtHR finds that it will tolerate a different level of human rights protection afforded by the CJEU as long as the provided human rights protection can be considered at least equivalent to that for which the ECHR provides. In that context, the ECtHR expressly stipulates that the equivalent does not mean "identical" but "comparable". It further underlines that any requirement that the organization's protection be "identical" could run counter to the interest of international cooperation and of the consequent

---

[13] Jonas Christoffersen, *Fair Balance, A Study of Proportionality, Subsidiarity and Primarity in the European Convention on Human Rights*, 2008, 335, www.humanrights.dk/files/pdf/Disputats%20_Endelig%202008%2004%2017_%20(2).pdf, accessed May 11, 2017.

[14] *Ibid.*, 338.

need to secure the proper functioning of international organizations.[15] In other words, the ECtHR also recognizes that full coherence is not achievable and that offering the equivalent human rights protection within the other human rights system is enough to avoid the review of the ECtHR on the compatibility of the given act with the ECHR.

Although the criterion of equivalent protection in terms of the *Bosphorus* wording *prima facie* seems realistically tailored, the ECtHR in its further elaboration fails to make needed clarifications. More specifically, the ECtHR introduces the presumption of "equivalent protection" stating that it can be rebutted provided that the ECtHR finds that the protection of ECHR's rights was "manifestly deficient" in the circumstances of a particular case.[16] The manifest deficiency concept produces legal uncertainty to the parties before the ECtHR as its content was not clarified by the ECtHR. Some authors further argue that the manifest deficiency threshold has been set too high by the ECtHR.[17] For that reason, the given high threshold has turned out to be unusable for human rights benefits of claimants. The hardly rebuttable character of the *Bosphorus* presumption on the doctrine of equivalent protection is proved by the fact that this presumption has so far never been rebutted in reality. It was rightly pointed out in the joint concurring opinion in the *Bosphorus* case that the introduction of hardly rebuttable presumptions demonstrates the intent of the ECtHR not to encroach deeply in the EU order unless grave human right violations occur.[18]

Moreover, this test of manifest deficiency was not consistently applied in the case law of ECtHR, which apparently has contributed to its vagueness. Although the ECtHR holds at the outset in *Bosphorus* that presumption could be rebutted only through *in concreto* review of the circumstances of

---

[15] European Court of Human Rights. "Bosphorus Hava Yollari Turizm ve Ticaret AS v. Ireland", application no. 45036/98, judgement of 30th June 2005, para. 155.

[16] *Ibid.*, para. 156.

[17] Sionaidh Douglas-Scott, "Tale of Two Courts: Luxembourg, Strasbourg and the Growing European Human Rights Acquis", *Common Market Law Review* vol. 43, no. 3 (2006): 638-639; Cathryn Costello, "The Bosphorus Ruling of the European Court of Human Rights: Fundamental Rights and Blurred Boundaries in Europe", *Human Rights Law Review* vol. 6. no. 1, (2006): 102-129.

[18] See Joint Concurring Opinion of Mr Rozakis, Mrs Tulkens, Mr Traja, Mrs Botoucharova, Mr Zagrebelsky and Mr Garlicki in "Bosphorus Hava Yollari Turizm ve Ticaret AS v. Ireland", para. 4.

a particular case, it takes a different approach later in this judgment.[19] Actually, it comes to the conclusion that the protection of human rights within the other system is not manifestly deficient applying only an abstract review of the EU (at that time Community) system.[20] This abstract review remained to exist in case law after *Bosphorus* undermining the efforts to approximate the human rights protections afforded by two supranational courts.

Finally, the scope of the doctrine of equivalent protection is limited as it relates only to those legal acts that have been, or that could have been, observed or reviewed by the EU judicial mechanisms with respect to their conformity with the EU human rights law.[21] In other words, the equivalent protection presumption immunizes only those legal acts that can be and are observed by the EU judicial mechanism including the CJEU. Accordingly, the EU primary law cannot be reviewed by the CJEU for its conformity with the human rights standards, as it has absolutely no power to invalidate any provision of the EU primary law.[22] The scope of application of this doctrine is also limited to member states' actions implementing EU law. Although some authors came up with proposals to broaden the given scope as to also include the EU acts not entailing national measures, the ECtHR, however, made it clear in *Connolly* case that member states can only be held responsible where there was a domestic act of some sort.[23] It means that in cases where only the EU acted, such action would be immune from ECtHR scrutiny. The reason for this is that the EU action could not be attributed to the member states and as such it could not fall into their jurisdiction under Article 1 of the ECHR.[24]

---

[19] European Court of Human Rights. "Bosphorus Hava Yollari Turizm ve Ticaret AS v. Ireland", para. 156.

[20] *Ibid.*, 161-166.

[21] Paul De Hert and Fisnik Korenica, "The Doctrine of Equivalent Protection: Its Life and Legitimacy Before and After the European Union's Accession to the European Convention on Human Right," *German Law Review*, vol. 13, nc. 7 (2012): 882.

[22] *Ibid.*, 883.

[23] See European Court of Human Rights. "Connolly v. 15 Member States of the European Union", application no. 73274/01, judgement of 9th December 2008.

[24] Tobias Lock, "Accession of the EU to the ECHR: Who Would Be Responsible in Strasbourg", 7, http://ssrn.com/abstract=1685785, accessed October 29, 2017.

3. Procedural Divergences between the Court of Justice of the European Union and the European Court of Human Rights

The ECtHR in *Bosphorus* specifies the shortcomings of concrete legal remedies which are available before the CJEU. It points to, *inter alia*, the limited access of individuals to the CJEU as there is restricted standing for filing an action for annulment under Articles 263 and an action for failure to act under Article 265 of the Treaty on the Functioning of the European Union (TFEU). Also, it mentions that their right to bring a plea of illegality under Article 271 is restricted. On the other hand, individuals have *no locus standi* to bring infringement actions under Articles 258 and 259 of the TFEU. Moreover, the ECtHR stressed that individuals have no right to bring an action against another individual.

However, after criticizing these remedies, the ECtHR replaced the criticism of the flaws of each specific procedural remedy with praise that the available set of procedural remedies taken in total do meet procedural protection standards which are equivalent to those guaranteed by the ECHR. Namely, the ECtHR concluded that the procedural "pillar" or aspect of equivalent protection is still met.[25] It justified its stance by stating that actions initiated before the CJEU (at that time European Court of Justice) by either the EU (at that time Community) institutions or a member state do constitute important control of compliance with the EU (at that time Community) norms to the indirect benefit of individuals. The ECtHR also underlines the relevance of actions for damages which are available to individuals in respect of the non-contractual liability of the institutions.[26] Furthermore, the ECtHR states that thanks to national courts, the EU system provides a remedy to individuals against a member state or another individual for a breach of EU law.[27] In addition, the CJEU maintains control over the application of EU law by national courts through the preliminary reference procedure under Article 267 of the TFEU.[28]

Although the ECtHR in its elaboration did not overlook any of available procedural remedies within the EU judicial system, it seems that the

---

[25] European Court of Human Rights. "Bosphorus Hava Yollari Turizm ve Ticaret AS v. Ireland", para. 163-165.

[26] *Ibid.*, para. 163.

[27] See Article 19 of the TEU.

[28] European Court of Human Rights. "Bosphorus Hava Yollari Turizm ve Ticaret AS v. Ireland", para. 164.

conducted assessment was not thorough, but superficial. A number of shortcomings of the procedural remedies before the CJEU were not brought up by the ECtHR both in *Bosphorus* and in its subsequent jurisprudence. Firstly, there are significant discrepancies when it comes to damage regimes falling under the competences of the CJEU and the ECtHR. The causal link, as well as other requirements for actions for damages, are formulated differently within these two systems which further leads to different levels of protection and awards provided by the two courts.[29]

Secondly, the ECtHR rightly mentions the existence of limited standing for bringing actions for annulment as well as actions for failure to act. However, it does not elaborate on it further. The full implementation of the principle of complementarity between an action for annulment and an action for failure to act is still not achieved, although the Lisbon Treaty brought some significant improvements while the CJEU made efforts to interpret Articles 263 and 265 of the TFEU in a parallel manner. It is important to eliminate lacunae by the treaty amendments or through the modification of the court's procedural rules in order to enhance their coherence. Although some gaps and flaws had already been partially improved through the case law of the CJEU, this method is not fully appropriate as it does not strengthen legal security.[30] The main shortcomings of an action for failure to act relate to omission of setting a time limit within which the applicant must bring the request for an action as well as to the failure to provide that an action for failure to act can be commenced against an EU institution even in a case when the institution exercises discretionary powers in the specific case.[31]

Thirdly, although the ECtHR in *Bosphorus* refers to the importance of a preliminary reference procedure, it failed to point out that it is not up to the parties to initiate this procedure. Therefore, **requests** for **preliminary rulings** cannot be considered as an effective legal remedy in the sense of Article 13 of the ECHR.[32] Moreover, due to the average duration of the preliminary reference procedure, it is apparent that the **requests** for

---

[29] Vesna Ćorić, *Compensation for Damages Before the European Supranational Courts*, (Republic of Serbia: Institute of Comparative Law, 2017), 123-131.

[30] European Court of Justice. "Sogelma v. EAR", no. T-411/06 ECR II 2008, 2771.

[31] Damian Chalmers, Gareth Davies, and Gorgio Monti, *European Union Law, Cases and Materials*, (United Kingdom: Cambridge University Press, 2010^2), 429-430.

[32] Vesna Ćorić, "Right to an Effective Remedy in the Light of the Recent Case Law of the Court of Justice of European Union", *Legal Review* no. 3, (2014): 128-137.

preliminary rulings also are not in line with the reasonable time requirement from Article 6 of the ECHR.

All these shortcomings of the CJEU procedural remedies have to be improved on the road of achieving more coherent approaches to human rights protection. The ECtHR's assessment of procedural remedies which are available before the CJEU proved to be superficial as it failed to address all these limitations.

4. Conclusion

The specific procedural improvements are needed in the judicial system of the EU as to achieve a level of protection which would be "equivalent" to the greatest possible extent with protection which is offered by the ECHR. Those procedural improvements will also prove sufficient to reach the needed level of "achievable coherence" in the meaning of the ILC's report. Furthermore, the proposed modifications of EU law are also needed in order to establish "a complete system of legal remedies and procedures designed to permit the European Court of Justice to review the legality of measures adopted by the institutions."[33]

However, the analyzed approaches of the ECtHR and the ILC do not sufficiently motivate either the CJEU or other competent bodies of the EU to improve the set of procedural remedies which are available before the CJEU. That lack of motivation on the side of the competent bodies of the EU to improve procedural remedies which are available before the CJEU to meet the ECHR standards and reduce the existing procedural divergences is attributable to several reasons.

Firstly, the scope of the doctrine of equivalent protection is limited as the conformity of EU primary law with human rights is out of the jurisdiction of the ECtHR. The given limitation is attributable to the fact that even the CJEU has absolutely no power to invalidate any provision of the EU primary law.[34] Moreover, as it was already mentioned, the application of this doctrine is limited only to member states' actions implementing EU law. Secondly, the incapability of the equivalent protection doctrine to contribute to the achieving more coherent human rights procedures is further caused by the abstract and lenient review which has been applied in assessing whether the manifest deficiency standard was met in a

---

[33] See. European Court of Justice. "Parti écologiste "Les Verts" v. European Parliament", no. 294/83, ECR 1986, 01339, para. 23.

[34] Paul De Hert and Fisnik Korenica, 883.

specific case. Moreover, the growing body of EU law and that of EU member states' law implementing EU law, further enhance the number of acts which are virtually unreviewable by the ECtHR, given the hardly rebuttable presumption of equivalent protection. Therefore, the equivalent protection doctrine, although continuing to operate even after Opinion 2/13, does not constitute enough strong instrument which will significantly contribute to reducing the level of procedural incoherence between two courts. Thirdly, the ILC failed to introduce specific criteria which should be applied in assessing whether the level of "achievable coherence" is reached between different legal systems.

In a nutshell, the lenient and abstract review of only limited number of EU legal acts in reality leads to creation of "virtually non-rebuttable" presumption of equivalent protection which literally creates a wide-spectrum immunity for the EU member states when they implement EU law, provided that a state "does not do more than implement legal obligations flowing from its membership to the organization".[35] Therefore, it would be recommendable for the ECtHR to modify the doctrine of equivalent protection as to introduce more concrete and stricter criteria when it assesses whether or not a procedural aspect of equivalent protection conditions is met. In the absence of its further improvement, the ECtHR will keep influencing the CJEU to follow ECHR standards only when they decide about legality or review national acts through which the EU acts are implemented, while the CJEU may continue to disregard the ECtHR "procedural" standards when it comes to the review of legality of EU acts which are not implemented by national acts.

In the absence of accession and the improvement of the equivalent protection doctrine, the alternative way for the CJEU will be to find internal motivation for improving the set of its procedural remedies. By doing so, it will not only meet the standards determined by the ECHR, but also those set forth by its own Charter. By meeting the standards of the Charter, the procedural divergences between the two courts will be apparently reduced as to include only exceptions which are declared as

---

[35] European Court of Human Rights. "Bosphorus Hava Yollari Turizm ve Ticaret AS v. Ireland", paras. 163-165.

[35] *Ibid.*, 163.

[35] See Article 19 of the TEU.

[35] European Court of Human Rights. "Bosphorus Hava Yollari Turizm ve Ticaret AS v. Ireland", para. 164.

[35] Paul De Hert and Fisnik Korenica, 882.

legitimate by the ILC as well as those stemming from the requirement of international cooperation as defined by the ECtHR.

Finally, the creation of more efficient and coherent European human rights protection system requires not only the removal of divergences of legal procedures but also the improved level of transparency of procedural rules of both courts. To that end, the respective courts' procedural rules should be amended as to incorporate a number of principles which are developed through the case law of the CJEU and the ECtHR. By doing so, the so-called *de facto* accession will take place thanks to the internal initiatives of both courts irrespectively of the uncertain future of *de jure* accession.

Bibliography

Chalmers, Damian Davies, Gareth, and Monti, Gorgio, *European Union Law, Cases and Materials*, (United Kingdom: Cambridge University Press, 2010^2);

Christoffersen, Jonas, *Fair Balance, A Study of Proportionality, Subsidiarity and Primarity in the European Convention on Human Rights*, 2008, 340-341, www.humanrights.dk/files/pdf/Disputats%20_Endelig%202008%2004%2017_%20(2).pdf, accessed May 11, 2017;

"Completion of the EU Accession to the ECHR", http://www.europarl.europa.eu/legislative-train/theme-area-of-justice-and-fundamental-rights/file-completion-of-eu-accession-to-the-echr, accessed October 21, 2017;

Costello, Cathryn, "The Bosphorus Ruling of the European Court of Human Rights: Fundamental Rights and Blurred Boundaries in Europe", *Human Rights Law Review* vol. 6. no. 1, (2006): 102-129;

Ćorić, Vesna, "Autonomy of the European Union Law in the Context of Signing an International Agreement Providing for Another Court", *Legal Review* no. 12, (2015): 257-272 [in Serbian]

Ćorić, Vesna, *Compensation for Damages Before the European Supranational Courts*, (Republic of Serbia: Institute of Comparative Law, 2017), 123-131 [in Serbian];

Ćorić, Vesna, "Right to an Effective Remedy in the Light of the Recent Case Law of the Court of Justice of European Union", *Legal Review* no. 3, (2014): 128-137 [in Serbian];

De Hert, Paul and Korenica, Fisnik, "The Doctrine of Equivalent Protection: Its Life and Legitimacy Before and After the European Union's Accession to the European Convention on Human Right", *German Law Review* vol. 13, no. 7 (2012): 874-895;

Douglas-Scott, Sionaidh, "Opinion 2/13 on EU accession to the ECHR: a Christmas bombshell from the European Court of Justice", *VerfBlog*, 2014/12/24, http://verfassungsblog.de/opinion-213-eu-accession-echr-christmas-bombshell-european-court-justice-2/, accessed October 19, 2017;

Douglas-Scott, Sionaidh, "Tale of Two Courts: Luxembourg, Strasbourg and the Growing European Human Rights Acquis", *Common Market Law Review* vol. 43, no. 3 (2006): 638-639;

European Commission of Human Rights. "M. & Co. v. Federal Republic of Germany", application no. 13258/87, decision on admissibility of 9th February 1990;

European Court of Human Rights. "Bosphorus Hava Yollari Turizm ve Ticaret AS v. Ireland", application no. 45036/98, judgement of 30th June 2005;

European Court of Human Rights. "Connolly v. 15 Member States of the European Union", application no. 73274/01, judgement of 9th December 2008;

European Court of Justice. "Parti écologiste "Les Verts" v. European Parliament", no. 294/83, ECR 1986, 01339;

European Court of Justice. "Sogelma v. EAR", no. T-411/06, ECR II 2008, 2771;

Joint Concurring Opinion of Mr Rozakis, Mrs Tulkens, Mr Traja, Mrs Botoucharova, Mr Zagrebelsky and Mr Garlicki in "Bosphorus Hava Yollari Turizm ve Ticaret AS v. Ireland";

International Law Commission, "Fragmentation of International Law: Difficulties Arising from the Diversification and Expansion of International Law", Report of the Study Group of the International Law Commission Finalized by Martti Koskenniemi, A/CN.4/L.682, 13 April 2006;

Lenaerts, Koen and De Smijter, Eddy, "The Charter and the Role of the European Courts," *Maastricht Journal of European and Comparative Law* vol. 8, no. 1 (2001): 90-101;

Lock, Tobias, "Accession of the EU to the ECHR: Who Would Be Responsible in Strasbourg", 7, http://ssrn.com/abstract=1685785, accessed October 29, 2017;

Lock, Tobias, "Oops! We did it again – the CJEU's Opinion on EU Accession to the ECHR", *VerfBlog*, 2014/12/18, http://verfassungsblog.de/oops-das-gutachten-des-eugh-zum-emrk-beitritt-der-eu-2/, accessed November 11, 2017;

Spielmann, Dean, "Human Rights Case Law in the Strasbourg and Luxemburg Courts: Conflicts, Inconsistencies, and Complementarities", in *The EU and Human Rights*, eds. Philip Alston, Mara R. Bustelo and James Heenan, (New York: Oxford University Press, 1999) 757-781.

Chapter 14

The ECHR's Influence on Convergence between Common Law and Civil Law Systems

Brice Dickson [1]

Abstract

The ECHR has been binding on the UK, Ireland, and Germany since 1953, and on France since 1974. Its impact on UK law was not very significant until 2000, when most Convention rights became part of domestic law, while its impact in Ireland has remained relatively insignificant even after Convention rights became part of domestic law at the end of 2003. With one noticeable exception, relating to prisoners' voting rights in the UK, both 14 countries have implemented adverse judgments of the European Court of Human Rights, though sometimes after a long delay and (in the case of the UK) considerable inter-judicial dialogue. Both countries now try to ensure that proposed new laws and policies are 'Convention proofed' before they are formally adopted. There has not yet been a serious clash between Ireland's Constitution and the ECHR and on some issues Ireland has been more willing than the UK to allow individual rights to outweigh societal interests when they appear to conflict. To some extent, the experience of France has mirrored that of the UK in that French judges largely ignored the ECHR until impelled to do so by the number of adverse judgments issued against France in Strasbourg. French constitutional law, like UK common law, proved inadequate to fully protect some Convention rights. For its part, Germany's constitutional law has demonstrated a larger capacity to protect Convention rights. Nevertheless, in 2004 the Federal Constitutional Court demonstrated that it was prepared to modify its interpretation of the

---

[1] Emeritus Professor of International and Comparative Law, Queen's University Belfast, Northern Ireland

Constitution in order to comply with judgments from Strasbourg. The net result is that across all four countries there has been a convergence both in the way national courts defer to Strasbourg and in the extent to which particular rights are protected. There is a risk, however, that after 2020 the UK might deviate from this convergence by, at best, weakening the authority of Strasbourg judgments within the UK or, at worst, denouncing the ECHR itself.

Introduction

The European Convention on Human Rights (ECHR) is the world's most successful human rights treaty. Over the course of the last 65 years, and in particular since the European Court of Human Rights became a permanent full-time institution in 1998, it has contributed very significantly to the enhanced protection of human rights throughout the whole of Europe, from the West of Ireland to the East of Russia. Within that area there are two principal types of legal system. Civil law systems predominate but the common law prevails in the United Kingdom (UK) and Ireland, and there are elements of it in the mixed legal systems of Malta and Cyprus. An obvious but rarely analyzed consequence of the Convention's success has therefore been a reduction in the differences between how common law and civil law systems protect human rights. The focus of this paper is on how and why that reduction has manifested itself. It begins with a stereotypical depiction of the features of common and civil law systems, observing that the differences between them are often exaggerated. It then considers the role of Constitutions within each type of system, noting the commonalities involved. This leads to an examination of the ECHR's effect on those Constitutions and of the constitutional position which the ECHR has acquired at the national level across Europe. The UK and Ireland are taken as representative common law systems, with France and Germany being representative of civil law systems. There is then a section on the interpretative principles which have been developed by the European Court when deciding cases brought to it in Strasbourg. Examples are given of how those principles have been applied by the Court in cases emanating from the four representative jurisdictions. The article ends with some conclusions about the nature and value of the convergent effect of the ECHR.

1. Common and Civil Law Systems: The Orthodox View

Traditionally common and civil law systems are portrayed very differently. In common law systems, judges do not just decide who should win a legal dispute and what remedy or sanction would be appropriate; they can also make law for the future, and they adhere to a doctrine of precedent in order to reinforce the applicability of such law. Common law systems supposedly make no distinction between the law which applies to private organizations and individuals on the one hand and that which applies to state organizations on the other. Albert Venn Dicey made much of this in his seminal work *An Introduction to the Study of the Law of the Constitution*, first published in 1885. Moreover, he stressed that the State, or Crown, could not be sued. Common law systems also treat international law as irrelevant unless and until the international norms have been incorporated into national law in ways prescribed by the country's Constitution. When it comes to human rights, the original English approach was that these did not exist under domestic law: rather than people having the 'right' to do something, the law recognized that people had the 'freedom' to do or say whatever they liked, provided that no law had been made disallowing it.

By way of contrast, civil law systems do not permit judges to make law. Their role is simply to interpret the law as set out by the legislators and to apply it to the facts of cases brought before them. They do not have to worry about rules of precedent because no single decision creates new law. As regards the categories within domestic law, civil law systems make a virtue out of recognizing that separate rules need to be devised to govern the way State bodies operate. They call this 'administrative law', and they usually create special courts to adjudicate disputes in this area. International law is looked upon more sympathetically than in common law systems, with many civil law countries adopting a 'monist' approach, meaning that, once the country's government has agreed to be bound by international norms, that is enough to make them binding on domestic courts.

We all know, however, that these stereotypical depictions are hugely inaccurate in this day and age. The forces of democratic politics, of international relations and of economic globalization have combined to diminish the differences between the two types of legal system almost to vanishing point. Thus, in common law systems the law-making powers of judges have been strictly confined, a wide-ranging set of principles has emerged which apply specifically to public bodies or to private bodies performing public functions, and in certain circumstances international norms can be applied even though they have not yet been formally incorporated into domestic law. These last two developments have meant that amongst the most litigated areas of law within the UK and Ireland in recent years have been administrative law (especially the law on judicial review of administrative action) and human rights law. On the civil law side judges now admit that they are significantly influenced in their decision-making by the way judges in previous similar cases have decided the matter, and in one or two situations judicial decisions are indeed binding on lower courts. In 2010 the Vice-President of France's Conseil d'État stated that in his country administrative courts almost always follow a precedent for fear of being overturned on appeal.[2] A purely monist approach to international law is now also rare even in civil law jurisdictions: they prefer to specifically adopt, or adapt, such norms to ensure that they do not contradict constitutional precepts within the legal system.

2. The Role of Constitutions

A feature which is present in every legal system is that of a Constitution, even if the degree to which it can be found in one single document varies greatly from country to country. It is often said that the UK and New Zealand, two prominent common law countries, get by without any written Constitution but of course this is inaccurate because in each of those countries there are numerous pieces of legislation, not to mention many court judgments, which have a clear constitutional status. All Constitutions do at least three things: they specify who in the country can make laws and who can enforce them, they specify which laws rank higher than other laws, and they guarantee fundamental rights. The provisions on each of these matters are often very similar, regardless of whether the country has a common law system or a civil law system. The power to make laws is usually given primarily to those who are elected to the national Parliament, with various lower-level bodies being empowered to make other laws provided certain conditions are satisfied. Laws are frequently ranked in a way which places provisions of the Constitution at the top of the hierarchy, Acts of the national Parliament as next in importance and then documents issued by the government or some other designated body as the least important (but still binding on all to whom they apply). The fundamental rights guaranteed are usually of the civil and political variety, such as the right to liberty, a fair trial, freedom of expression, freedom of association and voting. In recent years more and more Constitutions also require the protection of socio-economic and

---

[2] Jean-Marc Sauvé, speech in Hunter Valley, Australia, 4 March 2010, available in English at www.conseil-etat.fr/Actualites/Discours-Interventions/The-French-administrative-jurisdictional-system.

environmental rights, but this seems to be occurring more frequently in civil rather than common law systems.[3]

Each country that has ratified the ECHR has to work out for itself what status the ECHR thereby acquires within its own constitutional framework. Neither the Convention itself nor the European Court prescribes the nature of that status, so long as the net result is that Convention rights are adequately protected as a result. Notwithstanding the differences that exist between the legal systems of the 47 ratifying States, it is fair to say that the status of the Convention in each of them is roughly the same, in substance if not in form. In particular, no significant distinction can be made between typical common law countries on the one hand – such as the UK and Ireland – and typical civil law countries on the other – such as France and Germany. There is a definite convergence between the two types of legal system in this regard. It is not top-down in nature, that is, it is not imposed from outside. Instead, the convergence has emerged organically from the bottom up, as should be apparent from the following summary of what has occurred in the four jurisdictions just mentioned.

The United Kingdom

Famously the UK does not have a written Constitution, at least not one that can be found in a single document. Instead, the country's Constitution comprises a range of pieces of legislation, a set of judge-made rules and a collection of political traditions (sometimes called 'constitutional conventions').[4] The most fundamental aspect of the UK's Constitution is the idea of parliamentary sovereignty. It means that the Parliament at Westminster can do anything it likes. There are no constraints on how it can behave save those which, from time to time, it may impose upon itself. Thus, during the UK's membership of what is now called the European Union, laws derived from Brussels were enforceable in the UK only because Parliament had authorized this by passing the European Communities Act 1972 prior to the start of the UK's membership of the then Common Market on 1 January 1973. Likewise, public authorities in the UK have to comply with ECHR rights only because Parliament at Westminster required them to do this when it enacted the Human Rights Act 1998. Prior to 1998, going back as far as 1953 when the ECHR came into effect for the UK at the international level, Convention

---

[3] Or in a mixed system, such as that of South Africa.

[4] In France they would call such an amalgam of norms the *bloc de constitutionnalité*.

rights could not be directly relied upon in UK courts. People could fall back on domestic legislation and some common law precedents, but these were rarely as protective of human rights as the Strasbourg system.

Even after 1998, the power of UK courts to invalidate domestic laws because of their inconsistency with the ECHR has been limited. They can change judge-made precedents and strike down 'secondary legislation' made by agencies – such as government departments – authorized to do so by Acts of Parliament. But they cannot strike down Acts of Parliament. All they can do in that regard is issue a declaration that an Act, or part of it, is incompatible with the ECHR. This has no effect on the legality of the Act unless and until Parliament authorizes repeal or amendment of the offending statutory provision. The parties to the dispute which has led to the judicial declaration are not affected by it unless later legislation is expressly given retrospective effect, which is a rare phenomenon. An alternative course of action would be for a court to apply its duty to interpret all legislation in a way which makes it consistent with the ECHR. This it can do 'so far as it is possible to do so'.[5] In practice this means that courts can write words into or out of legislation, including Acts of Parliament, but not if the end result is a meaning which is inconsistent with a fundamental feature of the legislation in question or if the re-writing requires the making of decisions for which the judges are not equipped, presumably because they lack the expertise or evidence to come to a decision which they can fully justify.[6]

The status of the ECHR is therefore lower than that of EU law in the hierarchy of legal norms in the UK: courts can actually 'disapply' provisions in Acts of Parliament which infringe EU law, though of course that power will disappear once Brexit takes effect, possibly as early as March 2019.

Ireland

Ireland was the last of the 47 Council of Europe States to ensure that the ECHR could be called in aid by litigants in domestic courts. It did so by enacting the European Convention on Human Rights Act 2003. To a significant extent the Irish followed the British model in that, rather than

---

[5] Human Rights Act 1998, s 3(1).

[6] This is a summary of how the law was framed by the UK's House of Lords (the predecessor to today's Supreme Court) in *Ghaidan v Godin-Mendoza* [2004] UKHL 30, [2004] 2 AC 557. For further details see B Dickson, *Human Rights and the United Kingdom Supreme Court* (Oxford University Press, 2013) 64-70.

conferring power on courts to invalidate primary legislation because of its inconsistency with the ECHR, it authorized courts to make declarations of incompatibility.[7] As in the UK, such a declaration has no effect on the validity, continuing operation or enforcement of the statutory provision[8] but, unlike in the UK, a party in the case concerned can apply to the government for an *ex gratia* payment of compensation for an injury or loss suffered as a result of the incompatibility.[9] The Irish Act also imposes an interpretative duty comparable to that contained in the UK's Act: it requires legislation to be interpreted compatibly with the ECHR 'in so far as is possible'.[10] In both countries, the duty affects the interpretation of all legislation, whether enacted before or after the date when the duty was brought into force. In Ireland, however, the duty is imposed only on courts, whereas the UK duty applies more generally. On the other hand, Ireland's courts are exempt from the obligation imposed on all organs of the State to perform their functions in a manner compatible with the State's obligations under the ECHR.[11] In the UK that obligation is imposed on all 'public authorities', including courts.[12]

Ireland's 2003 Act makes no mention of the nations Constitution, which dates from 1937 and has been subsequently amended on 27 occasions.[13] Articles 40-44 of the Constitution guarantee certain 'fundamental rights', some of which overlap with those in the ECHR. Article 26 permits the country's President to ask the Supreme Court to rule on whether a Bill which he or she has been asked to sign contains any provisions which are repugnant to the Constitution and if the Supreme Court rules that it does then the President is not permitted to sign the Bill into law. The Constitution also permits the courts to invalidate already enacted legislation if it is repugnant to the Constitution,[14] and this has occurred on many occasions, often in cases where the repugnancy relates to one of the

---

[7] European Convention on Human Rights Act 2003, s 5.

[8] Ibid, s 5(2)(a).

[9] Ibid, s 5(4). In the UK compensation is payable only by a court which already has power to award damages in civil proceedings, and only if it is necessary to afford just satisfaction to the recipient: Human Rights Act 1998, s 8(2)-(4).

[10] Ibid, s 2(1).

[11] Ibid, s 3(1), read in conjunction with the definition of 'organ of the State' in s 1(1).

[12] Human Rights Act 1998, s 6(1), read in conjunction with s 6(3).

[13] See the useful summary of successful and failed attempt at amendment at https://en.wikipedia.org/wiki/Amendments_to_the_Constitution_of_Ireland.

[14] Arts 15.4, 34.3.2 and 34.5.5.

provisions in Articles 40-44.[15] The rights contained in the Constitution are therefore protected more strongly than those contained in the ECHR, but of course it is possible for a court to declare not only that a statutory provision is incompatible with the ECHR but also that it is repugnant to the Constitution. In formal terms the ECHR has the same status in Ireland as it does in the UK: ECHR rights are protected by ordinary Acts of Parliament and incompatibility of a provision in any other Act of Parliament with the ECHR will not *per se* invalidate that provision.

France

Like Ireland, France allows both *a priori* and (though only since 2010) *a posteriori* judicial review of legislation to assess whether it breaches the Constitution, which dates from 1958.[16] The body tasked with such reviews is the *Conseil constitutionnel*.[17] It is comprised primarily of serving or former politicians but, unlike the Irish President's Council of State,[18] its views have a binding effect. The French Constitution does not contain a list of rights as such but it does declare, in its Preamble, that the French people 'solemnly proclaim their attachment to the Rights of Man ... as defined by the Declaration of [the Rights of Man and the Citizen] 1789, confirmed and complemented by the Preamble to the Constitution of 1946, and to the rights and duties as defined in the Charter for the Environment of 2004'. The Preamble to the Constitution of 1946, in turn,

---

[15] By 2015 there had been 93 occasions on which a court in Ireland had declared a law to be unconstitutional, 58 of these being Supreme Court decisions: Gerard Hogan, David Kenny and Rachael Walsh, 'An anthology of declarations of unconstitutionality' (2015) 54 *Irish Jurist* 1.

[16] For a paper comparing the Irish and French constitutional approaches to implementing the ECHR (undated, but up-to-date as of mid-2009) see Marie-Luce Paris, *Implementing The European Convention on Human Rights: A Comparative Constitutional Perspective With References to Ireland and France*, available at www.ialsnet.org/meetings/constit/papers/ParisMarie-Luce%28Ireland%29.pdf.

[17] See generally Marie-Claire Ponthoreau and Fabrice Hourquebie, in Andrew Harding and Peter Leyland (eds), *Constitutional Courts: A Comparative Study* (Wildy, Simmonds and Hill Publishing, 2009) 81-101. The change made from 1 March 2010 (in line with an amendment to the Constitution dated 23 July 2008) is that the *Conseil constitutionnel* is now permitted to consider the constitutionality of a legislative provision already in force if this issue has been referred to it by the *Conseil d'État* or the *Cour de Cassation*. Such an application is treated as *une question prioritaire de constitutionnalité* (QPC), which means that it will be dealt with more quickly than other cases.

[18] Constitution of Ireland 1937, Arts 31-32.

provides that 'the people of France proclaim anew that each human being, without distinction of race, religion or creed, possesses sacred and inalienable rights'. It goes on to guarantee such rights as equality for women, the right of asylum for anyone persecuted because of their actions in favour of liberty, the right to employment and not to be discriminated against at work because of one's origins, opinions or belief, the right to strike, the right to health care and to social security, and the right to free, public and secular education at all levels.

France was the penultimate of the then 17 Member States of the Council of Europe to ratify the ECHR, with effect from 3 May 1974.[19] Amongst the reasons for its delay were, apparently, suspicions that the Convention was based on a common law approach to criminal justice,[20] which seems peculiar given that the main feature of common law criminal justice – the right to jury trial – does not feature in the Convention. France did not grant individuals in France the right to lodge applications in Strasbourg until 3 October 1981. Under Article 55 of France's Constitution, ratification of the ECHR meant that the Convention immediately acquired an authority superior to that of *lois* but, as in Ireland, inferior to the national Constitution. Nor does either country's Constitution require national courts to interpret domestic legislation in the light of ratified treaties.

A year after France's ratification of the ECHR the *Conseil constitutionnel* made it clear that it was no part of its remit to consider the consistency of a statute (in this case it was the Voluntary Interruption of Pregnancy Act) with the provisions of a treaty or an international agreement.[21] It said that a statute which is inconsistent with a treaty is not *ipso facto* unconstitutional. The Conseil staunchly maintains this stance, but it does now sometimes refer to the case-law of the European Court of Human Rights to support its interpretation of the constitutionality of French law.[22] On at least one occasion a decision by the *Conseil constitutionnel* that

---

[19] It was ratified by statute number 73-1227 of 31 December 1973 and published by a decree dated 3 May 1974.

[20] Elisabeth Lambert Abdelgawad and Anne Weber, 'The Reception Process in France and Germany' in Helen Keller and Alec Stone Sweet (eds), *A Europe of Rights: The Impact of the ECHR on National Legal Systems* (Oxford University Press, 2008) 107, 108.

[21] The *Interruption Voluntaire de Grossesse* case, decision of 15 January 1975, available in English at www.conseil-constitutionnel.fr/conseil-constitutionnel/root/bank_mm/anglais/a7454dc.pdf.

[22] Paris, n 15 above, 5;

French legislation is constitutional has later, in effect, been overturned by the Grand Chamber of the European Court on the basis that the legislation was in violation of one or more rights in the ECHR.[23] As regards the French law of 11 October 2010 prohibiting the concealment of one's face in public places, the *Conseil constitutionnel* found it to be constitutional[24] (while referring to the 1789 Declaration of the Rights of Man and the Citizen and to the Preamble to the 1946 Constitution, but not once mentioning the ECHR, despite the earlier Strasbourg decision on the ban on veils in Turkey[25]). On this matter, the European Court later upheld the compatibility of the law with the ECHR as well.[26]

Judging the compatibility of a *loi* with the ECHR has therefore been left to the ordinary courts, which are headed by the *Cour de cassation* (for civil and criminal matters) and by the *Conseil d'État* (for administrative matters). The *Conseil d'État* made this clear in 1990 in a case on an abortifacient drug,[27] while the *Cour de cassation* did so in 1996 in another criminal case relating to abortion.[28] In each case, the court held that the legislation in question was not incompatible with Article 2 of the ECHR, which protects the right to life. If a court does find an incompatibility, the legislation remains valid until amended or repealed, just as in the UK and Ireland (as regards primary legislation anyway). The doctrine of the separation of powers precludes an ordinary court from striking down a *loi*, the French equivalent to an Act of Parliament.

---

[23] *Zielinski v France* (2001) 31 EHRR 19, where the European Court found a violation of Art 6 of the ECHR when French legislation passed during the course of court proceedings purported to retrospectively abolish a 'special difficulties allowance' payable to social security staff. This was deemed to be in breach of the right to a fair trial.

[24] Decision no 2010-613 DC, of 7 October 2010, available in English at www.conseil-constitutionnel.fr/conseil-constitutionnel/root/bank_mm/anglais/en2010_613dc.pdf.

[25] *Sahin v Turkey* (2007) 44 EHRR 5 (GC).

[26] *SAS v France* (2015) 60 EHRR 11 (GC). Two of the 17 judges held that the law violated Arts 8 and 9 of the ECHR, which protect, respectively, the rights to a private life and to manifest one's religion.

[27] *Conseil d'État, Assemblée,* nos 105743, 105810, 105811 and 105812, 21 December 1990 (*Confédération nationale des associations familiales catholiques* case).

[28] *Cour de Cassation, Chambre criminelle,* pourvoi no 95-85118, 27 November 1996 (*Commandos anti-IVG* case).

Germany

In Germany, there is no system of *a priori* review of legislation, but there is a long-established system for *a posteriori* review. This is exercised by the Federal Constitutional Court (FCC) or *Bundesverfassungsgericht*. If other courts are asked to assess the constitutionality of a law during the course of litigation, they are obliged to refer the matter to the FCC. All courts, on the other hand, including the FCC, can assess the compatibility of laws with the ECHR. In 1987 the FCC held that it and other courts could also use the ECHR when interpreting domestic laws[29] and in 2004 the FCC further held it could use the ECHR when it is interpreting the German Constitution (the Basic Law, or *Grundgesetz*) of 1949. That document already contains a fairly comprehensive list of fundamental rights, set out in Articles 1-19,[30] and since 1951 people in Germany have been able to apply directly to the FCC to have their constitutional rights vindicated there. In 1955 they were given the additional right to petition the European Court in Strasbourg if they had exhausted their domestic remedies but were still dissatisfied.

As Germany adopts a largely dualist approach to international treaty law despite being a civil law country,[31] the ECHR had to be incorporated into domestic German law in order for it to be binding on German courts. This occurred in 1952.[32] This means that the ECHR has the same status as any other domestic federal *Gesetz* and that a breach of it is not *per se* a breach of the *Grundgesetz*. But Germany adopts a monist approach to the general rules of public international law, so one way of German courts according a higher status to the law incorporating the ECHR is for them to say that rights in that Convention are reflective of those general rules and therefore must trump even a *Gesetz* adopted by the German Parliament after the 1952 *Gesetz* incorporating the ECHR. In 2004, in the case of *Görgülü*,[33] the

---

[29] FCC 74, 358, decision of 26 March 1987.

[30] Art 1(1) famously imposes a duty on all State authorities to respect and protect human dignity. See generally Werner Heun, *The Constitution of Germany* (Hart, 2011) ch 8.

[31] *Grundgesetz*, Art 59(2).

[32] *Gesetz über die Konvention zum Schutze der Menschenrechte und Grundfreiheiten*.

[33] FCC 111, 307, decision of 14 October 2004, available in English at (2004) 25 *Human Rights LJ* 99; see too Gertrude Lübbe-Wolff, 'ECHR and national jurisdiction - the *Görgülü* Case', available at www.vaeter-aktuell.de/english/ECHR_and_national_jurisdiction_-_The_Goerguelue_Case.pdf. Also M Hartwig, Much ado about human rights: the Federal Constitutional Court

FCC went further than it had before by in effect holding that the ECHR had a status equivalent to that of the *Grundgesetz* itself.

In this case, the applicant was a father requesting custody of or access to his son, whose mother had given him up for adoption the day after he was born. As the German courts were not receptive to this request, Mr Görgülü lodged an application with the European Court of Human Rights and won a judgment holding that his right to a family life under Article 8 of the ECHR had been violated.[34] But when he came to enforce this victory in the German courts he again met resistance. He had to go as far as the FCC to be properly vindicated, but even at that level the judges were not unequivocal in their support for the European Court's authority in the matter. They emphasized that they were willing to side with the interpretation placed on Article 8 by the European Court in this case, but in doing so they asserted that the ECHR did not have a status which was superior to that of any other federal law in Germany. Some commentators saw this as a slight on the ECHR, but the then President of the European Court, Lucius Wildhaber, told *Der Spiegel* that he did not think it meant that the German courts would no longer implement the European Court's judgments.[35] Lübbe-Wolff was also firmly of the view that the decision in *Görgülü* indicated no change at all in the willingness of German courts to comply with European Court judgments. Indeed the *Görgülü* decision should instead be celebrated as the first occasion on which the FCC recognized that a person aggrieved by a public authority's alleged breach of the ECHR could then lodge a complaint at the FCC, under Article 93 of the *Grundgesetz*, alleging that Germany's Constitution had thereby been breached too.[36]

It is clear, then, that for all practical purposes the status of the ECHR in the four jurisdictions considered here is very similar. That two of them are common law jurisdictions and two of them are civil law jurisdictions does

---

confronts the European Court of Human Rights' (2005) 6 *German LJ* 868; F Hoffmeister, 'Germany: Status of the European Convention on Human Rights in domestic law' (2006) 4 *ICON* 722.

[34] *Görgülü v Germany* (2004) 25 *Human Rights LJ* 93, judgment of 26 February 2004.

[35] 'Wenn der Eindruck entsteht, daß das nun nicht mehr so ist, hat sich das Bundesverfassungsgericht keinen guten Dienst erwiesen' ('If the impression has arisen that that is no longer the case, the FCC has not performed a good service'); interview with Der Spiegel, 15 November 2004, available at www.spiegel.de/spiegel/print/d-36625709.html.

[36] Abdelgawad and Weber, n 19 above, at 118-9; Hoffmeister, n 32 above, 730-1.

not make any substantial difference. There is no space in this short paper for a consideration of how varied the status of the ECHR may be across other civil law jurisdictions. One has to recognize that in countries such as Austria and the Netherlands it is granted a constitutional or even higher status, but the fact that there is a uniformity of approach between the common law and at least two important civil law jurisdictions is evidence of the ECHR having had some congruential effect between the different families of law. It is striking that in both the UK and Germany the specific duty placed upon the domestic courts is to 'take account of' European Court jurisprudence when interpreting and applying all domestic laws.[37]

3. The European Court's interpretative Principles

It is significant that the status of the ECHR is similar in common law and some civil law countries, but that alone would not ensure that Convention rights are similarly protected within each of those countries. For that to occur, the European Court has to deal with the applications before it with as little regard as possible to the idiosyncrasies of the legal system from which the applications originate. Fortunately, that is precisely what the European Court has done through developing and applying a set of interpretative principles ensuring a considerable degree of uniformity in its approach, regardless of which national court's decisions it is reviewing. There are at least five of these principles, each of which has played a significant role in promoting congruence between common law and civil law approaches to the protection of human rights.[38]

First, the European Court insists that national 'laws' must be of a certain quality. They must be clear, consistent, accessible and properly made; if they leave people uncertain as to how to behave without breaking the law, they are not of the appropriate quality. Second, besides the word 'law', other words used in the ECHR are given an autonomous and evolving meaning by the European Court; it is not obliged to define 'criminal offense', 'civil rights', 'private life' or 'possessions', for example, in a way

---

[37] Human Rights Act 1998, s 2(1)(a) and the Berücksichtigungspflict referred to in the FCC's decision in Görgülü.

[38] See, generally, W Schabas, *The European Convention on Human Rights: A Commentary* (Oxford UP, 2015), 33-50; DJ Harris, M O'Boyle, EP Bates and CM Buckley, *Law of the European Convention on Human Rights* (Oxford UP, 3rd ed, 2014) 7-21; B Rainey, E Wicks and C Ovey, *The European Convention on Human Rights* (Oxford UP, 6th ed, 2014) 65-84; K Reid, *A Practitioner's Guide to the European Convention on Human Rights* (Sweet & Maxwell, 4th ed, 2011) 57-74.

which gels with the definition used in any national system, and the definition it prefers can develop over time. Third, and perhaps most importantly, if a State wishes to interfere with a Convention right it must provide the European Court with a justification for that interference which shows that it is legitimate, necessary and proportionate. Those too are terms which can be applied slightly differently as time goes on, but they remain as fundamental touchstones for the acceptability of interference with a right. Fourth, the Court interprets Convention rights in ways which ensure that they are protected effectively: it will not give purely formal recognition to a right without insisting that in practice the holder of that right can vindicate it in a way which makes it real, not illusory. Fifth, and this is a countervailing principle which admits that the ECHR is meant to be a last resort layer of protection for everyone in Europe, the European Court accepts that the primary responsibility for protecting human rights rests with national authorities. Hence its acceptance of the margin of appreciation doctrine, its assertion that it is not an appeal court or 'court of fourth instance', and its acknowledgment that its job is not to determine criminal guilt or civil liability. Its only function is to decide whether a State has failed to live up to the commitment to guarantee Convention rights which it gave when ratifying the document.

Taken together, these interpretative principles inevitably ensure that there is a great deal of similarity between the way in which human rights are protected across European legal systems. That such similarity would not have been attained without the influence of the European Court of Human Rights is clear from studies of how the UK's laws have changed as a result of judgments from the European Court countermanding those of the highest court in the UK – now the Supreme Court but until 2009 the Appellate Committee of the House of Lords.[39] The Supreme Court of Ireland has had its judgments reviewed on 20 occasions by the European Court between 1960 and 2017; in 14 of these the European Court found a violation of the ECHR where the Supreme Court had found none and in many of these domestic Irish law has had to be changed to bring it into line with the European norm.

---

[39] B Dickson, *Human Rights and the United Kingdom Supreme Court* (Oxford UP, 2013). App 3 in that book lists 133 decisions of the apex UK court which have been subsequently reviewed by the European Commission or Court of Human Rights since 1975. In 31 decisions the European Court did not agree with the national court's approach to the ECHR and found a violation of the Convention where the national court had found none.

4. Illustrative Examples of Congruence

This part of the paper attempts to provide indicative evidence for the congruential influence of the ECHR in each of the four jurisdictions under consideration. For each country, two examples drawn from the European Court's jurisprudence will be considered.

The United Kingdom

The two examples from the UK concern the right not to be searched and the right to vote in elections. The first illustrates how rapidly UK law can be altered to bring it into line with the requirements laid down by the European Court. The second concerns a more controversial issue which took more than 13 years to resolve. The process took so long precisely because the UK government was acutely aware that changing UK law would be an indication of the congruential effect of European Court judgments.

In *Gillan and Quinton v UK* the European Court had to rule on whether a police search of two people who were in the vicinity of an arms trade fair in London had been lawfully conducted under the UK's anti-terrorism legislation.[40] When the matter was before the nation's highest court, the House of Lords, the Senior Law Lord had held, with the concurrence of his four colleagues, that there had been no violation of the ECHR because there were no fewer than 11 respects in which the legislative power involved was constrained so as to make it compliant with human rights standards.[41] The European Court, however, completely disagreed: by seven votes to none it held that the searches had violated the right to a private life of those searched, despite the constraints in place. As a result of this ruling, the British government almost immediately suspended the operation of the relevant power and a year later replaced it with a new search power that was constrained in additional ways to those already in place for the earlier power.[42] That the UK should accept the need to alter its domestic law on such a sensitive issue as counter-terrorism laws, even though the country's own highest court had seen nothing wrong with it, is indeed a sign that one of the indirect effects of the ECHR is to bring

---

[40] (2010) 50 EHRR 45. Earlier a Chamber of the Court had reached a 7 v 0 decision against the UK: (2004) 38 EHRR 40.

[41] *R (Gillan) v Metropolitan Police Commissioner* [2006] UKHL 12, [2006] 2 AC 307.

[42] Terrorism Act 2000 (Remedial) Order 200, SI 631; Protection of Freedoms Act 2012, ss 61-62.

common and civil law jurisdictions closer together on an important aspect of human rights law.

The other decision of the European Court is that of the Grand Chamber in *Hirst v UK (No 2)*,[43] where the Strasbourg judges held (by 12 to 5) that the UK's ban on any convicted prisoner being allowed to vote in elections was a violation of the right to free elections guaranteed by Article 2 of Protocol 1 to the ECHR. The Court's position was confirmed in several subsequent cases.[44] The UK government and Parliament expressed their fundamental disagreement with these decisions,[45] but the UK Supreme Court accepted that it meant that UK law or policy would have to be changed.[46] There was significant political posturing over the issue for many years, and it remains the clearest example yet of a common law system standing in the way of the harmonization of European human rights law. Finally, in late 2017, the Committee of Ministers of the Council of Europe accepted a UK government plan as a satisfactory implementation of the judgments issued against it because the proposed administrative arrangements fell within the margin of appreciation allowed to each State.[47] Under the plan, prisoners who have been sentenced to short terms of imprisonment and who are being prepared for release through a temporary license, either for a day or under a Home Curfew Scheme, will be permitted to vote if they are registered to do

---

[43] (2006) 42 EHRR 41.

[44] *Greens and MT v UK* (2011) 53 EHRR 21; *Firth v UK* (2016) 63 EHRR 25; *McHugh v UK* App No 51987/08, judgment of 10 February 2015; *Millbank v UK* App No 44473/14, judgment of 30 June 2016.

[45] In the House of Commons on 3 November 2010 Prime Minister David Cameron said: 'It makes me physically ill even to contemplate having to give the vote to anyone who is in prison' (HC Debs, vol 517, col 921). See too House of Commons Resolution, 10 February 2011 (234 votes to 22).

[46] *R (Chester) v Secretary of State for Justice* [2013] UKSC 63, [2014] AC 271. In the meantime no compensation has been awarded to prisoners who have been denied the franchise.

[47] See the Committee's decision at its meeting on 5-7 December 2017: CM/Del/Dec(2017)1302/H46-39. This approach is in line with the European Court's pronouncements in *Scoppola v Italy (No 3)* (2013) 56 EHRR 19. For an insightful analysis of the *Hirst* case and its fall-out, see K Dzehtsiarou, 'Prisoner voting saga: reasons for challenges' in H Hardman and B Dickson (eds), *Electoral Rights in Europe: Advances and Challenges* (Routledge, 2017) 92-110.

so.[48] Once again we see that congruence, within the limits of the margin of appreciation doctrine, is the name of the game.

Ireland

The two examples from Ireland also comprise one good illustration of the country's readiness to adjust its laws to bring them closer to the European norm, even in a field as controversial as abortion, and another illustration of an apparent reluctance to do so in a much less controversial field.

The abortion case is *A, B and C v Ireland*, where the European Court held by 17 to 0 that one of three applicants who had been refused an abortion in Ireland had suffered a violation of her right to a private life under Article 8 of the ECHR.[49] Notwithstanding the political and religious sensitivities associated with abortion, the Irish legislators approved the Protection of Life During Pregnancy Act 2013, which clarifies the law so that a woman in the position of the successful applicant in Strasbourg is now able to obtain clear advice on whether she is entitled to an abortion or not. (It remains the case that the European Court has not yet held that a woman has a right to an abortion in any particular situation.)

The second case relates to vicarious liability for harm caused by child sex abuse. In 2008 the Irish Supreme Court held by 4 to 1 that no such liability should be imposed on the State for a school's failure to protect a girl at the school from molestation by a teacher.[50] It could see no justification for extending such liability in a situation where the teacher had acted so blatantly in contradiction with his job description and where the abuse had occurred in the 1970s when the law on vicarious liability was much less developed than it has since become. The European Court, however, found by 11 to 6 that vicarious liability should be imposed, despite the lapse of time since the 1970s.[51] In doing so the European Court was effectively adopting a common law position regarding the development of the law: a change to judge-made law represents a revealing of the underlying basis of the earlier law and so can be applied retrospectively (although other litigants who suffered under the earlier law are not

---

[48] See the Action Plan submitted to the Committee of Ministers on 2 November 2017: DH-DD(2017)1229.

[49] (2011) 53 EHRR 13; the applicant was awarded €15,000 as compensation.

[50] *O'Keeffe v Hickey* [2009] 2 IR 302.

[51] *O'Keeffe v Ireland* (2014) 59 EHRR 15; the applicant was awarded €30,000 as compensation.

permitted to have the judgments against them re-opened on the basis of this change). To date, Ireland has taken no legislative step to reflect the European Court's position, and it may not have to in view of the fact that in common law systems vicarious liability is traditionally an area of judge-made law. It should be noted that one of the judges who issued a judgment in the Supreme Court's hearing of this matter took the unusual step of later going into print to explain why he thought that the European Court had misunderstood the basis for the Supreme Court's conclusions.[52]

France

As already mentioned, since its revolution at the end of the eighteenth century France has prided itself on its system of administrative courts. One might say that these were as indicative of a civil law legal system as the right to jury trial was of a common law system. Nevertheless, France has had to modify its approach to administrative justice in order to bring its practices into line with the requirements of the ECHR. In *Kress v France*, in 2001, the Grand Chamber of the European Court ruled that France was in breach of Article 6 of the ECHR in allowing the lawyer acting for the government, the *commissaire du gouvernement*, to take part in the administrative court's deliberations on the outcome of a dispute.[53] In response to that judgment, the President of the Judicial Division of the *Conseil d'État* issued two directions which allowed the *commissaire* to be present at deliberations but not to address the court.[54] But a few years later, in *Martinie v France*,[55] the Grand Chamber built on *Kress* by ruling that Article 6(1) also meant that the mere presence of the *commissaire* at the deliberations was unacceptable. In doing so it expressly relied on the European Court's previous case law, where it had found a breach of Article 6(1) when the Deputy Attorney General of Portugal had attended the deliberations of the Portuguese Supreme Court[56] and when an Advocate

---

[52] A Hardiman, 'The jurisdiction of the European Court of Human Rights and the case of *O'Keeffe v Hickey*' in L Cahillane, J Gallen and T Hickey (eds), *Judges, Politics and the Irish Constitution* (Manchester UP, 2017) 94-107. The judge's views are countered in the same volume by James Gallen (84-83) and Conor O'Mahony (108-120).

[53] App No 39594/98, judgment of 7 June 2001.

[54] The directions were given legislative form in Decree 2005-1586, which inserted Art.R731-7 into the Code on Administrative Courts.

[55] *Martinie v France* (2007) 45 EHRR 15, judgment of 13 July 2006.

[56] *Lobo Machado v Portugal* (1997) 23 EHRR 79.

General in France had attended the deliberations of the Criminal Division of the French *Cour de cassation*.[57] The presence of all these officials violated the 'doctrine of appearances', whereby there must not only be actual fairness but also the appearance of fairness, the more so because the officials in question would all have publicly expressed their views on the case prior to the deliberations they were attending.[58]

The ruling in *Martinie* prompted the making of another law, Decree 2006-964, which denied the *commissaire* the right to be present in the room where the court's deliberations were taking place provided the complainant in the case did not object. This did not seem like a wholehearted implementation of the European Court's judgment and in *Étienne v France* it was challenged by a complainant who had not objected to the presence of the *commissaire* and had then lost her case at the *Conseil d'État*.[59] Surprisingly, her complaint was declared inadmissible by the European Court: her failure to expressly request the *commissaire* not to attend was, apparently, sufficient to remove any appearance of unfairness. It is doubtful if a common law country would in any circumstances tolerate the presence in the room where judges are deciding a dispute of a person who has already argued in favor of a particular solution to that dispute, but the position of the European Court is a reflection of its desire to ensure that where appropriate a *via media* between civil law and common law conceptions of fairness should be found.

France has had to make a comparable concession regarding its processes in the criminal justice arena. For decades it held the view that there was nothing objectionable, when detaining someone on suspicion of having committed a crime, for the police to have a 24-hour period during which to question that person without allowing him or her access to legal assistance. Additionally, it was not unusual for the police to treat a suspect merely as a witness and to insist that in that guise the person must supply investigators with testimony under oath. It was not until 2010, in *Brusco v France*, that the European Court declared both these practices to be in contravention of Article 6, thereby bringing French law into line with standard practice in common law countries.[60] While this might have led some French jurists to claim that their fears that France's ratification of the ECHR would lead to the infiltration of common law ideas had been

---

[57] *Reinhardt and Slimane-Kaïd v France* (1999) 28 EHRR 59.

[58] Note 54 above, paras 53-55.

[59] *Étienne v France* App No 11396/08, decision of 15 September 2009.

[60] *Brusco v France* App No 1466/07, judgment of 14 October 2010.

realized, legislation was duly passed in France to implement the European Court's judgment and the sky has not since fallen in.[61]

Germany

Germany, too, has changed its domestic law to bring it closer to the common law position. As an example we can refer again to the case of *Görgülü*[62] where, apart from the status of the ECHR within German domestic law, what was at issue was the right of a father to have access to his child. Such a 'rights' issue calls out for a uniform approach across all jurisdictions, if only to avoid situations where children are victims of a 'tug-of-love' between their parents living in different countries. In *Görgülü v Germany* the European Court tried to bring some harmony to European human rights law on this matter. It is clearly a very serious step to deny a father access to his child without even giving him a chance to be heard before that step is taken.

The second German example is the litigation brought by Princess Caroline of Monaco over alleged invasions of her privacy. She has now made three applications that have resulted in judgments of the European Court, one which she won and two which she lost. Together they have resulted in German law on privacy being harmonized with that in other European countries, including common law countries. In the first case, the Princess argued that the German press had violated her right to privacy by publishing photographs of her going about her daily business. Whilst she lost in Germany's Federal Constitutional Court[63] she won in the European Court of Human Rights, which held unanimously that the German Court had adopted the wrong test for deciding when a celebrity was entitled to privacy.[64] A few years later Princess Caroline and her husband again complained about the publication of photographs taken while they were on holiday, but on this occasion the European Court's Grand Chamber unanimously upheld the German courts' decision that there had been no violation of privacy.[65] The Court took special note of the

---

[61] Loi 2011-392 of 14 April 2011, amending the *Code de procedure pénale*, art 63(34).

[62] Note 32 above.

[63] BVerfG, judgment of the First Senate, 15 December 1999 (1 BvR 653/96). For a version in English see:
www.bundesverfassungsgericht.de/SharedDocs/Entscheidungen/EN/1999/12/rs19991215_1bvr065396en.html.

[64] *Von Hannover v Germany* (2005) 40 EHRR 1.

[65] *Von Hannover v Germany (No 2)* (2012) 33 EHRR 15.

fact that the German courts had reacted to the earlier Strasbourg judgment by adjusting the test to be applied when deciding whether privacy had been violated. In particular, they had paid great attention to whether the photographs had contributed to a debate of general interest.[66] The balance struck by the German courts, said Strasbourg, was within Germany's margin of appreciation. A third complaint from Princess Caroline, again about the publication of a holiday photograph, was also unsuccessful, because the press were able to show a link between the photograph in question and the public debate about wealthy people letting out their holiday homes.[67]

5. Conclusion

It is hoped that the principles and examples analyzed in this chapter have given a flavor of how the ECHR has operated almost surreptitiously as a unifying force between common and civil law systems in Europe. Even though human rights are primarily claims made against governments (though of course countries may also allow such claims at the horizontal level within the State) it is clear that what would otherwise be diverse approaches to human rights claims have been brought closer together through the judgments of the European Court of Human Rights. The rights protected by the ECHR are largely drawn from the Universal Declaration of Human Rights proclaimed in 1948, so it is entirely appropriate that the values enshrined in those rights are applied in practice in a similar way throughout the Council of Europe's 47 member states. *Realpolitik* has prompted the European Court to maintain some wriggle room for governments through its margin of appreciation doctrine, but in many states we have seen the killing of supposedly sacred cows without any profound damage occurring to the legal, political or cultural fabric of the nation. The fact that judges on the European Court are increasingly basing their decisions in novel cases on what is the consensus position amongst member states[68] is further evidence that for the foreseeable future

---

[66] BVerfG, order of the First Senate, 26 February 2008 (1 BvR 1602/07). For a version in English see:
www.bundesverfassungsgericht.de/SharedDocs/Entscheidungen/EN/2008/02/rs20080226_1bvr160207en.htm.

[67] *Von Hannover v Germany* App No 8772/10, judgment of 19 September 2013. Germany's Federal Constitutional Court rejected Princess Caroline's application for review on 23 September 2013 but issued no reasoned judgment (1 BvR 2678/08).

[68] Dzehtsiarou (2015).

convergence between common law and civil law systems will proceed steadily apace in this context.

Bibliography

(2010) 50 EHRR 45. Earlier a Chamber of the Court had reached a 7 v 0 decision against the UK: (2004) 38 EHRR 40.

A Hardiman, 'The jurisdiction of the European Court of Human Rights and the case of *O'Keeffe v Hickey*' in L Cahillane, J Gallen and T Hickey (eds), *Judges, Politics and the Irish Constitution* (Manchester UP, 2017)

Action Plan submitted to the Committee of Ministers on 2 November 2017: DH-DD(2017)1229.

App No 39594/98, judgment of 7 June 2001.

Brusco v France App No 1466/07, judgment of 14 October 2010.

BVerfG, judgment of the First Senate, 15 December 1999 (1 BvR 653/96). For a version in English see: www.bundesverfassungsgericht.de/SharedDocs/Entscheidungen/EN/1999/12/rs19991215_1bvr065396en.html.

BVerfG, order of the First Senate, 26 February 2008 (1 BvR 1602/07). For a version in English see: www.bundesverfassungsgericht.de/SharedDocs/Entscheidungen/EN/2008/02/rs20080226_1bvr160207en.htm.

Conseil d'État, Assemblée, nos 105743, 105810, 105811 and 105812, 21 December 1990 (*Confédération nationale des associations familiales catholiques* case).

Constitution of Ireland 1937, Arts 31-32.

Cour de Cassation, Chambre criminelle, pourvoi no 95-85118, 27 November 1996 (*Commandos anti-IVG* case).

Decision no 2010-613 DC, of 7 October 2010, available in English at www.conseil-constitutionnel.fr/conseil-constitutionnel/root/bank_mm/anglais/en2010_613dc.pdf.

Dickson, Brice.*Human Rights and the United Kingdom Supreme Court* (Oxford UP, 2013).

Dzehtsiarou Kanstantsin, 'Prisoner voting saga: reasons for challenges' in H Hardman and B Dickson (eds), *Electoral Rights in Europe: Advances and Challenges* (Routledge, 2017)

Elisabeth Lambert Abdelgawad and Anne Weber, 'The Reception Process in France and Germany' in Helen Keller and Alec Stone Sweet (eds), *A Europe of Rights: The Impact of the ECHR on National Legal Systems* (Oxford University Press, 2008).

Étienne v France App No 11396/08, decision of 15 September 2009.

European Convention on Human Rights Act 2003, s 5.

FCC 111, 307, decision of 14 October 2004, available in English at (2004) 25 *Human Rights LJ* 99

FCC 74, 358, decision of 26 March 1987.

Ghaidan v Godin-Mendoza [2004] UKHL 30, [2004] 2 AC 557. For further details see B Dickson, *Human Rights and the United Kingdom Supreme Court* (Oxford University Press, 2013)

Görgülü v Germany (2004) 25 *Human Rights LJ* 93, judgment of 26 February 2004.

Greens and MT v UK (2011) 53 EHRR 21; *Firth v UK* (2016) 63 EHRR 25; *McHugh v UK* App No 51987/08, judgment of 10 February 2015; *Millbank v UK* App No 44473/14, judgment of 30 June 2016.

Harris DJ, M O'Boyle, EP Bates and CM Buckley, *Law of the European Convention on Human Rights* (Oxford UP, 3rd ed, 2014)

Heun Werner, *The Constitution of Germany* (Hart, 2011) ch 8.

Hoffmeister F,'Germany: Status of the European Convention on Human Rights in domestic law' (2006) 4 *ICON*

Hogan Gerard, David Kenny and Rachael Walsh, 'An anthology of declarations of unconstitutionality' (2015) 54 *Irish Jurist*

Human Rights Act 1998, s 3(1).

Lobo Machado v Portugal (1997) 23 EHRR 79.

Loi 2011-392 of 14 April 2011, amending the *Code de procedure pénale*, art 63(34).

Lübbe-Wolff Gertrude, 'ECHR and national jurisdiction - the *Görgülü* Case', available at www.vaeter-aktuell.de/english/ECHR_and_national_jurisdiction_-_The_Goerguelue_Case.pdf.

Martinie v France (2007) 45 EHRR 15, judgment of 13 July 2006.

O'Keeffe v Hickey [2009] 2 IR 302.

O'Keeffe v Ireland (2014) 59 EHRR 15

Paris Marie-Luce, *Implementing The European Convention on Human Rights: A Comparative Constitutional Perspective With References to Ireland and France*, available at www.ialsnet.org/meetings/constit/papers/ParisMarie-Luce%28Ireland%29.pdf.

Ponthoreau Marie-Claire and Fabrice Hourquebie, in Andrew Harding and Peter Leyland (eds), *Constitutional Courts: A Comparative Study* (Wildy, Simmonds and Hill Publishing, 2009)

R (Chester) v Secretary of State for Justice [2013] UKSC 63, [2014] AC 271.

R (Gillan) v Metropolitan Police Commissioner [2006] UKHL 12, [2006] 2 AC 307.

Rainey, Bernadette E Wicks and C Ovey, *The European Convention on Human Rights* (Oxford UP, 6th ed, 2014)

Reid Karen, *A Practitioner's Guide to the European Convention on Human Rights* (Sweet & Maxwell, 4th ed, 2011)

Reinhardt and Slimane-Kaïd v France (1999) 28 EHRR 59.

Sahin v Turkey (2007) 44 EHRR 5 (GC).

SAS v France (2015) 60 EHRR 11 (GC).

Sauvé Jean-Marc, speech in Hunter Valley, Australia, 4 March 2010, available in English at www.conseil-etat.fr/Actualites/Discours-Interventions/The-French-administrative-jurisdictional-system.

Schabas William, *The European Convention on Human Rights: A Commentary* (Oxford UP, 2015)

Scoppola v Italy (No 3) (2013) 56 EHRR 19.

Terrorism Act 2000 (Remedial) Order 200, SI 631; Protection of Freedoms Act 2012, ss 61-62.

The *Interruption Voluntaire de Grossesse* case, decision of 15 January 1975, available in English at www.conseil-constitutionnel.fr/conseil-constitutionnel/root/bank_mm/anglais/a7454dc.pdf.

Von Hannover v Germany (2005) 40 EHRR 1.

Von Hannover v Germany (No 2) (2012) 33 EHRR 15.

Von Hannover v Germany App No 8772/10, judgment of 19 September 2013. Germany's Federal Constitutional Court rejected Princess Caroline's application for review on 23 September 2013 but issued no reasoned judgment (1 BvR 2678/08).

Zielinski v France (2001) 31 EHRR 19

Part 3
National implications

Chapter 15

Common Law and Civil Law Approaches to Excessive Group Crimes

Marjolein Cupido[1]

Abstract

This paper addresses the question of how common and civil law jurisdictions establish criminal responsibility for collective group crimes, and what they can learn from each other in addressing these crimes. Not only is this issue particularly topical in domestic criminal law, but it also constitutes one of the most fundamental challenges faced by international criminal courts. Indeed, it is at the international level, where the dichotomy between common and civil law approaches towards groups criminality emerges most clearly, and potentially generates unwanted fragmentation.

Against this background, this paper studies two liability theories that are used in the common and civil law to address group criminality: JCE and co-perpetration, respectively. In particular, the paper analyses how domestic courts apply these theories in practice. Specific attention is paid to the British Jogee case on JCE and the Dutch Nijmegen scooter case concerning co-perpetration. Following a thought-experiment, the paper appraises how

---

[1] LL.M. Leiden University (*summa cum laude*), PhD VU University Amsterdam. The author is currently assistant professor at VU University Amsterdam and fellow of the *Center for International Criminal Justice*. In addition, she is appointed deputy judge in the criminal law section of the District Court of Rotterdam. Parts of this chapter are based on the author's contribution to the national report of the Netherlands for the 2017 conference of the *International Association of Penal Law* (available online at Marjolein Cupido et al., "Individual Liability for Business Involvement in International Crimes," accessed November 20, 2018,
https://cicj.org/wp-content/uploads/2017/02/Cupido-Hornman-Huisman-2017-Individual-liability-for-business-involvement-in-international-crimes.pdf) and on Marjolein Cupido, Verhoogd Opzet bij Medeplegen?: Een Rechtsvergelijkende Analyse, *Ars Aequi* (2018) 28-40.

these cases would have been resolved, had the British and Dutch courts applied each other's liability theory – would that have resulted in a different outcome?

By taking such a practical approach, this paper clarifies the similarities and differences between common and civil law approaches to group criminality. Such insights are essential for developing a comprehensive understanding of domestic criminal justice, whilst they also help to harmonize international approaches to criminal responsibility.

Introduction

One of the characteristic features of criminal law is its focus on individuals. Criminal law attaches responsibility to *individual* persons based on their *personal* guilt and conduct.[2] Collective liability – i.e. liability based on mere group membership – is strictly prohibited. In principle, the notion of individual liability is universally recognized in common law and civil law jurisdictions.[3] Yet, in both legal traditions, courts struggle to apply this notion in cases of group criminality, in particular where it concerns so-called 'crimes of excess' or 'excessive crimes'. In these situations, a group plans to commit crime A, but one of the group members goes beyond this pre-established plan and on his own initiative commits a further crime – crime B – to which the other participants did not consent. The question then arises whether the participants can be held responsible for the commission of the further crime B despite their lack of agreement and direct involvement, or whether only the person who intentionally committed the excessive crime enjoys liability for it.

Both in the Netherlands and in England, courts have recently been challenged to address this question. It is noteworthy how these courts – that are part of the civil law and common law tradition, respectively – have adopted distinctive approaches to the issue of crimes of excess and in this way have given different meanings to the notion of individual liability. In this contribution, I will analyze the Dutch and English ways of dealing with crimes of excess in cases of group criminality. Moreover, I will compare these domestic approaches and assess what Dutch and English courts can learn from each other in dealing with excessive crimes. In this respect, it is important to take note of the broader framework of Dutch and English law and appraise the comparative findings in light of the legal

---

[2] Elies van Sliedregt, *Individual Criminal Responsibility under International Criminal Law* (Oxford: OUP, 2012): 17-18.

[3] Van Sliedregt, *Individual Criminal Responsibility*, 17-18.

traditions of both domestic systems. This does not mean that I will provide a comprehensive analysis of all parallels and unique features of Dutch and English law. My purpose is rather to draw attention to some typical characteristics of how crimes of excess are addressed by Dutch and English courts.

Where it concerns liability for group criminality, it is useful to draw inspiration from international criminal law (ICL). ICL is a hybrid system in which common and civil law notions of criminal responsibility come together in a unique way.[4] Thus, it is at the international level, where the dichotomy between common and civil law approaches, for example in relation to crimes of excess, emerges most clearly. Moreover, ICL relates to crimes that are inherently collective.[5] International crimes are generally committed by large groups of persons acting together pursuant to common plans and joint agreements. Therefore, debates about how to implement the notion of individual liability in relation to collective crimes are particularly prominent in ICL and provide valuable input for the analysis of domestic responses to group criminality. Again, it must be stressed that my analysis on this point is by no means intended to be exhaustive, but rather illustrative of the different ways in which crimes of excess can be addressed. As such, the analysis allows for adding new perspectives and for seeing domestic (case) law from a different perspective.

The contribution is structured as follows. First, I will discuss the Dutch and English law on crimes of excess by analyzing two landmark judgments in which Dutch and English courts have interpreted the law on crimes of excess in innovative ways (section 2 and 3). These judgments serve as the basis for a comparative analysis that depicts the parallels and unique features of the two domestic approaches, e.g. in terms of the rationale underlying the courts' reasoning and the implications of their findings (section 4). In appraising the domestic approaches to crimes of excess, I will draw inspiration from ICL by analyzing domestic (case) law in light of relevant international experience. As said before, the Dutch and English legal system are part of the civil law and common law tradition, respectively. This is not to say that their views on crimes of excess are characteristic for these two legal traditions and that all other domestic

---

[4] Van Sliedregt, *Individual Criminal Responsibility*, 8-9.

[5] Van Sliedregt, *Individual Criminal Responsibility*, 20-22; André Nollkaemper, "Introduction," in *System Criminality in International Law*, eds. Harmen van der Wilt and André Nollkaemper (Cambridge: CUP, 2010), 1.

systems that are part of the same traditions will take similar approaches. Having said that, the comparison of Dutch and English law is particularly useful. The way in which these legal systems deal with crimes of excess is connected to how the common law and civil law address criminal liability for group criminality – in particular the liability theories that they use in this respect – and relates to the *actus reus* (objective) and *mens rea* (subjective) requirements they distinguish for establishing criminal responsibility. Moreover, questions concerning crimes of excess are particularly topical in the Netherlands and England and have generated extensive debates. I will conclude with a number of evaluative observations concerning the implications of the comparative study (section 5).

1. The *Nijmegen Scooter*-Case and Dutch Law on Crimes of Excess

The issue of criminal responsibility for crimes of excess has recently generated an extensive debate in Dutch scholarship. This debate was particularly triggered by a landmark judgment of the Dutch Supreme Court in the so-called *Nijmegen scooter*-case.[6] In this case, two persons had planned to rob a hotel.[7] However – before even entering the hotel – they spotted a police surveillance car, and absconded, riding together on one scooter. In the course of their getaway, the two robbers exceeded the speed limit, ignored a red traffic light, and consequently hit a pedestrian, who later passed away as a result of his injuries.

One of the crucial points in this case concerned the lack of evidence about which of the two robbers was the driver of the scooter.[8] There were no recordings of the accident and witnesses had given contradictory statements as to who had actually driven the scooter. Moreover, it could not be established whether the robbers had deliberated during their escape about what to do and how to abscond from the police. It thus remained unclear how each of the robbers had actually contributed to the killing of the pedestrian. Considering these evidentiary uncertainties, the courts faced the difficult question of whether the pedestrian's death could be attributed to both robbers based on their joint planning of the robbery. In other words, was the accused's mutual agreement to rob a hotel and their joint participation in this plan sufficient for holding them criminally liable for the subsequent killing of the pedestrian? To answer this question,

---

[6] Dutch Supreme Court, 17 December 2013, ECLI:NL:HR:2013:1964 and 1966.

[7] Idem, para. 2.2.2.

[8] Idem.

the courts employed the notion of co-perpetration and assessed the accused's responsibility within this framework.

Co-perpetration is broadly regulated in Article 47 of the Dutch Penal Code (DPC) and has been interpreted more precisely in case law of the Supreme Court. Traditionally, the paradigm case of co-perpetration concerns a situation in which several persons together fulfill the *actus reus* – i.e. the objective elements – of a criminal offense and jointly act towards the completion of a crime.[9] Yet, in the landmark *Container theft*-case, the Supreme Court clarified that co-perpetrators do not necessarily have to fulfill a crime's *actus reus* elements physically – i.e. with their own hands – nor be present at the crime scene.[10] Rather, it suffices that the co-perpetrators 'intentionally and closely cooperate' in the commission of a criminal offense.[11] Today, the 'intentional and close contribution' test still constitutes the central requirement of co-perpetration and provides the legal test for assessing the criminal responsibility of co-perpetrators.

The *intentional* contribution requirement establishes a subjective criterion, which pertains to the accused's *mens rea*.[12] The accused must have intended to cooperate with the other co-perpetrators *and* intended to commit the crimes with which he is charged. The standard of intent is normally *dolus eventualis*, i.e. knowingly accepting the significant risk that crimes will be committed. The accused's intent is ideally based on his agreement and deliberation with others to commit a crime, but may also be proven by tacit approval, or be inferred from the accused's objective conduct.[13] In literature, it is therefore conceded that when the accused was willfully present at the crime scene, did not intervene, nor dissociate himself from the crimes, the totality of circumstances may imply that the accused silently accepted the commission of crimes by others.[14]

The *close* contribution requirement regulates the objective side of co-perpetration, i.e. it relates to the accused's *actus reus*. In particular, the close contribution requirement ascertains that the accused's involvement

---

[9] Harmen van der Wilt, "De Ontwikkeling van Nieuwe Deelnemingsvormen. Ben Ik mijn Broeders Hoeder?," *Delikt & Delinkwent* 10 (2007): para. 2.1.

[10] Dutch Supreme Court, 17 November 1981, ECLI:NL:HR:1981:AC7388, *NJ* 1983, 84.

[11] Idem.

[12] Jaap de Hullu, *Materieel Strafrecht: Over Algemene Leerstukken van Strafrechtelijke Aansprakelijkheid naar Nederlands Recht* (Deventer: Kluwer, 2015), 453.

[13] De Hullu, *Materieel Strafrecht*, 447.

[14] Idem, 465.

carries a certain weight – offering mere criminal assistance does not suffice.[15] For some time, courts applied the close contribution requirement rather broadly.[16] Accused were held responsible as co-perpetrators based on mere minor contributions to criminal offenses, e.g. standing at the look-out, or sharing in the criminal booty. On this account, scholars critically observed that co-perpetration essentially consists of sympathizing or consenting with the acts of the physical perpetrator, i.e. failing to prevent others from engaging in criminal conduct.[17]

In response to such critiques, the Dutch Supreme Court has recently emphasized that each co-perpetrator needs to make an *essential* contribution to the crimes charged that carries sufficient weight.[18] This entails that co-perpetrators should in principle contribute directly to the objective elements of crime by participating in the common execution of a criminal offense.[19] Giving moral support, being present at the scene of the crimes, or not-withdrawing from the commission of crimes are thus in themselves insufficient for establishing criminal responsibility for co-perpetration.[20] Yet, in combination with other contributions – such as the planning of crimes or the active encouragement of physical perpetrators – these limited and indirect contributions may nevertheless justify a conviction for co-perpetration.[21] Moreover, when liability is based on acts of assistance that are committed before or after the commission of crimes – such as, providing information, standing on the look-out, or driving the get-away car – courts have to explain precisely why the accused can be held liable as a co-perpetrator, despite his mere remote and limited involvement in the crimes charged.[22]

---

[15] Menno Dolman, "Doen Plegen, Uitlokken en Medeplegen," *Tekst & Commentaar Strafrecht* (Kluwer online resource, last modified July 1, 2018): para. 7.c. and 7.g.

[16] Van der Wilt, "De Ontwikkeling van Nieuwe Deelnemingsvormen," para. 2.1.

[17] Idem.

[18] Dutch Supreme Court, 2 December 2014, ECLI:NL:HR:2014:3474, para. 3.2.1. and 3.2.2.

[19] Idem, para. 3.2.3.

[20] Dutch Supreme Court, 16 December 2014, ECLI:NL:HR:2014:3637, para. 3.2.2; Dutch Supreme Court, 22 December 2009, ECLI:NL:HR:2009:BK3356, *NJ* 2010,193.

[21] De Hullu, *Materieel Strafrecht*, 455, fn. 129-133.

[22] Dutch Supreme Court, 2 December 2014, ECLI:NL:HR:2014:3474, para. 3.2.2.

At first sight, the 'intentional and close contribution' requirement excludes applying co-perpetration to crimes of excess, because in such cases the accused neither contributed nor agreed to the crime charged. Thus, it was to be expected that the accused in the previously discussed *Nijmegen scooter*-case would be acquitted from co-perpetrating the killing of the pedestrian, since there was no evidence of how each of them had participated in this crime, nor of the accused's agreement to co-perpetrate it. Yet, in its judgment of 17 December 2013, the Supreme Court adopted an innovative interpretation of co-perpetration that expanded the law beyond its traditional borders.[23] The Court considered that the accused's plan to rob the hotel could not be strictly distinguished from their escape from the police. Rather, these events should be assessed in connection with each other. In particular, the Court decided that when 'the commission of a crime is preceded by *another related* crime, the required cooperation between the co-perpetrators may have already existed when they contemplated committing the first crime'.[24] Following this thought, the Supreme Court held that it must be determined whether the plan to rob the hotel included the accused's escape from the police as a *probable possibility*.[25] When such a causal connection between the robbery and the accused's escape can be established, the deathly consequences of the escape may – according to the Supreme Court – be attributed to both accused, even in the absence of their specific contribution or agreement to this crime. By reasoning in this way, the Supreme Court in the *Nijmegen scooter*-case created a broad basis of criminal responsibility for crimes of excess based on a loose 'probable consequence' standard.

The Supreme Court referred the *Nijmegen scooter*-case back to the Court of Appeal in 's-Hertogenbosch that had to decide the case anew based on the established framework. On 20 June 2016, the Court of Appeal convicted the accused in the *Nijmegen scooter*-case to prison sentences of 4 years and 3 years and 9 months for co-perpetrating death by recklessness.[26] The Court accepted that the accused closely and intentionally worked together in planning an armed robbery of a hotel,[27] and held that by doing so had also contemplated cooperating in relation

---

[23] Dutch Supreme Court, 17 December 2013, ECLI:NL:HR:2013:1964 and 1966.

[24] Idem, para. 2.3.2.

[25] Idem, para. 2.3.3.

[26] Court of Appeal 's-Hertogenbosch, 20 June 2016, ECLI:NL:GHSHE:2016:2428 and 2429.

[27] Idem, para. 4.

to the pedestrian's death.²⁸ In this respect, the Court specifically noted that the accused supplied themselves with a fast motor vehicle to commit a robbery. Moreover, they had planned to execute their criminal plan on a Friday night at a time when many people were out on the streets and at a central location with ample traffic in the surrounding area. As soon as they sighted the police car, the accused immediately absconded. According to the Court of Appeal, these facts prove that the accused's escape from the police and their dangerous driving were a foreseeable element and the direct result of the preparation of a robbery.²⁹ The Court therefore concluded that the accused's cooperation in relation to the planned robbery included the way in which the accused absconded as a *probable possibility*,³⁰ which means that they did not only cooperate in a close and intentional way in relation to the armed robbery, but also co-perpetrated the crimes related to their escape from the police.³¹ The fact that the escape was not discussed during the planning of the robbery, and that the person sitting at the back of the scooter could not withdraw from the dangerous driving, could not alter this conclusion.³²

It is noteworthy that the Court of Appeal acquitted both accused of the primary charge of voluntary manslaughter (or second-degree murder).³³ Manslaughter requires that the accused acted with the intent to kill, which means that he must have at least *knowingly accepted the considerable risk* of the victim's death (*dolus eventualis*).³⁴ According to the Court in the *Nijmegen scooter*-case, there was insufficient evidence to establish that the accused had indeed *accepted* the risk of killing a pedestrian. The Court specifically noted that the act of driving into a pedestrian entailed a serious risk for the accused to be seriously injured or even killed themselves, in particular considering that they were not wearing helmets.³⁵ Moreover, an accident would have the effect that the accused

---

²⁸ Idem.

²⁹ Idem.

³⁰ Idem.

³¹ Idem.

³² Idem.

³³ Idem, para. 3.

³⁴ The crime of manslaughter is defined in Article 287 DPC. For a concise commentary, see Tineke Cleiren, "Doodslag," *Tekst en Commentaar Strafrecht* (Kluwer online resource, last modified July 1, 2018).

³⁵ Court of Appeal 's-Hertogenbosch, 20 June 2016, ECLI:NL:GHSHE:2016:2428 and 2429.

had to cease their escape and would be apprehended by the police.[36] The Court of Appeal considered it unlikely that the accused accepted the risk of hitting a pedestrian, and thereby also conceded to the risk of losing their own life. It rather seemed that the accused wrongfully assumed that their escape would be successful.[37] Under Dutch law, such a case of unjustly overestimating one's chances qualifies as *culpa* (rather than *dolus*), which is similar to recklessness.[38] Causing death by recklessness constitutes a separate, less serious crime than manslaughter and normally results in a lower sentence.[39]

2. The *Jogee*-Case and English Law on Crimes of Excess

Like the Netherlands, England has recently experienced a significant change in the law on criminal responsibility for crimes of excess. The starting point for this change was the landmark judgment of the UK Supreme Court in the *Jogee*-case.[40] This case concerned the conduct of two accused – Jogee and Hirsi – on the evening of 10 June 2011. Over the course of this evening, they visited a woman – named Naomi Reid – on at least three separate occasions, allegedly for the purpose of selling her drugs.[41] Their visits became increasingly hostile, and Jogee and Hirsi started harassing Ms. Reid, until at one point, Ms. Reid's partner – Mr. Fyfe – came home and confronted the two accused. An angry confrontation ensued, whereby Hirsi ultimately killed Mr. Fyfe inside the house by stabbing him with a kitchen knife. Jogee was not directly involved in this killing. In fact, he was not even in the house when Hirsi stabbed Mr. Fyfe but encouraged him from outside "to do something".[42] The critical question that consequently arose was whether the mere fact that Jogee

---

[36] Idem.

[37] Idem.

[38] In Dutch, this is known as *bewuste schuld*, which should be contrasted with *onbewuste schuld* that applies when the accused was unaware of the risk of causing a crime.

[39] Pursuant to Article 307 DPC, the maximum prison sentence for causing death by recklessness is 2 years. By contrast, manslaughter can be punished with a maximum sentence of 15 years imprisonment.

[40] *R v Jogee*, 18 February 2016, [2016] UKSC 8.

[41] "Jogee and Ruddock – cases at the UKSC and JCPC," ObiterJ, accessed August 8, 2017, http://obiterj.blogspot.nl/2016/02/jogee-and-ruddock-cases-at-uksc-and-jcpc.html.

[42] *R v Jogee*, 18 February 2016, [2016] UKSC 8, para. 102.

contributed to harassing Ms. Reid and encouraged Hirsi's conduct constitutes a sufficient basis for holding him responsible for the murder of Mr. Fyfe, even though he did not participate in this murder directly, nor agreed with Hirsi to kill Mr. Fyfe.

Under English law, criminal responsibility is regulated by different types of participation in crime, which all fall under the general notion of complicity. Complicity relates to *"an actor's participation in wrongdoing committed by another"* by his intentional support or intentional influencing of the perpetrator's decision to commit an offense.[43] The *Jogee*-case concerned a particular type of complicity, known as *joint enterprise liability*.[44] Based on joint enterprise liability the members of a group are accountable for crimes they jointly agreed to commit, regardless of their individual contributions to these crimes. The responsibility of the group members is based on their *affiliation*, rather than active participation:

> *Through entering into a joint criminal enterprise, [the accused] changes her normative position. She becomes, by her deliberate choice, a participant in a group action to commit a crime. (...) [The accused, MC] subscribes to a co-operative endeavor, one that is identified with a shared criminal purpose. As such, joint enterprise doctrines impose a form of collective responsibility, predicated on membership of the unlawful concert.*[45]

In case law, English courts have throughout the years developed a special type of joint enterprise liability, known as *parasitic accessorial liability*, or PAL. Based on PAL, the members of a group can be held responsible for excessive crimes that fall outside the scope of the joint enterprise. It is not required that the group members either intended or contributed to these crimes of excess. Rather, it suffices that they *foresaw* the excessive crime as a consequence of the crime they had planned to

---

[43] Miles Jackson, *Complicity in International Law* (Oxford: OUP, 2015), 10-12.

[44] Some scholars consider *joint enterprise liability* as an autonomous concept separate from *complicity*, see e.g. Elies van Sliedregt, "Joint Criminal Confusion – the rise and fall of the joint enterprise theory in English and international criminal law" (inaugural lecture School of Law of the University of Leeds, Leeds, UK, December 1, 2016).

[45] Andrew Simester, "The Mental Element of Complicity," *Law Quarterly Review* (2006): 598-599.

commit.⁴⁶ Thus, PAL allows for holding group members liable for the *collateral effects* of a joint criminal endeavor based on mere foresight.

In the *Jogee*-case, the PAL doctrine provided the primary basis for assessing Jogee's liability for the murder of Mr. Fyfe by Hirsi. The Nottingham Crown Court instructed the jury that: "*the appellant was guilty of murder if he participated in the attack on the deceased, by encouraging Hirsi, and* realised *when doing so that Hirsi* might *use the kitchen knife to stab the deceased with intent to cause him really serious harm*".⁴⁷ Indeed, the jury in Jogee "*was sure, at the very least, that the appellant* knew *that Hirsi had the knife and* appreciated *that he* might *use it to cause really serious harm*".⁴⁸ Thus, Jogee *foresaw* the murder of Mr. Fyfe as a collateral effect of the harassment of Ms. Reid. Following established case law on PAL, the jury consequently convicted Jogee of murder and sentenced him to life imprisonment, which – according to English sentencing guidelines – is the mandatory sentence in murder cases.⁴⁹ Jogee's conviction was upheld on appeal, where the Lord Justices confirmed that "*[t]he mental element, the* mens rea, *of the secondary party's crime is an* appreciation *that the primary actor* might *inflict grievous bodily harm and a* willingness *to lend his support notwithstanding*".⁵⁰

The jury's and courts' reasoning in Jogee followed established case law on PAL. Yet, interestingly, in a landmark judgment, the Supreme Court distanced itself from earlier judgments, rejected the general principle underlying the PAL doctrine, and accordingly held that Jogee's conviction could not stand. In particular, the Court ruled that Jogee could not be held liable for Mr. Fyfe's death based on his mere *foresight* of murder. According to the Court, the use of such a foreseeability standard in murder cases generates a "*striking anomaly*" between the intent requirements of perpetrators and PAL-participants:⁵¹ whilst the former must intend to kill or cause grievous bodily harm, a lower foreseeability standard suffices for the latter. To address this dichotomy, the Supreme Court formulated a new

---

⁴⁶ Andrew Simester, "Accessory Liability and Common Unlawful Purpose," *Law Quarterly Review* (2017): 74.

⁴⁷ *R v Jogee*, 18 February 2016, [2016] UKSC 8, para. 104 (emphasis added).

⁴⁸ Idem, para. 107 (emphasis added).

⁴⁹ "About guidelines," Sentencing Council, accessed September 12, 2017, https://www.sentencingcouncil.org.uk/about-sentencing/about-guidelines/.

⁵⁰ *R v Jogee*, 11 July 2013, [2013] EWCA Crim 1433, para. 23.

⁵¹ *R v Jogee*, 18 February 2016, [2016] UKSC 8, para. 84.

mens rea standard, which entails that each joint enterprise participant should at least *intend* to assist the crime committed by the perpetrator.[52] When a crime entails a particular type of intent – such as, in the case of murder, the intent to kill or cause grievous bodily harm – this intent must be established in relation to all participants in the joint enterprise. Thus, the intent requirements of joint enterprise liability cannot detract from the intent requirements of the crime in question.

This is not to say that the accused's foreseeability of the crime committed by another is completely irrelevant. By contrast, the Supreme Court in Jogee explicitly accepted that evidence of foresight may be used to infer an accused's intent. Yet foreseeability is by itself insufficient for establishing criminal responsibility under joint enterprise liability: "*if D2 continues to participate in crime A with foresight that D1 may commit crime B, that is evidence, and sometimes powerful evidence, of an intent to assist D1 in crime B. But it is evidence of such intent (or, if one likes, of 'authorization'), not conclusive of it*".[53] According to the Court, this stricter interpretation of joint enterprise liability complies with the regular common law rules on complicity according to which foresight of what *might* happen is no more than evidence – though possibly strong evidence – from which a jury may infer intent.[54]

The legal implications of the *Jogee*-case still remain somewhat uncertain and have not been crystallized completely. It is not entirely clear how courts will interpret the requirement of intent, in what ways they will use foresight as evidence of intent, and to what extent they will in fact restrain the scope of joint enterprise liability for excessive crimes. At least, the Supreme Court has stressed that:

> *The effect of putting the law right is not to render invalid all convictions which were arrived at over many years by faithfully applying the law (...). The error identified, of equating foresight with intent to assist rather than treating the first as evidence of the second, is important as a matter of legal principle, but it does not follow that it will have been important on the facts to the outcome of the trial or to the safety of the conviction.*[55]

---

[52] Idem, para. 90, 98.
[53] Idem, para. 66.
[54] Idem, para. 83.
[55] Idem, para. 100.

Moreover, it is noteworthy that the Supreme Court's rejection of the foresight standard appears to be limited to crimes of intent, such as murder. When the crime definition itself adopts a less stringent *mens rea* standard, such as recklessness or negligence, establishing criminal responsibility based on foreseeability is still permitted. The Supreme Court in Jogee accordingly recognized that an acquittal for murder because of lack of intent shall be without prejudice for a potential conviction for manslaughter.[56] The Court therefore rejected Jogee's submission that he was not only wrongly convicted for murder but should also be acquitted for manslaughter. According to the Court, *"[a]t a minimum, he (Jogee, MC) was party to a violent adventure carrying the plain objective risk of some harm to a person and which resulted in death; he was therefore guilty of manslaughter at least"*.[57] Indeed, after a retrial, the Nottingham Crown Court convicted Jogee for manslaughter.[58] Yet, in comparison to murder, manslaughter constitutes a less serious crime that is punished more leniently. Rather than having to impose a mandatory life sentence – as in the case of murder – judges have the discretion to sentence the accused as they deem fit. The Crown Court accordingly reduced Jogee's life prison sentence to 12 years.

Notwithstanding Jogee's ultimate conviction for manslaughter and the remaining uncertainties concerning the precise implications of the Supreme Court's judgment, the significance of the *Jogee*-judgment cannot be underestimated. It is clear that the Supreme Court in the *Jogee*-case in principle rejected PAL and conceptually abandoned the doctrine. This result is groundbreaking and has generally been well-received by scholarship, which has already criticized the PAL doctrine and its broad basis for establishing criminal liability for years.[59]

---

[56] Idem, para. 96, 107. Manslaughter entails that the accused caused or assisted in another person's death through recklessness, or negligence, see e.g. *R v Adomako*, (1994) 3 All ER 79 en *Caparo Industries PLC v Dickman*, (1990) 2 AC 605. See for a short and practical explanation "Homicide: Murder and Manslaughter," Crown Prosecution Service, accessed September 11, 2017, http://www.cps.gov.uk/legal/h_to_k/homicide_murder_and_manslaughter/#manslaughter.

[57] *R v Jogee*, 18 February 2016, [2016] UKSC 8, para. 107.

[58] "Joint Enterprise, Ameen Jailed for Manslaughter," BBC News, accessed August 8, 2017, http://www.bbc.com/news/uk-england-leicestershire-37336830.

[59] Beatrice Krebs, "Mens rea in joint enterprise: a role for endorsement?," *Cambridge Law Journal* 74 (2015): 486, 496; Simester, "Accessory liability and common unlawful purpose," 81-82.

3. Comparative Analysis

After having set out the reasoning of the Dutch and UK Supreme Court in the *Nijmegen scooter*-case and the *Jogee*-case, respectively, this section continues with a comparative analysis that elucidates some of the parallels and unique features of the courts' approaches to crimes of excess. As said before, the analysis in no way intends to provide an exhaustive overview, but rather points attention to a number of significant features that seem specifically important for appraising domestic law on crimes of excess. In particular, this section will elaborate upon four issues that help to explain and understand the courts' judgments in the *Nijmegen scooter*-case and the *Jogee*-case: (i) the rationale – i.e. the legal basis – underlying criminal responsibility for crimes of excess; (ii) the role of the common plan in establishing criminal responsibility for excessive crimes; (iii) the relation between the intent requirements of criminal liability theories, on the one hand, and the *mens rea* elements of the crimes charged, on the other; and (iv) the influence of sentencing laws on the assessment of liability. In discussing these issues, reference will be made to ICL and the case law of international courts and tribunals, where possible and useful.

3.1 The Rationale for Criminalizing Excessive Crimes

One of the most basic – yet fundamental – issues arising from the judgments of the Dutch and UK Supreme Court in the *Nijmegen scooter*-case and the *Jogee*-case, respectively concerns the basis or rationale underlying criminal responsibility for crimes of excess. In this respect, it is noteworthy that the Dutch and English courts use different criteria to assess and restrict criminal responsibility for excessive crimes. On the one hand, the Dutch Supreme Court focuses on the objective side of criminal responsibility. In its judgment in the *Nijmegen scooter*-case, the Court emphasizes the causal link between the excessive crime and the planned crime by formulating a *probability* standard.[60] By thus phrasing the accused's criminal responsibility for crimes of excess in terms of causality, the focus is placed on objective considerations, i.e. on the factual relationship between the crime that was planned and the crime that was ultimately committed.

By contrast, in the *Jogee*-judgment, the UK Supreme Court stresses the subjective limitations of joint enterprise liability. The Court rejects the PAL doctrine by holding that mere foresight is not an element of PAL, but may

---

[60] Dutch Supreme Court, 17 December 2013, ECLI:NL:HR:2013:1964 and 1966, para. 2.3.3.

only be treated as evidence of the accused's intent, i.e. for inferring intent.[61] Whilst the Court thus accepts that the accused is held liable for crimes in which he did not participate directly – i.e. to which he did not physically contribute – it refuses to establish criminal responsibility when the *mens rea* elements of the crime charged are not met. As such, it seems that the accused's criminal responsibility for crimes of excess primarily depends on whether the subjective elements of these crimes are met, and is thus essentially based on the accused's *mens rea*.

In this section, I will focus on the objective rationale adopted by the Dutch Supreme Court. The subjective rationale used by the UK Supreme Court will be discussed more elaborately in section 4.3. where the issue of intent is addressed. When analyzing the Dutch objective approach to co-perpetration, it is particularly useful to draw inspiration from ICL where the rationale for establishing criminal responsibility has been extensively debated.[62] In its early case law, the International Criminal Court (ICC) has expressed a preference for assessing criminal responsibility in objective terms following a so-called 'control over the crime' theory.[63] Pursuant to this theory, liability for co-perpetration depends on whether the accused made an essential – i.e. *conditio sine qua non* – contribution to the crime charged, i.e. whether the accused was able to frustrate the commission of crimes by withholding his contribution.[64] Because the essential contribution requirement focuses on facts and circumstances that are visible to the outside world, the control over the crime approach arguably

---

[61] *R v Jogee*, 18 February 2016, [2016] UKSC 8, para. 66, 83, 87, 94.

[62] Van Sliedregt, *Individual Criminal Responsibility under International Criminal Law*, 83-85; Lachezar Yanev, "*Theories of Co-perpetration in International Criminal Law*" (PhD diss., Tilburg University, 2016), 21-29; Jens Ohlin et al., "Assessing the Control Theory," *Leiden Journal of International Law* 26 (2013): 732-734.

[63] *Prosecutor v. Lubanga* (ICC-01/04-01/06-803-tEN), Decision on the Confirmation of Charges, Pre-Trial Chamber I, 29 January 2007, para. 328-329, 338, 343-367. This decision was later confirmed by the Trial and Appeals Chamber: *Prosecutor v. Lubanga* (ICC-01/04-01/06-2842), Judgment, Trial Chamber, 14 March 2012; *Prosecutor v. Lubanga* (ICC-01/04-01/06-3121-Red), Judgment, Appeals Chamber, 1 December 2014.

[64] E.g. *Lubanga* Decision on the Confirmation of Charges, para. 347; *Lubanga* Appeal Judgment, para 469.

presents a clear and principled basis for criminal responsibility.[65] In addition to requiring an essential contribution, the ICC also stipulates that the crime charged resulted from the common plan between the co-perpetrators *in the ordinary course of events*.[66] This entails that the crime charged was at least a *virtually certain* circumstance of the common plan between the co-perpetrators.[67]

At first sight, the standard of 'virtual certainty' establishes a higher threshold than the Dutch 'probable consequence' criterion, introduced in the *Nijmegen scooter*-case. Thus, ICC law – at least in theory – warrants a closer connection between the original plan of the co-perpetrators and the excessive crimes resulting from this plan, and accordingly sets stricter limitations on criminal responsibility. Moreover, under Dutch law, the essential contribution requirement of co-perpetration is applied leniently in relation to crimes of excess. Once it is established that the co-perpetrators' conduct was a probable consequence of their original plan, no evidence is required of how exactly each of the co-perpetrators contributed to the commission of the excessive crime. Accordingly, the Supreme Court in the *Nijmegen Scooter*-case accepted that responsibility for co-perpetration does not depend on conclusive evidence of which of the two robbers had driven the scooter and had thus killed the pedestrian. It is uncertain whether the ICC would likewise permit such a loose application of the essential contribution requirement. By stipulating that the accused must be able to frustrate the commission of the crime, the ICC arguably posits a higher threshold that depends on establishing whether and how the accused contributed to each of the crimes charged, including the crimes of excess.

As this comparison with international (case) law brings to light, the Dutch concept of co-perpetration allows for establishing criminal responsibility based on relatively low objective standards, both in terms of the accused's contribution, and in terms of the causal relationship

---

[65] Kai Ambos, *Treatise on International Criminal Law, Volume 1: Foundations and General Part* (Oxford: OUP, 2013), 152-153; Gerhard Werle and Boris Burghardt, "Establishing Degrees of Responsibility: Modes of Participation in Article 25 of the ICC Statute," in *Pluralism in International Criminal Law*, eds. Elies van Sliedregt and Sergey Vasiliev (Oxford: OUP, 2014), 316; Jens Ohlin, "Co-Perpetration: German *Dogmatik* or German Invasion," in *The Law and Practice of the International Criminal Court*, ed. Carsten Stahn (Oxford: OUP, 2015), 528.

[66] *Lubanga* Appeal Judgment, para. 447-451; *Lubanga* Trial Judgment, para. 983-986.

[67] *Lubanga* Appeal Judgment, para. 447-451.

between the planned crimes and the excessive crimes with which the accused is ultimately charged. Of course, Dutch courts are not bound by international case law and are in no way obliged to tailor their interpretation of co-perpetration to the ICC's findings. Yet, it would be worthwhile if Dutch courts become aware of their relative leniency and critically assess their use of co-perpetration in light of relevant international standards. By taking such a comparative approach, Dutch courts can gain new perspectives that potentially generate a more precise assessment of criminal responsibility for crimes of excess.

3.2 Role of the Common Plan

A typical feature of crimes of excess is that they go beyond the crime that participants initially planned to commit. In order to determine whether a crime constitutes a crime of excess, courts should thus first determine what the co-perpetrators' original plan was. Only by demarcating the plan's original scope, can it subsequently be established how the crime committed, is related to this plan. Indeed, English courts have paid close attention to the common plan, which forms the central basis for joint enterprise liability. As explained before, joint enterprise liability is based on group affiliation: by entering a joint enterprise, the accused deliberately chose to participate in a group action directed at criminal conduct.[68] The fact that the accused subscribes to a joint endeavor and identifies himself with a common criminal purpose justifies his liability for the acts of others who share this common purpose.

By contrast, under Dutch law, the common plan has so far not been recognized as a separate element of co-perpetration. Co-perpetration primarily depends on the close and intentional cooperation between two or more persons, not on their common plan. Yet, this is not to say that the common plan has no relevance for co-perpetration. In the *Nijmegen scooter*-case, Advocate-General Knigge suggested that the common plan actually plays a dual role: it (i) provides a starting point for determining whether the accused intentionally and closely cooperated in the commission of crimes to which he did not physically contribute, and (ii) constitutes a factor for assessing whether the accused intended to commit the crimes charged.[69] According to Knigge, if an accused pursued a plan

---

[68] Andrew Simester, "The Mental Element of Complicity,' *Law Quarterly Review* (2006): 598-599.

[69] Conclusion Advocate-General Knigge, 29 October 2013, ECLI:NL:PHR:2013:1080, para. 3.16.

together with others, he becomes a co-perpetrator of the crimes that are part of this plan and may be assumed to have intended the crimes following from it.

Admittedly, the Supreme Court has never endorsed or explicitly implemented Knigge's findings. Yet, the Court's reasoning in the *Nijmegen scooter*-case implicitly confirms the relevance of the common plan for establishing criminal liability under co-perpetration. The case illustrates how the common plan provides a context – a background – against which the accused's intentional and close cooperation in relation to specific crimes can be assessed. It even seems that when crimes are linked to a common plan, the 'intentional and close cooperation' criterion for co-perpetration can be applied in a looser way, because the co-perpetrators' cooperation does not have to be established individually in relation to each of the crimes charged. In this sense, the *Nijmegen scooter*-case shows parallels with the English concept of joint enterprise liability. Also in that respect, the accused's participation in a criminal plan – rather than his involvement in the commission of specific crimes – constitutes the basis for establishing criminal liability. The foundation of criminal liability is moved forward, towards the moment when the accused became part of a group and committed himself to the group's criminal purpose.

A similar development can be witnessed at the international level in relation to the so-called Joint Criminal Enterprise (JCE) doctrine, as developed in case law of the International Criminal Tribunal for the former Yugoslavia (ICTY). In the *Tadić* case – the first case before the ICTY – the Tribunal explained that JCE gives expression to the "*principle that when two or more persons act together to further a common criminal purpose, offences perpetrated by any of them may entail the criminal liability of all the members of the group*".[70] Based on this principle, the ICTY determined that JCE requires that (i) the accused and at least one other person (ii) formed a *common criminal plan* aimed at or involving the commission of a crime, and that (iii) the accused *significantly contributed* to the execution of this plan.[71] In addition, JCE liability

---

[70] *Prosecutor v. Tadić* (IT-94-1-A), Judgment, Appeals Chamber, 15 July 1999, para. 195.

[71] *Tadić* Appeal Judgment, para. 227. The concept has later been confirmed and further developed in e.g. *Prosecutor v. Brđanin* (IT-99-36-A), Judgment, Appeals Chamber, 3 April 2007, para. 430. For a scholarly discussion of JCE, see e.g. Antonio Cassese *et al.*, *Cassese's International Criminal Law* (Oxford: OUP, 2013), 163-164; Ambos, *Treatise on International Criminal Law*, 123-126; Robert Cryer *et al.*, *An*

expands criminal responsibility to excessive crimes. In *Tadić*, the ICTY introduced a so-called 'extended type' of JCE, which applies where the execution of the common plan resulted in the commission of an additional crime that falls outside the scope of the original plan, yet is a *natural and foreseeable* consequence of this plan.[72] In particular, extended JCE requires that the accused – in addition to sharing the intent to commit the original JCE crime(s) – (i) *foresaw* the commission of the excessive crime as a possible consequence, and (ii) *willingly* took this risk by continuing his participation in the common plan (*dolus eventualis*).[73]

It is noteworthy that – like the Dutch and English law on co-perpetration and joint enterprise liability – the international JCE concept allows for appraising criminal responsibility in light of the accused's joint criminal endeavor. JCE liability is essentially based on the accused's participation in a common plan, without requiring a precise determination of how he contributed to each of the crimes within this plan. Similar to the Dutch Supreme Court, the ICTY even accepts that criminal responsibility is expanded to crimes of excess. Yet, the ICTY in this respect requires a precise relation between the original and the excessive crime, which is phrased in terms of the accused's *foreseeability and acceptance* (*dolus eventualis*) of the crime of excess. By contrast, the Dutch Supreme Court in the *Nijmegen scooter*-case accepted the accused's liability for killing a pedestrian (excessive crime), because the *escape* from which this killing resulted, was a *probable possibility* of the accused's plan to commit armed robbery (original crime). From a comparative perspective, the Court thus formulated a loose standard that fails to establish a precise link between the planned crimes and the crimes charged, but rather focuses on the accused's – in itself legitimate effort – to escape from the police.[74] The basis of the accused's liability accordingly becomes rather weak. It is therefore recommendable that the Dutch Supreme Court takes account of international case law on extended JCE and considers whether this case law can be used to establish a more clear and well-founded basis for appraising criminal responsibility for crimes of excess in the future.

Introduction to International Criminal Law and Procedure (Cambridge: CUP, 2014), 357-359.

[72] *Tadić* Appeal Judgment, para. 204-213.

[73] Idem, para. 228.

[74] See also, Marjolein Cupido, "Van Kaping tot Doodslag: Medeplegen in Piraterijzaken," *Nederlands Juristenblad* 30 (2015): 2094.

Whilst the Dutch approach goes beyond ICTY case law, the UK Supreme Court in *Jogee* advanced a position that is considerably stricter than the Tribunal's case law on extended JCE. The Court rejected the foreseeability standard – which constitutes the minimum requirement for JCE liability – as an element of joint enterprise liability and presented the accused's foresight as mere relevant evidence of intent, instead. This limitation of the accused's *mens rea* will be further addressed in the next sub-section where the notion of intent is discussed.

3.3 Crimes of Excess and Intent

As said, the UK Supreme Court in *Jogee* rejected foreseeability as an element of joint enterprise liability and defined the accused's foresight as mere relevant evidence of intent, instead.[75] The Supreme Court's rejection of foreseeability specifically applies to the crime of murder, which requires that the accused intended to kill or cause grievous bodily harm. According to the Court, the use of a foreseeability standard for PAL participants in murder cases causes 'a striking anomaly' with the intent requirement of direct perpetrators.[76] Yet, in relation to manslaughter – a less serious crime that applies when the accused caused or assisted another person's death through recklessness or negligence – the foreseeability standard remains in place, and criminal responsibility may still be based on the accused's foresight of killing.[77] Thus, the Supreme Court does not reject the foreseeability standard in principle, but only in relation to specific crimes that require intent (e.g. the intent to kill). When the crime definition itself adopts a less stringent *mens rea* standard, like recklessness, criminal responsibility based on foresight is still accepted.

A similar use of intent can be witnessed in the *Nijmegen scooter*-case. In this case, the Dutch Court of Appeal concluded that the accused could not be held accountable for co-perpetrating voluntary manslaughter (or second-degree murder), which requires that the accused at least *knowingly accepted* the significant *risk* of killing (*dolus eventualis*), without necessarily premeditating such killing.[78] The Court considered it

---

[75] *R v Jogee*, 18 February 2016, [2016] UKSC 8, para. 83, 87, 94.

[76] Idem, para. 84.

[77] Idem, para. 96, 107.

[78] Cleiren, "Doodslag," para. 9a.

unlikely that the accused had indeed *accepted* the risk of killing,[79] in particular because driving into the pedestrian entailed a risk that the accused themselves would be seriously injured, or even killed, and would be apprehended by the police.[80] Instead, the Court held that the accused believed in the successful completion of their escape and could therefore 'only' be convicted for causing death by recklessness. By reasoning in this way, the Court of Appeal followed a series of previous judgments in which it has consistently been held that – apart from exceptional circumstances and subject to contrary evidence – it is unlikely that accused accept the risk of losing their own life in a traffic accident.[81] Admittedly, it can be questioned whether this line of thought generates reasonable outcomes and should be pursued in the future. Yet, leaving such questions aside, the Court of Appeal judgment in the *Nijmegen scooter*-case at least shows that the *mens rea* elements of the crime charged will be upheld, even when the requirements for co-perpetration are loosely assessed in terms of the 'probable consequence' criterion. Even though the Court accepted that the accused's responsibility for crimes of excess should be appraised in light of their joint criminal endeavor, this does not entail that the *mens rea* standards of the crimes charged may be lowered. The requirements of co-perpetration can thus not detract from the subjective elements of the crimes for which the accused stands trial.

Notably, the notion of intent carries a different meaning under Dutch and English law. Whilst Dutch courts accept *dolus eventualis* as the lowest standard of intent, which entails that the accused should at least have knowingly accepted the significant *risk* that a crime will be committed, under English law, intent relates to purposeful behavior, i.e. it applies when the accused had the desire to commit a crime, or at least foresaw such crime as a result of his conduct.[82] Acts of risk-taking do not belong to the realm of intent but are assessed under the notion of recklessness. Yet – notwithstanding this different understanding of intent – the observations above make clear that Dutch and English courts both accept the general idea that the *mens rea* elements of the crime charged should be

---

[79] Court of Appeal 's-Hertogenbosch, 20 June 2016, ECLI:NL:GHSHE:2016:2428 and 2429.

[80] Idem.

[81] Dutch Supreme Court, 15 October 1996, NJ 1997, 199; Dutch Supreme Court, 5 December 2006, ECLI:NL:HR:2006:AZ1668.

[82] Simon Parsons, "Intention in Criminal Law: Why Is it so Difficult to Find?," *Mountbatten Journal of Legal Studies* (2000): 5.

established in relation to all participants. The subjective requirements of a liability theory cannot be used to evade the *mens rea* standards of the crimes for which the accused is standing trial. In this sense, the English and Dutch courts thus take a similarly strict approach.

The domestic perspectives on intent are significant in light of ICTY case law on extended JCE, which presents a much more lenient view. In the *Brdanin*-case, the ICTY controversially held that modes of liability have their own *mens rea* elements, which should be distinguished from and cannot be conflated with the subjective elements of crimes.[83] This finding had significant implications for the use of extended JCE – which includes a standard of *dolus eventualis* – in genocide cases. Whilst genocide in principle requires that the accused acted with the specific *purpose* to physically or biologically destroy – i.e. exterminate – a protected ethnic, national, racial, or religious group,[84] when applying extended JCE to genocide, it only needs to be established that "*it was* reasonably foreseeable *to the accused that an act specified in Article 4(2) [concerning the crime of genocide, MC] would be committed and that it would be committed with genocidal intent*".[85] Thus, the Tribunal allows for convicting accused of genocide based on the *dolus eventualis* standard of extended JCE without having to prove their individual purpose to destroy.

Though the *Brdanin*-decision has been followed in later case law,[86] the practice of applying the *dolus eventualis* standard of extended JCE to special intent crimes remains highly controversial and has been widely criticized. The controversy particularly stems from the fact that JCE members are convicted and sentenced as principals. The accused's lower *mens rea* does thus not (necessarily) result in a different qualification of crime, nor in a lower punishment. This is particularly problematic in light of the principles of fair labeling and the fair discrimination of punishment, which basically require that the accused's conviction and sentence accord with his moral guilt and blameworthiness.[87] Indeed, the judgments of the

---

[83] *Prosecutor v. Brdanin* (IT-99-36-A), Decision on Interlocutory Appeal, Appeals Chamber, 19 March 2004, para. 5-10.

[84] Article II, Convention on the Prevention and Punishment of the Crime of Genocide, adopted on 9 December 1948, United Nations, Treaty Series, vol. 78.

[85] Idem, para. 6.

[86] E.g. *Prosecutor v. Milosevic* (IT-54-02-T) Decision on Motion for Judgment of Acquittal, Trial Chamber, 16 June 2004, para. 291.

[87] David Nersessian, "Comparative Approaches to Punishing Hate: The Intersection of Genocide and Crimes against Humanity," *Stanford Journal of International Law* 43

UK and Dutch Supreme Court stress the importance of respecting the *mens rea* elements of the crimes charged and of not letting modes of liability detract from these essential requirements when accused are qualified as perpetrators. Domestic practice thus provides convincing arguments that shed new light on the international case law on extended JCE and genocide. In particular the UK Supreme Court's rejection of PAL further explicates the objections against applying extended JCE to genocide and brings forward cogent reasons for taking a critical look at this practice. In this light, it significant that Jogee's defense counsel have recently submitted an *amicus curiae* brief to the ICTY in which they request the Tribunal to take note of the UK Supreme Court judgment in *Jogee* and to determine the relevance of this case for ICTY jurisprudence.[88]

3.4. Sentencing

The fourth and final observation of this contribution concerns the topic of sentencing. An important reason for the UK Supreme Court to reject PAL's foreseeability standard relates to the fact that foreseeability and intention generate different levels of blameworthiness. The Court's findings give expression to the thought that a person who *intends* to commit murder is more blameworthy than a PAL participant who merely *foresees* that murder will be committed. Following the notion of fair discrimination of punishment,[89] this difference in blameworthiness should be reflected in the sentence that is imposed on the accused, i.e. the accused's sentence must be tailored to his specific *mens rea*, be it intent or foresight.

Unfortunately, English law does not allow for such flexibility. Pursuant to the *Accessories and Abettors Act 1861*, all participants – including PAL participants – are tried, indicted, and punished as principals.[90] Thus, PAL participants acting with foresight are put on equal footing with

---

(2007): 255-256; Natalia Perova, "Stretching the Joint Criminal Enterprise doctrine to the Extreme: When Culpability and Liability Do Not Match,'" *International Criminal Law Review* 16 (2015): 761-795; James Stewart, "The end of 'modes of liability' for international crimes," *Leiden Journal of International Law* 25 (2012): 176; Antonio Cassese, "The Proper Limits of Individual Responsibility under the Doctrine of Joint Criminal Enterprise," *Journal of International Criminal Justice* 5 (2007): 121.

[88] *Prosecutor v. Karadžić* (MICT-13-55-A) Decision on a request for leave to make submissions as Amicus Curiae, Appeals Chamber, 25 September 2017.

[89] This principle is referred to in paragraph 74 of the *Jogee* judgment.

[90] "Accessories and Abettors Act 1861," Legislation Government United Kingdom, accessed September 8, 2017, http://www.legislation.gov.uk/ukpga/Vict/24-25/94/contents.

perpetrators and (can) receive the same sentence as the person who physically committed and personally intended a crime. In this way, the PAL doctrine (can) create(s) an unreasonable disparity between the accused's level of blameworthiness and the sentence that is imposed upon him. This disparity is particularly prominent in murder cases, which – pursuant to English sentencing guidelines – are punished with a mandatory life sentence.[91] PAL participants will thus receive a lifelong prison-sentence – just like physical perpetrators – notwithstanding their lower *mens rea* and their consequent reduced level of blameworthiness. Considering the strict English sentencing laws, the only way in which the Supreme Court could align the level of punishment with the moral guilt of PAL participants was by raising the mens rea requirement and by requiring that all participants should meet the *mens rea* elements of the crimes charged.

Under Dutch law, sentencing is regulated in a different way, and different choices have been made to tailor the accused's sentence to his level of personal guilt and blameworthiness. Dutch law does not entail strict sentencing guidelines that bind judges in determining the appropriate punishment. Whilst there are so-called 'judicial points of reference',[92] judges retain wide discretion to sentence the accused as they see fit, considering all relevant circumstances,[93] including the accused's level of intent and involvement. Thus, accused who played a minor role in the commission of crimes can receive a more lenient sentence. Where it concerns accessorial liability, this idea is explicitly regulated in the DPC. Accessorial liability stipulates relatively low *actus reus* (and *mens rea*) requirements, which only require that the accused assisted others in the commission of crimes by playing an ancillary role.[94] Since this results in a lower level of blameworthiness, Article 49(1) DPC provides that accessorial liability comes with a 1/3 sentence reduction. By thus adjusting the (maximum) sentence to the accused's role in the commission of crimes,

---

[91] "About guidelines," Sentencing Council, accessed September 12, 2017, https://www.sentencingcouncil.org.uk/about-sentencing/about-guidelines/.

[92] "Oriëntatiepunten voor straftoemeting en LOVS-uitspraken," De Rechtspraak, accessed September 12, 2017, https://www.rechtspraak.nl/SiteCollectionDocuments/Orientatiepunten-en-afspraken-LOVS.pdf.

[93] Geert Corstens, *Het Nederlands strafprocesrecht*, revised by Matthias Borgers (Deventer: Kluwer, 2014), 874.

Dutch law – like English law – tailors the level of punishment to the accused's reduced blameworthiness and brings the sentence for accessories in line with their personal guilt. Yet, this is not attained by raising the *mens rea* element and increasing the level of intent – as the English courts have done – but by adjusting the (maximum) sentence.

In light of the above, one could question whether the real objection against PAL was that it established criminal responsibility based on a relatively low foresight standard, or rather that the strict English sentencing guidelines – in particular in murder cases – do not allow that courts tailor the accused's punishment to his intent by lowering the sentence for persons with a reduced *mens rea*.[95] If sentencing laws had been more flexible, English courts would have been able to address the tensions that PAL creates in murder cases by recognizing that PAL generates a lower level of blameworthiness and therefore attracts a lesser sentence. In this way, the courts could have resolved the imbalance within PAL without completely dismissing the doctrine. PAL may thus have lost some of its punitive character, but at least it could have been retained as an effective means to appraise group criminality. Indeed, this approach follows the proposition of Van Sliedregt in relation to the use of extended JCE in genocide cases. In this respect, Van Sliedregt has explained that accused convicted for genocide based on *dolus eventualis* under extended JCE cannot be put on par with *genocidaires* who acted with the purpose to destroy a protected group. To express this difference in culpability, she proposes that '*participants in an extended JCE are held responsible for participating in genocide, which attracts a lower sentence*'.[96]

4. Conclusion

In this contribution, I have analyzed how Dutch and English courts – that are part of the civil and common law tradition, respectively – have addressed criminal responsibility for crimes of excess. After having discussed two landmark judgments in the *Nijmegen scooter*-case and the *Jogee*-case, I have conducted a comparative analysis in which I have pointed to four important features of the courts' assessment of excessive crimes. In this respect, I have also referred to ICL practice, which provided

---

[94] Menno Dolman, "Medeplichtigheid," *Tekst & Commentaar* (Kluwer online resource, last modified July 1, 2018): para. 4.C; De Hullu, *Materieel Strafrecht*, 488-492.

[95] Van Sliedregt, "Joint Criminal Confusion."

[96] Elies van Sliedregt, "Joint Criminal Enterprise as a Pathway to Convicting Individuals for Genocide," *Journal of International Criminal Justice* 5 (2007): 205.

further insights into the parallels between and distinctive characteristics of Dutch and English law, and which helped to put the domestic assessment of crimes of excess in perspective.

The comparative analysis makes clear that in some respects, Dutch and English (and international) courts adopt very distinctive approaches and present unique views on criminal responsibility for crimes of excess, such as in relation to the role and scope of the common plan. Yet, in other respects, important parallels can be drawn, for example where it concerns the notion of intent. It is interesting to see how these distinct and comparative features are connected to the structure and fundamentals of the Dutch and English legal system. For example, as became clear in section 4.4., the UK Supreme Court's rejection of the foreseeability standard in murder cases is related to English sentencing laws, which treat all participants equally and impose a mandatory life sentence in murder cases.

The linkage between the judicial assessment of crimes of excess and the structural features of the Dutch and English legal system raises the question of whether there is reason to speak of a distinct 'common law' and 'civil law' approach to crimes of excess. Structural features, such as sentencing, the distinction between different types of liability (e.g. principal and accessorial liability), and the requirements of intent (e.g. full intent, recklessness, *dolus eventualis*, and negligence) are strongly connected to the legal tradition that a legal system is a part of. Common law systems, for example, share largely similar views on criminal intent, which on some points differ from the civil law perspective. In this light, it would be interesting to conduct further research into whether domestic approaches to crimes of excess are typically 'common law' or 'civil law'. This requires a more comprehensive comparative study into the domestic laws of other countries like France, Germany, the United States of America, Canada, and Australia.

Bibliography

Ambos, Kai. *Treatise on International Criminal Law, Volume 1: Foundations and General Part*. Oxford: OUP, 2013.

BBC News. "Joint Enterprise, Ameen Jailed for Manslaughter." Accessed August 8, 2017. http://www.bbc.com/news/uk-england-leicestershire-37336830.

Cassese, Antonio. "The Proper Limits of Individual Responsibility under the Doctrine of Joint Criminal Enterprise." *Journal of International Criminal Justice* 5 (2007): 121.

Cassese, Antonio, and Paola Gaeta. *Cassese's International Criminal Law*. Oxford: OUP, 2013.

Cleiren, Tineke. "Doodslag." *Tekst en Commentaar Strafrecht* (Kluwer online resource, last modified July 1, 2018).

Corstens, Geert. *Het Nederlandse strafprocesrecht*, revised by Matthias Borgers. Deventer: Kluwer, 2014.

Crown Prosecution Service. "Homicide: Murder and Manslaughter." Accessed September 11, 2017. http://www.cps.gov.uk/legal/h_to_k/homicide_murder_and_manslaughter/#manslaughter.

Cryer, Robert, Hakan Friman, Darryl Robinson and Elizabeth Wilmshurst. *An Introduction to International Criminal Law and Procedure*. Cambridge: CUP, 2014,

Cupido, Marjolein. "Van Kaping tot Doodslag: Medeplegen in Piraterijzaken." *Nederlands Juristenblad* 30 (2015), 2094.

Cupido, Marjolein. *Verhoogd Opzet bij Medeplegen?: Een Rechtsvergelijkende Analyse*. (forthcoming).

Cupido, Marjolein, Mark Hornman and Wim Huisman. "Individual Liability for Business Involvement in International Crimes." Accessed November 20, 2018. https://cicj.org/wp-content/uploads/2017/02/Cupido-Hornman-Huisman-2017-Individual-liability-for-business-involvement-in-international-crimes.pdf.

De Hullu, Jaap. *Materieel Strafrecht: Over Algemene Leerstukken van Strafrechtelijke Aansprakelijkheid naar Nederlands Recht*. Deventer: Kluwer, 2015.

De Rechtspraak. "Oriëntatiepunten voor straftoemeting en LOVS-uitspraken." Acessed September 12, 2017. https://www.rechtspraak.nl/SiteCollectionDocuments/Orientatiepunten-en-afspraken-LOVS.pdf.

Dolman, Menno. "Doen Plegen, Uitlokken en Medeplegen." *Tekst & Commentaar Strafrecht* (Kluwer online resource, last modified July 1, 2018): para. 7.c. and 7.g.

Dolman, Menno. "Medeplichtigheid." *Tekst & Commentaar Strafrecht* (Kluwer online resource, last modified July 1, 2018): para. 4.C.

Jackson, Miles. *Complicity in International Law*. Oxford: OUP, 2015.

Krebs, Beatrice. "Mens rea in joint enterprise: a role for endorsement?" *Cambridge Law Journal* 74 (2015): 486, 496.

Legislation Government United Kingdom. "Accessories and Abettors Act." Accessed September, 8, 2017. http://www.legislation.gov.uk/ukpga/Vict/24-25/94/contents, accessed September 8, 2017.

Nersessian, David. "Comparative Approaches to Punishing Hate: The Intersection of Genocide and Crimes against Humanity." *Stanford Journal of International Law* 43 (2007): 255-256.

Nolkaemper, André. "Introduction." In *System Criminality in International Law*, edited by Harmen van der Wilt and André Nolkaemper. Cambridge: CUP, 2010.

ObiterJ. "Jogee and Ruddock – cases at the UKSC and JCPC." Accessed August 8, 2017. http://obiterj.blogspot.nl/2016/02/jogee-and-ruddock-cases-at-uksc-and-jcpc.html.

Ohlin, Jens. "Co-Perpetration: German *Dogmatik* or German Invasion." In *The Law and Practice of the International Criminal Court*, edited by Carsten Stahn. Oxford: OUP, 2015.

Ohlin, Jens, Elies van Sliedregt and Thomas Weigend. "Assessing the Control Theory." *Leiden Journal of International Law* 26 (2013): 732-734.

Parsons, Simon. "Intention in Criminal Law: Why Is it so Difficult to Find?" *Mountbatten Journal of Legal Studies* (2000): 5.

Perova, Natalia. "Stretching the Joint Criminal Enterprise doctrine to the Extreme: When Culpability and Liability Do Not Match." *International Criminal Law Review* 16 (2015): 761-795.

Sentencing Council. "About guidelines." Accessed November 20, 2018. https://www.sentencingcouncil.org.uk/about-sentencing/about-guidelines/.

Simester, Andrew. "The Mental Element of Complicity." *Law Quarterly Review* (2006): 598-599.

Simester, Andrew. "Accessory Liability and Common Unlawful Purpose." *Law Quarterly Review* (2017): 74, 81-82.

Stewart, James. "The end of 'modes of liability' for international crimes." *Leiden Journal of International Law* 25 (2012): 176.

Van der Wilt, Harmen. "De Ontwikkeling van Nieuwe Deelnemingsvormen. Ben Ik mijn Broeders Hoeder?." *Delikt & Delinkwent* 10 (2007): para. 2.1.

Van Sliedregt, Elies. "Joint Criminal Enterprise as a Pathway to Convicting Individuals for Genocide." *Journal of International Criminal Justice* 5 (2007): 205.

Van Sliedregt, Elies. *Individual Criminal Responsibility under International Criminal Law*. Oxford: OUP, 2012.

Van Sliedregt, Elies. "Joint Criminal Confusion – the rise and fall of the joint enterprise theory in English and international criminal law." Inaugural lecture School of Law of the University of Leeds, Leeds, UK, December 1, 2016.

Werle, Gerhard, and Boris Burghardt. "Establishing Degrees of Responsibility: Modes of Participation in Article 25 of the ICC Statute." In *Pluralism in International Criminal Law*, edited by Elies van Sliedregt and Sergey Vasiliev. Oxford: OUP, 2014.

Yanev, Lachezar. "*Theories of Co-perpetration in International Criminal Law.*" PhD diss., Tilburg University, 2016.

Chapter 16

The Concept of Fault in the Regulation of International Responsibility – Reception or Rejection of Domestic Law Analogy

Anna Czaplińska[1]

Abstract

Responsibility understood as the idea of legal reaction to a breach of a legal norm is the ultimate element of any legal order, a general principle confirming its legal nature. International law makes no exception in that respect. The study on responsibility in international law (international responsibility) is all the more intriguing when one realizes how it was possible within the system of equal subjects, not subordinated to any supreme authority, without legislator or judge upon them, to settle premises and consequences of their wrongful acts. These factors shaped the development of international responsibility as a uniform and universal regime. Unlike in the domestic (both civil and common law) legal orders, where the particular divisions of law (civil, criminal, constitutional, etc.) are usually governed by respective responsibility regimes, the international law determines the consequences of any breach of any of its norms, irrespective from its content or character. Because of the differences between the domestic and international legal orders and between their subjects, it is not possible to transfer automatically the solutions elaborated in domestic law in concerning the regulation of responsibility within particular branches of law (i.e. civil, criminal, administrative) to international law. International responsibility cannot be regarded as equivalent to any of the kinds of responsibility existing under international law. It must not be limited, e.g. to mere compensation for

---

[1] Faculty of Law and Administration, University of Lodz

the damage or punishment for wrongful conduct, since these notions and institutions may not have the same meaning or scope in international as in domestic law, or may turn out to be inapplicable on the international plane. Yet, domestic law analogies were and still may be used as a means for the development of the regulation of international responsibility, as long as it is applied with sensibility and temperance. Analogy assumes certain adjustment of adopted solutions to specific circumstances and conditions of international order. As already stated, in international law, there are no separate regimes of civil, criminal, constitutional and other responsibility. There is also no regulation corresponding to the civil/common law division into contractual and delictual (tort) responsibility. International responsibility therefore merges the objectives which on the internal plane are achieved through the various responsibility regimes of domestic law. Thus its regulation must cover all possible kinds of infringements of international law, their consequences and situations that may occur by such occasions. The regime of international responsibility actually developed through gradual simplification of rules defining its premises, forms, and means of implementation. This process was strongly influenced by references to principles and concepts elaborated in domestic responsibility regimes, such as fault, damage/injury, illegality, due diligence, appropriate reparation, etc. At different stages of the process, these concepts and principles were, to varied extent, adopted, modified or rejected in the regulation of international responsibility. The aim of the proposed paper is, therefore, to show how these principles and concepts, rooted in the civil and common law systems, contributed to the shaping of the uniform and universal regime of international responsibility and to assess what role (if any) they play in the present regulation.

Introduction

"It is a principle of international law, and even a general conception of law that any breach of an engagement involves obligation to make reparation."[2]

Responsibility in international law as well as in any other legal order may be described as the idea of a legal reaction to breach of a legal norm. As such it constitutes a general principle of law ultimately confirming the legal nature of the given order.

---

[2] *The Factory of Chorzów Case (Merits)*, PCIJ, A Series, No 17 (1928), 29.

Although the idea of responsibility is common to all legal orders, the particular regulations implementing this idea differ across the world. The states of both, civil and common law traditions, have developed complex systems of responsibility, consisting usually of various subsystems corresponding to the legal disciplines traditionally adopted under domestic law, civil liability and criminal responsibility being the most obvious of them. These domestic regulations differ in many ways and details, and the civil or common law nature of the particular order is one of the factors influencing these differences. However, they do share some basic concepts, present in both civil and common law tradition, such as fault, damage, forms of restitution, sanction, etc. – and from the perspective of international law precisely these common general concepts are the most relevant. As when it comes to the development of international law, it is not a question of adoption of a particular solution from a particular domestic legal order, but rather of whether a general concept of domestic law is transferable into international law.

The present paper aims to examine to what extent the domestic law concept of fault was suitable for the development of the law of international responsibility.

1. The Notion of "Fault" and the Subjective Theory of Responsibility in international Law

The acceptance of the violation of international law as the source of international responsibility entails two necessary premises: the violation of an international obligation of a state and the ability to attribute such behavior to the state.[3] But for a long time the question had been posed in the doctrine of international law whether, apart from these two conditions, by analogy to domestic law systems, the rank of a constitutive

---

[3] *Commentaries to the draft articles on Responsibility of States for internationally wrongful acts*, ILC Report 53rd Session (2001), Official Records of the General Assembly, Fifty-sixth session, Supplement No. 10 (U.N. Doc. A/56/10), commentary to art. 2, para 1-2, 68 ff. It should be noted that the contemporary doctrinal views and practice show that these premises are universal and apply also to the responsibility of non-state subjects of international law – for the exhaustive examination of this concept see Anna Czaplińska *Odpowiedzialność organizacji międzynarodowych jako element uniwersalnego systemu odpowiedzialności międzynarodowoprawnej*, Łódź, 2014. However, because of, the historical roots of the concept of international responsibility as state responsibility, on the one hand, and, on the other hand, the need to remain coherent, the present paper shall refer just to state responsibility.

premise of responsibility should also be attributed to fault. Two views competed in the academic discourse in this respect: the subjective theory of responsibility, also described as the fault theory and the objective theory of responsibility (otherwise - the result theory).[4] The older, primary one, was the fault theory, which dominated the doctrine of international law since the times of Grotius.[5] The two concepts of responsibility were confronted only at the beginning of the 20th century.

According to the subjective theory of responsibility, fault on the part of the state is a necessary condition for the rise of its international responsibility. Various advocates of this theory,[6] however, defined "fault" in different ways. Ricardo Pisillo-Mazzeschi distinguishes among them two basic trends, namely the concept of "psychological" fault and the concept of "normative" fault and the third one "psychological and normative" which constituted an attempt to reconcile the assumptions of the previous two.[7]

---

[4] Renata Sonnenfeld „Podstawowe zasady odpowiedzialności międzynarodowej państwa", in *Odpowiedzialność państwa w prawie międzynarodowym* edited by Renata Sonnenfeld, Warszawa 1980, 31; Malcolm N. Shaw *International Law*, Cambridge 2008, 782 ff.; Mohammed Bedjaoui "Responsibility of States: Fault and Strict Liability", in *Encyclopaedia of Public International Law* edited by Rudolf Bernhardt, Vol. IV, Elsevier 2000, 213.

[5] Paul Reuter "La responsabilité internationale – Problèmes choisis (cours de doctorat professé pendant l'année universitaire 1955-1956)", in Paul Reuter *Le développement de l'ordre juridique international – Ecrits de droit international*, Paris 1995, 386-388; Roberto Ago *Le Délit International*, RCADI, 1939 (II) vol. 68, 477-478; R. Sonnenfeld "Podstawowe zasady...", 32; Mansour Jabbari-Gharabagh "Type of State Responsibility for Environmental Matters in International Law", RJT 1999, vol. 33, 65; M. Bedjaoui "Responsibility...", 213.

[6] I.a. Lassa F.L. Oppenheim, Paul Fauchille, Franz von Liszt, Amos S. Hershey, Hersh Lauterpacht – after R. Ago *Le Délit...*, 482-483; M. Bedjaoui "Responsibility...", 213.

[7] Ricardo Pisillo-Mazzeschi "Due Diligence and the International Responsibility of States", GerYbIL 1992, vol. 35, 11-14. On the psychological and normative concept of fault in criminal and civil law e.g. Janina Dąbrowa *Wina jako przesłanka odpowiedzialności cywilnej*, Wrocław 1968; Biruta Lewaszkiewicz-Petrykowska "Wina jako podstawa odpowiedzialności z tytułu czynów niedozwolonych", *Studia Prawno-Ekonomiczne* issue 2/1969; Adam Szpunar "Czyny niedozwolone w kodeksie cywilnym", *Studia Cywilistyczne* vol. XV, 1970; G. Rejman *Teorie i formy winy w prawie karnym*, Warszawa 1980; Jarosław Majewski, Piotr Kardas "O dwóch znaczeniach winy w prawie karnym", *Państwo i Prawo* issue 10/1993, 69-79.

Most proponents of the subjective theory adopted the psychological concept of fault.[8] The author of the most precise definition of fault was Roberto Ago, who in 1939 wrote that this concept should be understood in the same way within all areas of law, including both internal and international order.[9]

The background for Ago's reflections on fault had been developed by generations of international law scholars. Already Grotius and his direct successors, had referred to the state's fault explained by using a concept of "complicity", meaning "participation" of the state in violations conducted by individuals acting on behalf of the state or in their private capacity, based on tolerating or even supporting (defined as *patientia*) of such acts. Due to the lack of appropriate preventive or repressive reactions, the state had become an "accomplice" to the violation, as if it had adopted the actions of individuals as its own (what was described as *receptus*). The end of this concept was put by Heinrich Triepel. As a proponent of dualistic theory, he argued that an individual, as not capable of being a subject of international law, could not infringe international law. Therefore the complicity of the state and the individual as entities belonging to two completely different legal orders had to be excluded. According to Triepel, the responsibility of the state was always direct and connected with the conduct of its organs. At the same time, Triepel did not exclude the responsibility of the state for its negligence in not preventing the conduct of individuals and continued to use the notion of fault in respect of state in that context.[10]

Consequently, Ago described fault as "a psychological relationship between a specific violation of the subjective right of another entity and the perpetrator of this violation".[11] This relationship is expressed by the subjective attitude of the perpetrator, which may take the form of intent to violate (*dolus*) or negligence (*culpa*). In the latter case the violation is not intentional but arises as a result of the improper conduct of the perpetrator, who did not anticipate, although he should have, the effects

---

[8] R. Pisillo-Mazzeschi "Due Diligence...", 11.

[9] R. Ago *Le Délit*..., 486; R. Pisillo-Mazzeschi "Due Diligence...", 11; R. Sonnenfeld "Podstawowe zasady...", 31.

[10] Heinrich Triepel *Völkerecht und Landesrecht*, Leipzig 1899, 334 ff.; P. Reuter "La responsabilité internationale...", 386, 396; R. Pisillo-Mazzeschi "Due Diligence...", 11, footnote 7.

[11] R. Ago *Le Délit*..., 486.

of his conduct or suspected that they would not occur.[12] Thus fault as a psychological category may only be the feature of a natural person who acts as a state organ or a member of such organ, or in another capacity acts on behalf of the state.[13] Accordingly, in Ago's opinion, one could speak in a literal sense of the state's fault, identified with this psychological attitude of the individual acting on its behalf.[14]

It seems, however, that such personification of the state, which provides its identification with a natural person also in the sphere of the psyche goes too far. The notion of "fault of the state" should only be used as a certain simplification, and actually it is the usual way it is applied by the doctrine. The inability to apply psychological categories, such as fault, to abstract entities such as the state is, moreover, one of the basic arguments in favor of the objective theory of international responsibility.

According to Ago, the correct approach to the problem of fault in international law is based on the consideration whether the existence of the psychological relationship between the perpetrator of a violation of international subjective right *(un droit subjectif international)* and the violation itself, manifested in one of the forms of fault (thus *dolus* or *culpa*) is a prerequisite for attributing a violation of international law to a state.[15] Ago stressed that the problem of fault appears at the stage of attribution; thus it is the premise of the very existence of the infringement, and not the condition for the state to bear the consequences.[16]

However, other eminent advocates of the subjective theory, among them Paul Fauchille and Gabriele Salviloli presented a different understanding

---

[12] Ibidem. Also: Oppenheim's *International Law* Vol. I *Peace – Introduction and Part 1*, edited by R. Jennings, A. Watts, London 1996, 508-509; M. Jabbari-Gharabagh "Type of State Responsibility...", 66; R. Sonnenfeld "Podstawowe zasady...", 31; Ian Brownlie *Principles of Public International Law*, Oxford 2008, 438 ff; M.N. Shaw *International Law...*, 783 ff; R. Pisillo-Mazzeschi "Due Diligence...", 9.

[13] R. Ago *Le Délit...*, 486; A. Gattini "La notion de faute à la lumière du projet de convention de la Commission du Droit International sur la responsabilité internationale", EJIL 1992, vol. 3, 253-286, 253; R. Sonnenfeld "Podstawowe zasady...", 49 ff.; Jean-Pierre Quéneudec *La responsabilité internationale de l'Etat pour les fautes personnelles de ses agents*, Paris 1966, 6-12.

[14] R. Ago *Le Délit...*, 486.

[15] Ibidem, 487.

[16] Ibidem, 486-487.

of fault (which Pisillo-Mazzeschi refers to as "normative fault").[17] They define it as any conduct different from that prescribed by the legal norm.[18] Accordingly, the term "fault" is used to describe the mere non-observance (violation) of the law. In effect, despite the persistent use of the notion of fault, this concept relates more to the assumptions of the objective theory of responsibility.[19] Considering this divergence in understanding of the concept of fault, one can agree with the authors of the leading French international law textbook that the whole dispute over fault in international law is, in fact, a matter of definition and not of actual substantial differences.[20]

In the earlier writings, there was no deeper theoretical justification for references to fault and for recognizing it as a constitutive premise of the international responsibility of the state. There is a strong presumption that fault occurred in international law through the almost automatic transposition of rules and terminology used in domestic legal order. As Karl Zemanek wrote, since the regulation of responsibility in internal (above all civil and criminal) law was largely based on the principle of fault the doctrine of international law simply had followed this example, and starting with Grotius, had adopted fault as the natural basis of international responsibility.[21] It seems all the more plausible if one considers the strong relationship between the ancient understanding of the notion of state and the person of the ruler who was regarded the personification of the state.[22]

The aforementioned lack of any theoretical examination of fault as the necessary premise of state responsibility can be explained by the fact that

---

[17] Paul Fauchille *Traité de droit international public* Vol. I, Paris 1921, 515; Gabriele Salvioli *Les règles générales de la paix*, RCADI 1933 (IV), vol. 46, 96; R. Pisillo-Mazzeschi "Due Diligence ...", 13

[18] R. Ago *Le Délit*..., 485; M. Bedjaoui "Responsibility...", 213; R. Sonnenfeld "Podstawowe zasady...", 31.

[19] Nguyen Quoc Dinh, Patrick Daillier, Allain Pellet *Droit international public*, Paris 2002, 766.

[20] Karl Zemanek "Responsibility of States: General Principles", in *EPIL* edited by R. Bernhardt, Vol. IV, Elsevier 2000, 222; Karl Zemanek "Responsabilité des Etats pour faits internationalement illicites, ainsi que pour faits internationalement licites", in Karl Zemanek, Jean Salmon *Responsabilité internationale*, Paris 1987, 36.

[21] R. Ago *Le Délit*..., 477. Por. A. Gattini "La notion de faute ...", 266 and literature quoted there.

[22] K. Zemanek "Responsibility of States...", 222.

until the publication of Dionisio Anzilotti's *Teoria generale della responsabilità dello stato nel dirtto internazionale*[23] at the beginning of the 20th century, there were no views in the doctrine of international law opposing to the subjective concept of responsibility. The proponents of the fault theory simply did not have the need to justify their position. Anzilotti's critique should have prompted them to do so. But still in 1939 Ago, although himself also (at that time) in favor of the subjective concept of responsibility,[24] accused its other supporters of the lack of any serious consideration and reply to Anzilotti's arguments against fault in international responsibility regulation.[25] Some limited themselves only to confirming their support for the fault theory, others resorted to some legal fictions, such as e.g. *culpa in eligendo*, which could not be applied in relation to the state.[26] Ago, as probably the first, attempted to substantively criticize the objective theory of responsibility.[27] However, despite his strict assessment of 1939, as time passed, he also revised his views and as the special rapporteur of the International Law Commission ultimately opted for the objective approach.[28]

Apart from the two concepts of fault mentioned above, in the doctrine and in the jurisprudence of international courts, fault was also defined as the lack of due diligence in the conduct of the state.[29] To recall the words of US Secretary of State Thomas F. Bayard, of 1887, due diligence is the diligence with which good governments used to act in certain circumstances.[30] Following this view, some scholars adopted the standard of diligence observed by the state in its own affairs and interests –

---

[23] Dionisio Anzilotti *Teoria generale della responsabilità dello stato nel dirtto internazionale*, Firenze 1902.

[24] R. Ago *Le Délit...*, 498.

[25] Ibidem, 482 ff.

[26] Ibidem, 483.

[27] R. Ago *Le Délit...*, 487-493. Also: A. Gattini "La notion de faute ..."; Andrea Gattini "Smoking / No Smoking: Some Remarks on the Current Place of Fault in the ILC Draft Articles on State Responsibility", EJIL 1999, vol. 10 issue 2, 398.

[28] R. Ago, Second report, U.N. Doc. A/CN.4/233 (YbILC, 1970, vol. II); Commentary to draft article 1 adopted by the ILC during its 25th session in 1973 (YbILC, 1973, vol. II, 173-176).

[29] R. Sonnenfeld "Podstawowe zasady...", 31; P. Reuter *La responsabilité internationale...*, 449-455; A. Gattini "La notion de faute ...", 260-265; R. Pisillo-Mazzeschi "Due Diligence...", 9-51.

[30] A. Gattini "La notion de faute...", 260.

diligentia quam in suis – as a reference point for the assessment of due diligence.[31] Krzysztof Skubiszewski, who was also one of the advocates of this concept, wrote:

> "Violation of international law (...) must always be at fault. In international relations, a culpable violation of law arises when a state in exercise of its international obligations does not observe the same standard of due diligence as it complies (or should comply) with while dealing with its own affairs."[32]

According to Gattini, application of the *diligentia quam in suis* standard does not lead in practice, as it might seem *prima facie*, to a kind of rewarding the worst organized and least self-respecting states by empowering them to treat in the very manner the entities with which they establish international relations.[33] For a state to exist requires a minimum degree of organization and possessing an apparatus of power (judicial and administrative) meeting at least the minimum efficiency criteria.[34] These minimum criteria are high enough in the international order that an entity which does not fulfill them cannot be classified as a state at all and that it is not possible to attribute any violation to it.[35]

Lack of due diligence on the part of the state is expressed in the conduct of the persons acting on its behalf. Thus it may be considered as an external manifestation of their mental condition defined as negligence (unintentional fault). On the basis of non-observance of the standard one would conclude what is happening in the perpetrator's psyche, assuming that if he does not act in the "right" way, at least he does not anticipate, though he should, the effects of his conduct. In this approach, the reference to the lack of due diligence seems to get close to the concept of negligence (unintentional fault) in the domestic legal order.[36] However, the very concept of due diligence is not a psychological category, it does

---

[31] Max Hubera 3rd report of 24 October 1924 *British claims in the Spanish zone of Morocco*, RIAA vol. II, 641; Otto Steiner "Spanish Zone of Morocco Claims", in EPIL edited by R. Bernhardt, Vol. IV, Elsevier 2000, 573.

[32] Krzysztof Skubiszewski "Odpowiedzialność międzynarodowa" in *Zarys prawa międzynarodowego publicznego* edited by Marian Muszkat, Warszawa 1956, vol. II, 240.

[33] A. Gattini "La notion de faute...", 265.

[34] Ibidem.

[35] Ibidem; P. Reuter "La responsabilité internationale...", 452.

[36] Władysław Czapliński, Anna Wyrozumska *Prawo międzynarodowe publiczne, zagadnienia systemowe*, Warszawa 2014, 747; A. Gattini "La notion de faute...", 264.

not describe the psychological experiences of the perpetrator, but it defines an objectified pattern of conduct.[37] We can talk about objectivization even when the reference criterion is *diligentia quam in suis*, as indicated by both, Gattini's argument of the minimum organization of the state and the Skubiszewski's mention of the diligence that states should observe. However, in contemporary literature there barely are references to the standard of *diligent quam in suis*, while the use of the notion of due diligence became widespread.[38]

Simultaneously, in the academic literature, there are proposals to define such a model as e.g. the average or ordinary conduct of a civilized state, similar to the patterns applied in domestic law, like the French "good father of the family".[39] However, these ideas are criticized as the possibility of sufficiently precise determination of such a general pattern, and the applicability of solutions analogous to domestic law on the international law plane are doubtful.[40] It must be stressed that it would be very difficult to create *in abstracto* a general model of due diligence applicable to all obligations of all states in all cases. Such a pattern of diligent conduct can be precisely defined only in relation to the content of the specific obligation arising from the specific norm of international law.[41] An appropriate (due) degree of diligence thus becomes an element of the obligation itself, and any failure to comply with this model will constitute a violation of this international obligation and accordingly the source of state responsibility.[42] It is a little bit of paradox, though, that the reference to the concept of due diligence, which originally was aimed to justify the subjective theory of international responsibility, in effect has brought us closer to the objective theory and to the contemporary solution of the problem of fault, which no more is regarded as a constitutive premise of

---

[37] R. Pisillo-Mazzeschi "Due Diligence...", 42.

[38] Ibidem, 41.

[39] R. Pisillo-Mazzeschi "Due Diligence...", 45; he notes however, that depending on the object of the obligation the standard may vary.

[40] A. Gattini, "La notion de faute...", 264.

[41] Gilles Cottereau "Système juridique et notion de responsabilité", in S.F.D.I. *La responsabilité dans le système international – Actes du XXIV Colloque de la F.D.I., 31 V – 2 VI 1990*, Paris 1991, 23; R. Pisillo-Mazzeschi "Due Diligence...", 41; James Crawford "Revising the Draft Articles on State Responsibility", EJIL 1999, vol. 10 nr 2, 438; K. Zemanek "Responsabilité des Etat..", 37-38.

[42] I. Brownlie *Principles* ..., 439.

responsibility, but as one of the eventual elements of the content of international obligation.[43]

2. The Objective Theory of International Responsibility

The development of the objective theory of state responsibility in international law began, as already mentioned, with Dionisio Anzilotti and the publication of his *Teoria generale della responsabilità dello stato nel dirtto internazionale*.[44] Anzilotti's theory is, as Paul Reuter writes "as simple as it is ingenious": the only source of responsibility is for him the violation of international law by the state. In other words, for the state to be held responsible, it is enough if it causes the violation.[45] Anzilotti described the issue of fault in the international responsibility theory as follows:

> "'Intent' and 'negligence', in their proper meanings, define the ways of expressing human will as a psychological fact, therefore they cannot be used in a different way than in relation to an individual (a natural person). It is, consequently, a matter of deciding whether a conduct contrary to international law, must be the result of intention or negligence of the person acting as an organ in order to be attributed to the state, in other words whether his/hers intentional or unintentional fault is a condition that the law requires so that certain events give rise to specific consequences for the state. "[46]

Since the concept of fault refers to the sphere of the human psyche, of the consciousness and will, it cannot be logically used in this sense in

---

[43] R. Pisillo-Mazzeschi "Due Diligence...", 21 oraz 41-46; J. Crawford "Revising the Draft ...", 438; A. Gattini "La notion de faute...", 258-259.

[44] Dionisio Anzilotti *Teoria generale della responsabilità dello stato nel dirtto internazionale*, Firenze 1902; Dionisio Anzilotti "La responsabilité internationale des Etats à raison des dommages souferts par des étrangers" RGDIP 1906, vol. 13, 5-29, 285-309; Dionisio Anzilotti *Corso di diritto internazionale*, Roma 1927, French translation by Gilbert Gidel *Cours de droit international* , Paris 1929. Also: W. Czapliński, A. Wyrozumska *Prawo międzynarodowe* ..., 737-738; Georg Nolte "From Dionisio Anzilotti to Roberto Ago: The Classical International Law of State Responsibility and the Traditional Primacy of a Bilateral Conception of Inter-State Relations", EJIL 2002, vol. 13, 5-6; Pierre-Marie Dupuy "Dionisio Anzilotti and the Law of International Responsibility of States", EJIL 1992, vol. 3, s 139.

[45] P. Reuter "La responsabilité internationale...", 397.

[46] D. Anzilotti *Cours de droit* ..., 498.]

respect of the abstract entity such as the state.[47] Moreover, recognizing the individual fault of a person acting on behalf of the state as a necessary premise of its international responsibility would result in making it dependent on a factor the examination and assessment of which would in practice face serious difficulties, on the one hand of technical nature, concerning the process of the examination of the individual's mental condition from the perspective of the international legal order.

On the other hand, also the problems of a legal character would occur, with regard to the mutual relations of domestic and international order, and concerning the interpretation and application in this context of the relevant norms of domestic law.[48] Anzilotti exclusion of fault as the constitutive premise of state responsibility is a consequence of its dualistic approach to law, assuming full autonomy of domestic and international legal order. With regard to responsibility, this means that domestic law norms determine whether and when a person (the actual perpetrator) acts on behalf of the state, as its organ or in another capacity. This includes all aspects of such relationships, including the psychological factor. However, the assessment of whether there has been a violation of international law by the state is carried out solely on the basis of the international legal order.[49] Fault, as the mental condition of the individual acting on behalf of the state, assessed according to the regulation of the internal order, cannot be considered a condition *sine qua non* for attributing to the state of responsibility in the sphere of international law. One of Anzilotti's favourite dualistic arguments was that an individual (e.g. an official) could behave in a manner that was perfectly consistent with domestic law and at the same time violate norms of international law, which would lead to a situation where, despite the obvious violation, one could not assign this person's fault (judged from the point of view of domestic law). Moreover, in many cases where the author of the violation may actually be a body composed of many people (an extreme example is the legislative body) a rather rhetorical question arises as to how to identify fault thereof.[50] Assigning responsibility to the state, according to Anzilotti, "(...) from the point of view of international law is nothing but the consequence of a

---

[47] R. Pisillo-Mazzeschi "Due Diligence...", 15.

[48] P.-M. Dupuy "Dionisio Anzilotti and the Law...", 141.

[49] D. Anzilotti *Cours de droit* ..., 468 ff.; P.-M. Dupuy "Dionisio Anzilotti and the Law...", 144.

[50] P. Reuter "La responsabilité internationale...", 397-398; R. Pisillo-Mazzeschi "Due Diligence...", 15.

causal relationship that exists between the act contrary to international law and the conduct of the state which is the author of this act."[51] And so for the rise of state responsibility, it is only necessary that the violation of international law is an objective consequence of the state's conduct.[52]

Anzilotti's concept gained a large group of supporters already in the first half the 20th century,[53] but also met with serious criticism, above all from the part of Ago. Anzilotti was charged with too far-reaching simplification in such absolute separation of the sphere of regulation of the international and the domestic order, of the "person" of the state as an international entity from the natural person acting on its behalf, as its agent.[54] His total negation of the subjective element was criticized as allegedly the objective premises of responsibility, could not be applicable to certain types of violations (for example in the event of responsibility for omission or for the actions of private persons).[55]

Nevertheless, Anzilotti's theory has become the basis for modern solutions adopted in the field of international responsibility. The simplification which was the main charge raised against it turned out to be its greatest advantage. Anzilotti cleared the theory of international legal responsibility from difficult to assess psychological elements and domestic law analogies. Simultaneously, he simplified as much as it was possible, reducing the premises to two completely basic and neutral, applicable to any situation, regardless of the content of the violation. But most

---

[51] D. Anzilotti *La responsabilité internationale des Etats*..., 291.

[52] P. Reuter "La responsabilité internationale...", 397-398. Reuter emphasizes that Anzilotti's objective theory should not be confused with the concept of responsibility based on risk in the domestic civil law, also called "objective responsibility", where the source of responsibility is not the violation of law, but damage caused even by a lawful conduct. Such terminological mistake is made by Shaw, who calls the objective theory of international responsibility the "risk theory" - M. Shaw *International Law*..., 782.

[53] With Hans Kelsen, Jules Basdevant and Clive Eagleton among them – for further reference R. Pisillo-Mazzeschi "Due Diligence...", 15-18 and literature quoted there and M. Bedjaoui "Responsibility...", 213.

[54] R. Ago *Le Délit*..., 490; P.-M. Dupuy "Dionisio Anzilotti and the Law...", 144.

[55] R. Ago *Le Délit*..., 493; P.-M. Dupuy "Dionisio Anzilotti and the Law..", 142. The critique was not fully deserved though. Anzilotti dismissed fault as a separate condition for international responsibility, but simultaneously considered that the subjective element (intended or negligent conduct) may constitute an element of contents of the violated legal norm and as such may be relevant for establishment of the violation – the view very similar to the contemporary solution adopted by the ILC.

importantly, he created a practical concept, which did not remain solely in the sphere of theoretical considerations. And the ILC draft articles on state responsibility constitute the ultimate final expression and confirmation of Anzilotti's objective theory of international responsibility.[56]

3. The Problem of Fault in International Practice

The diversity of views of the international law doctrine on the issue of fault was also directly related to the fact that international practice, especially until the end of the 2nd World War, was not uniform in this respect. Of course, supporters of each option tried to find arguments in support of their own position presented as "the only right" one. In fact, the international jurisprudence, in particular the arbitration, was based to some extent on both, the theory of fault, (variously understood) as well as the objective theory. Certainly the categorical statement of Ago, supported by just a few practical examples, that "the fault of the organ *lato sensu* (...) is a necessary condition for attributing the violation of international law to the entity" was unjustified.[57] All the more so, because actually most judicial or arbitral decisions have not referred to the premise of fault, in particular understood as a psychological category in the form of intent or negligence.[58]

The *Home Missionary Society* case, between the United States and the United Kingdom, may be recalled as one of the few exceptions. The arbitral tribunal rejected the US complaint against the UK regarding the damage suffered by the American Society as a result of insurgents' activities in Sierra Leone, stating that no government could be found responsible for such actions if it was not guilty of violating the principle of good faith or of negligence in suppressing the uprising.[59]

More frequently the international jurisprudence referred to fault understood as a failure to observe due diligence. A classic example thereof is the arbitral award in the *Alabama* case, in which the failure to comply

---

[56] P.-M. Dupuy "Dionisio Anzilotti and the Law...", 148; R. Sonnenfeld "Podstawowe zasady...", 34.

[57] R. Ago *Le Délit...*, 494-498. However, among the examples given by Ago to support the assertion about the prevalence of the fault theory the most concern exemption from responsibility due to non-culpable error or fortuity; there are just two cases where the very responsibility was based on fault.

[58] R. Sonnenfeld "Podstawowe zasady...', 31; M. Shaw *International Law...*, 546. R. Pisillo-Mazzeschi "Due Diligence...", 24; I. Brownlie, *Principles...*, 437.

[59] *Home Missionary Society Claim (USA v. UK)*, 1920 r., RIAA vol. VI, 42.

with the due diligence was considered the basis of the UK's liability.[60] It must be recalled, however, that the due diligence criterion had already been introduced in the arbitration agreement between the US and the UK as part of the contents of obligations resulting from state neutrality in an external conflict and the UK was charged with the violation thereof.[61] Article VI of the arbitration agreement provided:

> "In deciding the matters submitted to the Arbitrators they shall be governed by the following 3 rules, which are agreed upon by the High Contracting Parties as rules to be taken as applicable to the case, and by such principles of international law not inconsistent therewith as the Arbitrators shall determine to have been applicable to the case:
>
> RULES
>
> A neutral Government is bound -
>
> First. To use due diligence to prevent the fitting out, arming, or equipping, within its jurisdiction, of any vessel which it has reasonable ground to believe is intended to cruise or to carry on war against a Power with which it is at peace; and also to use like diligence to prevent the departure from its jurisdiction of any vessel intended to cruise or carry on war as above, such vessel having been specially adapted, in whole or in part, within such jurisdiction, to warlike use
>
> Secondly. Not to permit or suffer either belligerent to make use of its ports or waters as the base of naval operations against the other, or for the purpose of the renewal or augmentation of military supplies or arms, recruitment of men.
>
> Thirdly. To exercise due diligence in its own ports and waters, and, as to all persons within its jurisdiction, to prevent any violation of the foregoing obligation and duties."

The arbitrators stated that the UK by allowing the Confederation's caper ships to be stationed and docked in its ports during the American Civil

---

[60] Alabama Claims Arbitration (USA v. UK), award of 14 September 1872 r., published in History and Digest of the International Arbitrations to which the United States Has Been a Party edited by John B. Moore, Washington 1898, vol. I, 653 ff.; Peter Seidel, "The Alabama" in EPIL edited by R. Bernhardt, Vol. I, Elsevier 1992, 97-99.

[61] Art. VI, Treaty between Great Britain and the United States for the Amicable Setting of All Causes of Difference between the Two Countries, Signed at Washington, 8 May, 1871, [1871 Treaty of Washington], in The Consolidated Treaty Series edited by Clive Parry, New York 1977, vol. 143, 145.

War, violated the duty of a neutral state to exercise due diligence in preventing and counteracting the use of areas under its jurisdiction for such purposes by one of the parties to the conflict. The tribunal found that in such a situation the UK was liable for damage caused by these ships during military operations and awarded to the US compensation. This clearly indicates that due diligence was referred to as an objective standard and not as a subjective psychological factor. The broad analysis of arbitral awards presented by Pisillo-Mazzeschi confirms this assertion and leads to the general conclusion that the assessment of the due diligence standard is of the objective nature and does not constitute an attempt to examine the mental condition of the individual concerned.[62]

On the antipode, however, there is the judicial practice which distances from the fault theory in favor of the concept of objective responsibility. In the *Caire* case, Jan H.W. Verzijl, the Presiding Commissioner of the French-Mexican conciliation commission, interpreted the principles of state responsibility in the light of the objective theory:

> "En abordant l'examen des questions visées Sub 4 à la lueur des principes généraux que je viens d'indiquer, je déclare tout d'abord interpréter les dits principes dans le sens de la doctrine qui professe, en cette matière, la 'responsabilité objective' de l'Etat, c'est-à-dire une responsabilité pour les actes commis par ses fonctionnaires ou organes, qui peut lui incomber malgré l'absence de toute 'faute' de sa part. Il est notoire que, dans ce domaine, les conceptions théoriques ont beaucoup évolué dans les derniers temps et que notamment l'œuvre novatrice de Dionisio Anzilotti a frayé le chemin aux idées nouvelles qui ne subordonnent plus à une 'faute' quelconque de l'Etat sa responsabilité pour les actes de ses fonctionnaires. Sans entrer ici dans un examen du point de savoir si ces idées nouvelles, peut-être trop absolues, n'ont pas besoin de certaines corrections, par exemple dans le sens indiqué par le Dr Karl Strupp, je les considère en tout cas comme parfaitement correctes, en tant qu'elles tendent à grever l'Etat, en matière internationale, de la responsabilité pour tous les actes commis par ses fonctionnaires ou organes et qui constituent des actes délictueux au point de vue du droit des gens, n'importe que le

---

[62] R. Pisillo-Mazzeschi "Due Diligence...", 42. He presents broad digest of jurisprudence, in particular arbitral practice, in this respect – ibidem, 22-40.

fonctionnaire ou l'organe en question ait agi dans les limites de sa compétence ou en les excédant."[63]

The jurisprudence of the US-Mexican claims commission provides other significant examples of references to the concept of objective responsibility, i.a. the *Neer* and *Roberts* cases, in which the commission adopted the objective test of the state's compliance with "international standards".[64] In the *Neer* decision the commission determined when the state's conduct should qualify as a violation of law as follows:

"4. The Commission recognizes the difficulty of devising a general formula for determining the boundary between an international delinquency of this type and an unsatisfactory use of power included in national sovereignty. (...) Without attempting to announce a precise formula, it is in the opinion of the Commission possible (...) to hold (first) that the propriety of governmental acts should be put to the test of international standards, and (second) that the treatment of an alien, in order to constitute an international delinquency, should amount to an outrage, to bad faith, to willful neglect of duty, or to an insufficiency of governmental action so far short of international standards that every reasonable and impartial man would readily recognize its insufficiency."[65]

The quoted excerpt confirms that violation of international law (in this case in respect of the treatment of foreigners) may also result from a conduct objectively, clearly deviating from the international standard, not featuring any element of bad faith or intent.[66] Adoption of the objective

---

[63] *Caire Claim (France v. Mexico)*, 1929, RIAA vol. V, 529-531. Verzijl explained that he had chosen to follow the novel views of Anzilotti in determination of the principles of international responsibility in the *Caire* case because he considered it "perfectly correct" to hold the state responsible – on international level – for all the acts committed by its agents or organs, which constituted delicts in the light of international law, regardless whether they had acted within or outside the limits of their competence, without subjecting such responsibility to any kind of "fault".

[64] *Neer Claim (USA v. Mexico)*, 1926, RIAA vol. IV, 61-62; *Roberts Claim (USA v. Mexico)*, 1926, RIAA vol. IV, 80; *Chattin Claim (USA v. Mexico)*, 1927 RIAA, vol. IV, 284 ff.; cf. *Quintanilla Claim (Mexico v. USA)*, 1926 RIAA, vol. IV, 101 ff. Also M. N. Shaw *International Law...*, 783; I. Brownlie *Principles ...*, 437.

[65] 1926, RIAA vol. IV, 61-62.

[66] R. Sonnenfeld *Podstawowe zasady...*, 33; Yuko Matsui "The Transformation of the Law of State Responsibility", *Thesaurus Acroasium*, 1993, vol 20, 7-10.

concept of responsibility is even more clearly reflected in rulings rejecting the possibility of exclusion of state responsibility because of the good faith of the agents acting on its behalf.[67] as it was in the case *The Jessie, The Thomas F. Bayard & The Pescawha*.[68] The United States, though having acknowledged that the action of their officers against the three British ships was unlawful, claimed that the state in this case could not be held responsible, because they acted in good faith.[69] The arbitral tribunal rejected this argument:

> "It is unquestionable that the United States naval authorities acted *bona fide*, but though their *bona fides* might be invoked by the officers in explanation of their conduct to their own Government, its effect is merely to show that their conduct constituted an error in judgment, and any Government is responsible to other Governments for errors in judgment of its officials purporting to act within the scope of their duties and vested with power to enforce their demands."[70]

Also, the analysis of the jurisprudence of the Permanent Court of International Justice shows that it tended towards the objective concept of international responsibility. Perhaps it was the influence of the authority of Dionisio Anzilotti, who for several years had served as judge of the Court, but in its judgments the PCIJ examined only whether there was a breach of international obligation, without any reference to the subjective element of fault on the part of the perpetrator.[71]

---

[67] Eduardo Jiménez de Aréchaga "International Responsibility", in *Manual of Public International Law* edited by Max Sørensen, London 1968, 536 and jurisprudence quoted there.

[68] *The Jessie, The Thomas F. Bayard & The Pescawha Claim (Great Britain v. USA)*, 1921 RIAA vol. VI, 57.

[69] British ships were stopped and searched for seal skins on the high seas, in the protection zone where seal hunting was banned. The officers conducting the search, acting in good faith (in error as to the scope of their powers) sealed the weapons located on the vessels and banned breaking the seal until they leave the protection zone, which actually went beyond their powers and consequently constituted a violation of international law.

[70] 1921 RIAA vol. VI, 59.

[71] *The S.S. Wimbledon Case*, PCIJ, A Series, No 1 (1923), 30; *Certain German interests in Polish Upper Silesia Case (Merits)*, PCIJ, A Series, No 7 (1926), 24 ff.; *The Factory of Chorzów Case (Merits)*, 29 i 63; *Diversion of water from the Meuse Case*, PCIJ, A/B

4. Contemporary Solution to the Problem of Fault in the Regulation of international Responsibility

It seems that until the end of the 2nd World War, neither subjective nor objective theory of international responsibility could be considered as predominant.[72] However, after the War, the support for the fault theory was still visible. In this respect, one may recall the academic discussion on the ICJ ruling concerning the incident in the Corfu Channel.[73] Some scholars, including Hersh Lauterpacht regarded it a confirmation of the subjective theory,[74] along with the separate opinions of judge Krylov and judge *ad hoc* Ečer, explicitly expressing the authors' support for fault as a necessary premise of state responsibility.[75] Even contemporarily, there still are authors like Andrea Gattini, whose views are marked by a certain nostalgia for the fault theory in international responsibility law.[76]

Nevertheless, it needs to be admitted that from the beginning of the post-war period the objective theory started gradually but clearly prevailing over the subjective theory. Although the *Corfu Channel* judgment caused such positive reactions of the fault theory supporters, in fact there is nothing in it that could prejudge which concept of responsibility was applied. As Ian Brownlie rightly pointed out, the Court while considering whether Albania violated its international obligation by not having warned of the impending danger within its territorial waters (the presence of mines), accepted as the decisive factor for its responsibility not the fault (whether intentional or unintentional) but the

---

Series, No 70 (1937), 18-27 i 28-31. Also Remigiusz Bierzanek, Janusz Symonides *Prawo międzynarodowe publiczne*, Warszawa 2004, 152.

[72] R. Sonnenfeld "Podstawowe zasady..", 34.

[73] *Corfu Channel Case (UK v. Albania)*, ICJ Reports 1949.

[74] Hersh Lauterpacht *The Developement of International Law by the International Court*, London 1958, 88; Oppenheim's *International Law*, edited by Hersh Lauterpacht, 8th edition, London 1955, vol. I, 343. This view in the Polish doctrine was supported by K. Skubiszewski "Odpowiedzialność międzynarodowa...", 240; Alfons Klafkowski *Prawo międzynarodowe publiczne*, Warszawa 1966, 96-97; Marian Iwanejko "Świadomość jako przesłanka odpowiedzialności państwa w prawie międzynarodowym. Wypadek cieśniny Korfu", *Zeszyty Naukowe UJ* 1961, 57-76.

[75] ICJ Reports 1949, dissenting opinon of Judge Krylov, 71-72; dissenting opinon of Judge Ečer, 254.

[76] A. Gattini "La notion de faute…"; A. Gattini "Smoking / No Smoking: Some Remarks…".

knowledge about the threat, evaluated on the basis of objective facts.[77] It is also worth to mention the difference between the French and the English text of the judgment. The English version reads: "every State's obligation not to allow knowingly its territory to be used for acts contrary to the rights of other States" and the word "knowingly" seemed a key argument in favor of the Court's use of the subjective theory, according to its supporters. However in the French version the word for "knowingly" – "connaissant" – does not occur at all.[78] Probably the best comment to this whole controversy was expressed in the measured opinion of judge Azevedo, who argued that both theories were actually close to each other and equally present (and needed) in international practice.[79]

The reasons for the turn to the objective theory were, on the one hand, the practical advantages of the theory itself, on the other hand, some external circumstances that contributed to make these advantages appreciated. Among the latter factors, Zemanek notes the doubt in the possibility of the creation of a universal and obligatory judicial international dispute settlement system.[80] Under such a system it would be possible to apply the principles of responsibility similar to the domestic law ones, including investigation, in each case by an impartial body, of fault understood even as a psychological attitude of the individual perpetrator. However, relying on the subjective concept and the premise of fault in the absence of a uniform and effective process of its examination, would extremely complicate, if not at all frustrate the enforcement of state responsibility.[81] This was also one of the arguments which influenced the

---

[77] ICJ Reports 1949, 18-22; I. Brownlie *Principles...*, 442; M. N. Shaw *International Law...*, 784.

[78] Por. ICJ Reports 1949, 22 (English and French version); K. Zemanek "Responsabilité des Etats..." 44.

[79] They are close in the sense that their use, despite serious doctrinal differences, leads to similar results; ICJ Reports 1949, 82-83. Cf. dissenting opinions of: Judge Badawi Pasha, ibidem, 63-66; Judge Alvarez, ibidem, 44-45; Judge Winiarski, ibidem, 52-54.

[80] K. Zemanek "Responsibility of States...", 222; A. Gattini "La notion de faute...", 254.

[81] This reasoning is consistent with a position, quoted by R. Sonnenfeld, of Pranas M. Kuris, who believed that because of the principle of presumption of innocence and the principles of impartiality and sovereignty, it is only possible to prove fault (hence the requirement of fault is a condition of responsibility) when assessment of the facts of the case is made by an impartial body international (a court), otherwise fault is presumed on the basis of the conduct of the state-perpetrator objectively contrary to the law; P.M. Kuris *Mieżdunarodnyje prawonaruszenija i otwietstwiennost' gosudarstw*, Vilnius 1973, 236, after R. Sonnenfeld "Podstawowe zasady...", 33-34.

increase in support for the objective theory in the doctrine and its application in practice.[82]

The other relevant factors are: the overall increase in the number of states through the process of decolonization after 2nd World War and the associated expansion of UN membership through their accession; the very creation of the United Nations as well as the development of other international organizations (as fora for cooperation of the international community); and the prevalence of international agreements, bi- and multilateral, as a means of regulation of the mutual relations between states, also within new subject matters.[83] The consequence was a dramatic increase of mutual obligations of states – and the potential for violation thereof as well. Moreover, the responsibility ceased to be regarded as a purely bilateral relationship, arising only between the state-perpetrator and the state-victim. Along with the recognition of the categories of international obligations *erga omnes* and *erga omnes partes*, binding upon and towards the entire international community or all parties to a treaty, it was necessary to assume that the result of any breach of such obligations would also transgress the traditional bipartite offender-victim relationship; responsibility thus became, in these particular cases, a multilateral relationship.

Also, the character of the cases which constituted the basis of the formation of international legal standards of the responsibility of states had changed. While in the 19th and 20th century they were mainly the result of the exercise by the states of diplomatic protection in relation to own citizens in cases of violation of their rights by another state, in the second half of the 20th century the burden of interest moved to matters concerning the direct relations between states and the responsibility arising therein. Moreover, it was enforced not only through the traditional diplomatic methods, but increasingly also through arbitration or before permanent international organs (including courts and tribunals) under specific international dispute resolution schemes. As it seems, in the cases of this kind it was harder (than in the cases concerning damages caused to foreigners) to apply the general rules of responsibility applicable in the

---

[82] K. Zemanek "Responsibility of States...", 221-222; A. Gattini "La notion de faute...", 254.

[83] K. Zemanek "Responsibility of States...", 220; Shabtai Rosenne *The Perplexities of Modern International Law*, RCADI 2001, vol. 291, 385; G. Nolte "De Dionisio Anzilotti ...", 21.

domestic systems.[84] It was noted that the responsibility under international law had its own character, different than liability in domestic law; it could not be simply classified as "civil" or "criminal", and the domestic law solutions were not directly transferable to international law, in respect of both the conditions and the forms of responsibility.[85]

In the light of these circumstances, the change of views by Ago is not that much surprising. Ago, who primarily was a supporter of the fault theory, after the war verified his position. As the chairman (in 1962-1963) of the ILC subcommittee established to evaluate the results of previous research on the state responsibility and to prepare guidelines and objectives for subsequent work, he had the decisive influence on the radical revision of the Commission's approach to this subject. In the report summarizing the work of the subcommittee, Ago suggested that, not ignoring what has already been developed in various fields (mainly in cases of harm caused to foreigners), the ILC's main purpose and direction would be to

---

[84] Y. Matsui "The Transformation...", 11-13, 62; Sh. Rosenne *The Perplexities...*, 382, 412-414; R. Sonnenfeld "Podstawowe zasady...", 10-11. This approach was reflected in the work of the first rapporteur of the ILC on the topic State responsibility, Fernando Garcia-Amador. The situation changed, however, to the extent that the issue of diplomatic protection and responsibility for damage caused to foreigners since 1997 constituted a separate topic in ILC works, ILC Report, Official Records of the General Assembly, Fifty-second session, Supplement No. 10 (A/52/10), Ch. VII, paras 169-190.

[85] As noted by Georges Abi-Saab, responsibility system in the international law covers the entire sphere that in the domestic law is distributed between the criminal and civil liability (or, more broadly, public and private law), and even the attempt to introduce into the system of the distinction between international crimes and torts (a division which has not been fully preserved in the final version of the draft articles – A.Cz.) does not mean that it is identical to the existing divisions in the domestic order; Georges Abi-Saab "The Uses of Article 19", EJIL 1999, vol.10 issue 2, 350, footnote 42. Also James Crawford, Simon Olleson "The Nature and Forms of International Responsibility", in *International Law* edited by Malcolm D. Evans, Oxford 2003, 450-451. Cf. D. Anzilotti *Cours de droit ...*, 522-523. Also: *Commentaries ...*, (A/56/10), 126-127, para 4-5; James Crawford *First Report on State Responsibility, Addendum (1)*, (1998) UN Doc. A/CN.4/490/Add.1, para 60 (iv) Roberto Ago *Second Report on State Responsibility – Origin of International Responsibility*, U.N. Doc. A/CN.4/233, YbILC, 1970, vol. II, 194 ff.; K. Zemanek "Responsabilité des Etats ...", 15; G. Cottereau "Système juridique...", 6; Nguyen Quoc Dinh, P. Daillier, A. Pellet *Droit international ...*, 763-765; Henryk de Fiumel "W sprawie pojęcia odpowiedzialności państwa we współczesnym prawie międzynarodowym", *Państwo i Prawo* No 3/1976, 40; Ludwik Ehrlich *Prawo międzynarodowe*, Warszawa 1958, 638. Cf. P. Reuter "La responsabilité internationale...", 404-406; Krystyna Marek "Criminalizing State Responsibility", RBDI, vol. XIV, 1978-79, 461 ff.

determine the general principles of state responsibility. This would also require to settle whether the fault (in a broad sense) of the state organ was, and if so – to what extent, the necessary condition for rise and attribution of responsibility.[86] Implementing these recommendations as the special rapporteur for the ILC, Ago in effect argued for the objective theory of responsibility.[87] Subsequently the Commission adopted his position as the basic assumption for the prepared draft articles, consequently stating that the constitutive and sufficient premises of state responsibility in all cases are the breach of an international obligation and the attribution thereof to the state, while other factors could be relevant in particular case, however they were not the necessary conditions of responsibility.[88] This approach was clarified and explained in the commentary to the final draft, which stressed that these "other factors" depended on the content of the violated obligation.[89] It is therefore impossible to specify them *in abstracto*, as additional premises of responsibility; they are simply elements of the content of the obligation, and in this respect, their very occurrence (or lack of it) would result in the violation of the obligation.

---

[86] *Report by Mr. Roberto Ago, Chairman of the Sub-Committee on State Responsibility*, U.N. Doc. A/CN.4/152, YbILC 1963, vol. II, para 6; Sh. Rosenne *The Perplexities...*, 391 ff. Rosenne recognizes the decision of the ILC, accepting the conclusions of the report as a guide for future work of the Commission and conferring Ago as Special Rapporteur on the topic State responsibility and the decision of the UN General Assembly, calling on the Commission to continue its work on this topic, taking into account the opinions expressed on the GA forum and included in the report of the subcommittee, as the turning point in the codification of the principles of state responsibility, but also in the way of thinking about the concept of international responsibility in general. He writes that these decisions "drew it from its nineteenth-century form and put their straight in the international legal order established by the Charter of the United Nations", which confirmed the need to adapt the concept of responsibility to the new conditions of coexistence of states under the UN order.

[87] Roberto Ago *Second report* (1970), U.N. Doc. A/CN.4/233; *Third report*, U.N. Doc. A/CN.4/246 and Add.1-3 (YbILC, 1971, vol. II (1)).

[88] Commentary to draft article 3, ILC Report (1973), (A/9010/Rev.1 (A/28/10)), para 11-12; para 12 *in fine*:

> „The Commission was thus able to conclude that the two elements respectively described as the 'subjective' element and the 'objective' element are the only necessary components of any internationally wrongful act. Other elements may be present in any particular case, or even in most cases, but are not indispensable."

[89] *Commentaries...*, (A/56/10), 73, para 9.

These other factors include fault, but the commentary of 1973 did not refer to it directly. On the contrary, it rather gives the impression that the use of the term was avoided, as well as any formulation which might suggest that taking into account of the fault, the mental condition, the personal position of the perpetrator, was necessary to establish responsibility.[90]

However, the reports of the last special rapporteur James Crawford and the final ILC draft articles with commentaries largely based thereon do not leave any room for doubt in this respect. Crawford points out that the huge diversity of international obligations and the diversity of their contents and standards of conduct does not allow the adoption of any general (applicable to all cases) requirement to maintain a specified standard or of occurrence of a specific factor in the psyche of the perpetrator as necessary for establishing state responsibility.[91] Accordingly fault, regardless of whether it is understood as a psychological category, or as compliance with an objective pattern of conduct cannot constitute a general constitutive premise of responsibility, distinct from the breach and imputability.[92]

At the same time, this does not mean that fault disappeared from the concept of international legal responsibility. The position of fault is assigned just to the content of the original primary norm which

---

[90] See e.g. the explanations on the use of a more neutral term "attribution" instead of "imputation" (or "imputability"), which has connotations with criminal law, indicating the mental condition and the will of the offender; on the uniform treatment of violations involving the act and the failure to act; on the categorical statement that only two conditions are necessary for establishing responsibility – commentary to draft article, ILC Report (1973), (A/9010/Rev.1 (A/28/10)), para 4 and 14. Also Vilenas Vadapalas "Codification of the Law of International Responsibility by the International Law Commission: Breach of International Law and its Consequences"; *Polish YbIL,* (1997-1998) vol. 23, 41.

[91] James Crawford *First report on State responsibility* U.N. Doc. A/CN.4/490/Add.4, 10, para 122.

[92] Ibidem. Also *Commentaries* ..., (A/56/10), 73, para 10. What is worth noting, none of the states submitting remarks on the ILC draft after the first reading, spoke in favour of recognition and inclusion of fault as an additional general premise of responsibility. On the contrary, some of them (e.g. the Nordic states in their common position), clearly stated that the element of fault is important at the level of primary norm, but it is not a separate condition of responsibility. *Comments and observations received from Governments,* U.N. Doc. A/CN.4/488 and Add.1, 2-3.

constitutes the source of the obligation.[93] Fault, even variously understood, may be the element of the content of a particular obligation, but certainly not of every obligation or every international standard. It may be formulated so that the violation will be possible only as a result of e.g. the intended conduct of the direct perpetrator (fault within the psychological meaning), but it can also provide a specific procedure, assessed from the point of view of due diligence (fault as a failure to observe the objectified standard of due diligence).[94] Therefore the examination of fault is, in such cases, shifted to the level of determining whether the obligation was infringed and only as such it is essential for establishing responsibility. However, the content of the norm may equally contain no reference to any psychological factor, due diligence, etc. And then the element of fault will not have any relevance for the existence of the violation and, consequently, for establishing responsibility.[95]

The element of fault, however, appears in the ILC draft articles, also in a different context – namely within the rules concerning the form and the scope of reparation in respect of the possible contribution of the affected state (as well as another entity on behalf of which it claims reparation).[96] Should such contribution be a result of an intentional or grossly negligent act or omission of the victim, it must be taken into account while determining the reparation, which is fully compatible with the principle of fairness and full compensation for the damage.[97] From this perspective, fault becomes a factor of assessment of the consequences of the victim's

---

[93] R. Pisillo-Mazzeschi "Due Diligence...", 21; *Commentaries* ..., (A/56/10), 70, para 3 and 10.

[94] As was the case in the above cited classic *Alabama Claims Arbitration*, where the obligation to maintain the standard of due diligence was explicitly indicated as an element of the obligation of a neutral state in the conflict of other states.

[95] G. Cottereau "Système juridique ...", 24; *Commentaries* ..., (A/56/10), 70, para 3.

[96] Art. 39 – *Draft Articles on Responsibility of States for Internationally Wrongful Acts*, text adopted by the ILC at its fifty-third session, YbILC 2001, (U.N. Doc. A/56/10), vol. II (Part Two), 43-59. *Commentaries* ..., (A/56/10), 275 ff

[97] Bernard Graefrath, 'Responsibility and Damage Caused: relations between responsibility and damages", RCADI, vol. 185 (1984-II), 95; Brigitte Bollecker-Stern, *Le préjudice dans la théorie de la responsabilité internationale*, Paris, 1973, 265-300. On the other hand, the view was also presented that fault (in particular intent) of the direct perpetrator should be regarded as a factor likely to aggravate the responsibility at the stage of determining the form and scope of reparations – A. Gattini "Smoking / No Smoking ...", 402 ff.; G. Cottereau "Système juridique ...", 23.

contribution, and it should be noted that only such circumstances may justify limitations to the scope of the reparation.[98]

However it does not seem appropriate to refer to fault in another context – the circumstances justifying exemption from international responsibility, although the proponents of the subjective theory used to specify these circumstances (at least some of them) as "excluding fault".[99] Without going into the details concerning the nature of these circumstances and their classification on the plane of international law,[100] it is necessary to provide at least a few basic observations. First of all, it should be noted that the catalog contained in Chapter V of the ILC draft articles does not exhaust all the legal circumstances, the occurrence of which may result in the exclusion of responsibility known in domestic law.[101] In particular, it lacks the circumstances traditionally excluding – on the basis of criminal and civil law – fault in the psychological sense, namely, insanity or diminished accountability (of the direct perpetrator). Additionally, the force majeure which is frequently relied on by the proponents of the subjective theory to the support of their case, as "disabling fault" of the perpetrator, in the domestic civil law systems it is regarded as a circumstance excluding liability independent of fault and based on the principle of risk. Considering that the concept of responsibility based on fault was transposed to the international law by analogy to the domestic law, one may note that their arguments fell into, at least, inconsistency.

---

[98] *Commentaries...*, (A/56/10), 276, para 5.

[99] Chapter V of the ILC draft articles (art. 20-27) Circumstances precluding wrongfulness lists: consent, self-defence, countermeasures, force majeure, distress and necessity. The use of the term "circumstances excluding guilt" was most frequent in relation to the force majeure and the fortuitous event (the latter was dropped in the final text of the draft articles) – cf. Ago's arguments in favour of the fault theory in *Le Délit* ..., 939 ff.; A. Gattini "La notion de faute...", 268 ff.; A. Gattini "Smoking / No Smoking...", 401; K. Zemanek, "Responsabilité des Etats ...", 38.

[100] Vaughan Lowe "Precluding Wrongfulness or Responsibility: a Plea for Excuses", EJIL vol.10, issue 2, 405-411; Jean Salmon "Les circonstances excluant l'illiceité", in Karl Zemanek, Jean Salmon *Responsabilité internationale*, Paris 1987, 89-225. Also *Draft articles adopted on first reading - Text of articles with commentaries*, U.N. Doc. A/CN.4/L.528/Add.3, commentary to Chapter V, para 1-11; James Crawford *Second report on State responsibility* U.N. Doc. A/CN.4/498/Add. 2, para 221-229.

[101] W. Czapliński "Kodyfikacja prawa o odpowiedzialności międzynarodowej państw", *Studia Prawnicze* 4 (154) /2002, 39-40; *Commentaries* ..., (A/56/10), 172; Christian von Bar *The Common European Law of Torts*, Munich 2000, vol. II, 499-592.

Simultaneously, most of the international law scholars consistently use the concept of the circumstances excluding the unlawfulness of the conduct or the responsibility of the state (which, however, are not synonyms), without any references to "fault" in this respect.[102] This approach was also adopted in the work of the ILC on state responsibility: in the reports of the special rapporteurs from Ago to Crawford and in the subsequent versions of the draft articles up to the final 2001 text the notion of "circumstances precluding wrongfulness" is used.[103] Essentially none of the factors listed in Chapter V excludes responsibility, i.e. legalizes the consequences of the violation, but they primarily prevent qualification of the conduct which otherwise would be a source of responsibility as "unlawful".[104] The ILC also draws attention to the least theoretical possibility of constructing the circumstances excluding international responsibility, which would not repeal the unlawfulness of the act.[105] Actually, in the domestic legal order, these type of circumstances are such, that the occurrence thereof disables the capability to assign fault of the perpetrator – so they are essential in the system of responsibility based on fault.[106] However, after analyzing the Commission's position thereon, as expressed in the extensive commentary adopted to the first version of the draft articles, Crawford concludes:

---

[102] P. Reuter "La responsabilité internationale...", 554; J Salmon "Les circonstances ...", 89 ff.; V. Lowe "Precluding ...", 405 ff.; Julio Barboza "Necessity (Revisited) in International Law", in *Essays in International Law in Honour of Judge Manfred Lachs* edited by Jerzy Makarczyk, The Hague 1984, 31 ff.; Nguyen Quoc Dinh, P. Daillier, A. Pellet *Droit international* ..., 782 ff.; Alfred Verdross, Bruno Simma *Universelles Völkerrecht*, Berlin 1981, 627.

[103] Roberto Ago *Eighth report on State responsibility*, U.N. Doc A/CN.4/318, Add. 1-4 YbILC, 1979, vol. II (1); J. Crawford *Second report* ... U.N. Doc. A/CN.4/498/Add. 2; *Draft articles adopted on first* ..., U.N. Doc. A/CN.4/L.528/Add. 3; *Commentaries* ..., (A/56/10), 169 ff.

[104] *Draft articles adopted on first* ..., commentary to Chapter V, para 2; J. Crawford *Second report* ..., para 221.

[105] *Draft articles adopted on first* ..., commentary to Chapter V, para 2-4.

[106] In such a situation, the lack of fault and exemption from responsibility, mostly due to the insanity of the perpetrator (but not only), does not in itself set aside the illegality of the conduct, neither in criminal law (where it is possible to apply to such person a preventive measure e.g. in the form of detention in a mental institution), nor in civil law (where it is possible to bring claim for damages against another person or, in exceptional cases, against the direct perpetrator on the basis of *ex aequo et bono* principle).

"The commentary concedes that, despite the general language of article 1, there could be circumstances precluding responsibility which did not preclude the wrongfulness of the act in question, but which preclude the State in question from being held responsible for it. But it denies that there would be any point in characterizing an act as wrongful without holding some State responsible."[107]

It follows that, according to the ILC, there is no rational justification for the exclusion of international responsibility for an act which in fact is "unlawful". Traditional circumstances excluding fault are different in nature from those contained in the ILC draft articles, lack of fault does not constitute a negative premise of responsibility, neither explicit nor hidden under any of those listed in Chapter V. The use of the phrase "circumstances excluding fault" in reference to the factors which justify exemption from international responsibility is partly due to the problem with a clear definition of the concept of fault in international law which, as already discussed above, was sometimes used in the doctrine and the practice of international law as synonymous to the mere concept of breach of legal norm. In particular Jean Salmon notes, giving examples of references of this kind of fault in the judicial and arbitral practice, that in the light of the content of the examined decisions, "no fault" in essence means "no violation".[108] From this perspective, the problem is rather terminological, since on the merits one still has to deal with the circumstances excluding wrongfulness.

5. Conclusion

The eventual adoption of objective concept within the contemporary regulation of international responsibility does not lead – as it might seem at first glance – to the erasure of the element of fault from international law. Rather, the shift from the subjective to the objective theory of responsibility, which effectuated over the years, contributed to the determination of the proper status of fault within the system of international responsibility, taking also into account how diversely this notion may be understood. The "right place" of fault was found at the level of the primary international obligation: fault of the direct perpetrator, or rather lack thereof, can be a part of the content of the obligation. Therefore, the fault factor is depending just on the content of the

---

[107] *Draft articles adopted on first* ..., commentary to Chapter V, para 2-4; J. Crawford *Second report*..., para 221.

[108] J. Salmon "Les circonstances ...", 109-111.

obligation, and so it can be relevant or even decisive for determining whether there was a breach of this obligation. The basic premises of international responsibility – i.e. a breach of an international obligation and its attributability to the state – remain constant and independent of the content of the obligation. Thus the fault factor becomes an element of the conduct constituting the violation and in this way – but only in this way – in certain circumstances, it can affect the international responsibility of the state. This solution also has the huge advantage that takes into account the different meanings of the concept of fault, both as a psychological factor, as well as compliance with the objectivized standard of due diligence. It allows for a conflict-free, parallel operation of both of them, because the question which concept of fault is appropriate, is settled out case by case, depending on the content of the obligation. Moreover, both concepts of fault are not mutually exclusive as elements of the same obligation, as it may provide for both: a certain standard of conduct and a certain psychological attitude of the state's agent.

As the deliberations above show in respect of responsibility and fault, the concepts and rules of the domestic law are usually not easily transferable into international legal order. The use of the domestic law analogy in the international law always requires caution, sensibility and deep awareness of the particular characteristics of the international legal order. Nevertheless, even if the domestic law solutions , as in the case of fault, are not entirely suitable for the international plane, they still may inspire academic discourse and contribute to the development of specific theories and practical regulations to the legal issues of international law.

Bibliography

Abi-Saab Georges."The Uses of Article 19". EJIL 1999, vol.10 issue 2

Ago Roberto.*Le Délit International*.RCADI, 1939 (II) vol. 68

Anzilotti Dionisio.La responsabilité internationale des Etats à raison des dommages souferts par des étrangers.RGDIP 1906, vol. 13

Anzilotti Dionisio *Corso di diritto internazionale*, Roma 1927, French translation by Gilbert Gidel *Cours de droit international* , Paris 1929.

Anzilotti Dionisio. *Teoria generale della responsabilità dello stato nel dirtto internazionale.*Firenze 1902

Barboza Julio.Necessity (Revisited) in International Law.in *Essays in International Law in Honour of Judge Manfred Lachs* edited by Jerzy Makarczyk.The Hague 1984

Bedjaoui Mohammed .Responsibility of States: Fault and Strict Liability.in *Encyclopaedia of Public International Law* edited by Rudolf Bernhardt, Vol. IV, Elsevier 2000

Bierzanek Remigiusz.Symonides Janusz *Prawo międzynarodowe publiczne.*Warszawa 2004

Bollecker-Stern Brigitte. *Le préjudice dans la théorie de la responsabilité international*.Paris, 1973

Brownlie.Ian *Principles of Public International Law*.Oxford 2008

Crawford James and Simon Olleson."The Nature and Forms of International Responsibility".in *International Law* edited by Malcolm D. Evans, Oxford 2003

Czaplińska Anna. *Odpowiedzialność organizacji międzynarodowych jako element uniwersalnego systemu odpowiedzialności międzynarodowoprawne*.Łodź, 2014

Czapliński Władysław. "Kodyfikacja prawa o odpowiedzialności międzynarodowej państw".*Studia Prawnicze* 4 (154) /2002

Czapliński Władysław.Wyrozumska Anna *Prawo międzynarodowe publiczne, zagadnienia systemowe*. Warszawa 2014

Dąbrowa Janina.*Wina jako przesłanka odpowiedzialności cywilnej*.Wrocław 1968

de Fiumel, Henryk."W sprawie pojęcia odpowiedzialności państwa we współczesnym prawie międzynarodowym".*Państwo i Prawo* No 3/1976,

Dupuy Pierre-Marie."Dionisio Anzilotti and the Law of International Responsibility of States".EJIL 1992, vol. 3

Ehrlich, Ludwik.*Prawo międzynarodowe*.Warszawa 1958

Fauchille, Paul.*Traité de droit international public*.Vol. I, Paris 1921

Gattini, Andrea."La notion de faute à la lumière du projet de convention de la Commission du Droit International sur la responsabilité internationale".EJIL 1992, vol. 3

Gattini, Andrea."Smoking / No Smoking: Some Remarks on the Current Place of Fault in the ILC Draft Articles on State Responsibility".EJIL 1999, vol. 10 issue 2

Graefrath Bernard, "Responsibility and Damage Caused: relations between responsibility and damages". RCADI, vol. 185 (1984-II)

Iwanejko, Marian."Świadomość jako przesłanka odpowiedzialności państwa w prawie międzynarodowym. Wypadek cieśniny Korfu.*Zeszyty Naukowe UJ* 1961

Jabbari-Gharabagh, Mansour.Type of State Responsibility for Environmental Matters in International Law".RJT 1999, vol. 33

Jiménez, de Aréchaga Eduardo."International Responsibility".in *Manual of Public International Law* edited by Max Sørensen, London 1968

Klafkowski, Alfons.*Prawo międzynarodowe publiczne*.Warszawa 1966

Kuris, Pranas M.*Mieżdunarodnyje prawonaruszenija i otwietstwiennost' gosudarstw*.Vilnius 1973

Lauterpacht, Hersh. *The Developement of International Law by the International Court*.London 1958

Lewaszkiewicz-Petrykowska, Biruta."Wina jako podstawa odpowiedzialności z tytułu czynów niedozwolonych".*Studia Prawno-Ekonomiczne* issue 2/1969

Lowe, Vaughan."Precluding Wrongfulness or Responsibility: a Plea for Excuses".EJIL vol.10, issue 2

Majewski, Jarosław and Kardas, Piotr."O dwóch znaczeniach winy w prawie karnym". *Państwo i Prawo* issue 10/1993

Marek, Krystyna."Criminalizing State Responsibility". RBDI, vol. XIV, 1978-79

Matsui, Yuko."The Transformation of the Law of State Responsibility". *Thesaurus Acroasium*, 1993, vol. 20

Nguyen, Quoc Dinh, Patrick, Daillier and Allain Pellet.*Droit international public*.Paris 2002

Nolte, Georg."From Dionisio Anzilotti to Roberto Ago: The Classical International Law of State Responsibility and the Traditional Primacy of a Bilateral Conception of Inter-State Relations".EJIL 2002, vol. 13

Oppenheim's *International Law* Vol. I *Peace – Introduction and Part 1*, edited by R. Jennings, A. Watts, London 1996

Oppenheim's *International Law*, edited by Hersh Lauterpacht, 8th edition, London 1955, vol. I

Pisillo-Mazzeschi, Ricardo."Due Diligence and the International Responsibility of States". GerYbIL 1992, vol. 35

Quéneudec, Jean-Pierre.*La responsabilité internationale de l'Etat pour les fautes personnelles de ses agents*.Paris 1966

Rejman, Genowefa *Teorie i formy winy w prawie karnym*, Warszawa 1980

Reuter, Paul."La responsabilité internationale – Problèmes choisis (cours de doctorat professé pendant l'année universitaire 1955-1956)".in Paul Reuter *Le développement de l'ordre juridique international – Ecrits de droit international*, Paris 1995,

Rosenne, Shabtai.*The Perplexities of Modern International Law*. RCADI 2001, vol. 291

Salmon, Jean."Les circonstances excluant l'illiceité.in Karl Zemanek, Jean Salmon *Responsabilité internationale*, Paris 1987

Salvioli, Gabriele.*Les règles générales de la paix*. RCADI 1933 (IV), vol. 46

Seidel, Peter."The Alabama".in EPIL edited by R. Bernhardt, Vol. I, Elsevier 1992

Shaw, Malcolm.N. *International Law*.Cambridge 2008,

Skubiszewski, Krzysztof."Odpowiedzialność międzynarodowa".in *Zarys prawa międzynarodowego publicznego* edited by Marian Muszkat, Warszawa 1956, vol. II

Sonnenfeld, Renata."Podstawowe zasady odpowiedzialności międzynarodowej państwa".in *Odpowiedzialność państwa w prawie międzynarodowym* edited by Renata Sonnenfeld, Warszawa 1980

Steiner, Otto."Spanish Zone of Morocco Claims".in EPIL edited by R. Bernhardt, Vol. IV, Elsevier 2000

Szpunar, Adam."Czyny niedozwolone w kodeksie cywilnym".*Studia Cywilistyczne* vol. XV, 1970

Triepel, Heinrich.*Völkerecht und Landesrecht*.Leipzig 1899

Vadapalas, Vilenas."Codification of the Law of International Responsibility by the International Law Commission: Breach of International Law and its Consequences". *Polish YbIL*, (1997-1998) vol. 23

Verdross, Alfred and Bruno Simma. *Universelles Völkerrecht*.Berlin 1981
von Bar Christian. *The Common European Law of Torts*.Munich 2000, vol. II
Zemanek, Karl."Responsabilité des Etats pour faits internationalement illicites, ainsi que pour faits internationalement licites".in Karl Zemanek, Jean Salmon *Responsabilité internationale*, Paris 1987
Zemanek, Karl."Responsibility of States: General Principles".in *EPIL* edited by R. Bernhardt, Vol. IV, Elsevier 2000
The S.S. Wimbledon Case, PCIJ, A Series, No 1 (1923)
Certain German interests in Polish Upper Silesia Case (Merits), PCIJ, A Series, No 7 (1926)
The Factory of Chorzów Case (Merits), PCIJ, A Series, No 17 (1928)
Diversion of water from the Meuse Case, PCIJ, A/B Series, No 70 (1937)
Corfu Channel Case (UK v. Albania), ICJ Reports 1949
Alabama Claims Arbitration (USA v. UK), award of 14 September 1872 r., published in *History and Digest of the International Arbitrations to which the United States Has Been a Party* edited by John B. Moore, Washington 1898, vol. I
Home Missionary Society Claim (USA v. UK), 1920 r., RIAA vol. VI
The Jessie, The Thomas F. Bayard & The Pescawha Claim (Great Britain v. USA), 1921 RIAA vol. VI
Max Huber, 3rd report of 24 October 1924 *British claims in the Spanish zone of Morocco*, RIAA vol. II
Neer Claim (USA v. Mexico), 1926, RIAA vol. IV, 61-62;
Roberts Claim (USA v. Mexico), 1926, RIAA vol. IV, 80;
Quintanilla Claim (Mexico v. USA), 1926 RIAA, vol. IV
Chattin Claim (USA v. Mexico), 1927 RIAA, vol. IV
Caire Claim (France v. Mexico), 1929, RIAA vol. V
Treaty between Great Britain and the United States for the Amicable Setting of All Causes of Difference between the Two Countries, Signed at Washington, 8 May, 1871, [1871 Treaty of Washington], in *The Consolidated Treaty Series* edited by Clive Parry, New York 1977, vol. 143
Report by Mr. Roberto Ago, Chairman of the Sub-Committee on State Responsibility, U.N. Doc. A/CN.4/152, YbILC 1963, vol. II
Roberto Ago *Second Report on State Responsibility – Origin of International Responsibility*, U.N. Doc. A/CN.4/233, YbILC, 1970, vol. II
Roberto Ago *Third report on State Responsibility*, U.N. Doc. A/CN.4/246 and Add.1-3 (YbILC, 1971, vol. II (1))
Commentary to draft article 1 adopted by the ILC during its 25th session in 1973 (YbILC, 1973, vol. II)
Roberto Ago *Eighth report on State responsibility*, U.N. Doc A/CN.4/318, Add. 1-4 YbILC, 1979, vol. II (1)
James Crawford *First Report on State Responsibility, Addendum (1)*, (1998) UN Doc. A/CN.4/490/Add.1
James Crawford *First report on State responsibility* U.N. Doc. A/CN.4/490/Add.4

James Crawford *Second report on State responsibility* U.N. Doc. A/CN.4/498/Add. 2

Comments and observations received from Governments, U.N. Doc. A/CN.4/488 and Add.1 (1998)

Draft articles adopted on first reading - Text of articles with commentaries, U.N. Doc. A/CN.4/L.528/Add.3, YbILC 1996 vol. II (2)

Draft Articles on Responsibility of States for Internationally Wrongful Acts, text adopted by the ILC at its fifty-third session, YbILC 2001, vol. II (2)

Commentaries to the draft articles on Responsibility of States for internationally wrongful acts, ILC Report 53rd Session (2001), YbILC 2001, vol. II (2)

Chapter 17

A Mixture of Civil and Common Legal Systems? An Example of Trend of Taiwan's Legal Development on Information Technology

Chun Hung Lin[1]

Abstract

This essay aims to describe and examine the new trend of Taiwan's legal development especially Information Technology Law in Taiwan. The legal culture in Taiwan has not only ancient legal traditions but also stout foreign colors, as a result of the Western imperialism in the 16th century and from the late 19th to mid-20th centuries. The Portuguese, Dutch, and Japanese had sooner and later ruled the Island for a certain period and brought different legal traditions into Taiwan. The resulting legal system was then based on the Western European legal regime. From then on, the Taiwanese legal system, with substantial European traits, can be considered as a member of the family of "civil law" systems. After the end of World War II, the Nationalist government withdrew from mainland China and endeavored to create a freer market as well as democracy on this small island. The Nationalist government brought the new Chinese legal system from Mainland China to Taiwan, a landmark event in Taiwanese legal development in 1945. Due to both geographical advantages and the scarceness of natural resources, Taiwan has developed a trade-oriented economy with high speed and has inserted its market into the international community. However, under the strong influences and pressures of trade negotiations from the United States, the main economic regulations in

---

[1] Chairman & Professor Graduate Institute of Financial and Economic Law Feng Chia University

Taiwan has adjusted to fit into international requirements guided by the US administrations. Those legal adjustments include the laws for the protection of natural environment and intellectual property, as well as the liberalization of telecommunications, banking and financial services, etc. Those adjustments have led Taiwan legal system swift to common law by the US influences.

In addition, because of the rapid creation of new technology and the growth of economic development, the government has adopted a series of steps to restructure its legislation to fit international requirements. The globalization and deregulation of telecommunications have caused intense discussions and debates. Because Information Technology is one of the more strategic industries and also relates to national security, social order, and commercial transactions, its restructuring has been a politically highly charged issue. Reviewing the development of legal history and the formation of its economic market, one may conclude that Taiwan, in general, has been strongly touched by foreign influences and has tended toward internationalization. Does Taiwan's legislative development still follow this model, a mixture of Civil and Common Legal Systems? Or has the government already found a particular way to structure its own legal system especially on information technology law? If the legislature follows a particular pre-existing model to establish the legal system, which model of legislation will it adopt and why? This essay will discuss the role of international influences on the restructuring of the information technology industry in Taiwan. It will examine the impacts of foreign legislation on the reform process and review the background of the Taiwanese legal system as well as the development of the information technology industries in order to witness foreign effects on the Taiwanese legal adjustments.

Introduction

The Taiwanese legal culture had not only ancient Chinese influences but also stout foreign colors, as a result of the Western imperialism in the 16th and from the late 19th to mid-20th century. In 1945, the Nationalist government brought the new Chinese legal system from Mainland China into Taiwan and branded as the landmark event on Taiwanese legal development. The resulting legal system is based on the distinctive Chinese legal traditions and the Western European legal regime. From then on, the Taiwanese legal system has been Europeanized and can be ranked as one member of the family of civil law systems. In the following three decades, Taiwanese people and the Nationalist government endeavored to create a freer market as well as democracy on this small island. Due to geographical advantages as well as the scarceness of natural resources, Taiwan has developed a trade-oriented economy with high-speed and inserted its market into the international community. In addition, because of the rapid creation of new technology and the growth of economic development, the Taiwanese government has adopted a series of steps to restructure its legislation to fit international requirements. Those legal adjustments include the protection of natural environment and intellectual property, as well as the liberalization of telecommunication, banking, and financial services, etc. Meanwhile, the globalization and deregulation of telecommunications have caused intense discussions and debates. Because telecommunication is one of the most strategic industries and also relates to national security, social order, and commercial transactions, its restructuring has been a highly charged issue.

Reviewing the development of legal history and the formation of the economic market, Taiwan has been strongly influenced by foreign influences and tended to internationalization. Did Taiwan's telecommunication legislative development still follow this model or the government already find a particular way to structure its own telecommunication legal system? If Taiwan's legislatures follow the prior model to establish the telecommunication legal system, which country's legislation they will adopt and why? In addition, how did international telecommunication and trade agreements influence on Taiwan's telecommunication development? And how did the Taiwanese government adopt those agreements into its telecommunication regulations? Does the Taiwanese government also choose a freer economic environment and raise the percentage of foreign investment to make itself more competitive in the international telecommunication market? From historical reviews, this article will discuss the role of international influences on the restructuring of the telecommunications industry in Taiwan. It will examine the impact of international agreements and foreign legislation on the reform process. First, the article will review the background of the Taiwanese legal system and the development of telecommunication industries to witness international and foreign effects to the Taiwanese telecommunications sector. Secondly, the article will explore the effects of international agreements and foreign legislation on the legal codes of the current telecommunications regulations. Furthermore, it will survey the role of the regulatory authority, including the limitation of foreign ownership, the classification of services, the issues of labor participation, the prohibition of cross-subsidization and the establishment of the dispute resolution committee. Finally, the article will make a conclusion to prove the reality and strength of international effects on Taiwanese telecommunications regulations.

1. Taiwanese Legal System and the Impacts of International Regulations and Foreign Legislations

Taiwanese legal system is a blend of the distinctive Chinese heritage with strong Western influences. From the 18th and 19th centuries, thousands of Mainland Chinese had increasingly immigrated from Fujian and Guangdong Provinces to Taiwan Island supplanting aborigines as the dominant population group in this island. They brought not only the culture and lifestyle, but the Mainland Chinese also imported Imperial China's political and legal system to Taiwan. During that period, ancient Chinese legal tradition and customs ruled the old Taiwanese society. Within ancient Chinese society, Confucianism and the social order played the most important role in Chinese ethical thought and behavior. Legislation was simply complementary in Chinese social order, based as it was on the notion of social status. Chinese had followed other paths to search for justice rather than law.[2]

In 1896, Japan took Taiwan from the Ch'ing Dynasty as its first colony.[3] In order to completely control this island, the Japanese colonial government ruled Taiwanese by high-pressure rules. During fifty years of the colonial period, Japanese rule led to the "Japanization" of the island. In the beginning, the Japanese government kept the Taiwanese legal traditions intact.[4] They chose to recognize and respect some Taiwanese traditional social norms such as family practices in order to placate old Taiwan's society.[5] Since 1923, the Japanese legal system replaced the Imperial Chinese legal tradition to govern Taiwanese society.[6] Specifically, Japanese exerted their criminal and land legal system for control over Taiwanese society. There was a tendency to apply all Japanese laws to Taiwanese society during the 1920s. This change marked the point at which Taiwanese legal history separated from that of Imperial China. By 1945, most of the Imperial Chinese legal traditions and Taiwanese customs had been replaced with Japanese rules.

---

[2] Tung-Tsu, Chu, *Law and Society in Traditional China*, in: Hyperion Pr, (1979)

[3] In 1895, Ch'ing Dynasty was defeated by Japan in the first Sino-Japanese war and ceded Taiwan to Japan in the Treaty of Shimonoseki.

[4] Chaui-Ru, Chen, *The History of the Right to Divorce – The Establishment and Meaning of Taiwanese Women's Right to Divorce*, Source: LL.M. thesis, National Taiwan University, (1997), 69-79.

[5] Ibid.

[6] Tay-Sheng Wang, *The Westernization of Taiwanese Legal System for One Hundred Years*, in: *The Establishment of Taiwanese Legal History*, (1996), 343-78, 362.

At the end of World War II in 1945, Taiwan reverted to Chinese rule.[7] The Imperial Chinese Code and Taiwanese custom law prevailed in Taiwan until 1945, when the Japanese colonial period ended. In 1945, the Nationalist government from Mainland China took over Taiwan and brought the new Chinese legal system.[8] The new Chinese legal system was established following the Republic Revolution of 1911.[9] Due to the effects of domination, the republic regime of China had adopted a series of codes manifestly based on western models including the Civil Code in 1929, the Land Code in 1930, and the Civil Procedure in 1932. The current new Chinese legal system has been Europeanized and can be ranked within the family of laws deriving from the Romanist tradition.[10] Those codes are still in force in Taiwan.

Generally speaking, the Taiwanese legal system belongs to the civil law system and based largely on German, Swiss, and Japanese models. Taiwanese legal system also incorporates a good deal of Chinese legal traditions. In an effort to deal with modern economic development and adjusting itself toward the international community, Taiwanese government recently adopted and amended several regulations including intellectual property, environmental protection, telecommunication, maritime, banking and financial rules, immigration and emigration, as well as professional personnel laws for further deregulation and globalization. Obviously, Taiwanese legal system is rooted in Western European civil law system as well as Chinese traditional customs, but recently tends to adjust its legislative direction to conform rules and provisions of treaties and international agreements.

2. International Influences on Taiwan's Old Telecommunication Regulations Reform

Not only Taiwanese legislation but also its economic development is evolving toward internationalization. Beginning with the lifting of the ban on newspaper registration in January 1988, the related telecommunication liberalizations have been variously implemented in just a few years. The

---

[7] The Anti-Japanese War lasted eight years. Chinese people defeated Japanese and won the war.

[8] Wang, above n.5, 362.

[9] In the 1911 Revolution, Chinese people led by the KMT overthrew the Ch'ing Dynasty and the Republic of China (ROC) was established.

[10] Rene David & John E. C. Brierley, *Major Legal Systems in the World Today*, in: Stevens & Sons (3rd ed.), (1985), 523, London, England.

essential changes included the openness of cable TV, the release of broadcast frequencies, and the proliferation of the print media. For accession to the WTO, Taiwan had both significantly opened its telecommunication market to foreign investment and amended dozens of telecommunication regulations to fit the requirements of the WTO.[11] For example, the percentage of foreign ownership on cable TV networks also was increased from 20 to 50 percent in 1999. Satellite broadcasting was also opened to foreign investment and allowed up to 50 percent foreign ownership in the Satellite Broadcasting Law.

Changes in the international telecommunication regime as well as foreign legislations had a major impact on Taiwan's telecommunication development. In addition, the WTO members started to negotiate the liberalization of basic telecommunications services and proceeded negotiations on basic telecommunications services in Geneva in 1997. In early 1998, the European Union decided to liberalize telephone competition and introduced free and full competition among its members in basic telecommunications service. At the same time, the monopoly situation in Taiwan became undesirable, and the DGT began studies on liberalization.[12]

In the late 1980s, the old DGT began to permit private domestic companies to provide limited value-added telecommunications services. However, the process of liberalization was still slow. In the mid-1980s, under foreign trade pressure, the DGT made a decision about procurement of switching equipment that led to a three-way oligopoly. Each equipment supplier in northern, central, and southern Taiwan would set up as an international joint venture affiliated with DGT. In addition, under the old Telecommunications Act of 1958, foreign ownership of any type of telecommunications service was barred. If Taiwan had liberalized its telecommunications market for only domestic companies under the 1958 legislation without allowing foreign participation, it would have seriously violated the national treatment principle of the WTO. In this regard, the Taiwanese government had created several telecommunication bills to replace the 1958 Act. Under the mechanism of WTO, each member is required to treat other WTO members on "non-discriminatory" basis,

---

[11] After its long-run application over ten years, Taipei's entry to the WTO finally concluded in 2002, by the name of "the Separate Customs Territory of Taiwan, Penghu, Kinmen, and Matsu."

[12] Lawrence S. Liu, *Telecommunications Market Liberalization in Taiwan: Political and Legal Issues*, E. Asian Executive Reports, (1996), Taipei, Taiwan.

which is referred to the principles of "Most-Favoured-Nation" (MFN)[13] and "National Treatment" (NT).[14] MFN prohibits WTO Members from discriminating among themselves or treating other members less favorably than any other member. Based on such non-discriminatory rule, the GATS Annex on Telecommunication also regulated that each member shall ensure that any service supplier of any other WTO member is accorded access to and use of public telecommunications transport networks and services on reasonable and non-discriminatory terms and conditions in the telecommunications sector.[15] The principle of transparency is also regulated under the GATS to require members to make public their laws, rules and regulations affecting trade in services, so that service suppliers can know the rules under which they can do business.[16] Because transparency is one of the barriers in many telecommunications markets, this rule is one of the most important features of the Annex to achieve a fairer trade system on the telecommunication sector. To fit those requirements, the Taiwanese government began to introduce foreign operators into the telecommunications market and provide a freer competition environment.

Facing domestic demands and foreign pressures, the government had to adopt a series of legal adjustments on telecommunications. For example, the government made a formal policy to begin free competition and permit interregional investment in the mobile telecommunications

---

[13] Under GATS, MFN is defined "each Member shall accord immediately and unconditionally to services and service suppliers of any other Member treatment no less favourable than that it accords to like services and service suppliers of any other country." See GATS, art. 2(1).

[14] National treatment requires that each member "shall accord to services and service suppliers of any other member... treatment no less favourable than that it accords to its own like service and service supplies." See GATS art. 2(2).

[15] See GATS Annex on Telecommunications Paragraph 5(a). The term "non-discriminatory" is understood to refer to most-favoured-nation and national treatment as defined in the Agreement, as well as to reflect sector-specific usage of the term to mean "terms and conditions no less favourable than those accorded to any other user of like public telecommunications transport networks or services under like circumstances."

[16] Under the paragraph IV of the GATS Annex on Telecommunications states, "each Member shall ensure that relevant information on conditions affecting access to and use of public telecommunications transport networks and services is publicly available."

segment including mobile phones, paging, mobile data, and trunk radio.[17] Under the 1996 Act, foreign companies started to enjoy no ownership limitation on investing in Value-Added Services, which include Internet services, teleconferencing, the operation of automated cash machines, electronic bulletin boards and fax services. Afterward, foreign operators had raised twenty to forty-nine percent investment limit on wireless services, which include mobile phones, pagers, trunk radio communication, mobile data communications, and very small aperture satellite terminal (VSAT) services.[18]

Due to Taiwan's democracy and special status in the international community, political factors continue to add spice to further telecommunications reform initiatives in its dynamic economy.[19] For international firms and partners, such a specific political and economic background in Taiwan will also be an arduous challenge. As to Taiwan's telecommunications development, the 1996 telecommunications reform largely guided by the MOTC is still considered to be too conservative and fails to reflect current developments in global telecommunication industries. Therefore, how to speed the process of the telecommunication reform and adjust Taiwan into international telecommunications trends will determine the success of Taiwan's future ambitions in the international telecommunication market.

3. Changes of Taiwan's Telecommunication Act

After long discussions and domestic pressures, the original DGT had to change its functions, and the government adopted the US commission model – the creation of the National Communications Commission (NCC). The NCC is an independent statutory agency created in 2006 to regulate the information, communications and broadcasting industry in Taiwan. NCC was tasked with the responsibility to ensure a level playing field in competition in the communications industry, consumer protection, privacy

---

[17] There would be up to 8 regional mobile telephone operators, 8 regional paging operators, 24 trunk radio operators, and 21 regional mobile data operators to open for applications and registrations. The telecommunications legislation would allow the MOTC to schedule from March 1996 to begin receiving applications to provide those types of telecommunications whose liberalization had been promised in 1994 for implementation by the end of 1995.

[18] Anne Phelan, *Taiwan Passes Telecom Laws*, E. Asian Executive Reports, (1996).

[19] Lawrence S. Liu, *Aspiring To Excel--The Uneasy Case Of Implementing Taiwan's Asia — Pacific Regional Operations Center Plan*, Sp. Columbia JAL, (1996).

rights, and the development of universal service for remote and rural regions. It also developed new standards for emerging technologies that will improve access, lower cost and deliver services to remote areas. It landmarked the establishment of NCC a step of more independent and flexible communication environment. Not only the statutory agency, but the communication bill also has planned the fundamental changes after years of study and preparation.

The NCC had released the proposed text of a series of five new laws intended to promote digital convergence. The five draft acts cover electronic communication, telecom infrastructure and resources, cable systems, telecom services, and terrestrial television. The NCC designed them to replace the existing Radio and Television Act, Satellite Broadcasting Act, Cable Television Act, and Telecommunications Act. The new acts were drafted after reflection on the communication policies and trade agreements that have been implemented by the international community. The NCC had planned to merge the proposed provisions covering telecom services and telecom infrastructure, as well as conduct an additional review of the current Telecommunications Act, and then combined all of the proposed legislation into a single act to regulate the telecom sector. For the purpose, the government announced its Digital Convergence Development Policy in 2010, designed to create new legislation to reflect technological changes that blurred the lines between services offered by different types of telecom platforms. But the complexity of the task made it a long and drawn-out process. The NCC also had addressed longstanding industry concerns about unregulated over-the-top content (OTT) – media content delivered directly to viewers over the Internet that bypasses traditional cable and satellite TV services. The telecom and media industry has long urged the NCC to take on the OTT issue because unfair competition is hitting their bottom line. The NCC thus would enact "relatively light" regulation of OTT while relaxing restrictions on the cable industry to ensure fair competition. Possible changes to existing regulations may include a loosening of the rate cap on cable providers, so they are able to charge a higher fee to subscribers as well as a move to charge cable subscribers by set-top box rather than household. Those proposal changes mark the Taiwan future telecommunication legislation would be still under the international requirements.

4. Conclusion

Following the creation of advanced technology and the openness of the telecommunications market, the telecommunication reforms in North

America and Europe had gradually been liberalized and internationalized. The WTO also required its members to fit the rules of GATS and Annex on the basic telecommunications. The European Union decided to liberalize telephone competition and introduce full competition among its members in basic telecommunications services. Facing such changes, the Taiwanese government has restructured its legislation for further deregulation and globalization since the early 1980s. The monopolistic telecommunications situation in Taiwan became undesirable and demanded legal adjustments to fit international requirements. Subsequently, Taiwan has both significantly opened its telecommunication market to foreign investment and amended many provisions of telecommunication regulations to avoid the violation of the principle of non-discrimination under the WTO agreement.

To conform to foreign legislation, Taiwan's TA had separated operational businesses from old regulatory authority. For the role of the regulatory authority, the American inter-ministry communications commission model and European ministerial telecommunications directorate model had been mixed and adopted in Taiwan on a certain period, but finally adopt the US way – commission model. In addition, the Act also has removed the limitation of foreign investment and gave increased preferential treatments to foreign telecommunications investors time by time. To meet the ITU's missions and the meaning of the right to telecommunication, the act also incorporated the provision concerning universal access and prohibition of service discrimination. In the Taipei-Washington bilateral trade negotiations, Taiwan's telecommunication regulatory authority followed the US requirements to adopt the merits of price capping and amending the pricing formula for the tariff. Considering the failure of the privation of the Japanese NTT Company, the Act had conducted a rate-rebalancing program to reduce cross-subsidization. As to the issues of labor participation and board qualifications, Taiwan's labor activists specifically referred to employee participation legislation in certain European and socialist countries including German and French Telecommunications regulations to strive for labor rights. Those implementations all show Taiwan's Telecommunication Act is blends of international agreements and foreign legislation. Furthermore, due to Taiwan's special status and current politic dilemma, the telecommunication reforms yielded to domestic pressures and included some special provision such as posterior audit, the formation of the Dispute Resolution Committee, and the twenty percentage of foreign investment limitation.

Generally speaking, Taiwan's Telecommunication Act has adopted several steps to fit the goals of a much more competitive market, universal access, and nondiscrimination services. It tends to not only correspond to international requirements but also domestic demands. These include independent regulatory authority, release of the limit of foreign ownership, protection of privacy and confidentiality, prohibition of cross-subsidization and service discrimination, as well as tariff liberalization, etc. Obviously, the major factor that impacts Taiwan's current telecommunications developments is the change of international telecommunications regime and foreign legislation. It is believed that not only foreign legislations but also multinational corporations will increase their influences on Taiwan's telecommunications development, reform, and legislation. Although the current Telecommunications legislation went through several legal adjustments, it is still considered too conservative and failed to reflect current developments in the global telecommunications industries. Taiwan is one of the highest teledensity areas in the Asia-Pacific region. Related telecommunications infrastructure in Taiwan is also well developed and efficient. Because of the rapid creation of new technology and the growth of economic development, the government has adopted a series of steps to restructure its legislation to fit international requirements. The globalization and deregulation of telecommunications have caused intense discussions and debates. Reviewing the development of legal history and the formation of its economic market, one may conclude that Taiwan in general has been strongly touched by foreign influences and has tended toward internationalization. Thus Taiwan's legislative development still follow this model, a mixture of Civil and Common Legal Systems, but due to the new domestic demands, the government already had found a particular way to structure its own legal system especially on information technology law.

Bibliography

Chaui-Ru, Chen, *The History of the Right to Divorce – The Establishment and Meaning of Taiwanese Women's Right to Divorce.*National Taiwan University, 1997.

GATS - General Agreement on Trade and Services

Lawrence S. Liu.*Aspiring To Excel--The Uneasy Case Of Implementing Taiwan's Asia — Pacific Regional Operations Center Plan.*Sp. Columbia JAL,1996.

Lawrence S. Liu, "Telecommunications Market Liberalization in Taiwan: Political and Legal Issues.*E. Asian Executive Reports.*1996.

Phelan, Anne."Taiwan Passes Telecom Laws".E. Asian Executive Reports.1996.

Rene David & John E. C. Brierley, *Major Legal Systems in the World Today*, in Stevens & Sons (3rd ed.), (1985), 523, London, England.

Wang, Tay-Sheng."The Westernization of Taiwanese Legal System for One Hundred Years". *The Establishment of Taiwanese Legal History* (1996): 343-378.

Tung-Tsu, Chu.*Law and Society in Traditional China*. Hyperion Pr, 1979.

Chapter 18

Conceptions of Contract in German and English Law and their Legal Traditions

Marin Keršić[1]

Abstract

The topic of this paper is the comparative analysis of the conception of contract in German and English legal systems. The main questions of the paper are: what are the defining elements of the conception of contract and what is their relation to the legal traditions of Germany and England? In terms of structure, after a brief introduction (Part I), the work starts with theoretical considerations about 'concept' and 'conception' of contract and their 10 relation, followed by exposition of some of the key characteristics of contracts in Germany (Part II), followed by exposing such key characteristics of contracts in England (Part III). The paper concludes with providing an answer to the main question, in the form of summaries, through key characteristics and differences about the defining elements of the conceptions of contract in German and English law, thus providing comparative insight between the specifics of the representatives of the Civil law and the Common law legal traditions.

Introduction

The topic of this paper is the comparative analysis of the conception of contract in German and English legal systems. The main question of the paper is: what are the defining elements of the conception of contract and what are their relations to the legal traditions of Germany and England? How do legal systems in question and their characteristics influence contract law, and particularly the conception of contract? This relation can be seen also from the other way – how do conceptions of the contract generally fit with the legal systems in question? The relevance of the topic

---

[1] Assistant at the Faculty of Law, University of Split, Croatia

stems from the contract law itself, which deals with one of the foundations of the society – exchange in its broad meaning. In the context of the world becoming more integrated, differences between legal systems and their comparison become an even more relevant issue. In terms of structure, after a brief introduction, the paper starts with theoretical considerations about "concept" and "conception" of contract and their relation (Part 2), followed by some of the key characteristics of contract law in German law (Part 3), continuing with such key characteristics of contract law in English law (Part 4). Through exposition of the key characteristics and differences about the defining elements of the conceptions of contract in German and English law (in the form of summaries), the paper concludes with remarks regarding the main question, thus providing some comparative insight from the representatives of the Civil and Common law legal traditions. The conclusions could then be used as a starting point for other comparisons between legal systems, particularly the interpretation of contracts. The practical importance of interpretation comes from the fact that it ultimately has to lead to the solution of the problematic legal situations which involve unclear meaning or contested understanding, usually through judicial decisions. The paper aims to develop a starting framework for that research.

1. "Concept" and "Conception" of Contract

A concept can be defined as "something conceived in the mind" or "an abstract or generic idea generalized from particular instances".[2] A contract is an example of a legal concept. But what is the contract as a concept, looked beyond merely its definition? Whittaker and Riesenhuber suggest three possible usages of the word "contract"[3]: firstly, the word can be used for a "relationship between two or more persons recognized and regulated by law." In this sense, the contract is defined as the way of how a particular legal system sees the legal relationship in question. Secondly, the word can be used for describing the "factual circumstances which, taken together, are recognized by a particular law constituting the legal relationship of contract." In this sense, the contract is seen as an agreement between the parties. Thirdly, in a situation where the parties' agreement is put into

---

[2] Merriam-Webster, "concept", accessed October 30, 2017, www.merriam-webster.com/dictionary/concept

[3] Whittaker, Simon; Riesenhuber, Karl: "Conceptions of Contract", in *The Common European Sales Law in Context: Interactions with German and English Law*, edited by Gerhard Dannemann and Stefan Vogenauer (Oxford [u.a.], Oxford University Press, 2013), pp. 120-122.

written form, the word contract is used for the written document itself. Authors sum up the relationship between these three possible uses of the word contract: contract, in the sense of an agreement between the parties (second meaning), may result in a particular legal relationship recognized and regulated by law (first meaning), which may or may not be expressed in the written form (third meaning).

Conception can be defined as the "capacity, function or process of forming or understanding ideas or abstractions or their symbols"; "a general idea (concept)"; "a complex product of abstract or reflexive thinking"; "the sum of person's ideas and beliefs concerning something".[4] Dworkin proposed an explanation of the relation between the terms "concept" and "conception" in *Law's Empire* on the example of "courtesy" and "respect"[5]: people will mostly agree about the general propositions regarding courtesy – for example, that the courtesy is a matter of respect, but they will also usually disagree about the interpretation of the idea of "respect", with some people considering that people of certain rank or group should be shown respect because of their belonging to certain rank or group, while others might think that respect should be earned by individual acts. Respect provides the concept of courtesy, as he says, but the competing conceptions about what the respect is are "different conceptions of that concept".

"Conception of contract" can be defined as the "understanding" (or understandings, where conception is unsettled or controversial) about the nature of the legal relationship of contract."[6] Whittaker and Riesenhuber differentiate between the three types of conception or aspects of the conception of contract: first, the analytical or definitional one; second, the one linked to fundamental characteristics and third, the functional one. The first, analytical or definitional aspect of the conception of contract consists of definition and formal conditions for the existence of the contract; the second aspect consists of the fundamental characteristics of contract, such as its formation, interpretation, performance, non-performance, and enforcement, while the third, functional aspect of the conception of contract, as the name suggests, focuses more on the functions of the contract.[7] The conception or aspect of conception which

---

[4] Merriam-Webster, "conception", accessed October 30, 2017, www.merriam-webster.com/dictionary/conception

[5] Dworkin, Ronald: *Law's Empire* (Oxford, Hart Publishing, 1998), pp. 70-71.

[6] Whittaker, Riesenhuber, "Conceptions of Contract", p. 122.

[7] Ibid., pp. 122-124.

is prevailingly relevant for this paper is the second one, which focuses on the fundamental characteristics of the contract because it is the most plausible for comparative approach, but also the deepest one in terms of the scope of inquiry.

The introductory remarks about the concept and conception of contract and the relation between them serve as the starting points, establishing key terms for the work; the following part deals with some of the key characteristics of contract law in German and English legal systems so that the respective conceptions of contract can be established. The paper continues with analyzing the contract as a legal relationship between the persons and the factual circumstances which constitute it by focusing on its fundamental characteristics. The characteristics analyzed for this purpose are: 1) the position of contract in the legal system; 2) its constitutive elements; 3) its formation and 4) general principles, where applicable.

2. Germany

2.1. Contract and the German Civil Code

Since the German Civil Code (*Bürgerliches Gesetzbuch*, BGB) is the main source of private law in Germany, it is natural to take it as a starting point of contract analysis. The German legal system is highly structured and characterized by a systematic approach to law, which "considers the numerous rules to constitute a 'whole' which follows an 'inner order' as expressed by the underlying principles."[8] The civil law in Germany in general is considered to be the "law of the system", where "the emerging contingencies of life readily find themselves being subsumed under one or other of the categorical umbrellas", with special significance given to the act of the categorization and to the criteria which allow the separation of the categories.[9] The BGB is characterized as logical and precise.[10] Because of these reasons and in order to have a clear and coherent structure to follow,

---

[8] Riesenhuber, Karl: "English common law versus German Systemdenken? Internal versus external approaches", *Utrecht Law Review*, Vol. 7, No. 1, 2011, p. 119, in relation with pp. 122-125.

[9] Legrand, Pierre: "Against a European Civil Code", *Modern Law Review*, Vol. 60, No. 1, 1997, p. 50.

[10] Rückert, Joachim: "Das BGB und seine Prinzipien: Aufgabe, Lösung, Erfolg", in *Historisch-kritischer Kommentar zum BGB – Band 1: Allgemeiner Teil*, §§ 1-240, edited by Matthias Schmoeckel, Joachim Rückert and Reinhard Zimmermann (Tübingen, Mohr Siebeck, 2003), p. 35.

the structure of the BGB and the fundamental terms of contract law are presented. These terms are a contract (*Vertrag*), the contractual relationship of obligation (*vertragliches Schuldverhältnis*), legal transaction (*Rechtsgeschäft*) and declaration of intent (*Willenserklärung*).[11]

The general structure of the BGB consists of the following elements, starting with more general and ending with less general: Book (*Buch*) as the broadest category, Division (*Abschnitt*), Title (*Titel*), Subtitle (*Untertitel*) and Chapter (*Kapitel*). Out of the five books of the BGB, the general rules regulating contract law are located in the Book 1 (General part, *Allgemeiner Teil*, §§ 1-240) and Book 2 (Law of obligations, *Recht der Schuldverhältnisse*), Division 1-7 (§§ 241-432). Division 8 (§§ 433-853), the last in the Book 2 regulates particular types of obligations.[12]

2.2. Contract

The contract is usually defined as a "legal act consisting of two or more declarations of intent (offer, *Angebot* or *Antrag*, and acceptance, *Annahme*), both corresponding with one another and aiming at bringing about a particular legal effect."[13] The definition of a contract is not given in the BGB; it is derived from the systematic structure of the BGB and the position of contract in it, classified as a bilateral or two-sided legal transaction (*zweiseitges Rechtsgeschäft*) which requires two corresponding declarations of intent.[14] Contract is a source of voluntary obligation and can also be seen as "contractual relationship of obligation" (*vertragliches*

---

[11] These terms are identified as key in Markesinis, Basil; Unberath, Hannes; Johnston, Angus: *The German Law of Contract: A Comparative Treatise* (2nd ed., Oxford [u.a.], Hart, 2006), p. 25, but their importance can be also seen directly from their position in the BGB and in the literature, where they are presented immediately after the introductory chapter. See, for example, *Allgemeiner Teil* from Boemke, Burkhard; Ulrici Bernhard: *BGB Allgemeiner Teil* (2nd ed., Berlin, Heicelberg, Springer, 2014); Bork, Reinhard: *Allgemeiner Teil des Bürgerlichen Gesetzbuch* (4th rev ed., Tübingen, Mohr Siebeck, 2016) and Brox, Hans; Walker, Wolf-Dietrich: *Allgemeiner Teil des BGB* (39th rev ed., München, Verlag Franz Vahlen, 2015).

[12] Federal Ministry of Justice and Consumer Protection (*Bundesministerium der Justiz und für Verbraucherschutz*), Bürgerliches Gesetzbuch, accessed October 30, 2017, https://www.gesetze-im-internet.de/englisch_bgb/index.html

[13] Foster, Nigel; Sule, Satish: *German Legal System and Laws* (4th ed., Oxford, [u.a.], Oxford University Press, 2010), p. 428. Similarly, Boemke, Ulrici, *BGB Allgemeiner Teil*, pp. 99-100; Bork, *Allgemeiner Teil des Bürgerlichen Gesetzbuch*, pp. 256-257 and Brox, Walker, *Allgemeiner Teil des BGB*, p. 43.

[14] Whittaker, Riesenhuber, "Conceptions of Contract", p. 134.

Schulverhältnis), which forms the first important difference in the conception of contract in German and English law: "contract", in the terminology of English law should be equated with "contractual relationship of obligation" in German law in order to analyze it from a comparative perspective.[15]

§ 311 (1) BGB states that to create a relationship of obligation by legal transaction or to alter the contents of an obligation, a contract is necessary unless provided otherwise by the statute. When the parties have concluded a contract, a relationship of obligation arises, and the parties are under obligation, according to the terms of the contract they have concluded, following the general principle of *pacta sunt servanda*.[16] An agreement is considered binding for the parties as *lex contractus*, with the parties agreeing, while acting in their self-determination, that the contract has the force of law between them; the binding nature of the obligations of the parties is considered "autonomously rooted in the contract itself, whose effect is overtly analogized to the effect of the law."[17] The contract in contemporary German law is seen as a consensus or an agreement: by contracting, through their declarations of will, the parties intentionally agree to some legal consequences, which occur because they are agreed upon.[18] Furthermore, the law itself often directly refers to the contract as to an agreement (*Einigung*), for example in the §§ 873 and 929 BGB; also §§ 154 and 155 speak of an agreement in the sense that contract is formed by a mutual agreement of the contracting parties.[19]

The essential element of the contract lies in the "parties' self-commitment as an expression of their autonomy (*Privatautonomie*) or self-determination (*Selbstbestimmung*)", with the contract being "an act of expression of one's own autonomy and at the same time a recognition of the autonomy of one's contracting partner."[20]

---

[15] As noted by Markesinis, Unberath, Johnston, *The German Law of Contract: A Comparative Treatise*, p. 25.

[16] Ibid., p. 26. See also Boemke, Ulrici, *BGB Allgemeiner Teil*, pp. 119-120.

[17] Whittaker, Riesenhuber, "Conceptions of Contract", p. 135.

[18] Translated from the German original Bork, *Allgemeiner Teil des Bürgerlichen Gesetzbuch*, pp. 256-257.

[19] Whittaker, Riesenhuber, "Conceptions of Contract", pp. 133-134.

[20] Ibid., p. 135.

2.3. The Legal Transaction, Declaration of Intent and Offer

Legal transaction (also translated as "legal act") is usually defined as "general term comprising all legal acts that bring about a legal consequence or effect."[21] With the legal transaction, which consists of at least one declaration of intent, a person is given power by the law to "determine his relationship with others through mutual conduct."[22] The legal transaction is broader and more fundamental concept than "contract" or "contractual relationship of obligation", with the contract being "one incidence of legal transaction".[23] Previously mentioned § 311 (1) BGB refers to the legal transaction by stating that a relationship of obligation is created by the legal transaction.

Declaration of intent can be defined as a "private expression of will, directed at achieving specific, intended legal consequences which are recognized by the legal system"[24] or as "any statement or action aimed to achieve a distinct legal outcome".[25] German theory distinguishes between two aspects of intent, the external or objective aspect (*objektiver Tatbestand*) and the internal or subjective (*subjektiver Tatbestand*): the external aspect is the expressed declaration and the internal aspect is the real intent of the person which consists of three elements: first, the general intention to act (*Handlungswille*) – the intent to physically move; second, conscious declaration of intent (*Erklärungsbewußtsein*) – the awareness that the action has legal effect and third, business intent (*Geschäftswille*) – the awareness of the particular effect of the action.[26] The problem of the necessity of *Erklärungsbewußtsein* for valid declaration of intent was disputed by academics and courts, as Kramer and Probst note, where the traditional German doctrine, influenced by the will theory (which gives primacy to the intention rather than to the expression) held the position that if *Erklärungsbewußtsein* was lacking, the declaration of intent would be ineffective and thus the contract would be void; the position changed towards treating the issue as an *error in expression*, with the consequence that the declaration of intent and contract are only voidable and in the

---

[21] Foster, Sule, German Legal System and Laws, p. 427.

[22] Markesinis, Unberath, Johnston, The German Law of Contract: A Comparative Treatise, pp. 26-27.

[23] Ibid., p. 26.

[24] Translated from the German original Boemke, Ulrici, BGB Allgemeiner Teil, p. 65.

[25] Foster, Sule, German Legal System and Laws, p. 424.

[26] Ibid., p. 424. Similarly, Brox, Walker, Allgemeiner Teil des BGB, pp. 44-45.

case of successful avoidance, the person who acted in good faith could claim the compensation for his reliance loss.[27]

The offer is the presupposing element of the contract, referred to in the § 145 BGB – the first paragraph of the Title 3 (Contract) and defined as a "declaration of intent which must be received by the other party".[28] The revocability of the offer, before the contract comes into existence through the acceptance of the other party is identified as a major point of difference between the legal systems.[29] What is relevant for the conception of contract regarding offer is its binding nature in the case of so-called 'distant contracts', where the offeree is not immediately present at the time when the offeror made the offer: the question here is about the possibility of the offeror to revoke his offer and the conditions under which he could do it.[30] The relevance of this question comes from the fact that it shows the significance which the legal system gives to the offer, and through it to the intent or will since offer is a declaration of it. In the German legal system, as § 145 BGB states, the offeror is bound by his offer to an absent offeree, unless stated otherwise, with the consequence being that the offer, after received by the offeree, cannot be withdrawn for the period of time specified in the offer or, if no time is specified, for a "reasonable period", with the sanction being that the withdrawal would be without legal effect, rather than resulting in liability in damages.[31] The resulting conclusion regarding the offer in German law, as it will also be seen when compared to the offer in English law (see 4.2.), that German law gives binding effect to the unaccepted offer, as opposed to the English law; furthermore, that idea is even characterized as "inconceivable in systems such as the English".[32]

---

[27] Kramer, Ernst August; Probst, Thomas: "Defects in the Contracting Process", in *International Encyclopedia of Comparative Law*, vol 7 – *Contracts in General*, part 1, edited by Arthur Taylor von Mehren and René David (Tübingen, Mohr, 2008), p. 41.

[28] Ibid., p. 428.

[29] Farnsworth, Edward Allan: "Comparative Contract Law", in *The Oxford Handbook of Comparative Law*, edited by Reimann, Matthias (Oxford, Oxford University Press, 2008), p. 915.

[30] Zweigert, Konrad; Kötz, Hein: *Introduction to Comparative Law* (3rd rev end rpt, Oxford, Clarendon Press, 2011), p. 357.

[31] Ibid., p. 361.

[32] Markesinis, Unberath, Johnston, *The German Law of Contract: A Comparative Treatise*, p. 64.

2.4. General Principles

Since the BGB came into force in the time when classical individualism and *laissez-faire* doctrines were dominant, it was infused with the idea that the state should generally not get involved in the individual decisions and their autonomy in respect of the agreements that were made between them.[33] The principle of personal autonomy (*Privatautonomie*) means that the individual has the freedom to self-determine his legal relations, for which he is responsible and therefore the individual himself knows what is most beneficial for him and he can decide without the interference from the state.[34] The principle is protected by the German constitution: Article 2 (1) of the Basic Law for the Federal Republic of Germany (*Grundgesetz*, GG) protects personal freedoms by stating that "Every person shall have the right to free development of his personality insofar as he does not violate the rights of others or offend against the constitutional order or the moral law."[35] Freedom of contract (*Vertragsfreiheit*) is considered the most important practical aspect of the principle of personal autonomy, having three different aspects: first, the freedom to conclude contracts (*Abschlussfreiheit*); secondly, the freedom to decide the content of the contract (*Inhaltsfreiheit* or *Gestaltungsfreiheit*), and thirdly, the freedom of form (*Formfreiheit*).[36] The detailed analysis, classification, and systematization of abstract notions such as freedom of contract show how important the principle of *Privatatonomie* – the freedom of individual to self-determine his legal relations, deriving from its will, is important in German law.

The other two important principles which need to be mentioned are the principle of separation (*Trennungsprinzip*) and the principle of abstraction (*Abstraktionsprinzip*). Through the principle of separation, German law distinguishes between legal transactions that create a relationship of obligation (*Verpflichtungsgeschäft*) and legal transactions which transfer, alter, extinguish or encumber the right (*Verfügungsgeschäft*), and through the principle of abstraction the validity of the second transaction (*Verfügungsgeschäft*) is considered independent from the validity of the first

---

[33] Foster, Sule, German Legal System and Laws, p. 412.

[34] Translated from the German original Boemke, Ulrici, BGB Allgemeiner Teil, pp. 47-48.

[35] Federal Ministry of Justice and Consumer Protection (Bundesministerium der Justiz und für Verbraucherschutz), Grundgesetz, accessed October 30, 2017, https://www.gesetze-im-internet.de/englisch_gg/englisch_gg.html#p0030

[36] Boemke, Ulrici, BGB Allgemeiner Teil, p. 50; Brox, Walker, Allgemeiner Teil des BGB, pp. 41-42 and Foster, Sule, German Legal System and Laws, pp. 412-414.

one (*Verpflichtungsgeschäft*).³⁷ To illustrate on an example, the principle of separation distinguishes the contract of sale (§ 433 BGB) as *Verpflichtungsgeschäft* from the transfer of the property (§ 929 BGB) as *Verfügungsgeschäft*, and the principle of abstraction makes their validities independent from each other.³⁸ Zweigert and Kötz argue that these principles are so distinctive that they give a characteristic style to the German legal system.³⁹ These principles, among other functions, show how the notion of "contract" is related to and rooted in the wider notion of "obligation".

2.5. Summary

As it can be seen from this short exposition of the basic characteristics about the conception of contract and its surroundings in German law, the following observations stand out: the German legal system is highly systematized and coherent, with the Civil Code having a central position in the area of private law, with a complex interrelation of concepts of the law of obligations (*Willenserklärung* – *Rechtsgeschäft* – *Vertrag*); this abstract and conceptual thinking is projected on the facts, which are viewed through it (*Erklärungsbewußtsein* and valid declaration of intent); principles and notions (*Privatautonomie*, *Verpflichtungsgeschäft*, and *Verfügungsgeschäft*) have strong importance and practical consequences; contract is viewed as an agreement (*Einigung*), often directly, and special theoretical consideration and importance is given to the will of the parties and their declarations of intent.

3. England

3.1. The Contract in English Law

If there is a comparison to be made with German law regarding the stance towards the concepts, facts, and system, several illustrative quotes can be mentioned: "For the common law lawyer, any construction of an ordered account of the law firmly rests on the disorder of fragmented and dispersed facts.";⁴⁰ "The common law is a historical development rather than a logical whole, and the fact that a particular doctrine does not

---

³⁷ Markesinis, Unberath, Johnston, The German Law of Contract: A Comparative Treatise, p. 27.

³⁸ Ibid., pp. 29-30.

³⁹ Zweigert, Kötz, Introduction to Comparative Law, p. 71.

⁴⁰ Legrand, "Against a European Civil Code", p. 50.

logically accord with another or others is no ground for its rejection."[41]; "Arguments based on logical consistency are apt to mislead for the common law is a practical code adapted to deal with the manifold diversities of the human life (...)";[42] Markesinis, Unberath, and Johnston mention the "continental search for a principle which contrasts with the common law attachment to casuistry."[43] Consequently, English law, unlike German law, does not have a code which would regulate contract law or obligations in general.

There are two main, competing definitions of contract in English law: in the first one, a contract is seen as a promise (or similarly, as a bargain), and in the second one, a contract is seen as an agreement.[44] In the first view, a contract can be defined as "a promise or set of promises which the law will enforce."[45] The view of contract as a bargain, which is linked to the definition of contract as a promise, is considered to be in line with the commercial understanding of the contract law in England while also stressing the significance of the requirement of consideration, a specific trait of English law.[46]

In the second view, a contract can be defined as "an agreement giving rise to obligations which are enforced or recognized by the law".[47] This view emphasizes the importance of the intention of the parties, tending to minimize the importance of consideration, but it allows consideration to

---

[41] Lord Porter in *Best v Samuel Fox & Co. Ltd.* [1952] AC 716, 727 (H.L.), Riesenhuber, "English common law versus German Systemdenken? Internal versus external approaches", pp. 122-123.

[42] Lord Macmillan in *Reads v Lyons & Co.* [1947] A.C. 156, 175 (H.L.), Riesenhuber, "English common law versus German Systemdenken? Internal versus external approaches", p. 123.

[43] Markesinis, Unberath, Johnston, *The German Law of Contract: A Comparative Treatise*, p. 55.

[44] Atiyah, Patrick, Smith, Stephen: *Atiyah's introduction to the law of contract* (6th ed., Oxford [u.a.], Clarendon Press, 2006), p. 22 see contract as an agreement. Chitty, Joseph (Begr.); Beale, Hugh (Hrsg.): *Chitty on Contracts, Volume I – General Principles* (31st ed., London, Sweet & Maxwell, 2012), pp. 12-13 see contract as a promise.

[45] Chitty, Beale, *Chitty on Contracts*, p. 12. This view was adopted by the 26th edition of the book.

[46] Whittaker, Riesenhuber, "Conceptions of Contract", p. 128.

[47] Chitty, Beale, *Chitty on Contracts*, pp. 12-13. This view was taken by the 2nd edition of the book.

be kept as a feature of the positive law, as a factor which determines will the contract be enforced or not by the law.[48] The idea of contract as an agreement was strongly influenced by the civil law legal scholars in the 19th century, following the systematic and classificatory tendencies in the civil law, as Atiyah and Smith note, but this structure was never seen as fully fitting for the English contract law.[49] It can be seen from this that the influence of civil law on the common law in this aspect was raising the importance of the intention of the parties and bringing a more systematic approach to the law.

Before the mentioned influence of the civil law on the conception of contract in England in the 19th century, English conception of contract relied on three elements: promise, consideration, and breach of promise, with the main question being whether a promise (not a contract) has been broken, and the reciprocity of the promises was established by making them conditionally dependent upon the performance of the other promise.[50] What happened in the 19th century, as Whittaker and Riesenhuber note, was that the idea of the importance of the agreement as a condition for the formation of contract appeared through the elements of "offer" and "acceptance", with the will theory gaining roots in English law.[51] Today, the contract is analyzed in terms of offer and acceptance, intention to create legal relations and the doctrine of consideration, as requirements for its existence, which is a result of the change from the pre-civil law influence which saw the promise being broken to the contemporary notion that the contract is broken.[52]

Atiyah identifies two main characteristics which influenced common law's history[53]: first, the organic development, meaning that the contract

---

[48] Whittaker, Riesenhuber, "Conceptions of Contract", p. 129.

[49] Atiyah, Smith, Atiyah's introduction to the law of contract, p. 22.

[50] Whittaker, Riesenhuber, "Conceptions of Contract", p. 126.

[51] Ibid. The acceptance of the "will theory" is noted by Atiyah, Smith, Atiyah's introduction to the law of contract, fn 31, in relation with the previously mentioned Robert Joseph Pothier and his Treatise on Obligations (Traité des obligations, 1761). Regarding the historical influence from the continental Europe, see also Furmston, Michael Philip: Chesire, Fifoot and Furmston's Law of Contract, ch 2, p. 2.

[52] Simpson, Alfred William Brian: Legal theory and legal history: essays on the common law (London, [u.a.], Hambledon Press, 1987), p. 181; Zimmermann, Reinhard: The Law of Obligations: Roman Foundations of the Civilian Tradition (Oxford, Oxford University Press, 1996), p. 571.

[53] Atiyah, Smith, *Atiyah's introduction to the law of contract*, pp. 21-22.

law developed without any special structure or conscious design, with little or no regard from judges when it came to the structure or the organization of law and, secondly, the commercial setting, which means that most cases which came before the court dealt with commercial matters regarding medium to large companies, with judges themselves often having a commercial law background.

The result of different approaches to the contract had as a result two competing conceptions of contract which are still visible today in English law, with authors basically as a rule mentioning and elaborating both approaches and then opting for one of them, resulting in authors analyzing contract both from the perspective of an agreement (offer and acceptance) and of a promise (because consideration is given for a promise, and not for an agreement or a contract).[54] From the functional perspective (see 2.), contract in English law is seen as "fundamentally commercial in its approach, seeing contracts primarily as market transactions", with the main role of contract law being the "facilitation of these transactions".[55] Similarly, Furmston stresses the "commercial flavor" of contract in English law.[56] What strikes out as a difference from the German law is the explicit position of English law on the issues of assent or agreement between the parties: "Agreement, however, is not a mental state, but an act, and, as an act, is a matter of inference from conduct. The parties are to be judged not by what is in their minds, but by what they have said or written or done. While such must be, to some degree, the standpoint of every legal system, the common law, preoccupied with the bargain, lays particular emphasis upon external appearance."[57]

3.2. Offer

An offer in English law can be defined as "an expression of willingness to contract on specified terms made with the intention (actual or apparent) that it is to become binding as soon as it is accepted by the person to whom it is addressed."[58] Regarding the revocability of the offer, the general rule of English law is that an offer can be withdrawn at any time before it is accepted, and this rule applies even if the offeror has promised to keep the offer open for a specified time, because that promise is

---

[54] Whittaker, Riesenhuber, "Conceptions of Contract", p. 128.

[55] Ibid., p. 123.

[56] Furmston, *Chesire, Fifoot and Furmston's Law of Contract*, ch. 3, p. 3.

[57] Ibid.

[58] Chitty, Beale, *Chitty on Contracts*, p. 172.

unsupported by consideration and is therefore not legally binding.[59] This position is in sharp contrast with the position the offer and its revocability has in German law, where it is considered as binding (as elaborated in 3.3.).

3.3. Consideration

Since consideration was already mentioned, its content and importance need to be briefly presented here. The general rule of English law is that the promise is binding as contract only if it is either made in a deed or supported by some "consideration", with the purpose of the doctrine of consideration being to legally limit the enforceability of some agreements (the ones which do not contain factors such mistake, misrepresentation, duress or illegality), even if they were intended to be legally binding.[60] The basic idea behind the doctrine of consideration is reciprocity, giving something for something, meaning that "something of value in the eyes of the law" must be given for a promise in order to make it enforceable as a contract.[61] Consideration, more precisely the "doctrine of consideration" was the basis of the enforcement of the contract developed in common law, historically identifying promises which were considered important enough, in the eyes of the law, to be legally enforceable.[62]

In the German legal system, there is no requirement comparable to consideration: it is sufficient that the "promise is made with an intention to be bound".[63] To follow the terminology used in German law, it would be more precise to say here that it is sufficient that there is a valid declaration of intent. From a comparative perspective, the question falls under the question of the evidence of seriousness: how do legal systems decide which promises are legally binding and how the seriousness and binding nature of the declared will are determined.[64]

---

[59] Ibid., p. 221.

[60] Ibid., p. 293.

[61] Ibid., p. 294.

[62] Farnsworth, "Comparative Contract Law", p. 908. See also Furmston, *Chesire, Fifoot and Furmston's Law of Contract*, ch. 4, pp. 2-3.

[63] Ibid., p. 910.

[64] Markesinis, Unberath, Johnston, The German Law of Contract: A Comparative Treatise, p. 87.

3.4. Summary

This brief exposition of key characteristics of contract in English law resulted in the following conclusions: it is based on casuistry rather than conceptual thinking, which allows it to exist in a more diverse but also potentially more conflicting environment, but the one which also allows great flexibility in the absence of strict conceptual thinking. The conception of contract in English law is strongly influenced by commercial setting and needs ("commercial flavor"), reinforcing what one could call a more pragmatic approach to the contract law. From the original position of contract as promise, through the influence of the continental thought, two competing conceptions of contract have been established (contract as promise and contract as an agreement), but in a way specifically fused, since the analysis of the contract includes, among others, both the doctrine of consideration but also agreement through offer and acceptance. The conception of contract in English law is characterized strongly by an "objective" approach to the agreement, emphasizing what was expected ("external appearance").

4. Conclusion

After presenting the relation between the "concept" and the "conception", particularly through "conception of contract", defined as the understanding(s) of the nature of the legal relationship of contract (2.), and some of the key characteristics of the German and English legal system, the respective conceptions of contract in German (3.5.) and English (4.4.) law were established. The characteristics with a defining influence on the conception of contract in German law are: the systematic and coherence of its system of private law; complex interrelation between the concepts of the law of obligations (*Willenserklärung – Rechtsgeschäft – Vertrag*); abstract and conceptual thinking; special significance of the principles and notions (*Privatautonomie* and *Treu und Glauben*); perception of contract as an agreement, with special theoretical significance given to the phenomenon of the will and its declaration. Conception of contract in English law, on the other hand, is strongly influenced by the casuistic approach rather than conceptual thinking, which allows it to develop a diverse environment; a strong commercial note; a specific perception of the nature of the contract (either as a promise or as an agreement, with the perception of contract as a promise being native to English law, and the perception of contract as an agreement coming from the later civil law influence), and a strongly "objective" approach to the agreement of the parties, with an emphasis on the external appearance, followed by a unique feature of the English contract law – the doctrine of consideration.

What has shown to be the defining aspect of the conceptions of contract, influencing the approach in each of the legal systems analyzed, was the theoretical treatment of the will or intention of the parties and its expression. This comes as a no surprise since the wills of the parties are the building blocks of the contract. The theoretical treatment of will follows the distinct marks of the legal traditions of Germany and England; a high level of abstraction and an elaborated conceptual approach, marked by a strong internal coherence versus casuistic, more flexible and pragmatic approach. Undoubtedly, as it is here also the case, general characteristics of the legal traditions influence practically every aspect of concepts and their conceptions in a given legal system, and that is one of the strongest values of the comparative approach.

The idea behind this inquiry is to set a framework for an analysis of the approaches to the interpretation of contracts in German and English law. How do conceptions of contract and interpretation interrelate? To answer this question, it was necessary to present the conceptions of contract derived from some of the characteristic elements of the contract in the legal systems in question. The next step should proceed to the analysis of the methods of interpretation of contracts in German and English law. The conclusion to be taken from this paper is that the theoretical treatment of the will or intention of the parties has shown to be the defining aspect of the conception of contract. It is thus the natural starting point for further research on the topic, combining conceptions of contract with interpretation and resulting, after these theoretical considerations, also in ones with practical implications.

Bibliography

Atiyah, Patrick; Smith, Stephen: *Atiyah's introduction to the law of contract* (6th ed., Oxford [u.a.], Clarendon Press, 2006)

Boemke, Burhard; Ulrici, Bernhard: *BGB Allgemeiner Teil* (2nd ed., Berlin, Heidelberg, Springer, 2014)

Bork, Reinhard: *Allgemeiner Teil des Bürgerlichen Gesetzbuch*, (4th rev ed., Tübingen, Mohr Siebeck, 2016)

Brox, Hans; Walker, Wolf-Dietrich: *Allgemeiner Teil des BGB* (39th rev ed., München, Verlag Franz Vahlen, 2015)

Chitty, Joseph (Begr.); Beale, Hugh (Hrsg.): *Chitty on Contracts, Volume I – General Principles* (31st ed., London, Sweet & Maxwell, 2012)

Dworkin, Ronald: *Law's Empire* (Oxford, Hart Publishing, 1998)

Farnsworth, Edward Allan: "Comparative Contract Law", in *The Oxford Handbook of Comparative Law*, edited by Reimann, Matthias (Oxford, Oxford University Press, 2008)
Foster, Nigel; Satish, Sule: *German Legal System and Laws* (4th edn, Oxford [u.a.], Oxford University Press, 2010)
Furmston, Michael Philip: *Chesire, Fifoot and Furmston's Law of Contract* (16th ed., Oxford, Oxford University Press, 2012)
Kramer, Ernst August; Probst, Thomas: "Defects in the Contracting Process", in *International Encyclopedia of Comparative Law*, vol 7 – *Contracts in General*, part 1, edited by Arthur Taylor von Mehren and René David (Tübingen, Mohr, 2008)
Legrand, Pierre: "Against a European Civil Code", *Modern Law Review*, Vol. 60, No. 1, 1997.
Markesinis, Basil; Unberath, Hannes; Johnston, Angus: The German Law of Contract: A Comparative Treatise (2nd ed., Oxford [u.a.], Hart, 2006)
Riesenhuber, Karl: "English common law versus German Systemdenken? Internal versus external approaches", *Utrecht Law Review*, Vol. 7, No. 1, 2011.
Rückert, Joachim: "Das BGB und seine Prinzipien: Aufgabe, Lösung, Erfolg", in *Historisch-kritischer Kommentar zum BGB – Band 1: Allgemeiner Teil*, §§ 1-240, edited by Matthias Schmoeckel, Joachim Rückert and Reinhard Zimmermann (Tübingen, Mohr Siebeck, 2003)
Simpson, Alfred William Brian: *Legal theory and legal history: essays on the common law* (London, [u.a.], Hambledon Press, 1987)
Whittaker, Simon and Riesenhuber, Karl: "Conceptions of Contract", *The Common European Sales Law in Context: Interactions with German and English Law*, edited by Gerhard Dannemann and Stefan Vogenauer (Oxford [u.a.], Oxford University Press, 2013)
Zimmermann, Reinhard: *The Law of Obligations: Roman Foundations of the Civilian Tradition* (Oxford, Oxford University Press, 1996)
Zweigert, Konrad; Kötz, Hein: *Introduction to Comparative Law* (3rd rev end rpt, Oxford, Clarendon Press, 2011)

Chapter 19

Institutional Transplants in Serbia – the Stories of Success and Failure

Ana Knežević Bojović[1]

Abstract

As Alan Watson once pointed out, law is different from bread because in all its manifestations it is an element of the state – and hence, the transplanted rule is not the same thing as it was in its previous home.[2] The same can be said of transplanted institutions. This, however, does not mean that a transplanted rule or a transplanted legal institution cannot fulfill the same purpose as in the country of their origin. But what does the effectiveness of a legal transplant depend on?

The author will examine several examples of institutional transplants in Serbia, analyze their effectiveness in accomplishing the purpose for which they were introduced in the Serbian legal system, and examine the reasons of their success or lack of success. The criteria for selecting the examples was the purpose with which they were introduced – to address the deficiencies in the national legal system that were repeatedly criticized by the international community, mainly the European Union, in a wider context of EU conditionality. The author will focus on reviving the legal norms by which these transplants were introduced and the wider regulatory context in which they operate. The author will analyze the institutes of the National Convention on the European Union, the civil monitor in public procurement proceedings and the High Judicial Council, and assess to what extent they have succeeded in achieving their intended purpose. Based on the analysis, the author will identify the key requirements for the success of legal transplants in Serbia.

---

[1] Research Fellow, Institute of Comparative Law, Belgrade

[2] Alan Watson, *Law out of context* (Athens, GA: University of Georgia Press, 2000), 1.

1. Institutional transplants in Serbia – to work or not to work?

"Legal transplants", a term devised in the 1970s by Alan Watson, implies "the moving of a rule or a system of law from one country to another".[3] While Watson believes that legal transplantation is at the top of the fertile sources of legal development, Pierre Legrand is one of the sharpest opponents of legal transplants.[4] In between these two academic opinions stands a plethora of research on legal transplants, with the intermediate position such as that taken by Kahn-Freud[5] who finds it is dangerous to transplant a law that is culturally and vitally attached to a particular society because all jurisdictions have a unique and different social constitution. This paper will take the position that legal transplants are possible, and focus on examining their success in a Serbian context in the last two decades.

When it comes to the success of legal transplants, legal scholars point out that it is important to make a distinction between those legal transplants that are based on simple copy-pasting, and others, that are a result of harmonization of legal ideas with existing waves and fashions.[6] In this respect, little can be objected to Miller's position that the majority of unsuccessful legal transplants can be considered as blind copy-paste acts, which are not truly motivated by a transition process and the chance of improving and developing the legal system.[7] This position could further be elaborated by acknowledging that the success of legal transplants depends

---

[3] Alan Watson, Legal Transplants: An Approach to Comparative Law (Edinburgh, 1974).

[4] Pierre Legrand, "The Impossibility of 'Legal Transplants'", Maastricht Journal of European and Comparative Law 4, no. 2 (1997): 111-124, doi:10.1177/1023263x9700400202.

[5] Otto Kahn-Freund, "On Uses and Misuses of Comparative Law", The Modern Law Review 37, no. 1 (1974): 1, 2 ff. For a detailed overview of various positions on legal transplants see Maria Reyes, "The Challenges of Legal Transplants in a Globalized Context: A Case Study on 'Working' Examples.", SSRN, November 26, 2014, accessed December 07, 2017, https://papers.ssrn.com/sol3/papers.cfm?abstract_id=2530811.

[6] Jonathan M. Miller, "A Typology of Legal Transplants: Using Sociology, Legal History and Argentine Examples to Explain the Transplant Process", The American Journal of Comparative Law 51, no. 4 (2003): 839-885, doi:10.2307/3649131.

[7] Ibid.

on the receptivity of the transplanting legal system[8] and that transplants are more likely to succeed provided that the resources, political orientations, and values of the source country and country to which the transplant is transferred are similar.[9] But most importantly, successful legal reforms require a relatively strong state and political stability[10], and hence legal transplants that are meant to bring about reforms should be viewed in this context. Institutional transplantation, in this context, is a conscious attempt to alter existing institutions and replace or complement them with new institutions (the transplants) borrowed from another country or another context.[11]

Serbia is a country that has still not fully completed its transition and is in the process of EU accession and approximation of its law with Union acquis. While the country has a long established practice of legal and institutional transplants,[12] in the recent decades, particularly in the context of EU conditionality, seems to often resort to institutional transplantation as a method of "quick fix for quick wins" in its reformatory efforts. However, this institutional transplantation is often not preceded by a society-wide dialogue nor accompanied by the necessary transfer of the underlying dogmatic approach. As a result, their success is limited.

---

[8] Daniel Berkowitz, Katharina Pistor and Jean-Francois Richard, "The Transplant Effect", The American Journal of Comparative Law 51, no. 1 (2003): 163-203.

[9] Linda Hantrais, International comparative research: theory, methods and practice (New York: Palgrave Macmillan, 2009), 45.

[10] Randall Peerenboom, "Toward a Methodology for Successful Legal Transplants", The Chinese Journal of Comparative Law 1, no. 1 (2013): 4-20.

[11] Martin De Jong, Virginie Mamadouh, Konstatinos Lalenis, Drawing Lessons About Lesson Drawing, The Theory and Practice of Institutional Transplantation De Jong M., Lalenis K., Mamadouh V. (eds.) (2002) The GeoJournal Library, vol 74, 283-299.

[12] For illustrative examples of the practice of legal transplants and underlying transfer of relevant dogmatic approaches see, for instance: Stefan Pürner. ""Dug i krivudav put" srpskog prava (nazad) u Evropu", Zbornik radova Pravnog fakulteta u Nišu, 68:607-625; Miroslav Đorđević. "Pravni transplanti i Srbijanski građanski zakonik iz 1844". Strani pravni život 1:62-84; Aleksandra. Rabrenović et al, „Istorijski razvoj mehanizama za sprečavanje korupcije u zemljama Jugoistočne Evrope", Pravni mehanizmi sprečavanja korupcije u Jugoistočnoj Evropi, Institut za uporedno pravo, Beograd 2013, 13-37; Luka Breneselović, „O zaštiti osnovnih prava u Srbiji u svetlu loše ocene Evropske komisije – razlozi niskog stepena stvarne zaštite osnovnih prava u republici Srbiji i neophodne mere za njeno poboljšanje", Evropsko zakonodavstvo, 43-44/2013, 335-360.

The paper shall analyze three recent examples of institutional transplants - The National Convention on the EU, the civil monitor in public procurement procedures and the High Judicial Council - which were introduced to the Serbian legal system in an attempt to i. The paper will examine their success or failure in achieving the desired reform goals. Based on the three case studies, a set of prerequisites for future institutional transplantation efforts in Serbia will be formulated.

2. Transplanting the National Convention on the EU as a Platform for Cross-Sectoral Dialogue on EU Accession

2.1. National Convention on the EU in Slovakia

Ever since the mid 1990ies, the relationship between the European Union and the civil sector has become one of the key issues within a wide debate on democratic deficit, that is, on the EU's lack of legitimacy.[13] In 2001, the EU issued a White paper, in which it underlined the importance of dialogue with the civil sector in the process of development of policies and regulations on EU level – however, this dialogue was primarily understood as a task that is effected on the state level.[14]

After the fall of the Berlin wall and active contribution of the civil sector in ensuring the legitimacy of the EU accession process,[15] the EU has recognized the importance of the civil sector and started to support and encourage its work through specific programmes. As O'Brenan points out,[16] this was an attempt on the part of the Commission to facilitate the accession process. This approach has been since then followed in the accession of the Western Balkan countries, given the need to strengthen democratic institutions and put in place democratic processes in all countries, particularly those that were subjected to autocratic regimes for

---

[13] Beate Kochler-Koch, "Civil society and EU democracy: 'astroturf' representation?" *Journal of European Public Policy* 17, no. 1 (2010): 101.

[14] John O'Brennan, "The European Commission, Enlargement Policy and Civil Society in the Western Balkans", in *Civil society and transitions in the Western Balkans*, eds. V. Bojičić-Dželilović, J. Ker-Lindsay, D. Kostovicova (Houndmills, Basingstoke, Hampshire: Palgrave Macmillan, 2013), 30.

[15] *Ibid.*, 34.

[16] *Ibid.*, 35.

long periods of time.[17] Even though the Commission's approach to the development of the civil sector in the Western Balkans is undoubtedly significant, it is also subject to criticism – the Commission is sometimes perceived as including in the dialogue only a small number of "favorite" civil sector organizations;[18] it is sometimes difficult to assess to what extent does this constitute a platform for expressing the true needs and positions of the civil sector. The author's direct experiences[19] corroborate these claims to a certain extent. The process through which an NGO becomes recognized as a relevant partner of the Commission is a lengthy one, and often depends on whether that same NGO is also recognized as a partner of the government in the reform, which sometimes dulls the blade of criticism of government actions. While this by no means minimizes the importance of the contributions provided by NGOs selected in this manner to the advancement of national policies in the EU accession context, it does show that an NGO has to dispose of considerable resources in order to find itself in a position to provide such a contribution and be heard.

In addition to top-down efforts of civil sector development supported by the EU,[20] some countries have attempted to integrate their own approach

---

[17] On the need for advanced civil sector participation in the accession process see European Commission. "Enlargement strategy and main challenges 2011-2012: Communication from the Commission to the European Parliament and the Council", 5.; European Commission. "Enlargement Strategy and Main Challenges 2012-2013", accessed November 8, 2017, http://ec.europa.eu/enlargement/pdf/key_documents/2012/package/strategy_paper_2012_en.pdf; European Commission. "Communication from the Commission to the European Parliament, the Council, the European Economic and Social Committee And the Committee of the Regions Enlargement Strategy and Main Challenges 2014-15", accessed November 8, 2017, http://ec.europa.eu/enlargement/pdf/key_documents/2014/20141008-strategy-paper_en.pdf.

[18] O' Brennan, "The European Commission, Enlargement Policy and Civil Society in the Western Balkans", 35.

[19] Working as policy coordinator at the National Alliance for Local Economic Development (www.naled.rs) the author participated in dialogues with the representatives of the EU Commission and of the European Parliament.

[20] PHARE Programme of Community aid to the countries of Central and Eastern Europe (Phare) was the main financial instrument of the pre-accession strategy for the Central and Eastern European countries (CEECs) which have applied for membership of the European Union programme. PHARE democracy programme was launched in 1992. Currently, financial support is provided primarily through

to civil sector participation in the EU integration process, taking into account the needs and programmes of local NGOs. One such successful model is the National Convention on the European Union (hereafter: the National Convention).

The National Convention is a platform that was first set up in Slovakia, and then replicated in Serbia, Montenegro, Albania, Ukraine and Moldova. The National Convention was based on the idea that all key stakeholders and decision-makers in one country should participate in a structured debate on the country's European future. The initiative for setting up such a platform came from the Slovak Foreign Policy Association (SFPA)[21] and the Slovakian Ministry of Foreign Affairs. Slovakia was therefore the first candidate country to institutionalize the debate on the future of the EU. In three years preceding Slovakian accession to the EU, the National Convention served as an open platform for professional and focused debate on relevant EU-related issues. In order to ensure the participation of all relevant stakeholders, the composition of the Convention had to be wide, and open. The Convention in Slovakia gathered the representatives of political parties, the government and the public administration, the parliament, civil sector organizations, interest groups, religious organizations and representatives of local self-government bodies. This model of the National Convention was operational in Slovakia until 2007, and it is this model that, to an extent, had been replicated in Serbia.[22] It is interesting to note that Slovakia has chosen the 'transition experience' as a major realm of its foreign policy towards East European countries and also its contribution to the EU and its foreign policy – where the National Convention holds a prominent place.[23]

2.2. Replication of the Slovakian Model of the National Convention on the EU in Serbia and its Practical Effects

In Serbia, the National Convention was set up under the auspices of the European Movement in Serbia, with the assistance of the Slovakian

---

the Civil Society Facility, particularly in organising and supporting conferences aimed at including CSOs in the enlargement process and facilitating dialogue with CSOs from EU member states. Also see. Maja Bobić and Relja Božić, *Civilno društvo u procesu evropske integracije – od konstruktivnog dijaloga do uspešnih pregovora* (Beograd: Evropski pokret u Srbiji, 2012), 6.

[21] www.sfpa.sk.

[22] The National Convention was re-launched in Slovakia in 2013.

[23] Lucia Najšlová, "Slovakia in the East: Pragmatic Follower, Occasional Leader", *Perspectives: Central European Review of International Affairs* 19, no. 2 (2011): 102.

SFPA.[24] It became operational in 2006, with the aim to present and showcase the idea of establishing a partnership between state bodies, CSOs, academia and political parties in the EU accession negotiations.[25] The setup of the Serbian National Convention largely resembled that of the Slovakian National Convention – it had a Presidency and a number of Working groups, which had their chairs and co-chairs. In this phase of the National Convention's work, the working group meetings were held 2 to 4 times on average. The chairs of the working groups were mainly nominated from among line ministries, which testifies of the need for the EU Convention to obtain its legitimacy primarily through having representatives of the state participate in its working groups. At the time the National Convention in Serbia was initially formed, the EU negotiation process was not particularly advanced, which resulted in the platform having a limited outreach and success. However, the National Convention was re-launched when Serbia became a candidate country for membership in the EU and when the bilateral screening had commenced.[26] This meant that the National Convention had more potential to be truly utilized as a platform for civil sector participation in the EU accession negotiations. This was particularly important given the Croatian experience of the absence of institutionalized participation of CSOs in their accession process.[27] The structure of the re-launched Serbian National Convention[28] had departed from both the Slovakian

---

[24] http://eukonvent.org/.

[25] Vojislav Milošević, ed., *Nacionalni konvent o Evropskoj uniji – Knjiga preporuka* (Beograd: Evropski pokret u Srbiji, 2008), 8.

[26] European Council confirmed Serbia as a candidate country on March 1, 2013. The accession negotiations between Serbia and the EU formally began by the 1st EU-Serbia Intergovernmental Conference held in Brussels on January 21, 2014. See Council of the European Union, "First Accession Conference with Serbia", Brussels, January 21, 2014, accessed accessed on November 8, 2017, http://www.consilium.europa.eu/uedocs/cms_data/docs/pressdata/EN/genaff/14 0676.pdf. The screening commenced on September 25, 2013, with Chapter 23 Judiciary and fundamental rights.

[27] See Gordan Bosanac, "Civil Society and EU Accession: The Croatian Experience", *EU-Monitoring.ba*, April 03, 2015, accessed December 07, 2017, http://eu-monitoring.ba/en/gordan-bosanac-civil-society-and-eu-accession-the-croatian-experience/.

[28] For more on the Serbian National Convention see: Ana Knežević Bojović "Učešće civilnog sektora u procesu pridruživanja Evropskoj uniji i praksa nacionalnog konventa o EU", *Strani pravni život* no. 2 (2015):131-144

model and from the previous composition of the National Convention in Serbia, by giving the civil sector the key role in managing the work of the Working Groups – the Working groups are chaired by representatives of the civil sector, while the representatives of the state bodies (government, public administration) are only participants in thematic discussions. It could be claimed that this approach in fact serves to additionally legitimize the National Convention as a platform for cooperation between the civil and the public sector, as its work is led and modeled in accordance with the needs of the civil sector rather than by following the public sector agenda.

This approach has also resulted in the recognition of National Convention by the CSOs as a platform that can help them amplify their voices and policy reform efforts, and be used as a complementary mechanism to advocate for change. It has also rendered the work of the National Convention more flexible, effective and prolific.

Currently, the Serbian National Convention gathers over 600 civil sector organizations, which monitor the EU negotiation process in all 35 negotiation chapters. National Convention maintains a relatively high intensity of activities, with 2 to 10 events of different working groups on a monthly basis. So far, the National Convention was most active in the adoption of Action Plans for Chapter 23 and 24, through extensive comments and direct meetings with the relevant government working groups. The National Convention has succeeded in becoming recognized by the legislative and the executive:

- the European Integration Committee of the National Assembly has adopted a decision stating that, before this Committee considers the proposal of a negotiation position in the EU accession negotiations, it will first consider the suggestions and recommendations of the National Convention;[29]
- Serbian EU accession Negotiation has committed itself to requesting the opinion of the National Convention on the EU

---

[29] Narodna skupština Republike Srbije. *Odluka o postupku razmatranja predloga pregovaračke pozicije u procesu pregovora o pristupanju Republike Srbije Evropskoj uniji*, No. 02-1864/14 of June 4, 2014, http://eukonvent.org/wp-content/uploads/2014/08/Odluka.pdf (accessed on November 8, 2017).

and informing it of its final negotiation position[30] by adopting Guidelines for the cooperation of the Negotiation team with the civil sector, the National Convention on the EU and the Chamber of Commerce.

The National Convention seems to have succeeded in becoming the most comprehensive platform for dialogue between the public and the civil sector on EU accession negotiations. More importantly, it does respond to the needs of the civil sector to initiate and maintain dialogue rather than on the need of the government and the public administration to ensure the legitimacy of their reform efforts. In departing from the original model, in Serbia this transplant was responsive and adaptive to the local setting and local needs, which are precisely what had geared it towards success.

3. Civil Monitor in Public Procurement Proceedings – a Transplant Aimed at Curbing Corruption

3.1. Civil Monitoring of Public Procurement

Public procurement is the activity of the public administration that is most susceptible to corruption, as it implies an interaction between the public and the private sector, where the potential for abusing public funds is abundant.[31] This is a challenge that Serbia has decided to face by introducing additional independent control mechanism in the public procurement processes in the 2012 Public Procurement Act. [32] Namely, Article 28 of this Act introduces the institute of civil monitor sets out the mandate of the civil monitors in public procurement procedures, while Article 148, paragraph 3 of the Law vests the civil monitor with authority to file a motion for the protection of rights. Based on Article 28, the Serbian

---

[30] Pregovarački tim za vođenje pregovora o pristupanju Republike Srbije Evropskoj uniji. Smernice za saradnju Pregovaračkog tima za vođenje pregovora o pristupanju Republike Srbije Evropskoj uniji i pregovaračkih grupa sa predstavnicima organizacija civilnog društva, Nacionalnog konventa o Evropskoj uniji i Privredne komore Srbije nakon dostavljanja Rezultata skrininga, http://eukonvent.org/wp-content/uploads/2016/04/smernice_za_saradnju_pregovarackog_tima_civilnim_dr ustvom.pdf (accessed on November 8, 2017).

[31] OECD, "OECD Principles for Integrity in Public Procurement", 9, accessed November 8, 2017, http://www.oecd.org/gov/ethics/48994520.pdf.

[32] Zakon o javnim nabavkama, Službeni glasnik RS, No. 124/2012. The statute started to be applied on April 1, 2013.

Public Procurement Office has adopted a Rulebook on Civil Monitors,[33] regulating the issues related to the appointment and work of civil monitors in more detail. It is worth noting that the new Public Procurement Act was the first statute adopted after the Serbian Progressive Party took power in 2013, as their contribution to curbing corruption.

The institute of a civil monitor of public procurement procedure is a legal and institutional transplant. This was acknowledged in the text of the Bill, by stating that the idea of having independent experts in the field of public procurement, who are experienced and renowned, monitor the most valuable contracts awarded in public procurement procedures and, as representatives of the public, exert pressure that may prove to be instrumental in curbing corruption.[34] The example after which this ex ante monitoring transplant was modeled is that of the Polish Public Procurement Office, which has the mandate to control the procurement procedure for awarding most valuable contracts.[35] However, unlike the solution adopted in Serbia, the Polish model implies that the public procurement process is controlled by a body that is a part of the public administration. On the other hand, the role of civil sector representatives in scrutinizing public procurement was developed in a similar fashion in some other countries: comparative studies show the existence of systems based on integrity pacts, such as the one in the Philippines,[36] monitoring groups, such as *veedurías*

---

[33] Pravilnik o građanskom nadzorniku, Službeni glasnik RS, No. 29/2013.

[34] Predlog Zakona o javnim nabavkama, http://www.sns.org.rs/lat/novosti/narodna-skupstina/predlog-zakona-o-javnim-nabavkama, accessed on November 8, 2017.

[35] See Katarina Jovičić, "Sistem kontrole javnih nabavki u Poljskoj", in *Građanska kontrola javnih nabavki*, ed. Milorad Bjeletić (Prokuplje: Toplički centar za demokratiju i ljudska prava; Beograd: Institut za uporedno pravo, 2013), 27-40.

[36] V. Ramkumar, W. Krafchik, The Role of Civil Society Organisations in Auditing and Public Finance Management, 2006, 17, http://www.internationalbudget.org/wp-content/uploads/The-Role-of-Civil-Society-Organizations-in-Auditing-and-Public-Finance-Management1.pdf, 20.8.2013. Aleksandra Rabrenović, "Učešće civilnog sektora u nadgledanju javnih nabavki u zemljama Aziji", in *Građanska kontrola javnih nabavki*, ed. Milorad Bjeletić (Prokuplje: Toplički centar za demokratiju i ljudska prava; Beograd: Institut za uporedno pravo, 2013), 11-27.

ciudadanas in Columbia, Ecuador and Peru and mechanism similar to the Serbian civil monitor – *testigo social* – in Mexico.[37]

---

[37] Veedurías cidudadanas were introduced in Columbia in 1994 by the Law 134 – Ley 134 de 1994 (Mayo 31) Por la cual se dictan normas sobre mecanismos de participación ciudadana, available at http://pdba.georgetown.edu/Electoral/Colombia/ley134-94.html, accessed on July 19, 2018. In 2015 a new law governing the principles of civic participation was adopted: *Ley estatutaria por la cual se dictan disposiciones en materia de promoción y protección del derecho a la participación democrática*, available at http://www.alcaldiabogota.gov.co/sisjur/normas/Norma1.jsp?i=62230#0, accessed on July 5, 2018. In 2003, Columbia adopted the Law which expressly regulates veedurías: LEY 850 de 2003 (noviembre 18) Por medio de la cual se reglamentan las veedurías ciudadanas, available at http://www.secretariasenado.gov.co/senado/basedoc/ley_0850_2003.html., accessed on July 19, 2018. For an overview see: S. C. González, „Las veedurías ciudadanas en cuanto mediaciones/mediadores de las relaciones Estado-sociedad en el ámbito local", *Administración & Desarrollo*, Vol. 40, Nº. 55, 2012, 19-32. In Ecuador, the process of establishing the regulatory framework was spearheaded by the Commission for the Civil Control of Corruption (*Comisión de Control Cívico de la Corrupción*), which has initially adopted a bylaw governing their work. Once introduced, and following good practical experiences, Ecuador has adopted a special law establishing a Council for Civic Participation and Social Control - *Ley Orgánica del Consejo de Participación Ciudadana y Control Social*, available at http://www.amevirtual.gob.ec/wp-content/uploads/2017/05/ley-organica-del-consejo-de-participacion-ciudadana-y-control-social.pdf, accessed on July 8, 2018. Once established, the Council has adopted a new ruebook on the said mechnism: *Reglamento General De Veedurías Ciudadanas*. The rulebook was last updated in 2016, and is available at http://www.cpccs.gob.ec/wp-content/uploads/2017/01/REGLAMENTO-2017.pdf, accessed on July 19, 2018. More information on the work of veedurias in Ecuador is avaliable at http://www.cpccs.gob.ec/es/participacion-ciudadana-y-control-social/control-social/veedurias-ciudadanas/, accessed July 5, 2018.

The key issues related to the civil monitor and the capacity of this mechanism to truly curb corruption in public procurement procedures include the following:

- the contract value threshold, if any, for the participation of civil monitor in the public procurement procedure
- the process of appointment of civil monitors

In Peru, veedurías are formally regulated as of 2017, following the adoption of a Ministerial Resolution- Resolución ministerial N° 0173-2017-MINAGRI Crean Veedurías Ciudadanas en Contratación Pública para ejercer vigilancia en las contrataciones realizadas en el marco de la Ley N° 30556, Ley que aprueba disposiciones de carácter extraordinario para las intervenciones del Gobierno Nacional frente a desastres y que dispone la creación de la Autoridad para la Reconstrucción con Cambios, available at https://busquedas.elperuano.pe/normaslegales/crean-las-veedurias-ciudadanas-en-contratacion-publica-para-resolucion-ministerial-n-0173-2017-minagri-1518676-1/. accessed July 5, 2018. For information on how the veedurías functioned de facto, based on the general principles established in the Constitution and laws governing access to information, see:
http://www.osce.gob.pe/red/default.asp?pin=h7.htm, accessed July 5, 2018.

In Mexico, civil monitors in public procurement procedures were first introduced on federal level in 2004, as a result of activities of Transparency International Mexico (see: APEC Procurement Transparency Standards in Mexico Time to Engage the Private Sector", Transparency International-USA and Center for International Private Enterprise., 2011, 14. available at
https://www.coalitionforintegrity.org/?ddownload=534, accessed on July 19, 2018). Namely, in 20014 the federal Ministry of Public Administration (Secretaria de la Función Publica) has issued Guidelines governingthe participation of civil monitors in public procurement procedures of federal authorities *(Lineamientos que Regulan la Participacion de los Testigos Sociales en las Contrataciones que Realicen las Dependencias y Entidades de la Administracion Publica Federal)*. In 2009, the laws governing procurement in the public sector were amended to formally regulate the role of civil monitors in public procurement procedures (the two laws changed were *Ley de Adquisiciones, Arrendamientos y Servicios del Sector Público* and *Ley de Obras Públicas y Servicios Relacionados con las Mismas*). For more information see: Ana Knežević Bojović, "Građanski nadzornik – Testigo Social – u Meksiku i drugi mehanizmi građanske kontrole javnih nabavki u Latinskoj Americi", in *Građanska kontrola javnih nabavki*, ed. Milorad Bjeletić (Prokuplje: Toplički centar za demokratiju i ljudska prava; Beograd: Institut za uporedno pravo, 2013), 41-60. Also see: OECD Public Governance Reviews Public Procurement Review of Mexico's PEMEX Adapting to Change in the Oil Industry: Adapting to Change in the Oil Industry, available at http://www.oecd.org/gov/public-procurement-review-of-mexico-s-pemex-9789264268555-en.htm, accessed on July 19, 2018.

Institutional Transplants in Serbia 393

- civil monitor's powers in case misfeasance is identified and subsequent response of the relevant authorities
- incentives for the work of civil monitors.

Since none of these issues are regulated in a uniform manner in comparative practice, it would be very difficult to investigate whether the statutory setup of the civil monitoring mechanism is in line with what can be considered good or best comparative practices. Some indications as to the potential drawbacks of the Serbian regulatory framework were rather apparent from the onset and then confirmed in Serbian practice.

3.2. Civil Monitors of Public Procurement in Serbia – Regulatory Framework, its Drawbacks and Practice

The threshold set out in the Public Procurement Act for the civil monitor to participate in public procurement process requires that the estimated value of the contract exceeds 1 billion dinars. At the time the Act was adopted, this amounted to around 9 million EUR, and currently amounts to 8.443.662 EUR. The setting of such a high threshold is not uncommon in comparative practice. For example, in Mexico, one of the thresholds amounted to over 19 million EUR. In Poland, the threshold for mandatory control was set at 10 million EUR. However, both these, and other regulatory frameworks that institutionalized the *ex-ante* monitoring of public procurement have also envisaged the possibility for certain procedures to be monitored regardless of their value - if so requested by the procuring entity or based on a decision of a relevant state body. In Serbia, this was as still is not the case. The Serbian statute does not leave any room for flexibility and does not encourage the use of the mechanism in other cases, e.g. if the goods or services purchased are of particular interest to the public (for instance, the contract for renting street Christmas decorations in a city) or if the value of the contract is considerable in proportion to the annual budget of a local self-government. This regulatory inflexibility was not mitigated by having any of the key stakeholders on the part of the state systematically advocating for an ad hoc voluntary implementation of this mechanism. As a result, the scrutinizing mechanism targets a very small number of public procurement procedures in Serbia – according to Serbian Public Procurement Office data, only 0.027% of contracts awarded are covered by this mechanism, while the average value of contracts remains considerably below the threshold, amounting to 27.121 EUR.

Table 19. 1. Comparative Overview of Contracts Concluded in Public Procurement Procedures in Serbia

Comparative overview of concluded public procurement contracts			
Year	Total No. of Contracts	Total value (in thousands of dinars)	Average value (in thousands of dinars)
2003	231 661	98 777 652	426
2004	215 815	109 282 212	506
2005	148 758	124 753 207	838
2006	152 485	168 914 947	1 108
2007	122 587	187 559 752	1 530
2008	109 910	234 028 744	2 129
2009	91 992	190 655 028	2 073
2010	83 693	273 055 306	3 263
2011	111 249	293 324 810	2 637
2012	92 710	303 694 136	3 276
2013	83 121	262 938 735	3 163
2014	87 712	298 374 363	3 401
2015	104 527	354 982 753	3 396
2016	104 370	335 268 082	3 212

Source: Serbian Public Procurement Office Report, 2016

Having this in mind, it is quite clear that the potential for civil monitors to curb corruption is highly limited.

Conditions for the appointment of civil monitors, as set out in the Act, target a very small circle of natural and legal persons. Article 28, paragraph 2 of the Act envisages that persons eligible to be appointed as civil monitors are:

- individuals, renown experts in the field of public procurement or in a field related to the goods, services or works being procured

- associations whose scope of work includes public procurement, corruption prevention or conflict of interest prevention.

There is no registry or list of civil monitors[38] – rather, they are appointed on a case-to-case basis by the Public Procurement Office, within 30 days

---

[38] As the case is, for instance, in Mexico. See Knežević Bojović, "Građanski nadzornik – Testigo Social – u Meksiku i drugi mehanizmi građanske kontrole javnih nabavki u Latinskoj Americi", 41-60.

from the day the public procurement procedure is initiated.[39] The civil monitors are not entitled to remuneration for their work, nor to reimbursement of expenses related to participation in the procedure. The incentives for the work of civil monitors are, therefore, sparse, particularly when it comes to individuals. In fact, it is only the associations, or rather, the CSOs that already monitor public procurement processes and fight corruption that have a vested interested and sufficient resources to be appointed as civil monitors in Serbia. This is perhaps the reason why the Public Procurement Office has adopted a pragmatic approach and opted for not regulating the procedure for the appointment of civil monitors in more detail, but has reiterated, in the relevant rulebook, the very general wording included in the Act . In this way, the Public Procurement Office is free to directly negotiate with potential civil monitors and appoint them based on their availability, enabling them to regroup their internal capacities in order to the job properly. Although a not a very transparent solution, it has proven to be a realistic and effective one, particularly having in mind the fact that over the past four and half years, the number of appointed civil monitors was under 100, and the Public Procurement Office has most often resorted to appointing CSOs that actively pursue an anti-corruption and transparency agenda.[40]

How did the appointed civil monitors fare in their work and were they able to prevent corruption? It should first be borne in mind that the powers and the method of work of civil monitors are set out in the Act in rather laconic terms. The civil monitor monitors the public procurement process and has permanent insight into the procedure, documents, and communication between the procuring entity and the bidders. If the civil monitors have doubts as to the legality of the procedure, it will inform the competent bodies and the public thereof. In addition, the civil monitor can submit the motion for the protection of rights, which is one of the legal remedies envisaged by the Act to protect the rights of the bidders – it triggers a second-instance process before the Republican Commission for the Protection of Rights in Public Procurement Procedure.[41] Finally, once the procedure is completed, the civil monitor submits a report on his work

---

[39] Zakon o javnim nabavkama, Službeni glasnik RS, No. 124/2012, 14/2015 and 68/2015, art. 28.

[40] The 34 civil monitors' reports submitted so far, including the information on the appointed civil monitor, are available at Public Procurement Office's webpage http://www.ujn.gov.rs/ci/izvestaji/izvestaji-gn.

[41] Zakon o javnim nabavkama, article 148, paragraph 3.

to the National Assembly Committee in charge of finance and to the Public Procurement Office.[42] This report should also be published on the webpage of the procuring entity.

In the 2014-2016 period, a total of 90 civil monitors were appointed, and a total of 32 civil monitor's reports were submitted. The civil monitor has filed criminal charges in 1 case (they were dismissed) and was also thrown out of the National Assembly Finance Committee session in which the monitor's report was discussed under the accusation that the report was "political".[43] Civil monitors have initiated and won administrative disputes against the decisions of the second-instance authority in public procurement procedures in at three cases.[44]

Within the limited reach that has been awarded to them, civil monitors in Serbia have performed their task conscientiously. They have prevented, halted or brought into the public spotlight some serious corruption cases, such as that of the award of the contract to, halted or brought into the public spotlight some serious corruption cases, such as the one related to the reconstruction of an underground railway station in Belgrade.[45] Despite the fact that the political party that was instrumental in the adoption of the new Public Procurement Act and the adoption of this mechanism – the Serbian Progressive Party – is still in power, over the past years the lack of political support to the work of civil monitors was more than evident. So far, although the initial intention for the introduction of

---

[42] Zakon o javnim nabavkama, article 28, paragraph 9.

[43] "Arsić izbacio građanskog nadzornika sa sednice: Nema politike na sednicama Odbora", *Blic.rs*, November 25, 2015, accessed November 08, 2017, http://www.blic.rs/vesti/politika/arsic-izbacio-gradanskog-nadzornika-sa-sednice-nema-politike-na-sednicama-odbora/e3wgxkd.

[44] Judgments of the Serbian Administrative Court No. II-9 U. 10959/14 II-2 U.1367/16 and II-3 U. 4790/15 all sustained the argumentation provided by the civil monitor and ordered the second-instance authority, namely, the Republican Commission for the Protection of Rights in Public Procurement Procedu, to repeat the procedure and re-assess their position that there had been no violation of the regulations governing public procurement..

[45] "Izveštaj građanskog nadzornika: Šta je sporno u Prokopu," Nedeljnik Vreme, February 12, 2015, , accessed November 08, 2017, http://www.vreme.co.rs/cms/view.php?id=1271012. In this case the civil monitor concluded there was no competition in award of the 26-million euro contract and that, moreover, anti-corruption provisions were at hand since one of the representatives of the bidding consortium who won the contract used to work in Serbia as the director of the one of the sectors.

this legal transplant was good, the government has done nothing to advance either the regulatory framework or the practice of civil monitoring of public procurement.

It seems that, for the government, the civil monitors remain a nice box to be ticked when it comes to ensuring public scrutiny over public procurement procedures. The civil monitors, to their credit, when given the opportunity, have seized the opportunity to carry out the tasks that were requested from them with integrity and competence. This is why, despite very general and laconic regulatory framework and almost no political support to the idea of civil monitoring of procurement procedures, this transplant could still be assessed as partially successful.

4. High Judicial Council – Asserting Judicial Independence?

4.1. High Judicial Council as a Model for Asserting Judicial Independence

During the XX century an increasing number of states accepted a specific autonomous body as the constitutional or statutory representative of judicial power - the *judicial council*. Judicial council is not an institute that is generally accepted – either in Europe or globally. The existence of a judicial council is not an international obligation of the states attempting to establish the rule of law – quite to the contrary, there are many European and non-European states that are considered to have a model judiciary, but which do not have a judicial council or a similar body.[46]The construction of the judiciary has never been the result of legislative activity alone. Quite to the contrary, it is more often than not the result of political battles rather than of successful legal formulas. Until 1989, judicial independence in East European socialist/communist countries was severely influenced by the executive branch of government. In an attempt to affirm judiciary as a third branch of power after major political changes a number of Central and Eastern European Countries have introduced judicial councils. [47] In other countries, particularly in Latin America, the introduction of the High Council of the Judiciary was common following the change of political

---

[46] Vesna Rakić-Vodinelić, Ana Knez˘ević Bojović, and Mario Reljanović, *Judicial reform in Serbia 2008-2012* (Belgrade: Center for Advanced Legal Studies, 2012), 18.

[47] Ramona Coman and Jean-Marc De Waele, eds., *Judicial Reform in Central and Eastern European Countries* (Bruges: Vandenbroele, 2007); Vesna Rakić-Vodinelić et al., *Pravosudni saveti* (Beograd: Institut za uporedno pravo, 2003).

regime or as a part of a broader reform aiming at judicial independence.[48] This approach was subsequently indirectly imposed by the European Commission, as a normative model of judicial governance, in the absence of a specific blueprint of judicial independence – this is particularly true for Western Balkan countries.[49]

Serbia was no exception in this respect.

4.2. High Judicial Council in Serbia– the New Institution and its Impact on Judicial Independence

Aiming at setting solid foundations for the operation of a truly independent judiciary, completely equal to the other two branches of power, the first step taken was to introduce the High Council of the Judiciary[50] into the existing legal system. The introduction of the High Council of the Judiciary was coupled with the adoption of the new Organization of Courts Act and the Judges' Act.[51] Both legal scholars and judicial practitioners and Serbia generally welcomed[52] the introduction of an independent and autonomous

---

[48] Linn Hammergren, "Do Judicial Councils Further Judicial Reform? Lessons from Latin America", *Rule of Law Series* no. 28 (2002): 1-44, http://www.law.wisc.edu/gls/lhdjc.pdf; also Linn A. Hammergren, *Envisioning reform: improving judicial performance in Latin America* (University Park, PA: Pennsylvania State University Press, 2007) Carlos Manuel Rosales García, "El consejo de la magistratura como órgano de gobierno del poder judicial", *Pensamiento Jurídico* 44: 83-134; Agustín Grijalva, "Novo constitucionalismo, democracia e independência judicial", Cálamo: Revista de Estudios Jurídicos Quito – Ecuador, 3:27-38.

[49] Denis Preshova, Ivan Damjanovski, Zoran Nechev, "The Effectiveness of the "'European Model" of Judicial Independence in the Western Balkans: Judicial Councils as a Solution or a New Cause of Concern for Judicial Reforms", *CLEER PAPERS* 1(2017), 11; Ramona Coman, "Quo Vadis Judicial Reforms? The Quest for Judicial Independence in Central and Eastern Europe", *Europe-Asia Studies* 66, no. 6 (2014): 899;

[50] Zakon o Visokom savetu pravosuđa, Službeni glasnik RS, No. 63/2002, 42/2003, 39/2003, 44/2004 and 61/2005.

[51] Zakon o uređenju sudova, Službeni glasnik RS No. 63/2001, 42/2002, 17/2003, 25/2003, 27/2003, 29/2004, 44/2004, 61/2005, 101/2005 and 46/2006.

[52] Dušan Pavlović, "Srbija za vreme i nakon Miloševića", Sociološki pregled 39, no. 2 (2005): 183–196; Jasminka Hasanbegović, "Ostvarivanje i zaštita ljudskih prava u Srbiji – normativni okvir i pravna stvarnost", *Zbornik radova Pravnog fakulteta u Splitu* 42, no. 1-2 (2005): 55-65; Marko Žilović, "Demokratska neizvesnost i nezavisnost pravosudja u Srbiji nakon 2000. godine", *Sintezis* 4, no. 1 (2012): 87-108.

judicial body, which would contribute to overall judicial independence.[53] Despite this, the solutions of the actual legislative text, particularly those concerning the composition of the High Council of the Judiciary, have raised some concern.[54] The rules on the competence of this body often have been changed both by amendments to the High Council of the Judiciary Act[55] and by frequent changes of the Judges' Act.[56] Furthermore, the existing constitutional framework at the time — Constitution of the Republic of Serbia of 1990[57] — mandated that the tasks usually assigned to judicial councils in comparative law[58] be divided between the High Council of the Judiciary Council and the High Personnel Council, a body of the Supreme Court of Serbia.[59] The 2006 Constitution has brought some important changes to the Serbian judiciary, the most important of which lay in the fact that the High Judicial Council (hereinafter: HJC), together with another body, the State Prosecutor's Council (hereafter: SPC), have become

---

[53] For comparative analysis and critical review regarding the introduction of judicial councils and ensuing effects on judicial independence and rule of law see Nuno Garoupa and Tom Ginsburg, "Guarding the Guardians: Judicial Councils and Judicial Independence", *American Journal of Comparative Law* 57, no. 1 (2009): 103-134. The Romanian experience is analyzed in detail in Cristina Parau, "Beyond Judicial Independence: What Kind of Judiciary is Emerging in Post-Communist Eastern Europe?" (paper presented at the Social Foundations of Constitutions Workshop, Wolfson College, Oxford, 8-9 December 2009), http://ssrn.com/abstract=1523285.

[54] This was mainly due to the hierarchical organization of the HJC – three out of its eleven members were ex officio members – the president of the Supreme Court of Cassation, the Minister of Justice and the chairperson of the Parliamentary Committee for the Judiciary, all with full voting rights. The critics feared that the representatives of two other branches of power will be able to exert political pressure on the other members (appointed among judges, prosecutors, barristers and legal scholars).

[55] Adopted in 2001, amended in 2002, 2003, 2004 – two times, and 2005.

[56] Adopted in 2001, amended in 2002, 2003, 2004 – three times, 2005 and 2006.

[57] Ustav Republike Srbije, Službeni glasnik RS, No. 1/90.

[58] Selection, recruitment, appointment, promotion, disciplinary liability and termination of office of judges, as recommended by Recommendation CM/Rec(2010)12 of the Committee of Ministers to member states on judges: independence, efficiency and responsibilities. For a detailed comparative analysis of judicial councils see: Rakic Vodinelic *et al.*

[59] Article 101 of the 1990 Serbian constitution envisaged that the Supreme Court of Serbia establishes the reasons for termination of judicial office and informs the National Assembly thereof.

constitutional categories.⁶⁰ Their competences were formulated so as to encompass all those usually vested with similar bodies in comparative law and that are in line with the requirements of the relevant international documents.⁶¹ In short, the composition and the competences of the High Judicial Council in Serbia correspond to what W. Voermans and P. Aleber⁶² classify as the Southern European Model of judicial council, as found in France, Italy, Spain, and Portugal.

However, there were some concerns as to how this model was transplanted in Serbia from the very beginning, and the 2006 Constitution and a set of judicial acts adopted in 2008 - including Judges' Act, High Judicial Council Act, Public Prosecutor's Office Act, State Prosecutor's Council Act, Organization of Courts Act, Seats and Territories of Courts and Public Prosecutor's Offices Act and Act on Amendments to Petty Offences Act – did not mitigate those concerns fully.

Firstly, the solution of the former HJC Act whereby the HJC is comprised of permanent members (members by virtue of their office) and elected members is preserved in the new regulatory framework, despite criticism.⁶³ Namely, in both the HJC and the SPC⁶⁴ the Minister of Justice and president of the competent Parliamentary board are two of three so-called "permanent" HJC members, together with the President of the Supreme Court of Cassation and the Republican Public Prosecutor, with full voting rights. In comparative law, and in transition countries in

---

⁶⁰Article 153 of 2006 Serbian Constitution (Ustav Republike Srbije, SGRS 98/2006).

⁶¹ See: Rakić-Vodinelić *et al*. It is worth noting that the idea of judicial appointments by judicial collegiate bodies is not a novel one in Yugoslav theory. For instance, I. Krbek wrote about the benefits of introducing such a body. Ivo Krbek, „Garancije sudske nezavisnosti", in *Spomenica sedme glavne skupštine Kongresa pravnika Kraljevine Jugoslavije*, ed. Stojan Jovanović (Beograd: Kongres pravnika, 1935).

⁶² Wim Voermans and Pim Albers, *Councils for the Judiciary in EU Countries* (Leiden, The Hague 2003), http://www.drb.de/fileadmin/docs/sv_councils_for_the_judiciary_voermans_albers_2003.pdf (accessed on November 8, 2017).

⁶³ See: Rakić-Vodinelić *et al*.

⁶⁴ HJC is comprised of 11 members. Three members are so-called permanent members, ex officio – the President of the Supreme Court of Cassation, the Minister of Justice and the chairperson of the Parliamentary Committee for the Judiciary. The remaining eight members are so-called "elected members" – who are nominated and elected by their peers, by secret ballot. One member is selected among professors of law and one member is selected among the members of the Serbian Bar Association. The SPC has a similar composition, *mutatis mutandis*.

particular, representatives of the executive are either not members of the HJC at all or do not have voting rights, in order to avoid the potential or the appearance of potential for undue political influence.[65]

Following the constitutional reform, a set of judicial Acts was adopted in 2008. The major changes introduced by these statutes are the following:

- HJC and SPC composition and member selection, and HJC and SPC competences. Certainly, the most important new competencies of this body are those related to the election of judges/prosecutors to permanent office, determining the number of judges/prosecutors and lay judges, deciding on termination of office, and drafting the relevant budget.
- Comprehensive reorganization of court and prosecutorial network, effective as of 1 January 2010, including the establishment of Appellate courts, Administrative courts and the Supreme Court of Cassation, alongside the existing municipal and district courts and commercial courts, and the redistribution of their competences both in terms of subject-matter and territory
- General appointment (or reappointment) of all judges and prosecutors, in all instances and termination of all existing judicial and prosecutorial offices, coupled with an introduction of a three-year probation period for judges and prosecutors appointed to such office for the first time.[66] The general

---

[65] See: Rakić-Vodinelić *et al.*

[66] The term appointment refers to the process of selection and appointment of judges and as prescribed by the 2008 reformatory statutes The process entailed the following steps:
- /HJC/SPC announced a concourse for all judicial/prosecutorial posts in the Republic
- Applications were sent to the HJC/SPC
- HJC/SPC selected candidates, according to the prescribed criteria, based on the documents attached to the application. The candidates were not interviewed, although interview was an option, according to relevant statutes.
- if a judge/prosecutor did not hold a judicial or prosecutorial office before, the HJC/SPC proposed, by way of a reasoned decision, one or more candidates for the post to the National Assembly and the National Assembly then appointed one of those candidates by majority vote.

appointment was to be completed by the end of 2009, so as to enable the functioning of the new judicial network.

The general re-appointment of all judges and prosecutors was first contested from the standpoint of its constitutionality, since the constitution proclaimed the permanence of judicial office.[67] In addition, there was an underlying concern that the re-appointment will be heavily influenced by the executive power and used as an opportunity to ensure that those appointed to judicial offices are those who are loyal to the current government or political coalition. The manner in which the re-appointment process was carried out has clearly shown that such concerns were not unfounded and that the entire exercise had been carried out with a considerable degree of undue influence of the executive power over the process, coupled with a considerable disregard of due process standards.[68] Three years after the re-appointment process began, it was practically restored to a status quo by two decisions of the Constitutional Court of Serbia – all the judges and prosecutors who have appealed against the decision on their non-appointment were reinstated.

The decision was perceived as a major success of the fight that the members of the judicial profession had fought against undue influence of the executive power over their appointment process and over the judiciary as the third branch of power in general. The step that was perceived as a potential beginning of discontinuity with undue influences over the HJC was the election of the HJC and SPC members from among judges and prosecutors, which took place in December 2015. The new composition meant that the judges and prosecutors who were involved in the general re-appointment procedure and the procedure for re-examining the decisions on non-appointment of judges and prosecutors are not going to be further involved in making the decisions on appointment, promotion, and termination of office of judges and prosecutors.

Unfortunately, the High Judicial Council, however, does not seem to take clear steps in re-affirming its position as the body that guarantees judicial

---

- if the candidate already held a judicial/prosecutorial office, he/she was appointed to the given post by the HJC/SPC.

The term general appointment refers to the 2009 process, where the concourse was announced for all judicial and prosecutorial posts in Serbia, with the simultaneous termination of office of all judges and prosecutors who had exercised them thus far.

[67] Article 101 of the Serbian Constitution of 1990.

[68] For more details on the entire process see: Rakić Vodinelić, Knežević Bojović, Reljanović, *Judicial Reform in Serbia 2008-2012*.

independence. Quite to the contrary, it seems to be taking a rather passive course in this respect, when the HJC has refrained from examining the substance of the case it was supposed to deal with (disciplinary sanctions against judge Vučinić and judge Trešnjev, both initiated by the same court president, in politically sensitive cases).[69] This means that the HJC has refrained from examining the substance of the case and resorted to formality as a means of dealing with a sensitive situation.

The Serbian HJC has also taken a curious position towards judicial appointments, particularly when it comes to first-time judicial appointments and the underlying conflict between the Judicial Academy and the members of judicial professional organizations. Namely, the Judicial Academy was established in 2009 and was intended to be a single entry point to the judicial and prosecutorial profession. In February 2014, the Constitutional court had decided that the provision of the Law on the Judicial Academy whereby the HJC and the SPC would be obligated to nominate Judicial Academy trainees as candidates for judicial and prosecutorial offices was unconstitutional, as it violated the principles of equality of citizens and the right to assume a public office under equal conditions. This put the HJC in the position to decide on whether to nominate candidates who have completed the training within the Judicial Academy or those who had previously worked as judicial assistants and not having attended the Judicial Academy, without having any formal mechanisms to cross-compare their respective competencies. The HJC had so far appointed a relatively small number of Judicial Academy trainees (under 10) and at the same time had maintained a discouraging lack of transparency with regards to its decisions on concrete nominees for judicial function coming from the ranks of judicial assistants or other qualified candidates who did not attend the Judicial Academy. Even though the Decision prescribes relatively detailed and quantified standards for judicial appointments, the actual nominations are not, contrary to what may be expected, accompanied by any comparative rankings of all the candidates. Quite to the contrary, the HJC member Miroljub Tomić even openly spoke about what can only be characterized as false professional solidarity within the judicial profession - judges always award the highest marks for work to their judicial assistants - and

---

[69]For a more detailed elaboration see: Ana Knežević Bojović, *Continuity and discontinuity in Serbian legislation and practice – Selected Aspects*, Institut za uporedno pravo, 2018. For a detailed analysis and documents related to the case of judge Trešnjev visit http://www.cepris.org/slucaj-cepris/, accessed on July 22, 2018.

de facto confirmed the prevalence of the subjective criteria and the opinion of the courts on deciding whether someone should be appointed as a judge over the quantifiable criteria set out in the Decision. The HJC still preserves elusive and subjective criteria for initial judicial appointments, which raises concerns as to the possibility of undue influence being exerted on them in the process - which was a general impression related to judicial appointments before the democratic changes in 2000.

When it comes to the HJC's impact on reducing undue influence on the judiciary, it seems to be minimal. According to a study conducted by the Judge's Association of Serbia[70], including an anonymous survey of the opinions of 1585 judges, 44% of participants have responded they had felt pressured to pass a certain decision. Out of those who had sustained pressure, 43% of judges also reported they feel an atmosphere of general and systematic pressure within the judiciary. According to this survey, 27% of judges reported they sustained pressure from the executive power – 18% stated this pressure was indirect, whilst 9% stated that this pressure was open. A total of 22% of judges stated they were pressured by the court president – 16% reported indirect pressure (the president of the court inquired about a case) whilst 8% stated that the pressure was clear and direct.

It seems that, contrary to expectations and despite the introduction of a judicial council, the judiciary in Serbia has become a victim of the ineffective democratic consolidation – it is subjected to pressures mainly from the executive, but also from the legislative power, with limited capacities to internally build its independence. In this respect, the judicial council as a legal transplant must be assessed as a failure.

5. Are there Lessons to be Learned for Serbia?

The above analysis shows that in Serbia, despite the previous well-established practice of legal transplants, in recent years, the institutional transplants have had very limited social and political support. This is perhaps to an extent a result of the external conditionality of the EU

---

[70] "Predstavljanje rezultata istraživanja u okviru projekta Jačanje nezavisnosti i integriteta sudija u Srbiji", Predstavljanje rezultata istraživanja u okviru projekta Jačanje nezavisnosti i integriteta sudija u Srbiji | Medija centar Beograd, January 30, 2017, accessed December 07, 2017, http://www.mc.rs/predstavljanje-rezultata-istrazivanja-u-okviru-projekta-jacanje-nezavisnosti-i-integriteta-sudija-u-srbiji.4.html?eventId=10423.

accession process,[71] the approach which, though initially assessed by some authors as a rock-solid anchor for genuine political reforms,[72] has also started to show some deficiencies. Namely, recent studies show that the EU policy focuses on institutions and tends to define the legal system's problems and cures legalistically, in terms of courts, prosecutors, law reforms and processes.[73] This means that it is relatively easy for the national government and legislator to introduce the needed reforms first, while not fully engaging in their implementation.[74] On the other hand, the justification of the reform efforts through the EU conditionality does not necessarily secure the needed support to the newly introduced institutions – it may even induce resistance to change.

In addition, there seem to be some deeply rooted practices and path dependencies that are difficult to overcome, and that slow seep their way in even in the best of regulatory setups – as the case was with the High Judicial Council in Serbia.

The success of institutional transplant in this complex Serbian setting of an incomplete transition and effort to catch up with ever-evolving Union acquis in practice seems to depend heavily on the transplant's main protagonists or champions, and on the existing sectorial capacities. Out of

---

[71] Zoran Nechev et al, Embedding rule of law in the enlargement process—a case for EU political conditionality in the accession of the Western Balkan Countries (Skopje: Association for Development Initiatives – Zenit, 2013), www.kas.de/wf/doc/kas_36352-1522-1-30.pdf (accessed on November 7, 2017). Also see Frank Schimmelfennig and Ulrich Sedelmeier, "Governance by conditionality: EU rule transfer to the candidate countries of Central and Eastern Europe", Journal of European Public Policy 11, no. 4 (2004): 661-679, doi:10.1080/1350176042000248089.

[72] Zoran Nechev et al.

[73] Kalypso Nicolaidis and Rachel Kleinfeld, "Rethinking Europes « Rule of Law » and Enlargement Agenda", SIGMA Papers 49 (2012), accessed November 8, 2017, doi:10.1787/5k4c42jmn5zp-en.

[74] The EU has made an attempt to mitigate these issues through the new reporting system in its annual Progress reports, where, in pilot areas, it assesses both the state of play and progress made over the last year. The impact of this style of reporting is yet to be seen, but, judging by the pace with which reforms in the Chapter 23, Rule of law and fundamental rights are implemented in Serbia, EU seems to be on the losing end, as the focus of regulatory and practice reforms over the past several years in Serbia was on business-enabling environment, with transnational and national companies and business association and the Government's political and economic agenda being the drivers of reform.

the two of the cases analyzed in this paper where the CSOs were the reform champions, the National Convention had a wider pool of potential protagonists to draw from then the case was with civil monitors. This seems to be precisely what enabled the National Convention to ensure a consistent track record of activity and pursuit of its goals and its ultimate success. The number of civil sector organizations who acted as civil monitors, on the other hand, was under 10, and their task was a more engaging one in terms of use of time and resources, which may eat away from their additional advocacy and institution-building potential. As a result, the institution of the civil monitor has remained on the outskirts of practical and policy efforts to curb corruption in public procurement.

Institutional transplants promoting independence and integrity in Serbia function better and gain ownership faster in the civil sector, while public sector support to them is usually lagging. This should not come as a surprise, as the civil sector is generally more flexible and open to change. However, it is precisely the support to institutional transplants in the public sector and particularly by the key political actors that makes or breaks them as success stories. And support is not always systematically provided in a country that is not politically stable and is still on a transition path, as Serbia is. So what can be done to advance this support in future similar efforts?

Based on the analysis presented in this paper, the following necessary prerequisites for success in institutional transplanting can be formulated:

1. **Conduct regulatory impact analysis** prior to the introduction of institutional transplants. Particular attention should be given to the analysis of whether to regulate or not. In this way, it will be clear not only to the legislator whether the introduction of the transplanted institution is necessary in the reform context, but also ensure that both the legislator and relevant stakeholders fully understand the implications of the functioning of the new institution and its position in the national legal system.
2. **Ensure an inclusive strategic policy dialogue on the proposed reform.** This is critical in creating a wider sense of ownership over the institution and overcoming path dependence.
3. **Step away from the introduction of an institutional transplant as a box-ticking reform exercise to implementation of the entire reform package.** If an institutional transplant is transferred from another legal system by regulatory copy-pasting, it will have little chance for success. It is necessary to also transfer the underlying dogmatic approach and streamline

the reform efforts not towards setting up of the new institution, but towards its practical reform achievements and effects.
4. **Conduct ex-post RIA.** Even though ex-post RIA is not systemically introduced nor mandatory in most countries,[75] when it comes to the assessment of effects of institutional transplants, it would be most useful to conduct it after a three-year period of functioning of the institutional transplant, particularly in a country that still lacks overall political and institutional stability. This exercise would not only help assess the impact of the institutional transplant and enable its fine-tuning but would also provide valuable lessons for future efforts.
5. **Ensure pre- and post-introduction support to** the key actors. Reformatory efforts, particularly those that entail transplanting of legal norms and institutions, must not be reduced to legislative interventions. If institutional transplants are to be given at least a chance at success, it is necessary to ensure sufficient pre-introduction support to the key actors in the process, through awareness raising and training campaigns, in order to enable them to exercise their duties properly and ensure as uniform an application and understanding of the legal norms as possible. This support should be extended over at least one year of the functioning of the institutional transplant, thus supporting fine-tuning and uniformity even prior to the conducting of ex-post RIA, and also ensuring consistent practice and interpretation of relevant legislation.

Bibliography

"Arsić izbacio građanskog nadzornika sa sednice: Nema politike na sednicama Odbora." Blic.rs. November 25, 2015. Accessed November 08, 2017. http://www.blic.rs/vesti/politika/arsic-izbacio-gradanskog-nadzornika-sa-sednice-nema-politike-na-sednicama-odbora/e3wgxkd.

"Izveštaj građanskog nadzornika: Šta je sporno u Prokopu." Nedeljnik Vreme. February 12, 2015. Accessed November 08, 2017. http://www.vreme.co.rs/cms/view.php?id=1271012

"Predstavljanje rezultata istraživanja u okviru projekta Jačanje nezavisnosti i integriteta sudija u Srbiji." Predstavljanje rezultata istraživanja u okviru projekta Jačanje nezavisnosti i integriteta sudija u Srbiji | Medija centar Beograd. January 30, 2017. Accessed December 07, 2017. http://www.mc.rs/predstavljanje-rezultata-istrazivanja-u-okviru-

---

[75] OECD, "Ex post evaluation of regulation", *Government at a Glance Government at a Glance 2015*, 2015, 130, doi:10.1787/gov_glance-2015-40-er.

projekta-jacanje-nezavisnosti-i-integriteta-sudija-u-srbiji.4.html?eventId=10423.

Berkowitz, Daniel, Katharina Pistor, and Jean-Francois Richard. "The transplant effect." *The American Journal of Comparative Law* 51, no. 1 (2003): 163-203.

Bobić, Maja, and Relja Božić. *Civilno društvo u procesu evropske integracije – od konstruktivnog dijaloga do uspešnih pregovora.* Beograd: Evropski pokret u Srbiji, 2012.

Bosanac, Gordan. "Civil Society and EU Accession: The Croatian Experience." *EU-Monitoring.ba.* April 03, 2015. Accessed December 07, 2017. http://eu-monitoring.ba/en/gordan-bosanac-civil-society-and-eu-accession-the-croatian-experience/.

Breneselović, Luka „O zaštiti osnovnih prava u Srbiji u svetlu loše ocene Evropske komisije – razlozi niskog stepena stvarne zaštite osnovnih prava u republici Srbiji i neophodne mere za njeno poboljšanje", Evropsko zakonodavstvo, 43-44/2013, 335-360.

Coman, Ramona, and Jean-Marc De Waele, eds. *Judicial Reform in Central and Eastern European Countries.* Bruges: Vandenbroele, 2007.

Coman, Ramona. "Quo Vadis Judicial Reforms? The Quest for Judicial Independence in Central and Eastern Europe." *Europe-Asia Studies* 66, no. 6 (2014): 892-924.

De Jong Martin, Mamadouh Virginie, Lalenis Konstatinos, "Drawing Lessons About Lesson Drawing, *The Theory and Practice of Institutional Transplantation,* De Jong M., Lalenis K., Mamadouh V. (eds.) (2002) The GeoJournal Library, vol 74, 283-299

Đorđević, Miroslav "Pravni transplanti i Srbijanski građanski zakonik iz 1844". Strani pravni život 1:62-84;

European Commission. "Enlargement strategy and main challenges 2011-2012: Communication from the Commission to the European Parliament and the Council".

European Commission. "Enlargement Strategy and Main Challenges 2012-2013". Accessed November 8, 2017. http://ec.europa.eu/enlargement/pdf/key_documents/2012/package/strategy_paper_2012_en.pdf

European Commission. "Communication from the Commission to the European Parliament, the Council, the European Economic and Social Committee and the Committee of the Regions Enlargement Strategy and Main Challenges 2014-15". Accessed November 8, 2017. http://ec.europa.eu/enlargement/pdf/key_documents/2014/20141008-strategy-paper_en.pdf.

Garoupa, Nuno, and Tom Ginsburg. "Guarding the Guardians: Judicial Councils and Judicial Independence." *American Journal of Comparative Law* 57, no. 1 (2009): 103-34. doi:10.5131/ajcl.2008.0004.

González, S. C, " Las veedurías ciudadanas en cuanto mediaciones/mediadores de las relaciones Estado-sociedad en el ámbito local", Administración & Desarrollo, Vol. 40, Nº. 55, 2012, 19-32

Hammergren, Linn A. "Do Judicial Councils Further Judicial Reform? Lessons from Latin America", *Rule of Law Series* no 28 (2002): 1-44, http://www.law.wisc.edu/gls/lhdjc.pdf.

Hammergren, Linn A. *Envisioning reform: improving judicial performance in Latin America.* University Park, PA: Pennsylvania State University Press, 2007.

Hantrais, Linda. *International comparative research: theory, methods and practice.* New York: Palgrave Macmillan, 2009.

Hasanbegović, Jasminka. "Ostvarivanje i zaštita ljudskih prava u Srbiji- normativni okvir i pravna stvarnost." *Zbornik radova Pravnog fakulteta u Splitu* 42, no. 1-2 (2005): 55-65.

Jovičić, Katarina. "Sistem kontrole javnih nabavki u Poljskoj." In *Građanska kontrola javnih nabavki,* edited by Milorad Bjeletić, 27-40. Prokuplje: Toplički centar za demokratiju i ljudska prava, Beograd:Institut za uporedno pravo, 2013.

Kahn-Freund, Otto. "On uses and misuses of comparative law." *The Modern Law Review* 37, no. 1 (1974): 1-27.

Knežević Bojović, Ana. "Učešće civilnog sektora u procesu pridruživanja Evropskoj uniji i praksa nacionalnog konventa o EU", *Strani pravni život* no. 2 (2015):131-144

Knežević Bojović Ana. "Građanski nadzornik – Testigo Social – u Meksiku i drugi mehanizmi građanske kontrole javnih nabavki u Latinskoj Americi." In *Građanska kontrola javnih nabavki,* edited by Milorad Bjeletić, 41-60. Prokuplje, Beograd: Toplički centar za demokratiju i ljudska prava, Institut za uporedno pravo, 2013.

Knežević Bojović, Ana. *Continuity and discontinuity in Serbian legislation and practice – Selected Aspects,* Institut za uporedno pravo, 2018

Kohler-Koch, Beate. "Civil society and EU democracy:'astroturf'representation?." *Journal of European Public Policy* 17, no. 1 (2010): 100-116.

Krbek, Ivo. „Garancije sudske nezavisnosti". In *Spomenica sedme glavne skupštine Kongresa pravnika Kraljevine Jugoslavije,* edited by Stojan Jovanović. Beograd: Kongres pravnika, 1935.

Legrand, Pierre. "The Impossibility of 'Legal Transplants'." *Maastricht Journal of European and Comparative Law* 4, no. 2 (1997): 111-24. doi:10.1177/1023263x9700400202.

Levy, Ron. "Judicial Selection: Trust and Reform." *U.B.C Law Review* 40, no. 1 (2007): 195-250.

Miller, Jonathan M. "A Typology of Legal Transplants: Using Sociology, Legal History and Argentine Examples to Explain the Transplant Process." *The American Journal of Comparative Law* 51, no. 4 (2003): 839-85. doi:10.2307/3649131.

Milošević, Vojislav, ed. *Nacionalni konvent o Evropskoj uniji – Knjiga preporuka*. Beograd: Evropski pokret u Srbiji, 2008.

Najšlová, Lucia. "Slovakia in the East: Pragmatic Follower, Occasional Leader." *Perspectives: Central European Review of International Affairs* 19, no. 2 (2011): 101-22.

Nechev Zoran, Gordana Vidovic Mesarek, Nikola B. Saranovich and Aleksandar Nikolov. *Embedding rule of law in the enlargement process— a case for EU political conditionality in the accession of the Western Balkan Countries.* Skopje: Association for Development Initiatives – Zenit, 2013, www.kas.de/wf/doc/kas_36352-1522-1-30.pdf

Nicolaidis, Kalypso, and Rachel Kleinfeld. "Rethinking Europe's «Rule of Law» and Enlargement Agenda." *SIGMA Papers* 49 (2012). Accessed November 8, 2017. doi:10.1787/5k4c42jmn5zp-en.

O'Brennan, John. "The European Commission, Enlargement Policy and Civil Society in the Western Balkans." In *Civil Society and Transitions in the Western Balkans*, edited by V. Bojičić- Dželilović, J. Ker-Lindsay, D. Kostovicova, Houndmills, Basingstoke, Hampshire: Palgrave Macmillan, 2013: 29-46.

OECD. "Ex post evaluation of regulation." *Government at a Glance Government at a Glance 2015*, 2015, 130-31. doi:10.1787/gov_glance-2015-40-en.

OECD. "OECD Principles for Integrity in Public Procurement." Accessed November 8, 2017. http://www.oecd.org/gov/ethics/48994520.pdf

OECD. "OECD Public Governance Reviews Public Procurement Review of Mexico's PEMEX Adapting to Change in the Oil Industry: Adapting to Change in the Oil Industry", http://www.oecd.org/gov/public-procurement-review-of-mexico-s-pemex-9789264268555-en.htm. Accessed July 19, 2018.

Parau, Cristina. "Beyond Judicial Independence: What Kind of Judiciary is Emerging in Post-Communist Eastern Europe?". Paper presented at the Social Foundations of Constitutions Workshop, Wolfson College, Oxford, 8-9 December 2009, http://ssrn.com/abstract=1523285

Pavlović, Dušan. "Srbija za vreme i nakon Miloševića." *Sociološki pregled* 39, no. 2 (2005): 183-196.

Peerenboom, Randall. "Toward a Methodology for Successful Legal Transplants." *The Chinese Journal of Comparative Law* 1, no. 1 (2013): 4-20.

Preshova, Denis, Ivan Damjanovski, and Zoran Nechev. "The Effectiveness of the 'European Model'of Judicial Independence in the Western Balkans: Judicial Councils as a Solution or a New Cause of Concern for Judicial Reforms." *CLEER PAPERS* 1 (2017).

Pürner, Stefan. ""Dug i krivudav put" srpskog prava (nazad) u Evropu", Zbornik radova Pravnog fakulteta u Nišu, 68:607-625;

Rabrenović et al, „Istorijski razvoj mehanizama za sprečavanje korupcije u zemljama Jugoistočne Evrope", Pravni mehanizmi sprečavanja korupcije u Jugoistočnoj Evropi, Institut za uporedno pravo, Beograd 2013, 13-37;

Rabrenović Aleksandra. "Učešće civilnog sektora u nadgledanju javnih nabavki u zemljama Azije." In *Građanska kontrola javnih nabavki*, edited by Milorad Bjeletić, 11-27. Prokuplje, Beograd: Toplički centar za demokratiju i ljudska prava, Institut za uporedno pravo, 2013.

Rakić-Vodinelić, Vesna, Ana Knežević Bojović, and Mario Reljanović. *Judicial reform in Serbia 2008-2012*. Belgrade: Center for Advanced legal Studies, 2012.

Rakić-Vodinelić, Vesna, Ana Knežević, Ljubinka Kovačević, Milena Vujović, Predrag Vukasović, Ilidio Saccarao Martins, Vladimir Cvijan, Katarina Jovičić, and Marija Karanikić-Mirić. *Pravosudni saveti*. Beograd: Institut za uporedno pravo, 2003.

Ramkumar V., Krafchik W., The Role of Civil Society Organisations in Auditing and Public Finance Management, 2006, http://www.internationalbudget.org/wp-content/uploads/The-Role-of-Civil-Society-Organizations-in-Auditing-and-Public-Finance-Management1.pdf. Accessed 20.8.2013

Reyes, Maria. "The Challenges of Legal Transplants in a Globalized Context: A Case Study on 'Working' Examples." SSRN. November 26, 2014. Accessed December 07, 2017. https://papers.ssrn.com/sol3/papers.cfm?abstract_id=2530811.

Schimmelfennig, Frank, and Ulrich Sedelmeier. "Governance by conditionality: EU rule transfer to the candidate countries of Central and Eastern Europe." *Journal of European Public Policy* 11, no. 4 (2004): 661-79. doi:10.1080/1350176042000248089.

Transparencia Mexicana. "APEC Procurement Transparency Standards in Mexico Time to Engage the Private Sector", Transparency International-USA and Center for International Private Enterprise, 2011, https://www.coalitionforintegrity.org/?ddownload=534. Accessed on July 19, 2018

Voermans Wim and Pim Albers. *Councils for the Judiciary in EU Countries*. Leiden, The Hague 2003, http://www.drb.de/fileadmin/docs/sv_councils_for_the_judiciary_voermans_albers_2003.pdf

Watson, Alan. *Law out of context*. Athens, GA: University of Georgia Press, 2000.

Watson, Alan. *Legal Transplants: An Approach to Comparative Law*. Edinburgh, 1974.

Žilović, Marko. "Demokratska neizvesnost i nezavisnost pravosuđa u Srbiji nakon 2000. godine," *Sintezis* 4, no. 1 (2012): 87-108.

Chapter 20

Supreme Audit Institutions of the Republic of Serbia and the United Kingdom – Comparative Legal Analysis

Jelena Kostić[1]

Abstract

One of the most important public finance control mechanisms, at the national level, is the Supreme Audit Institutions. In the United Kingdom, public finance control is performed by the National Audit Office. This office has developed from the former Exchequer and Audit Department, which had been founded in 1866. Its primary function is to examine and match the quantitative allocation with the qualitative purpose.

Unlike internal financial control in the public sector, in the region of former Yugoslavia, external control of budget expenditure has a longstanding tradition. It was embodied in the General Control of the Kingdom of Yugoslavia, which was authorized to carry out ex ante and ex post controls of budget execution. After the Second World War, the control of budget expenditures was executed by the Social Accounting Service, which did not have a status of a Supreme Audit Institution. The State Audit Institution of the Republic of Serbia was founded in 2006.

The national Supreme Audit Institutions are members of the International Organization of Supreme Audit Institutions (INTOSAI). The Framework of International Standards of Supreme Audit Institutions has been established by INTOSAI. These standards are relevant to the practice of the national Supreme Audit Institutions, and they are accepted in all INTOSAI member states. It appears that national legislations on financial control in the civil law and the common law systems are very similar. Therefore, the subject of

---

[1] Research Fellow, Institute of Comparative Law, Belgrade

the analysis in this paper is the functioning of the Supreme Audit Institutions of the Republic of Serbia and the United Kingdom.

Introduction

The accession of the Republic of Serbia to the European Union depends on the fulfillment of both political and economic conditions. These conditions are contained in the Stabilisation and Association Agreement and have previously been specified by the Copenhagen Criteria. One of the economic criteria specified in the Negotiations Chapter 32 is the establishment of the public sector financial accountability, i.e. the development of the mechanisms for its enhancement.[2] Financial discipline in the public sector is ensured also by the existence of an external audit. The Copenhagen Membership Criteria set the condition of the existence of an independent and functional state audit institution of the candidate country.[3]

The objective of the public sector institutions' operations is not profit. It is reflected in the creation of public goods to meet general needs. Those assets are not unlimited, and neither are the assets used to secure them (which are, to a large extent, the public revenues). That is exactly why the rational use of public funds is important to all citizens.[4]

The Supreme Audit Institution in the Republic of Serbia was established in 2005, under the State Audit Institution Law.[5] In accordance with the International Standards of Supreme Audit Institutions, it reports on its activities to the National Parliament of the Republic of Serbia. The State Audit Institution is an independent body in charge of auditing public funds. It is authorized to report on the performed audits to the National Parliament

---

[2] Jelena Šuput, "Interna finansijska kontrola u javnom sektoru" in *Usklađivanje prava Republike Srbije sa pravnim tekovinama EU, prioriteti, problemi, perspektive*, eds. Aleksandra Rabrenović and Jelena Ćeranić, (Beograd: Institut za uporedno pravo, 2012), 247.

[3] Aleksandra Tekijaški, "Ustanovljenje funkcije eksterne revizije u javnom sektoru," in *Usklađivanje prava Republike Srbije sa pranim tekovinama EU, prioriteti, problemi, perspektive*, eds. Aleksandra Rabrenović and Jelena Ćeranić, (Beograd: Institut za uporedno pravo, 2012), 262.

[4] Jelena Šuput, "Usaglašenost propisa koji uređuju internu reviziju sa međunarodnim standardima, primer Makedonije, Crne Gore i Srbije" in *Dobra uprava i interna revizija*, ed. Dejan Šuput, (Beograd: Insititut za uporedno pravo, 2012), 97.

[5] The Law on the Supreme Audit Institution ("Official Gazette of the Republic of Serbia" Number 101/2005, 54/2007 i 36/2010).

of the Republic of Serbia, and to the local self-government assemblies. In addition to audit, it may also have the advisory function in relation to the Government and other state institutions when it comes to undertaking specific activities or major projects, but only to the extent that it does not limit the independence of the Institution. As part of its advisory role, the State Audit Institution may give its opinion on draft legislation and other legal acts, and on the matters of relevance to the public sector finances. It may also make recommendations for changes to the existing regulations, based on the information received during the auditing process, to prevent any negative effects or in case the existing solutions would lead to undesired results. In addition to the above activities, it cooperates with the international auditors' and accountants' organizations in the field of public sector accounting and auditing.[6] The establishment of the independent Supreme Audit Institution has contributed to strengthening the parliamentary control over public expenditure, as well as to strengthening the principles of good governance.

The national law of the Republic of Serbia had been developed originally under the influence of the Germany and Austrian law, and not under the influence of the Anglo-Saxon legal system. However, in the recent period, in the legislation of the Republic of Serbia, there has been an increasing influence of the solutions applied in the Anglo-Saxon countries.[7] This influence is also present in the public sector finances, by way of a strengthened parliamentary control over public expenditure. Although the public expenditure external control system existed even at the time of the Kingdom of Serbia, as well as in the period of the Kingdom of Yugoslavia, the competent institution that carried out these duties reported to the executive power. This means that the control over public expenditure was under the authority of the King. Such a situation existed until 1931, when parliamentary control over public expenditure was established in accordance with the September Constitution and was carried out through the General Control institution.[8] Subsequently, that was replaced by the

---

[6] Its powers are specified by Article 5 of the State Audit Institution Law.

[7] Such influence is very present in criminal law matters. For example, *plea barging* and *liaison officers* are legal transplants from American law.

[8] The September Constitution ("Official Gazette of the Kingdom of Yugoslavia", Number 215, 3 September 1931). The jurisdiction of the General Control was specified in the 10th article in the aforementioned Constitution, which defined issues of importance for allocation and distribution of the state budget . According to the article 107. of the Constitution, the aforementioned body was in charge of auditing state accounts as well as monitoring the distribution of State and self-

activity of the Social Accounting Service, which was an effective form of the public expenditure external control. However, while the Service performed its activities to an exceptionally high standard, it did not have the status of a Supreme Audit Institution in line with international standards.[9]

The need to establish control over public expenditures prevailed in the Republic of Serbia only after 2000. However, it appears to have been driven by the European Union accession intentions. The establishment of this mechanism should contribute to the public sector organizations operating in accordance with the regulations, in an efficient and effective manner, and to maintaining assets and minimizing the possibility for the destruction or damage of assets. As it has already been stated, the adoption of the 2005 Law created a legal basis for the establishment of an effective public expenditures parliamentary control system. Taking into account the legal provisions governing the operations of the State Audit Institution, specific solutions in the national legislation appear to be similar to a certain extent to the solutions that exist in the UK. One of the reasons for that could be the exchange of best practices, which takes place at the level of the International Organisation of Supreme Audit Institutions, as the State Audit Institution of the Republic of Serbia is its member.

---

governing bugdets. Its authority was more expansive and very much different in comparison with that of the current State Auditing Institution of the Republic of Serbia. Under the provisions of the Septembre Constitution this body was responsible for not only controlling, but also auditing and liquidation of general administrative accounts and other chief accounts of the State Treasury. Text is available on the following web-site:
http://digitalna.nb.rs/wb/NBS/Tematske_kolekcije/Srpski_ustavi/RA-ustav-1931#page/16/mode/1up accessed June 30 2018.

[9] Bearing in mind that Serbia once used to be a Kingdom, and that she used to be a part of the Kingdom of Serbs, Croats and Slovenes, and subsequently the Kingdom of Yugoslavia, this referes to the General Control that existed in the territory of the today's Republic of Serbia. The Social Accounting Service was established in 1959, at the time of the Federal People's Republic of Yugoslavia, which later became the Socialist Federal Republic of Yugoslavia in 1963, and which after the breakup of the Socialist Federal Republic of Yugoslavia became the Federal Republic of Yugoslavia, and subsequently, in 2003, the State Union Serbia and Montenegro. After the secession of Montenegro from the State Union, and in accordance with the Constitutional Charter, Serbia maintained the state and legal continuity as the Republic of Serbia.

Even though Serbia has had for some time the General Control Institution, which, after the adoption of the September 1931 Constitution, reported on its activities to the Parliament, it did not have continuity in its operations. The UK Supreme Audit Institution has not only a longstanding tradition but also the continuity. Because of that, some authors consider mentioned institution is one of the world's leading Supreme Audit Institutions.[10]

1. The Historical Development of the Public Finances External Control in Serbia

The mechanism of external financial control of public spending has existed since the time of the Kingdom of Serbia. The Law on the General Control of 1892 defined the control of the state budget. According to this Law, the General Control was in charge of controlling that the budget credits are not exceeded and that the amounts are not transferred from one party to another. In addition, the annual account was submitted to the Assembly with the remarks of the General Control. According to this Law, only the annual account was to be controlled. The National Assembly did not establish a preventive control. Nevertheless, the Law gave independence to the General Control over the execution.[11]

The new Law on General Control was passed in 1922 and was later amended in 1929 and 1930. Immediately prior to the adoption of the said Law, the Vidovdan Constitution was passed, by which the Yugoslav state was organized as parliamentary. The Law on General Control defines its functioning, organization, and relation towards the legislative and

---

[10] Kennet M. Dye and Rick Stepenhorst, "Pillars of Integrity: The Importance of Supreme Audit Institutions" in *Curbing Corruption*, (Washington: Economic Development Institute of the World Bank, 1998), 6. According to mentioned authors the UK National Audit Office is one of the leading Supreme Audit Institution and emphasizes rigorous audits, quality assurance and objectivity.

[11] Slobodan Jovanović, *Vlada Aleksandra Obrenovića*, knjiga prva (1889–1897), (Beograd: Izdavačka knjižarnica Gece Kona, 1929), 27-8, quoted according to Nadežda D. Tošić, *Budžetksa kontrola*, (Beograd: Pravni fakultet Univerziteta u Beogradu, 2013), 55-6. Article 16 of the Law on the General Control ("Serbian Gazette", Number 103, 10 May 1892). In the Article 1 of the aforementioned Law it was specified that the body was State Accounting Court, and that it was empowered to review and audit all State accounts and other accounts which were under the State supervision. By Article 15 it was defined that the body was authorised for auditing, reviewing and liquidation of general administrative accounts and other chief accounts of the State Treasury.

administrative authorities. The territorial jurisdiction of the General Control included the entire country.[12] This body represented the supreme court of accounts and was in charge of auditing the state accounts and supervising the execution of the budget. The General Control assessed and authenticated the state annual account and produced reports for the king. It controlled whether the funds from the budget were spent beyond the permissible limitations, whether the funds were transferred from one budgetary party to another, whether the budget funds were spent on activities that were not planned by the budget.[13] Hence, one of its important tasks was to prevent the unlawful use of state resources, as well as to determine the responsibility for abuse and to establish procedures for compensation for damages. The General Control consisted of a president and eleven members. They were appointed by the king. As can be concluded, at the time, the mechanism of external control of public spending was not responsible to the parliament. The king appointed the presidents and members, and they also submitted to him reports on performed control.[14]

---

[12] Milan P. Radojkovič, *Kontrola budžeta*, doktorska rasprava, (Beograd: Pravni fakultet Univerziteta u Beogradu, 1940), 57, quoted according to: Nadežda D. Tošić, *Budžetska kontrola*, 57. The Vidovdan Constitution ("Official Gazette of the Kingdom of Serbs, Croats and Slovenes", Number 142a, 28. Jun, 1921).

[13] Article 26, paragraph 1, item 13 of the Law on the General Control ("Official Gazette of the Kingdom of Serbs, Croats and Slovenes", Number 125, 10 June 1922) and the Law on the General Control ("Official Gazette of the Kingdom of Serbs, Croats and Slovenes", Number 9, 11 January 1929).

[14] The Law on the General Control (May the 30th 1922, DSKJ, Belgrade, 1930, reprinted issue, ZZUP, Belgrade, 2008, 5-7, quoted according to Nadežda D. Tošić, *Budžetska kontrola*, 57. Under the provision 5 of the Law on the General Control ("Official Gazette of the Kingdom Serbs, Croats and Slovenes", Number 7, 8 January 1929), by which the Article 2 of the Law on the General Control was amended ("Official Gazette of the Kingdom of Serbs, Croats and Slovenes", Number 125, 10 June 1922) the members and the president of the General Control were appointed and dismissed by the King, to whom they were held accountable for their work. The Article 1 which specified the authority of the General Control was replaced by the Article 1 of the General Control dating from 1930. and according to which the aforementioned body was responsible for reviewing state, bannat and general formal decisions and supervising the distribution of their budgets. Apart from that, the General Control was, as a General Accounting Court, in charge of eliminating illegal usage and damaging material, state-owned, bannat and general goods, and by auditing the accounts it recorded correctness, malpractices or irregularities , and related to that

The Law on the General Control was amended in 1929, but the president and members of the General Control continued to be accountable to the king for their work. He appointed and dismissed them upon a proposal from the Prime Minister. The reports on the state annual account were also submitted to the king. However, with the adoption of the September Constitution of 1931, the General Control became a constitutional category and an institution that is responsible to the Parliament for its work.[15] The president and members were elected by the National Assembly of the Kingdom of Yugoslavia on the proposal of the National Council. The General Control was in charge of auditing government accounts and supervising the execution of state and self-government budgets. Although in Serbia external control of public spending existed in the past, it was not embodied in a supreme audit institution. Nevertheless, it is often pointed out that a high quality control of the public spending was performed by the Social Accounting Service, which was responsible for the external control and supervision of financial operations of users of budget funds and business entities. It was independent and autonomous in its functioning and performed social accounting and payment operations.[16] To some extent, it was the same as today's budgetary inspection. Should the existence of unlawfulness and irregularities be established during the control procedure, the authorized person was obliged to issue a decision requiring the undertaking of certain actions for the elimination of these illegalities.[17]

Unlike the Social Accounting Service, the General Control was the supreme audit institution. It performed almost all the functions of a supreme audit institution. Therefore, it can be said that, in contrast to internal audit, the external audit had a long tradition in the territory of today's Serbia.[18] However, one can speak of the existence of an

---

also legal responsibility for malpractices and compensation for the damage.("Official Gazette of the Kingdom Yugoslavia", Number 244, 24 October 1930).

[15] Article 104 of the September Constitution („Official Gazette of the Kingdom of Yugoslavia", Number. 215, 3. September, 1931.

[16] Article 4 of the Law on the Social Accounting Service, Službeni list SFRJ, No. 70/83, 16/86, 72/86, 74/87, 61/88, 57/89, 79/90, 84/90 and 20/91.

[17] Aleksandra Rabrenović et al, "Istorijski razvoj mehanizama za sprečavanje korupcije u zemljama Jugoistočne Evrope", in: *Pravni mehanizmi sprečavanja korupcije u zemljama Jugoistočne Evrope sa posebnim osvrtom na sektor odbrane*, ed. Aleksandra Rabrenović, (Beograd: Institut za uporedno pravo, 2013), 25.

[18] *Ibid.* 26.

independent supreme audit institution only as of 2005, when the Law on State Audit Institution was adopted, whose standards are fully harmonized with the International Standards of Supreme Audit Institutions. These standards were passed by the International Organization of Supreme Audit Institutions (INTOSAI), and therefore there is a similarity of national regulations of different countries, which regulate the field of external audit. Although the legal tradition of some of them is quite different, there is a lot of similarities in terms of organizing independent external control.

2. The International Standards of Supreme Audit Institutions

The International Organization of Supreme Audit Institutions was established for the purpose of cooperation between the supreme audit institutions of various countries. This institution is an independent, non-governmental organization with special consultative status with the Economic and Social Council of the United Nations. It was founded in 1953 at the initiative of Emilio Fernandez Camus, President of the Supreme Audit Institution of Cuba. 34 countries participated in the 1st Congress of the International Organization of Supreme Audit Institutions held in Cuba. Today, this organization counts 194 full members and 5 associate members.[19]

For more than 50 years, this organization has ensured an institutionalized framework for supreme audit institutions necessary to improve external auditing. The reasons for interconnecting the supreme audit institutions at the international level are the exchange of knowledge, the improvement of the audit of public funds and the exchange of experience in order to establish and improve the functioning of supreme audit institutions at the national level.[20] The International Organization of Supreme Audit Institutions has issued guidelines for the best auditing practice in both the public and private sectors.[21] These guidelines are not binding, but their

---

[19] Information about the International Organization of Supreme Audit Institutions can be found on the following web-site: http://www.intosai.org/en/about-us.html, accessed December 1, 2017.

[20] Ibid.

[21] These guidelines are general and specific (specific refer to certain fields, such as guidelines for IT-auditing). The general guidelines are: ISSAI 100-2999 General Auditing Guidelines of Financial Audit, ISSAI 3000-3999 General Auditing Guidelines on Performance Audit, ISSAI 4000-4999 General Auditing Guidelines on Compliance Audit. The more detailed list is given on the web-site: www.intosai.org/issai-executive-summaries/4-auditing-guidelines/general-auditing-guidelines.html, accessed December 1, 2017.

implementation depends on the attitude and the needs of a specific country. They contain the basic principles of the Lima Declaration: preconditions for the adequate functioning of supreme audit institutions, and professional standards of audit.[22] The guidelines detail the above-mentioned principles. They are applied during the audit procedure. In addition, the Code of Ethics that INCOSAI passed in 2001 is of particular importance for the functioning of the audit.[23]

A supreme auditing institution of a country should also improve the life of its citizens. That is why it is necessary to ensure its independence, which is provided by predicting its accountability to the parliament, as a national representation. A national supreme audit institution should improve the accountability of public sector institutions in relation to the spending of public funds. It is therefore of particular interest that employees of these institutions act in accordance with the recommendations of a supreme audit institution. One of the mechanisms for increasing the accountability of public sector institutions is the obligation to publicize the reports of the supreme audit institution. In order to realize these goals, it is necessary to ensure the transparency of the work of the supreme audit institution, good governance within it, as well as the treatment of its employees in accordance with the Code of Ethics. In addition, capacity building is also required through the improvement of knowledge and sharing of experience. One way of accomplishing this is membership in international and regional organizations of supreme audit institutions.[24]

---

[22] The basic principles contained in the Lima Declaration are available on the following web-site: http://www.issai.org/en_us/site-issai/issai-framework/, accessed December 1, 2017.

[23] The Code of Ethics was adopted by the Congress of the International Organization of the Supreme Audit Institutions. More information about this document can be found on the following web-site: http://www.intosai.org/issai-executive-summaries/view/article/issai-30-code-of-ethics.html, accessed December 1, 2017.

[24] ISSAI 12 – The Value and Benefits of Supreme Audit Institutions – making a difference to the lives of citizens. More about this can be found on the following web-site: http://www.intosai.org/issai-executive-summaries/view/article/issai-12-the-value-and-benefits-of-supreme-audit-institutions-making-a-difference-to-the-liv.html, accessed December 1, 2017.

The INTOSAI operates on the basis that there can only be the one Supreme Audit Institution for each country.[25] The mentioned organization encourages the exchange of good practice of national supreme institutions. It is quite realistic that countries that have a long tradition of external control of public spending have developed the best practice. Lasting presence of such mechanisms makes it possible to observe any possible error in the previous period and to improve the existing system. One of these countries is the United Kingdom. In this country, the external audit as an important mechanism for controlling public spending has a very long tradition. In the Republic of Serbia, the system of external control of public spending also has a long tradition. The external audit function was once performed by the General Control. Although the external control of public spending was also carried out by the Social Accounting Service, it did not have the authority of a supreme audit institution. Such an institution was only established in 2005 by the Law on State Audit Institution. This Law was amended twice and harmonized with the International Standards of Supreme Audit Institutions. These standards also contain the best practices at the national level of the member states of INTOSAI. The UK Supreme Audit Institution has a rich tradition of external control of public spending. This is probably one of the reasons why the national legislation regulating the field of external audit in the public sector of the Republic of Serbia adopted some solutions similar to the national regulations of the United Kingdom, which regulate the same matter. According to INTOSAI standards, the Supreme Audit Institution of each country should be responsible for public sector monitoring, which provides information that highlights both good government as well as inefficient administrative structures.[26]

3. The Supreme Audit Institution of the United Kingdom

The National Audit Office of the UK is the supreme audit institution of public funds without jurisdictional responsibility and has as objective "to

---

[25] Good Practices in supporting Supreme Audit Institutions, OECD 16. This document is available on the following web-site:
https://www.oecd.org/dac/effectiveness/Final%20SAI%20Good%20Practice%20Note.pdf, accessed July 1, 2018.

[26] Belén González, Antonio López, Roberto Garcia, "How do Supreme Audit Institutions measure the impact of their work?", *Implementing Reforms in Public Sector Accounting*, ed. Susana Jorge, (Coimbra: Coimbra University Press, 2008) 503.

help the nation spend wisely".[27] The legal basis for its status as well as the status of its employees is contained in three laws: the Exchequer and Audit Departments Act of 1866, the Exchequer and Audit Departments Act of 1921, which amended the Exchequer and Audit Departments Act of 1866, and the National Audit Act of 1983, which amended numerous provisions of the previous two laws.[28]

The task of the National Audit Office is the control of public spending for Parliament. This form of public auditing facilitates the Parliament in controlling the public expenditure in the public sector, which contributes to its improvement. This office audits all institutions – government institutions, agencies, and other public bodies, and reports the results to the Parliament. The head of the audit institution is the Comptroller and Auditor General. He or She is an officer of the Parliament and in the light of his statutory position has a high degree of independence.[29]

The supreme audit institution of the United Kingdom has existed for a very long time and has had continuity in its functioning. In the XIV century, the supreme audit institution of the United Kingdom was established as a body in charge of supervising government expenditure and was embodied in the Auditor of the Exchequer of 1314. Later it became the Auditors of the Imprest, established under Queen Elizabeth I in 1559, which was responsible for auditing state budget payments. The fact that in 1780 Commissioners for Auditing the Public Accounts were appointed, also contributed to the improvement of the financial accountability system. As of 1834, the Commissioners worked in tandem

---

[27] Cornelia Dobre, "Great Britain and Germany Supreme Audit Institutions", *Annals of Faculty of Economics, University of Oradea*, Number 1, (2012), 698.

[28] The Exchequer and Audit Documents Act (1866 Chapter 39 29 and 30, 28th of June 1866. Text is available on the following web-site:
http://www.legislation.gov.uk/ukpga/Vict/29-30/39), The Exchequer and Audit Departments Act (1921 Chapter 5211 and 12 Geo, 19th of August, 1921, Text is available on the following web-site:
https://www.legislation.gov.uk/ukpga/Geo5/11-12/52) and The National Audit Act (1983 Chapter 44, 13th of May 1983. Text is available on the following web-site:
https://www.legislation.gov.uk/ukpga/1983/44/pdfs/ukpga_19830044_en.pdf) accessed July 1 2018.

[29] Cornelia Dobre "Great Britain and Germany Supreme Audit Institutions", 698.

with the Comptroller of the Exchequer, who was in charge of controlling the public expenditure of the government.[30]

From 1960, parliamentary control of public spending has been gradually improved. The first reforms were undertaken thanks to William Ewart Gladstone, Chancellor of the Exchequer between 1859 and 1866. The Exchequer and Audit Departments Act was adopted in 1866, and it stipulated that the public institutions must submit to the parliament their annual accounts for the approval. This legal document also established the position of Comptroller and Auditor General, who was authorized to perform *ex-ante* financial control. This authorization consisted in approving the use of public funds after verifying that this was in accordance with the law, i.e. in accordance with the amounts approved by Parliament. Besides, he was also in charge of *ex-post* control through the audit of all government accounts and was obliged to report to Parliament.[31]

In the meantime, the public administration expanded, and it became almost impossible for the Comptroller and the Auditor General to examine every budget transaction. Public spending has increased, especially during the First World War. This is why the new Exchequer and Audit Departments Act was passed in 1921, which made it possible to control public spending on the basis of a sample of transactions – a selection of a certain number of transactions. It also stipulated submitting a report to Parliament on the audit carried out in accordance with the limits of public spending that it defined.[32]

Although in the 1960s parliamentarians and academics believed that modernization of the state audit was necessary, its role was reformed only in the 1980s. First of all, it was argued that it was necessary to establish the so-called value for money audit, on which the Comptroller and the Auditor General would inform the Parliament. Also, it was argued that it was necessary to establish greater independence of the national audit institution from the executive authorities. All these arguments were adopted in the National Audit Act of 1983. Based on this act, the Comptroller and the Auditor General formally became an official of the

---

[30] Some information about the historical development of the supreme audit institution can be found on the following web-site: https://www.nao.org.uk/about-us/our-work/history-of-the-nao/ accessed December 1, 2017.

[31] See: https://www.nao.org.uk/about-us/our-work/history-of-the-nao/ accessed December 1, 2017.

[32] *Ibid.*

House of Commons, an audit of the effectiveness of public spending was established, and the National Audit Office was founded. Also, the Public Accounts Commission was established, whose task was to oversee the work of the National Audit Office, provide financial means for its functioning, appoint its auditors and consider their reports.[33] The Comptroller and the Auditor General may carry out examinations into the mentioned principles with which any department, authority or other body uses its resources in discharging its functions. In essence, The National Audit Office is concerned with value for money. In addition to executing its historical role of ensuring that delivery of public goods and services maintain proper accounts.[34]

After 2000, several other legal acts of importance for the work of the National Audit Office were adopted. Pursuant to the Government Resources and Accounts Act of 2000, cash-based accounting in the public sector was established, as well as the preparation and audit of consolidated annual accounts for the whole public sector. According to this act, the audit of these accounts was entrusted to the National Audit Office. In addition, if public bodies are established as companies and use public funds, in accordance with the new provisions of the Companies Act of 2006, the audit of public funds expenditure in these companies is performed by the National Audit Office. The Budget Responsibility and National Audit Act of 2011 established a collective management body for the said institution. This management body is a Board consisting of four executive members (including the Comptroller and Auditor General as Chief Executive of the Board) and five non-executive members (including a Chairman). The Board's task is to adopt the strategic programme of the National Audit Office and support the Comptroller and Auditor General, who retains his independence in terms of his statutory functions. The Comptroller and Auditor General remains independent in terms of his responsibility to the House of Commons but now has a limited term. According to the Act of 2011, his term is limited to ten years. In addition to the aforementioned acts, the Local Audit and Accountability Act was adopted in 2014. It stipulated the obligation to introduce new mechanisms for the audit of local public bodies, including policing bodies. This act also envisages the obligation of the Comptroller and Auditor

---

[33] Ibid.

[34] Simon D. Norton and L. Murphy Smith, "Contrast and Foundation of the Public Oversight Roles of the US. Government Accountability Office and the U.K. National Audit Office", Public Administration Review, Vol. 68, Number 5, (2018), 924.

General to prepare the Code of Audit Practice, which would regulate local auditors' procedures in accordance with their responsibilities under the Act.[35] Although the aforementioned acts, except the Budget Responsibility and National Audit Act of 2011, do not regulate the work of the supreme audit institution, they extended its jurisdiction. The audit of the annual account for the whole public sector is also one of the basic functions of the State Audit Institution of the Republic of Serbia. In addition, the national auditing institution of the Republic of Serbia may also perform audits of business entities under the conditions stipulated by the Law on the State Audit Institution.[36] The supreme body of the supreme audit institution in the Republic of Serbia is the Council, as a collegial body. In accordance with the law, it supports the General State Auditor, who at the same time is the President of the Council and the President of the Institution.[37] When it comes to auditing the users of public funds of local self-government units, it is carried out not by special bodies, but by the State Audit Institution of the Republic of Serbia. Nevertheless, regardless of this difference, there are still many similarities in the functioning of the said supreme audit institution and the UK National Audit Office.

4. Similarities in Functioning of the Uk and Serbian Supreme Audit Institutions

The Comptroller and Auditor-General (CAG) in the UK Supreme Audit Institution has a specific function. It includes both *ex ante* and *ex post*

---

[35] Ibid.

[36] Pursuant to Article 10 of the Law on State Audit Institution, the auditees may include public enterprises, business associations, and other legal entities, established by direct or indirect beneficiary of public funds, legal entities within which direct or indirect beneficiaries participate in capital or in management, legal entities established by legal entities in which the state participates in capital or in management, legal and physical entities which receive subsidies and other grants or guarantees from the Republic, territorial autonomies and local authorities, and subjects dealing with acceptance, maintenance, issuing and use of public reserves. Also, pursuant to Article 11 of the Law, the State Audit Institution may conduct audit of operations of the legal entities having business dealings with the aforementioned auditees. In this case, the audit is conducted only in relation to their business dealings with the auditees.

[37] Article 15 of the Law on State Audit Institution stipulates that members of the Council participate in the work and decision making of the Council, monitor the activities of certain auditing units in the Institution, participate in the working process of auditing services and perform other duties, entrusted by President of the Council.

financial control. The first function is reflected in the authorization, i.e. transfer, of budget allocations to departments and other administrative authorities. The above function relates exclusively to checking whether the requested amount is in accordance with the approved budget framework.[38] The second key function is the audit of the final budget account. The CAG is responsible for controlling the final account reliability, regularity, and accuracy, as well as to control the value for money element. In other words, the CAG is authorized to perform two types of audits: financial audits and performance audits. On behalf of the House of Commons, the CAG scrutinizes all financial reports. In doing that, the CAG must be assured that the money has been spent for the purpose or purposes for which it had been approved by the Parliament and that the expenditures are in accordance with the regulations governing those expenditures.[39] The CAG report is considered by the Public Accounts Committee, which holds the responsible persons in the administration authorities accountable for the irregularities committed. Although there are virtually no legal sanctions for being held accountable by the Public Accounts Committee (if no criminal offense has been committed), this may have an adverse impact on the future career of the responsible person. Therefore, that is a serious sanction for senior officers.[40] With respect to the State Audit Institution of the Republic of Serbia, it performs exclusively *ex post* control of public expenditures. It is not authorized to check whether the requested amount is in accordance with the approved budget framework. However, it is obligated to make sure that the money is spent for the purpose or purposes for which it was approved by the Parliament, as well as to check that the expenditures are in accordance with the regulations governing those expenditures. The reports on the audit of the Republic of Serbia final budget account, as well as the reports on the audit of the financial plans of the mandatory social insurance organizations and the Republic of Serbia consolidated financial statements are furnished by the Supreme Audit Institution to the

---

[38] Fidelma White, Kathryn Hollingsworth, *Audit, Accountability and Government*, (Oxford: Clarendon Press, 1999), 60-61.

[39] The 1921 Exchequer and Audit Department Act (1921 Chapter 5211 and 12 Geo, 19th of August, 1921) in section 1 (1) lists what is meant by financial audits. Text is available on the following web-site: https://www.legislation.gov.uk/ukpga/Geo5/11-12/52 accessed 30 June 2018.

[40] Ian Harden, Fidelma White, Kathryn Hollingsworth, "Value for Money and Administrative Law", *Public Law*,1986. 670-681.

Parliament.[41] The above institution audits financial statements also by examining documents, papers, reports, and other information in order to collect sufficient, adequate, and reliable evidence for investigating whether the financial statements of the audited entity reflect accurately and objectively its financial position, performance outcomes, and cash flows, in accordance with the accepted accounting principles and standards.[42]

The Value for Money aspects of public sector auditing are important steps towards assuring taxpayers concerning the accountability of Government to elected representatives and public official for the receipt and spending of public money. In the light of this assertion, external auditors concerned with assessing value for money.[43] This option is prescribed in Section 2 of the UK National Audit Act 1983, while Section 6 provides that the CAG may carry out examinations of the economy, efficiency, and effectiveness of the use of resources in discharging its functions.[44] The same type of audit is carried out by the Supreme Audit Institution of the Republic of Serbia as part of a performance audit. It involves the examination of the budget expenditures and other public expenditures to obtain sufficient, adequate, and reliable evidence for reporting on whether the audited entity has used the resources in accordance with the principles of economy, efficiency, and effectiveness, and in accordance with the specified objectives.[45]

The UK National Audit Act 1983 in Section 8 specifies that the CAG has the right of access to all documents that are under the supervision or control of the department or other authority that is subject to audit.[46] The

---

[41] The obligation to submit a report to the National Parliament is prescribed by Article 43 of the Republic of Serbia State Audit Institution Law.

[42] Article 2, para. 1, sub-para. 1 of the Republic of Serbia State Audit Institution Law.

[43] Nwosu M. Eze , Mshelia M. Ibrahim, "Value for Money Audit: A Veritable Tool for Expenditure Management", *International Journal of Financial Research*, Vol. 6, Number 3, 2015. 151.

[44] Text of the UK National Audit Act 1983 (1983 Chapter 44, 13th of May 1983) is available on the following web-site:
https://www.legislation.gov.uk/ukpga/1983/44/pdfs/ukpga_19830044_en.pdf accessed 30 June, 2018.

[45] The term "performance audit" is defined by Article 2, para. 1, sub-para. 4) of the State Audit Institution Law.

[46] Text of the UK National Audit Act 1983 is available on the website:
https://www.legislation.gov.uk/ukpga/1983/44/section/8 accessed June 30, 2018.

state auditors in Serbia also have free access to the documents of the audited entity. Accordingly, the audited entity is obliged to make available to the auditors all the required information and documents, including confidential information, which are necessary for the planning and execution of the audit. In addition, he/she is obliged to submit the requested information to the State Audit Institution in the course of the year, or in accordance with the schedule specified in the detailed audit plan, and within the timelines specified by the authorized person in the Institution. At the request of the auditor of the Institution, the auditing entity is also obliged to submit a copy of their database.[47]

Each report of the UK National Audit Office includes a high-level statement on the extent to which the government has achieved value for money and also includes recommendations and improvements.[48] After the report has been drafted, it is adopted and presented to the audited entity, which should respond to it within four weeks. This procedure is called "the approval procedure". The objective of this procedure is to achieve a sort of a consensus between the National Audit Office and the audited entity in relation to the facts and to ensure that both the parties agree that the report covers all the material and relevant facts. In the event that no consensus can be reached, the report may include both parties' opinions. The final stage is the publication of the value for money report, which usually includes recommendations addressed to the audited entity.[49] One of the problems in practice is that the reports of the National Audit Office are usually to a large extent in line with the views of the audited entities. The procedure may take a long time, and in addition, it involves a great deal of compromise. The recommendations are more open to discussion, and therefore less authoritative. That is why there is also a high probability that they will not be accepted.[50] The same procedure has been adopted also by the Serbian State Audit Institution, in

---

[47] Article 36 of the State Audit Institution Law stipulates free access of auditors to the documents of the audited entity.

[48] David Goldsworthy, Ian Rogers, *The Role of a Modern Supreme Audit Institution: the experience of the United Kingdom*, (UKAID from the British People, GIZ Deutsche Gesellschaft für Internazionale Zusammenarbeit (GIZ) GmbH, UK National Audit Office, 2014), 3. Text is available on the following web-site: http://gogov.org.ua/wp-content/uploads/2016/05/The-role-of-a-modern-Supreme-Audit-Institution-the-experience-of-the-United-Kingdom.pdf accessed June 30, 2018.

[49] Fidelma White, Kathryn Hollingsworth, *Audit, Accountability and Government*,77.

[50] Aleksandra Rabrenović, "Status i funkcije Nacionalne revizorske institucije Velike Britanije", *Strani pravni život*, Number 3, 2007, 126.

their operations. After the auditing procedures have been carried out at the audited entity, the Institution drafts the audit report and submits it to the audited entity and the persons responsible for the operations during the audited period. The audited entity may submit an objection to the draft audit report, including justifications, within the legal timeline. The State Audit Institution should consider the justifications of objections from the complaint within the legal timeline, after which it would invite the responsible persons in the audited entity to discuss the draft audit report, during which the audited entity may submit new evidence. The discussion of the audit findings is not mandatory if the audited entity, after having received the draft conclusions, declares in writing that it does not dispute any of the findings contained in the draft report. Reaching agreement on the audit report may require a long period of time, as there can be several draft audit report discussions. The law does not limit the number of such discussions, providing only that the last such discussion must be held no later than within 30 days from the date of delivery of the draft audit report. If the Institution is satisfied that the objections to the audit findings are justified, such findings would be omitted from the audit report. However, prior to that, additional audit checks may be carried out.[51] Therefore, as well as in the case of the UK audit, an objection can be made that the audit opinion and audit findings are based on numerous compromises. In addition, the audit process in Serbia takes a very long time. This could also have a negative impact on the effectiveness of the prosecution of the perpetrators of offenses that may be discovered during the auditing activities.

The UK National Audit Office is required in a way to take into account the needs of the Public Accounts Committee Members and Members of Parliament. In the event that the National Audit Office touches upon some sensitive state policy issues, the Public Accounts Committee may be divided along the political lines, which could jeopardize both its work and the work of the Supreme Audit Institution itself. One of the objectives of the activities of the above institution is the reduction in crime. In addition, it often has an advisory role in relation to the government.[52] There are a number of ways in which Supreme Audit Institution can encourage input from citizens and civil organizations as well. For example, fraud hotlines are used by the UK National Audit Office to encourage to public and

---

[51] Article 39 of the State Audit Institution Law.

[52] Aleksandra Rabrenović, "Status i funkcije Nacionalne revizorske institucije Velike Britanije", 127.

whistle-blowers to provide information on suspected irregularities in the management of public funds.[53] Even though that is not its core activity, the role of the Supreme Audit Institution in detecting criminal offenses that might have a widespread impact on public finances is of great importance. Prescribing severe penalties in criminal legislation alone is not a sufficiently effective means of preventing crime, and it is also necessary that there is a high likelihood that the criminal acts will be revealed.[54] The law governing the operations of the Republic of Serbia State Audit Institution stipulates that if a certain act or document is discovered at the audited entity, which indicates the existence of a criminal offense, the authorized person in the Institution is obliged to inventory, seize and secure such documents no later than within eight days. A certificate must be issued to the audited entity on the seizure of such documents.[55] The law stipulates the obligation of the Institution to inform immediately the competent authorities, as well as the competent public attorney who is authorized to represent the legal property interests of the state.[56]

An important link in the establishment of parliamentary control over public expenditures in the Republic of Serbia is also the work of the Committee on Finance, Republic Budget and Control of Public Expenditures, which is responsible to consider both draft legislation and other general acts, as well as other issues in the fields of state functions financing system, taxes, fees and other public revenues, the republic budget, and financial plans of mandatory social security organisations, the final budget account, the final accounts of the financial plans of mandatory social insurance organisations, and the audits of the final accounts, loans, guarantees and games of chance, public debt and financial assets of the Republic of Serbia, public procurements, credit and monetary, banking, foreign exchange and customs systems, property and personal insurance, legal property relations and expropriation, payment and payment

---

[53] Albert van Zyl, Vivek Ramkumar and Paolo de Renzio, *Responding to challenges of Supreme Audit Institutions: Can legislatures and civil Society help?*, (Bergen: U4 Anti Corruption Resource Centre, Chr Michelsen Institute, 2009), 23. Such mechanizam also exist in the United States and South Korea.

[54] Jelena Šuput, "Državna revizorska institucija i prevencija kriminaliteta belog okovratnika u javnom sektoru," *Zbornik radova pravnog fakulteta Univerziteta u Nišu*, no. 67, year LIII, (2014), 336.

[55] Article 38, para. 8 and Article 41 of the State Audit Institution Law.

[56] Article 38, para. 9 and Article 41 of the State Audit Institution Law.

transactions, property relations and expropriation, payment and payment transactions, securities and capital markets, anti-money laundering activities, and the fight against corruption, accounting and auditing, as well as other issues in the field of finance. It is competent also to review the reports by the State Audit Institution, and reports on its findings and recommendations to the National Parliament. The Committee on Finance, Republic Budget and Control of Public Expenditures controls the implementation of the republic budget and the accompanying financial plans in terms of the legality, performance, and efficiency of public expenditures, and reports on its findings and proposed measures to the National Parliament.[57] In this way, in line with the solution adopted in the UK, more efficient cooperation has been established between the State Audit Institution and the National Parliament, as the representatives of the citizens.

5. Conclusion

In all democratic countries, there is a need to improve the public expenditure control mechanisms. The public sector institutions are responsible to all citizens for their spending, as these public expenditures are financed largely from the public revenues. By paying taxes and contributions, the citizens give up a portion of their income for the benefit of the state. However, in return, they expect a certain level and quality of public goods in which they have invested a portion of their money. Accordingly, public expenditures should be efficient, economical, and effective. However, in some cases, it is possible that the responsible persons in the public funds' user institutions act contrary to the above principles. By establishing adequate control mechanisms, the possibility of such behavior can be minimized to a certain extent. The reason for that is, above all, the fear of sanctions, which do not necessarily have to be criminal sanctions.

The public finance control mechanisms can be internal or external. With respect to the internal mechanisms, they were established in the Republic of Serbia much later than the external financial control mechanisms. Serbia had them in place as early as in the 19th century. The institutional public expenditure external control was first developed in the form of the General Control, during the Kingdom of Serbia. However, it initially

---

[57] The competence of the Committee is regulated by Article 46, para. 1, sub-para. 8 of the Rules of Procedure of the National Parliament of the Republic of Serbia ("Official Gazette of the Republic of Serbia," Number 14/2009).

reported on its activities to the King. The parliamentary accountability of the executive power for the use of public funds was established only after the adoption of the September Constitution, at the time of the Kingdom of Yugoslavia, in 1931.

Subsequently, the Social Accounting Service was established, which carried out the control of financial and material operations of budget user institutions and business entities to a high standard. However, it did not have the status of a Supreme Audit Institution. The State Audit Institution of the Republic of Serbia was established only by the 2005 State Audit Institution Law.

The United Kingdom has a longstanding tradition and continuity of parliamentary control over public expenditures. Today, this control is carried out through the National Audit Office. Like similar institutions in other countries, it is a member of the International Organization of Supreme Audit Institutions (INTOSAI).[58] One of the goals behind the establishment of INTOSAI is the exchange of knowledge and practical experiences, i.e. best practices, between the INTOSAI Member States. These practices are contained in the International Standards of Supreme Audit Institutions, which have become part of the legislation governing external audit of public expenditures by INTOSAI Member States. That is one of the reasons why the solutions regulating the organization and functioning of the Republic of Serbia Supreme Audit Institution are similar to those regulating the same area in the UK. However, that also testifies that the needs of the practice imply similar solutions in the European continental law and the Anglo-Saxon law countries. In addition, this also speaks about the fact that membership in international organizations contributes to taking over solutions from other legal systems, which have already shown good results in practice.

Bibliography

Dobre Cornelia."Great Britain and Germany Supreme Audit Institutions", *Annals of Faculty of Economics, University of Oradea*, Number 1, (2012), 695-701.

---

[58] Supreme Audit Institutions of the following countries are members of the INTOSAI: Argentina, Australia, Austria, Belgium, Bosnia and Herzegovina, Bulgaria, Canada, Croatia, Cyprus, Denmark, France, Germany, Italy, Norway etc. The complete list of members of the said organization is available on the following website: www.intosai.org/about-us/organisation/membership-list.html.

Eze M. Nwosu, Ibrahim M. Mshelia."Value for Money Audit: A Veritable Tool for Expenditure Management", *International Journal of Financial Research*, Vol. 6, Number 3, 2015, 150-162.

Goldsworthy David, Rogers Ian. *The Role of a Modern Supreme Audit Institution: the experience of the United Kingdom*, UKAID from the British People, GIZ Deutsche Gesellschaft für Internazionale Zusammenarbeit (GIZ) GmbH, UK National Audit Office, 2014.

González Belén, López Antonio, Garcia Roberto."How do Supreme Audit Institutions measure the impact of their work?", *Implementing Reforms in Public Sector Accounting*, ed. Susana Jorge, Coimbra: Coimbra University Press, 2008, 503-517.

Good Practices in supporting Supreme Audit Institutions, OECD 16. This document is available on the following website: https://www.oecd.org/dac/effectiveness/Final%20SAI%20Good%20Practice%20Note.pdf, accessed Jun 1, 2017.

Harden Ian, White Fidelma and Hollingsworth Kathryn."Value for Money and Administrative Law", *Public Law*, 1986, 661-681.

http://www.intosai.org/issai-executive-summaries/view/article/issai-12-the-value-and-benefits-of-supreme-audit-institutions-making-a-difference-to-the-liv.html

ISSAI 12 – The Value and Benefits of Supreme Audit Institutions – making a difference to the lives of citizens, last modified December 1, 2017

Kennet M. Dye and Stepenhorst Rick.*Pillars of Integrity: The Importance of Supreme Audit Institutions in Curbing Corruption*, Washington: Economic Development Institute of the World Bank, 1998.

Norton D. Simon and Smith L. Murphy."Contrast and Foundation of the Public Oversight Roles of the US. Government Accountability Office and the U.K. National Audit Office", *Public Administration Review*, Vol. 68, Number 5, 2018. 921-931.

Rabrenović, Aleksandra et al."Historical development of Corruption prevention Mechanisms in Southeast European Countries", in *Legal Mechanisms for prevention of Corruption in Southeast Europe with special focus on the Defence sector*, edited by Aleksandra Rabrenović, 13-35, Belgrade: Institute of Comparative Law, 2013 [In Serbian].

Rabrenović, Aleksandra."The Status and Functions of the National Audit Office in Great Britain", *Foreign Legal life*, Number 3, 2007, 116-28 [In Serbian]

Šuput, Jelena."Harmonization of National Internal Audit Legislation with International Standards," in Good Governance and Internal Audit, edited by Dejan Šuput, 96-110, Belgrade: Insititute of Comparative Law, 2012 [In Serbian].

Šuput, Jelena."Public internal financial control," in Alignment of the Serbian law with acquis communautaire, priorities, problems, perspectives, edited by Aleksandra Rabrenović and Jelena Ćeranić, 247-61, Belgrade: Institute of Comparative Law, 2012 [In Serbian].

Šuput, Jelena."The Role of the State Audit Institution in Prevention of White-Collar Crime in the Public Sector," Collection of papers, Faculty of Law, Niš, no. 67, (2014): 331-46 [In Serbian].

Tekijaški, Aleksandra."Establishment of the External Audit Function in the Public Sector" in *Alignment of the Serbian Law with Acquis Communautaire, priorities, problems, perspectives,* edited by Aleksandra Rabrenović and Jelena Ćeranić, 262-81, Belgrade: Institute of Comparative Law, 2012 [In Serbian].

The Law on the General Control ("Official Gazette of the Kingdom of Serbs, Croats and Slovenes", Number 125, 10 June 1922) [In Serbian].

The Law on the General Control ("Official Gazette of the Kingdom of Serbs, Croats and Slovenes", Number 9, 11 January 1929) [In Serbian].

The Law on the General Control ("Official Gazette of the Kingdom Jugoslavija", Number 244, 24 October 1930.) [In Serbian].

The Law on the General Control ("Serbian Gazette", Number 103, 10 May 1892) [In Serbian].

The Law on the Social Accounting Service, Službeni list SFRJ, No. 70/83, 16/86, 72/86, 74/87, 61/88, 57/89, 79/90, 84/90 and 20/91 [In Serbian].

The Law on the Supreme Audit Institution ("Official Gazette of the Republic of Serbia," Number 101/2005, 54/2007 i 35/2010) [In Serbian].

The September Constitution ("Official Gazette of the Kingdom of Yugoslavia, Number 215, 3 September 1931) [In Serbian].

The Vidovdan Constitution ("Official Gazette of the Kingdom of Serbs, Croats and Slovenes", Number 142a, 28. Jun, 1921) [In Serbian].

Tošić, D. Nadežda.*Budget control,* Belgrade, Faculty of Law, University of Belgrade, 2013 [In Serbian].

Van Zyl Albert, Ramkumar Vivek and De Renzio Paolo.*Responding to challenges of Supreme Audit Institutions: Can legislatures and civil Society help?*, Bergen: U4 Anti Corruption Resource Centre, Chr Michelsen Institute, 2009.

White Fidelma, Hollingsworth Kathryn.*Audit, Accountability and Government,* Oxford: Clarendon Press, 1999.

Chapter 21

Influence of the Eurasian Integration Process on the Legal System of the Russian Federation

Dmitriy V. Galushko[1]

Abstract

The research is focused on a study of relationships between the Russian legal system and one of the most significant trends of modern International law — the phenomena of regional integration. For the Russian Federation, regional integration found its expression as the Eurasian integration process. Eurasian integration is characterized by attempts at the interaction of states which are combined by common history, economic and demographic links within the post-Soviet space to create new associations by building common institutions and norms. The initial steps for formation of an effective mechanism for interstate and then for supranational cooperation in the post-Soviet space has been implemented in different structures and associations, being very politicized as the process, to some extent, has been strongly influenced by political motives, which often contradict with everyday, practical needs of the participating countries.

The author starts from the evolution of the process of Eurasian integration and development of the relevant international legal basis. As the Eurasian integration process now faces both internal and external-global threats, relevant law, developments of its different spheres and branches, particularly its interrelations with the legal system of the Russian Federation, are explored. Features of the influence of Eurasian integration on developments of the Russian legal system are identified and analyzed. The author finally gives his view on prospects of Russian law, its development in the light of existing and

---

[1] PhD, Associate Professor of the International and European Law Department, Voronezh State University

future changes in the Eurasian integration process, particularly regarding the Eurasian Economic Union's (EAEU's) functioning, relations with its member-states and in relations with other subjects of International law. The factor of Russia's EAEU membership is considered as it gives rise to new learning opportunities while at the same time posing new legal challenges, that demand further exploration.

Introduction

International law, as known, is the most important regulator of international relations between states and between states and other subjects. Due to the fact, that in the modern world the international legal system and the domestic legal systems are closely connected, international law has a serious impact on states' national legislation. International relations of the Russian Federation are quite extensive, and therefore we may see the active influence of international legal norms on Russian legislation. At present, all branches of Russian law are more or less subject to the influence of international legal norms. Via the implementation of international legal obligations, the state is improving and modernizing its legislation. This fully applies to the integration processes taking place in the Eurasian region, and to those international legal norms that are formed as a result of this.

More than twenty-five years of the existence of states formed after the collapse of the USSR showed that each of them nowadays has its own legal culture and legal system. Nevertheless, modern development processes point to increasing globalization and integration tendencies, and, as a consequence, there appears a need to establish a balance between the functioning of national legal systems, legal families and international law. The creation of international organizations of a supranational type is a response to the challenges of the corresponding historical period as scientific and technological progress develops.[2] An example of such integration is the Eurasian Economic Union (hereinafter — the EAEU).

Created in 2014, the Eurasian Economic Union is often perceived as a kind of «second edition of the Soviet Union». However, the reality is quite obvious

---

[2] Myslivskij P.P. Mezhdunarodno-pravovoe regulirovanie sozdanija Evrazijskogo jekonomicheskogo sojuza i sposoba razreshenija sporov: dissertacija ... kandidata juridicheskih nauk: 12.00.10. Moskva, 2016. - S. 12.

that as the model for the EAEU is acted not the Soviet Union, gone forever in the past as, but modern European and other regional integration entities.[3]

The process has been very chaotic with the creation of different international organizations, dealing with issues of economy, security, etc. And therefore there have been examples for different approaches to the integration process: both functionalist and transactionalist. The initial entity, created just after USSR, has been the Commonwealth of Independent States (CIS). And within this basic organization there were initiated further «multi-speed» integration processes.[4]

1. Legal and historical Aspects of Eurasian Integration

In the 90s, due to a complex combination of objective and subjective reasons after the collapse of the Soviet Union and the formation of the post-Soviet newly independent states, the idea of the Eurasian integration process were first taken up by the head of Kazakhstan Nursultan Nazarbaev, who in 1994 proposed a detailed and comprehensive project of creation of a new integration entity by the CIS member states — the Eurasian Union as the Union of equal independent states, aimed at the implementation of national interests of each of the participating countries and their overall integration potential.[5] And that can be regarded as a good characteristic of sensitivity of the integration process for the post-Soviet Republics with their young statehoods.

The presidents of Belarus, Kazakhstan, Russia and Ukraine, based on the concept of multi-level integration, under the CIS framework concluded the Agreement on the formation of the Common Economic Space, 2003, with the aim of creation conditions for stable and efficient development of the states' economies and raising standards of living of their people. In 2007 Belarus, Kazakhstan and Russia signed the Agreement on the Creation of the Common Customs Territory and Establishing of the Customs Union. Then the governing body of the Customs Union defined stages and terms for the formation of the single customs territory of the Customs Union, marking January 1, 2010 as the beginning of the first stage

---

[3] Balytnikov V., Boklan D. Evrazijskij jekonomicheskij sojuz: predposylki sozdanija, problemy formirovanija, perspektivy razvitija // Sravnitel'noe Konstitucionnoe Obozrenie. 2015. №3 (106). P. 69-82.

[4] See: Glotov S., Grigoriev I. The legal system of the Eurasian Economic Union: stating the problem // Vestnik MGOU. Serija: Jurisprudencija 2015. №3. S. 12-29.

[5] See: Ivanova E.M. Evrazijskaja integracija: put' ot SNG k EAJeS // Rossijskij vneshnejekonomicheskij vestnik. 2015. Vol. 2015, issue 6. S. 112-119.

of its formation. On the basis of the Customs Union, the states moved further to the formation of the Single Economic Space.

On November 18, 2011, the Presidents of Belarus, Kazakhstan and Russia signed the Declaration on Eurasian Economic Integration and determined January 1, 2012 as the date for the launch of the Single Economic Space, which should ensure the free movement of goods, services, capital, and labour. The heads of the three states proclaimed, that the development of the Customs Union and the Single Economic Space should lead to the creation of the Eurasian Economic Union. On the same day — November 18, 2011 — the Presidents of Belarus, Kazakhstan, and Russia signed the Treaty on the Eurasian Economic Commission, which became a single, permanent, regulative body of the Customs Union and the Single Economic Space. The Eurasian Economic Commission began its work on February 2, 2012.

The Supreme Eurasian Economic Council enacted international treaties forming the Single Economic Space on December 19, 2011. The implementation of these and other international treaties on balanced macroeconomic, budgetary and competitive policies, structural reforms of labor markets, capitals, goods and services, and the creation of Eurasian networks in the energy, transport and telecommunications sectors was defined as the basis for the creation by January 1, 2015 of the Eurasian Economic Union.

In general, within the process of Eurasian integration, politics has always been ahead of law as the process is highly politicized. An understanding of the transition to the practical formation of Eurasian integration associations, which took place at the turn of the 20th and 21st centuries, was formulated by President Vladimir V. Putin. In his famous article «The New Integration Project for Eurasia — the future that is born today» the head of the Russian state, summarizing his earlier ideas, emphasized that during the search for a way out of the global system crisis, that began in 2008 and was associated with the development of new models of global development, «a solution might be found in devising common approaches from the bottom up, first within the existing regional institutions, such as the EU, NAFTA, APEC, ASEAN inter alia, before reaching an agreement in a dialogue between them. These are the integration bricks that can be used to build a more sustainable global economy».[6] For example, the two

---

[6] Putin V. A new integration project for Eurasia: The future in the making. URL: http://www.europarl.europa.eu/meetdocs/2009_2014/documents/d-ru/dv/dru_2013_0320_06_/dru_2013_0320_06_en.pdf

largest associations of our continent — the European Union and the emerging Eurasian Union — based on their interaction on the rules of free trade and the compatibility of regulatory systems, objectively, via relations with third countries and regional structures, are able to extend these principles to all the way from the Atlantic to the Pacific Oceans. The space will be harmonious in its economic nature, but polycentric in terms of specific mechanisms and management solutions. Then it will be logical to begin a constructive dialogue on the principles of interaction with the states of the Asia-Pacific region, North America, and other regions. Thus, this [Eurasian] integration project ... opens wide prospects for economic development, creating additional competitive advantages.[7]

This statement of President Putin on the creation of the Eurasian Union can be regarded as a kind of political manifesto, a Russian view on the integration process and its future development. It was proposed to establish a regional integration entity with a comprehensive competence in its future perspective – the Eurasian Union, not just «Economic». But this comprehensiveness was partly rejected as it was decided to concentrate integration efforts in the economic sphere.

Finally, on May 18, 2014, the leaders of Belarus, Kazakhstan, and Russia signed the Treaty on the Eurasian Economic Union [8] In December 2014, the Union was joined by Armenia and, in May, 2015, by Kyrgyzstan. Since January 1, 2015, the process of practical implementation of the Treaty has begun.

The Treaty on the Eurasian Economic Union (hereinafter — the EAEU Treaty) is based on the codification of international treaties signed within the framework of the Eurasian Economic Community (EurAsEC), the Single Economic Space (SES) and the Customs Union (CU). The use of such a conventional codification mechanism during the work on the EAEU Treaty was extremely difficult, since there was a problem of different depths of economic integration of the future EAEU member states, as it was envisaged by the systematized treaties. In addition, not only the initial

---

[7] Putin V. Novyj integracionnyj proekt dlja Evrazii — budushhee, kotoroe rozhdaetsja segodnja. URL: https://iz.ru/news/502761

[8] Treaty on the Eurasian Economic Union. URL: http://www.un.org/en/ga/sixth/70/docs/treaty_on_eeu.pdf

EAEU member states, but also some other states (for example, Kyrgyzstan and Tajikistan), were parties to a significant number of these treaties.[9]

At the same time, a number of provisions of the EAEU Treaty are beyond the scope of provisions of earlier international treaties as it provides much deeper integration among the member states. These provisions were formulated on the basis of existing political documents, draft treaties and comments by representatives of the EAEU member states. As a whole, the EAEU Treaty has been a result of a very subtle compromise between its parties.

2. The EAEU Treaty as the Basis for the Eurasian Integration Legal Order

The EAEU Treaty is a constituent agreement for the Eurasian Economic Union. It consists of four parts (the main text) and 33 annexes, which concretize its main provisions.[10]

Part one «Establishment of the Eurasian Economic Union» contains general provisions, basic principles, objectives, provisions on the competence and law of the EAEU, its organizational structure and its budget.

Of particular importance are the main objectives of the Union, formulated in Article 4 of the Treaty. It is necessary to emphasize that the Parties to the Treaty have approached the formulation of its main goals with caution, taking into account the need for progressive economic integration without sacrificing the economy of each of the states-participants. An example of this delicate approach is the formulation of the goal as «the desire to form a single market for goods, services, capital, and labor resources within the Union». The treaty is ambitious to the extent that it introduces the concept of «the law of the Union»,[11] the content of which is disclosed in Article 6 of the Treaty.

The second part of the EAEU Treaty is devoted to the legal regime of the Customs Union: information interaction and statistics, functioning of the

---

[9] Roberts S.P., Marin A, Moshes A, Pynnöniemi K. The Eurasian Economic Union: breaking the pattern of post-Soviet integration? FIIA Analysis 3. The Finnish Institute of International Affairs, 2014. P. 6.

[10] See: Kapustin A.Ya. Treaty on the Eurasian Economic Union — a new page of legal development of eurasian integration // Zhurnal rossijskogo prava. 2014. № 12.

[11] Wolczuk K., Dragneva R, The Eurasian Economic Union: Deals, Rules and the Exercise of Power. Chatham House Research Paper, Royal Institute of International Affairs, London, 2017. P. 4.

Customs Union, regulation of drug circulation, customs regulation, foreign trade policy, technical regulation, sanitary, veterinary-sanitary and quarantine phytosanitary measures and consumer protection.

Within the framework of the Customs Union, member states implement a generally common policy: within the customs territory of the Union the unified Goods Nomenclature for Foreign Economic Activity of the EAEU and the Unified Customs Tariff (UCT) are applied, unified import customs taxes and unified mandatory technical regulation requirements are established. That is one of the areas with the deepest economic integration in the EAEU. An exception is the scope of application of sanitary, veterinary and sanitary and quarantine phytosanitary measures and protection of consumer rights, where the EAEU member states conduct an agreed policy.[12]

Common exceptions to the Customs Union regime, which give the right to apply restrictions in mutual trade, are cases specified in Article 29 of the Treaty, which almost completely correspond to the regime provided for in Articles XX and XXI of the GATT, namely: the need to protect human life and health; protection of public morality and legal order; environmental protection; protection of animals and plants, cultural values; fulfillment of international obligations and ensuring a country's defense and security.

The third part of the EAEU Treaty is devoted to the Single Economic Space (SES) regime. It codifies norms of agreements previously concluded within the SES, namely, the provisions on the implementation of macroeconomic and monetary policy, trade of services, provisions for investments, for regulation of financial markets and taxation, general principles and rules of competition, the legal regime of natural monopolies and the legal regime for energy policy, transport policy and the state procurement regime, protection of intellectual property, industrial and agro-industrial policy, and labor migration.

In almost all these areas, the EAEU member states carry out economic integration at the level of coordinated policy. The only exception is the scope of granting industrial subsidies, where unified rules for granting subsidies for industrial goods exist in the territories of the member states.

At the same time, in some areas, the Treaty imposes on the participants an obligation to pursue a coordinated policy, in contrast to too vague provisions of the earlier agreements on the process of «determination of

---

[12] See: Malinovskaya V.M. Legal and Institutional Bases of Functioning of the Eurasian Union // Vestnik MGIMO. 2012. 4(25). S. 197-202.

directions of the coordinated policy». These areas include areas of macroeconomic and monetary policy. The provisions on the trade of services are aligned with the provisions of the GATS, which provide four modes of supply of services, providing of regimes of national treatment and most-favored-nation in all service sectors.

In the areas of competition regulation, the natural monopoly regime, energy, transport policy, public procurement, intellectual property protection, agro-industrial policy and labor migration, the economic integration of the EAEU member states as a whole remained at the level of the codified agreements. At the same time, novellas of the Treaty include norms on access to services of natural monopoly subjects; a task of forming of the «Single Transport Space» and expanding the scope of regulation in the field of railway and other types of transport: road, air and water; the idea of introducing of a single intellectual property registry.

The fourth part of the Treaty contains transitional and final provisions. In particular, the procedure for joining the Union and the possibility of granting the status of a candidate country for accession and an observer state are envisaged. The working language of the EAEU institutions is Russian. Clauses to the Treaty are not allowed. The Treaty does not prevent the conclusion of bilateral international treaties between member states that provide for a deeper level of integration, in comparison with the provisions of the Treaty or international treaties within the Union.

The provisions of the four main parts of the Treaty are supplemented and specified in 33 annexes to the Treaty, which are an integral part of the latter. The annexes concern the competence of the Eurasian Economic Commission; activities of the Court of the Eurasian Economic Union (Statute of the Court); cooperation in the field of information technology and statistical information; order of enrollment and distribution of amounts of customs duties and uniform customs and tariff regulation; measures of non-tariff regulation in relation to third countries; application of special protective, anti-dumping and countervailing measures to third countries; technical regulation; coordinated policy in the field of measurement uniformity; application of sanitary, veterinary-sanitary and quarantine phytosanitary measures; coordinated policy in the field of consumer protection; coordinated macroeconomic policies; coordinated monetary policy; trade of services and investments; access to services of natural monopolies, development of oil and oil products markets; coordinated transport policy; regulation of procurement; protection of intellectual property rights; industrial cooperation and industrial subsidies; state support of agriculture; medical care, social guarantees, privileges and immunities.

3. Features of EAEU Law

The EAEU Treaty is aimed at solving the main task of the international integration entity - the creation of the single legal space in technical and economic fields,[13] having features that form the legal space of the integration entity.[14] And according to the provisions of the Treaty and its annexes, along with provisions of other acts, forming EAEU law, their influence on domestic legal systems of EAEU member states is potentially and legally very serious. And thus, in conditions of the Eurasian integration process, there arise issues related to the functioning and development of the national legal systems of the member states, in particular of the Russian Federation, their interrelations with the norms of the Union's law. And for implementation of relevant international norms and adaptation of a national legal system to the integration of legal demands, there should be created relevant national legal mechanisms.

According to Art. 2 of the EAEU Treaty main mechanisms for building the legal system of the Union and relations with the member states in the legal sphere, and thus further development of their legal systems, are unification and harmonization.

In general, use and application of these tools for alignment between international and domestic law is a characteristic feature of the modern level of inter-state integration. From one point, unification of law consists in removing differences in the legal regulation of similar relations in laws of individual states, creating uniform rules of law, despite different national legal traditions, influencing its further development. And from another point, unification predetermines removing obstacles to international cooperation and development of relations regulated by national law.[15]

In fact, the legal systems of the member states of the Union (Armenia, Belarus, Kazakhstan, Kyrgyzstan, Russia) historically belong to the Romano-German legal family, definitely with some influence of Soviet Unions legal traditions as a part of its legacy.

---

[13] Bekjashev K.A., Moiseev E.G. Pravo Evrazijskogo jekonomicheskogo sojuza. M.: Prospekt, 2015. S. 33.

[14] Volova L.I. Pravovoj status regional'nyh integracionnyh ob'edinenij // Rossijskij ezhegodnik mezhdunarodnogo prava. 2012. SPb. : Rossija-Neva, 2013. S. 98.

[15] See: Kapustin A.Ya. The Law of Eurasian Economic Union: International Legal Discourse // Zhurnal rossijskogo prava. 2015. № 11. S. 59–69.

Harmonization of law, as one of the ways of its convergence, is characterized by the absence of an obligation to achieve complete uniformity in legal regulation. It does not mean a rejection of the specifics of national legal traditions, reflecting the diversity and uniqueness of the order of life in different states. Harmonization of law implies a duty of states during the process of developing national legislation to follow certain principles of legal regulation in accordance with a massif of legal norms of a relevant international organization. The ultimate goal of harmonization of law is the establishment of a single result of a legal norm's operation. Harmonization, as a simpler process, which does not bind a state with strict legal obligations, is often preferable and actually promotes convergence of law. As a way to ensure unity in diversity, it involves alignment of concepts and programs of legal development, development of common normative definitions and assessments, as well as the orderliness of legal actions.

The desire for convergence, unification, and harmonization of law is supplemented in the EAEU Treaty by key concepts of common, coordinated and agreed policies within the Eurasian Economic Union. These provisions were developed in the light of the different readiness of member states for a certain level of depth of economic integration, namely, a common policy highlights a deep level of integration, coordinated and agreed policies — less deep integration.[16]

A common policy is understood as «the policy implemented by the Member States in certain spheres as specified in this Treaty and envisaging the application of unified legal regulations by the Member States, including on the basis of decisions issued by Bodies of the Union within their powers». A coordinated policy means «policy implying the cooperation between the Member States on the basis of common approaches approved within Bodies of the Union and required to achieve the objectives of the Union under this Treaty». An agreed policy pursued by member states in various fields presupposes «policy implemented by the Member States in various areas suggesting the harmonization of legal regulations, including on the basis of decisions of the Bodies of the Union, to the extent required to achieve the objectives of the Union under this Treaty».

---

[16] Shumilov V.M., Boklan D.S., Lifshic I.M. Pravovye novelly Dogovora o Evrazijskom jekonomicheskom sojuze // Rossijskij vneshnejekonomicheskij vestnik. 2015. Vol. 2015, issue 4. S. 90.

It is obvious that the very processes of globalization prompted means for optimal legal regulation for EAEU activities. The EAEU Treaty is built on international legal principles as the Union carries out its activities and participates in international relations on the rights of an international organization, granted relevant international legal personality by states-creators. But the realization of effective inter-state integration within the Eurasian Economic Union necessarily involves the creation of relevant domestic legal mechanisms within the member states to let them fulfill their obligations.

In general, to run this, there are favorable geographic, economic, legal, and political prerequisites: closeness of territories, political will, friendly attitude between peoples inhabiting the territories of the member states. The confirmation of this is contained in Art. 2 of the EAEU Treaty, which defines the concept of a «common economic space» as consisting of the territories of the member states implementing similar (comparable) and uniform economy regulation mechanisms based on market principles and the application of harmonised or unified legal norms, and having a common infrastructure. Thus, the Treaty created the legal basis for the convergence of the legal systems of the EAEU member states.

Paragraph 1 of Art. 6 of the EAEU Treaty establishes the following hierarchy of legal acts of the Union:

1. the Treaty;
2. international treaties within the Union;
3. international treaties of the Union with a third party;
4. decisions and dispositions of the Supreme Eurasian Economic Council, the Eurasian Intergovernmental Council, and the Eurasian Economic Commission adopted within the powers provided for by this Treaty and international treaties within the Union.

Despite the uncertainty of a place in the hierarchy of acts of the Union, the existing international treaties continue to be applied exclusively in a part that does not contradict the EAEU Treaty, which in this respect acts as *lex superior*.

The Treaty (P. 2-4 Art. 6) establishes a parity of sources of EAEU law that is rather positive from the side of legal certainty, uniformity of its interpretation and application.[17] The clarification of the legal force and

---

[17] See: Bakaeva O.Yu. Acts of the Eurasian Economic Commission as a source of law EAEU // Russian journal of legal studies. 2016. № 3 (8). S. 73-76.

the hierarchy in a separate article, especially in one of the first articles of such a big act, indicates many different points: the desire of the parties to clearly define forms of legal regulation of relations, which are acceptable to them in the context of the integration project, importance of the agreed legal mechanisms, built into an effective system of law.

The acts of the EAEU bodies are also hierarchically structured: decisions of the Higher Eurasian Economic Council take precedence over decisions of the Eurasian Intergovernmental Council and the Eurasian Economic Commission; the decisions of the Eurasian Intergovernmental Council take precedence over the decisions of the Commission.

Thus, the EAEU law includes sources of different legal nature, different in the time of adoption. These are international treaties (the Treaty itself, as well as international treaties within the Union and with a third party), and acts of the EAEU bodies. At the same time, such sources are also of several types: some require domestic measures (these are decisions of the Higher Eurasian Economic Council, the Eurasian Intergovernmental Council), which is explicitly provided by the Treaty, while others don't need and are applied directly.

4. EAEU Law and the Russian Legal System

For proper implementation of the EAEU legal acts as sources of international law, in any case, a national legal system must still be able to «perceive» them. Now there is no such special regulatory mechanism for all types of sources of EAEU law in the legal system of the Russian Federation.

P. 4 Art. 15 of the Russian Constitution states, that «the universally-recognized norms of international law and international treaties and agreements of the Russian Federation shall be a component part of its legal system. If an international treaty or agreement of the Russian Federation fixes other rules than those envisaged by law, the rules of the international agreement shall be applied».[18]

For the Russian Federation, this constitutional provision is crucial for an issue of effective interaction of international and domestic legal regulation, as well as the influence of international legal norms on the development of the national legal system. In this regard, we can note that, at the constitutional level in the Russian Federation, has been established

---

[18] Constitution of the Russian Federation. URL: http://www.constitution.ru/en/10003000-01.htm

a very general mechanism for the application of international legal norms, including those adopted and operating under the auspices of interstate integration entities in the post-Soviet space.

However, at present in the Russian legislation, there are quite a lot of gaps related to the implementation of acts of international entities and organizations on the domestic level. One of them is the implementation of mandatory acts of international organizations, which place in the legal system of Russia is not legally defined, raising many questions, including those that appeared in the light of the interpretation of Part 4 of Article 15 of the Constitution of the Russian Federation. Moreover, that is also due to the young and developing nature of EAEU law itself.

Implementation of norms of international law, including norms of international treaties, related to specific relations among states, should be implemented by special means of «coming into» of the international legal norms into a massif of national legislation, which is primarily conditioned by observance and protection of the national interests of a state in correspondence with international legal institutions. This circumstance requires the state-specific legislative regulation of issues, related to ways of implementing the state's international obligations.

However, legislative regulation of the issue of implementation of legally binding decisions of bodies of international organizations on the domestic level in Russia is actually absent, only general issues of the implementation process of the international treaties have been settled at the level of the Russian Constitution and the Federal Law «On International Treaties of the Russian Federation».[19]

At present, they are applied by mediating a direct action of such sources through obligations, came from international treaties, in other words, having assumed obligations of a particular international treaty, Russian legislation provides a condition of their direct action within its legal system. The doctrine indicated that the international agreements «paved the bridge» between acts of inter-state entities, including the Eurasian Economic Union, and domestic acts.

Thus, for effective implementation of international obligations arising from decisions of the bodies of the Eurasian Economic Union, a national regulatory framework is highly needed.[20]

---

[19] Federal Law No101-FZ of July 15, 1995 «On International Treaties». URL: https://www.wto.org/english/thewto_e/acc_e/rus_e/WTACCRUS48_LEG_56.pdf

[20] See: Morozov A.N. Implementation of International commitments undertaken by

As Russian legislation does not prejudge legal issues of resolving conflicts between decisions of bodies of the Union and domestic legal acts. In this connection, there should be mentioned the Ruling of the Constitutional Court of the Russian Federation of March 3, 2015, N 417-O.[21]

In its ruling, the Constitutional Court, on the one hand, recognized the exclusive competence of the EurAsEC Court to review cases on the compliance of acts of the Customs Union bodies with international treaties constituting the legal basis of the Union, and on the other, indicated that these legal positions alone cannot by themselves serve as the basis for derogation from the requirement contained in the Constitution of the Russian Federation, to recognize and guarantee the rights and freedoms of persons and citizen not only in accordance with generally recognized principles and rules of International law, but also in accordance with the Constitution of the Russian Federation. In other words, it was concluded that if the Constitution of the Russian Federation provides for a higher level of protection than an international treaty, the relevant provisions of the Constitution are subject to application. The Constitutional Court of the Russian Federation has announced, that it is only authorized to decide the issue of the operation of a particular EAEU norm, including decisions of the Eurasian Economic Commission, in the legal order of Russia.

It was found that at this stage, the priority of law of an integration entity is not absolute, but is dependent on the conditions established by the Constitution of the Russian Federation as an EAEU member state.

Thus, while establishing in Article 6 of the EAEU Treaty[22] the internal hierarchy of sources of the Union's law, the EAEU Treaty nevertheless doesn't give an answer to the question of how the normative conflict between a norm of EAEU law and a contradictory norm of national legislation will be resolved, and whether in this case the rule of EAEU law has a priority. The conflict between a normative act adopted by the

---

member states within the framework of the Eurasian Economic Union // Zhurnal zarubezhnogo zakonodatel'stva i sravnitel'nogo pravovedenija. 2017. №3. S. 111-120.

[21] Opredelenie Konstitucionnogo suda Rossiiskoi Federacii po zaprosu Arbitrazhnogo suda Central'nogo okruga o proverke konstitucionnosti punkta 4 Porjadka primenenija osvobozhdenija ot uplaty tamozhennyh poshlin pri vvoze otdel'nyh kategorii˘ tovarov na edinuju tamozhennuju teritoriju Tamozhennogo sojuza. URL: http://doc.ksrf.ru/decision/KSRFDecision190708.pdf

[22] Treaty on the Eurasian Economic Union. URL: http://www.un.org/en/ga/sixth/70/docs/treaty_on_eeu.pdf

Eurasian Economic Commission (EEC) (an EAEU secondary legal act, which, according to the Treaty, is directly applicable within territories of member states) and an internal normative act, regardless of time of its adoption, is particularly complex. Obviously, the question arises as to how important the hierarchical status of the national norm (be it the norm of the constitution, the law or the bylaw), as well as the time of its adoption (for example, after the entry into force of the EEC decision), are important in this case. The treaty bypasses these issues with silence, and most likely they should be resolved by the EAEU Court.

In accordance with the EAEU Treaty, decisions of the EEC are directly applicable within the territories of the member states. For the EAEU Court, as well as for national courts of the member states, including their constitutional courts, this category of the Union's acts is of particular interest. Moreover, the further destiny of this integration entity will largely depend on efficiency, as well as on the stable and uniform practice of application EAEU law as a whole at the national level. At the same time, the Court has already started to solve this problem by starting to build its doctrine of priority of EAEU law in its recent decision on the dispute between Russia and Belarus,[23] as well as the direct action doctrine in its Advisory Opinion of April 4, 2017.[24]

In the judgment on the dispute between Russia and the Republic of Belarus of February 21, 2017, the Court stated that norms of the Agreement on Mutual Administrative Assistance of Customs Authorities of the Customs Union's Member States of May 21 2010[25] (hereinafter referred to as the Agreement) take precedence over conflicting national legal acts. This is a dispute between the Russian Federation and the Republic of Belarus initiated by Russia in September 2016. In its

---

[23] Reshenie Bol'shoj kollegii Suda ot 21 fevralja 2017 goda po delu po zajavleniju Rossijskoj Federacii po sporu o sobljudenii Respublikoj Belarus' Dogovora o Evrazijskom jekonomicheskom sojuze, stat'i 125 Tamozhennogo kodeksa tamozhennogo sojuza, statej 11 i 17 Soglashenija o vzaimnoj administrativnoj pomoshhi tamozhennyh organov gosudarstv–chlenov tamozhennogo sojuza. URL: http://courteurasian.org/doc-17943

[24] Konsul'tativnoe zakljuchenie Bol'shoj kollegii Suda po zajavleniju Ministerstva justicii Respubliki Belarus' ot 4 aprelja 2017 goda. URL: http://courteurasian.org/doc-18093.

[25] Soglashenie o vzaimnoj administrativnoj pomoshhi tamozhennyh organov gosudarstv-chlenov tamozhennogo sojuza ot 21 Maya 2010 goda. URL: http://www.eurasiancommission.org/docs/Download.aspx?IsDlg=0&ID=4183&print=1

application to the Court, Russia argued that Belarus does not fulfill its obligations arising from the Treaty establishing the EAEU.

The essence of the dispute was that the customs authorities of Belarus repeatedly detained and confiscated household appliances produced by Russian companies in the Kaliningrad region and transported by road in transit through Lithuania and Belarus to the «mainland» territory of Russia. At the same time, transit documents issued by Kaliningrad customs officers met all the requirements, as well as the conclusion of the Chamber of Commerce that the goods were produced in Russia. However, according to the Belarusian side, instead of Russian goods, produced in Kaliningrad, imported goods were actually of foreign production. In the materials submitted to the Court, the Russian side insisted on the unconditional acceptance by the Belarusian side of Russian documents and argued that in case of suspicion of the Belarusian customs officers they had to send an instruction to the Russian customs authorities to control cargoes as required by the above-mentioned Agreement.

In its turn, the respondent proceeded from the fact, that the transit of goods was stopped in accordance with the norms of the national legislation, namely within the procedure of customs control in connection with the established fact of an administrative offense (an attempt to transport goods produced in a foreign country under the flag of the goods of the Union). A very important conclusion made by the EAEU Court in its decision is to recognize the norms of the Agreement as a priority over existing and applicable domestic regulations (literally "in connection with its special character have priority in conducting customs control"). This means that the customs authorities of the EAEU member-states should be guided and apply directly the norms of the Agreement that take precedence over the national legal acts that conflict with it (literally «are imperative, do not contain exceptions or references and in this connection should be applied directly»).[26] If we proceed from this logic of the Court, then this should be done not only by the customs authorities but also by other authorities of the member states of the Union, including national courts, as well as by individuals — subjects of customs legal relations.

---

[26] Reshenie Bol'shoj kollegii Suda ot 21 fevralja 2017 goda po delu po zajavleniju Rossijskoj Federacii po sporu o sobljudenii Respublikoj Belarus' Dogovora o Evrazijskom jekonomicheskom sojuze, stat'i 125 Tamozhennogo kodeksa tamozhennogo sojuza, statej 11 i 17 Soglashenija o vzaimnoj administrativnoj pomoshhi tamozhennyh organov gosudarstv–chlenov tamozhennogo sojuza. URL: http://courteurasian.org/doc-17943

In essence, the Court proposes its own version of a solution to the normative conflict between an EAEU law norm and an applicable rule of national law. In its opinion, in cases when the application of the domestic rule will lead to a conflict with the norm of EAEU law, the domestic norm should not be applied at the national level, but it does not cease to operate and is not declared invalid (this can only be done by authorized authorities of a member-state of the Union). However, questions remain unanswered as to whether the status of the national norm will be important in the case of a normative conflict, as well as regarding time of its adoption. In this respect, the special opinion of the judge from Russia, K. Chaika, seems very remarkable. He stated that the EAEU member states, having concluded the EAEU Treaty, thereby created an «autonomous set of legal norms binding for all member states».[27] Drawing an analogy with arguments of the EU Court of Justice in the decisions on Costa / Enel[28] and Simmenthal II,[29] Judge K. Chaika insists on the absolute priority of the EAEU legal order over any national norm, regardless of whether they were adopted before the creation of the Union or later, not specifying, however, if we are talking only about laws and subsidiary legislation or also about constitutions of the Union's member-states.[30] In any case, these words, so expected by many, still sounded, albeit not yet in the Court's decision, but in a special opinion.

The EAEU Court continued to discuss the priority of the Union's law in the Advisory opinion of April 4, 2017, responding to the request of the

---

[27] Osoboe mnenie sud'i Chajki K.L. po delu po zajavleniju Rossijskoj Federacii po sporu o sobljudenii Respublikoj Belarus' Dogovora o Evrazijskom jekonomicheskom sojuze, stat'i 125 Tamozhennogo kodeksa tamozhennogo sojuza, statej 11 i 17 Soglashenija o vzaimnoj administrativnoj pomoshhi tamozhennyh organov gosudarstv – chlenov tamozhennogo sojuza. URL: http://courteurasian.org/doc-17993

[28] Judgment of the Court of Justice, Costa v ENEL, Case 6/64 (15 July 1964). URL: http://eur-lex.europa.eu/legal-content/EN/TXT/?uri=CELEX%3A61964CJ0006

[29] Case 106/77 Amministrazione delle Finanze dello Stato v. Simmenthal SpA (Simmenthal II) (1978) ECR 629. URL: http://eur-lex.europa.eu/legal-content/EN/TXT/?uri=CELEX:61977CJ0106

[30] Osoboe mnenie sud'i Chajki K.L. po delu po zajavleniju Rossijskoj Federacii po sporu o sobljudenii Respublikoj Belarus' Dogovora o Evrazijskom jekonomicheskom sojuze, stat'i 125 Tamozhennogo kodeksa tamozhennogo sojuza, statej 11 i 17 Soglashenija o vzaimnoj administrativnoj pomoshhi tamozhennyh organov gosudarstv – chlenov tamozhennogo sojuza. URL: http://courteurasian.org/doc-17993

Ministry of Justice of the Republic of Belarus to clarify precisely those provisions of the EAEU Treaty that regulate competition in cross-border markets (the geographical boundaries of the markets cover the territory of two or more EAEU member states). Article 76 of the EAEU Treaty in paragraph 4 prohibits so-called «vertical» agreements between enterprises (these are agreements where one party sells goods and the other party purchases goods). However, such agreements are allowed if they meet the eligibility criteria. In turn, these criteria are established by the Protocol on General Principles and Rules of Competition (Annex No. 19 to the Treaty on the EAEU), according to which, «Vertical» agreements shall be permitted if: 1) they constitute commercial concession agreements; 2) the share of each economic entity (market participant) that is a party to such an agreement in the commodity market of the goods covered by the vertical agreement does not exceed 20 percent.[31]

The Court's Opinion notes that the applicant requested clarification of these provisions with regard to the possibility of establishing in the national legislation of the EAEU member states of other criteria for the admissibility of the «vertical» agreements. However, from the Special opinion of Judge E. Hayriyan, it becomes clear that it was a question of the Belarusian draft law providing for the introduction of a new, more stringent upper threshold for the market share in such agreements — 15% instead of 20%, and the use of such a threshold not for the commodity market, which is the subject of a vertical agreement, but for «any commodity market», which is clearly broader than the wording of the Protocol, that is, the adoption of a later national act that contradicts the provisions of the Treaty.[32] The Court came in general to an obvious conclusion — the Treaty does not contain provisions allowing to establish in the norms of the legislation of the Member States other criteria for the admissibility of the «vertical» agreements, rather than those, that are clearly and unequivocally provided for in the Treaty. This can also be understood as the Court's conclusion that it implicitly assumes that the time for the adoption of an internal rule that is contrary to the Union's law (whether before or after the adoption of a norm of EAEU law) does not matter. Incidentally, it is in this area that the Court's opinion can be

---

[31] Treaty on the Eurasian Economic Union. URL: http://www.un.org/en/ga/sixth/70/docs/treaty_on_eeu.pdf

[32] Osoboe mnenie sud'i Ajrijan Je.V. po delu po konsul'tativnomu zakljucheniju po zajavleniju Ministerstva justicii Respubliki Belarus' ot 4 aprelja 2017 goda. URL: http://courteurasian.org/doc-18153.

interpreted from the judgement on the dispute between Russia and Belarus that «actions of any of the member states that go beyond the requirements of the Union's customs legislation and are broad in interpretation of their rights do not correspond to the principles of the functioning of the Customs Union, creating unlawful obstacles to the proclaimed freedom of movement of goods between the territories of the Member States».[33]

It can be assumed that these words hide another conclusion of the Court, this time that the EAEU member states should refrain from adopting normative acts that directly contradict the norms of the Union's law. It should be noted that it cannot establish a prohibition for states to adopt such legal acts (nevertheless, it concerns sovereign states and powers of their national parliaments expressing the will of the people). But if such acts are adopted, this will be a violation of the state's obligations under EAEU law, which should entail the responsibility of this state under the law of the Union. The words «should refrain from adopting such acts» would be a wording that suits everyone and does not encroach upon powers of the legislature of the EAEU member states. Even if it is assumed that such norms will be adopted at the national level (or they already exist), then according to the doctrine of the priority of the Union's law, they simply should not be applied in a national legal order by both legal subjects and national courts.

5. Principles of EAEU and EU Legal Systems in Comparative Perspective

A distinctive feature of regional integration entities is the transfer by Member States of their sovereign powers to the institutions of these entities, including powers on the adoption of generally binding legal acts, governing relevant relations between all subjects of domestic law and applying in resolution of disputes by national courts. It is this feature of the integration entities that distinguishes them from other forms of interstate economic and political cooperation, such as international organizations and free trade zones. The action in the national legal order of generally binding acts and decisions adopted by the institutions of integration entities is designed to be used by an unlimited circle of

---

[33] Reshenie Bol'shoj kollegii Suda ot 21 fevralja 2017 goda po delu po zajavleniju Rossijskoj Federacii po sporu o sobljudenii Respublikoj Belarus' Dogovora o Evrazijskom jekonomicheskom sojuze, stat'i 125 Tamozhennogo kodeksa tamozhennogo sojuza, statej 11 i 17 Soglashenija o vzaimnoj administrativnoj

subjects of national law and raises the question of the correlation and interaction of these acts with the already existing (or later adopted) norms of domestic law that regulate the same issues. The success of regional integration depends, ultimately, on how, and by how convincingly the question of ways to resolve normative conflicts and the priority of the norms of law of integration entities over the contradictory norms of national law will be decided.

As the practice of regional integration entities shows, member states are not fond of the normative consolidation of the principle of priority of law of an integration entity in establishing treaties (even in the European Union such attempts to do this eventually failed), in fact granting the right to resolve these issues to the court of the entity. However, the efforts of the court of any integration entity (and, in this respect, the EAEU is not an exception) in this direction will depend not only on the credibility and quality of its arguments, but also on the willingness of the national authorities of the member states to follow its decisions and practice. The overall effect of EAEU law within the national legal orders of member states is unclear. The EAEU Treaty does not specify the relation of legal force between Union acts and national legislation. The regulation on the Eurasian Economic Commission provides that decisions of the Commission are binding on Member States. However, there is nothing on the supremacy of Commission decisions over national law.[34] The recent decisions of the EAEU Court show that the Court not only realized the fundamental importance of this problem but also began to build its doctrine of the priority of the EAEU law.

The EU Court, finding itself in a similar situation in the already mentioned judgment in the case of Simmenthal II, stated that in accordance with the principle of the priority of EU law, an EU legal norm automatically makes all contradictory provisions of national law inapplicable to it (Para. 17): «in accordance with the principle of the precedence of Community law, the relationship between provisions of the Treaty and directly applicable measures of the institutions on the one hand and the national law of the Member States on the other is such that those provisions and measures not only by their entry into force render automatically inapplicable any conflicting provision of current national

---

pomoshhi tamozhennyh organov gosudarstv–chlenov tamozhennogo sojuza. URL: http://courteurasian.org/doc-17943

[34] Karliuk M. Russian Legal Order and the Legal Order of the Eurasian Economic Union: An Uneasy Relationship , Russian Law Journal. 2017. 5(2). P. 37.

law but — in so far as they are an integral part of, and take precedence in, the legal order applicable in the territory of each of the Member States — also preclude the valid adoption of new national legislative measures to the extent to which they would be incompatible with Community provisions».[35] This does not mean the invalidity of the internal norm: it is still valid and applies in cases where it does not conflict with the norms of the EU. However, if such a normative conflict is still present, national courts should be guided by EU legal norms, leaving aside the contradictory norm of national legislation.

However, it should be noted that such a concept of absolute priority of EU law came up against objections of the constitutional and supreme courts of the EU member states, which, in response to such a practice, formulated the doctrine of the relative and conditional priority of EU law over the laws of EU member states, but not on national constitutions. In a series of decisions of constitutional and supreme courts of most of the EU member states, the courts went along the path of the Constitutional Court of Germany and, in general recognizing the priority of EU law over national legislation except over fundamental provisions of constitutions, established conditions and limits of such priority of EU law, reserving their rights in exceptional cases and under certain circumstances (ultra vires decisions of EU institutions, infringements of constitutional identity) to consider the issue of the non-use of EU legislation in national legal systems.[36]

In its Advisory Opinion of April 4, 2017, the EAEU Court reached a very serious conclusion: «The general rules of competition in the cross-border markets of the Union have direct effect and should be directly applied by the member states as norms enshrined in an international treaty».[37] This provision highlights notions of «direct applicability» and «direct effect», that have already been firmly established and widely used in the European

---

[35] Case 106/77 Amministrazione delle Finanze dello Stato v. Simmenthal SpA (Simmenthal II) (1978) ECR 629. URL: http://eur-lex.europa eu/legal-content/EN/TXT/?uri=CELEX:61977CJ0106

[36] See: C. Mayer, Franz. (2013). Constitutional comparativism in action. The example of general principles of EU law and how they are made-a German perspective. International Journal of Constitutional Law. 11. 1003-1020.

[37] Konsul'tativnoe zakljuchenie Bol'shoj kollegii Suda po zajavleniju Ministerstva justicii Respubliki Belarus' ot 4 aprelja 2017 goda. URL: http://courteurasian.org/doc-18093.

Union law.[38] Direct applicability is understood to mean the situation when EU norms are addressed and applied by private persons, state bodies and national courts directly, without issuing any internal normative act authorizing the application of these norms. This meaning seems very similar to the first understanding of the meaning of «direct application» used in the EAEU Treaty. And the position of the EAEU Court also followed the practice of the EU Court of Justice, in particular, the Van Gend en Loos case,[39] when the Dutch court, following the explanations of the EU Court, for resolving the dispute between the plaintiff (a private company) and the local customs authority, according to which the plaintiff was obliged to pay increased customs duties, applied not the national law, but Article 12 of the EEC Treaty. The EU Court recognized its direct effect, as it prohibited the member states unilaterally to increase import duties without any reservations and conditions. If we apply these EU Court's doctrines to the EAEU law, it appears, that Eurasian Economic Commission's decisions have both direct application and a direct effect, that is, their action in the national legal orders does not need the adoption of a national act, and their provisions can be used by private persons in national courts, including in disputes between themselves. Previously, EAEU law had not contained the 'direct effect' principle that is common in EU Law and other supranational legal orders. The introduction of this concept in the EAEU Court decision has become a serious breakthrough for the EAEU legal order and its future development.[40]

The EAEU Court calls on the member states to find «a reasonable balance between the development of their domestic market and the effective functioning of the cross-border market» and «to harmonize the legislation in such a way as to avoid the formation of various law enforcement practices». The Court draws this conclusion on the basis that the EAEU member states in Article 4 of the EAEU Treaty declared their desire to form a single market for goods, services, capital, and labor resources within the Union, and this will not be possible without creating fair competition in the market.

---

[38] See: Law of the European Union: a Textbook for Master Students / ed. P. Biriukov and V. Tuliakov. – Voronezh: VSU Publishing House, 2016. – 476 p.

[39] Case 26/62 Van Gend en Loos (1963) ECR 1. URL: http://eur-lex.europa.eu/legal-content/EN/TXT/?uri=CELEX%3A61962CJ0026

This problem is not unique, but is also a characteristic of other integration entities, first of all, of course, of the European Union, which legal system has passed a very long way of its development. In this respect, the large and difficult work was done by the Court of Justice of the European Union regarding building relations with its member states, in particular, with Germany and Italy.

So, it took the Constitutional Court of Italy more than twenty years to change its approach: from denying the supremacy of communitarian law to recognizing that in the event of a conflict between national and supranational law, Community law should be applied.[41]

Relations between the EU Court and the Federal Constitutional Court of Germany were even more complicated. The latter in 1974 in the Solange I case confirmed its right to assess the constitutionality of acts of the European Communities until the list of basic human rights protected by communitarian law becomes comparable to those guaranteed in the German Constitution. The Court of Justice, responding to the decision of Solange I as a kind of challenge, gradually expanded the range of basic human rights, which provided protection with its decisions. The result of this process was recognition in 1986 by the Federal Constitutional Court of Germany in the Re Wunsche case (better known as Solange II) that the Court will no longer re-examine the communitarian law for compliance with the Constitution, «since the European Communities have effectively protected basic human rights, comparable to the level of protection guaranteed by the German Constitution».[42]

Moreover, within the process of development of communitarian law and the integration entity itself, there were developed mechanisms to avoid questions of the operation of acts of European institutions in the national legal systems of its member states and their legal force. First of all, it concerns states that joined the European Community, and then — the

---

[40] Kalinichenko P. A Principle of Direct Effect: The Eurasian Economic Union's Court pushes for more Integration, VerfBlog, 2017/5/16. URL: http://verfassungsblog.de/the-principle-of-direct-effect-the-eurasian-economic-unions-court-pushes-for-more-integration/

[41] See: Craig P. The ECJ, national courts and the supremacy of community law. URL: http://www.ecln.net/elements/conferences/bookrome/craig.pdf

[42] See: Pollicino O. The New Relationship between National and the European Courts after the Enlargement of Europe: Towards a Unitary Theory of Jurisprudential Supranational Law? // Yearbook of European Law, Volume 29, Issue 1, 1 January 2010. P. 65–111.

European Union. Acceding countries throughout the history of enlargements of the European Communities / Union and nowadays should adapt their national legal systems and state mechanisms for EU membership, for operation of its law at the national level and for other requirements for meeting membership criteria. Usually this happens by making relevant amendments to their Constitutions and national legislation. And it can be both acts changing existing legislation and sometimes completely new laws, which, in some cases, repeal existing legal acts.[43]

And all these legal mechanisms should be perceived in relations between the Eurasian Economic Union and its member states, particularly Russia.

6. Conclusion

This analysis shows that EAEU law's relations with national legal systems of the member states, in particular of the Russian Federation, are quite inconsistent as there are a number of sources for possible tensions between the legal orders of the EAEU and Russia. Some of the developments have already scratched the surface of such tensions.

In any case, in our opinion, EAEU law's influence on the Russian legal system along with legal systems of other EAEU member states will grow. This process is predetermined by developments within the EAEU itself as its law will be developed within its competence and the powers possessed by the organs of the Union, especially the development of those features that are inherent to legal systems of other integration entities, in particular the European Union. In addition, it also depends on the position of authorities of the EAEU member states, especially higher courts, and through this, the perception of the essence of EAEU law and its relationships with the national legal system. The problem is further complicated by the fact that there is no single mechanism for implementing the acts of the EAEU bodies in the legal system of the Russian Federation, which still needs to be determined if the Russian authorities want the continuation of the development of the Eurasian integration process and its intensification. Much will depend on the willingness and readiness of the national government to take the priority of EAEU law, agreeing with the logic and arguments of the EAEU Court. For the unleashing of the integration potential, it is now necessary to

---

[43] See e.g. in Ireland: European Communities Act 1972 // Acts of the Oireachtas. - № 27/1972.

create a foundation for the development and implementation of long-term integration measures and projects that specify and develop the provisions of EAEU law especially at the national level.

Bibliography

Bakaeva O.Yu. Acts of the Eurasian Economic Commission as a source of law EAEU // Russian journal of legal studies. 2016. № 3 (8). S. 73-76.

Balytnikov V., Boklan D.Evrazijskij jekonomicheskij sojuz: predposylki sozdanija, problemy formirovanija, perspektivy razvitija // Sravnitel'noe Konstitucionnoe Obozrenie. 2015. №3 (106). P. 69-82.

Bekjashev K.A., Moiseev E.G. Pravo Evrazijskogo jekonomicheskogo sojuza. M.: Prospekt, 2015. S. 33.

C. Mayer, Franz. (2013). Constitutional comparativism in action. The example of general principles of EU law and how they are made-a German perspective. International Journal of Constitutional Law. 11. 1003-1020.

Case 106/77 Amministrazione delle Finanze dello Stato v. Simmenthal SpA (Simmenthal II) (1978) ECR 629. URL: http://eur-lex.europa.eu/legal-content/EN/TXT/?uri=CELEX:61977CJ0106

Case 106/77 Amministrazione delle Finanze dello Stato v. Simmenthal SpA (Simmenthal II) (1978) ECR 629. URL: http://eur-lex.europa.eu/legal-content/EN/TXT/?uri=CELEX:61977CJ0106

Case 26/62 Van Gend en Loos (1963) ECR 1. URL: http://eur-lex.europa.eu/legal-content/EN/TXT/?uri=CELEX%3A61962CJ0026

Constitution of the Russian Federation. URL: http://www.constitution.ru/en/10003000-01.htm

Craig P. The ECJ, national courts and the supremacy of community law. URL: http://www.ecln.net/elements/conferences/bookrome/craig.pdf

Federal Law No101-FZ of July 15, 1995 «On International Treaties». URL: https://www.wto.org/english/thewto_e/acc_e/rus_e/WTACCRUS48_LEG_56.pdf

Glotov S., Grigoriev I. The legal system of the Eurasian Economic Union: stating the problem // Vestnik MGOU. Serija: Jurisprudencija. 2015. №3. S. 12-29.

Ivanova E.M. Evrazijskaja integracija: put' ot SNG k EAJeS // Rossijskij vneshnejekonomicheskij vestnik. 2015. Vol. 2015, issue 6. S. 112-119.

Judgment of the Court of Justice, Costa v ENEL, Case 6/64 (15 July 1964). URL: http://eur-lex.europa.eu/legal-content/EN/TXT/?uri=CELEX%3A61964CJ0006

Kalinichenko P. A Principle of Direct Effect: The Eurasian Economic Union's Court pushes for more Integration, VerfBlog, 2017/5/16. URL: http://verfassungsblog.de/the-principle-of-direct-effect-the-eurasian-economic-unions-court-pushes-for-more-integration/

Kapustin A.Ya. The Law of Eurasian Economic Union: International Legal Discourse // Zhurnal rossijskogo prava. 2015. № 11. S. 59–69.

Kapustin A.Ya. Treaty on the Eurasian Economic Union — a new page of legal development of eurasian integration // Zhurnal rossijskogo prava. 2014. № 12.

Karliuk M. Russian Legal Order and the Legal Order of the Eurasian Economic Union: An Uneasy Relationship , Russian Law Journal. 2017. 5(2). P. 37.

Konsul'tativnoe zakljuchenie Bol'shoj kollegii Suda po zajavleniju Ministerstva justicii Respubliki Belarus' ot 4 aprelja 2017 goda. URL: http://courteurasian.org/doc-18093.

Konsul'tativnoe zakljuchenie Bol'shoj kollegii Suda po zajavleniju Ministerstva justicii Respubliki Belarus' ot 4 aprelja 2017 goda. URL: http://courteurasian.org/doc-18093.

Law of the European Union: a Textbook for Master Students / ed. P. Biriukov and V. Tuliakov. –Voronezh: VSU Publishing House, 2016. – 476 p.

Malinovskaya V.M. Legal and Institutional Bases of Functioning of the Eurasian Union // Vestnik MGIMO. 2012. 4(25). S. 197-202.

Morozov A.N. Implementation of International commitments undertaken by member states within the framework of the Eurasian Economic Union // Zhurnal zarubezhnogo zakonodatel'stva i sravnitel'nogo pravovedenija. 2017. №3. S. 111-120.

Myslivskij P.P. Mezhdunarodno-pravovoe regulirovanie sozdanija Evrazijskogo jekonomicheskogo sojuza i sposoba razreshenija sporov: dissertacija ... kandidata juridicheskih nauk: 12.00.10. Moskva, 2016. - S. 12.

Opredelenie Konstitucionnogo suda Rossiiskoi Federacii po zaprosu Arbitrazhnogo suda Central'nogo okruga o proverke konstitucionnosti punkta 4 Porjadka primenenija osvobozhdenija ot uplaty tamozhennyh poshlin pri vvoze otdel'nyh kategorii ˇ tovarov na edinuju tamozhennuju territoriju Tamozhennogo sojuza. URL: http://doc.ksrf.ru/decision/KSRFDecision190708.pdf

Osoboe mnenie sud'i Ajrijan Je.V. po delu po konsul'tativnomu zakljucheniju po zajavleniju Ministerstva justicii Respubliki Belarus' ot 4 aprelja 2017 goda. URL: http://courteurasian.org/doc-18153.

Osoboe mnenie sud'i Chajki K.L. po delu po zajavleniju Rossijskoj Federacii po sporu o sobljudenii Respublikoj Belarus' Dogovora o Evrazijskom jekonomicheskom sojuze, stat'i 125 Tamozhennogo kodeksa tamozhennogo sojuza, statej 11 i 17 Soglashenija o vzaimnoj administrativnoj pomoshhi tamozhennyh organov gosudarstv – chlenov tamozhennogo sojuza. URL: http://courteurasian.org/doc-17993

Osoboe mnenie sud'i Chajki K.L. po delu po zajavleniju Rossijskoj Federacii po sporu o sobljudenii Respublikoj Belarus' Dogovora o Evrazijskom jekonomicheskom sojuze, stat'i 125 Tamozhennogo kodeksa tamozhennogo sojuza, statej 11 i 17 Soglashenija o vzaimnoj administrativnoj pomoshhi tamozhennyh organov gosudarstv – chlenov tamozhennogo sojuza. URL: http://courteurasian.org/doc-17993

Pollicino O. The New Relationship between National and the European Courts after the Enlargement of Europe: Towards a Unitary Theory of Jurisprudential Supranational Law? // Yearbook of European Law, Volume 29, Issue 1, 1 January 2010. P. 65–111.

Putin V. A new integration project for Eurasia: The future in the making. URL: http://www.europarl.europa.eu/meetdocs/2009_2014/documents/d-ru/dv/dru_2013_0320_06_/dru_2013_0320_06_en.pdf

Putin V. Novyj integracionnyj proekt dlja Evrazii — budushhee, kotoroe rozhdaetsja segodnja. URL: https://iz.ru/news/502761

Reshenie Bol'shoj kollegii Suda ot 21 fevralja 2017 goda po delu po zajavleniju Rossijskoj Federacii po sporu o sobljudenii Respublikoj Belarus' Dogovora o Evrazijskom jekonomicheskom sojuze, stat'i 125 Tamozhennogo kodeksa tamozhennogo sojuza, statej 11 i 17 Soglashenija o vzaimnoj administrativnoj pomoshhi tamozhennyh organov gosudarstv–chlenov tamozhennogo sojuza. URL: http://courteurasian.org/doc-17943

Reshenie Bol'shoj kollegii Suda ot 21 fevralja 2017 goda po delu po zajavleniju Rossijskoj Federacii po sporu o sobljudenii Respublikoj Belarus' Dogovora o Evrazijskom jekonomicheskom sojuze, stat'i 125 Tamozhennogo kodeksa tamozhennogo sojuza, statej 11 i 17 Soglashenija o vzaimnoj administrativnoj pomoshhi tamozhennyh organov gosudarstv–chlenov tamozhennogo sojuza. URL: http://courteurasian.org/doc-17943

Reshenie Bol'shoj kollegii Suda ot 21 fevralja 2017 goda po delu po zajavleniju Rossijskoj Federacii po sporu o sobljudenii Respublikoj Belarus' Dogovora o Evrazijskom jekonomicheskom sojuze, stat'i 125 Tamozhennogo kodeksa tamozhennogo sojuza, statej 11 i 17 Soglashenija o vzaimnoj administrativnoj pomoshhi tamozhennyh organov gosudarstv–chlenov tamozhennogo sojuza. URL: http://courteurasian.org/doc-17943

Roberts S.P., Marin A, Moshes A, Pynnöniemi K. The Eurasian Economic Union: breaking the pattern of post-Soviet integration? FIIA Analysis 3. The Finnish Institute of International Affairs, 2014. P. 6.

Shumilov V.M., Boklan D.S., Lifshic I.M. Pravovye novelly Dogovora o Evrazijskom jekonomicheskom sojuze // Rossijskij vneshnejekonomicheskij vestnik. 2015. Vol. 2015, issue 4. S. 90.

Soglashenie o vzaimnoj administrativnoj pomoshhi tamozhennyh organov gosudarstv-chlenov tamozhennogo sojuza ot 21 Maya 2010 goda. URL: http://www.eurasiancommission.org/docs/Download.aspx?IsDlg=0&ID=4183&print=1

Treaty on the Eurasian Economic Union. URL: http://www.un.org/en/ga/sixth/70/docs/treaty_on_eeu.pdf

Volova L.I. Pravovoj status regional'nyh integracionnyh ob'edinenij // Rossijskij ezhegodnik mezhdunarodnogo prava. 2012. SPb. : Rossija-Neva, 2013. S. 98.

Wolczuk K., Dragneva R, The Eurasian Economic Union: Deals, Rules and the Exercise of Power. Chatham House Research Paper, Royal Institute of International Affairs, London, 2017. P. 4.

European Communities Act 1972 // Acts of the Oireachtas. - № 27/1972.

Chapter 22

Convergence and Divergence of International Law in Slovak Judicial System

Lucia Mokrá[1]

Abstract

The court system in the Slovak Republic is based on the principle of general jurisdiction. In practice, it means that all the courts, including the District Courts (courts of first instance), Regional Courts (appellate courts) and the Supreme Court are obliged to follow the principle of international law supremacy, as stated in the Constitution of the Slovak Republic and also as stated in international treaties adopted and ratified in national law. Direct supremacy is given to the international human rights treaties. This research deals with the diversified implementation of the positive obligation on Slovakia, resulting from imprecise constitutional regulation of human rights treaties.

Introduction

National constitutions used to have some reference to international law and international treaties. As Anne Peters states, "*State constitutions have traditionally included references to foreign affairs and to international law. Classic examples are constitutional clauses on the powers of state organs in foreign affairs, especially with regard to the conclusion of international*

---

[1] Dean of Faculty of Social and Economic Sciences of Comenius University in Bratislava

treaties".[2] As Peters and others confirm, the development of international law in recent decades has shifted its status within the national system. It has become more clearly identified as a source of law and very often the supremacy of international law and international treaties is recognized over national law. Often, however, international and national law converge.

The principle of supremacy of international law means the supreme position of international law over national legislation. Gerald Fitzmaurice confirmed, that the principle of supremacy is *"one of the great principles of international law, informing the whole system and applying to every branch of it"*.[3] Generally, *"the principle of supremacy of international law seeks to subordinate the sovereignty of states to international law."*[4] One of such manifestations is that *"international law is supreme over, and takes precedence in the international legal order, national law."*[5] In case of conflict between international law and domestic law, the international law prevails. *"This aspect is at the heart of the law of treaties and the law of international responsibility"*.[6]

In the broadest sense, the supremacy of international law is the rule, which establishes the obligation on nation states to supervise, that the way state authorities exercise their powers, conforms to international law. Nevertheless, as Nollkaemper states: *"Allowing states to prioritize fundamental rules of domestic law over international law would undermine the efficacy of international law and the international rule of law."* [7]

---

[2] e.g. Article 2 § 2 US Constitution of 17 September 1787, art. 59 German Basic Law of 23 May 1949. In: Ann Peters, Supremacy Lost: International Law Meets Domestic Constitutional Law. Vienna Journal of International Constitutional Law. Vol. 3/2009, p. 170. Online:
https://ius.unibas.ch/uploads/publics/8830/20100219153347_4b7ea14b06261.pdf

[3] Gerald Fitzmaurice, the General Principles of International law Considered from the Standpoint of the Rule of Law (1957), RdC, 85 ff

[4] Gerald Fitzmaurice, the General Principles of International law Considered from the Standpoint of the Rule of Law (1957), RdC, p. 6

[5] Dominique Carreau: Droit International (2004), 43 ff, Fitzmauriece, General PRinciples (Fn 3) 68 ff. Santulli Carlo: Le Satuts International de LÓrdre Juridique Étatique (2001) 427.

[6] Articles 27 and 46 of the Vienna Convention on the Law of Treaties
Articles 3 and 32 of the Articles on the Responsibility of States for Internationally Wrongful Acts – UN Doc A/Res/56/83 (28 January 2002)

[7] Nollkaemper, André: Rethinking the Supremacy of Internaitonal Law. Online:
https://link.springer.com/content/pdf/10.1007%2Fs00708-010-0044-4.pdf, p. 67

Supremacy clauses in constitutions are very often used to enshrine the status and legal power of international human rights treaties; however, these constitutional provisions do not necessarily lead to an increased efficiency in the application of the positive obligation. However, the clear and precise constitutional provision of the supremacy of international law respecting minimum international standards, is the condition sine qua non of the proper application of international obligations.

1. The Position of International Law in the Slovak Legal System

1.1. The Principle of Supremacy in the Constitution of the Slovak Republic

The principle of international law supremacy was originally stated, in a general way, in the Constitution of the Slovak Republic [Constitutional Act No. 460/1992 Coll.[8]] The sovereign Slovak Republic recognized international law and its fundamental principles as stated in the United Nations Charter. It is explicitly stated in article 1, para 2 of the Constitution: *"The Slovak Republic recognizes and honours general rules of international law, international treaties by which it is bound and its other international obligations."*[9] However whilst the Slovak Republic from its beginning recognized international obligations, a more precise definition became part of the constitution later mainly due to the development of the position of the country in international relations, its membership of international organizations, and integration ambitions in the European regional context.

The most visible change of the Slovak Constitution in its recent history was its amendment through the adoption of Constitutional Act No. 90/2001 Coll. of laws. This constitutional amendment was important not only from the point of future accession to the European union, but also that it stated more concretely the position of international law and international human rights treaties within the Constitution of the Slovak Republic.

The reason for this significant amendment of the Constitution of the SR was in part legal terminology but also to modernize some provisions connected with previous constitutional legal acts of a socialistic character. The, last but not least, reason for the initiating of this constitutional amendment was the harmonization of basic constitutional provisions

---

[8] Legal acts adopted before 1993 were published in the Collection (abb. Coll.). Legal acts adopted after 1993 are published in the Collection of Laws (abb. Coll. of laws)

[9] Constitutional Act No. 460/1992 Coll. – Constitution of the Slovak Republic. Online: https://www.prezident.sk/upload-files/46422.pdf

with European Union Law, in accordance with the association agreement the Slovak Republic had signed.

The amendment contained several crucial changes and modifications. One of the most important points, was regularising the relationship of international law and European law with national law. This was enabled by the change of article 1 of the constitution with the by adding a new paragraph '(2)' to the article:

> *"(2) The Slovak Republic recognizes and honours general rules of international law, international treaties by which it is bound and its other international obligations."*[10]

Recognition of the international treaties and of the supranational communitarian legal approach was enabled by the new text of article 7, mainly paragraphs 2, 4 and 5 of the Constitution:

> *"(2) The Slovak Republic may, by an international treaty ratified and promulgated in a manner laid down by law, or on the basis of such treaty, transfer the exercise of a part of its rights to the European Communities and European Union. Legally binding acts of the European Communities and European Union shall have primacy over the laws of the Slovak Republic. Undertaking of legally binding acts that require implementation shall be executed by law or a government ordinance pursuant to Article 120, paragraph 2.*
>
> *(4) In order for any international treaties on human rights and fundamental freedoms, international political treaties, international treaties of military nature, international treaties establishing the membership of the Slovak Republic in international organizations, international economic treaties of general nature, international treaties whose execution requires a law and international treaties which directly constitute rights or obligations of natural persons or legal persons to be valid, an approval of the National Council of the Slovak Republic is required prior to their ratification.*
>
> *(5) International treaties on human rights and fundamental freedoms, international treaties whose executions does not require a law and international treaties which directly establish rights or obligations of natural persons or legal persons and which were ratified and*

---

[10] Constitutional Act No. 460/1992 Coll. – Constitution of the Slovak Republic. Online: http://www.slovakia.org/sk-constitution.htm

promulgated in a manner laid down by law shall have primacy over the laws."[11]

The amendment also modified competences and jurisdiction of the Constitutional Court of the Slovak Republic in a way to establish competences of the Court to decide on the conformity of important international treaties with the Constitution, as well as to increase the efficiency and enforceability of its decisions on conformity. The text of the new article 125a of the Constitution, was enacted as follows:

"Article 125a

(1) The Constitutional Court decides on compliance of the concluded international treaties for which consent of the National Council of the Slovak Republic is required with the Constitution or a constitutional law.

(2) The petition for a decision pursuant to paragraph 1 may be filed with the Constitutional Court by the President of the Slovak Republic or the Government before submitting of the concluded international treaty for a deliberation to the National Council of the Slovak Republic.

(3) The Constitutional Court decides on the petition pursuant to paragraph 2 within the period laid down by law; if the Constitutional Court by its decision expresses that the international treaty is not in compliance with the Constitution or a constitutional law, such international treaty may not be ratified." [12]

1.2. The Principle of Supremacy of International Human Rights Treaties in the Slovak Constitutional System – A Legal Dilemma between Legislative and Executive Power?

The recognition of fundamental rights and freedoms in Slovakia is guaranteed by two parallel legal provisions:

  a) in the form of relevant constitutional provisions on the protection of fundamental rights and freedoms (Chapter II of the Constitution),

---

[11] Constitutional Act No. 460/1992 Coll. – Constitution of the Slovak Republic. Online: http://www.slovakia.org/sk-constitution.htm

[12] Constitutional Act No. 460/1992 Coll. – Constitution of the Slovak Republic. Online: http://www.slovakia.org/sk-constitution.htm

b) in the Bill of fundamental rights and freedoms, adopted on 9th January 1991 by the Federal Assembly of the Czech and Slovak Federal Republic. This was enacted as constitutional Act No. 23/1991 Coll., becoming valid and efficient (coming into force) on the 8th February 1991. It was transposed into the legal order of the Slovak Republic through article 152 of the Constitution of the Slovak Republic.

The Bill of fundamental rights and freedoms established, together with the Constitution of the Slovak Republic, the constitutional framework for the protection of human rights. Another fundamental source of human rights protections in the Slovak Republic are international treaties on human rights and fundamental freedoms, adopted and ratified regarding to article 7 para 4 and 5 of the Constitution of the Slovak Republic, and also those adopted and ratified regarding to article 154c para 1 of the Constitution of the Slovak Republic.

In article 7 para 4 of the Constitution, different types of international treaties are identified: "*international treaties on human rights and fundamental freedoms, international political treaties, international treaties of military nature, international treaties establishing the membership of the Slovak Republic in international organizations, international economic treaties of general nature, international treaties whose execution requires a law.*" All these treaties require the consent of the National Council of the Slovak Republic (the parliament) before its ratification. We have to add, that while the validity of any international treaty is judged through international treaty law and does not depend on national law, in relation to adoption, ratification and publication of an international treaty the rules are expressly stated in national law. When using logic and a systematic interpretation approach in relation to article 7 para 4 of the Constitution, we can conclude, that the purpose of this provision is to connect ratification of relevant international treaties with the approval of parliament, mainly because of parliamentary democracy in the country. Any international treaty, as defined in article 7 para 4, has to be approved by absolute majority in the Parliament, i.e. by a minimum of 76 MPs. However, this approval is not a condition for the validity of an international treaty, but it is a condition of its ratification (and treaty publication requires ratification) and in time a condition of its efficiency.

The legal recognition of the different international treaty cycle in national and international law does not influence the legal effects of an international treaty. The subsidiary legislative regulation states in §3 para 3 of the Act No. 1/1993 Coll. of laws on the Collection of Laws as amended, that an "international treaty becomes valid by the way and on the day set in its provisions or by other ways stated in the rules of international law. International treaty is published in the Collection of laws immediately after its submission for publication (§ 10 para 3), at the latest on the day of its validity to the Slovak republic; by this publication it becomes of obligatory effect for natural and legal persons, if there is not stated later day of efficiency in the treaty explicitly." According to §10 para 3 of the Act on the Collection of laws, "international treaties have to submitted by the Ministry of Foreign Affairs of the Slovak Republic to its publication in the Collection of Laws 15 days before its efficiency for the Slovak Republic".

According to article 7 para 5 of the Constitution, some of the international treaties named in article 7 para 4, are supreme to national law: *"international treaties on human rights and fundamental freedoms, international treaties whose executions does not require a law and international treaties which directly establish rights or obligations of natural persons or legal persons and which were ratified and promulgated in a manner laid down by law shall have primacy over the laws."*[13]

A pre-condition of the approval of the National Council SR is connected to international treaties identified in article 7 para 4, from the point of its content and the form of its execution. A particular international treaty may fulfil several criteria stated in article 7 para 4 of the Constitution. A problematic situation may occur, if an international treaty was be considered as a treaty on human rights and fundamental freedoms, which establishes the membership of Slovakia in an international organizations which directly establish rights or obligations to natural persons or legal persons, whilst at the same time it is capable of being interpreted as an international economic treaty of general character, whose execution requires adoption of a national law, etc.

According to this, it is necessary to underline the importance of the provision of article 86 letter d) of the Constitution, which gives the power to the National Council of the Slovak Republic to prior to ratification, approve international treaties on human rights and at the same time to make a determination whether these are international treaties stipulated in Article 7, paragraph 5.

The purpose of this provision is to enable the National Council of the SR to decide, whether an international treaty according to article 7 para 4 of the Constitution, is simultaneously an international treaty according to

---

[13] Constitutional Act No. 460/1992 Coll. – Constitution of the Slovak Republic. Online: http://www.slovakia.org/sk-constitution.htm

article 7 para 5 of the Constitution, i.e. whether it is an international treaty on human rights and fundamental treaty whose executions does not require a law (so-called "self-executive treaty") or if it is an international treaty, which directly establish rights or obligations of natural persons or legal persons (considered as "treaty with direct effect").

In using this provision, the National Council of the SR does not decide to make a legal determination, whether a finalized international treaty should be classified as a treaty on human rights with a self-executive character or a treaty with direct effect to the national legislation or not. The parliament instead decides on its classification, i.e. whether a finalized human rights treaty will be identified in the national legal system as self-executive or one with direct effect. In the case where the National Council of the SR classifies the treaty as the one with direct effect, this treaty becomes *ex constitutione* supreme to the laws. The content of the supremacy clause published in the Collection of laws should be the classification of a finalized international treaty, which then becomes supreme to national law, as a direct result of the provisions of the Constitution.

At the initial interpretation, if the National Council of the SR wishes to avoid international treaty supremacy to national law, then it should not decide, that a treaty is human rights treaty, self-executive treaty or a treaty with direct effect and notify this decision explicitly as the published supremacy clause. The decision on the classification of an international treaty based on article 86 letter d) of the Constitution has no influence on the international legal status of the treaty and does not limit state responsibility for any breaches of obligations stated in the international treaty.

It is important to underline, that in the decision-making process according to article 86 letter d) of the Constitution, the National Council of the SR do not decide, whether it is an international treaty according to article 7 para 4 of the Constitution, but it may exclusively decide about expressing of the consent to the treaty and may as well decide on classification of this treaty as stated in article 7 para 5 of the Constitution. That decision, whether it is an international treaty according to article 7 para 4 of the Constitution, is the matter for the institution responsible for the negotiation of the international treaty, and it has to be proposed in only one way: presenting the treaty for discussion and subsequent express consent by the National Council of the SR. This procedure may be considered as insufficient, especially in relation to the position of the National Council of the SR and its position as the sole constitutional and legislative body of the Slovak Republic, when exercising its competence to decide on the structure of legal order of the Slovak Republic and the character of international obligations. Its competence looks limited when discretion is moved to another body authorized to conduct the negotiation of the treaty.

The Parliament does not have any specific power to prevent the limitation of its prerogative by the executive power bodies. The existence of the SR Constitutional Court's competence according to article 125a in the form of the deciding on the compatibility of an international treaty adopted according to article 7 para 4 and article 7 para 2 of the Constitution, does not establish competence of the Constitutional Court to evaluate either the procedural aspects of expressing consent or the procedural aspects of the ratification of an international treaty. Parliament's competence to submit an application to the Constitutional Court for an interpretation according to article 128 of the Constitution is questionable in its effect, in light of the extensive interpretation of Constitutional Court's competence made by itself. Constant case-law of the Constitutional Court concerning active legitimation of state bodies, in proceeding according to article 128 of the Constitution, indicate the Court takes a restrictive interpretation of its own competence. (see Finding of the Constitutional court, ref. No. II. ÚS 804/00).

Similarly, there is limited ability to act at the disposal of the President of the Slovak Republic, whose ratification competence is more of notarial character. The question may arise, as to whether the president could refuse ratification of an international treaty, which the National Council of SR had not dealt with through the process of expressing consent according to article 86 para d) of the Constitution, if the President's opinion was that it should follow this process. In any case, such a conclusion would not influence the fact that the Parliament would not be a direct actor with the possibility of influencing the process of treaty negotiation and its result.

Neither legal acts nor the Constitution in the Slovak Republic contain explicit interpretation of criteria, as to whether particular international treaties should be classified in accordance with article 7 para 4 or article 7 para 5 of the Constitution. Full interpretation of such criteria is in the competence of bodies authorised to negotiate and adopt international treaties, usually reflecting the diplomatic or international relations practice. There is also no regulated mechanism, that gives the National Council of the SR competence to decide, whether individual international treaty fulfil criteria stated in article 7 para 4 of the Constitution, during the process of expressing consent with the treaty. As stated in the current form of the constitution, it is the exclusive competence of the body responsible for the negotiation of an international treaty (in majority of the cases this is the Government), whether the treaty is submitted to the National

Council of the SR for proceeding according to article 7 para 4 of the Constitution or not.

Interconnected with this disputable issue is the fact, that while article 7 para 4 conditions the ratification of international treaties whose execution is requires the adoption of a law, to the consent of the National Council of SR, article 7 para 5 recognizes the supremacy or direct effect of international treaties for whose execution it is not necessary to adopt a law.

The majority of international treaties of self-executive character as stated in article 7 para 5 are international treaties on human rights. However, some self-executive treaties may not be treaties on human rights and may not constitute rights or obligations of natural persons or legal persons. These treaties may however establish obligations on state bodies, the exercise of which requires the adoption of finalized law. In the sense of article 7 para 4, the ratification of such a treaty is not dependent on the National Council of the Slovak Republic expressing consent. The state body implementing the law may recognize the supremacy of the international treaty to law; however, the National Council of the SR would not have expressed consent to the treaty. Such process would not reflect to the basic characteristics of the democratic process and the rule of law, including the sovereignty of the legislative body in the decision-making when the finalized rule is transformed into the law as the part of the legislative order.

This problem may be neutralized by the fact, that the international treaty's supremacy to national law is recognized only for international treaties on which the National Council of the SR explicitly decides, that it is self-executive treaty, treaty on human rights or treaty with direct effect, concretely in proceeding when the National Council of the SR expresses consent with international treaty according to article 7 para 4 of the Constitution. There cannot exist the situation, where a self-executive treaty is supreme to national law without the expressed consent of the National Council of the SR. From the literal interpretation of article 86 letter d) of the Constitution, it results, that the situation cannot exist, where any self-executive treaty (which is not treaty on human rights or treaty with direct effect) is supreme to national law, where the National Council of the SR does not express consent with self-executive treaty (as it is defined in the article 7 para 5 of the Constitution) or decides about its character as self-executive treaty as stated in the article 7 para 5 of the Constitution.

International treaties which may otherwise fulfil the criteria of a self-executing treaty according to article 7 para 5 of the Constitution, the President is entitled to ratify; however, the National Council of the SR does not have the competence to express the supremacy of the treaty to national law. This provision does not reflect its basic purpose which is to prevent, as much as is possible, the state's liability for non-fulfilment of the obligations resulting from international treaties.

According to this we may conclude with the interpretation, that the National Council of the SR may classify any international treaty according to article 7 para 4 as a self-executive treaty in accordance to article 7 para 5 of the constitution, except for a human rights treaty, treaty with direct effect and also treaty whose execution requires a law. Using this interpretation, the National Council of the SR may also classify as a self-executive treaty according to article 7 para 5 of the Constitution an international political treaty, an international treaty of military nature, an international treaty establishing the membership of the Slovak Republic in international organizations, and international economic treaties of general nature whose execution does not require a law.

Noting these facts, the Slovak national legal framework has "*preferential position only to international treaties according to article 7 para 5. This is, in fact, however, contrary to the issue, that in case of applications for violation of the fundamental rights and freedoms guaranteed also by international treaties (constitutional proceeding according to article 127 of the Constitution), the Constitution does not make any difference between these two categories of international treaties*".[14]

This explanation and interpretation of the status of international treaties in the national legal system and its regulation in the Constitution of the Slovak Republic would not be complete, if we did not mention the recognition of human rights and the protection of fundamental freedoms within the European Union. It is important to underline the position of the fundamental principle of the protection of human rights, given the supremacy of European Union law, despite being limited by the constitutional traditions of the member state. The positive impact of this is mainly visible in the existence of the rights of the fourth generation[15]

---

[14] Kamil Baraník: Interakcia medzinárodného, supranacionálneho a ústavného práva pri ochrane ľudských práv v SR (2017). Bratislava: Justičná revue, 10/2017, p. 1127

[15] In relation to fourth generation of human rights as right for sustainable development, see more in: Derek G. Evans: Human Rights: Four Generations of

which are not included in the national constitution. The Constitution of the Slovak Republic states in article 7 para 2, that "*legally binding acts of the European Communities and European Union shall have primacy over the laws of the Slovak Republic. Undertaking of legally binding acts that require implementation shall be executed by law or a government ordinance pursuant to Article 120, paragraph 2.*" The principle of direct effect should also be considered. This is defined by the European Court of Justice, that according to the founding treaties, a treaty provision may have a direct effect, when fulfilling stated criteria[16] (such as clear and precise rights or obligations, un-conditionality and legal perfectness), and then it is also supreme to national constitutions.[17] In this sense, we should consider as a relevant international human rights treaty the Charter of the Fundamental Rights of the EU, but in relation to the purpose of this article, we are not analysing its position in the legal system of the Slovak Republic.

2. Decision-Making In Practice in Slovakia – Is International Law Supreme in Jurisdiction?

2.1. Human Rights Treaties, Treaties with Direct Effect and Self-Executive Treaties

In Slovakia the recognition of treaties as human rights treaties according to article 7 para 5 of the Constitution is limited to only those international treaties, which are classified as human rights treaties by the National Council of the Slovak Republic. The decision-making of the Parliament as to the classification of a treaty is not limited by specific attributes the treaty has to fulfil. The fundamental principle for classification is the free will of contracting parties reflected in the text of the international treaty and within the travaux preparatoires.

Practice and Development. In: Abdi, A. And L. Shults, eds., Educating for Human Rights and Global Citizenship. Albany: State University of New Yor Press, 2007

[16] ECJ judgement – case 26/62 NV Algemene Transport- en Expeditie Onderneming van Gend & Loos v Netherlands Inland Revenue Administration of 5 February 1963. ECLI:EU:C:1963:1 online: http://eur-lex.europa.eu/legal-content/EN/TXT/PDF/?uri=CELEX:61962CJ0026&from=EN

[17] see more in: ECJ judgement – case 11/70 Internationale Handelsgesellschaft mbH v Einfuhr- und Vorratsstelle für Getreide und Futtermittel of 17 December 1970. ECLI:EU:C:1970:114 online: http://eur-lex.europa.eu/legal-content/EN/TXT/PDF/?uri=CELEX:61970CJ0011&from=EN

An International treaty may be classified as a **human rights treaty**, when fulfilling the following characteristics:

1) the content of the treaty regulates fundamental rights and freedoms as guaranteed in the second chapter of the Constitution or is connected with it,
2) or it is connected with fundamental rights or freedoms regulated by international treaties to which the Slovak Republic is bound,
3) or is explicitly named as a treaty on human rights,
4) or according to its preamble, text or travaux preparatoires it results, that it is a treaty on human rights

and any other treaty:

5) whose primary purpose is the protection of fundamental rights and freedoms, i.e. a treaty which does not contain only incidental regulation of fundamental rights and freedoms, but was concluded with the aim of regulating its protection,
6) and whose provisions are liable to be directly implemented by the authorities responsible for the implementation of law, i.e. contains regulation of human rights or fundamental freedoms sufficiently clear and concrete enough, and precise for the decision in merit,
7) or at least the provisions of human rights and fundamental freedoms are capable of having direct applicability or are not contrary to the direct applicability of the treaty.

While attributes 1 to 4 are alternatives, usually in practice, an international treaty will fulfil several of them simultaneously. In the case of characteristics 5 to 7 these are required to be filled cumulatively. The international human rights treaties should be classified as such treaties in the Slovak legal order, as they fulfil at least one of the characteristics in point 1 to 4 and all three of characteristics 5 to 7.

According to the Constitution, there exist two other types of international treaty that also regulate human rights:

a) a treaty with direct effect
b) a self-executive treaty.

These may have a different character in relation to its provision and also a different form of execution.

When Parliament decides, according to article 86 letter d) of the Constitution, about the classification of an international treaty (either a human rights treaty, a treaty with direct effect or a self-executive treaty), the international treaty is supreme only in that part which is capable of direct execution by a national authority, and only in relation to the provisions which are sufficiently clear and precise to be used as the basis for a decision in merit.

An international treaty may be classified as a **treaty with direct effect**, when fulfilling all the following characteristics:

(a) it directly recognises rights and establishes obligations to natural and legal persons, which are of an innovative normative character in relation to the legal order of the Slovak Republic or its content is different to the existing one in Slovakia; and

(b) these rights and obligations are in the competence of the legislative power of the Parliament or the Government according to article 120 para 2 of the Constitution, in conjunction with article 13 para 1, letter c) of the Constitution; and

(c) these rights are not of a fundamental right or a fundamental freedom in their character, and

(d) the State authorities are not considered as legal persons governed by the treaty.

Simultaneously, only a treaty:

1) whose provisions are liable to be directly implemented by the authorities responsible for the implementation of law, i.e. contains regulation of human rights or fundamental freedoms sufficiently clear and concrete enough, and precise for the decision in merit; or

2) at least the provisions effecting human rights and fundamental freedoms are capable of having direct applicability or are not contrary to the direct applicability of the treaty.

is considered as a treaty with direct effect. All these characteristics are required to be filled cumulatively.

An international treaty may be classified as a **self-executive treaty**, when fulfilling the following characteristics:

(a) it contains obligations, which do not require adoption of additional legislation for execution in the form of an individual legal act or amendment and

(b) it is not a human rights treaty or a treaty with direct effect.

Simultaneously, only a treaty:

1) whose provisions are liable to be directly implemented by the authorities responsible for the implementation of law, i.e.

contains regulation of human rights or fundamental freedoms sufficiently clear and concrete enough, and precise for the decision in merit; or
2) or at least the provisions effecting human rights and fundamental freedoms are capable of having direct applicability or are not contrary to the direct applicability of the treaty.

is considered as self-executive treaty. All these characteristics are required to be filled cumulatively.

The differences between different types of international treaties are quite small, therefore the precise classification of an international treaty is really important and usually problematic .All three of the above-mentioned treaty types are, however, supreme to national legislation, and this is a condition sine qua non for proper and constant implementation.

2.2. Case Analysis and Conclusion

The Constitution of the Slovak Republic recognises generally the supremacy of the international treaties to national law but not above the Constitution of the Slovak Republic and constitutional laws. The Constitutional Court of the Slovak Republic has several times ruled and justified the importance of the international treaties in the process of interpretation and implementation of the Constitution:

"The Constitutional Court has working from the beginning of its existence according to the principle pacta sunt servanda and constantly rules, that fundamental rights and freedoms as stated in the Constitution have to be interpreted and implemented conform to international treaties on human rights and fundamental freedoms."[18]

When considering the relationship between the Constitution of the Slovak Republic and international treaties, the Constitutional Court has ruled and clearly stated, that *"International treaties on human rights have specific position in the system of legal sources in the Slovak Republic. According to conditions stated in article 11 of the Constitution of the SR, these are supreme to national law, not to the Constitution of the SR."*

---

[18] Findings of the Constitutional Court of the SR No. PL. ÚS 5/93, PL. ÚS 15/98, PL. ÚS 17/00. In: Drgonec, J.: Constitution of the Slovak Republic. Comments. Bratislava: C.H.Beck, 2015, p. 333

Findings of the Constitutional Court of the SR No. II. ÚS 55/98. In: Drgonec, J.: Constitution of the Slovak Republic. Comments. Bratislava: C.H.Beck, 2015, p. 333

We have to stress the important role of the judges in providing such interpretation of the Slovak Constitution and also in determining its relationship to international law. This implementation practice, including the above-mentioned interpretation rules of the Constitutional Court rely on article 144, para 1 of the Constitution, *"Judges are independent in execution of their function and bound solely by the Constitution, constitutional laws, international treaties stipulated in Article 7, paragraphs 2 and 5 and laws."* According to article 144, para 2 of the Constitution, *"If the court is of the opinion that another generally binding legal regulation, its part or a particular provision related to the subject-matter of the proceeding contravenes the Constitution, constitutional laws, international treaties stipulated in Article 7, paragraphs 2 and 5 or laws, it will interrupt its deliberations and submit a motion that a proceeding under Article 125, paragraph 1 is initiated. The finding of the Constitutional Court of the Slovak Republic is binding for all courts."*

According to § 162 para 1 letter b) of the Code of Civil Contentious Litigation, a court postpones proceedings, if it concludes before it makes a decision on the merits of the case, that the general legally binding act which should be applied to the case, is contrary to the Constitution, to the law or to an international treaty to which the Slovak Republic is bound. In such cases, the Court forwards the proposal to the Constitutional Court to deal with the issue of compatibility.

As stated in the article 125 para 1, letter a) of the Constitution,

„*The Constitutional Court decides on the compatibility of:*
a) laws with the Constitution, constitutional laws and international treaties to which a consent was given by the National Council of the Slovak Republic and which were ratified and promulgated in a manner laid down by law...."

International human rights treaties are an important source of the arguments before the national courts in Slovakia. Sometimes, however, the national courts use national legislation, where the international law is already incorporated sufficiently into the national legislation and there's no need to explicitly follow the international treaty provisions:

In the Finding of the Constitutional Court No. I. ÚS 28/01-29 of 13 December 2001 the Court stated, that: "*If the applicant is claiming the violation of the fundamental rights and freedoms guaranteed in the Constitution and in the same time violation of human rights and fundamental freedoms guaranteed by international human rights treaty by which the Slovak Republic is bound, and if there is not difference in the content of these rights and freedoms, by the determination and confirmation of the violation of fundamental right or freedom, there is filled the purpose of protection provided by the Constitutional Court to the right or freedom also according to international treaty. The Constitutional Court in such cases in the part of the application dealing with the reference to the concrete international human rights treaty's provision usually do not comply (mutatis mutandis II. ÚS 55/98)."*[19]

The Constitutional Court in another case PL. ÚS 25/01-45 of 7 November 2002 dealt with the supremacy of the Convention on the protection of the human rights and fundamental freedoms as international human rights treaty. In the proceedings on the conformity of the claimed provision §200i of the Code of Civil Procedure with the Convention, *"the Constitutional Court after the review of the claimed provision's conformity with the article 6 para 1 the first sentence of the Convention, had ruled that the Convention as international human rights treaty has to be interpreted based on the interpretation rules of international law (articles 31 to 33 of the Vienna Convention on the Law of Treaties of 23 May 1969) and not on the interpretation rules of national law (PL. ÚS 5/93). Also the European Court for Human Rights, exercising the exclusive competence for all questions connecting to interpretation and application of the Convention and its protocols (article 32 of the Convention) had claimed, that the Convention must be interpreted in the way to be conform to other rules of international law as the integral and indivisible part of it (ECtHR judgement Al-Adsani of 21 November 2001). The ECtHR repeatedly underlined, that according to the Convention and its special character of normative treaty on the collective guarantee of human rights, it is necessary to endeavour to its most proper interpretation to achieve its goal and implementation of the treaty purpose".*[20]

While the European Court of Human Rights' case law became an integral part of the inspiration for national court's decision-making, some other international treaties including human rights treaties are in the opposite position. The divergence is visible in the view of the UN CEDAW

---

[19] Finding of the Constitutional Court No. I. ÚS 28/01-29 of 13 December 2001. Online: https://www.ustavnysud.sk/ussr-intranet-portlet/docDownload/abf57423-a027-4ee8-9d13-5d72f3536a26/Rozhodnutie%20-%20Rozhodnutie%20II.%20%C3%9AS%20499_2012.pdf

[20] Finding of the Constitutional Court of the SR No. PL. ÚS 25/01-45 of 7 November 2002. Online: https://www.ustavnysud.sk/ussr-intranet-portlet/docDownload/d353f739-7b83-46dd-95da-d0fc5262f2e6/Rozhodnutie%20-%20Rozhodnutie%20PL.%20%C3%9AS%2025_01.pdf

Committee, when adopting its view of 7 November 2016, in the case of Ms D. versus the Slovak Republic, on discrimination based on gender and family and marital status in employment. The UN CEDAW Committee in its View of 7 November 2016, concerning communication No. 66/2014, ruled that *"Slovakia violated the rights of Ms. D. guaranteed by the Convention on the Elimination of All Forms of Discrimination against Women. Specifically, the State party violated her rights by not providing her protection from discrimination on grounds of gender and family and marital status in employment. The Committee considered that the arguments presented by Ms. D. before domestic courts were sufficient to make prima facie claim of discrimination and that requesting additional proof of discriminatory behaviour by the employer put a disproportionate burden to the discriminated person."*[21] The national courts, including the Constitutional Court had dismissed her claim as inadmissible; however, the CEDAW is considered as an international human rights treaty according to article 7 para 5 of the Constitution of the Slovak Republic.

It is apparent that the problems of the status and implementation of the international treaties often become the object of the interpretation competence of the Constitutional Court. Practice and case-law is sometimes giving bi-directional guidelines and may lead to divergence within the system. However, the Constitutional Court has clearly stated, that international treaties, while they are considered as the source of law, have to always be used as for the interpretation of the principles of national constitutional regulation. It is confirmed by the ruling of the Constitutional Court in the finding of 2001: *"In the proceeding of the interpretation of the constitution, the human rights and freedoms guaranteed by the international treaties on human rights and fundamental freedoms are of subsidiary support importance, at the same time the Constitution cannot be interpreted in the way it establishes breach of international treaty, to which the Slovak republic is signatory party (also in finding II. ÚS 48/97, PL ÚS 15/98) and at the same time in definition of the content of constitutionally guaranteed human rights and fundamental freedoms, the Constitutional Court has to take into account, if not excluded*

---

[21] According to the UN CEDAW Committee Slovakia failed to provide adequate protection against discrimination to a woman after parental leave. Poradna prava, 2016. Online: https://www.poradna-prava.sk/en/news/according-to-the-un-cedaw-committee-slovakia-failed-to-provide-adequate-protection-against-discrimination-to-a-woman-after-paren/

by the Constitution, the text and provisions of relevant international treaties and case-law connected (see also II. ÚS 55/98)."[22]

A somewhat different situation is the case of the EU Charter of Fundamental rights, as this fundamental rights treaty is considered by the Constitutional Court as the international treaty which as has supremacy to national law according to article 7 para 5 of the Constitution, as it is the integral part of primary law of the European Union (article 7 para 2 of the Constitution). The Constitutional Court has ruled and interpreted, that "*to the sub-category of international treaties according to article 7 para 5 of the Constitution may by integrated also Association treaty and through it also Treaty on European Communities and Treaty on European Union as well as Lisbon Treaty, which re-named Treaty on European Communities to the Treaty on Functioning European Union. According to article 6 para 1 of the Treaty on European Union, which guarantee the same legal power to Charter as to the founding treaties, the Charter is recognised to have the same legal power in the legal order of the Slovak Republic as international treaties according to article 7 para 5 of the Constitution. These treaties are without any doubt treaties, which fulfil criteria stated in article 125 para 1 of the Constitution.*"[23]

3. Conclusion

The relationship between national and international law is developing and varying overtime. From the national point of view, the constitution with its highest legal power creates the basic legal framework. However, sovereign states exist in a globalised world, where multilevel governance and international organisations set international standards, particularly in the area of human rights protection. The principles of democracy, rule of law, good governance, human rights, dignity are leading principles of international human rights treaties and often have been incorporated in the constitutions. In this sense, international treaties are contributing to the legal framework. However, we should be aware of the status of international treaties, is based on the consent of the state and following

---

[22] Finding of the Constitutional Court of the SR No. I. ÚS 3/2001 of 20 December 2001. Coll. of findings of the Constitutional Court of the SR 2001, p. 537 – 538. In: Drgonec, J.: Constitution of the Slovak Republic. Comments. Bratislava: C.H.Beck, 2015, p. 336

[23] Finding of the Constitutional Court of the SR No. PL. ÚS 10/2014-78. Coll. of findings of the Constitutional Court of the SR 2014. In: Drgonec, J.: Constitution of the Slovak Republic. Comments. Bratislava: C.H.Beck, 2015, p. 335-336

ratification. "*Once a State assumes a treaty commitment, it is bound by that commitment and the principle set in article 27 of the Vienna Convention on the Law of Treaties provides that a State may not invoke the provision of its internal law as justification for its failure to perform a treaty.*"[24] This approach should prevail over any tendency towards divergence from international law in the national practice.

Bibliography

According to the UN CEDAW Committee Slovakia failed to provide adequate protection against discrimination to a woman after parental leave. Poradna prava, 2016. Online: https://www.poradna-prava.sk/en/news/according-to-the-un-cedaw-committee-slovakia-failed-to-provide-adequate-protection-against-discrimination-to-a-woman-after-paren/

Ann Peters, Supremacy Lost: International Law Meets Domestic Constitutional Law. Vienna Journal of International Constitutional Law. Vol. 3/2009, p. 170. Online: https://ius.unibas.ch/uploads/publics/8830/20100219153347_4b7ea14b06261.pdf

Articles on the Responsibility of States for Internationally Wrongful Acts – UN Doc A/Res/56/83 (28 January 2002)

Constitutional Act No. 460/1992 Coll. – Constitution of the Slovak Republic. Online: http://www.slovakia.org/sk-constitution.htm

Daniel Bethlehem, The Supremacy of International Law? – Part One. European Journal of International Law (blog), 2016. Online: https://www.ejiltalk.org/the-supremacy-of-international-law-part-one/

Derek G. Evans: Human Rights: Four Generations of Practice and Development. In: Abdi, A. And L. Shults, eds., Educating for Human Rights and Global Citizenship. Albany: State University of New Yor Press, 2007

Dominique Carreau: Droit International (2004), 43 ff, Fitzmauriece, General PRinciples (Fn 3) 68 ff. Santulli Carlo: Le Satuts International de LÓrdre Juridique Étatique (2001) 427.

ECJ judgement – case 11/70 Internationale Handelsgesellschaft mbH v Einfuhr- und Vorratsstelle für Getreide und Futtermittel of 17 December 1970. ECLI:EU:C:1970:114

ECJ judgement – case 26/62 NV Algemene Transport- en Expeditie Onderneming van Gend & Loos v Netherlands Inland Revenue Administration of 5 February 1963. ECLI:EU:C:1963:1

Finding of the Constitutional Court No. I. ÚS 28/01-29 of 13 December 2001. Online: https://www.ustavnysud.sk/ussr-intranet-

---

[24] Daniel Bethlehem, The Supremacy of International Law? – Part One. European Journal of International Law (blog), 2016. Online: https://www.ejiltalk.org/the-supremacy-of-international-law-part-one/

portlet/docDownload/abf57423-a027-4ee8-9d13-5d72f3536a26/Rozhodnutie%20-%20Rozhodnutie%20II.%20%C3%9AS%20499_2012.pdf
Finding of the Constitutional Court of the SR No. PL ÚS 10/2014-78. Coll. of findings of the Constitutional Court of the SR 2014. In: Drgonec, J.: Constitution of the Slovak Republic. Comments. Bratislava: C.H.Beck, 2015

Finding of the Constitutional Court of the SR No. PL ÚS 25/01-45 of 7 November 2002. Online: https://www.ustavnysud.sk/ussr-intranet-portlet/docDownload/d353f739-7b83-46dd-95da-d0fc526cf2e6/Rozhodnutie%20-%20Rozhodnutie%20PL.%20%C3%9AS%2025_01.pdf

Findings of the Constitutional Court of the SR No. I. ÚS 3/2001 of 20 December 2001. Coll. of findings of the Constitutional Court of the SR 2001, p. 537 – 538. In: Drgonec, J.: Constitution of the Slovak Republic. Comments. Bratislava: C.H.Beck, 2015

Findings of the Constitutional Court of the SR No. II. ÚS 55/98. In: Drgonec, J.: Constitution of the Slovak Republic. Comments. Bratislava: C.H.Beck, 2015

Findings of the Constitutional Court of the SR No. PL. ÚS 5/93, PL. ÚS 15/98, PL. ÚS 17/00. In: Drgonec, J.: Constitution of the Slovak Republic. Comments. Bratislava: C.H.Beck, 2015

Gerald Fitzmaurice, the General Principles of International law Considered from the Standpoint of the Rule of Law (1957), RdC, 85 ff

https://www.ustavnysud.sk/ussr-intranet-portlet/docDownload/abf57423-a027-4ee8-9d13-5d72f3536a26/Rozhodnutie%20-%20Rozhodnutie%20II.%20%C3%9AS%20499_2012.pdf

Kamil Baraník: Interakcia medzinárodného, supranacionálneho a ústavného práva pri ochrane ľudských práv v SR (2017). Bratislava: Justičná revue, 10/2017

Nollkaemper, André: Rethinking the Supremacy of Internaitonal Law. Online: https://link.springer.com/content/pdf/10 1007%2Fs00708-010-0044-4.pdf

online:http://eurlex.europa.eu/legalcontent/EN/TXT/PDF/?uri=CELEX:61962CJ0026&from=EN

online:http://eurlex.europa.eu/legalcontent/EN/TXT/PDF/?uri=CELEX:61970CJ0011&from=EN

Vienna Convention on the Law of Treaties

Index

A

abuse of rights, 221, 222, 224, 225, 226, 229, 230, 231, 232, 233, 234, 235, 238, 239, 240, 241, 243
Arbitration, 37, 221, 225, 231, 233, 235, 238, 240, 242

B

Brexit, 105, 268

C

civil law, 1, 2, 3, 6, 7, 10, 14, 15, 17, 18, 19, 20, 21, 24, 55, 63, 64, 65, 70, 203, 205, 214, 221, 222, 224, 232, 234, 264, 265, 266, 267, 273, 274, 275, 278, 280, 281, 283
common law, 1, 2, 3, 6, 7, 10, 11, 12, 14, 15, 17, 18, 19, 20, 21, 24, 27, 36, 38, 49, 55, 56, 57, 58, 59, 60, 61, 62, 63, 64, 65, 66, 69, 70, 94, 198, 201, 203, 205, 206, 207, 210, 214, 216, 221, 224, 231, 232, 234, 263, 264, 265, 266, 267, 268, 271, 274, 275, 278,279, 280, 281, 282, 284
comparative international law, 1, 2, 3
Constitution, 9, 18, 29, 34, 37, 57, 60, 68, 263, 265, 266, 267, 269, 270, 271, 272, 273, 274, 280
Continental, 61, 205, 231
Contract, 224, 363
Convergence, 1, 27, 55, 263, 465
customary law, 22, 223

D

Divergence, 1, 55, 465

E

European Court of Human Rights, 11, 247, 263, 264, 271, 274, 276, 280, 282, 283
European Court of Justice, 201, 203, 210
European Union, 17, 20, 197, 199, 200, 201, 202, 203, 204, 205, 206, 207, 210, 213, 214, 216, 247, 267

G

globalization, 93

I

International Court of Justice, 2, 7, 24, 206, 223
international law, 2, 3, 4, 5, 6, 7, 9, 11, 12, 13, 14, 15, 17, 21, 23, 24, 25, 27, 28, 29, 31, 32, 34, 37, 42, 45, 49, 93, 201, 221, 223, 231, 234, 235, 241, 243, 244, 265, 266
Italy, 11, 12, 19, 224, 278

L

language, 32, 39, 45, 47, 94, 240, 244
legal culture, 3, 37, 42, 211
legal transplants, 93

P

protection of human rights, 137, 264, 275
public international law, 5, 6, 28, 29, 49, 273

R

Roman law, 59, 70, 224
Russian Federation, 5, 12, 15

S

separation of powers, 13, 39, 57, 64, 272
Serbia, 381, 413
supranational, 21, 93, 214
Supreme Audit Institutions, 413

U

UK Supreme Court, 69, 70, 278
United Nations, 13, 22, 31, 34, 35
United States, 1, 4, 7, 8, 9, 11, 12, 13, 14, 30, 37, 39, 56, 57, 58, 60, 61, 64, 65, 68, 70, 137, 224, 233, 234

Lightning Source UK Ltd.
Milton Keynes UK
UKHW021555080223
416650UK00005B/917/J